THE SECURITY OF FREEDOM:
ESSAYS ON CANADA'S ANTI-TERRORISM BILL

EDITORS

Ronald J. Daniels is the seventh Dean of the modern Faculty of Law at the University of Toronto. He has written extensively on the law and economics of corporate law, securities law, and government regulation. He is founder and current Chair of Pro Bono Students Canada. He has served as Chair of the Ontario Task Force on Securities Regulation, Chair of the Ontario Market Design Committee, and member of the Toronto Stock Exchange Committee on Corporate Governance. He is past-President of the Canadian Council of Law Deans.

Patrick Macklem is Professor of Law at the University of Toronto. After articling with a Toronto law firm specializing in labour law, he served as Law Clerk for Chief Justice Brian Dickson of the Supreme Court of Canada. He served as a constitutional advisor to the Royal Commission on Aboriginal Peoples, and was a Visiting Scholar at Stanford Law School in 1988 and at U.C.L.A. School of Law in 1992, and a Visiting Professor at Central European University in 2001. He is the author of *Indigenous Difference and the Constitution of Canada* (2001), and co-editor of *Canadian Constitutional Law* (1997).

Kent Roach is Professor of Law and Criminology at the University of Toronto. Professor Roach is the author of *Constitutional Remedies in Canada* (1994), which won the Walter Owen Prize as the best English language law book published in 1994 and 1995, and *Due Process and Victims' Rights: The New Law and Politics of Criminal Justice* (1999), which was short-listed for the 1999 Donner Prize for best book on public policy. He is also the author of *Criminal Law* 2nd ed. (2000), and *The Supreme Court on Trial: Judicial Activism and Democracy* (2001). He is also the editor-in-chief of the *Criminal Law Quarterly*.

Edited by Ronald J. Daniels, Patrick Macklem,
and Kent Roach

The Security of Freedom: Essays on Canada's Anti-Terrorism Bill

UNIVERSITY OF TORONTO PRESS
Toronto Buffalo London

© University of Toronto Press Incorporated 2001
Toronto Buffalo London
Printed in Canada

ISBN 0-8020-8519-9

Printed on acid-free paper

National Library of Canada Cataloguing in Publication Data

Main entry under title:

The security of freedom : essays on Canada's anti-terrorism bill

Papers presented at a conference entitled: The security of
freedom: a conference on Canada's anti-terrorism bill, held
Nov. 9–10, 2001, and sponsored by the University of Toronto
Faculty of Law.
ISBN 0-8020-8519-9

1. Terrorism – Canada – Prevention. 2. Civil rights – Canada –
Congresses. I. Daniels, Ronald J. (Ronald Joel), 1959–
II. Macklem, Patrick III. Roach, Kent, 1961–   IV. University of
Toronto. Faculty of Law.

KE9007.S42 2001   344.71'0532   C2001-903772-4

University of Toronto Press acknowledges the financial assistance to its publishing
program of the Canada Council for the Arts and the Ontario Arts Council.

University of Toronto Press acknowledges the financial support for its publishing
activities of the Government of Canada through the Book Publishing Industry
Development Program (BPIDP).

Contents

The Charter and Democratic Accountability

Criminalizing Terrorism

Terrorism and Criminal Justice

Information Gathering

Financing Terrorism

International Dimensions of the Response to Terrorism

Administering Security in a Multicultural Society

ACKNOWLEDGMENTS

The organization of the Security of Freedom conference, and the production of this book, took place in the space of less than three weeks. Such an achievement in such a short time is the result of the incredible energy and dedication of a number of people.

First and foremost, we want to thank Kate Hilton, the Director of Special Projects at the Faculty, for serving as Conference Coordinator. The task of successfully mounting the conference, of coordinating with the University of Toronto Press, of working with our numerous authors fell to Kate, who discharged all of these responsibilities with her characteristic skill, diligence, commitment, and good cheer.

We want to also thank the staff of University of Toronto Press for embracing the challenge of delivering a finished book one week after the beginning of the conference. George Meadows and Bill Harnum, along with Melissa Pitts, Roy Schoenberger, Molly Schlosser, Malgosia Halliop, Bruce Peters, and Virgil Duff, all worked long and hard to make the impossible possible. In this they were motivated, as so many others were, to demonstrate the capacity of the academy to contribute to public debate and deliberation on a pressing policy issue in a timely and effective manner.

We also want to thank Robert Birgeneau, President of the University of Toronto, and Adel Sedra, Vice-President and Provost of the University of Toronto, for lending financial support for the publication of the proceedings of the conference. On very short notice, Paul Gooch, the President of Victoria University, and his staff, graciously allowed us to hold our conference in the Isabel Bader Theatre when we found our registrations had soared beyond what we could accommodate at the Faculty of Law.

Members of the administrative staff at the Faculty of Law worked tirelessly to put on a major conference with little notice. We wish to thank Jennifer Tam, the Events Coordinator at the Faculty, and Cheryl Sullivan, Director of Communications, for their invaluable assistance. We also want to thank Ivana Kadic and Jill Given-King for lending support when it was needed. We also want to thank Marylin Raisch and Shikha Sharma of the Faculty's Law Library, who were responsible for compiling on-line research materials and the Appendix to this book. We also want to express our appreciation to Susan Barker who was responsible for creating the conference website.

In mounting the conference, we were ably assisted by the support and participation of several prominent members of the legal and academic communities who agreed to chair panels at the conference. Specifically, we wish to thank Ronald Atkey, Alan Borovoy, Michael Code, Nathalie Des Rosiers, Allan Gotlieb, Andrew Petter, and Peter Russell for their invaluable contributions.

Many of the chapters of the book were critical of certain aspects of the proposed legislation (some of the entire legislative project), but we were struck by the commitment, decency, and good faith of members of the Department of Justice who traveled to Toronto to participate in the conference. We are particularly appreciative of the involvement of Messrs. Richard Mosley and Stan Cohen of the Department of Justice who offered their comments at the end of the conference.

Finally, we want to express our deepest gratitude to our academic colleagues in and outside of the University of Toronto who participated in this endeavour. By elevating this enterprise to the top of their research priorities, and for embracing so readily the challenges and the opportunities for contributing to public debate on this most urgent of public policy matters, they demonstrated in vivid terms their collective and enduring commitment to the public weal.

Ronald Daniels, Patrick Macklem, and Kent Roach
Toronto, November 12, 2001

THE SECURITY OF FREEDOM:
ESSAYS ON CANADA'S ANTI-TERRORISM BILL

Introduction
Ronald J. Daniels

This collection of essays is the product of an extraordinary two-day conference – The Security of Freedom – that was held at the Faculty of Law, University of Toronto on November 9th and 10th, 2001. The conference was open to the public, and attracted the active participation of more than 350 individuals representing the academy, the legal profession, the federal and provincial governments, and various local community groups.

The purpose of the conference was to enlist the assistance of Canada's leading academic experts in law, criminology and political science in analyzing the federal government's proposed omnibus anti-terrorism legislation – Bill C-36.[1] The Bill, which was introduced by Justice Minister Anne McLellan on October 15th, 2001, was crafted in the aftermath of the tragic events that unfolded in the United States on September 11th, 2001, and was designed to enhance the federal government's capacity to protect Canada from terrorist threats, as well as allowing it to contribute more effectively to international efforts aimed at combating global terrorism. The Bill seeks to do this by amending 10 different statutes and by ratifying two different United Nations Conventions – the *International Convention for the Suppression of the Financing of Terrorism* and the *International Convention for the Suppression of Terrorist Bombings*. The Bill is 175 pages long, and is scheduled to be adopted into law well before the end of the calendar year. A bill of this magnitude could not be adequately assessed and evaluated by any one or several persons; it would require the type of effort that was undertaken by the 24 commentators whose names appear in this volume.

As is discussed in some detail within the volume, the Bill seeks to achieve its stated goals of enhanced security for Canadians by conferring a number of new powers on the federal government and federal and provincial security forces. Significantly, Bill C-36:

- Defines, for the first time in Canadian law, a terrorist activity;
- Defines several new terrorism offences, and provides stringent penalties for persons convicted of committing these offences;
- Facilitates enhanced used of electronic surveillance against terrorist groups;
- Allows police to invoke judicially supervised investigative hearings which require individuals who are alleged to have information related to a terrorist group or offence to appear before a judge to provide that information;
- Creates criminal sanctions for persons who knowingly collect or give funds, either directly or indirectly, in order to carry out terrorism;
- Enhances the federal government's capacity to deny or remove charitable status from those who support terrorist groups;
- Allows for certain information of national interest to be suppressed during courtroom or other judicial proceedings; and
- Provides for the arrest of people on the grounds of reasonable suspicion that the arrest or recognizance is necessary to prevent the carrying out of a terrorist activity.

In view of the magnitude of the changes proposed to the federal government's various powers, authors who presented papers at the Conference sought to assess the proposed legislation by addressing two basic issues. First, what is the impact of expanded governmental powers on individual rights and liberties? This question, as numerous authors have argued, transcends singular focus on the Bill's capacity to withstand judicial scrutiny under the *Charter of Rights and Freedoms*. Rather, the question posed was a more fundamental one of whether the enhanced powers being sought for the state are congruent with our core democratic traditions and values, and consistent with bedrock ideas of the rule of law. The second issue identified relates to the Bill's efficacy, namely how likely is the proposed legislation to achieve its avowed goals? In other words, will the expanded powers contemplated by the Bill materially reduce the risks of terrorism borne by citizens in and outside of Canada?

The first section of the conference addressed the *Security of Freedom*. Drawing on the work of Ulrich Beck[2], Professor David Schneiderman in his chapter, 'Terrorism and the Risk Society', details the impact of new global risks, such as international terrorism, on the social environment. Schneiderman invokes Beck's framework to demonstrate the new risks posed by globalization and technology, and their pervasive impact on society. Schneiderman also relies on Beck to express concern over the capacity of enhanced security states, nurtured and encouraged by technocratic advice, to deal effectively with these risks. To temper the expansion of the security state, Schneiderman argues for heightened democratic deliberation and participation in fashioning the new security arrangements.

The need for enhanced democratic deliberation in fashioning an effective response to terrorism is echoed in the chapter written by Professor Mariana Valverde, 'Governing Security, Governing Through Security'. Valverde further argues that in undertaking such deliberation, society needs to be cognizant that security and freedom are not a zero sum game. Society can have increased security, but can do so without reducing our fundamental freedoms. To address society's security needs, Valverde proposes an 'evidence-based approach' to national security issues. Such evidence, Valverde believes, would provide invaluable discipline to public debate and deliberation over new laws and institutional arrangements designed to increase security.

In Professor Janice Stein's chapter, 'Network Wars', the evidence surrounding the character of the threat posed by Bin Laden's al-Qa'aeda network, as well as the strategy proposed to reduce its threat value, is discussed. According to Stein, al-Qa'aeda is a complex, decentralized, multi-nodal network that spans several different countries and is, in her words, 'designed for redundancy'. Cutting off one node of the network does not destabilize the entire network just as our international financial network was not destroyed by the destruction of the World Trade Centre. Nevertheless, even global terrorist networks require a host state environment that offers finance and a secure environment. To undermine these global terrorist networks, Stein eschews conventional military and security analysis, and proposes a multi-dimensional strategy that seeks to make it more costly and complex for its members to access the network, while suffocating the host state from needed resources.

The challenge then for architects of laws and legal institutions is to design arrangements that equip the state to deal effectively with terrorist threats, but without undermining its democratic core. According to Professor Gross, however, review of the experience of other liberal democratic states in responding to threatened security risks is not encouraging. In his chapter, 'Cutting Down Trees' Law-Making Under the Shadow of

Great Calamities', Gross notes that limited government, separation of powers, and the rule of law are often casualties when states confront terrorist threats. States grossly overstate the risk of terrorism, even to the point where it is mistakenly believed that terrorists can pose existential risks to the state. In this environment, citizens are willing to accord state officials greatly expanded emergency powers that become the baseline for even greater distributions of power from citizen to state.

This theme of the willingness of citizens to sacrifice liberty for security is the subject of Professor Dyzenhaus' contribution to the volume, 'The Permanence of the Temporary: Can Emergency Powers be Normalized?' Like Gross, Dyzenhaus is skeptical of the transfer of emergency powers to the state in conventional domestic legislation. The fear is that states will become addicted to the expanded powers, and that citizens will become steadily inured to their exercise – despite the impact on individual rights and liberties. To constrain this threat, Dyzenhaus argues that the state should be forced to defend the exercise of emergency powers against normal rule of law justificatory criteria. Further, the laws providing for such expanded powers should be created in advance of the emergency, should be carefully confined in duration and scope, and should ensure effective legislative and judicial control over the exercise of augmented executive powers. To do otherwise is, in Dyzenhaus' terms, to create 'legal vacuums'. In this respect, Dyzenhaus urges the judges who will be charged with interpreting the legislation to refrain from adopting a deferential approach that unduly elevates national security concerns over individual rights.

The concern over the enactment of permanent emergency powers is given expression in the chapter written by Professor Weinrib, 'Terrorism's Challenge to the Constitutional Order'. Weinrib observes that Canada's track record in relation to the adoption of emergency powers which seek to imbue the Executive with enhanced powers unsettles the traditional balance struck across different branches of government that ensure strong but limited government. She laments the treatment of Japanese Canadians during the Second World War and the excesses perpetrated in the aftermath of the FLQ Crisis in 1970. Weinrib does not have much confidence in the constraints imposed by judicial oversight on the exercise of executive powers under the Bill. Not only are judicial challenges 'slow, expensive and piecemeal', but they are also beset by undue judicial deference to government in times of emergency. Preferable from Weinrib's perspective is the enterprise of ensuring enhanced legislative and public scrutiny of the exercise of powers under the Bill. In this respect, Weinrib suggests regular bi-cameral, multi-party examination of government policy in relation to the legislation (including enhanced access to information). Interestingly, such a regime is already found in the provisions contained in the federal *Emergencies Act*[3] which seeks to regulate governmental conduct in a declared emergency, but which are noticeably (and perplexingly) absent from the Bill.

In the next section of the volume, *The Charter and Democratic Accountability,* the congruence of Bill C-36 with fundamental rule of law concerns is explored. Professor Roach's first contribution to the volume, 'The Dangers of a *Charter*-Proof and Crime-Based Response to Terrorism' critiques the Government's reliance on the Bill's avowed *Charter* compatibility as allaying fears over its fundamental consistency with basic liberal democratic values. Based on a review of the proposed legislation against Supreme Court jurisprudence, Roach concludes that the Minister is probably correct when she declares the Bill is consistent with the *Charter*. Nevertheless, by focusing only on the Bill's *Charter* compatibility, the polity's capacity to assess the broader soundness and wisdom of the proposed legislation is correspondingly reduced.

Roach's concerns over the Bill's wisdom are further heightened by its highly symbolic character. As Roach observes, everything that the 19 terrorists did on September 11th – murder, assault, highjacking – would have constituted crimes under our *Criminal Code*, and would have subjected the terrorists to criminal sanction had they survived the attack. Roach argues that legislatures often enact highly symbolic criminal laws in response to tragic crimes, but that creating new criminal laws and tougher penalties will not by themselves prevent such crimes. In this, Roach notes the Bill's consistency with other legislative enactments (like the introduction of new offences relating to organized crime and sexual assault) that divert attention from more promising avenues of reform involving improved intelligence gathering and enforcement. Roach also argues that justifying criminal laws in the nature of human rights does not take away from the coercion of the criminal law and may make unwarranted assumptions about the ability of the criminal law to protect human rights.

In a provocative contribution, 'Thinking Outside of the Box: Foundational Principles for a Counter-Terrorism Law and Policy', the Honourable Irwin Cotler argues that the Bill should be evaluated against a 'converging and inclusive domestic and international perspective anchored in the notion of human security – itself a people-centred rather than state centred approach'. Cotler states that the Bill protects both national security – or the security of democracy if not the democracy itself – and civil liberties'. In contrast to other contributors who argue against the permanence of emergency legislation, Cotler is firm in his view that the Bill is 'legacy legislation' that will 'likely be with us for a long time'. Nevertheless, despite Cotler's confidence in the enterprise of the Bill, he identifies several civil liberties concerns over specific provisions in the Bill which, he argues, require amendment. Notably, Cotler argues for the inclusion of sunset clauses on the most controversial powers contained in the Bill – a suggestion endorsed and expanded upon by many other speakers in the Conference, as well as a narrowing of the definition of terrorist activities.

In the next section of the volume, *Criminalizing Terrorism*, the breadth and operation of the new terrorism offence provisions are given exacting scrutiny. In this respect, although varying in tone and emphasis, there is a remarkable convergence of the analysis set out in the four chapters written by Professors Roach ('The New Terrorism Offences and the Criminal Law'), Schneiderman and Cossman ('Political Association and the Anti-Terrorism Bill'), Shaffer ('Effectiveness of Anti-Terrorism Legislation: does bill C-36 Give Us What We Need?'), and Stuart ('The Dangers of Quick Fix Legislation in the Criminal Law: The Anti-Terrorism Bill C-36 Should be Withdrawn').

To begin with, each of the authors is skeptical, if not hostile, to the claim that the enhanced criminal law powers claimed by the federal government in the proposed legislation will have a discernable effect on enhancing the impact of existing criminal law sanctions on terrorist activity. Professors Shaffer and Stuart, for instance, both caution that the Bill will not make us safer, and stress that its myriad shortcomings expose the frailties of 'quick fix' legislation. Professor Shaffer notes, if the target, *in extremis,* is religious fanatics who are prepared to commit suicide to achieve their ends, escalating the stringency of sanctions imposed will be unlikely to have any marginal impact on the propensity to engage in such acts.

Perhaps the greatest concern surrounding the Bill relates to section 83.01(1) which defines the terrorist activities as they are prohibited in a number of new offences contained in the Bill. As Professor Roach notes, the definition is the most important provision in the Bill because all of the investigative powers, enhanced sanctions, and the definition of terrorist groups are predicated upon it. Regrettably, Roach laments, the definition is 'not nearly as clear, careful or restrained as it should be'. Indeed, Roach finds that the definition of terrorism embedded in the Bill is broader than definitions found in similar legislation enacted in both the United States and the United Kingdom and even in some respect than the definition of terrorism in the regulations enacted in response to the October Crisis of 1970.

Specifically, section 83.01(1)(b) states that 'terrorist activity' includes an act or omission, in or outside of Canada 'committed in whole or in part for a political, religious or ideological purpose, objective or cause' and 'with the intention of intimidating the public, or a segment of the public, with regard to its security, including its economic security, or compelling a person, a government or a domestic or international organization to do or to refrain from doing any act, whether the person, government or organization is inside or outside of Canada'. The act must also be intended:

A. to cause death or serious bodily harm to any person by the use of violence,
B. to endanger a person's life,
C. to cause a serious risk to the health or safety of the public or any segment of the public,
D. to cause substantial property damage, whether public or private, if causing such damage is likely to result in the conduct or harm referred to in any of clauses (A) to (C) and (E), or
E. to cause serious interference with or serious disruption of an essential service, facility or system, whether public or private, other than as a result of lawful advocacy, protest, dissent or stoppage of work that does not involve an activity that is intended to result in the conduct or harm referred to in any of clauses (A) to (C).

A terrorist group is, in turn defined as including 'an entity that has one of its purposes of activities facilitating or carrying out any terrorist activity' or 'an entity' listed by the Solicitor General.

The greatest concern over the Bill's definition section arises in relation to Clause (E). Here, as Professors Scheiderman and Cossman note, the risk is that individuals or groups engaged in political protest aimed at compelling government to do or to refrain from doing something by disrupting 'essential services'. They argue that the inclusion of the word 'lawful' would enable police to arrest, and the courts to convict, those individuals who were engaged in unlawful advocacy, protest, dissent or stoppage of work *as terrorists*. The authors stress that they do not seek to condone such unlawful acts – indeed the authors point out their lack of effectiveness and their existing criminal character – but rather to demonstrate how far such unlawful activity is from accepted definitions of terrorism. In these terms, the concern is that Clause (E) will cast a pall over forms of political protest that have recently been engaged in by domestic anti-globalization groups, poverty coalitions, and Aboriginal protesters. In fact, the authors even speculate that the new offence provisions could have been used to subject domestic supporters of foreign national liberation movements such as the anti-apartheid struggle waged by the ANC in South Africa or the anti-Pinochet movement in Chile to sanction. This concern is echoed by virtually all of the other others in this section of the volume.

Although there is a growing chorus of support in favour of the removal of the word 'lawful' from Clause (E), many of the participants in the conference argued that the most prudent course of action is simply to remove Clause (E) in its entirety. In this respect, Professors Scheiderman and Cossman note that it is even possible that lawful or unwaful protests that would otherwise be exempted from the provision of terrorist activities in Clause (E) would still be within the ambit of Clause (D) if they were caused by the intentional property damage targeted in that clause. The authors argue that if there are 'particular concerns regarding essential services that the government would like to see addressed, it can do so more precisely'. In this respect, reference to similar anti-terrorism legislation in the United Kingdom which sets out more finely honed provisions dealing, for instance, with serious interference or disruption of an electronic system is apposite.

Professor Roach's chapter points to other defects in the definitional section of the Bill. His concern is that the Bill's definitional section 'piles inchoate liability on top of inchoate crimes', thereby stretching the chain of criminal activity to 'absurd lengths'. Roach notes that the Bill covers not only complete terrorist activities, but a 'conspiracy, attempt or threat', or being an accessory after the fact or counseling in relation to any such act or omission. The problem Roach identifies is that many of the offences that are set out in the Bill are already inchoate crimes (financing, facilitating and instructing) that are done in preparation for the commission of any complete terrorist offence. His chapter includes a careful and systematic analysis of the new offences of participating, facilitating, instructing and harbouring in relation to terrorist activities. Professor Stuart extends this analysis to the new offence of knowingly participating or contributing to terrorist activities. Although Roach's analysis suggests that many of these provisions are vague and overbroad, he is not optimistic that courts will actually strike down the legislation on these grounds. Professor Shaffer, however, is somewhat more optimistic that the definition as presently conceived could be struck down under s. 7 of the *Charter* for failing to provide the accused with fair notice and for failing to limit law enforcement discretion.

The next section of the volume, *Terrorism and Criminal Justice*, addresses the enforcement of the proposed legislation. Professor Stewart's contribution, 'Rule of Law or Executive Fiat? Bill C-36 and Public Interest Immunity', notes that the Bill amends the *Canada Evidence Act*[4] by conferring new (and, in Stewart's terms, extraordinary) powers on the Attorney General of Canada surrounding the disclosure of information relevant to a wide range of judicial proceedings. Specifically, proposed section 38.13 would allow the Attorney General to prohibit the disclosure of information in connection with a proceeding for the purpose of 'protecting international relations or national defence or security'. Stewart observes that 'the power would be available to the Attorney General irrespective of the nature of the information suppressed, regardless of the outcome of any judicial determination of a claim of public interest immunity, and regardless of the effect of the prohibition on the proceeding to which it applies.' Moreover, the Bill provides no recourse to the courts for review of the Minister's exercise of this power. Against this backdrop, Stewart argues forcefully that the proposed amendments to the *Canada Evidence Act* are inconsistent with our core rule of law values, although, as in the case of other controversial provisions of the proposed legislation, Stewart is equivocal that the legislation will necessarily be found to be constitutionally infirm. Stewart's view is that the best course of action is to refrain from adopting the proposed amendments to the *Canada Evidence Act*, particularly in light of a failure on the part of the government to demonstrate any defect in the existing sections of the statute which allow a minister of the Crown and other certain persons to object to disclosure of information in proceedings on grounds relating to the public interest or cabinet security.

Professor Trotter's chapter, 'The Anti-Terrorism Bill and Preventative Restraints on Liberty', focuses on three components of the new criminal law regime envisaged by the Bill, namely preventative arrests and peace bonds for terrorists, stricter bail laws, and harsher sentences. The preventative arrest provisions contemplated by the Bill would allow an individual to be detained for no more than 72 hours prior to a bail hearing. Trotter finds that the 72 hour detention period is not, when compared to other democracies having enacted anti-terrorism legislation, particularly problematic. However, Trotter is concerned about legislative expansion of this period, as well as with the protections to be accorded detained individuals during the detention period. Similarly, Trotter does not find the new peace bond provisions 'particularly offensive', but does worry about the awkwardness of the legislative drafting and urges clarification. He is also dubious of the efficacy of recognizance in thwarting terrorist offences. Trotter's greatest concern is over the ambit of the offences created in the Bill, and their connection to enhanced criminal sanctions. Trotter is concerned that the longer minimum terms and consecutive sentences contemplated by the Bill will result in disproportionate sanctions. In the end, like many other criminal law academics, Trotter is dubious that there is much deterrence value offered by the proposed provisions.

The seventh section of the volume deals with *Information Gathering*. Given the widely shared view among speakers at the Conference that the first line of defence in responding to the new terrorist threat (at least for North America) is information gathering, Professor Wark's chapter, 'Intelligence Requirements and Anti-Terrorism Legislation' offers instructive insight on the likely impact of the Bill on our intelligence apparatus. Wark identifies the daunting challenges posed to security officials in penetrating clandestine terrorist organizations that have developed operational techniques based on the 'compartmentalization of operations, the 'need to know principle', the use of operational cut-outs to shield different components of a terrorist mission, and the employment of 'deep cover' or 'sleeper' agents'.' Most distressingly, the lessons of September 11th demonstrate that facilitation of terrorist activities can occur without the full knowledge of those who are directly involved in the operations.

Against this backdrop, Wark argues that the Bill is a 'mixed bag'. Wark finds concludes that many of the 'front line' legislative provisions – for instance, preventative detention and investigative hearings – are necessary in responding to terrorist threats. However, Wark is concerned that several of the institutional changes proposed to the security establishment present problems of overlap and coordination across different agencies that need to be addressed. Wark also discusses other defects in the provisions dealing with official secrets, the interception of communications, and tracking of financial activities of terrorist groups. He is concerned with the wisdom of moving the Communications Security Establishment to the Department of National Defence. However, Wark warns that no matter how Bill C-36 is drafted, good laws are only part of the checklist of what makes for effective and democratic functioning of a security and intelligence community, and that governments need to be attentive to other issues such as resources, talent, and legitimacy of the information gathering community.

Professor Austin's chapter, 'Is Privacy a Casualty of the War on Terrorism', addresses the threat to privacy posed by the proposed legislation. Austin observes that the Bill's expansion of information gathering and information suppressing powers pose significant risks to citizen privacy. Austin acknowledges that a new balance is being stuck between citizen privacy and the state's interest in promoting enhanced security, and the critical question to ask is 'what kind of balance is permissible and desirable'. Austin finds that amendments to several statutes dealing with privacy – the *Privacy Act*, the *Personal Information Protection and Electronic Documents Act*, and the *Access to Information Act* are not consistent with the principles of a free and democratic society, and should be revoked. In developing this analysis, Austin is sensitive to the scope for massive privacy violations posed by new technologies that facilitate aggregation of widely dispersed and fragmented pieces of information into detailed individual profiles. These concerns are most acute in relation to information warehousing of electronic data, collection of DNA information, and the Attorney General's powers in relation the suppression of information. In these areas, Austin is concerned that citizen rights of privacy are not balanced but are completely swamped by national security concerns.

Professor Friedland's chapter, 'Police Powers in Bill C-36', raises several interesting and important concerns surrounding the scope of powers contemplated by the Bill. Friedland's systematic review of police powers is significant for his finding that some police powers should in fact be added to the Bill, such as the power to deal with encryption and to make undercover operatives more effective by permitted some illegal acts. He finds that other powers, notably investigative hearings, although probably legal, are unnecessary in light of the availability of other existing incentives that will persuade parties with information to cooperate with police. Yet other powers, such as wiretapping and arrest on suspicion, are justified to deal with the very serious problem of terrorism. However, as in the case of other contributors, Friedland expresses concern over the breath of the offence provisions, and, argues for the removal of Clause (E) in the definition section set out in 83.01(1)(b).

Importantly, Friedland is concerned with ensuring adequate safeguards on the exercise of new police powers set out in the Bill, and argues that the consent of the Canada Security Intelligence Service or the Solicitor

General of Canada should be required as a prior condition to their exercise. In an effort to guard against the infiltration of the new measures contemplated by the Bill into other areas of the criminal law, Friedland argues that the new police powers should be included in CSIS's enabling legislation, not the *Criminal Code*. A further suggested safeguard that follows in train from the augmented role to be played by CSIS is to ensure that the Security Intelligence Review Committee (established to oversee CSIS) enjoys a correspondingly increased role in supervising the exercise of authority conferred by any proposed legislation.

The theme of section 8 of the volume is *Financing Terrorism*. In this section, we seek to evaluate proposed changes to existing laws that will support efforts aimed at thwarting the transfer of funds to terrorists. Professor Davis' contribution, 'Cutting off the Flow of Funds to Terrorists: Whose Funds? Which Funds? Who Decides' focuses on proposed changes to money laundering legislation in Canada. These changes are inspired by the Bill's adoption of United Nations Conventions relating to the financing of terrorism. Davis notes that the effort to limit financial support to terrorists involves two components. The first component is designed to prosecute the financiers, i.e., the individuals or organizations that provide money or property to support terrorist activities. The second component involves freezing, seizing and forfeiting property that has been or might be directed toward terrorist activities. Davis' analysis indicates that it is difficult to implement these goals through legislation. In part, this is because of threshold definitional issues in determining the appropriate level of risk that a certain economic activity will contribute to terrorist activity. In part, it is because of uncertainty defining the relationship between economic activity and terrorist activity, and the consequent difficulties in specifying appropriate criminal standards. Davis' comprehensive review of the changes proposed in the Bill reveals several problems relating to the scope of sanctioned activity. Davis argues that the Bill goes well beyond what is necessary for Canada to adopt under the UN Conventions, and would prefer that Parliament give the courts more authority to participate in the process of determining the appropriate scope of the financing provisions.

The chapter by Professor Duff, 'Charitable Status and Terrorist Financing: Rethinking the Proposed *Charities Registration (Security Information) Act*' discusses the marginal value of conferring power on the executive to de-register charities (meaning the denial of favourable income tax treatment for donors) in light of the various new financing offences specified in the Bill and discussed in detail in the Davis chapter.

Duff is concerned with the breadth of ministerial power to de-register or to prevent registration of charitable organizations. Duff, as Sossin does in his chapter, argues that there is a need to impose more effective procedural and judicial safeguards on the exercise of executive discretion. However, Duff's concerns extend to the new substantive criteria for offences involving charities. Duff, in particular, worries about the mental element (or lack thereof) in triggering the Bill's sanctions. He argues that an organization that negligently permits the financing of terrorist activities should be subject to lesser sanctions. This is particularly relevant given the 'useful and important work that … organizations and foundations perform, both domestically and internationally, particularly in countries that have been devastated by the kinds of political, religious, ethnic and/or ideological conflicts which frequently foster the kinds of activities that are regarded as terrorist'.

In section 9 of the volume, the *International Dimensions of the Response to Terrorism* are discussed. Professor Brunnée's chapter, 'Terrorism and Legal Change' An International Law Lesson', examines the international framework governing the response to terrorism. Brunnée observes that while there is considerable debate over the desirability or legitimacy of domestic laws designed to combat terrorism, the polity is insufficiently attentive to significant changes that are occurring in the international law arena in relation to terrorism, and which have important and far-reaching implications for customary international law. Brunnée focuses on the changing nature of the self-defence rationale in relation to the use of force on foreign states and citizens. Customary rules of international law are framed on new norms that are established by claims that are asserted and not challenged in the international arena. Brunnée believes that there has been a noticeable lack of diligence in understanding how the existing international norms have been invoked in support of the actions taken against the Taliban regime, and that there is the risk that the pursuit of ends will enable an 'uncritical justification of means'. This is, she argues, an important lesson to bear in mind when analyzing the scope of Bill C-36.

Professor Macklem's chapter, 'Canada's Obligations at International Law', addresses the role of international obligations in requiring states to prosecute and punish individuals for actions which amount to international criminal behaviour, and seeks to assess the enterprise of Bill C-36 on this basis. Macklem notes that international human rights law focuses on two species of international crime: one which involves trans-national criminal activity and the other which by its very nature 'shock the conscience of mankind and threaten peace and security in the world'. For Macklem, in contrast to commentators such as Stuart and Gross, see King to define a clear offence of international terrorism in the criminal law framework of Canada is a laudable legislative goal. Unlike 'ordinary' criminal offences, an international offence of terrorism enables the prosecution and punishment of terrorist activity regardless of where it occurs. Although the task of defining the unique character of international terrorism is not easy, Macklem asserts that it is a task which must be done. Macklem declines to accept the moral relativism embedded in the idea that 'one man's terrorist is another man's freedom fighter'. For Macklem there is a need to grapple with the difficulties in reconciling the concept of terrorism with civil disobedience, human security and national liberation, and although Bill C-36's definition is doubtless flawed and ought to be revised, its assertion of universal jurisdiction over crimes of terrorism is an important starting point for mature discussion and deliberation on these matters.

In section 10 of the volume, we discuss *Administering Security in a Multicultural Society*. The chapter by Professor Choudhry, 'Protecting Equality in the Face of Terror: Ethnic and Racial Profiling and S. 15 of the *Charter*', addresses the vexing issues surrounding the use of racial profiling in the response to terrorism. Choudhry states that in the wake of September 11th, there is little doubt that security forces in Canada and abroad will train their enforcement efforts under existing and the proposed legislative provisions contained in Bill C-36 on Arabs, persons of Middle Eastern appearance, or Muslims. Choudhry bemoans the scarce public attention that has been devoted to profiling, particularly in relation to its constitutionality. In part, he attributes this oversight to the informal and less visible means which will be used to support such conduct. Choudhry argues against both broad and narrow uses of profiling – the latter involving the use of race or ethnicity along with other factors, such as suspicious behaviour. Given the adverse impact that profiling has on minority groups, Choudhry advocates the adoption of new strategies to be deployed in the response to terrorism which would subject *everyone* to intrusive investigation both by airport security personnel and immigration officers. Although Choudhry acknowledges the costs of such an approach, he believes that they are worthy in light of the respect that it would accord basic equality commitments.

The chapter by Professor Macklin, 'Borderline Security', is significant for the contrasts drawn between the approaches to terrorism contemplated in Bill C-36 (which apply to all) and in Canada's existing (and recently revised) immigration regime. Whereas the former at least seeks (albeit in a flawed manner) to articulate a definition of terrorism, the latter does not, thereby conferring significant discretion on immigration officials. Although Macklin believes that the immigration regime in Canada will benefit from the Bill's specification of a terrorist offence, Macklin is concerned that the national security apparatus will still invoke immigration measures as the principal means of disciplining the threat perceived to be posed by international terrorism. This is because the more elaborate safeguards set out in Bill C-36 will encourage police and security officials to rely on more flexible and discretionary immigration measures. In this respect, Macklin laments that society is moving in a parochial and ineffectual way to shore up borders precisely at a time when the border has less efficacy than ever in constraining terrorist threats (e.g., use of antharax and other biological weapons that do not require a corporeal presence in the target jurisdiction).

Professor Morgan's chapter, 'A Thousand and One Rights' focuses on the challenges posed for courts in reviewing the exercise of executive authority. Morgan's analysis is based on the labyrinthine and complex processes involved in immigration proceedings. Morgan details the long, complex and indeterminate process used by the federal government to expel Mohammed Issa Mohammed, a Palestinian terrorist who was convicted of participating in an airport highjacking in Greece in which one passenger was killed. Mohammed was sentenced to a 17 year prison term, but was released after four months to secure the release of hostages seized in another terrorist incident. Mohammed entered Canada in 1987 without disclosing his past conviction, but efforts commenced in 1988 to deport him are still not resolved. For Morgan, the delays in the process are in part attributable to the difficulties innate in reconciling national and international rights and the international struggles of persons everywhere with the imperative for domestic community's peace.

Professor Sossin's contribution, 'The Intersection of Administrative Law with the Anti-Terrorism Bill', discusses the problem of procedural fairness in the context of national security decision-making and the problem of accountability in relation to ministerial discretion in matters of national security. Sossin expresses concern (as others have in the volume) with the number of discretionary ministerial powers that are immunized from review. Sossin also echoes Duff's concerns over the capacity of the Solicitor General and the Minister of National Revenue to sign a certificate which, in effect, denies charitable status to certain organizations. Sossin notes that it is possible that a certificate can be signed and upheld by the courts without the affected applicant or charity ever knowing what activity it is alleged to have participated in, or having an opportunity to test the veracity of the evidence relied upon. In the end, Sossin argues that there is a need to incorporate standard administrative law type protections into Bill C-36, and believes that these protections can be squared with the imperatives of an effective response to terrorism. Indeed, Sossin asserts that the 'safeguards and supervisory scrutiny imposed by administrative law may well lead to more accurate, more effective, and more just decision-making in matters of national security'.

• • •

In conclusion, the essays in this book contain important contributions to the very necessary democratic debate about Bill C-36. This robust democratic process honours our free and democratic society and distinguishes it from those who would use violence and weapons, not essays and speeches, for political ends. The commentators in this book have brought their varied expertise, experience and perspectives to bear on the many parts of the government's omnibus bill in an incredibly short time. They have discharged their duties as both citizens and academics in a most admirable way. I am very proud to have been associated with the collective effort necessary to produce such learned and thoughtful commentary that can contribute so directly to debates that are fundamental to both our security and our freedom.

Notes

1 First Session Thirty–seventh Parliament 49-50 Elizabeth II, 2001.
2 Ulrich Beck, *Risk Society: Towards a New Modernity* (London: Sage Publications, 1992).
3 *The Emergencies Act*, S.C. 1988, c. 29.
4 *Canada Evidence Act*, R.S.C. 1985, c. C-5.

The Security of Freedom

The Permanence of the Temporary:
Can Emergency Powers be Normalized?

DAVID DYZENHAUS[1]
Faculty of Law
University of Toronto

I view with apprehension the attitude of judges who on a mere question of construction when face to face with claims involving the liberty of the subject show themselves more executive minded than the executive. Their function is to give words their natural meaning ... In this country, amid the clash of arms, the laws are not silent. They may be changed, but they speak the same language in war as in peace. It has always been one of the pillars of freedom, one of the principles of liberty for which on recent authority we are now fighting, that the judges ... stand between the subject and any attempted encroachment on his liberty by the executive, alert to see that any coercive action is justified in law. In this case I have listened to arguments which might have been addressed acceptably to the Court of King's Bench of Charles I.

> Lord Atkin, dissenting, in *Liversidge* v *Anderson* [1942] AC 206, 244.

Postscript – I wrote this speech some three months before the recent events in New York and Washington. They are a reminder that in matters of national security, the cost of failure can be high. This seems to me to underline the need for the judicial arm of government to respect the decisions of ministers of the Crown on the question of whether support for terrorist activities in a foreign country constitutes a threat to national security. It is not only that the executive has access to special information and expertise in these matters. It is also that such decisions, with serious potential results for the community, require a legitimacy which can be conferred only by entrusting them to persons responsible to the community through the democratic process. If the people are to accept the consequences of such decisions, they must be made by persons whom the people have elected and whom they can remove.

> Lord Hoffman, concurring, in *Secretary of State for the Home Department* v. *Rehman*, [2001] UKHL 47.

The Anti-Terrorism Bill,[2] says the *Globe and Mail,* is 'the exception, not the norm.' The *Globe* goes on to argue that, because the bill deals with an emergency by stripping Canadians of civil liberties, it should have an expiry date, subject to 'Parliament's considered renewal.' A crisis, it says, is 'by definition finite.'[3]

In talking of the 'exception' and the 'norm,' the *Globe*'s editorial writer uses, perhaps deliberately, language that was coined by Carl Schmitt. Schmitt was one of the leading legal and political theorists of Weimar Germany. He wrote extensively and brilliantly on emergency powers and the problems they pose for a state committed to the rule of law. It is not surprising that his work seems highly relevant when our government seeks to respond to an emergency by crafting a law that both recognises the emergency and seeks to contain it.

But it is important to know that Schmitt thought that it followed from his analysis of the relationship between legal norm and political exception that a state committed to the rule of law could *not* limit its response to an emergency. In short, an effective response has to be outside of the rule of law, and so cannot be limited by the rule of law. Schmitt also concluded that liberal democratic states could not respond effectively to fundamental challenges, unless they were to give up on their fundamental commitments, which is to say, unless they were to forego liberal democracy.

As we will see, Schmitt is wrong that a liberal democratic state is incapable of responding effectively to a political emergency. Moreover, it can do so on its own terms – without stepping outside of the rule of law. But Schmitt's analysis remains relevant when a liberal democratic government does step outside of the rule of law, as I will argue is inevitably the case when anti-terrorism legislation is the means adopted to deal with an emergency. Once that step is taken, we have to hope that the judges who interpret the anti-terrorism statute will take seriously the idea that, as judges, they are committed to upholding the rule of law. We have to hope that our judges will be able to reduce the extent to which our government is seeking to make Canada into a state where the rule of law is a luxury, rather than one of the fundamental commitments of our society.

It is important to keep in mind here that the idea of the rule of law means more than the fact that a statute has been validly enacted according to the rules of 'manner and form' observed by Parliament. For example, judges in Canada will hold that a statutory provision that seeks to immunise totally an administrative agency against judicial review is invalid because the rule of law requires that judges be able to ensure than an agency stays within the limits of its authority.[4] Moreover, the Supreme Court has stated that the rule of law consists of principles that are part of the unwritten or common law constitution of Canada, for example, principles that protect judicial independence.[5] In short, a formally valid statute can offend against the rule of law because there is more to compliance with the rule of law than compliance with formal criteria of validity.

I want to begin by noting that much of my title is not original – it comes from an article written in 1966 in the *South African Law Journal* by a lawyer, AS Mathews and a psychologist, RC Albino – 'The Permanence of the Temporary: an Examination of the 90- and 180-Day Detention Laws.'[6] The statutes to which they were reacting permitted the detention of opponents of apartheid whom a policeman suspected of being involved in the activities of outlawed organisations, especially the African National Congress led by Nelson Mandela. The detention orders were protected from judicial review by draconian privative clauses – statutory provisions that oust the review authority of the courts. The particular case to which they were reacting was a decision by South Africa's highest Court, the Appellate Division, *Rossouw* v. *Sachs*,[7] where in issue was the conditions of detention of Albie Sachs – now a judge of South Africa's Constitutional Court and a revered figure in Canada – under section 17 of the 90–Day statute.[8]

The case came to the Appellate Division by way of the government's appeal against the decision of two judges of the Cape Provincial Division, which had said that to deprive Sachs of reading matter would amount to 'punishment' and that it would be 'surprising to find that the Legislature intended punishment to be meted out to an unconvicted prisoner.' The discretion of the officer in charge of detention in regard to such issues, was the judges said, 'at all times subject to correction in a court of law.'[9]

The Appellate Division found that it could not order that Sachs be given reading and writing materials, since the purpose of the detention provision was clearly to use psychological pressure to 'induce the detainee to speak.'[10] Moreover, the Court said that it was influenced by the fact that subversive activities of various kinds directed against the public order and the safety of the State are by no means unknown, and sec. 17 is plainly designed to combat such activities. Such being the circumstances whereunder sec. 17 was placed upon the Statute Book, this Court should, while bearing in mind the enduring importance of the liberty of the individual, in my judgment approach the construction of sec. 17 with due regard to the objects which that section is designed to attain.[11]

Mathews and Albino argue that the Appellate Division, in contrast to the Cape Provincial Division, declined to impose any constraints of legality on the detention, even though the statute was silent as to the particular constraints sought. And, in so declining, the Court accepted the permanence of the temporary, the government's sense that South Africa was in a permanent state of emergency, so that a declaration of a state of emergency – an intrinsically temporary exception to the norm – did not suffice. Instead, one enacts ordinary common or garden statutes that permit government to respond outside of the rule of law.

Now the 90–Day detention provision had to be renewed each year and detentions were for a limited period. However, not only did the Appellate Division later hold that there was no limit on successive periods of detention, but in any case new terrorism statutes followed which permitted indefinite detention and which did not require annual renewal. Generally, the Appellate Division took its cue from the statutory barrage of security legislation and sedulously followed the line of reasoning first set out in *Rossouw* v. *Sachs*. Thus, as Mathews and Albino predicted, the Court set the stage for much of the gross human rights abuse that occurred in police detention, abuse which has now been documented in the Truth and Reconciliation Commission's *Final Report*. And, it should be noted, the judges' role in permitting such abuse to happen also came under the spotlight of the Truth and Reconciliation Commission during its special Hearing into the role of the legal profession during apartheid. The judges were, as I argued in my own submission to that Hearing, accountable for having facilitated the shadows and secrecy of the world in which the security forces operated. Thus they bear some responsibility for the bitter legacy of hurt which was the focus of the Truth and Reconciliation Commission.[12]

The Bill we are considering at this conference is far less draconian than the South African security statutes. It is free of formal privative clauses which seek to oust judicial review, though there are some official decisions that are immunised against review – the decision by the Attorney

General to withhold information – and some official certificates, while subject to the scrutiny of the Federal Court for reasonableness, are not reviewable by any further court. Generally, the Bill has been drafted with an anxious eye on the potential for successful challenges under the *Charter*. At the same time, cabinet ministers, most notably the Minister of Justice, are warning judges that they might have to rethink their approach to adjudication in the wake of September 11th, and I want now to argue, this warning is of a piece with the very idea of terrorism.

Put differently, the stripping of our civil liberties in the cause of combating terrorism is relatively speaking quite minor, minor, that is, compared to what happens in fascist and quasi-fascist regimes. But the fact that this stripping happens under the rubric of combating terrorism suffices to bring our legal order closer than we should like to the 'legal' orders of such regimes. This is so especially when the warning to judges can only be interpreted as a government signal that the judges should change their understanding of the *Charter*, at least in so far as they rethink their approach to section 1 and so to the question of what justifies limits on our rights and freedoms in a free and democratic society.[13] To explain this, I return to Schmitt.[14]

Schmitt's early work on states of emergency makes a useful distinction between the two kinds of 'dictatorship' – rule outside of the rule of law – for which a society faced with an emergency might opt.[15] There is 'sovereign dictatorship,' where the government is utterly unconstrained by any limits, whether on the facts that justify the claim that there is an emergency, on the time limits of the emergency, and on the means that may be used to respond to the emergency. In contrast, a 'commissarial dictatorship' is dictatorship on commission of the people, and the terms of that commission are legally limited in respect of all three of the issues just listed – justification, time, and means of response. In contemporary parlance, the commissarial dictatorship is a 'reference model' of emergency powers, in that it seeks to bring the response to the emergency into line with democratic principles.[16] Requirements in this regard include that the emergency legislation predate the crisis, that the legislation contains controls on the exercise of emergency powers, and that the legislation and powers are to be applied as provisional, temporary measures.[17]

In later work, during the disintegration of the Weimar Republic, Schmitt's arguments presuppose that the distinction between the two kinds of dictatorship is illusory. The declaration of a state of emergency, as he points out, indicates that the state is compelled to respond to a political challenge to its existence that is so grave that the ordinary criminal law and ordinary mechanisms of law enforcement do not suffice. But, says Schmitt, if we are to understand the nature of such a challenge, we have to understand the nature of politics. The fundamental distinction of the political is between friend and enemy, where what matters is not the basis of the distinction – ethnic, religious, economic – but its intensity. The distinction arises when one political entity regards another as its 'existential negation' – as threatening its very existence – so that the appropriate response is whatever means will bring about the death of the enemy.[18]

Before September 11th, these ideas would have had little resonance at a Canadian Conference on some legal issue. They would have seemed plucked from the overheated terms of the debates of late Weimar, where the forces of the right were squaring up to the left, the middle ground seemed to be vanishing, and the stage was set for the Nazi seizure of power. But if one thinks back to the initial response of President Bush, the ideas do resonate. At the time when Bush was visibly reeling from the shock of the attack on his country, we were told that at stake was the very existence of Western democracy, that the West would have to embark on a 'crusade' of 'infinite justice,' that other countries had to see that they were either 'with us or against us,' and that the rules of the response were those of the Wild West, that is, anything goes.

Now it is important to take into account that the enemy here, the networks of Islamist terror, see the West in just these terms.[19] Schmitt's understanding of politics describes exactly their view of the West, especially of the United States of America. Since they already understood United States foreign policy as a 'crusade' designed to destroy Islam, Bush's initial response simply accepted the terms of their Schmittian view of politics.

Since then reality and *realpolitik* have led to a shift in the rhetoric of the Bush administration, including a description of the armed intervention in Afghanistan as a military police action, rather than total war. But this is a shift, not a change. In both the USA and Canada, we seem by and large to accept Bin-Laden's own understanding of the threat he and other Islamists pose to us – that the nature of his challenge is both fundamental and without a foreseeable end, since there is no end without total victory.[20] Politicians and newscasters on both sides of the border intone their mantra that the world changed on September 11th and talk of the threat as one posed to 'the homeland' – a phrase designed to evoke images of alien invasion.[21]

This Conference is about the Bill on terrorism, not about foreign policy. But one cannot understand that Bill without seeing that it is designed to deal with that same mysterious enemy, though on home ground because his soldiers, whoever they are, are already within our walls and more might seek to enter. It is worth recalling that within Canada, the initial official rhetoric, at least from the Prime Minister, was designed to avoid Schmittian terms. But the Anti-Terrorism Bill shows that Canadian official rhetoric has changed.[22] And in defending her opposition to calls for 'sunset clauses' in the Bill, Anne McLellan, Federal Minister of Justice, says the following:

> Furthermore, placing a sunset clause on new Criminal Code offences and new investigative and prosecution tools will impair efforts to identify and prosecute terrorists and their supporters. A sunset clause for the entire bill would lead to a legislative vacuum. We cannot expect terrorism to disappear in a few years, so it would be irresponsible to suspend our legislation in three years, thereby running the risk of not having effective laws in place for extended periods[23]

Now we would not, of course, have anything like a vacuum. The Criminal Code already supplies law-enforcement officials with a battery of offences. And no-one is arguing against vastly improved resources for both law-enforcement and for intelligence-gathering, although my argument assumes that we should not let security be defined by the government or by agencies such as CSIS.

However, it is crucial to see that the *point* of the Bill is to *create* a legal vacuum. The Bill is designed to remove, in so far as the *Charter* permits this, law-enforcement and intelligence-gathering activities from the discipline of the rule of law. And by rule of law here I mean simply the general principles of the common law of judicial review that require openness and accountability of officials when they make decisions affecting important individual interests.

The reference model of emergency sketched above has been developed along lines that accord with this understanding of the rule of law. Many versions of the model go far beyond strict temporal controls and legislative oversight of executive action. They require in addition that the invocation of the emergency, the regulations promulgated under emergency legislation, and action done under such regulations be subject to effective control by the courts.

The central idea of the model is that it complies with democratic principles. Hence, even – indeed especially – in the direst of political circumstances, we have a right as citizens, or simply as individuals subject to the coercive authority of the state, to demand that, as Lord Atkin put it, 'any coercive action is justified in law.' As he argued in his dissent in *Liversidge* v. *Anderson*, the phrase 'justified in law' is emptied of all meaning if we take executive officials at their word. What we have is rule by men, not the rule of law. Moreover, these are often the least visible and thus least accountable of our civil servants – the men who are attracted to and who live in the strange and shadowy world of the security services.

The most serious derogation from the rule of law in the Bill is inherent in all anti-terrorism statutes. The target is 'terrorism,' an offence which is undefinable since it presupposes that there is an internal *political* enemy, someone so existentially different that that we cannot name him in advance in order to deal with him either through the ordinary criminal law, or by relaxing the rule of law to some extent for a definable and carefully supervised period. The Anti-Terrorism Bill is no exception here, nor could it be. Nor will attempts to refine the definitions help, as they will pile definition on top of definition, leading to the same vague result. For this reason, those who think that the statute is likely to end up being used against targets other than the Islamist terrorists are absolutely right. It will be for the agents of law-enforcement and security to tell us who the terrorist is, when they have him in their grasp.

'Sovereign is he,' said Schmitt, 'who decides on the state of exception,'[24] which is to say that the sovereign is the one who decides on the nature of the emergency as well as on how to respond to it. Our Anti-Terrorism Bill gives to the executive virtual sovereignty in the first respect and a lot of slack in the second. Most notable in respect of response are the provisions that require an individual to answer questions and permit his or her detention while subject to interrogation[25] and the provisions that give to the Attorney General an unreviewable authority to withhold information, because he deems it necessary to protect 'international relations or national defence or security.'[26]

But even if changes are made to such provisions as the Bill makes its way into law, and even if sunset clauses are introduced, the fact that what we have is not emergency legislation but a terrorism law – an emergency law masquerading as an ordinary statute – means that we have stepped outside of the rule of law. Terrorism legislation, because it seeks to normalize the exception by declaring a permanent state of emergency, is inherently a deviation from commissarial dictatorship or the reference model of emergency. The rule of law is relaxed, though not totally, and there is no clearly defined threat. We have the permanence of the temporary, an attempt to normalize the exception.

Schmitt would have said of our Anti-Terrorism Bill that it exemplifies the inability of liberal democracies to deal with fundamental political threats. If they seek to defend themselves, they have to give up on their own fundamental commitments, including their commitment to the rule of law. That goes to show, he thought, that liberal democracy is a sham. My view is that Schmitt was wrong, as was the Baron de Montesquieu when he said that 'The practice of the freest nation that ever existed induces me to think that there are cases in which a veil should be drawn for a while over liberty, as it was customary to cover the statues of the gods.'[27] For, as the reference model of emergency law shows, liberty – and its protection through the rule of law – is not an all-or-nothing sacred object which we either worship or veil. We can still require that government act in accordance with the rule of law, and thus protect our liberty, even when there is an emergency. However, our own government's response to September 11th – at least for the moment – seeks to prove Schmitt right.

It is crucial to note in this respect that the government is well aware that the point of the Bill is in fact to create a rule of law vacuum to the extent that this is possible without using section 33 to explicitly override the *Charter*. Their awareness is this regard is, as I suggested, signaled in the messages to the judiciary that judges will have to interpret the law differently because of the way that the world has changed. In other words, judges are now supposed to give greater weight than they would have done in the past to government arguments that national security considerations should weigh more heavily in the justification both of statutory limits on *Charter*-protected right or freedoms and of decisions by executive officials that do the same. If there were no damage done to the rule of law, then judges would not need to rethink their interpretative practices.

Need we worry about Canadian judges' commitment to the rule of law? This is a very uncomfortable question to ask, not least because the judges who will have to interpret the statute that is coming their way did not invite being placed in the predicament they will soon face. But because they will find themselves in that predicament, we cannot avoid asking the question.

My fear, to be blunt, is that our government is quite deliberately seeking to do what the South African government achieved during apartheid. The government introduces legislation that is inherently suspect from the perspective of the rule of law, but avoids in so far as this is possible provisions that seem in flagrant violation of rule of law principles. The dirty work is done by those charged with implementing the law and the government expects that judges who hear challenges to the validity of particular acts will put aside their role as guardians of the rule of law because in issue is the security of the state. In short, the government – and the Parliament under its control – can avoid responsibility for stepping too far outside of the rule of law, since they leave that job to the security services, and rely on judges to be either cowed or convinced into a stance of relaxing the discipline of the rule of law.[28]

If we take our cue from the recent path-breaking decision in *Baker* v. *Canada* the answer to my question about concern in regard to judicial commitment to the rule of law would be an emphatic 'no.'[29] In that case, the Supreme Court held, relying on the common law of judicial review, that an act of discretion that would in the past have been thought by many judges and administrative lawyers to be pretty much 'unfettered' by rule of law considerations was subject to the rule of law.[30] The Court said that:

> [D]iscretion must ... be exercised in a manner that is within a reasonable interpretation of the margin of manoeuvre contemplated by the legislature, in accordance with the principles of the rule of law (*Roncarelli* v. *Duplessis*, [1959] SCR 121), in line with general principles of administrative law governing the exercise of discretion, and consistent with the Canadian Charter of Rights and Freedoms (*Slaight Communications Inc.* v. *Davidson*, [1989] 1 SCR 1038).[31]

In addition, the Court established a common law duty to give reasons for decisions whenever an official decision affected important interests, so that the onus fell on the official who made the decision to show he or she had taken rule of law values as well the statutory considerations properly into account.

Similarly, in *United States of America* v. *Burns*, the issue was the discretion of the Minister of Justice whether to seek assurances that the United States of America would not execute extradited individuals who had been or might be found guilty of offences which are punished by death. The Court found that the discretion was not itself inconsistent with the *Charter*, but that *Charter* considerations radically tilted the balance in favour of requiring assurances.[32] In other words, the Minister of Justice retained her discretion but she would have to have extremely strong reasons to justify a decision not to seek an assurance. As the Court held in an earlier decision, courts should in general defer to administrative expertise, but expertise has to be justified by supplying coherent reasons for conclusions.[33]

In sum, the dominant trend in the Court has been to defer to the Legislature's delegation of authority to an official, as well as to the fact that such officials are more likely expert in a way that courts are not when it comes to policy and politics. And of course national security considerations are eminently political. But at the same time, the Court has required that official decisions are justified, not only by reference to the objectives of the statute, but by reference to fundamental legal values, including the rule of law. On the basis of established legal principles, it follows that the more important the interest affected by the decision, the more heavy the onus of justification. It also follows that, to the extent that the Anti-Terrorism statute will give to officials the authority to avoid discharging that onus, that authority is in violation of both the rule of law and the *Charter*. Finally, it should follow that the legitimate exercise of such authority is conditional on officials' preparedness to demonstrate that their decisions are reasonable in the sense that they are justified by reasons before a court of law, even if that justification takes place in *in camera* proceedings.

However, there is cause for concern. First, even the Supreme Court of Canada, has shown itself to think that the rule of law does not discipline the decision of security matters. Take for example Sopinka J's 1992 judgment for the Court in *Chiarelli* v. *Canada (Minister of Justice)*.[34] Not only did he suggest there that Canadian citizens are entitled to more protection under section 7 of the *Charter* than non-Canadians, but he emphasized the need for judges to recognize the state's 'considerable interest in effectively conducting national security investigations and in protecting police sources.' Here he quoted from a judgment by Lord Denning in *R*. v. *Secretary of State for Home Department, Ex parte Hosenball*.[35]

The point here is not that state has no such interests, but whether the state is – to use Schmitt's terms – a sovereign dictator when it comes to defining those interests. In evaluating Sopinka J's judgment in this regard, one should not underestimate the importance of his approving quotation from *Hosenball*. In that decision, Lord Denning upheld the deportation of an American journalist from the United Kingdom, after a process in which the journalist was told only that he was a threat to security and public safety. In the passage quoted approvingly by Sopinka J, Lord

Denning concluded that the Secretary of State could decide to keep his information secret if he deemed that to be in the public interest. In a passage Sopinka J did not quote, but which offers the justification for that conclusion, Lord Denning said that in national security cases – when the 'state is itself endangered' – 'our cherished freedoms may have to take second place ... Time after time Parliament has so enacted and the courts have loyally followed.'[36]

Lord Denning cited among the judicial authority for this proposition, the decision of the House of Lords during the Second World War, *Liversidge* v. *Anderson*.[37] But the majority judgments in that case are not only regarded as the low-water mark in British judges' fidelity to the rule of law in the twentieth century, they also formed the foundation stone for the South African, Appellate Division's judgment in *Rossouw* v. *Sachs*. Other Canadian Supreme Court decisions from the 1990s might lead to a similarly pessimistic conclusion.[38]

To a large extent, the issues will turn on whether judges, in reaching what Rand J called in *Roncarelli* v. *Duplessis* 'a reasonable interpretation of the margin of manoeuvre contemplated by the legislature,'[39] regard the context for interpretation as set by the Anti-Terrorism statute or by the commitment of the Canadian legal order to the rule of law, in which each particular provision or act of discretion has to be evaluated.

If they take the statute as setting the limits of the interpretative context, their understanding of each particular provision will be that it is to be interpreted in light of the fact that an anti-terrorism statute is a step away from the rule of law. They will then regard the statute as setting up a twenty first century equivalent of Charles I's 'Court' of Star Chamber, which gave both the power to detain and the authority to determine the legality of the detention to the king.

The very recent decision of the House of Lords from which the second epigraph to this chapter is taken is troubling in this respect. There the Law Lords unanimously approved the line of reasoning that goes from *Liversidge* to *Hosenball* that in effect exempts the executive from rule of law controls when, in the view of the executive, national security demands this.[40] Moreover, as Lord Hoffman indicates, the judges will be even more resolute in this tack in the wake of September 11th.

Lord Hoffman seems to hold the curious, even contradictory, view that democracy is served by exempting very important official decisions from the general democratic requirement that decisions that affect important interests have to be justified by reasons if they are to be legitimate. And he goes well beyond what I recall any apartheid era executive-minded judge doing. For he announces in advance his readiness to reduce himself, as one judge at the time described the majority in *Liversidge*, to one of the 'mice squeaking under a chair in the Home Office.'[41] If the Law Lords adopt this approach in the wake of the statutory incorporation of the *European Convention of Human Rights*, and when two of the judges – Lords Steyn and Lord Hoffman – are former South Africans with a record of being enthusiasts of human rights, what can we expect of our own highest Court?

If, on the other hand, our judges insist that they will not impute an intention to the Legislature to step outside of the rule of law, unless on every occasion the Legislature very explicitly says this is the particular provision's purpose, they will uphold the commitment of their legal order to the rule of law. Their choice will be between, as Lord Atkin described it in his dissent in *Liversidge*, being 'more executive minded than the executive,' or being judges who understand that, unless they are forced by explicit legislative statements to do otherwise, their obligation as judges is to uphold the rule of law.

This last point raises my second worry. The Supreme Court might well require that the Anti-Terrorism statute be interpreted in what our present Chief Justice has agreed is a legal culture of 'justification,' one in which all official decisions have to be shown to be demonstrably justified in accordance with a principle of legality or the rule of law.[42] But, as things stand, the first and sometimes the last port of call for those affected by official decisions is often the Federal Court, some of whose judges have a reputation for being 'more executive minded than the executive.'

Moreover, the Anti-Terrorism Bill provides for fifteen additional judges to be appointed to a Court whose total complement presently is somewhere around twenty nine, including the appellate branch.[43] While this provision might just indicate how much more work the government thinks is coming that Court's way, that the work will have to be done in the context of an Anti-Terrorism statute should raise public alarm bells about the possibility of court-packing.

This is not just a point about the personality of judges. The ambiguities that necessarily attend both the 'legal' definition of terrorism and the 'legal' response to it require a very frank public discussion of the interpretative approaches we can expect of our judges. What we might get in Canada is the reverse of South Africa where it was much more likely that judges of first instance would uphold the rule of law than the Appellate Division. And it will be small comfort for someone to know that he has to wait for rescue from the Supreme Court, when in issue, for example, is that his supposedly limited detention period for an investigative hearing has turned into indefinite detention because, as in South Africa, he is released only to be immediately rearrested; and the official says to the court: 'trust me, it's necessary.'[44]

In conclusion, I want to recall that the idea that the rule of law can be productively understood as establishing a culture of justification was coined by a South African administrative lawyer to describe the terminus of the journey away from the apartheid culture of legal authoritarianism.[45] That journey was begun in the light of an experience of violence, virtual civil war, and terrorism (on both sides), which I still trust will not afflict Canadians.

When societies with such experience deliberately turn their backs on 'legal' instruments such as our Anti-Terrorism Bill, one has to wonder about the wisdom of embracing such measures. And since they will be embraced, we will have to trust that our judges will not so much accept the normality of the exception, but try to make it less exceptional, that is, more subject to legal norms.

Notes

1 Professor of Law and Philosophy, University of Toronto. I thank Nicholas Blake, Murray Hunt, Audrey Macklin, Kent Roach, David Schneiderman, Rabinder Singh, Lorne Sossin, Michael Taggart, and Mariana Valverde for comments on a draft. The final version does not take into account any changes after November 5th, 2001 to the Bill.

2 First Session Thirty-Seventh Parliament 49–50 Elizabeth II, 2001 (Bill C-36). All references in bold below are to sections of this Bill.

3 *Globe and Mail*, lead editorial, October 23rd, 2001, A16.

4 See *Crevier v. Attorney General of Quebec* [1981] 2 SCR 220.

5 *Reference re Remuneration of Judges of the Provincial Court of Prince Edward Island* [1997] 3 SCR 3.

6 (1966) 83 *South African Law Journal* 16.

7 1964 (2) SA 551 (A).

8 The '90–day detention law' was the name given to section 17 of Act 37 of 1963, enacted to assist the government in countering the underground activities of the African National Congress and other liberation organisations. Section 17(1) provided that

> Notwithstanding anything to the contrary in any law contained, any commissioned officer ... may ... without warrant arrest ... any person whom he suspects upon reasonable grounds of having committed or intending ... to commit any

offence under the Suppression of Communism Act ... , or the Unlawful Organizations Act ... , or the offence of sabotage, or who in his opinion is in possession
of information relating to the commission of such offence ... , and detain such
person ... for interrogation ... , until such person has in the opinion of the Commissioner of Police replied satisfactorily to all questions at the said interrogation,
but no such person shall be so detained for more than ninety days on any particular occasion when he is so arrested.

Section 17(2) provided that no person was to 'have access' to the detainee except
with the consent of the Minister of Justice or a commissioned officer, though the
person had to be visited not less than once a week by a magistrate. Section 17(3)
provided that, 'No court shall have jurisdiction to order the release from custody
of any person so detained ...'

The section was effective for twelve months and thereafter was subject to annual
renewal by proclamation of the State President.

9 The decision is unreported. For detailed analysis of the Appellate Division's decision, see my *Hard Cases in Wicked Legal Systems: South African Law in the
   Perspective of Legal Philosophy* (Oxford: Clarendon Press, 1991), chap. 4.

10 *Rossouw v. Sachs*, 560–1.

11 Ibid., 563.

12 See *Truth and Reconciliation Commission of South Africa Report* (Cape Town: Juta
   & Co., 1998, 5 volumes) vol. 4. For my account of this Hearing, see *Judging the
   Judges, Judging Ourselves: Truth, Reconciliation and the Apartheid Legal Order*
   (Oxford: Hart Publishing, 1998); for the point about judges, see 150–77, at 160.

13 I should mention that, as a former South African whose academic interests have
   focused on situations where the rule of law is under deep stress – apartheid South
   Africa and Germany between the wars, it was until very recently literally unimaginable to me that my work on 'wicked legal systems' could become relevant to Canada.

14 I rely in what follows on my *Legality and Legitimacy: Carl Schmitt, Hans Kelsen
   and Hermann Heller in Weimar* (Oxford: Clarendon Press, 1997), and on 'Legal
   Theory in the Collapse of Weimar: Contemporary Lessons?' (1997) 91 *American
   Political Science Review* 121. I also rely on Gabriel L Negretto and José Antonio
   Aguilar Rivera, 'Liberalism and Emergency Powers in Latin America: Reflections
   on Carl Schmitt and the Theory of Constitutional Dictatorship,' (2000) 21 *Cardozo
   Law Review*, 1797, as well – indeed especially – on Oren Gross, 'The Normless and
   Exceptionless Exception: Carl Schmitt's Theory of Emergency Powers and the
   "Norm-Exception" Dichotomy' (2000) 21 *Cardozo Law Review* 1825.

15 Carl Schmitt, *Die Diktatur: Von den Anfaengen des Modernen Souveraenitaets-
   gedankens bis zum Proletarischen Klassenkampf* (Berlin: Dunckler & Humblot,
   1990, first pub. 1922).

16 See Gross, 1855.

17 My list is taken pretty well *verbatim* from Gross, ibid.

18 Carl Schmitt, *The Concept of the Political* (New Jersey: Rutgers University Press,
   1976, George Schwab trans., first pub. 1932).

19 See the numerous *fatwas* reproduced in Yossef Bodansky, *Bin-Laden: The Man Who Declared War on America* (New York: Random House, 2001).

20 Bodansky, ibid, argues convincingly that there is a system of overlapping networks with each particular network and its leadership designed to be 'redundant,' that is, the elimination of either the network as a whole or its leadership will not eliminate this source of terrorism.

21 To be fair, Peter Mansbridge of the CBC news is the only Canadian I've heard use 'homeland' talk, but given his position, that is of some significance.

22 For an egregious, early example of this kind of overblown language, see the abstract of the article by Irwin Cotler, a Liberal Member of Parliament, and former Law Professor, 'Towards a Counter-Terrorism Law and Policy' (1998) 10 *Terrorism and Political Violence* 1.

23 *Globe and Mail*, October 25, 2001, A18.

24 Carl Schmitt, *Political Theology* (Cambridge, Mass.: MIT Press, 1988, George Schwab trans., first pub. 1922), 1.

25 See *Investigative Hearing*, 83.28.

26 See *Prohibition Certificate*, 38.13.

27 I take this quotation from Negretto and Aguilar Rivera, where it is the epigraph.

28 See my *Judging the Judges*, 150–77, for full analysis of this strategy,

29 [1999] 2 SCR 817. For more analysis of the issues raised here, see, this volume, Lorne Sossin, 'The Intersection of Administrative Law with the Anti-Terrorist Bill.'

30 The discretion was to stay a deportation order if, in the discretion of the official, this was required on 'humanitarian and compassionate' grounds.

31 *Baker*, 853–4.

32 2001 SCC 7.

33 *Canada (Director of Investigations and Research)* v. *Southam Inc.* [1997] 1 SCR 748, para. 62.

34 [1992] 1 SCR 711.

35 [1977] 1 WLR 766.

36 Ibid., 778.

37 [1942] AC 206. The issue between the judges was simply whether the Home Secretary's say so was conclusive of the necessity to detain under Regulation 18B of the Defence (General) Regulations, 1939, or whether reasons were required. The regulation provided that 'If the Secretary of State has reasonable cause to believe any person to be of hostile origins or associations or to have been recently concerned in acts prejudicial to public safety or the defence of the realm or in the preparation or instigation of such acts and that by reason thereof it is necessary to exercise control over him, he may make an order against that person directing that he be detained.' For analysis, see *Hard Cases in Wicked Legal Systems*, chaps 4 and 8. For a devastating account of the damage to civil liberties under this detention provision, with no apparent benefit for security, see AW Brian Simpson, *In the Highest Degree Odious: Detention without Trial in Wartime Britain* (Oxford: Clarendon Press, 1992).

38 For example, *Thomson* v. *Canada (Deputy Minister of Agriculture)* [1992] 1 SCR 385, L'Heureux-Dubé J dissenting.

39 See text to note 31, above.

40 In *Secretary of State for the Home Department* v. *Rehman*, [2001] UKHL 47, in issue was a decision of the Special Immigration Appeals Commission which had sought to widen the definition of state security so that the question of when a matter of state security is not determined by the say so of the minister. The House of Lords reaffirmed the narrow definition.

41 Stable J, quoted in RVF Heuston, '*Liversidge* v. *Anderson* in Retrospect,' (1970) 86 *Law Quarterly Review* 33, at 51.

42 The Honourable Madame Justice Beverly McLachlin, 'The Roles of Administrative Law and Courts in Maintaining the Rule of Law,' (1999) 12 *Canadian Journal of Administrative Law and Practice* 171, at 174, 1867.

43 See 95.

44 Here it is provincial court judges who are charged with supervising the provision but I am not sure that this is less of a cause for concern. Notice in this regard that the investigative hearing provision, just because it allows for detention, seems designed to put psychological pressure on the detainee to speak, as the Appellate Division interpreted the statutory provision at stake in *Rossouw* v. *Sachs*. That is, it will be interpreted in this way if the context for interpretation is set by the statute rather than the rule of law. In Canada, judges have a legal resource in the *Charter* which South African judges lacked during apartheid. Hence, it sometimes it might be best for Canadian judges to interpret a statute in its worst possible light, since that interpretation will make of the statutory provision in question something that not only limits the *Charter*, but cannot be justified as a legitimate limitation. Analogous issues are explored in Kent Roach, *The Supreme Court on Trial: Judicial Activism or Democratic Dialogue* (Toronto: Irwin Law, 2001).

45 For an exploration of the late Etienne Mureinik's ideas, see my 'Law as Justification: Etienne Mureinik's Conception of Legal Culture' (1998) 14 *South African Journal on Human Rights*, 11.

Cutting Down Trees: Law-Making Under the Shadow of Great Calamities

OREN GROSS[1]

Benjamin N. Cardozo School of Law

ROPER: So now you'd give the Devil benefit of law!

MORE: Yes. What would you do? Cut a great road through the law to get after the Devil?

ROPER: I'd cut down every law in England to do that!

MORE: Oh? And when the last law was down, and the Devil turned round on you – where would you hide, Roper, the laws all being flat? This country's planted thick with laws from coast to coast – man's laws, not God's – and if you cut them down – and you're just the man to do it – d'you really think you could stand upright in the winds that would blow then? Yes, I'd give the Devil benefit of law, for my own safety's sake.[2]

[L]et us not deceive ourselves as to the nature of the threat that faces us; that it can be defeated easily or simply with one swift strike. We must be guided by a commitment to do what works in the long run not by what makes us feel better in the short run.[3]

Desperate measures have a way of enduring beyond the life of the situations that give rise to them.[4]

I. Introduction

In many respects the world post the September 11th terrorist attacks on the World Trade Center and the Pentagon is not similar to the one we lived in before that tragic Tuesday. Yet in some important respects nothing is really new, or at least not conceptually new. Much of the discussion around legal matters pertaining to dealing with terrorism and the structuring of counter-terrorism measures and extraordinary governmental powers to answer to future threats falls into that latter category. It is not only countries such as my own, Israel, that have grappled with terrorism and counter-terrorism for decades, but other democracies as well. Whether you focus on such issues as the definition of 'terrorist activity,' the incorporation of a sunset clause into the proposed *Anti-terrorism Act* (*'Bill C-36'*), the issue of investigative hearings, combating the financial infrastructure of terrorism, or preventive detentions, there is much to learned from past experience in order to avoid repeating old mistakes. Unfortunately history also tells us that it is quite likely that old mistakes will, indeed, be repeated. Speaking in Jerusalem in 1988, Justice William J. Brennan stated that:

> There is considerably less to be proud about, and a good deal to be embarrassed about, when one reflects on the shabby treatment civil liberties have received in the United States during times of war and perceived threats to its national security. ... After each perceived security crisis ended, the United States has remorsefully realized that the abrogation of civil liberties was unnecessary. But it has proven unable to prevent itself from repeating the error when the next crisis came along.[5]

This paper explores some of the reasons that explain why it is that we seem unable to prevent ourselves from repeating past errors when dealing with acute emergencies and terrorist threats. It draws attention to some fundamental challenges that may skew the judgment and legal decision-making processes involving law-makers, the government and judges.

II. A Tension of 'Tragic Dimensions'

There exists a tension of 'tragic dimensions' between democratic values and responding to terrorism.[6] Democratic nations faced with serious terrorist threats must 'maintain and protect life, the liberties necessary to a vibrant democracy, and the unity of the society, the loss of which can turn a healthy and diverse nation into a seriously divided and violent one.'[7] At the same time, exigencies and acute crises directly challenge the most fundamental concepts of a constitutional democracy. The question then arises to what extent, if at all, can violation of fundamental democratic values be justified in the name of survival of the democratic-constitutional order itself? and if so, to what extent can a democratic, constitutional government defend the state without losing its democratic nature and transforming into an authoritarian regime? Frequently it is precisely the strengths of democracy that are considered its weaknesses in times of exigency and hence as something to be dispensed with, at least until the threat is over.

Take, for example, the notion that a government must be of limited powers, a government of laws, not of men (or women).[8] When an extreme exigency arises it leads, almost invariably, to the strengthening of the executive branch of government at the expense not only of the other two branches, but also that of the citizenry at large. The government's ability to act swiftly, secretly and decisively against the threat to the life of the nation becomes superior to the ordinary principles of limitation on governmental powers and individual rights.[9] Crises tend to result in the expansion of governmental powers, concentration of powers in the hands of the executive and the concomitant contraction of individual freedoms and liberties.[10] Enhanced and newly created powers are given to, or asserted by, the government as necessary to successfully meet the challenge to the community. Concepts such as separation of powers and federalism (where applicable) are likely to be among the first casualties when a nation goes to war against terrorism.[11]

Two seemingly antithetical vectors are in a constant tug-of-war. The existence of restrictions and limitations on governmental powers is a fundamental attribute of democratic regimes. Ideas of democracy, individual rights, legitimacy and accountability, and the rule of law suggest that even in times of acute danger government is limited, both formally and substantively, in the range of activities that it may pursue in order to protect the state.

However, serious terrorist threats directly challenge this organizing principle. The concept of the 'reason of state' (*raison d'état*) advocates the exercise of an unrestricted panoply of measures by the state faced with such existential challenges.[12]

The basic dilemma is nowhere nearer a resolution when one considers that terrorist threats are, for the most part, far from being existential in nature in the sense of threatening the actual physical survival of the nation. To be sure, terrorism poses physical and psycho-logical threats to the state and to its individual members. A successful terrorist campaign, met by a hesitant governmental counter-action, may lead to the elimination of inhibitions against using force and violence in order to accomplish political, social and economic goals by other committed groups and individuals within the community. If the state is expected to guarantee the 'liberty' of its citizens, surely it is supposed to protect and guarantee their 'life.' However, it is generally accepted that terrorist groups and organizations are no real physical or military match to well organized states. Where terrorism does seem to pose a real threat is in its tendency to push a democratic regime to react to perceived threats by employing authoritarian measures. A major goal of terrorist orga-nizations is to bring about precisely that sort of response by the chal-lenged government in order to (i) weaken the fabric of democracy, (ii) discredit the govern-ment domestically as well as internationally, (iii) alienate more segments of the population from their government and push more people to support (passively if not outright actively) the terrorist organizations and their cause, and (iv) undermine the govern-ment's claim to its holding the moral higher ground in the battle for survival against the terrorists while gaining legitimacy for the latter.[13] The danger from terrorism is 'not that democracies would fail to defend themselves, but rather that they would (and did) do so far too well and, in so doing, [become] less democratic.'[14]

III. Rush to Legislate

Extravagant terrorist attacks tend to bring about a rush to legislate. As Kent Roach correctly notes, the prevailing belief may be that if only we add new offenses to the criminal code and broaden the scope of existing offenses, and if only we extend the arsenal of law enforcement agencies by putting at their disposal more sweeping powers to search and seize, to interrogate, to detain without trial, to deport and so on, the country will be more secure and better able to fight against the terrorists.[15] The need to respond quickly to future threats (as much as to assure the public that government is not sitting idly by but is rather acting with a vengeance against the terrorists who committed attacks) frequently results in rushed legislation, often without much debate and at times foregoing normal legislative procedures.

Thus, for example, the *Defence of the Realm Act* of 1914 ('DORA'), perhaps the most important emergency legislation in English history, was rushed through parliament without any meaningful debate.[16] A similar story can be told of the enactment of the first *Prevention of Terrorism Act* of 1974 ('*PTA*') immediately after a bombing, on November 21, 1974, in a pub in Birmingham which killed twenty-one and injured more than 180 people. The *PTA* brought, for the first time, emergency legislation related to the Northern Irish conflict to Great Britain proper. The PTA marked a watershed in legal responses to terrorism related to Northern Ireland in as much as it deviated from the previous set pattern of enacting special emergency legislation for Northern Ireland that did not apply in the rest of the United Kingdom.[17] Claims that the legislative process which resulted in the enactment in the United States of the *Uniting and Strengthening America By Providing Appropriate Tools Required To Intercept and Obstruct Terrorism Act* of 2001 (the '*USA PATRIOT Act*') was 'terribly flawed' have also been made.[18]

In the haste to defend the state, governmental authorities may be all too willing to forego safeguards against abuse of power. Moved by perceptions of substantial physical threat, motivated by growing personal fear of being the next victim and by hatred towards the terrorists as well as frustration at the continuance of terrorist activities, the general public may 'rally 'round the flag'[19] by supporting and calling on the government to employ more radical measures. The sense that curtailment of freedoms and implementation of authoritarian measures are to be, more or less, temporary (until the threat is removed) and are, for the most part, directed against 'outsiders,'[20] may allow a smooth transition to dictatorship, whether constitutional or not. Panic, fear, hatred and similar emotions frequently carry the day pushing aside rational discourse and analysis and taking over the direction of the state's response. In paraphrasing von Clausewitz it may be said that 'terrorism and counter-terrorism have their own language but not always their own [rational] logic.'[21]

Under such circumstances, governments may opt for draconian, authoritarian measures. All too frequently they may over-react against the terrorist threat. Such over-reaction may, in turn, result in the 'barbarization'[22] of society not only in that terrorism from 'below' may be transplanted by institutionalized terror from 'above,'[23] but also in that use of power and force is legitimated as a means for the settlement of disputes.[24] All uses of power are then regarded as found on the same moral plain. The state will be unable to claim a higher moral ground against the terrorists.[25]

IV. The Exception Becomes the Norm

Counter-terrorism and emergency measures, whatever their particular features, share certain basic assumptions. Perhaps the most important one concerns the nature of the challenge facing the nation.

Emergencies are conceptualized in terms of a dichotomized dialectic.[26] The term 'emergency' connotes a sudden, urgent, usually unforeseen event or situation that requires immediate action,[27] often without time for prior reflection and consideration. The notion of 'emergency' is inherently linked to the concept of 'normalcy' in the sense that the former is considered to be outside the ordinary course of events or anticipated actions. To recognize an emergency, we must, therefore, have the background of normalcy. Furthermore, in order to be able to talk about normalcy and emergency in any meaningful way, the concept of emergency must be informed by notions of temporariness and exception. For normalcy to be 'normal,' it has to be the general rule, the ordinary state of affairs, whereas emergency must constitute no more than an exception to that rule[28] – it must last only a relatively short time and yield no substantial permanent effects. Traditional discourse on emergency powers posits normalcy and exigency as two separate phenomena and assumes that emergency is the exception. Thus, the governing paradigm is that of the 'normalcy-rule, emergency-exception.'[29]

A similar assumption underlies our discussion of counter-terrorism measures. Such measures are perceived as extraordinary in nature. Yet we may be willing to allow government to wield such awesome powers so that it is able to deal with threats that are extraordinary in nature. The broad scope of such powers is linked to our belief that they will not be normalized but rather will, somehow, stand outside and not affect ordinary law which applies to ordinary decent folk, *i.e.*, to ourselves.

Indeed, counter-terrorism measures and emergency powers are often considered to be directed against a clear enemy of 'others' namely the terrorists. The contours of conflict are drawn around groups and communities rather than individuals. The clearer the distinction between 'us' and 'them' and the greater the threat 'they' pose to 'us,' the greater in scope may the powers assumed by government (with the cooperation of the legislature and frequent acquiescence of the courts) and tolerated by the public be. A bright-line separation of 'us' and 'them' allows for the piercing of the veil of ignorance.[30] We allow for more repressive emergency measures when we believe that we possess the key to peek beyond the veil and ascertain that such powers will not be turned against us.

Certainly, the distinction between us and them is not unique to the sphere of emergency powers. Such notions are fundamental to the understanding of our individual as well as group consciousness. An integral part of our definition as individuals or as members of certain distinct groups is tied to the drawing of boundaries between the ins and the outs.[31] Group consciousness is, to a large extent, about an affirmative, internal organizing communitarian symbol which serves as the core around which the identity of the group is constructed.[32] It is also about distinguishing those who are in – members of the group – and those left outside.[33]

Crises inevitably lead to heightened individual and group consciousnesses. Allegiance to the community and the willingness to sacrifice (in certain situations, the willingness to sacrifice one's own life) for its sake receive a higher premium and attention in times of peril that endanger the group.[34] The lines of *ins* and *outs* are more clearly and readily drawn and marked. Stereotyping is often employed both with respect to insiders (emphasizing good, noble, worthy attributes) and outsiders (pointing out contrary traits). Collective derogatory name calling and identification of the others as 'barbarians,' are symptoms of that trend.[35] Internal conformities within the community are exaggerated while divergence from 'outsiders' is emphasized.[36]

In times of crisis when emotions run high the dialectic of 'us–them' may serve several functions. It allows people to vent fear and anger in the face of (actual or perceived) danger and direct negative emotional energies towards groups or individuals clearly identified as different. The same theme also accounts for the greater willingness to confer emergency powers on the government when the 'other' is well-defined and clearly separable from the members of the community.

The theory of emergency powers and counter-terrorism is, therefore, a theory of separation and bright-line distinctions. The clearer the distinctions and divisions and the brighter the dichotomies, the stronger are the arguments for the use of emergency powers based, first and foremost, on the ability to confine the use of those powers to times of true emergency and to direct them against 'real' terrorists.

However, our belief in the ability to separate emergency powers from the return to normalcy, counter-terrorism measures from the ordinary set of legal rules and norms, is misguided and dangerous. It is dangerous because it undermines our vigilance against excessive and unnecessary transgressions against human rights and civil liberties. It is also dangerous because it channels our vision to the immediate affects of counter-terrorism legal mechanisms, but hides from view the long-term detrimental effects of such measures. Thus, the calculus of cost-benefit with respect to enhancing the powers of government is likely to be skewed and misguided, not according adequate weight to the competing interests at stake.

The remainder of this section highlights, albeit briefly, some of the ways in which dichotomies and bright-line distinctions between emergency and normalcy, counter-terrorism and 'normal' law, are illusory.[37]

A. *Defining 'Terrorism' and 'Terrorist Activity'*

Article 83.01(1) of *Bill C-36* contains definitions of 'terrorist activity' and 'terrorist group.' While a detailed analysis of the specific elements of those definitions are beyond the scope of this paper, some general comments may be made here.[38]

The very attempt to define 'terrorism' is problematic. Attempts to arrive at an agreed upon definition of 'terrorism' on the international level have failed consistently.[39] However, this author believes that despite such definitional difficulties and their ideological underpinnings, 'easy cases' of activity that can be considered 'terrorist' by the vast majority of democratic-minded people and societies may be identified. In my mind there is no doubt that the September 11 attacks were a terrorist attack. There is no doubt that Palestinian suicide bombers are terrorists.[40] Yet, what is more significant in this context is the shared belief of members of the general public that counter-terrorism acts target terrorists that fall into such easy-to-make-out categories and classifications and not be turned against 'us.' As mentioned above, this is the major premise, even if unstated, behind the willingness to allow government expansive 'counter-terrorist' powers. The problem here is that too narrow a definition of terrorism may prove useless in the real world of fighting against terrorism. On the other hand, a broad definition is bound to blur the basic distinction between easy-case-terrorists and the rest of society and will enable government to use its extraordinary powers against individuals and groups who may hardly be considered 'terrorist' in the common sense inter-pretation of this term. Such a definition may, for example, enable government to garner political support for repressive measures against anti-governmental groups. If we suspect the state's ability to adequately balance its needs in times of crisis against the protection of human rights, we ought to be even more circumspect when the rights of 'others' are at stake. The political price to be paid for infringing on their rights may seem negligible when viewed against the perceived benefits of being seen as protecting the nation from threat and danger. At the same time, one cannot ignore the fact that emergency situations bear a disproportionately heavier burden on political outsiders, minorities, critics of the government, trade unionists, defense lawyers and even critical insiders.[41]

We should (but rarely are) also be aware of the danger that exigencies may lead to a redefinition, over time, of the boundaries of groups, even those which were deemed well defined in the past, making certain members of the original 'non-terrorist' group into outsiders against whom emergency powers may be 'properly' exercised.

Blind belief in the protective shield of the us–them dichotomy makes us ill-prepared to take notice of the fact that the boundaries between the categories become permeable rather than hermetically closed. We may not realize the collapse of the dichotomy until it is too late.[42]

B. *Extension of Extraordinary Legislation: will the Sun ever Set?*

Under the traditional understanding of the relationship between normalcy and emergency, the latter is to be no more than a temporary, transient phenomenon. Accordingly, emergency legislation and powers should be available to government only for short, well-defined, periods of time. The duration for which such legislation may be kept operative ought to be as short as possible and must not extend beyond the termination of the emergency. Even in cases where some transition period is required beyond the emergency before a complete (or close to a complete) return to normalcy may be obtained[43] such a period must be as brief as possible and the effects of the emergency must not spill over to the restored normalcy.

As a matter of practice, however, emergency legislation tends to have a life of its own. Once made it is not so readily terminated. The State of Israel has been under a continuous declared emergency regime since its establishment in May 1948. As originally authorized, the declaration of a state of emergency was considered a temporary necessary evil, a transition mechanism to be operative only as long as war was being fought.[44] This transition mechanism became, however, a permanent feature in the life of the state.

Similarly, time-bound emergency legislation, or indeed statutes such as *Bill C-36*, are quite often the subjects of future extensions and renewals beyond their original (relatively) initial duration, despite Lord Devlin's caution that '*[i]t would be very unfortunate if the public were to receive the impression that the continuance of the state of emergency had become a sort of statutory fiction which was used as a means of prolonging legislation initiated under different circumstances and for different purposes.'*[45] It is not uncommon to find on the statute books laws which had originally been enacted as temporary emergency or counter-terrorism measures but which were subsequently transformed into permanent legislation.

When originally enacted, the *Civil Authorities (Special Powers) Act (Northern Ireland)* of 1922 ('*Special Powers Act*') was meant to last for no more than one year.[46] It was renewed annually several times until, in 1928, it was extended for a five year period. Upon the expiration of that additional period the Act was made into permanent (emergency) legislation.[47] The story of the series of *Prevention of Terrorism (Temporary Provisions) Acts* ('*PTA*') was much the same. Originally introduced in 1974, it was amended in 1975, 1983 and re-enacted in 1984. In 1989 the *PTA* became a permanent statute with the passage of the *PTA* of 1989.[48]

Maintenance of extended emergency powers or counter-terrorism mechanisms is often accompanied by expansion overtime of the normative provisions concerning such powers and mechanisms. At the same time, built-in limitations on the exercise of emergency authority and powers may wither away. Koh and Yoo, for example, indicate the trend of presidential sidestepping congressional statutory restrictions incorporated into legislation such as the *International Emergency Economic Powers Act*, 1977, gaining access to statutory broad grants of authority without the built-in limitations on the use of that authority.[49]

A related phenomenon concerns the use of emergency and counter-terrorism legislation for purposes other than those for which it had originally been promulgated. It may be said that the likelihood for such use is in direct relation to the length of time during which a particular piece of legislation is maintained. The farther we get from the original situation that precipitated the enactment of such legislation, the greater are the chances that the norms and rules incorporated therein will be applied in contexts not originally intended. The use of the American *Feed and Forage Act* of 1861 to allocate funds for the invasion of Cambodia in 1971 is but one example in this context.[50]

C. Counter-Terrorism and 'Ordinary' Law

The longer are counter-terrorism laws, broadly understood, on the statute book, the greater is the likelihood that the extraordinary powers made available to government under them will infiltrate into the ordinary, normal legal system.[51] Such an infiltration is apparent, for example, when examining the relatively recent history of the curtailment of the right to silence in Northern Ireland and eventually in the United Kingdom.[52]

On August 25, 1988, in response to a series of massive terrorist attacks – including an August 20 bombing in County Tyrone, Northern Ireland, of a military bus returning soldiers from a vacation in Britain leaving eight British soldiers dead and twenty injured – the British government decided to adopt a package of security measures. Included in the package was a decision to limit the right to silence of suspects and defendants, both with respect to their interrogation by the police and to their silence in court during trial. The explanation given by the government for the suggested deviation from a well established principle was based on the claim that the wide and systematic lack of cooperation by those suspected of involvement in terrorist activities in Northern Ireland was critically hampering interrogations regarding serious offenses linked to terrorist activity.[53] The factual background against which the new limitations on the right to silence were introduced, as well as specific declarations made by senior public officials, created a clear impression that the measures were designed to bolster the state's powers needed to wage a comprehensive war on Northern Irish terrorism.[54]

The public debate on the new order focused on 'terrorist activities.'[55] The general perception was that the proposed measures were necessary in the fight against paramilitary terrorism in Northern Ireland.[56] Furthermore, such measures were supported on the assumption that they were going to target a well-defined group. Not only were they to be limited in their geographic application to Northern Ireland, but even within this territorial framework they were aimed at 'terrorists' alone.

Despite repeated declarations and assurances to the effect that the new limitations were meant to strengthen law enforcement authorities in their war on terrorism, once the *Criminal Evidence Order (Northern Ireland)* (the '*1988 Order*') was approved, its language was not confined to acts of terrorism.[57] Moreover, the *1988 Order* was not enacted within the framework of emergency legislation already existing in Northern Ireland, but rather as part of the ordinary, regular criminal legislation. Any mention or indication of the Order's relation to terrorist acts disappeared. Thus, the Order's jurisdiction and the limitations it set on the right to silence were not limited to those suspected of serious crimes related to terrorism,[58] but were expanded and interpreted as relating to every criminal suspect or defendant in Northern Ireland.[59] It is also worth noting that the *1988 Order* was quickly approved by the British Parliament, forsaking traditional legislative procedures *en route*.[60]

Six years later the British government decided that the time was ripe for a similar move in other parts of the United Kingdom.

On November, 1994, parliament approved the *Criminal Justice and Public Order Act* ('*CJPOA*').[61] Articles 34–37 of the Act reproduced, almost verbatim, the relevant provisions of the *1988 Order*. In fact, While proposing and explaining the new act, the British Home Secretary relied specifically on the example of the *1988 Order*.[62] Once again the claim that the new piece of legislation was necessary because terrorists were abusing the right to silence was heard. Similarly to its Northern Irish prototype, the *CJPOA* was presented as part of a more comprehensive plan for a war against terrorism and organized crime, and similar to the *1988 Order*, these new-old limitations on the right to silence were incorporated into the regular criminal legislation, and were expanded so as to apply to every suspected offender, not just those suspected of terrorist activities.

The story of the curtailment of the right to silence in the United Kingdom, only briefly described above, clearly substantiates the claim that '[t]here is no reason to think that investigative hearings [incorporated into Bill C-36], especially if enacted without a sunset clause, will not expand outside the terrorism context.'[63] In fact, it is quite likely that they be so expanded.

D. *Increasing Dosages*

Governmental conduct during a crisis creates a precedent for future exigencies as well as for 'normalcy.' Whereas in the 'original' crisis the situation and powers of reference were those of normalcy and regularity, any future crisis government takes as its starting point the experience of extraordinary powers and authority during previous emergencies. What might have been seen as sufficient in the past (judged against the ordinary situation) may not be so regarded at present. Much like a medication whose dosage may need to be increased to have the same effect along time, so too with respect to emergency powers the perception may be that new, more extreme, powers are needed to fight developing emergencies. New extraordinary emergency measures confer additional degree of post-facto legitimacy, respectability and normality to previously used, less drastic, emergency measures. What was deemed to be exceptional emergency measures in the past may now be regarded normal, routine and ordinary in light of more recent and more dramatic emergency powers.

A related phenomenon is the 'piling up' of available emergency powers and legislation.[64] An important feature of both complex and institutionalized states of emergency,[65] this piling up could be detected, for example, in the United States in 1976 when more than 470 pieces of emergency legislation were on the statute books and no less than four declared states of emergency were still in force.[66]

E. *One Can Get Used to This*

The pattern of normalization of the exceptional described above as a result of subsequent expansion of the scope of governmental powers is likely to add to the drive to incorporate some extraordinary powers into the normal legal system, making them available to government in times of normalcy as well as in times of emergency. Another driving force behind the government's push in that direction is the fact that government and its agents grow accustomed to the convenience of emergency powers. Once they have tasted the taste of operating with less limitations and shackles curbing their actions, they are unlikely to be willing to give it up.

One possible pattern of such normalization and routinization may be described as follows: first, emergency legislation designed to deal with a terrorist threat is promulgated. Second, the police 'stretches' the scope of application and coverage of the emergency provisions within the framework of its counter-terrorist activity. Third, both the general public and the legal profession (and, more importantly, the judiciary) give their seal of approval to such police activity and claims of authority. Fourth, the police exercises its broad emergency powers outside the confines of 'emergency.' Finally, the legislature 'enacts reality,' that is normalizes those police powers by explicitly incorporating them into the ordinary legislation.[67]

In Israel, the administrative authority to issue emergency regulations under Article 9(a) of the *Law and Administration Ordinance* of 1948 was originally used mainly in the context of security issues and in a relatively restrained fashion.[68] During the 1950s, 60s and early 70s there were few cases in which use was made of the powers accorded under that article. However, this pattern has changed dramatically after the Yom Kippur War of 1973.[69] Since 1974 the emergency powers under Article 9(a) have been exercised in an almost routine fashion in non-emergency situations relating to labor disputes and monetary issues.[70] Thus, for example, after surveying the history of using Article 9(a) in the context of labor disputes in Israel, one scholar concluded that the emergency-related mechanism of compulsory work orders had been frequently used in situations where no special urgency was present or when other, less drastic means, were available. Such a relatively easy-to-use mechanism for an imposed solution of labor disputes has had a 'narcotic effect' on government officials, allowing them to by-pass the more burdensome process of negotiations between employers and employees. [71]

One ought not to disregard the tranquilizing effect that the 'growing used to' phenomenon has on the public's critical approach towards dictatorial emergency regimes. As John Stuart Mill put it,

> [e]vil for evil, a good despotism, in a country at all advanced in civilization, is more relaxing and enervating to the thoughts, feelings, and energies of the people. The despotism of Augustus prepared the Romans for Tiberius. If the whole tone of their character had not first been prostrated by nearly two generations of that mild slavery, they would probably have had spirit enough left to rebel against the more odious one. [72]

F. *The Persistence of Judicial Precedents*

Courts' rulings in emergency-related issues may be subsequently used as precedents and their impact expanded to other matters. [73] This can happen in two ways. Either an emergency precedent is applied to 'normal' cases, or such a precedent is applied to other cases which have certain emergency or national security components. When we recall that the spectrum of 'national security' and 'emergency' has increased substantially [74] and that '[i]t would, it seems, have to be a manifestly hopeless claim to national security before the courts would turn nasty,' [75] the potential wide scope of such precedents can be fully appreciated. Furthermore, '[c]oncessions made to necessity in a special, largely unknown context might be later generalized to apply to other contexts.' [76]

G. *Structural and Institutional Changes*

Institutional and structural modifications which were put in place as a result of the necessities of crisis management may continue long past the termination of the original crisis. There is a direct relation between emergencies and the strengthening of the executive branch of government. In times of national crisis, governments enjoy an unparalleled concentration and expansion of powers. More often than not the executive enjoys a substantial, if not overwhelming, support of the public and of the other branches of government. Structural shifts are not confined to the duration of a particular emergency. They often carry over into the subsequent period of 'normalcy.' Surely, the aggrandizement of executive power is not solely the product of emergency. The growing complexity of modern society and of the needs of its members and the inability to regulate the multifaceted aspects of modern life solely through legislative action have played an important role in the expansion of executive authority. However, emergencies have been a catalyst leading to quantum leaps in this process of aggrandizement. The clearest examples in this respect are the non-linear explosions of executive powers following the 'economic war' against the Great Depression[77] and the New Deal[78] (and later on, the Second World War)[79] in the United States, the transformation from the Fourth Republic to the Fifth Republic in France (closely linked to the Algerian War),[80] and the fundamental changes in the governmental structure of Great Britain during and after the First World War.[81]

H. *The (Warning) Bells Do not Toll*

Instances of crossing the line separating emergency from normalcy (assuming for the moment its existence) may go unnoticed without any warning bells sounding off. It is not unusual that when emergency legislation is initially adopted no meaningful debates (if at all) take place either within the executive or the legislative branch of government. Once introduced, emergency provisions may pass into the ordinary legal system, again without invoking much debate and discussion.[82]

V. Conclusion

Fighting against terrorism is a messy business. Trees will be cut down and the face and shape of the legal forest will change. This paper draws attention to certain dangers that tend to be over-looked and underestimated in the process of crafting legal responses to terrorism. It sounds a warning about our ability to separate, effectively, between the normal and the extraordinary, between temporary and permanent measures, between measures aimed at the 'other' and measures targeting 'us.' It is about the need for rational, calm and reasoned discourse even when contemplating changes to the legal system in the face of great calamities.

Notes

1 Associate Professor, Tel Aviv University Faculty of Law; Visiting Professor, Benjamin N. Cardozo School of Law; Visiting Scholar, Woodrow Wilson School of International and Public Affairs, Princeton University.

2 Robert Bolt, A Man For All Seasons 66 (Vintage International ed., 1990).

3 Address by Prime Minister Jean Chrétien on the occasion of a Special House of Commons Debate in response to the terrorist attacks in the United States on September 11, 2001 (Sept. 17, 2001).

4 John E. Finn, Constitutions in Crisis: Political Violence and the Rule of Law 54 (1991).

5 William J. Brennan, Jr., *The Quest to Develop a Jurisprudence of Civil Liberties in Times of Security Crises*, 18 Isr. Y.B. Hum. Rts. 11, 11 (1988).

6 Pnina Lahav, *A Barrel Without Hoops: The Impact of Counterterrorism on Israel's Legal Culture*, 10 Cardozo L. Rev. 529, 531 (1988) (noting the 'tragic dimensions of the tension between terrorism, counterterrorism, and justice in any democratic society.')

7 Philip B. Heymann, Terrorism and America – A Commonsense Strategy for a Democratic Society xvii (1998).

8 This idea traces its origins to Aristotle who suggested that '[w]here laws do not rule, there is no constitution.' Aristotle, The Politics, Bk. IV (Ernest Barker trans., rev. ed. 1995).

9 *See, e.g.*, Michael Linfield, Freedom Under Fire – U.S. Civil Liberties in Times of War (1990); Itzhak Zamir, *Human Rights and National Security*, 23 Isr. L. Rev. 375 (1989); Jules Lobel, *Emergency Power and the Decline of Liberalism*, 98 Yale L. J. 1385, 1386 (1989); Frederick M. Watkins, *The Problem of Constitutional Dictatorship*, 1 Pub. Pol'y 324, 343–344 (C. J. Friedrich & E. S. Mason eds., 1940).

10 *See* Arthur S. Miller, *Constitutional Law: Crisis Government becomes the Norm*, 39 Ohio St. L.J. 736, 738–41 (1978); Harold H. Koh, The National Security Constitution 117–49 (1990); Clinton Rossiter, Constitutional Dictatorship – Crisis Government in the Modern Democracies 288–90 (1948).

11 Edward S. Corwin, Total War and the Constitution 70–77 (1947); Peter Rosenthal, *The New Emergencies Act: Four Times the War Measures Act*, 20 Manitoba L.J. 563, 576–580 (1991) (noting a long history of encroachment by the Canadian federal parliament on provincial jurisdiction in times of emergency, under the aegis of the 'emergency doctrine').

12 Carl J. Friedrich, Constitutional Reason of State – The Survival of the Constitutional Order 4–5 (1957). Friedrich explains considerations of 'reason of state' to exist when 'whatever is required to insure the survival of the state must be done by the individuals responsible for it, no matter how repugnant such an act may be to them in their private capacity as decent and moral men.' *id. See also* Maurizio Viroli, From Politics to Reason of State – The acquisition and transformation of the language of politics 1250–1600, 238–280 (1992).

13 *See* Yehezkel Dror, *Terrorism as a Challenge to the Democratic Capacity to Govern, in* Terrorism, Legitimacy, and Power 65 (Martha Crenshaw ed., 1983).

14 David A. Charters (ed.), The Deadly Sin of Terrorism 1 (1994); *see also* Lahav, *supra* note 6, at 559 ('Counterterrorism may be tamed, but too much domestication may render it ineffective. ... Undomesticated counterterrorism on the other hand, when challenged by the state, responds by attempting to tame the legal system rather than be tamed by it.').

15 Kent Roach, *The Dangers of a Charter-Proof and Crime-Based Response to Terrorism* (in this book).

16 *See,* John Eaves, Jr., Emergency Powers and the Parliamentary Watchdog: Parliament and the Executive in Great Britain 1939–1951 8–9 (1951).

17 Clive Walker, The Prevention of Terrorism in British Law 31–33 (2d ed. 1992); Finn, *supra* note 4, at 118; Oren Gross & Fionnuala Ni Aolain, *To Know Where We Are Going, We Need to Know Where We Are: Revisiting States of Emergency, in* A Human Rights Agenda for the 21st Century 79 (A. Heggarty & S. Leonard eds. 1999).

18 Thus, for example, in a letter to U.S. Senators, sent by the American Civil Liberties Union on Oct. 23, 2001, the process was described as follows:

> After bypassing a Judiciary Committee mark-up, a few Senators and their staffs met behind closed doors, on October 12, 2001 to craft a bill. The full Senate was presented with anti-terrorism legislation in a take-it-or-leave-it fashion with little opportunity for input or review. No conference committee met to reconcile the differences between the House and Senate versions of the bill. We find it deeply disturbing that once again the full Senate will be forced to vote on legislation that it has not had the opportunity to read. Senate offices are closed and staff cannot even access their papers to fully prepare you for this important vote. Regular order is being rejected and it is an offense to the thoughtful legislative procedures necessary to protect the Constitution and Bill of Rights at a time when the rights of so many Americans are being jeopardized.

American Civil Liberties Union, Letter to Senators (Oct. 23, 2001) «www.aclu.org/congress/1102301k.html»

19 Bruce Russett, Controlling the Sword – The Democratic Governance of National Security 34 (1990)(the 'rally 'round the flag effect' describes the phenomenon by which 'a short, low-cost military measure to repel an attack – is almost invariably popular at least at its inception. So too are many other kinds of assertive action or speech in foreign policy.'). *See also* Gad Barzilai, A Democracy in Wartime: Conflict and Consensus in Israel 248–60 (1992).

20 Oren Gross, *'Once More unto the Breach': The Systemic Failure of Applying the European Convention on Human Rights to Entrenched Emergencies*, 23 Yale J. Int'l L. 437, 487 (1998) ['Gross, *Entrenched Emergencies*']; Oren Gross, *On Terrorists and Other Criminals: States of Emergency and the Criminal Legal System, in*

Directions in Criminal Law: Inquiries in the Theory of Criminal Law 409 (Eli Lederman ed. 2001) ['Gross, *Terrorists and Criminals*']; W.A. Elliott, Us and Them: A Study of Group Consciousness 9 (1986) (suggesting that crises lead to heightened individual and group consciousness such that internal conformities within community are exaggerated while divergence from 'outsiders' is em-phasized); Ilena M. Porras, *On Terrorism: Reflections on Violence and the Outlaw*, 1994 Utah L. Rev. 119.

21 'War has its own language but not its own logic.' *Quoted in* Paul Wilkinson, Terrorism and the Liberal State 52 (2nd ed. 1986).

22 Yehezkel Dror, *supra* note 13, at 65, 73–74 (barbarization of the international global system as a result of counterterrorism measures invoked against the challenge of international terrorism).

23 Grant Wardlaw, Political Terrorism 69 (2nd ed., 1989).

24 *See, e.g.*, Benjamin Constant, *The Spirit of Conquest and Usurpation and Their Relation to European Civilization*, in Political Writings 133, 136 (Biancamaria Fontana ed. & trans., 1993) (*quoted in* Gabriel L. Negretto & José Antonio Aguilar Rivera, *Liberalism and Emergency Powers in Latin America: Reflections on Carl Schmitt and the Theory of Constitutional Dictatorship*, 21 Cardozo L. Rev. 1797, 1801 (2000)) ('Power, by emancipating itself from the laws, has lost its distinctive character and its happy pre-eminence. When the factions attack it, with weapons like its own, the mass of the citizens may be divided, since it seems to them that they only have a choice between two factions.').

25 Wardlaw, *supra* note 23, at 69; Ronald Crelinsten, *Terrorism as Political Communi-cation: The Relationship between the Controller and the Controlled*, in Contem-porary Research on Terrorism 9 (Paul Wilkinson & Alasdair Stewart eds., 1989).

26 Gross, *Entrenched Emergencies, supra* note 20, at 453–55.

27 *See* New Shorter Oxford English Dictionary 806 (5th ed. 1993)

28 A reversed image of the relationship between normalcy and emergency arises out of Carl Schmitt's theory of the 'state of exception' ('*Ausnahmezustand*'). *See, e.g.*, Oren Gross, *The Normless and Exceptionless Exception: Carl Schmitt's Theory of Emergency Powers and the 'Norm-Exception' Dichotomy*, 21 Cardozo L. Rev. 1825 (2000).

29 Gross, *Entrenched Emergencies, supra* note 20.

30 John Rawls, A Theory of Justice 17–22 (1971).

31 Jean-Paul Sartre, Being and Nothingness: a Phenomenological Essay on Ontology (Hazel E. Barnes trans., 1992).

32 Frederick Schauer, *Community, Citizenship, and the Search for National Identity*, 84 Mich. L. Rev. 1504, 1513–17 (1986).

33 W.A. Elliott, Us and Them: a study of group consciousness 6–10 (1986) ('People only display attitudes of *us* due to an acquired sense of *we-ness* determined largely by a sense of *they-ness* in relation to others. So-called ingroup and outgroup behaviour therefore merely reflects the two sides of group consciousness.' *Id*. at 8.).

34 Schauer, *supra* note 32, at 1504 ('a meaningful sense of community exists only insofar as the individuals who comprise that community are willing to take actions on behalf of the community not only that they would not take on their own behalf, but that are quite possibly detrimental to their own interests ... we cannot think about a meaningful sense of community without thinking of some sense of sacrifice.').

35 Elliott, *supra* note 33, at 9 (mentioning the use, by the Allies during WWII of such nicknames as Krauts, Nips, Wops, Wogs, and Gooks). *See also* J. Glenn Gray, The Warriors: Reflections on Men in Battle, ch. 5 (1967).

36 Elliott, *supra* note 33, at 9.

37 *See also* David Dyzenhaus, *The Permanence of the Temporary: Can Emergency Powers be Normalized?* (in this book).

38 For a critical analysis of the relevant definitions *see* Brenda Cossman & David Schneiderman, *Associational Life and the Anti-Terrorism Bill* (in this book).

39 *see, e.g.,* GAOR, 28th Sess., Supp. 28, 1973, at 7–8; Antonio Cassese, Terrorism, Politics and Law (1989).

40 The statement that 'one man's terrorist is another man's freedom fighter' should not be allowed to undermine a firm stance against the clear cases of terrorism. There are simply some things that are not relative.

41 Oren Gross & Fionnuala Ni Aolain, *From Discretion to Scrutiny: Revisiting the Application of the Margin of Appreciation Doctrine in the Context of Article 15 of the European Convention on Human Rights*, 23 Hum. Rts. Q. (2001).

42 I am reminded here of the powerful words of Martin Niemöller copied at the entrance to the Yad Va-shem (the Holocaust Memorial Museum in Jerusalem, Israel):

They came for the Communists
>   and I didn't object for I wasn't a Communist;
They came for the Socialists
>   and I didn't object for I wasn't a Socialist;
They came for the Labour leaders
>   and I didn't object for I wasn't a labour leader;
They came for the Jews
>   and I didn't object for I wasn't a Jew;
Then they came for me
>   and there was no one left to object.

43 For discussion of transition periods between war and peace *see, e.g.,* Christopher D. Gilbert, *'There Will be Wars and Rumours of Wars': a Comparison of the Treatment of Defence and Emergency Powers in the Federal Constitutions of Australia and Canada*, 18 Osgoode Hall L.J. 307, 320–324 (1980); Christopher N. May, In the Name of War – Judicial Review and the War Powers since 1918 (1989).

44 See statement by David Ben-Gurion in Provisional State Council, Minutes, vol. 1, meeting of May 19, 1948, at 5.

45 Willcock v. Muckle [1951] 2 K.B. 844, 853 (per Devlin J.).

46 The radical nature of this piece of legislation was best reflected in section 2(4) which provided that, '[i]f any person does any act of such nature as to be calculated to be prejudicial to the preservation of the peace or maintenance of order in Northern Ireland and not specifically provided for in the regulations, he shall be guilty of an offence against those regulations.' The South African Minister of Justice was quoted to refer to section 2(4) when he said, at the time, that he 'would be willing to exchange all the [south African] legislation of that sort for one clause in the Northern Ireland Special Powers Act' *quoted in* Committee on the Administration of Justice, *No Emergency, No emergency Law* 6 (1993).

47 *See* Gross & Ni Aolain, *supra* note 17. In 1973, following the bloodiest year of the 'troubles' and the introduction of 'direct rule' over Northern Ireland in March 1972, the UK Parliament enacted the *Northern Ireland (Emergency Provisions) Act*, 1973 which replaced the *Special Powers Act*.

48 Walker, *supra* note 17, at 33–39; E.C.S. Wade & A.W. Bradley, Constitutional And Administrative Law 591 (11th ed., 1993).

49 Harold H. Koh & John C. Yoo, *Dollar Diplomacy/Dollar Defense: The Fabric of Economics and National Security Law*, 26 Int'l Lawyer 715, 742–46 (1992). Thus, the *International Emergency Economic Powers Act* has been invoked with little regard to whether a real emergency existed, in order to allow the pursuit of policies which Congress had failed to approve). *See also* Dames & Moore v. Regan, 453 U.S. 654 (1981).

50 Note, *The National Emergency Dilemma: Balancing the Executive's Crisis Powers with the Need for Accountability*, 52 S. Cal. L. Rev. 1453, 1453 (1979)('*The National Emergency Dilemma*').

51 Dermot P.J. Walsh, *The Impact of the Antisubversive Laws on Police Powers and Practices in Ireland: The Silent Erosion of Individual Freedom*, 62 Temple L. Rev. 1099 (1989) (describing the move in the Republic of Ireland from the emergency-type *Offences Against the State Act*, 1939 to the regular criminal code, the *Criminal Justice Act* of 1984).

52 The discussion below is based on Gross, *Terrorists and Criminals, supra* note .

53 Hansard, *col.*, 8 Nov. 1988, 185.

54 Explaining the reasoning behind the government's decision, the Secretary for Northern Ireland, Mr. Tom King, emphasized that:

> 'It will help in convicting guilty men. I don't think it will undermine standards of justice. In Northern Ireland, *the whole system of justice is under sustained attack by terrorists* and their aim is to destroy the whole system. They intimidate and murder witnesses and judges, and they train people not to answer any questions at all.'
>
> E. Moloney, *Britain Seeks to Abolish Key Civil Liberty in Ulster; London's Move Aimed at Thwarting IRA*, The Washington Post, Oct. 21, 1988, at A1 (quoting

Tom King) [emphasis added]. C. Hodgson, *Plan to Curb Silence Approved*, Fin. Times, Nov. 9, 1988, at 15.

55 *See* Susan M. Easton, The Right to Silence 60 (2nd ed., 1998) ('The debates of the early seventies focused on the "abuse" of the right to silence by professional criminals, but by the late eighties this concern was overshadowed by anxieties over professional terrorists, such as members of the Irish Republican Army and other sectarian para-military groups.')

56 *See*, for example, *Review of the Operation of the Prevention of Terrorism (Temporary Provisions) Act 1984* (HMSO, Cmnd. 264) (1987), in which Viscount Coleville declared his support for the annulment of the right to silence as terrorists are using this right to hide behind a wall of silence, thus causing difficulties for police interrogators and prosecution authorities in bringing terrorists to justice.

57 Easton, *supra* note 55, at p. 69 ('It was also expected that any changes to the right to silence in Northern Ireland ... would be incorporated into emergency legislation, and restricted to terrorist offences, rather than becoming part of the ordinary criminal law ... it seems unlikely that this route will be taken now that the curtailment of the right to silence is a feature of the English criminal justice system applicable to all suspects').

58 Antonio Vercher Terrorism in Europe 121–25 (1992).

59 Gregory W. O'Reilly, *Criminal Law: England Limits the Right to Silence and Moves towards an Inquisitorial System of Justice*, 85 Nw. J. Crim. L. & Criminology 402, 425 (1994).

60 Michael Mansfield, *Reform that Pays Lip Service to Justice*, The Guardian, Oct. 6, 1993, at 22.

61 *See generally* Paul Tain Criminal Justice and Public Order Act 1994 (1994).

62 In his speech to the annual convention of the Conservative party on October 6, 1993, Michael Howard announced that:

> '[t]he so-called right to silence is ruthlessly exploited by *terrorists*. What fools they must think we are. It's time to call halt to this charade. The so-called right to silence will be abolished. The innocent have nothing to hide and that is exactly the point the prosecution will be able to make in future."

> *The Guardian*, October 7, 1993, at p. 6. *See also* Heather Mills, *Tougher Policies Aimed at Helping Victims of Crime*, The Independent, Nov. 19, 1993, at p. 6; Hansard, *col. 26* ,1 Nov. 94, (Michael Howard, Home Secretary) [emphasis added]

63 Roach, *supra* note .

64 N. Questiaux, *Study of the Implications for Human Rights of Recent Developments Concerning Situations Known as States of Siege or Emergency*, U.N. ESCOR, 35th Sess. §§ 118–128, at 16, U.N. Doc. E/CN.4/Sub.2/1982/15 (1982).

65 *Id.* §§ 129–145.

66 *The National Emergency Dilemma, supra* note 50, at 1453.

67 Walsh, *supra* note .

68 I. Hans Klinghofer, *On Emergency Regulations in Israel, in* Jubilee to Pinchas Rosen 86 (Haim Cohen ed., 1962).

69 Menachem Hofnung, Israel - Security Needs vs. The Rule of Law 57–59 (1991).

70 *Id*. at 58–59.

71 Mordechai Meroni, *Back-to-Work Emergency Orders: Government Intervention in Labor Disputes in Essential Services*, 15 Mishpatim 350, 380–86 (1986).

72 John Stuart Mill, Three Essays – On Liberty, Representative Government, The Subjection of Women 185 (Oxford University Press, 1975)(1859–1869).

73 George J. Alexander, *The Illusory Protection of Human Rights by National Courts During Periods of Emergency*, 5 Hum. Rts. L.J. 1, 26–27 (1984) ('In evaluating the role of courts in emergencies it is important to consider not only the fact that bad decisions such as Korematsu may infest law long after the emergency has passed, but also the fact that they provide an imprimatur for military-executive decisions which might otherwise draw more political disfavor. The absence of court approval, as for example during the war in Vietnam, allows the questions of legitimacy full sway in public discussion.').

74 Gross, *supra* note , at 1857–63.

75 Graham Zellick, *Official Information, National Security and the Law in Britain*, 98 Studi Senesi 303, 317 (1986).

76 Harold Edgar & Benno C. Schmidt, Jr., *Curtiss-Wright Comes Home: Executive Power and National Security Secrecy*, 21 Harv. C.R.-C.L. L. Rev. 349, 389 (1986).

77 The fight against the Great Depression was thought of, and spoken about, in terms of 'war,' and 'emergency.' *See* W. Leuchtenburg, *The New Deal and the Analogue of War, in* Change and Continuity in Twentieth Century America 81–82 (John Braeman ed., 1964); Michal R. Belknap, *The New Deal and the Emergency Powers Doctrine*, 62 Tex. L. Rev. 67, 70–76 (1983). In his inaugural address President Roosevelt set the tone for regarding the economic crisis as analogues to the War against the German army in the World War. *See* Inaugural Address of President Roosevelt (Mar. 4, 1933), *quoted in* Clinton Rossiter, Constitutional Dictatorship – Crisis Government in the Modern Democracies 256–57 (1948).

78 The New Deal resulted in an enhancement of presidential power and authority vis-a-vis the other branches of the federal government as well as the strengthening of the federal government at the expense of the states. Executive leadership in the legislative process as well as the creation of numerous administrative actors are two of the main outcomes of the era. *See generally* Cass R. Sunstein, *Constitutionalism After the New Deal*, 101 Harv. L. Rev. 421 (1987).

79 *See* Rossiter, *supra* note , at 266–75; Edward S. Corwin, Total War and the constitution 35–77 (1947). Expansion of the power and authority of the Executive has been facilitated by the following means: first, expansive presidential claims of inherent constitutional emergency powers; Second, broad delegations of power from Congress to the President; Third, establishment of various war agencies under

the president's assumed constitutional war powers; finally, legislative leadership by the President.

80 Oren Gross, Theoretical Models of Emergency Powers 328–48 (SJD Dissertation, Harvard Law School, 1997).

81 Rossiter, *supra* note 77, at 151–170 (noting especially the rise of the Cabinet and the parallel decline in the power and prestige of the Parliament).

82 *See*, *e.g.*, Walsh, *supra* note 51, at 1129 (passage of the Criminal Justice Act – 'enacting reality' – with hardly any notice of the incorporation of emergency-related provisions into the ordinary criminal legislation).

Terrorism and the Risk Society

DAVID SCHNEIDERMAN
Faculty of Law
University of Toronto

The scene of twin crumbling towers is seared forever in our minds. Endless hours of 'Die Hard' and 'Terminator' movies could not prepare us for the depth of destruction and loss of life we viewed in a couple of hours that Tuesday morning. The common wisdom is that the world forever has changed, at least its North American variant.[1] The event simply was beyond the capacity of anyone to imagine.

The Anti-terrorism Act must be situated in this context.[2] Consider the chilling testimony of RCMP Commissioner Zaccardelli to the House Committee on Justice and Human Rights. 'Terrorist activity is indiscriminate, global in scope, and destabilizing in effect,' he advises. Terrorists 'have no respect for human life' and they 'will stop at nothing in their effort to achieve their goals.' Terrorists 'think nothing of strapping a bomb around their waist and detonating it and themselves in a location strategically selected to result in the greatest possible loss of life and destruction of property.' Terrorist groups are 'intricate, complex, sophisticated, and clandestine criminal organizations.' They have 'long-term goals, to infiltrate and assimilate in society and establish individuals with sleepers' roles.' They, in short, can be anyone and are everywhere (though their skin colour may be of a certain hue). Terrorist activity, he concludes, 'poses an extraordinary threat to society,' consequently, the 'fight against terrorist activities calls for extraordinary action.'[3] Terrorism now poses a danger of global proportions which cannot be contained or controlled but through extraordinary measures.

All that we have known becomes obsolete and so the routine methods of law enforcement are portrayed as ineffective in this new context.

Citizens, moreover, cannot be expected to comprehend the real magnitude of this threat. Justice Minister Anne McLellan advised *The Globe and Mail* that her experience in cabinet has been sobering. In response to naive critics of the bill, she says: 'I wish you knew what I know.'[4] According to this account, police and security forces have the expertise, but are inadequately equipped, to cope with the threat and insecurity generated by the mechanisms of modern terrorism.

The rush to respond to the events of September 11th in this manner fits well sociologist Ulrich Beck's important work on 'risk society.'[5] If it is correct to say that social relations shape legal institutional forms, it should be the case that social theory will contribute to an understanding of the legal response to the threat of terrorism in Canada. Here we draw on an influential strand within social theory in order to comprehend better the implications of our response to that threat.

The Risk Society

According to Beck, modernity has moved from a phase where it safely could ignore the 'side-effects' of industrialization – the threat of radioactive fallout, cancer-causing toxins and pollutants[6] – to a new phased called the 'risk society.' In this era, society no longer has the ability to control, through the usual techniques, the 'hazards and insecurities induced and introduced by modernization itself' (21). In the not too distance past, risks conceivably could be brought under control. A variety of techniques were available – health or life insurance for individuals and investment insurance for business firms – with the help of actuarial tables. Risk, however, no longer can be tamed in the old ways.

In order to cope with the risks produced by processes of industrialization, society turns 'reflexive:' we become attuned to the potential 'unintended consequences' of the modernization process.[7] In this new phase, professional knowledge elites – the mass media, scientific and legal professionals – emerge as key figures in defining risks (23). At the same time, the margin for diagnostic error decreases as risk no longer is a personal concern but a global danger (21).The threat of ecological devastation 'knows no frontiers,' Beck writes, and so contributes to the accelerating phenomenon of globalization.[8]

In the pages that follow, we take up a few of the features associated with the risk society: (i) the universalizing tendency of risks; (ii) reliance on professional expertise; and (iii) the coping mechanisms risks generate, particularly legal institutional responses.

Now it may be that Beck overstates the advent of risk society as a 'new' feature on the global scene. It certainly is the case that the devastating threat of environmental crisis is not new to many communities around the world. Upon the arrival of European settler societies in North America, Aboriginal peoples suffered environmental catastrophes which nearly 'wiped out entire populations.'[9] The claim of risk-as-paradigm-shift figures less large in this analysis. It also is a limiting feature of Beck's analysis that it is confined mostly to ecological risks associated with the modernization process (though he generalizes from the fallout of these risks to all dimensions of society). In this way, his thesis could be read as a paean the German Green party and the transnational environmental social movement. Yet there are interesting parallels between the world out-of-control that he describes and the contemporary scene in the wake of the Twin Towers disaster.

There are, of course, some very direct parallels. Among the threats we feasiblely now can imagine are suicide bombings of nuclear facilities or acts of bio-terrorism exposing civilians to anthrax bacteria or the small pox virus.[10] There are other less obvious parallels that have to do with the political and legal responses to the fear and anxiety generated by threats previously unimaginable and now beyond our capacity to control. 'Intentionally or not,' Beck writes, 'through accident or catastrophes, in war or peace, a large group of the population faces devastation and destruction today, for which language and the powers of imagination fail us' (52). I consider here the political and legal consequences of this challenge.

The Local and the Global

The dangers that we face are global in scope. Risk society operates on a world-wide scale and so risk positions are 'somehow universal and unspecific' (53). Yet, Beck writes, risks do not abolish entirely class distinctions, rather, risks also may adhere to existing class patterns (35). Some are more affected by the distribution of risk, and these patterns may replicate, even strengthen, class positions. Consider that, after finding traces of anthrax on high-speed sorting machines in New York's largest mail sorting facility, the facility remained open. The postal workers' union rightly asked why the U.S. Senate, State Department, and Supreme Court buildings were closed immediately while their place of employment remained open. 'They treat us like we're worthless' one mail sorter remarked.[11]

Class nevertheless increasingly is irrelevant in a global risk society.

'Poverty is heirarchic; smog is democratic' Beck writes (36). As the growing threat of global ecological hazard 'equalizes and universalizes,' the advent of the risk society signals an accelerating process of globalization. Risk society speaks to globalization in at least two dimensions: as a growing awareness of vulnerability in relation to global hazards without frontiers; and as an increasing feeling that a common destiny lies with others and not merely with one's national community. Risks arouse a 'cosmopolitan everyday consciousness which transcends' borders.[12]

The Anti-terrorism Act aims to address the global hazard of terrorism in both of these dimensions. As a threat that lies both within and without the borders of the national state, the preamble to the Act speaks to the 'trans-border nature' of terrorism. Foreign Affairs Minister John Manley, in an address before a New York audience, declared that 'terrorism globalizes us.' We must ensure, he added, 'that it also globalizes a sustained commitment to fight terrorism.'[13] The Anti-terrorism Act should be understood, then, as contribution to a global response to the events of September 11. The Bill's preamble declares that Canada 'must act in concert with other nations' which requires that we implement domestically a variety of U.N. conventions and international instruments concerning terrorism.[14]

There also is a particular North American variant to the idea of 'cosmopolitan' consciousness. The discourse of globalization often addresses very specific state interests but in the language of the universal.[15] It would be unrealistic, then, to suggest that the Act is directed only at a Canadian audience or to only a global one. Rather, it also is directed at a more specific, U.S. audience. So when Barbara Crossette of the *New York Times* described Anti-Terrorism Bill C-36 as 'the most stringent anti-terrorism legislation in the country's history' and a 'first step toward dealing with a new sense of danger across North America,'[16] the government of Canada will have achieved, in part, its objective of enhanced feelings of security not only at home but in the United States. To be sure, discussions about a North American 'security perimeter' began in late summer 2001,[17] while debates around dollarization and increased integration under NAFTA and the proposed FTAA began well before then. Nevertheless, one cannot but situate our response to the events on September 11th within the larger movement toward continentalization.

There is another uncomfortable sense in which post-September 11 events prompt feelings of a common destiny with humankind. This is the sense in which some people in Afghanistan, Pakistan, or the Palestinian authority understand these events: as finally having (North) Americans share in the sense of danger and insecurity felt daily in their own countries. One tailor in Kabul is reported to have seen 'God's justice in America's pain.' 'So they at least now know how it feels in their own country,' he remarked.[18] In the environmental context, Beck would call this the 'boomerang effect.' This is when the producers of hazardous risks – the affluent countries of the North – have the adverse affects of risks return to them from overseas (44). Having supported the Afghan Mujahideen against the Soviet Union, here is a case, Eqbal Ahmed writes, of 'the chickens of the Afghanistan war coming home to roost.'[19]

Government by Experts

As we become aware of the production of risk caused (directly and indirectly) by the advance of technology, we turn increasingly to experts. In the eyes of the technological elite, Beck writes, 'the majority of the public still behaves like engineering students in their first semester.' We are 'ignorant' but 'well intentioned; hard working but without a clue' (58). In the era of risk, the technocratic and scientific elites make important determinations about how we should live and the acceptable levels of poisoning. That level of poisoning is determined to be normal, and then the normal disappears behind the rhetoric of 'acceptable' levels (65). By controlling this feature of our lives, then, experts make determinations about 'how we want to live' (65).

One of the startling features of Anti-terrorism Act is the extent to which authority is delegated to a professional core of cabinet ministers, police, and security officials. The consent of federal or provincial attorneys general is required to prosecute a terrorism offence (s. 83.24). The Minister of Justice may prohibit disclosure of information or conceal evidence in any proceeding for the 'purpose of protecting international relations or national defence or security.'[20] On the recommendation of the Solicitor General, organizations may be added to a list of entities deemed 'terrorist'(s. 83.05). The Canadian security apparatus may listen in on the conversations of Canadian citizens without warrant while tracking conversations abroad. Police officers are endowed with authority to arrest and detain persons based on an expansive definition of the term 'terrorism' (s. 83.01).[21]

Speaking to the matter of enforcement, RCMP Commissioner Zaccardelli, in his testimony to the House of Commons Standing Committee, admitted that the legislation was meant to be used 'in the most severe cases' and 'applied in very rare circumstances by highly skilled officers in full consultation not only with senior officers, but with the legal system.' Application of the law would not be of concern to the ordinary cop on the beat, rather, 'chances are that most of the people who will be working on this type of activity tend to be more sophisticated and well-qualified people who make their living working in this area.'[22] In the hands of the experts, feelings of safety are expected to ensue.

This diagnosis is in accord with Ericson and Haggerty's findings that contemporary police work calls for professional 'risk management' in the place of traditional crime control. Police practices in the risk society require a particular kind of rationality: the collection and classification of risks and the dissemination of that assembled knowledge to other sectors of state and society. In order for police work to appear effective, police communication strategies must dramatize danger while portraying the police as 'efficient risk managers.'[23]

We might acknowledge that the statutory recognition of the Canadian Security Establishment (CSE) is a positive development – until now it merely has been a creature of Order-in-Council. CSE now is authorized to target 'foreign entities' and to intercept communications conducted abroad (s. 273.64). The Anti-terrorism Act, however, expands CSE authority to include the interception of communications that originate abroad but that make contact with persons in Canada (s. 273.65).[24] Though these interceptions would require only authorization from the Minister of Defence applying certain criteria, surveillance of electronic communications in Canada always has required judicial warrant.[25]

Taking account of this new expansive authority delegated to political, police, and security officials – some of it of the most intrusive kind – requires a great deal of time and expertise. Over 10 pieces of legislation are proposed to be amended and a variety of marks are intended to be hit: from investigative hearings (s. 83.28) to hate propaganda on the internet (s. 320.1). The omnibus style of the Act makes it inaccessible to most citizens. We are assured, however, that the Act does not overreach. According to the Minister of Justice, the draft text is the product of a team of government lawyers with the single-minded mission of ensuring that the Act does not trench unreasonably on Charter rights and freedoms.[26] The dominant theme that emerges from a reading of the legislation is: trust us as you have no one else left to trust.

While we need not adopt Beck's radical skepticism of scientific elites – in his account, the authority of governance by experts loses most of its legitimacy – we are warranted in reserving some skepticism for exercises of authority by ministers, police, and security officials. And while we might admit that we are in need of enhanced vigilance post-September 11th, we legitimately should worry about having official authorities define acceptable levels of toxicity to democratic practice. We need to evaluate and weigh more critically the impact of the Act on our democratic health. We might begin by democratizing deliberation about appropriate limits to rights – despite the rhetoric of Charter-proofing – and resisting the idea that these are matters over which citizens are too naive to come to grips. As Valverde suggests, law-and-order officials 'ought not to be the main voice defining our security needs.' There is nothing more urgent, she declares, than to facilitate public participation in debating and defining what we mean by 'security.'[27]

The (In)Security State

Where risks have been processed through the consciousness of civil society, 'the order of the world changes' (76). The highest priority is given over to seeking solutions which will eliminate the threat of hazardous consequences from our daily lives. The manner in which we eliminate these hazards then become political 'hot potatoes' (78).[28] Beck describes the process in this way:

> As the threat grows, the old priorities melt away, and parallel to that the interventionist policy of the state of emergency grows, drawing its expanded authorities and possibilities for intervention from the threatening condition. Where danger becomes normalcy, it assumes permanent institutional form. In that respect, modernization risks prepare the field for a partial redistribution of power (78)

The challenge to democracy is to resist the tendency toward what Beck calls the 'totalitarianism of hazard prevention' (80). By taking effective action to resist modernity's 'side-effects' we generate other side effects that amount to risks to the political process itself. Either we fail to respond meaningfully to risks or, in the process of responding, we threaten fundamental democratic principles. Beck suggests that breaking through this either-or dilemma is among the principle tasks of democratic thought (80).

To the extent that the Anti-terrorism Act threatens due process rights, inhibits associational life, and chills democratic expression, our response to the threat of terrorism will have melted away the 'old priorities.' We have entered a danger zone to democratic practice where, in order to reduce the threat of terrorism and associated anxieties and insecurities, we may be institutionalizing a legal regime (with or without a sunset clause) that is repressive of civil liberties. The challenge here is to test the limits of proposed action and ask to what extent such broad powers truly are necessary. As Alan Borovoy has asked, 'if the police have no interest in exercising certain powers,' – such as invoking the terrorism provisions so as to clamp down on merely 'unlawful' protest – 'why in the world should the law make it possible for them to do so?'[29]

Conclusion

If one accepts that the insecurity and anxiety generated by threats of terrorism can be likened to the threat of extraordinary ecological disaster, a number of avenues of inquiry are opened up. By undertaking this study with the tools provided by risk society analysis, we can identify a number of clear tendencies. The first is the fostering of the idea of 'globality': that there is such a thing as a cosmopolitan consciousness transcending national borders.[30] The second is an overreliance on expert and professional knowledges. The third is a tendency to overreach in response to the threat of risk. Legislation is broadly drafted to promote feelings of security, but other priorities, like the exercise of rights and freedoms, are, in turn, threatened.

This is not to deny the fact that terrorist acts are a direct assault on human rights and human dignity, as Cotler maintains. Rather, it is to say that our reaction to that assault can threaten these very values.[31] If our primary responses tend to rely on management techniques and expanded legislative authority, we might consider it our task to counteract these tendencies by democratizing knowledge about risk while checking the likelihood of legislative overreach.

Notes

* Faculty of Law, University of Toronto. Many thanks to Patrick Macklem, Trish McMahon, Pratima Rao, Kent Roach, and Mariana Valverde who provided helpful comments on an earlier draft.
1 Martin Mittelstaedt, 'Attack Has Changed the World Forever, US Pollsters Told' *The Globe and Mail* (13 September 2001) A7.
2 The following comments are based on Bill C-36, 1st Sess., 37th Parl. tabled for First Reading on 15 October 2001.

3 Canada, House of Commons, Standing Committee on Justice and Human Rights, *Evidence* (23 October 2001) 09:32–09:35.

4 Shawn McCarthy, 'Anne McLellan's New Ideals' *The Globe and Mail* (22 October 2001) A7.

5 Ulrich Beck, *Risk Society: Towards a New Modernity* (London: Sage Publications, 1992). All further references to this book appear in parentheses in the body of this text.

6 Malcolm Waters, *Globalization* (London: Routledge, 1995) at 59.

7 Ulrich Beck, *Democracy Without Enemies* (Cambridge: Polity Press, 1998) at 84. Also see Beck, *The Reinvention of Politics: Rethinking Modernity in the Global Social Order* (Cambridge: Polity Press, 1997).

8 Ulrich Beck, *What is Globalization?* (Cambridge: Polity Press, 2000) at 38.

9 Bryan S. Turner, *Orientalism, Postmodernism and Globalism* (London: Routledge, 1994) at 181.

10 See the very frightening list of potential threats in William J. Broad, Stephen Engelberg, and James Glanz, 'Assessing Risks, Chemical, Biological, Even Nuclear' *The New York Times* (1 November 2001) A1.

11 Steven Greenhouse and Eric Lipton, 'Possible Anthrax Case Shuts Down a New York Hospital' *The New York Times* (30 October 2001) A1, B7 at B7.

12 Beck, *What is Globalization?*, *supra* note 8 at 38.

13 Canada, Department of Foreign Affairs and International Trade, 'Notes for an Address by the Honourable John Manley, Minister of Foreign Affairs to the U.S. Foreign Policy Association,' New York, November 5, 2001 at http://www.dfait-maeci.gc.ca/mina-e.asp (accessed 11 November 2001).

14 See Patrick Macklem, 'Canada's Obligations at International Criminal Law' in this volume.

15 Boaventura de Sousa Santos, *Toward a New Common Sense: Law, Science and Politics in the Paradigmatic Transition* (New York: Routledge) at 262–3.

16 Barbara Crossette, 'Canada Pushes Broad Antiterror Measure, Alarming Some Who Fear Erosion of Rights' *The New York Times* (18 October 2001). Also see the testimony of CSE head Keith Coulter that Bill C-36 has been 'extremely well received south of the border.' In Canada, House of Commons, Standing Committee on Justice and Human Rights, *Evidence* (23 October 2001) 16:15–16:20.

17 See National Post ...

18 Barry Bearak, 'Taliban Plead for Mercy to the Miserable in the Land of Nothing' *The New York Times* (13 September 2001) A18.

19 Eqbal Ahmed, 'Why Practise Double Standards? The Genesis of International Terrorism II' *The Dawn* (Internet Edition) (6 October 2001) at:http://www.dawn.com/2001/10/06/op/htm (accessed 11 November 2001).

20 See Hamish Stewart, 'Rule of Law or Executive Fiat? The Effect of Bill C-36 on Public Interest Immunity in the Trial Process' in this volume.

21 See David Schneiderman and Brenda Cossman, 'Political Association and the Anti-terrorism Act' in this volume.

22 Canada, House of Commons, Standing Committee on Justice and Human Rights, *Evidence* (23 October 2001) 10:40–10:45.

23 Richard V. Ericson and Kevin D. Haggerty, *Policing the Risk Society* (Toronto: University of Toronto Press, 1997) at 430.

24 See Bill C-36, Part V.1 and the testimony of the Minister of National Defence, Art Eggleton, in Canada, House of Commons, Standing Committee on Justice and Human Rights, *Evidence* (23 October 2001) 15:40–15:45.

25 The Senate of Canada recommends, therefore, that 'judicial authorization be obtained where appropriate and feasible.' See Canada, Senate, Special Senate Committee on the Subject Matter of Bill C-36, *First Report* (1 November 2001) at A.III.(e).

26 See Kent Roach, 'The Dangers of a Charter-Proof and Crimes-Based Response to Terrorism' in this volume.

27 See Mariana Valverde, 'Governing Security, Governing Through Security' in this volume.

28 These phenomenon for Beck are associated with the 'dynamics of reflexive politicization' (at 77).

29 A. Alan Borovoy, *When Freedoms Collide: The Case for our Civil Liberties* (Toronto: Lester & Orpen Dennys, 1988) at 9.

30 On idea of globality, see Martin Albrow, *The Global Age* (Stanford: Stanford University Press, 1997).

31 Irwin Cotler, 'Towards a Counter-Terrorism Law and Policy' *Terrorism and Political Violence* (1998) 10: 1–14 at 3.

Network Wars

JANICE GROSS STEIN*
Munk Centre for International Studies
University of Toronto

I. War by a Network

That we in North America face a new kind of threat is beyond question. The attacks against the heartland of the United States, its corporate and military icons, and the killing of over 3,000 civilians, mark a watershed in thinking about security. It is almost two hundred years since civilians in North America have been the object of systematic attack, and even longer since the core of the hegemonic power was struck from the periphery. It is no surprise that the public is anxious and threatened. The important analytical and political question is: what kind of threat, and from whom? And, what is the appropriate response?

President Bush claims that the threat is from 'evil doers' who seek to destroy western civilization. This is a struggle of good against evil, of the forces of darkness against light. These forces of darkness are themselves threatened by the openness, the affluence, and the cultural diversity of post-industrial democratic society. Here, we come close to an argument of a clash of civilizations, even if that clash is not between Islam and the West. Others claim that the attacks are the work of a small, maniacal group of terrorists, unrepresentative of the mainstream of their societies, and isolated in small, disorganized, conspiratorial groups. While both analyses capture part of the more complex character of the current threat, neither analysis can stand close scrutiny and the weight of evidence. And, more important, the conceptual language is wrong.

We are in a new kind of struggle, one against a network with global reach. We need to understand who organizes and manages this particular network. And, we need appropriate conceptual language to understand what a network is, how it operates, how it thrives, and how it withers. Without appropriate conceptual language, we will misunderstand the threat and misconceive the response.

2. The Network as the Basic Form of Post-Industrial Organization

We have witnessed the first large-scale violent attack against post-industrial society, using its signature form of organization: the network. The network has become the most pervasive organizational image and the dominant form of social organization in post-industrial society. 'As a historical trend,' observes Manuel Castells, 'dominant functions and processes in the information age are increasingly organized around networks. Networks constitute the new social morphology of our societies, and the diffusion of networking logic substantially modifies the operation and outcomes in processes of production, experience, power, and culture.'[1] Networks also shape processes of terror and violence, and we need to understand the structure of a network, its application, and its resiliency in the face of disruption.

A network is a collection of connected points or nodes, generally designed to be resilient through redundancy. It can be one terminal, connected to the Internet, or one expert communicating with another expert in a common network devoted to a shared problem. The design of the network determines its resilience, its flexibility, its capacity to expand, and its vulnerability. The computer network originally designed by the Department of Defense in the 1960s was made invulnerable to nuclear attack, because no single computer or computer site was the centre for the transmission of communications. Every message was broken into 'packets' that could take alternative routes to their destination. Were one node to be destroyed, the message would reroute toward another. The network was resilient because of its built-in redundancy. So were the financial networks headquartered within the World Trade Center. Within hours, many had resumed operations because of the redundancy they had built into their information systems.

No single approach against a single site – even the headquarters, to the extent they exist – will be effective. The implications are clear: removing a single node, or even several, will not destroy the network. The attack on the World Trade Center, the symbolic seat of global corporate finance, failed; it did not succeed in disrupting network financial transactions. In the pure model of a network, eliminating one node of a network does not imperil other nodes. The network adjusts, reroutes, and reforms.

Networks generally are also highly decentralized, with different leadership branches that operate with a large degree of autonomy. Unlike the tight pyramids of command-and-control structures, the hallmark of industrial society, networks are 'flat,' with leaders who are empowered to act under a minimum of direction and supervision.

3. Global Networks

Networks are a characteristic organizational form in post-industrial society in an era of globalization. Using advanced electronic forms of communication, global networks of every kind have multiplied in the last decade: civil society networks, journalists, scientists, physicians, lawyers, scholars, and environmentalists. These networks differ in how they are organized and, consequently, in their flexibility and resilience.

Most generally do not approximate the pure form of network. A study of global knowledge networks found, for example, that the most successful networks require a centre or a 'hub,' financial support, and a secure environment for the 'host' which serves as the temporary organizational focus. There is an element of 'place,' even if that place is temporary, within almost all successful networks work.[2] Most networks build some elements of a 'web' into their design. Analysts have suggested, for example, that one of the reasons why complex financial networks were able to resume operations so quickly after the attack on September 11th was that the 'corporate headquarters' of many of the firms had been moved off site after the first attack in 1993.

4. Global Networks of Terror

Global networks of terror bear an uncanny resemblance to their generally benign and productive counterparts. Unlike legitimate global networks, of course, they work in secrecy and through illegitimate practices and violence to advance their political purposes. Often with life-cycles of decades, networks of terror thrive on the openness, flexibility, and diversity of post-industrial society, crossing borders almost as easily as do goods and services, knowledge and cultures. They have global reach, particularly when they can operate within the fabric of the most open and multicultural societies, and through post-industrial organizational forms.

Global networks of terror are enabled by conditions unique to our times. They are conceivable only in a world that is tightly interconnected and in societies that are moving through the processes of post-industrialization. Without global markets and communications, the widespread mobility of people, and multicultural, diverse societies, these networks of terror could not survive, much less succeed.

Many hosts of networks of terror, although not all, cling to weak states that can provide a secure environment for the infrastructure and resources that they need. They often depend on states for infrastructure, logistics, and training sites. In exchange for the shield provided by a state, a network delivers complex political and financial rewards that help a regime to stay in power. An ideal environment for a 'host' of a network of terror is a weak or fractured state where a network can provide critically needed assets in exchange for the capacity to operate 'in place.' Even without a secure physical environment, however, networks can survive; a host can use mobile headquarters but operations and recruitment become more difficult.

5. Who is this Network?

The existence of al-Qa'eda was well-known to intelligence analysts and experts on the region long before September 11th. Its organizational structure, according to the best available knowledge, in large part resembles a network. It is organized in self-contained nodes that function autonomously, with limited communication and support from the centre. Responsibility and decision making power is devolved down to the lowest possible level. Unlike open networks, however, each node is unaware of the identities and attributes of others.

The name of al-Qa'eda means base. Historically, it has had only temporary bases, first in Sudan and now in Afghanistan. It is better described as 'a distributed, roaming, non-territorial network, operating through its combined use of advanced information technologies and traditional *halawa* exchanges.'[3] Its nodes communicate through the Internet, funds are transferred through local exchanges with global connections, and its members move freely across the borders of multi-cultural, diverse societies.

Al-Qa'eda is also a network of networks. In the last three years, it successfully interlinked with other networks like Gama'at el-Islamiya, a network led by Egyptian dissidents and exiles, the Armed Vanguard of Conquest, and the Islamic Group from Algeria. The Egyptian network brought a significance increase in the level of operational planning, competence and logistics to the broader network. As al-Qa'eda connects with other networks, it more closely approximates a pure network with very flexible, insulated, and redundant connections.

It does, however, have a centre, the equivalent of a small corporate headquarters, and it operates in place. Both these attributes merit some attention. It has a hub, which is led by Saudi and Egyptian dissidents and is organized in a corporate structure. 'It has a financial committee, an operations committee, a committee on Islamic study, and a military committee.'[4] Leaders are important, but, as in other network structures, not all-important. It is consequently misleading to personalize the threat as Osama bin-Laden, for in this kind of hybrid network-corporate structure, he can be replaced by others were he to disappear. On the other hand, it is also misleading to claim, as some do, that bin-Laden is a social construction, that he is the creation of those who seek to personalize and demonize the enemy. His leadership, and his charisma – expressed in part through piety, asceticism, and commitment – has been significant. As in other kinds of social and political organizations, leaders matter in networks. They may matter far less than they do in command-and-control hierarchies, but, even in networks, they still matter. Al-Qa'eda approximates 'a hybrid peer-to-peer network, in which a central source triggers the actions that are carried out by individual nodes.'[5] Destroying the centre and removing the leader would weaken but not necessarily disable the network.

Al-Qa'eda is a network that also functions partly 'in place.' In its very earliest phase of development, it used Sudan as a host. When bin-Laden was expelled by Sudan, he secured his headquarters behind the shield provided by the Taliban in Afghanistan. Here, the network becomes a more familiar and vulnerable organizational form as it organizes training camps, recruits members, and draws on a pool of sympathizers to form a guard around its assets. These assets are potential targets and can be disrupted more easily than a pure network without the organizational apparatus of a corporate headquarters.

Paradoxically, this network organized in post-industrial form, is committed to a pre-industrial project of religious monopoly and intolerance. It rejects the post-industrial project even as adapts its organizational forms and technology to pursue its purpose. Al-Qa'eda rejects not only post-industrial society but even the hierarchical command-and control state characteristic of the industrial era. It seeks a return to an earlier community of the faithful uninterrupted by the borders and the divisions of the modern state.

6. The 'Roots' of the Network

The roots of any network of terror are complex. The Soviet invasion of Afghanistan and the funding of Afghani groups by the United States to fight against Soviet forces set the context for this network. After the Soviet Union withdrew, some of those who had come to the assistance of the Afghani resistance turned their attention to the overthrow of governments in Saudi Arabia and Egypt. If there are 'roots' of al-Qa'eda, they can be found largely in the closing of political space in Saudi Arabia and Egypt in the last two decades.

Political challenges to both regimes were dealt with through the politics of deflection. Both Egypt and Saudi Arabia exported their problem to other weaker, less stable societies, with less well embedded states. Stronger regimes exported the threats to their stability to weaker states. Dissidents were jailed or exiled but the government of Saudi Arabia funded Islamic groups causes that operated beyond territorial borders to provide a safety valve for political opposition at home. To mute protest, governments adapted some of the language of the dissidents and strengthened Islamic iconography and discourse for political purposes. The only safe way to express opposition to the government became Islam and the only safe place to do so became the mosque.

This strategy of political deflection has enabled al-Qa'eda in important ways. It creates a context in which the discourse of militant Islam is gradually legitimated, even while those who pose a threat to the regime are expelled or jailed. A climate permissive of increasingly militant Islam makes it easier for al-Qa'eda to recruit members, to raise funds, and to enlist support for training and operations.

The opening of political processes in these societies will not happen quickly, especially in the face of active networks of terror. The closing of space for 'normal' politics and the growth of networks of terror are mutually and positively reinforcing. Were greater political space to open, it would make it more difficult to recruit new members, but the commitment of current members of the network would in all likelihood remain. There is no escape from the struggle with a network of terror.

7. The Challenge of a War against a Network

A struggle against a network is different. It is asymmetric: states must fight a global network that is not designed around dominant power centres, but is dispersed, flat, and flexible. It is easier, for example, to destroy a web-like structure, with a controlling hub, connected through strands to the points of the web. Destroy the hub and the web is fatally weakened. Not so with a network.

When we think about al-Qa'eda as a network, it becomes clear that existing military doctrine, based on concepts of mass-and-maneuver, reinforced by heavy strikes from the air, is a poor fit with the target. Military doctrine will have to change to decentralize intelligence and command to the lowest possible levels, and provide as much flexibility as possible to give local area commanders the capacity to launch continuous pin-prick attacks from multiple directions to confuse and overwhelm the network.

A military attack to disable those who provide safe haven for the host and the assets of the network is a first but largely inadequate and limited response to a network of terror. Its purpose is to deprive al-Qeida, the host, of the secure geographic environment that the Taliban has provided. Conventional military attacks against the environment that fail to disable the host enhance the status of network leaders and their capacity to recruit among those outraged by the attacks. Military attacks, conducted through a command and control structure are designed to be effective against hierarchical state structures with conventionally structured forces. Here the purpose must be to destroy the capacity of this host to find a secure environment in which it can continue to act as a server to the network. A blunt military instrument may not succeed in performing even this limited task well.

To return to the analogy of computer networks, they often have more than a single host server. Increasingly, application processing is distributed across a network of hosts that are geographically dispersed. Client work stations, or nodes within the network, access the network for application software and communication with other end-user work stations and with databases that are themselves often distributed. This analogy is a reasonably good fit with the way the hijackers communicated with nodes of the network that were dispersed. Although the node has no knowledge of which server is supporting which part of the task at any moment, it still needs to have sufficient servers intact and in touch to continue its work.[6]

How then can the capacity of the network be impaired? It is unlikely that networks, organisms with rudimentary central nervous systems, can be destroyed. A network has no powerful central 'brain,' that can be surgically targeted to lead to quick death. Paradoxically, actions designed to 'kill' a part of the network directly identifies for the organism the part that has been damaged. Like other lower-order organisms, it then sheds that part and regenerates.

The capacity of the network must be degraded over time, through suffocation and starvation. The capacity of the servers must be degraded, the connections among nodes must be slowed, and the connections between the work-stations, or the cells on the ground, and the servers must be interrupted and eventually damaged.

How does this analogy of a computer network translate into a strategy against a network of terror? Let me suggest just three ways in which the analogy can be suggestive of strategy. The objective is to make it more difficult, more time-consuming, more expensive, for users in the field to get what they need from the 'hosts.' More rigorous requirements for documentation, more frequent checks on existing documentation, more frequent checks on compliance with existing regulations, all increase the transactions costs for users. This kind of strategy does not necessarily require new powers of enforcement, but a different approach to the implementation of existing regulations. The objective is to complicate life for the end user.

A useful analogue may be a virus that invades, disrupts, confuses, and overwhelms communication within a network through a multiplier effect. The strategic use of disinformation, misleading signals about possible targets, frequent and at times deliberately misleading messages about information at hand, can all make it more difficult for end users to communicate with hosts. This kind of strategy both increases the risks for end users, and simultaneously encourages them to communicate with the network for clarification. In the process, they become easier to identify and target.

A third strategy is to starve and suffocate the hosts. Depriving the host of a secure environment is only one way to make it more difficult for the host to perform its network function. Careful monitoring of resource transfers can reduce the capacity of the host to function efficiently and in a timely way. When network reaction time is slowed, the user finds it more difficult to complete tasks and co-ordination becomes more difficult. Gradually, fewer users qualify as active participants and the network begins to decline. Networks that lack redundancy, as we have seen, are inefficient. The strategic objective in a struggle against a network of terror is to reduce its redundancy.

All these strategies depend critically on intelligence, but our intelligence systems are not properly configured to wage this battle. Within the intelligence community, the emphasis is on secrecy, control, and a command and control structure. The structure is poorly suited to the struggle ahead, as is the emphasis on closed channels and secrecy. To disrupt a network of terror, we will need a reconfigured system of intelligence, one that is decentralized, network based, with a capacity to communicate and confuse in real time. Sharing information across nodes, rather than controlling and limiting information in a hierarchical structure, increases its value and impact.

Network-like thinking is suggestive for the reconfiguring of strategies of military and intelligence. It privileges flexibility and local initiative over centralization and command and control, openness rather than secrecy, and partnering rather than monopoly. Legislators preparing new guidelines for the war against the network would do well to keep these imperatives in mind.

Notes

*   Janice Gross Stein is the Harrowston Professor of Conflict Management and the Director of the Munk Centre for International Studies at the University of Toronto. She is the Massey Lecturer in 2001 and her most recent book is *The Cult of Efficiency*.

1   Manuel Castells, *The Rise of the Network Society*, Vol. 1 of *The Information Age: Economy, Society, and Culture* (Oxford: Blackwell, 1996), p. 469. See also Jessica Lipnack and Jeffrey Stamps, *The Networking Book: People Connecting with People* (New York: Routledge and Kegan Paul, 1986), and Barry Wellman and S.D.Berkowitz, ed. *Social Structures: A Network Approach* (Cambridge: Cambridge University Press, 1988).

2   Janice Gross Stein, Richard Stren, Joy Fitzgibbon, and Melissa MacLean, *Networks of Knowledge: Collaborative Innovations in International Learning* (Toronto: University of Toronto Press, 2001).

3   Ronald J.D. Deibert, 'Wars of The Wide-Area Networks,' http://www.watsohninstitute.org/infopeace/911/deibert_wide.html

4   From Obscurity to Most Wanted: A Failure to Heed al-Qa'eda's Telling Signs of Terror, New York Times, October 14, 2001, B6.

5   John Arguilla and David Ronfeldt, 'Fighting the Network War,' *Wired*, December 2001, p.150, and *Networks and Netwars: The Future of Terror, Crime, and Militancy* (Santa Monica, CA.: Rand, 2001).

6   I am indebted to Philip Siller for the elaboration of the computer network model to a network of terror. The reasoning in the following paragraphs draws on the logic he elaborated in a written memo to me. Email from Philip Siller, 10 November 2001.

Governing Security, Governing Through Security

MARIANA VALVERDE
Centre of Criminology
University of Toronto

This conference is primarily about law – about the antiterrorism bill, about existing law (including the Charter), and more fundamentally about the rule of law. But in democratic discussions of laws it is always important also to discuss and analyze the entity, the condition, or perhaps more accurately the utopian ideal for the sake of which laws like Bill C-36 are written – and that is, of course, 'security.'

The debate about civil liberties and Bill C-36 that already exists in civil society and to which this conference makes an important contribution has shown an unfortunate tendency to reproduce unthinkingly the assumption that the relation between 'security' and civil liberties – or even worse, security and freedom – is a zero-sum game. That is, people seem to think that it goes without saying that if we want to have more security we will just have to lose something from our democratic rights, and that if we decide to hold on to these rights and to our democratic traditions more generally, then our collective security may suffer.

This assumption is simply incorrect. The original theorist of security, Thomas Hobbes, first elaborated the zero-sum model in his prediction that even totally free and equal individuals would always, when push came to shove, trade in their natural freedoms for security. He may have been correct about some elements of human psychology: we see all around us, particularly if we look south of the border, plenty of re-enactments of Hobbes' original social contract.[1] But whatever the psychological accuracy of Hobbes' pessimistic individualism, Hobbes turned out to be wrong about *collective* human history, particularly about political history.

Throughout the 19th and 20th centuries, the development of totalitarian regimes with new capacities to control and monitor populations has shown that Hobbes was incorrect in equating the security of the 'Commonwealth' or state with the security of *citizens*. One need not have lived in the Soviet Union under Stalin to have learned from our collective historical inheritance that measures that enhance the security of the state are often inimical not only to the rather abstract freedoms we call civil liberties but even to that fundamental good that criminologists call 'primary security,' that is, the basic physical safety of oneself and one's loved one's.

1. Assessing Security Needs and Security Solutions: Democracy in Action

Research by criminologists and urban-studies scholars has amply demonstrated that both primary security and other basic democratic goods are more likely to be achieved, maintained, and (the most difficult part) guaranteed by measures that rely on and build up horizontal links among citizens, rather than vertical state-citizen relations of surveillance. Although social research often produces results that are counter-intuitive, in this case research tends to back up what we know from our own experience. For example, we don't deal with our fear of child abduction by posting armed guards at playgrounds, and we don't decide to cancel Hallowe'en trick-or-treating as a measure to reduce the risk of child sexual abuse. Both of these dangers are extremely serious, involving some of the worst things that could ever happen to human beings. But Canadians don't generally govern the many risks that surround our lives, our families, our households, and our neighbourhoods by deploying the most high-tech and most military solutions. We do indeed take all kinds of precautions that maximize security: but we don't usually act on the basis of the worst fear or the worst risk. We govern our safety and security risks by quickly performing a complex non-numerical calculation through which we consider that preventing one risk often creates a different kind of risk, and that measures to enhance security (such as recourse to armed guards) often create new safety risks, as well as risks to the social relations of community life that are the bedrock of democracy. There are two steps in this process: first, we assess our security needs,[2] often in ways that differ from what a 'professional' assessment would generate; and secondly, we evaluate different means of meeting those needs. Having decided just how far we are willing to go in putting other values and other risks aside for the sake of 'security, we choose carefully among the diverse array of possible "security solutions".'

In choosing among the array of possible 'security solutions,' we don't necessarily take the advice of those who sell security services, or of those who are employed by the state to provide security. We understand that professionals in all walks of life tend to give advice that is highly coloured by their own work. We don't go to a rape crisis centre to get positive sex education materials for our teenagers; and we don't ask a civil-liability specialist whether we should hold a large, fun New Year's Party. This does not mean we are naive about risks. It simply means that we are cautious about letting the risk specialists, and in the case of 'security' the professionals of traditional, heavy-handed 'security,' dominate our lives. We are aware of alternative ways of providing and guaranteeing security that do less harm to our other goals and values.

All of this underlines the dangers inherent in committing the fallacy – a political as well as grammatical fallacy – of mistaking 'security' for a concrete noun. 'Security' is not something we can have more of or less of, because it is not a thing at all. It is – as Hobbes tells us – the name we use for a temporally extended state of affairs characterized by the calculability and predictability of the future.[3] This condition of predictability, this experience of temporality, does not actually exist anywhere – as Hobbes implies when he compares war not to actual fighting but to something like foul weather, that is, a general condition of insecurity over a long period of time, a metaphor that has the effect of reminding us that, like fair weather in England, security can never be successfully guaranteed. The impossibility of guaranteeing security is rooted in the fact that like justice, and like democracy, 'security' is not so much an empirical state of affairs but an ideal – an ideal in the name of which a vast number of procedures, gadgets, social relations, and political institutions are designed and deployed.

Each of the constellations or ad hoc assemblages of material and social relations that constitute the never-ending quest for security has certain social and political effects. In many instances research on the effects of this or that security 'assemblage'[4] exists. To give one example: surveillance cameras are supposed to reduce the risk of crime and increase both the reality and the feeling of security by announcing to offenders that they will be caught, and by making law-abiding citizens feel that someone is watching. But in Britain, which has by far the highest per capita number of surveillance video cameras, scholars have shown that criminals are not necessarily deterred, in part because (as criminals well know) there is often no human eye behind the camera, there is nobody that actually watches the video being recorded.[5] If the effect of security cameras on crime is not clear, so too law-abiding citizens do not necessarily *feel* safer under the anonymous gaze of the surveillance video. In Toronto, the not yet build Yonge-Dundas public square was designed not to have surveillance cameras precisely because the focus groups conducted by the firm that won the contract for the square showed that people felt that the presence of cameras made them feel they were in a high-crime, dangerous area. An interesting example of the contestation of security needs assessment occurred when, recently, Police Chief Julian Fantino, who like police generally sees the city exclusively as a vast scene of crime,[6] insisted that surveillance cameras be added to the square's design.[7]

2. Governing Security

At the Centre of Criminology we have conducted many empirical and theoretical studies of what we call 'the governance of security.'[8] These studies show that it is indeed possible to devise mechanisms that maximize democracy, cultural pluralism, and neighbourliness while at the same time increasing safety and security. Internationally, research on contemporary law-and-order initiatives, such as the much-trumpeted zero-tolerance policing programmes in New York City and in Chicago, shows that passing harsher laws and municipal ordinances, giving the security professionals the gadgets they like (such as police helicopters) and increasing the number of criminal charges does not reduce crime any better than the community-based, antimilitary strategies involved in what is known as 'problem-oriented community policing.'[9]

The point here is that Big Brother does not have a monopoly on the provision of the means of urban safety and citizen security, as a matter of empirical fact. Therefore, Big Brother ought not to be the main voice defining our security needs and devising the mechanisms by which thes needs are to be met. By 'Big Brother' I am mainly referring to CSIS and to law-and-order oriented police chiefs. There is a great deal of expertise in Canada on democratic forms of domestic security; but these grasroots-oriented experts tend not to be in federal agencies. These experts are in neighbourhood safety projects, and to some extent also among police units trained in community policing and crime prevention.

Some might say that democratic security mechanisms are all right for playgrounds and to prevent burglaries, but are not appropriate for terrorism. In response to this, one would have to engage in an unpacking of the umbrella term 'terrorism,' breaking it up, analyzing it into its various components. Unpacking the term, forcing users of the word 'terrorism' to employ more concrete words instead, makes it very clear that there are some activities that 'terrorists' engage in that require something like a military response – but on the other hand, there are many other activities that cannot be either monitored or prevented by conventional high-tech, top-down military-style or spy-agency style measures and for which community-based responses based on horizontal social bonds rather than on vertical state powers are adequate responses.

Let me give an example. In response to the anthrax cases, New York's Grand Central Station now features soldiers in camouflage uniforms brandishing M-16 rifles. The research on gun control shows that accidents and suicides make up a large proportion of guns going off (indeed, in Canada, there are more accidents and suicides with rifles than there are homicides). This demonstrates that the decision to post soldiers trained for war holding battlefield-grade weapons is not evidence-based, as they say in medical sciences. And whatever the causes of the decision, which are in some ways irrelevant, the *effects* of that decision are clear: citizens taking the train will feel that America is indeed at war, that the enemy is within, that ordinary procedures and freedoms are suspended, that the army is our best friend ... and so on. These political effects provide comfort and benefit to certain interests, while undermining other values like multiculturalism and civil freedoms. But whether one knows the statistics about gun-related deaths, and whether one is an expert on the political semiotics of guns, it should be obvious to the reasonable person that having a lot of automatic weapons in a very crowded place that is distinguished by a high number of transient mentally ill people is not a good security measure, if citizen security (as opposed to state security) is what we prioritize.

In other words: there is neither expert evidence nor reasonable-person-type evidence to support the decision to deploy troops with battlefield weapons in crowded urban centres. But the decision was taken, and as far as I know there has been very little dissent. That shows that the incredibly important task of defining security needs and engaging in a process to meet those needs has been pretty successfully monopolized by a certain group of people – people who are of course honestly interested in security, but who have a professional bias in favour of top-down military style solutions. The high-tech military-style professionals cannot be faulted for giving the advice they give; but politicians can be faulted for assuming that they are the only source of wisdom. We don't get all our health advice or meet all our health needs from high-tech surgery specialists; for some things we go to them, but for others we go to nurse practitioners, chiropractors, psychotherapists, or any one of a number of alternative sources of knowledge. Security is like health: an abstract noun, a term hovering above a very diverse array of different types of knowledge, different procedures, different solutions. Surgery is not always the only or the best solution, in security as in health matters. The rise of 'evidence-based medicine' in recent years could serve as an inspiration to think about the urgent need for evidence-based security solutions.

The professionals of security, who in relation to Bill C-36 are primarily interested in enhancing state security, not citizen security, are thus not necessarily the experts on what works, on the most effective ways of minimizing the risks of politically motivated crime. But my argument for a democratic process of assessing security needs and choosing among a range of possible security solutions is normative as well as pragmatic. In a democracy, the police don't write the Criminal Code, and they don't set out the rules of procedure and the rules of evidence. What counts as a crime; what penalty should be attached to that crime; and what the police can or cannot do when in pursuit of criminals are all issues that in a democracy are governed by a combination of elected representatives and independent courts, with considerable public input. The police of course claim that they are the real experts on crime. But if democracy means anything, it means that the police do not get to monopolize either the public process by which the Criminal Code is written and interpreted or the parameters within which the Code is enforced. The criminal defence bar has for many years been a strong voice to provide an alternative view on questions of defining crimes and enforcing the law; and other groups in civil society have of course been very active as well, as we have seen in situations like the decriminalization of homosexuality and abortion.

In the area of 'security,' however, there is not much by way of organized public debate. Alternative voices, both among academics and around communities, do exist; but they are not being heard. This is in part because the debate about the antiterrorism bill and the broader debate about 'security' has been conducted from the start as if we all knew what security is and where it can be purchased, as if the only questions to be decided was how much money to spend and how much of our freedom to sacrifice. This way of posing the debate concedes far too much to the Hobbesian model favoured by state security professionals. Since do not live under Hobbes' Leviathan, or at least, not yet, the process of assessing security needs and evaluating different potential solutions needs to be as democratic as possible.

3. Governing Through Security

The governance of security is only one of the issues calling out for urgent democratic participation. A related discussion, one which will be furthered by some papers given here tomorrow, concerns how matters such as immigration and charitable giving are coming to be governed in the name of security. The American criminal law scholar Jonathan Simon has eloquently argued that in the US immigration and poverty have increasingly come to be 'governed *through* crime,' with rather nasty consequences in both cases.[10] Similarly, in Canada as in other parts of the world, we are seeing not only worrying moves in the governance *of* security but also moves that amount to 'governing through security' – namely, the governance of other areas of public life from the standpoint of a Hobbes-defined notion of security. Immigration procedures and other areas of law and policy affected by Bill C-36 and other 'security' measures are examples of the direct governance of other areas of life through security. There are, however, other areas in which one can see a very worrying *indirect* governance of other things, other values and other budget items, through security. In the province of Ontario, for example, there is a good chance that the primary security and well being of people with cancer becomes severely damaged by longer treatment waiting lists that are the indirect result of 'security' budgets being maintained while health care budgets are cut back. This example shows the importance of thinking concretely, of refusing to go along with nice-sounding abstractions like 'security.' Any citizen-driven assessment of primary security needs would conclude that unnecessary waits for cancer treatment pose a very serious risk to Ontarians. At the same time, if Ontario citizens were encouraged to democratically scrutinize the 'security' budget, they would find that most of the money Ontario taxpayers spend on 'security' goes to the Ontario Provincial Police, a body which is mainly responsible for highway traffic and crime control in towns that are too small to have their own police force. Now, traffic accidents on Highway 400 are a real danger; but how do they rate if we compare them to the risks posed by longer cancer treatment waiting lists?

The point here is that in a democracy it is absolutely necessary for citizens to become acquainted with the details of governance and the particularities of government budgets. When politicians wave abstractions around like flags – abstractions like 'security,' or for that matter 'freedom' – citizens should be immediately suspicious. It was the philosopher Hegel, somewhat ironically given his notoriously obscure writing style, who gave us the most rigorously argued warnings about the dangers of the politics of abstractions. The freedom sincerely advocated by French revolutionary activists turned into the unfreedom of the Terror precisely because it was an abstraction; the rationality sought by Enlightenment philosophers turned into the irrationality of Romanticism because it was not sufficiently concrete; and so on. And in our own day, the security sought by the Minister of Justice is likely to turn into insecurity for large numbers of Canadian citizens unless we all pay close attention to the concrete details and get involved in defining our security needs and participating in the debate about how we want to meet those needs. The insecurity I refer to is not simply a lack of civil liberties; it is also a deficit in basic primary security – in physical safety (particularly in relation to such innovative practices of citizen insecurity as detention without charges), in what the UN calls food security, which will suffer as social services are cut back even more for the sake of military and police budgets, and, as my example of the indirect governance of the health budget through 'security,' in the basic health and well-being of the population as a whole.

The abstract noun 'security' is an umbrella term that both enables and conceals a very diverse array of governing practices, budgetary practices, political and legal practices, and social and cultural values and habits. There cannot be a more urgent task at this moment than facilitating public participation in a broad debate about what we mean by 'security,' how we think 'security' should be governed, who should be involved in defining security needs and choosing security solutions, and how a whole range of needs and values may be affected by measures taken in the name of security. Democratic discussions about security needs and solutions already exist, but unfortunately these have tended to remain local. What we desperately need at this point is to have national authorities listen to local experience, and to international experience as well; we need our politicians to recall the basic principle of security provision in liberal democratic societies, namely, that the security of the state and the security of citizens do not necessarily coincide, and have often been at odds; and we need to demand opportunities for significant grassroots involvement in the definition of security needs and the provision of security solutions.

In conclusion, I am not appealing to you to listen to my expertise on security matters rather than listening to CSIS – an appeal which would substitute one undemocratic authority for another. Instead, I appeal to you to reflect upon your own experiences and your own knowledge of security issues and to immediately get involved in the process of concretely assessing security needs and security solutions.

Because of this dissemination of security rationales to areas of life far removed from both terrorism and crime, it is absolutely imperative for all citizens to take an active part in the democratice process of defining our security needs and discussing which particular means we want to use to meet this or that security need. Expert evidence from those who know about forms of democratic security will be useful, but I would suggest that we can also draw from our own experiences of managing our own security risks. In our own lives, we usually prefer to manage and govern security provision democratically rather than giving it up to either commercial or military 'experts'; and we do not usually govern any and all domestic and workplace risks and conflicts under the banner of security, in the name of security. So we already have the resources that are needed to engage in the much-needed debate on security needs and security measures.

Notes

1 In parts of the United States as in many cities in the Third World, the Hobbesian contract is particularly visible in the context of private for-profit security providers. Upper-class whites who migrate to gated communities would not give up their natural freedoms to the state, but they have little hesitation to embrace stringent systems of commercially run surveillance and control that curtail their own freedom, not just that of potential intruders or 'criminals.' See among other sources Mike Davis, *City of Quartz* (New York, Vintage, 1992, especially chapter 4).

2 There is a highly sophisticated literature on the ways in which economic and social needs are subject to a complex process of 'needs interpretation' through which some needs become politically visible and are deemed legitimate, whereas other needs fall below the political radar. The American political theorist Nancy Fraser is one of the key contributors to this literature.

3 'For Warre, consisteth not in Battell only, or the act of fighting; but in a tract of time, wherein the Will to contend by Battell is sufficiently known: and therefore the notion of Time is to be considered in the nature of Warre; as it is the nature of Weather. For as the nature of Foule weather, lyeth not in a shower or two of rain, but in an inclination thereto of many dayes together: so the nature of War, consisteth not in actuall fighting; but in the known disposition thereto, during all the time there is no assurance to the contrary ... Whatsoever therefore is consequent to a time of Warre, where every man is Enemy to every man; the same is consequent to the time wherein men live without other security than what their own strength, and their own invention shall furnish them withall.' T. Hobbes, *Leviathan* [1651] Part I chapter 13, Penguin 1968 ed. pp. 185–186.

4 I borrow the term 'assemblage' from the French sociologist of science Bruno Latour, who emphasizes that science is not a body of textual knowledge but rather a set of practice-driven assemblages of instruments, measuring practices, people, and ideas. Elsewhere I argue that in legal contexts the production and authorization of different knowledges can be usefully studied as a question of the construction of various assemblages from elements usually borrowed from elswhere: M. Valverde, *Law's dream of a common knowledge* (forthcoming Princeton University Press.)

5 See the analysis of surveillance videos in the James Bulger murder case in A. Young, *Imagining crime* (London, Sage, 1996). See also S. Zukin, *Landscapes of power* (Berkeley, University of California Press, 1991) and S. Herbert, *Policing space: territoriality and the LA Police Department* (Minneapolis, University of Minnesota, 1997).

6 Allan Sekula's brilliant study of police photography borrows Walter Benjamin's comment on a Paris photographer, namely, that a certain style of photography makes the city feel like a 'vast scene of crime' (Sekula, 'The body and the archive' *October* Vol 39, 1986, 1–64). We could apply this to current events by pointing out that by giving the Toronto police money to buy a helicopter, Toronto city council was perpetuating the 'city as a vast scene of crime' model.

7 This information is drawn from Evelyn Ruppert's PhD thesis in progress, 'The moral economy of crities: security, consumption, aesthetics' (York University, Sociology Department).

8 M. Valverde, R. Levi, et al, *Democracy in governance: A socio-legal framework* (Report to the Law Commission of Canada, May 1999); M. Brogden and C. Shearing, *Policing for a new South Africa* (New York and London, Routledge 1993); J Wood and C Shearing, 'Reflections on the governance of security: a normative inquiry' forthcoming in *Police research and practice: an international journal*; M Valverde and M Cirak, 'Governing bodies, creating gay space: policing and security in Toronto's gay village' forthcoming in *British J of Criminology*.

9 For an overview see B Harcourt, *Illusion of order: the false promise of broken windows policing* (Cambridge Mass., Harvard 2001). For New York, see J Greene, 'Zero tolerance: a case study of police practices in New York City' *Crime and Delinquency* 1999 (April), 45 (2), 171–187, and M Felson et al, 'Redesigning hell: preventing crime and disorder at the Port Authority bus terminal' in *Preventing mass transit crime*, ed. RV Clarke (New York, Criminal Justice Press, 1996). For Chicago see R J Sampson, SW Raudenbusch and F Earls, 'Neighborhoods and violent crime: a multilevel study of collective efficacy' *Science* 277, 15 (August 1997), 918–924. See also the Oakland study in LG Mazerolle, C Kadleck, and J Roehl, 'Controlling drug and disorder problems: the role of place managers' *Criminology* 1998 , 36 (2), 371–403.

10 J Simon, 'Governing through crime' in L Friedman and G Fisher, eds., *The crime conundrum: essays on criminal justice* (New York, Westview Press, 1997), 171–189.

Terrorism's Challenge to the Constitutional Order

LORRAINE E. WEINRIB*
Faculty of Law
University of Toronto

Terrorists seek to undermine the rule of law and the preservation of human rights. The real test of our values is how they guide us in times of crisis. Quite frankly, in the past as a country we did not always pass that test. We must be vigilant today to make sure that we do not repeat past mistakes.[1]

I. Introduction

The proposed *Anti-Terrorism Act*, Bill-36, embodies Canada's legislative response to the terrorist attacks upon the United States on September 11, 2001. It reflects the realization that fundamentalist, internationally directed terrorist groups have the ability to effect massive loss of life, devastation and disruption of basic public services within North America. It also reflects the fact that the standard approaches to criminal activity – deterrence, detection and punishment – will not satisfy the government's commitment, in concert with other western countries, to prevent further attacks and ultimately dismantle these groups.

In introducing the Bill, Justice Minister McLellan described it as 'the most rigorously scrutinized piece of legislation' of her political career. She recounted the mobilization of extraordinary resources within a tight time frame. She ensured the Canadian public that (a) the Bill conformed to the strictures of the *Canadian Charter of Rights and Freedoms, 1982*, (b) complied with Canada's international obligations, and (3) compared favourably with the legislation of other countries.[2] The government made it a high priority to shape the debate on the *Charter* issues with a strong affirmative statement of *Charter* compliance.

The Minister mentioned, but did not produce, documentation setting out the detailed analysis prepared by her legal experts on the *Charter* issues. While conceding the unprecedented powers created, she emphasized their companion safeguards. She noted in particular the safeguards integrated in the Bill that had not been included in Canada's original emergency legislation, the discredited *War Measures Act* of 1914.[3] The Minister supported her prediction that the Supreme Court of Canada would uphold the Bill against any future *Charter* challenge with the observation that the 'balance between individual rights and collective security shifted after the attacks.'[4]

The government's initial defense of the Bill thus has four branches, none of which invoke emergency circumstances or powers explicitly. In fact, the government has denied that Bill C-36 is emergency legislation. Paramount is the claim that the Bill has been 'Charter-proofed.' This means that its expert legal advisers have considered possible legal challenges based on the *Charter* and determined that courts will uphold the legislation. This is the primary line of defense. Second, the government argued that the Bill is necessary to bring Canada into compliance with its international obligations to fight terrorism. Third, the government pointed out that its partners in fighting terrorism have implemented similar measures in their domestic legislation. Fourth, the government gave assurance that the Bill provides greater safeguards than did the *War Measures Act* – the statute that authorized some of the most egregious incursions upon basic rights and freedoms in Canadian history. Notably absent from this catalogue was any favourable comparison to the *Emergencies Act*, the statute that replaced the *War Measures Act* in 1988.[5]

The government's defense of the Bill to date has taken place in the forum of public opinion and within parliamentary proceedings, not in a court of law. Nonetheless, this multi-faceted anticipatory defense of the Bill reveals the government's understanding of the legal regime in which it would have to defend it. This paper challenges that understanding. I outline the rule of law framework that the government appears to presuppose and to which it has tailored its response to the new terrorist threat. It is within this framework that the government has expressed confidence as to the constitutionality of the Bill and, to date, resisted trenchant criticism as to its general and particular failings. The paper suggests that this understanding may not be the most appropriate basis on which to evaluate the merits or the constitutionality of Bill C-36.[6]

II. The *Charter* Framework: Rights, Justified Limits and Legislative Override

The government's confidence in the *Charter* compliance of the Bill appears to rest on the understanding that the Supreme Court of Canada would apply a less rigorous standard of review to Bill-36. It is possible, however, that the Court would consider the less rigorous approach inappropriate to challenges to the terms or operation of Bill C-36 because of its important public purposes.

The standard of review is a structural component of judicial review under the Charter. When our courts deliberate upon a claim of infringement of *Charter* rights, they first consider the issue of infringement and then, as a separate and distinct second question, analyze whether the infringement is justified. The party claiming an infringement by the state of a right or freedom guaranteed by the *Charter* bears the burden of proving the specific content of the guarantee and the fact of infringement. The government then bears the burden of establishing that an infringement is prescribed by law, a matter of form, and justified, a matter of substance. The stipulation of prescription by law requires that the measure be intelligible and accessible to those to whom it applies. Justification requires satisfaction of a sequenced inquiry into the super-ordinate objective of the impugned measure and then its proportionality to that objective. This analysis includes consideration of rational connection between ends and means as well as minimal impairment of the guarantee in question.

The government's second, third and fourth claims are relevant to this second stage – the justification of limitation on *Charter* rights. Justification of limitation upon a *Charter* guarantee often draws on the content of Canada's international obligations. This analysis may also take account of the ways in which other free and democratic countries have dealt with the problem at hand. From the point of view of domestic law, it may be relevant that the impugned legislation or state action cures constitutional defects in earlier enactment or practice.

The government's defense of the Bill-36 thus anticipates the analysis that would engage a court of law deliberating upon the question whether the Bill on its face or in application, in whole or in part, breached the Charter. The government's prediction that the Supreme Court would be more deferential in this context, because the 'balance between individual rights and collective security has shifted', reveals its underlying understanding of the applicable legal rules. It amounts to a concession that certain, perhaps most, of the Bill's provisions would fail the first step, i.e., that a court of law would find that these features breached *Charter* guarantees. The government's professed optimism rests upon the second stage of *Charter* analysis. The government's legal advice must therefore be that the courts would uphold the impugned legislative provision – or action taken thereunder – at this second stage. Such a determination would follow from judicial analysis concluding that, despite its breach of a *Charter* guarantee, the impugned provision or action was justified nonetheless.

The public discussion of the Bill has not included explicit attention to the specific tests for prescription by law or justification. It stresses the importance of the fight against terrorism, not the more specific types of analysis that a court of law would apply. Emphasis on the purposes of the Bill makes sense in the court of public opinion. It constitutes, however, only one part of the analysis relevant to the second stage of Charter analysis.

Public opinion polls across the country reveal strong support for Bill C-36. These findings reflect our horror and fears in the aftermath of the wanton destruction and loss of life inflicted by terrorists on September 11, 2001. They also reflect our increased awareness of the possibility of biological, chemical or nuclear attacks. In this context, Canadians naturally focus on the paramount need to secure basic personal safety rather than the precise measures taken to achieve that goal. This would explain the government's repeated statements of openness to constructive comment on the Bill combined with its refusal to date to accept any recommended changes, including a sunset provision.

Acceptance of the broad purposes of a set of legislative proposals by the public or even by a majority of parliamentarians in a period of exceptional shock and fear is not an adequate benchmark for constitutionality. Moreover, it does not meet the legal tests stipulated for limitations on *Charter* rights and freedoms. In fact, the Canadian public expressly rejected such a test for permissible limits on rights in the context of a more focused debate on constitutional principles and state powers.

The penultimate draft of the formula for limitations on *Charter* guarantees would have permitted 'reasonable limits as are generally accepted in a free and democratic society with a parliamentary system of government.'[7] This compromise formula, put forward to make the *Charter* palatable to the eight provincial premiers who opposed its adoption, met scathing criticism when it came before the Special Joint Committee that deliberated upon the Charter's text in 1981–2. Dubbed the 'Mack Truck' clause, connoting the expansiveness of permissible limitation on rights that it would afford, it was condemned as worse that the *status quo* by a wide cross-section of Canadians.[8] Of particular importance was the generally held view that past breaches of fundamental freedoms in Canada under the *War Measures Act* would pass muster under this standard. One of the primary legal purposes of the *Charter* was to ensure that emergency conditions no longer authorizes unjustifiable encroachements on these fundamental freedoms.

The more stringent standard adopted in s. 1 of the *Charter* emerged as the product of deliberation upon the appropriate limitation formula in parliamentary hearings that constituted the most extensive public engagement on the terms of the relationship between the individual and the state in Canadian history. Its models were the postwar bills of rights at the national and international levels, which (unlike earlier instruments such as the U.S. Bill of Rights) make express provision for limitation on rights. The purpose of these clauses is to restrict the scope of permissible limitation on guaranteed rights and freedoms.[9] Then Justice Minister Chretien welcomed the narrowing of the limitation formula. He acknowledged that the final wording made it much more difficult for governments to persuade courts to limit *Charter* rights by insisting upon reasonableness, prescription by law, and demonstrable justification – not just general acceptance. Moreover, he acknowledged that the 'Mack Truck' clause, with its standard of general acceptability, would have permitted such extensive limitation on rights as to render the *Charter* guarantees 'useless.'[10] This view accords with the general view that the effectiveness of modern rights-protecting instruments is a function of the stringency of the permitted limitations on guaranteed rights and freedoms.

The eight premiers who opposed the Charter's adoption could not continue to oppose a *Charter* that had the widespread public approval demonstrated in the parliamentary hearings. Accordingly, they declined the invitation to test their opposition to the *Charter* in a national referendum. Instead, they made their acceptance of the Charter, including the more stringent limitation clause, conditional on the adoption of the legislative notwithstanding clause. This clause enables Parliament and the provincial legislatures to expressly, by statute, suppress the operation of selected *Charter* rights for a maximum, renewable, five-year period. They did not intend frequent or easy resort to this clause to suppress *Charter* rights at large or to overrule court decisions. Their models for this clause were in domestic federal and provincial statutes. They had come into operation very rarely if at all. The features that, as we have learned, exact a high political cost for using the notwithstanding clause were features that they, as seasoned politicians, knew would ensure its exceptional character.[11]

While Canadian governments may invoke the notwithstanding clause to suppress *Charter* rights in time of emergency, that was not its purpose. If it had been, the architects of the clause would have emulated the derogation clauses in the postwar rights-protecting systems which serve this end. They presumably decided not to do so because their complaint against the *Charter* was its restraint on political power generally, not specifically in times of emergency.

The postwar derogation clauses impose a regimen upon states when exceptional circumstances necessitate extraordinary measures that may encroach on fundamental rights and freedoms.[12] There must be a formal declaration of emergency by the government, including a detailed account of the derogations implemented. The threat must be exceptional, the measures adopted must be proportional to the threat, and international obligations must continue in force. Most importantly, these clauses stipulate that certain rights are not subject to derogation, even in times of declared emergency. While these clauses have attracted considerable criticism in their application, many of the problems noted have to do with their weak enforcement in the supra-national context.

Canada's *Charter* thus followed the pattern of the postwar rights-protecting instruments in providing a narrow, express, limitation clause.[13] It departed from these instruments in including a general notwithstanding clause, rather than a narrower and more circumscribed emergency derogation clause. One can therefore infer from the Charter's structure of rights protection that the exercise of state power under exceptional circumstances would be subject to judicial review under the *Charter* according to the regular arrangements. To displace these arrangements – whether in emergency circumstances or not – Parliament or a legislature would have to take the formal steps necessary to invoke the notwithstanding clause.

The terms of Bill 36 as well as the government's emphasis upon its compliance with the *Charter* make clear that any challenge to its constitutionality will fall to the courts for deliberation in the two stage analytic sequence. The Bill contains no invocation of the notwithstanding clause. The Minister of Justice has indicated that there is no plan to invoke this clause in the future to overrule a judicial ruling invalidating any part of Bill 36.[14] In any event, the Supreme Court of Canada has ruled that the notwithstanding clause may not be used retrospectively.[15] The rigour of the judicial analysis to be applied is therefore of paramount importance.

What standard of review should the judiciary apply when, in exceptional but not emergency circumstances, the government does not invoke the override to shelter its law from *Charter* challenge? Should the judiciary apply the rigorous standard appropriate to serious encroachments on fundamental rights or should it defer to the state in light of its political accountability, access to information and developed expertise? The institutional roles that emerged from an intense and prolonged debate on the Charter's remedial purposes suggest the need for stringent review. Reference to the evolution of the statutory structure that authorizes the exercise of emergency powers in Canada may provide some direction in answering this question.

III. The Statutory Framework for Emergency Powers

The framework of the derogation clause is not wholly absent from Canadian law. There is a statutory framework for the exercise of emergency powers by the federal government that possesses some of the same formal structure. This framework emulates the arrangements under the derogation instruments in the international rights-protecting instruments in requiring formal invocation, oversight and termination when the emergency conditions abate. Moreover, since it lacks any invocation of the notwithstanding clause, this regime remains fully subject to the Charter. It is also subordinated to the statutory *Canadian Bill of Rights, 1960*. These statutory arrangements shed light on the adequacy of the safeguards afforded under Bill C-36, which the government does not consider emergency legislation. It may also assist in the delineation of the appropriate standard of review under the *Charter* for Bill C-36.

The 1988 *Emergencies Act* replaced earlier discredited arrangements under the *War Measures Act* of 1914.[16] The latter statute had provided the authorization for government action inimical to our current understanding of legitimate state power. In the public debate leading to the adoption of the Charter, the excesses of power authorized by the *War Measures Act* became the standard example demonstrating the need for constitutional protection of basic rights and freedoms. This history also provided the benchmark for evaluating the effectiveness of various proposals for the Charter's structure of rights protection, especially the limitation clause. As Herbert Marx has observed: 'Nothing has stirred the disquietude of Canadians on civil liberties more than the treatment of Japanese Canadians in World War II. It is the skeleton in the closet that stalks out to haunt all our discussions on civil liberties.'[17]

The *War Measures Act* remained on the books from 1914 to 1988 when the *Emergencies Act* replaced it. The primary purpose of the *War Measures Act* was to concentrate power in the hands of the federal cabinet in times of emergency, with minimal oversight by Parliament or the courts. In effect for about 40% of that period, it constituted a parallel legal universe, i.e., a separate and distinct legal regime that empowered the federal government to exercise powers that were unthinkable in peacetime.[18] A.R.M Lower described its operation as 'the most complete surrender of parliamentary power made in any English-speaking country (except Newfoundland) since Henry VIII' and described Canada as having, in wartime, 'not parliamentary government, but "Order in Council" government.'[19]

Professor Patricia Peppin provides this description of these powers:

> The *War Measures Act* was used to impose censorship, to outlaw socially unacceptable organizations, to legalize retroactively the actions taken by the military during the Quebec City conscription riots, to impose preventive detention, to allow the deportation of Canadian-born people of Japanese ancestry, to permit the internment of thousands of Japanese Canadians, to authorize the confiscation of Japanese Canadians' property under the guise of expropriation for compensation, the registration and internment of alien enemies in both World Wars, and the detention of persons who belonged to 'unlawful associations' like the Communist Party. Citizenship, the right to hold property, freedom to contract, the right to bring a civil suit, freedom of speech, freedom of the press, freedom of association, *habeas corpus*, equality before the law, due process, the right to a fair trial, the presumption of innocence and the rule of law itself have all been denied in greater and lesser measure under the War Measures Act.[20]

The excesses reached their peak, as is often the case with grants of plenary emergency power, when the emergency conditions had abated. At the end of World War II, after hostilities had ceased, the government proposed to disperse within Canada and deport persons of Japanese ancestry on the view that they were disloyal. The deportation order was to apply to Japanese nationals in Canada, to naturalized and Canadian born Japanese, and to their wives and young children. Although the deportations were characterized as voluntary, there was evidence of coercion and revocation of the request for deportation was restricted. The Privy Council upheld the orders as falling within the plenary power accorded to government under the Act, despite the fact that the war was over. Members of Supreme Court of Canada would have exempted wives and children from the deportation order. Justice Rand, in a prescient dissent, excluded British subjects.[21]

The peacetime invocation of the *War Measures Act* also stirred enormous controversy. In 1970, the Trudeau government invoked the Act to respond to the terrorist activity that came to be known as the October Crisis. One can defend the invocation of the powers under the Act, especially since there was no other legislative framework that would have authorized a more limited intervention by the federal government. Failure to respond to the demands for assistance from the premier of Quebec, the mayor of Montreal and the Chief of Police was unthinkable. Commentators agree, however, that the powers exercised were excessive. In a recent interview, Marc Lalonde, who was Senior Secretary to the Prime Minister at the time noted that Trudeau was shocked at the number and extent of the arrests and searches. He attributed this excess to the lack of training and information available to the police.[22] As is often the case with emergency powers, there was controversy as to the cessation of the emergency conditions.[23]

These two historical episodes changed the course of Canadian legal history, marking the need for alteration of the basic legal framework. The concentration of power in the executive, lack of independent checks and balances in the legislative arena or the courts, and continuation of emergency powers long after the cessation of the emergency conditions were no longer acceptable. The adoption of the *Charter* secured protection of rights at the constitutional level through judicial review, without any concession for emergency conditions. The need for constraint on the powers available in time of emergency and oversight of their exercise by elected representatives prompted the specific terms of the *Emergencies Act*.

The preamble of the Act marks a strong departure from its predecessor by invoking the *Charter* and the Bill of Rights, as well as the International Covenant on Civil and Political Rights. It also emphasizes the exceptional and temporary character of emergency powers in the hands of the executive. The Act delineates separate sets of rules for different types of emergency. The category of 'international emergency' can serve as an example against which to evaluate the procedure and safeguards in Bill 36 since one could easily imagine its terms falling under that part of the Act.

An international emergency may involve Canada and one or more other countries. Its definition stipulates 'acts of intimidation or coercion or the real or imminent use of serious force or violence.' The Governor General in Council (Cabinet) proclaims such an emergency, after consultation with the provinces as is deemed appropriate and practicable. The declaration must include specification of the situation as well as the temporary measures necessary to respond. The declaration takes effect immediately; it expires automatically in 60 days unless previously revoked by Parliament or the Cabinet or extended by the Cabinet. Both Houses of Parliament must confirm the proclamation and consider any motion to revoke the declaration where supported by ten members of the Senate or twenty members of the House of Commons. All orders or regulations made under the authority of the proclaimed emergency must be laid before Parliament within two sitting days and are subject to revocation. The legislation calls for an all-party joint committee of the Senate and House of Commons to review, in secret, any orders or regulations exempted from publication. It also falls to this committee to review the exercise of powers and other activity under the declaration, with power of revocation or amendment over orders and regulations issued. The committee must report on its review function at intervals of at least sixty days.

The Act authorizes the Cabinet make orders or regulations under the authority of the proclamation of emergency. These powers are extensive and as invasive of existing rights and liberties as the provisions made a permanent component of Canadian law under Bill 36. The powers are however temporary. They are also subject to the ongoing involvement of Parliament. This oversight includes authorizing the continuity of the declaration from time to time. It also includes the responsibility of reviewing and reporting upon the exercise of the powers – in detail and on a timely basis. Moreover, it includes access, for some parliamentarians, to information not available to the public. The classic model of emergency power in Canada, previously exemplified by *the War Measures Act*, had concentrated power in the executive. This was both its strength and its weakness. The *Emergencies Act* reverses that tendency by reconstructing and intensifying the role of elected representatives, not merely those who sit in Cabinet or in the ruling party's caucus.

This model of parliamentary oversight, review and approval can provide safeguards over and above those afforded by judicial review under the *Charter* or the Canadian Bill of Rights. While *Charter* review is an important protection of our rights and liberties, it is slow, expensive to the claimant, and usually piecemeal rather than comprehensive in scope. Moreover, as our pre-*Charter* history and the experience of other countries makes clear, domestic courts tend to defer to governmental judgment in times of emergency. This deference rests on the view that the democratic arm of government bears political responsibility and accountability, has access to more information and better expertise.[24] Judicial bodies overseeing the exercise of emergency powers under international rights-protecting instruments display the same tendency.

Canadian history also makes clear, however, that such deference is often unwarranted and misplaced: 'crisis governments seldom remain limited governments.'[25] It is not unusual for the emergency powers to prove more dangerous than the emergency itself. For this reason it is important to provide ample checks and balances. The possibility of excessive breaches of rights is especially strong when the structures of government do not afford ample checks and balances. Both of these conditions prevail in Canada at this time. Canada's tradition of two strong national parties vying for power has abated. The Liberal Party has a strong hold on the levers of power, enjoying its third majority government, and popular support. The other parties are relatively small, divided and regionally based.

Moreover, our system of government concentrates an exceptional amount of power in the national executive. Other states, whether unitary or federal, have established checks on executive power. Canada, in contrast, vests extraordinary control over the available checks on executive power in the executive itself. Thus, the executive has command of Parliament, at least when there is a majority government, through the application of strict party discipline. Parliament, in turn, can legislate to contract the powers of the appointed Senate in a number of ways that do not fall afoul of the Constitution. The executive makes appointments to the Senate as well, an unusual arrangement in a federal state. In addition, and perhaps most importantly, the executive controls appointments to the superior courts in the provinces, the Federal Court and the Supreme Court of Canada.

The concentration of political power in the executive at the federal level in Canada is the product of a number of provisions in Canada's constituent instrument, the *Constitution Act, 1867*. Attempts to introduce more checks and balances as well as to increase the participation of the provinces at the center by means of constitutional amendment have failed. There is no reason to expect that initiatives along these lines will take shape in the foreseeable future.

Judicial review under the Constitution generally, or under the *Charter* in particular, remains the primary check on the exercise of state power, unless the executive or Parliament chooses to impose restrains upon itself. The *Emergencies Act* stipulates a strong role for Parliament when emergency powers are necessary. Bill C-36 does not. In this respect, Bill C-36 emulates the *War Measures Act* more than the two regimes, constitutional and statutory, adopted to prevent repetition of its abuses.

IV. Political Self-Restraint and Judicial Review

The Justice Minister may be right in her prediction that the 'balance has shifted' in the aftermath of the terrorist attacks on the United States on September 11, 2001. As a result, courts may well defer to the government when *Charter* challenges to Bill C-36 arise. One cannot deny that the Bill is both urgent and important or that the courts lack the political accountability, expertise and experience that one might insist upon for stringent review of the state's response to emergency situations. Moreover, it is the tendency of courts to defer in these types of circumstances.

On the other hand, good reasons militate against judicial deference in this context as well. The Supreme Court has not laid down a clear and consistent directive as to when it will defer, rather than engage in a stringent review of impugned state action that encroaches on guaranteed rights and freedoms. It has indicated, however, that some types of cases merit rigorous review. These include cases that pit the state against the individual. They also include cases that raise doubts as to whether the state respects the full equal dignity of those who are different from the majority in terms of their personal characteristics, including race, religion and ethnicity. Even the Charter's strongest critics concede that the courts should not defer when such basic rights and liberties are in jeopardy.

Canada's political history offers too many examples of the abuse and prolongation of emergency powers to assume that the government's assurances of high purpose and careful execution merit automatic deference. Indeed, this is the sorry story of emergency powers in most countries.[26] The legal purposes of the *Charter* included commitment to a reformed legal system, in which the rule of law would prevail over the exercise of emergency power through judicial review of infringements of guaranteed rights and freedoms. While the government would have us think that the exceptional circumstances in the aftermath of September 11th call for deference to its response, the opposite claim is not without merit.

While judicial review is of imperative importance, the *Emergencies Act* demonstrates the advantages of public policy that engages the institutional strengths of legislatures in their many different capacities. Bicameral, multi-party examination of government policy, including systematic review of its application in individual cases with access to confidential information and a reporting mechanism can prevent and remedy abuses long before they would come to the attention of the judiciary. The insights and evaluation offered by seasoned politicians are invaluable. It is important that the possibility of success in the courts, under a deferential standard of review, not distract us from the advantages of exploiting the protection of rights available from imaginative use of the representative arm of the state. It is, after all, the benchmark of our legal tradition, inherited from the United Kingdom, that legislatures refrain from exercising their full powers in recognition of the rights and freedoms of their constituents.

The institutional structure of the *Charter* supports this approach. It does not elevate super-courts over ordinary legislatures. It creates super-courts and super-legislatures, both charged to the extent of their institutional mandate and strengths, to forward the values of the rights-protecting polity. If Bill C-36 contained a notwithstanding clause it would preclude judicial review, with the attendant political responsibility for this step registered. In the absence of the notwithstanding clause, judicial review should be as stringent as is appropriate to the constitutional guarantees that stand imperiled.

The availability of judicial review does not leave the other arms of government free of responsibilities under the Constitution. On the contrary, all government actors bear the burden of discharging their responsibilities consistent with constitutional principles.[27] If they fail to do so, the courts may well create the institutional structure that compels compliance.

The government should assume that it might have to defend Bill C-36 under a stringent standard of review. This discipline will likely make the safeguards put forward by the Bill's critics look more attractive, even though they diminish executive power. These safeguards will go a long way to satisfying the courts that any *Charter* infringements are prescribed by law, reasoned and sufficiently narrow.

V. Conclusion

Our common law tradition, in theory if not always in practice, provides us with the paradigm of self-restraint and self-regulation by the executive and the legislature to ensure the enjoyment of our fundamental rights and freedoms. The greatest judges in this tradition supported this approach, but had ultimately to cede to their more deferential colleagues.[28] The rejection of their wisdom produced the need to adopt the Charter. The *Emergencies Act* marks continuity with this vision.

The paradigm of the post-Second World War constitutional state, reflected in the institutional structure of the Charter, provides us with the advantage of constitutionally guaranteed rights and freedoms, protected by judicial review. Our rights are subject only to justified limits in courts of law or express denial through the exceptional invocation of the notwithstanding clause.

These two approaches, one constitutional and one statutory, to the rule of law offer different modes of protection for our most fundamental interests. We need not choose between them just as we need not consider anti-terrorism law as inimical to respect for the most basic principles of liberal democracy. We can enjoy the advantages of each mode of protection. We can enjoy the creative tension of both.

Notes

* Louise James and Roy Lee provided valuable research assistance for this paper.

1 National Post, October 16, 2001, A01.

2 National Post, October 16, 2001, A03. She mentioned specifically the United States, the United Kingdom, Australia, New Zealand and France.

3 5 Geo. 5, c.2 (Can).

4 The Globe and Mail, October 6, 2001 A1 and October 22, 2001, A7.

5 S.C. 1988, c. 29. See text, infra, at note 15.

6 The Minister of Justice has recently added a fifth line of defense to the Bill. In her presentation on October 29th, 2001 to the Special Senate Committee examining Bill c-36, the Minister stressed that the Bill does not pit terrorism against civil liberties, as her earlier statements suggested. Rather, the Bill works to protect the most basic human right – the right to peace and security. This at right, she pointed out, is essential to the protection of all *Charter* rights, such as freedom of expression and association. This statement echoes that of the Home Secretary David Blunkett on the occasion of outlining the government's legislative package to combat terrorism to the U.K. Parliament. News Release, Home Office, dated October 15th, 2001.

7 Anne F. Bayefsky, *Canada's Constitution Act, 1982 & Amendments: A Documentary History* (Toronto: McGraw-Hill Ryerson Ltd., 1989) at 766.

8 Proceedings of the Special Joint Committee of the Senate and of the House of Commons on the Constitution of Canada 1980–1, 38:42. See Lorraine Weinrib, 'Canada's *Charter* of Rights: Paradigm Lost?,' forthcoming in Review of Constitutional Studies.

9 Alexandre C. Kiss, 'Permissible Limitations on Rights,' in Louis Henkin, ed., *The International Bill of Rights: The Covenant on Civil and Political Rights* (New York: Columbia University Press, 1981) 290 at 310: '... the ultimate objective of the limitation clauses is not to increase the power of a state or government but to ensure the effective enforcement of the rights and freedoms of its inhabitants.'

10 Proceedings, *supra* note 6, 38:42.

11 Bayefsky, *supra* at 904–5. Bayefsky provides the text of the First Ministers' Agreement, dated November 2–5, 1981, which sets out the other elements of the final compromise, and an accompanying fact sheet. See Lorraine Weinrib, 'The Activist Constitution' in Paul Howe and Peter H. Russell eds., *Judicial Power and Canadian Democracy* (Montreal: McGill-Queen's University Press, 2110) 80.

12 Venkat Iyer, 'States of Emergency – Moderating their Effects on Human Rights,' (1999) 22 Dalhousie L.J. 125.

13 Lorraine Weinrib, 'The Supreme Court of Canada in the Age of Rights,' [2001] 80 Can. Bar Rev. 699.

14 The *Globe and Mail*, October 16, 2001, A5.

15 *Ford v. A.G. Quebec*, [1988] 2 S.C.R. 712; 54 D.L.R. (4th) 577. For discussion, see Lorraine Weinrib 'Learning to Live with the Override' (1990) 35 McGill Law Journal 541.

16 *The Emergencies Act*, S.C. 1988, c. 29.

17 Herbert Marx, 'The Emergency Power and Civil Liberties in Canada,' (1970) 16 McGill Law Journal 39 at 83. See also, Lorraine Weinrib, 'Situations of Emergency in Canadian Constitutional Law,' (1990) *Contemporary Law: Canadian Reports to the 1990 International Congress of Comparative Law* (Montreal: Yvon Blais, 1991); and Peter Rosenthal, 'The New Emergencies Act' (1991) 20 Man. L.J. 563.

18 Marx, *supra* at 40. D.G. Creighton, *Dominion of the North* (Boston: Houghton Mifflin, 1944) at 439.

19 A.R.M. Lower, *Colony to Nation* (Toronto: Longmans, Green and Co., 1946) at 469–70.

20 Patricia Peppin, 'Emergency Legislation and Rights in Canada: The War Measures Act and Civil Liberties,' (1993) 18 Queen's Law Journal 129 at 131.

21 *Co-operative Committee on Japanese Canadians v. A.G. Canada*, [1947] A.C. 87.

22 Max and Monique Nemni, 'The October Crisis Revisited: A Conversation with Marc Lalonde,' (2000) 28 Cite Libre 40 at 46.

23 Legislation enacted to replace the *War Measures Act* two months after the October Crisis included a sunset clause, causing it to lapse on April 30, 1971. The sunset clause was included at the insistence of Justice Minister John Turner. There are reports that Premier Bourassa of Quebec, Prime Minister Trudeau and others insisted upon continuation of the measures outlawing the FLQ when the sunset was about to take effect. Turner prevailed, sustaining the view that the Criminal Code provided an adequate basis for dealing with criminal activity, including revolutionary violence. Toronto Star, November 4, 1990, B4.

24 George J. Alexander, 'The Illusory Protection of Human Rights by National Courts During Periods of Emergency,' (1984) 5 Human Rights Law Journal 1 and

Daniel C. Kramer 'The Courts as Guardians of Fundamental Freedoms in Times of Crisis,' (1980) 2 Universal Human Rights 1.

25 Edward A. Harris, 'Living with the Enemy: Terrorism and the Limits of Constitutionalism,' (1992) 92 Columbia Law Review 984.

26 The Independent, Oct 2, 2001 9: 'Lawyers know that the statute books are littered with laws brought in during times of national crisis but which have been used to achieve results not intended by the lawmakers. The Public Order Act 1936, rushed through Parliament to combat Mosley's blackshirts, but later used to stop gay men holding hands in public is a good example.' The Guardian, Oct 16, 2001 (no page): [Parliament] has learned the lessons of earlier hasty legislation – the way in which the temporary 1974 Prevention of Terrorism Act lasted for 16 years ...'

27 *Reference re Secession of Quebec*, [1998] 2 S.C.R. 217 and *Reference re Remuneration of Judges*, [1997] 3 S.C.R. 3.

28 'The Supreme Court of Canada in the Age of Rights,' *supra*, note 13.

The Charter and Democratic Accountability

Thinking Outside the Box: Foundational Principles for a Counter-Terrorism Law and Policy

IRWIN COTLER[*]
Faculty of Law
McGill University

Introduction

It has been said that the world changed on September 11. I do not know whether the world changed – or whether the darker side of the universe was exposed – but what is clear is that September 11 was a transformative event, impacting on our psyches as well as on our politics, on our priorities as on our purposes. It has been a central motif of public and Parliamentary discourse – whether in the public square or the halls of Parliament – while the 'war on terrorism' has become a centrepiece of the daily media.

Indeed, while the threat of terrorism – or any legislative response to it – was not even on the Parliamentary or political radar screen before September 11, not a day has passed since Parliament convened on September 17 that has not been dominated by the cataclysmic events of September 11. Every party caucus, every meeting of the House Standing Committee on Justice and Human Rights, every Question Period, has been organized around the terrorist threat and the appropriate response. If nothing else – and at the risk of extrapolating irony from this horrific tragedy – September 11 has clearly raised the level of political and Parliamentary discourse, if not also that of the media, academe, and civil society in general.

As it happens, however, the discourse and discussion of Bill C-36 (the proposed *Anti-terrorism Law*, hereinafter referred to as 'the Bill') in the public square and before our Commons Justice and Human Rights Committee – some of which has been very good indeed – has been somewhat beset, if not burdened, by a 'conventional wisdom' perspective in what is an unconventional, if not extraordinary, time. In particular, analysis of the legislation has often proceeded from the juridical optic of the domestic criminal law/due process model, while a more inclusive model would be that of an international criminal justice system counteracting a transnational and existential threat. Similarly, the legislation has been characterized, if not sometimes mischaracterized, in terms of national security versus civil liberties – a zero sum analysis – when what is involved here is 'human security' legislation that purports to protect both national security and civil liberties.

Accordingly, an analysis of the proposed Bill invites us to 'think outside the box' – to go beyond the conventional domestic optics, to re-think and re-configure the legislation in terms of a converging and inclusive domestic and international perspective anchored in the notion of human security – itself a people-centred rather than State-centred approach. This paper, then, will be organized around two parts: first, the analysis of the foundational principles that underpin the Bill; second, the identification of the rights-based concerns generated by this *projet de loi*, while offering recommendations that seek to address, if not redress, these legitimate civil libertarian concerns.

I. Foundational Principles Underpinning the Counter-Terrorism Law

Principle 1: Human Security Legislation

The configurative analysis of this Bill in terms of national security versus civil liberties may be as misleading as it is inappropriate in its framing of the issues. It appears to suggest – however inadvertently – that those who are against the legislation are the true civil libertarians, while those in favour of it are somehow indifferent to, if not insensitive to, civil liberties. The point is that there are good civil libertarians on both sides of the issue – and the civil libertarian issues should be considered on the merits and not as a function of the labelling of one's position as being for or against the legislation.

The better approach from a conceptual and foundational point of view is to regard the legislation as human security legislation, which seeks to protect both national security – or the security of democracy if not democracy itself – and civil liberties. As the United Nations puts it, terrorism constitutes a fundamental assault on human rights and, as such, a threat to international peace and security, while counter-terrorism law involves the protection of the most fundamental of rights, the right to life, liberty, and the security of the person, as well as the collective right to peace.

This does not mean that the legislation raises no civil liberties concerns, or that it cannot be critiqued from a human rights perspective. On the contrary, in Part Two of this paper – *The Civil Liberties Principle* – I will identify 11 rights-based concerns; but these concerns must be examined within the framework of these foundational principles, and in particular, this generic principle of human security.

Principle 2: Jettisoning 'false moral equivalencies': Towards a 'Zero Tolerance' Principle re Transnational Terrorism

One of the more important, yet oft ignored, dynamics inhibiting the development of a counter-terrorism law and policy has been the blurring of the moral and juridical divides occasioned by the mantra that 'one person's terrorist is another person's freedom fighter.' Indeed, the repeated invocation of this moral and legal shibboleth has not only undermined intellectual inquiry, but its moral relativism, or false moral equivalence, has blunted the justificatory basis for a clear and principled counter-terrorism law.

In a word, the underlying principle here should be that terrorism from whatever quarter, for whatever purpose, is unacceptable; that there must be a Zero Tolerance Principle for transnational terrorism, just as there is a Zero Tolerance Principle for racism.

Also, the oft-invoked analogy with the proclamation of the *War Measures Act* in 1970 – suggesting that this Bill is a replay of the repressive content and context of the 'war measures' attending that proclamation – is as inappropriate as it is inapplicable. There was no *Canadian Charter of Rights and Freedoms* as a constitutional filter to pre-test the proclamation of the *War Measures Act* in 1970 and the issuance of *Public Order Regulations* pursuant thereto; equally, the new legal regime occasioned by the proclamation of a state of emergency was unfettered by any Charter accountability. There was no capacity for principled judicial review of this exercise of State power, nor were there any restraints or safeguards on the exercise of executive, as distinct from Parliamentary, power, such as the *Public Order Regulations* authorizing prolonged preventive detention for up to seven days, and with authorization for further prolongation for up to 21 days. Nor, from the point of view of context, was there any transnational terrorist threat, or domestic threat akin to the dimensions of the contemporary transnational terrorism.

As one who counselled accused under the *War Measures Act* and who later acted as Special Counsel to the Canadian Civil Liberties Association before the McDonald Commission of Inquiry into Certain Activities of the RCMP, I can say that there was nothing tantamount to the remedial constitutional and juridical framework as exists today. If, as is alleged, the context – factual and juridical – of the Bill is like that of the *War Measures Act*, then the context – factual and juridical – of the *War Measures Act* is like the Bill. That is simply a false analogy.

Principle 3: Terrorism and Human Rights: The Contextual Principle

As the Supreme Court of Canada stated, a fundamental 'building block' of Charter jurisprudence is that Charter rights, and any limits imposed upon them, must be analyzed not in the abstract but in terms of the factual context. Accordingly, any counter-terrorism law and policy, such as the Bill, must factor in the nature and dimensions of this transnational terrorist threat.

As Professor Paul Wilkinson stated in his testimony before the Parliamentary Standing Committee on Justice and Human Rights, '[w]e passed a strategic watershed on September 11.' I would add that we passed a juridical watershed, domestically and internationally. The anti-terrorism law therefore must be appreciated and assessed in the context of the existential threat of this terrorism, including the increasingly lethal face of terrorism as in the deliberate mass murder of civilians in public places; the increasing incidence of terrorism associated with or driven by political, ideological, or religious extremism; the growth and threat of economic and cyber terrorism; the teaching of contempt and demonizing of the 'other' (as in the Japanese terrorist cult reference to their targets as 'bourgeois vermin'); a standing incitement against the demonized target; the dangers of microproliferation; the potential use of weapons of mass destruction; and the increased vulnerability of open and technologically advanced democratic societies like Canada to this genre of terror.

As former Canadian Foreign Minster Lloyd Axworthy stated, '[t]he new face of international terrorism may be one in which whole communities' – indeed, as he put it, 'the community of nations' – are held 'hostage' to this existential threat. So it is, then, that the profile of the terrorist existential threat at the *fin de siècle*, as the U.S. State Department Report put it:

is the transnational super-terrorist who benefits from modern communication and transportation, has global sources of funding, is trained and anchored in transnational networks, enjoys base and sanctuary in rogue or pariah states, is knowledgeable about modern explosives, and is more difficult to track down and apprehend than members of old established groups, or those sponsored by state terrorism.

Principle 4: The Proportionality Principle

These features of contemporary transnational terrorism and the transnational super-terrorist, nearly all of which found expression in the cataclysmic terrorism of September 11, must be factored into any assessment of a counter-terrorism law and policy such as that of the Bill. Indeed, the invocation or application of the principle of proportionality – that the juridical response to terrorism must be proportional to the threat – requires that we have an appreciation of this cluster of dynamics that characterize the increasingly lethal face of contemporary transnational terrorism.

The features and face of this transnational terrorism may underpin the 'necessity' criterion for a juridical response – a response that meets the first prong of a Charter and rights-based proportionality test: that the legislation exhibit a substantial and pressing objective. While the existential threat gives rise to a 'compelling State interest' or people-centred interest, such legislation must still pass constitutional and policy muster in respect of the three prongs of the 'remedial means' part of the proportionality test: that there be a rational basis for the remedy tailored specifically to the objective; that the remedy intrude upon Charter rights as little as possible (the 'minimum impairment' component of the proportionality test); and that the effect or cost of the legislation, particularly in its impact on our civil liberties, not outweigh its purposive and remedial character.

Principle 5: The International Criminal Justice Model

In brief, we are not dealing here with your ordinary or domestic criminal but with the transnational super-terrorist; not with ordinary criminality but with Crimes Against Humanity; not with your conventional threat of criminal violence but with an existential threat to the whole human family. In a word, we are dealing with Nuremberg crimes and Nuremberg criminals – of *hostes humanis generis* – the enemies of humankind.

Accordingly, the domestic criminal law/due process model standing alone is inadequate, if not inappropriate. The juridical war on terrorism cannot be fought here or won by one country alone. Rather, one has to 'think outside the box' and invoke an international criminal justice model having regard to both the nature of the threat and the proportionality of the response. Simply put, combating the transnational super-terrorist suicide-bomber will require transnational investigative and procedural mechanisms that are as preventive as they are punitive; that support a global justice system anchored *inter alia* in the related principle of universal jurisdiction, which gives the domestic criminal justice system a global jurisdictional reach. Universal jurisdiction over terrorism, when joined with the Treaty for an International Criminal Court and the implementing domestic *War Crimes and Crimes Against Humanity* legislation, the centrepiece of the human security agenda, underpins this international criminal justice model.

Principle 6: The Domestication of International Law: The Complementarity Principle

At the core of the Bill – and without which the Bill could be assimilated into the ordinary criminal law regime – is the domestic implementation of international law undertakings, in particular, the domestic implementation by Canada of 12 international anti-terrorism issue-specific treaties. It is not enough that these treaties be ratified. Canada has already ratified 10 of these and intends to ratify the two most recent ones. Rather, Parliament must enact domestic implementing legislation, as will be accomplished by the Bill, to give effect to these treaties for prosecutorial and jurisdictional purposes. Indeed, the two most recent of the anti-terrorism treaties are the most important: the International Convention on the Suppression of Terrorist Bombing and the International Convention on the Suppression of Terrorist Financing.

As well, the legislation seeks to implement the undertakings as mandated by the recent United Nations Security Council Resolution, which authorizes, *inter alia*, the creation of new and specific anti-terrorism offences including Participating in the Activities of a Terrorist Group (s.83.18); Facilitating a Terrorist Activity (s.83.19); Instructing the Carrying Out of a Terrorist Activity (s.83.22); Instructing Activities for Terrorist Groups to Enhance their Ability to Carry Out Terrorist Activities (s.83.21); Harbouring or Concealing Terrorists (s.83.23).

The Canadian government has regarded the implementation of the comprehensive undertakings in the U.N. Security Council Resolution, including these new and specific anti-terrorism offences, as obligatory. Moreover, the Resolution required that member states report back within 90 days as to their compliance with the Resolution thereby inducing the 'fast-tracking' of the Bill. As Rick Mosely, Assistant Deputy Minister of Justice, and one of the architects of the Bill, put it, 'We thought we had at least several months – maybe even years – to implement the International Convention on the Suppression of Terrorist Financing. We now found ourselves obliged to enact implementing legislation for this Treaty – even leaving aside the undertakings mandated by the Resolution – within 90 days.' If one adds to the obligation to implement the two international treaties the obligation to enact new and specific terrorist offences in the Bill itself, one can appreciate not only the impact of the domestication of international criminal law as set forth in the international treaties, but also the enactment of these new and specific terrorist offences pursuant to a Security Council Resolution – and all within 90 days.

This domestication of international obligations – and Canada is a leader in this field as exemplified also by the enactment of the *War Crimes and Crimes Against Humanity Act* pursuant to the ratification of the ICC Treaty – may result in the incorporation by reference of the United Nations treaty language – let alone the language of the U.N. Security Council Resolution. This language is at a higher level of generality than the specificity required for its adaptation as a domestic criminal law offence and may account somewhat for the breadth of the new offences such as the financing of terrorism.

Principle 7: The Comparativist Principle

In determining the justificatory basis for the Bill, resort may be had not only to the *Canadian Charter of Rights and Freedoms* and the values and principles of a free and democratic society such as Canada, but to the legislative experience of other free and democratic societies. Indeed, the drafters of the Bill engaged in a comparative inquiry that drew upon *inter alia* the recent anti-terrorism legislation of the United Kingdom and the United States.

Indeed, an examination of the legislative framework of other free and democratic societies supports the view that not only is anti-terrorism legislation representative of free and democratic societies, but its very purpose is to ensure that such societies remain free and democratic while the rights of its citizenry to live in peace and security are safeguarded. Moreover, a comparative study from a civil libertarian perspective of the Canadian legislation with that of other free and democratic societies, particularly the U.S. and the U.K., reveals a set of safeguards and protections for civil liberties that do not find expression in comparable legislation. Admittedly, this may not satisfy those who argue, and not incorrectly, that Canada must meet Canadian normative and juridical standards; but the comparativist principle has been invoked by the Supreme Court to help determine whether the legislation is compatible with what a free and democratic society would do. In that sense, it is a relevant principle, even if the comparativist perspective may be found wanting by some.

Principle 8: The Prevention Principle

One of the *raisons d'être* for the Bill – having regard to the character of the transnational terrorist, existential threat – is organized around a culture of prevention and pre-emption, as distinct from reactive 'after the fact' law enforcement. This includes the range of incorporated offences pursuant to ratified international treaties so as to establish a global justice network; the new and specific offences, mainly pursuant to the implementation of the U.N. Security Council Resolution, that seek to disable and dismantle the terrorist network itself; the novel investigative and procedural mechanisms, such as preventive arrest, that seek to detect and deter rather than just prosecute and punish; the provisions for international co-operation respecting law enforcement and information gathering that seek to counteract the super-terrorist utilization of transnational technologies, communications, and transportation networks; the spectrum of provisions, aimed at what the Paris Ministerial Conference regarded as the lynchpin of the transnational terrorist network, prohibiting the financing of terrorism in all its forms; the specific changes in the law relating to wiretapping, including eliminating the requirement of a finding that 'other investigative procedures have been tried and have failed,' or are 'unlikely to succeed'; and the provision for wiretaps for judicial approval for up to a year for terrorist offences, rather than the normal 60–day limit, reflecting the 'time lines.' As Professor Martin Friedland put it, 'One would have thought that where there is a serious threat to national security, wiretapping with a judicial authorization should be at or near the top of the list of techniques that could be used.'

Principle 9: Criminal Due Process Safeguards

In the course of representing political prisoners over the years, including those falsely accused by repressive (e.g., former Soviet Union, or China today), authoritarian (e.g., Argentina under the Junta or Tunisia today), or racist (e.g., former apartheid South Africa) regimes, as well as those accused in democratic societies (the U.S., Canada), I have resorted to a 'checklist' of due process safeguards, including some which may be particularly relevant having regard to the Bill as follows:

- the overbreadth or vagueness of the offence so as to deny the accused the right to know the particulars of the offence and charges laid;
- the suppression of information such that the accused is denied the basic right to information including the right to know the nature of the adverse evidence, the right to access the evidence collected against him or her, the right to be able to confront witness testimony, and the right to be able to rebut adverse evidence;
- the right to retain and instruct counsel and the right to confer with counsel before a police interrogation, during the trial and at any other critical stage in the proceedings against him or her;
- the protection of the right to counsel and the solicitor-client privilege and confidentiality;
- the right to remain silent;
- the right against self-incrimination. In a word, as the burden of proof in a criminal case is on the prosecution, the accused do not have to supply the police or prosecution with any evidence that could be used against them – a right that protects the defendant from having to reveal incriminating facts;
- the right to protection against coercive interrogation;
- the right to a fair and public trial.

Principle 10: The Minority Rights Principle

This principle is organized around the rights of visible minorities to protection against differential and discriminatory treatment in the application and enforcement of Bill C-36. Accordingly, it is recommended that a non-discrimination principle prohibiting the arrest, investigation, detention and imprisonment of any person on any prohibited ground of discrimination be expressly included in the legislation as follows: [that nothing in the Bill] provide for the detention, imprisonment or internment of Canadian citizens, or permanent residents as defined in the *Immigration Act*, on the basis of race, national or ethnic origin, colour, religion, sex age or mental or physical disability.

Principle 11: The Anti-Hate Principle

The Bill includes important provisions that would allow the courts to order the deletion of publicly available hate propaganda from computer systems such as an Internet site. As well, there are *Criminal Code* amendments that would create a new offence of mischief motivated by bias, prejudice or hate based on religion, race, colour, or national or ethnic origin committed against a place of religious worship or associated religious property.

In addition, there are amendments to the *Canadian Human Rights Act* to make it clear that using telephone, Internet, or other communications tools for hatred purposes or discrimination is prohibited. As the Canadian Human Rights Commission enunciated in its testimony before the Standing Committee on Justice and Human Rights, 'We strongly support the proposed amendments to section 13 of the *Canadian Human Rights Act* ... the Internet has fast become a forum for hate – extending the potential reach of hate messages to millions. For a number of years, the Canadian Human Rights Commission has been interpreting the *Canadian Human Rights Act* to include hate messages over the Internet and we are pleased that Bill C-36 makes this explicit.'

The Commission added:

> The Commission is also pleased that the Bill proposes to extend the hate propaganda provisions of section 320 of the *Criminal Code* to allow for a court to order the removal of hateful material on the Internet pending a final decision by the Court. Although these new Criminal Code provisions would operate outside the complaints procedures of the *Canadian Human Rights Act* they would allow potential complainants to seek interlocutory removal of alleged hate messages, and we support this change.

Principle 12: The Chartering of Rights

The proposed anti-terrorism legislation has been 'pre-tested' under the Charter. This does not mean that the legislation is 'Charter-proof' as much as it means that the legislation is Charter bound. In a word, the legislation is not immune from a Charter challenge, and any limitation on a Charter right will have to comport with the requirements of Section 1 and the proportionality test as developed by the courts, and summarized earlier under Principle 4.

Principle 13: The Oversight Principle

An appropriate oversight framework is germane to the integrity and efficacy of anti-terrorist legislation, and should include the following instruments and mechanisms for monitoring, review, and redress:

- Application of the *Canadian Charter of Rights and Freedoms*;
- Enhanced capacity for judicial review;
- Annual Report by the Attorney General to Parliament on the operation of the Act;
- A Parliamentary Officer in the ongoing monitoring and supervision of the legislation, or perhaps more preferably, a review by SIRC (the Security Intelligence Review Committee) which has developed a repository of experience and expertise in these security-related matters;
- Sunset clauses for the provisions respecting preventive arrest and judicial investigative hearings;
- Media scrutiny and sunshine;
- NGO monitoring; and,
- An engaged civil society.

II Rights-Based Concerns: The Civil Liberties Principle

While the Bill may be said to be inspired by, and anchored in, the principle of human security – both domestic and international – and while the Bill was subjected to a rigorous Charter scrutiny, this does not obviate civil libertarian concerns as set forth below, all of which were referred to in the course of witness testimony before the Justice and Human Rights Committee.

1. Definition of 'Terrorist Activity'

A persistent and pervasive concern adduced before the Justice Committee related to the arguable overbreadth of the definition of terrorist activity as set forth in s.83.01(2) in the Bill. A 'terrorist activity' is defined as an action that takes place either in or outside Canada, 'committed in whole or in part for a political, religious or ideological purpose, objective or cause' and intended to intimidate the public 'with regard to its security, including its economic security' or compelling people, governments or domestic or international organizations 'to do or to refrain from doing any act' whether those targets are in or outside of Canada.

As well, a terrorist activity must also intend:

(A) to cause death or serious bodily harm to a person by the use of violence,
(B) to endanger a person's life,
(C) to cause a serious risk to the health or safety of the public or any segment of the public,
(D) to cause substantial property damage, whether to public or private property, if causing such damage is likely to result in the conduct or harm referred to in any of clauses (A) to (C) and (E), or
(E) to cause serious interference with or serious disruption of an essential service, facility or system, whether public or private, other than as a result of lawful advocacy, protest, dissent or stoppage of work that does not involve an activity that is intended to result in the conduct or harm referred to in any of clauses (A) to (C).

The government has argued that 'this definition is carefully circumscribed to make it clear that disrupting an essential service is not a terrorist activity if it occurs during a lawful protest or a work strike and is not intended to cause serious harm to persons.'

Many witnesses, including the Canadian Bar Association, however, submitted that 'section (b)(ii)(E) of the proposed definition is particularly problematic in that it might catch unlawful activity – such as a wildcat strike or demonstration – that is not terrorist conduct, even though there may be "serious disruption of an essential service, facility or system."'

Indeed, the brief of the CBA raised a number of questions in this regard which are generally reflective and representative of the concerns expressed before the Committee as follows:

- Does this definition include protest activities by Aboriginal people which disrupt an 'essential' service or block a road, as a protest against development activities on Aboriginal lands?
- At Burnt Church, protestors disrupted the use of the highway and waterways to protest the lobster fishery and to compel government to recognize an Aboriginal fishery. Were they terrorists?
- What about those involved in recent nurses' or truckers' strikes, or

the protestors at the Québec City summit or the Asia-Pacific Economic Cooperation (APEC) conference in Vancouver?

- What about political activists who may have appeared as 'terrorist' to those in power at a given time, but who are ultimately remembered as champions of freedom, such as Louis Riel or Nelson Mandela?

The definition of a 'terrorist activity' is a crucial issue as it is determinative and dispositive of the terrorist offences as set forth in the Act. Accordingly, having regard to the definition in the Act and the witness testimony before the Committee, I would recommend the following:

- Consideration should be given to removing the motivational elements (i.e., 'act ... committed for a political, religious, or ideological purpose') as requisite elements for the offence, while insuring that they cannot serve as exculpatory grounds for the defence; admittedly, the motivational elements have been included to distinguish the genre of terrorist activity from other criminal offences, but it could end up being not only a superfluous but burdensome obstacle to a successful prosecution in that the Crown would have to establish the presence of these motivational elements; as well, while most terrorist acts are indeed driven by politics, religion, or ideology, some may be unrelated to these elements. Finally, the inclusion of some motivational elements and the exclusion of others may prompt a Charter challenge under section 15.
- The word 'unlawful' in section 83.01(b)(ii)(E) should be deleted;
- This section (b)(ii)(E), as set forth above, is particularly problematic in that it might be stretched to characterize as 'terrorist,' activity which was never intended to be characterized as such.
- Accordingly, given what might be called 'the law of unintended consequences,' it might be prudent to remove (E) entirely so as to preclude any untoward application of the Act to civil disobedience or even violent conduct that is clearly not terrorist activity.
- Since, however, there is legitimate concern about terrorist attacks intended to paralyse or destroy the civilian electronic infrastructure, one might well adopt the recommendation of Professor Martin Friedland to add the words 'or seriously interferes with or seriously disrupts and electronic system' after the words 'substantial property damage' in clause (D). This would ensure that such disruption would only be caught by section (D) if it was 'likely to result in the conduct

or harm' referred to in the previous sections (A) to (C), and whose validity does not appear to be in doubt.

2. Listing of Terrorist Organizations

In clause 4 of Bill C-36, section 83.05(1) authorizes the Governor in Council to make regulations to establish a list of entities believed to be involved in terrorist activities, with all the ensuing consequences of listing an entity as a terrorist group. In particular, if considered a terrorist group, it is subject to the ensuing provisions in the Bill that criminalize involvement with, or support of any sort for a terrorist group, and all its property is frozen or subject to forfeiture.

Admittedly, there are safeguards including the requirement of reasonable grounds to believe that an entity should be included in a list, provisions for removal, judicial review, and redress for cases of mistaken identity in that an entity can apply to be removed from the list. As well, the list must be reviewed every two years by the Solicitor-General.

However, these safeguards are 'after the fact' – that is, the listing has taken place. Consideration should be given for 'prior notice' to the prospective 'listed entity,' with an opportunity for a hearing prior to the 'listing' taking place.

3. Requirement of a Mens Rea Threshold

The Supreme Court of Canada has clearly stipulated that where the penalties for a criminal offence are serious and stigma is attached to the offence, such as in the present legislation, *mens rea* – or guilty intent – should always be a requisite element of the criminal offence. This is not always clear in Bill C-36. For example, under the definition of 'facilitation,' (section 83.01)(2) clause 4), a terrorist activity is deemed to be 'facilitated' whether or not the facilitator knows that such terrorist activity is taking place. Accordingly, the legislation must make it clear that the prosecution must prove criminal intent to find anyone guilty of a terrorist offence. In particular, the *mens rea* requirement for the facilitation offence must be made clear.

4. Access to Information and the Right to Privacy

Bill C-36 authorizes the Attorney General to issue a Certificate prohibiting disclosure of certain information in order to protect international relations, national defense, or national security. This would apply to prohibiting disclosure under the *Access to Information Act* (clause 87), the *Privacy Act* (clause 103), and the provisions of the *Personal Information Protection and Electronic Documents Act* (clause 104). But these three statutes protect important values in terms of information access and the right to privacy in a democracy. At the same time, they have also prevented disclosure of information concerning security-related matters, and there has not been any instance of disclosure by the judiciary of 'prohibitory' information.

Regrettably, Bill C-36 would exclude the application of each of these Acts, as well as the involvements of the Information Commissioner and the Privacy Commissioner, respecting any oversight role regarding the Attorney General's Prohibitory Certificate. Indeed, the public would even be prevented from knowing that a Prohibitory Certificate had been issued. Consequently, the exclusion of oversight creates a basis for the exercise of unfettered and unreviewable discretion.

In a word, Bill C-36 does not provide a mechanism for review of the Attorney General's certificate, whether by the Privacy Commissioner or otherwise. Accordingly, one might well argue that clauses 87, 103, and 104 should be deleted, or that Bill C-36 should at least be amended to provide for the necessary safeguards and oversight. For example the Privacy Commissioner, George Radwanski has recommended that the following amendment to the *Privacy Act* could address the necessary oversight requirement:

New subsections 51(4), (5) and (6) should be added as follows:

(4) The Attorney General of Canada may at any time following an application to the Federal Court under section 41 or 43 personally issue a certificate that prohibits the disclosure of information for the purpose of protecting international relations or national defence or security.

(5) The Attorney General shall cause a copy of the certificate to be served on
   (a) the person presiding or designated to preside at the proceeding to which the information relates or, if no person is designated, the person who has the authority to designate a person to preside;
   (b) every party to the proceeding;
   (c) any other person who, in the opinion of the Attorney General of Canada, should be served,

(6) The *Statutory Instruments Act* does not apply to a certificate mark under subsection (4).

5. *Preventive Arrest and Investigative Hearing: Provision for a Sunset Clause*

These two procedural and investigative techniques should be subject to a sunset clause as they represent novel demarches in criminal investigation and procedure.

Admittedly, there are safeguards with respect to these provisions in the Bill. For example, in the matter of preventive arrest, police may invoke this power to arrest without warrant, and bring the suspected terrorist before a judge,

- where there are reasonable grounds to suspect that a terrorist activity will be carried out, and reasonable grounds to suspect that imposing conditions or arrest is necessary to prevent the carrying out of terrorist activity.
- The threat must be specific and involve a specific individual.
- Except in exigent circumstances, the Attorney General must consent to the arrest.
- In all cases, the detention after arrest must be subject to judicial review within 24 hours.
- In addition, the consent of the Attorney General is required before a judge can be asked to impose supervisory conditions on the release of the person, or detain the person for any longer period (up to a maximum of an additional 48 hours).

Given the nature of the terrorist threat, the 'preventive' aspect of this provision may yet prove its worth, even allowing for a lower standard of proof. At the same time, however, the Bill in its present form would allow warrantless arrest and detention on a mere suspicion that a terrorist activity is planned, without the need for a reasonable belief that the activity is in any way imminent. It would appear, therefore, that the best option to determine both the legitimacy and efficacy of this novel procedure is to subject it to a sunset clause, allowing for reassessment—and re-enactment where it has proven itself—after some three years' time.

Under the investigative hearing provisions in section 83.28 in clause 4 of the Bill, a judge may order a person to appear to give evidence as a material witness, and to be arrested with a warrant if he or she fails to appear. Once again, there are a number of safeguards respecting these provisions in the Bill:

- the judge must be satisfied that the consent of the Attorney General was obtained and
- that there are reasonable grounds to believe a terrorist offence has been or will be committed;
- during the hearing, people are protected from self-incrimination and
- laws relating to privilege and the non-disclosure of information as well as the right to counsel, continue to apply.
- The legislation also provides the judge with the authority to include terms and conditions to protect the interest of the witness, third parties and any ongoing investigations.

Nor are these provisions respecting an investigative hearing as exceptional as critics have suggested. For example, there are a number of cases where persons are compelled to give evidence under oath including various public inquiries such as the *Coroner's Act* in Quebec, and the *Public Inquiries Act* in Ontario; the *Fire Protection* Acts; and securities Acts. As well, compellable testimony is not unknown in the criminal law. For example, under section 545 of the *Criminal Code*, persons who have knowledge of a criminal offence can be summoned to a preliminary hearing; if they refuse to answer, they can be jailed for successive eight-day periods; also, persons who are subpoenaed for a trial and who refuse to give evidence can then be held in contempt of court. Finally, there is precedent for an investigative hearing in *Competition Act* matters, and in mutual legal assistance treaty requests (MLATs).

Once again, the virtue of these provisions lies in their potential to prevent and pre-empt the commission of terrorist offences. At the same time, there is a risk of prejudice to the right to remain silent as guaranteed under section 7 of the Charter. Accordingly, this provision should also be subject to a sunset clause, while protection for the right against self-incrimination is ensured.

6. Interception of Foreign Communications

In fulfilling its mandate in collecting foreign intelligence, the Communications Security Establishment must receive authorization from the Minister of National Defence to intercept any communication involving a foreign target located outside Canada that originates or ends in Canada.

The Minister must be satisfied before issuing such authorization that measures are in place to protect the privacy of Canadians.

Consideration should be given to providing for judicial rather than Ministerial authorization, or at least providing that the Ministerial authorization be subject to judicial confirmation. It might also be advisable, as some have recommended, to empower SIRC review the work of the CSC, as the SIRC is dependent on knowing what the CSC is doing in order to effectively discharge its own role.

7. The Right of visible minorities to protection against differential discriminatory treatment

There is a potential in the expansive powers of the Act for the possible singling out of visible minorities for differential treatment. The inclusion of a non-discrimination clause respecting the application of the Act in matters of arrest, detention, and imprisonment would have important symbolic as well as substantive value. Such a provision now exists in section 4 (b) of the *Emergencies Act* – as set forth in Principle 10 of Part I above – and it would seem desirable to include such a provision in this Bill.

8. Scrutiny of Registered Charities

Part 6 of Bill C-36, which incorporates most of the prior Bill C-16 on charities registration, could 'chill' the charitable activities of Canadian charities, both in their domestic and international operations. In a word, the Bill imposes significant liability on charities, including criminal liability, without providing appropriate defences and protections for these charities, including norms of procedural fairness prior to criminalization.

Accordingly, Part 6 should be amended to provide, *inter alia*, for a 'due diligence defence' for Canadian charities which may inadvertently be distributing funds to a foreign entity which is identified or qualified as a terrorist group. Also, the charitable organization should be advised of the foreign information being considered in any case against them, lest they be unable to challenge the credibility of that information, which would prejudice the charity's right to be heard and to rebut the case against it.

9. Civil Forfeiture Process

There are certain procedural safeguards here, including, court protection of the interests of family members and the principal residence, access to the property in order to meet reasonable living/business needs and legal expenses and appeal procedures. Provision should be made for the protection of innocent third parties.

10. *Legal Representation, Solicitor-Client Privilege and Solicitor-Client Confidentiality*

Several provisions of the Bill (e.g., sections 83(1), 83(03), 83(08)) might prejudice the right to retain and instruct counsel, and should be amended to protect solicitor-client privilege and solicitor-client confidentiality.

11. *Oversight Mechanisms*

Bill C-36 is one of the most important, comprehensive, yet complex pieces of legislation to have been introduced – involving juridical considerations of a criminal, constitutional, international, evidentiary, procedural, and technological character. Accordingly, consideration should be given to an oversight mechanism involving:

- Annual Report by the Attorney General to Parliament on the operation of the Act;
- A Parliamentary Officer in the ongoing monitoring and supervision of the legislation, or the delegation of this superintending power to SIRC;
- Enhanced capacity for judicial review; and,
- Sunset clauses for the provisions respecting preventive arrest and judicial investigative hearings.

Nor should one ignore the significant oversight role played by NGOs, the media, academe, and the various constituent elements of civil society.

Conclusion

Bill C-36 is legacy legislation. It is likely to be with us for a long time. We should try to get it right—or as right as possible.

Note

* I am grateful to Helen Elliot for her assistance in the preparation of this paper.

The Dangers of a Charter-Proof and Crime-Based Response to Terrorism

KENT ROACH[*]
Faculty of Law
University of Toronto

It is not, what a lawyer tells me I *may* do; but what humanity, reason and justice tells me I ought to do ... I am not determining a point of law; I am restoring tranquillity ...[1]

... the classic pattern of unthinking, unscientific legislation [is] 'If you want to stop something from happening, make it a crime.'[2]

We have been told countless times that everything changed on September 11, 2001. The idea that everything changed should, however, make us deeply uneasy. A great strength of our free and democratic society is its traditions of freedom, democracy and the rule of law. Those such as the September 11 terrorists who have nothing but contempt and hatred for these traditions would be only too happy to hear that everything has changed as a result of their evil deeds. They do not deserve that pleasure.

The best thing that has happened since September 11 is not Bill C-36, the comprehensive *Anti-terrorism Act*,[3] which in my view contains some provisions that are dangerous and others that are unnecessary. Rather, it is the increasingly robust democratic process that has surrounded the introduction of the bill. It is this process, rather than the contents of the bill, that best honours our traditions. The bill was quite properly introduced for debate and discussion before enactment. Unlike the invocation of the *War Measures Act* in the early morning hours of October 16, 1970,[4] we are not responding to an assertion of an emergency after it has been declared and acted upon. In this sense, the form of Bill C-36, although perhaps not its spirit, follows the rule of law. More importantly, newspapers, legislative committees, civil society groups, and academics have broken the silence of a collective shock, grief and revulsion at the events of September 11 that was producing a war-like solidarity.[5] Debate about Bill C-36 has helped us get back into the loud and pluralistic practice of democracy as we assess and often criticize the bill. The exercise of reason and dissent in evaluating this bill is in the long run far more important than any of its provisions.

Many of the essays in this collection will be devoted to understanding the possible ambit of the many provisions of Bill C-36 and whether they comply with the Canadian Charter of Rights and Freedoms. This is important work and work well-suited for academics who possess independence and some, albeit not sufficient, time to evaluate the bill before it is enacted into law. Nevertheless, I want to suggest that there are some dangers in this very necessary process that we are about to undertake.

The first danger is that citizens and elected representatives may be too quick to accept as wise or necessary what the government's lawyers conclude is permissible to do. This is what Edmund Burke meant when he warned the House of Commons in London that their guide in responding to American grievances about taxation without representation should not be 'what a lawyer tells me I *may* do; but what humanity, reason and justice tell me I ought to do.'[6] In today's language, Burke's point is that just because a bill can be presented as 'Charter-proof' does not mean that it should be enacted. Charter-proofing is now an entrenched part of the legislative process in Canada, but it presents dangers especially if governments become more concerned about avoiding invalidation of legislation under the Charter than living up to its broader purposes and spirit. Charter-proofing can be a matter of shrewdly predicting what the courts will be prepared to do. Concerns exist, however, that courts, especially on sensitive matters such as security, will be reluctant to strike legislation down.[7] In short, a conclusion that Bill C-36, or for that matter any other piece of legislation, should survive Charter review does not mean that it is a good law.

The second danger is the great reliance that Bill C-36 places on a crime-based approach to terrorism. What happened on September 11 was a horrific crime and those who commit, attempt, conspire, counsel or assist such crimes must be prosecuted to the full extent of the law. Nevertheless, the terrible acts of September 11 were crimes long before that fateful morning. We failed to apprehend the September 11 terrorists not because the criminal law was inadequate, but because law enforcement and co-ordination, including intelligence gathering, was inadequate.[8] Bill C-36 responds to this failure by creating many new offences, increasing the investigative powers of the police and increasing punishments for terrorist offences. As Hart and Sacks observed, society is instinctively drawn to the naive belief that: 'If you want to stop something from happening, make it a crime.' We routinely ratchet up an already broad and severe criminal law in response to horrific crimes. If anything, this process of relying on the criminal law has become more attractive as the state retreats in other areas of governance and as our ability to predict, record and broadcast the risk of crime outstrips our ability to prevent it. There is little reason to think that this reliance on the criminal law makes us more safe and secure even though it can threaten fundamental values.

Charter Proofing Bill C-36

The claimed consistency of Bill C-36 with the Charter has been one of its main selling points. Minister of Justice Anne McLellan has repeatedly stressed that Bill C-36 has received the most rigorous Charter scrutiny of any bill and that 'numerous safeguards have been included to ensure that nothing in this proposed act unreasonably infringes on civil liberties and Charter rights.'[9] Some in these proceedings will take issue with the Minister's repeated insistence that 'the legislature fully complies with the Charter of Rights and Freedoms.'[10] Nevertheless, I want to warn of a danger of playing that game. Quite simply, the Minister and her many Charter experts,[11] may be right.

The courts might uphold most of Bill C-36 as consistent with the Charter. They reject a large majority of Charter claims and the Supreme Court has already indicated in one of its very first Charter cases that the protection of national security was a particularly compelling objective that would affect the manner in which it would determine both the content of Charter rights and reasonable limits on those rights.[12] Courts have frequently deferred to governments in times of strain and perceived crisis with judicial approval of the war-time internment of Japanese-Canadians and Japanese-Americans being the most famous example. One of the dangers of an unsuccessful Charter challenge to Bill C-36 would be that it would give the legislation a sense of permanency and legitimacy that it might not otherwise have or deserve.[13]

As the Minister of Justice has stressed, the rights in the Charter are not absolute. The Charter protects basic liberal rights such as freedom of expression and due process, but also allows legislatures under s .1 to prescribe by law reasonable limits that are demonstrably justified in a free and democratic society. The test for determining what constitutes a reasonable limit on a Charter right is evolving and increased judicial deference to the legislature has frequently been extended into the criminal law. The Charter can accommodate and even enable and legitimate much crime control.[14]

The Charter also allows legislatures to enact laws notwithstanding most Charter rights for a renewable five year period. This ensures sober second thoughts before rights are overridden and requires the legislature to re-affirm its commitment to override rights when the immediate crisis has passed. The federal government, however, has never used the override power even when it has enacted several 'in your face' replies to Supreme Court's decisions articulating broad Charter rights for the accused. The constitutional five year sunset provision in the s.33 override,[15] may also explain some of the Prime Minister's apparent reluctance to follow the American example of including statutory sunset provisions in its anti-terrorism legislation or the Canadian example of sunsetting the legislative response to the October Crisis. To employ a statutory sunset provision in Canada, as recommended by the Special Senate Committee on Bill C-36,[16] may seem too close to admitting that the legislation may override or make emergency exceptions to Charter rights, something that the federal government emphatically denies will occur under Bill C-36. At the same time, the refusal to sunset some provisions of Bill C-36 because they are Charter-proof is troubling. It raises fears of perhaps not a permanent *War Measures Act*, but at least a permanent expansion of the criminal law and extraordinary investigative powers of the state.

Charter-proofing has become standard operating procedure for the federal government. All departments receive legal advice on the Charter implications of upcoming legislation[17] and federal legislation has made increasing use of preambles which attempt to frame and influence Charter analysis.[18] When legislation has been struck down under the Charter, the federal government has frequently responded with new legislation that it claims (and frequently has been held) to be Charter- proof. Examples include the enactment of new restrictions on the admissibility of evidence of both a sexual assault complainant's prior sexual conduct and her private records after the Supreme Court declared that the accused's rights to full answer and defence could require the use of such evidence. Parliament has also responded to a Supreme Court Charter decision recognizing a defence of extreme intoxication with legislation abolishing the defence in many cases and it has responded to the Court's decision striking down the denial of bail on the vague basis of the 'public interest' with the equally vague, but possibly Charter-proof, basis of 'just cause.' The Court has responded to virtually every major Supreme Court decision striking down warrantless searches with new legislation authorizing a wide variety of searches with and without warrants.[19] Over the last decade, the Department of Justice has become very adept in creating Charter-proof legislation. It has also become bolder over the years and enacted legislation that many commentators have seen as 'in your face' replies reversing Charter decisions. The fact that the boldest such legislative reply was upheld by the Supreme Court in a decision[20] that indicated it would respect legislative interpretations of the Charter and legislative attempts to hold the Court accountable creates conditions in which the government can, with considerable confidence, push the envelope of permissiveness under the Charter. My concern is that the question of whether legislation has been Charter-proofed by careful drafting and strategic use of precedent is replacing more fundamental and traditional questions about the need for restraint in the criminal law.[21]

Charter-Proofing Investigative Hearings

The unfortunate consequences of Charter-proofing can be seen in one of the more controversial provisions of Bill C-36, namely the provisions in s.83.28 regarding investigative hearings or orders for gathering evidence. Compelling a person to talk to the police in an investigation in which he or she may well be implicated[22] offends our traditions of respect for the right of silence during police investigations. These traditions date back to the abolition of the Star Chamber in 1641 and the compensation given to John Lilburne who was imprisoned for more than 2 years because he would not testify under oath to the Attorney's General clerk or to the Star Chamber about whether religious books he shipped from England to Holland were seditious.[23] Nevertheless, s.83.28(8) providing that a person 'shall answer questions put to the person by or on behalf of the peace officer who applied for the order' has been carefully and cleverly crafted to abrogate fundamental rights to silence and against self-incrimination. It may well be Charter-proof in the sense that courts would not strike the section down.

First, there is a requirement that a provincial or superior court judge authorize in his or her discretion the extraordinary procedure. In the context of searches and seizures at least, the Supreme Court has stressed the importance of prior judicial authorization and Parliament has responded with a raft of new warrants that allow judges to authorize the seizure of dna samples, body impressions, and even the use of 'any device or investigative technique or procedure or do anything described in the warrant that would, if not authorized, constitute an unreasonable search or seizure'[24] The fact that investigative hearings are authorized by judges on the basis of reasonable grounds to believe that a terrorism offence has or will be committed and that reasonable and less drastic efforts to obtain the evidence have failed assist the government's case that this controversial and innovative provision is Charter-proof.

Although a person subject to an investigative hearing can refuse to answer on the basis of other forms of privilege, section 83.28(10) abrogates the right against self-incrimination by providing that no person subject to an investigative hearing 'shall be excused from answering a question or producing a thing ... on the ground that the answer or thing may tend to incriminate the person or subject the person to any proceeding or penalty.' By itself, this odious provision would likely offend the Charter, but it is accompanied by what lawyers call use and derivative use immunity. This means that any answer or document compelled from the accused could only be used if the person was charged with perjury (as contemplated in s.13 of the Charter) and the police will have to demonstrate that evidence on subsequent charges against the witness would have been obtained independently without reliance on the compelled statements. These immunity provisions in s.83.28(10) build on a number of Supreme Court cases concluding that the right against self-incrimination is not absolute.[25]

The final Charter-proofing measure is the provision in s.83.28(11) of the right to retain and instruct counsel at any stage of the investigative proceedings. The lawyer, however, may often only inform the client that he or she is legally obliged to talk and remain in attendance until excused by the presiding judge or that he or she may even face prosecution under s.127 of the *Criminal Code* or contempt of court for refusing to obey a court order for the gathering of evidence. The bells and whistles of Charter-proofing – judicial authorization, derivative and use immunity and the right to counsel – may ensure that the provision for investigative hearings is not struck down under the Charter, but it does not remove the danger of abrogating the right of silence that potential suspects have long enjoyed in our adversarial system of criminal justice.

A conclusion that investigative hearings have been 'Charter- proofed' in Bill C-36 does not mean that they are necessary or wise. Introducing investigative hearings into the Criminal Code will produce pressures to abrogate the right to silence and the right against self-incrimination in other pressing situations. If judges can require a person to talk about terrorism, why not about the sexual abuse of children or criminal organization offences? The criminal law has a tendency to replicate itself and language and law designed to deal with terrorism has been applied to street gangs and street gang legislation applied to terrorism.[26] There is no reason to think that investigative hearings, especially if enacted without a sunset clause, will not expand outside the terrorism context. We can expect that the incursions on fundamental values in Bill C-36 will be a model the next time another menace becomes pressing, especially if they are found to be Charter-proof. The minimum standards of conduct in the Charter are quickly becoming the maximum standards of restraint that we can expect from our governments.

And then there is the question of efficacy. In most cases, legal compulsion to talk should not be necessary and it may be counter-productive. People with information, including those involved with crime, frequently volunteer to talk especially if their co-operation can be rewarded in various ways. Some terrorist suspects including Ahmed Ressam have co-operated with authorities in the hope of a lighter sentence. Others have not, but it is unlikely that a court order or even the threat of a prosecution for not talking would change their minds. If it did change their minds, they may only provide misinformation and they may not be overly impressed by the threat of a perjury prosecution. Compelled interrogations can be a risky shortcut to labour intensive and expensive police work and intelligence gathering.

At one level, the attempt to codify procedures for compelling people to talk is laudable. It can be argued that it is better that such dangerous procedures be set out in legislation for all the world to see than to be undertaken illegally and at the discretion of state officials. It may even be that such extraordinary procedures could be justified to stop imminent mass terrorism or destruction[27] as opposed to the broad definition of terrorist activity in Bill C-36 that includes property damage that endangers life and illegal attempts to disrupt essential public and private services.[28] Nevertheless, it is significant that neither the American *Patriot Act* enacted in response to September 11 or the United Kingdom's *Anti-terrorism Act, 2000* provide for investigative hearings of the type contemplated in Bill C-36 This may indicate that investigative hearings are a disproportionate response at least with respect to the broad definition of terrorism in Bill C-36. Nevertheless, it is far from clear that the courts will insist on such exacting principles of proportionality.

But you see how easy it is to fall into the trap of Charter-proofing. Regardless of whether investigative hearings can or cannot survive Charter review, there is a strong case that they are unnecessary, unprincipled and unwise. Those who will talk will do so without the threat of prosecution. Those who refuse to talk or who lie will likely not be deterred by the threat of continued detention or prosecutions for failing to obey a judicial order or for perjury. More fundamentally, it is unworthy to abrogate centuries of respect for the right to silence and the right against self-incrimination during police investigations. Attempts at Charter proofing, in the form of judicial authorization, right to counsel and use and derivative use immunity, should not take away from the fundamental damage that investigative hearings will do to our long traditions of adversarial criminal justice.

The Criminalization of Tragedy and of Politics

The expansion and toughening of the criminal law contemplated in Bill C-36 is a common response to tragic crimes. The criminalization of tragedy has regularly followed horrific acts of terrorism in the United Kingdom[29] and the United States.[30] New offences, new investigative powers and more severe punishments are added to our *Criminal Code* literally every year and often in direct response to horrific crimes. Bill C-36 for example follows Bill C-24[31] which added crimes, investigative powers and punishments in an attempt to combat organized crime in the wake of the shooting of a journalist. Bill C-24 in turn toughens 1997 amendments to respond to biker gang wars in Quebec which resulted in a boy being killed by a bomb.[32] Bolstering already broad and powerful criminal laws and increasing punishment[33] produces strong, symbolic and relatively inexpensive statements denouncing crime and promising safety and security. Unfortunately, there is little evidence that our continuing enthusiasm for enacting new criminal laws makes us safer and more secure. We should not confuse our debates about the expansion and toughening of the criminal law with the actual prevention of terrorism.

The criminalization of politics occurs when issues of criminal justice and in particular the creation of new offences, new investigative powers and more severe punishment are given priority in political discourse over issues of social and economic justice, even when those larger issues may play a role in crime. This process could be described as a politicization of crime or a legalization of politics, but the concept of the criminalization of politics best describes the particular pressures that are leading the state to place more and more reliance on the criminal law. The criminalization of politics occurred throughout the 1990's as restrictions on government spending[34] gave criminal justice greater prominence. For example, feminists in the 1990's found it easier to secure criminal law reform than pay equity and child care. It was also easier and cheaper to amend the criminal law to facilitate prosecutions of child abuse than to address child poverty. Aboriginal people were able to win some modest criminal justice reforms, but not self-government or better living conditions. Groups representing the disabled won a successful defensive battle to prosecute and punish Robert Latimer, but not their battle to decrease very high unemployment rates among their numbers. The criminalization of politics thrived as the state retracted in other areas.

Part of the criminalization of politics is what has been called the rise of the new political case. The old political case pitted the accused against the state. The new political involves not only the accused and the state, but also the victim, potential or actual. In a number of cases, the Supreme Court has upheld criminal laws such as laws against hate propaganda and obscenity on the basis of the rights of the victims or groups such as women and minorities who are disproportionately harmed by such crimes. The new political case is well-represented in the court room by the fact that progressive groups representing women and minorities now often line up on the side of the state in the defence of the criminal sanction.[35] The new political case has aided and abetted the criminalization of politics and concerns about the rights of victims have become the new legitimating face of crime control.[36]

The above phenomenon seems to be occurring in the anti-terrorism context. Irwin Cotler, a law professor and currently a Liberal Member of Parliament, has called for a conceptualization of the fight against terrorism and hate crimes as part of a human rights agenda. He has argued that 'the conventional conceptualization of counter-terrorism in terms of the needs of national security versus civil liberties, has resulted in concern for the rights of terrorist suspects – as there should be – but not for the rights of victims, be they individuals, groups or the very danger to democracy itself.' He urges governments and non-governmental organizations to embrace anti-terrorism as part of their human rights agenda.[37] Professor Cotler's 1998 essay has been influential in the government's defence of Bill C-36. The Minister of Justice has explained that her colleague's arguments have helped distinguish the bill from 'a law and order agenda'[38] There is much truth to the new victims' rights perspective on criminal justice. Victims cannot be ignored and crime can threaten human and equality rights. At the same time, however, a law and order agenda remains a law and order agenda even when it is defended and legitimated in the name of human rights. The new defence of the criminal sanction in the name of victims' and human rights presents a danger that we will discount the coercive reality of using the criminal law. It also presents a danger that we will make unwarranted assumptions about the ability of criminal sanctions to contribute to human rights and equality.

The criminalization of politics affects all ends of the political spectrum. It was well represented by neo-liberal parties such as the Reform Party and the Harris Conservatives which advocated drastic reductions in government spending, but also an expensive law and order agenda. It also has an appeal to more progressive groups. Bill C-36 advances a progressive law and order agenda – one that stresses that the criminal sanction is necessary to protect human rights – by incorporating various United Nations conventions against crimes into domestic law and by creating a hate crime for mischief to religious property. The moral leadership of those such as President Bush and Prime Minister Chretien who rightly warned of the evils of racial and religious prejudice has been bolstered by a new offence punishable by up to 10 years in prison for hate-motivated mischief to religious property. This new crime goes beyond the current law which recognizes hate as an aggravating factor in sentencing and has been defended as reaffirming 'the equal right of every citizen of whatever religion, race or ethnic origin to enjoy the security, protections and liberties shared by all Canadians.'[39] Hate crimes themselves are not sufficient to guard against the dangers of racial and religious prejudice and stereo-typing and they may have unanticipated effects.

Another example of the criminalization of tragedy and politics has been recent expansions of the category of first degree murder. Everyone convicted of murder in Canada is subject to a mandatory sentence of life imprisonment but those subject to first degree murder are not eligible (barring a successful faint hope application to a jury after 15 years) for parole for 25 years – one of the longest periods of incarceration for murder in the western world. First degree murder has traditionally applied to planned and deliberate killings, killings of police officers and prison guards and killings during a short list of serious crimes including hijacking an airplane, kidnapping and forcible confinement and hostage taking. The list, however, is getting longer. In response to a well-publicized killing of a woman stalked by her former spouse, Parliament added killings during the commission of the new offence of criminal harassment to the list. In response to a well-publicized death of a child in a bombing linked to biker gangs, Parliament added killings for a criminal organization by the use of explosives to the list. Now Bill C-36 proposes that killings during terrorist activities be added.[40] The criminalization of tragic events such as September 11 values the expressive, narrative and symbolic functions of the criminal law above its rationality and coherence. This is unfortunate because, as the many moving memorials and acts of generosity towards the many victims of September 11 demonstrate, there are more direct and humane ways to recognize tragedy.

The criminalization of politics will also affect political discourse. Criminal law focuses on intentional misconduct, not the social and political factors that may contribute to crime. This focus, especially when applied to the evil events of September 11, is quite appropriate in a criminal trial. But what may be more problematic is when the focus on individual fault and evil dominates political discourse. For example, New York mayor Rudolph Giuliani was widely praised when he returned a $10 million donation from a Saudi Prince after the donor attempted to link September 11 with the treatment of Palestinians in the Mid-East.[41] Mayor Giuliani is absolutely correct that the killing of innocent civilians can never be justified or excused for political reasons and his return of the donation made a strong statement to this effect. Nevertheless, it would be troubling if linkages between terrorism and foreign policy were seen as inherently improper. As Thomas Homer-Dixon has argued the task of explaining terrorism should be distinct from the task of assigning criminal responsibility for it.[42] One of the unfortunate side effects of the criminalization of politics, however, is a refusal to understand crime by reference to its broader social, cultural and political context. This may mean that we will focus on the investigation and punishment of terrorism and ignore some of the conditions that may contribute to terrorism. Moreover, there is a danger that even the act of calling attention to the context in which terrorism emerges will be seen as illegitimate and akin to attempting to excuse the horrible and inexcusable crimes that terrorists commit.

The use of the criminal law is necessary to deal with crimes, but one problem with the criminalization of politics is a tendency to see it as a sufficient response. September 11 may well trigger an increased criminalization of politics in which more and more attention and spending is directed towards security matters. Bill C-36 is heavily weighted towards criminal justice matters in the creation of new offences and investigative powers and enhanced penalties. A second omnibus bill may be in development, but it is unclear the extent to which it will focus on criminal justice matters or involve other ministries such as health and transportation that may have a role to play in preventing terrorism and dealing with its aftermath. In any event, increased spending on policing, security and the military, combined with tax cuts and declining governmental revenues, may preclude major social and economic re-investment in the next federal budget.[43] September 11 may stimulate a re-evaluation of neo-liberal reforms such as the privatization of airports and the contracting out of security.[44] Nevertheless, if the state comes back in a post-September 11 world, it will be a more repressive state with increased emphasis on the investigation and punishment of crime.

Conclusion

It is important that we use our skills and knowledge to evaluate whether Bill C-36 complies with the Charter and to understand the scope of the many additions it proposes to our criminal law. At the same time, however, we should heed the warnings of Burke that what is legal, or today what is Charter-proof, is not necessarily wise or necessary. The evil that was committed on September 11quite naturally makes us reach for the criminal law. Nevertheless we should also remember that our existing criminal law is already broad and that expanding and toughening the criminal law, however easy and satisfying that may be, is unfortunately not an effective means to prevent crime.

Notes

* Faculty of Law, University of Toronto. I thank (without implicating) a number of colleagues including Lisa Austin, David Dyzenhaus, Marty Friedland, Jonathan Rudin, David Schneiderman, Lorne Sossin, Hamish Stewart, Don Stuart and Gary Trotter for helpful comments on earlier drafts. I also thank Julian Jubenville for his enthusiastic research assistance.

1 Edmund Burke *Burke's Speech on Conciliation with America* (London: MacMillan, 1961) at 35

2 Henry Hart and Albert Sacks *The Legal Process Basic Problems in the Making and Application of Law* (Westbury: Foundation Press, 1994) at 35.

3 First Session Thirty-seventh Parliament 49–50 Elizabeth II, 2001. (henceforth Bill C-36)

4 The *War Measures Act* and the Public Orders Regulations, 1970 SOR 70-444, making the FLQ an unlawful association, was declared at 4.00 am on October 16, 1970. By the time Parliament met later that day, 150 of the almost 500 people who would be arrested during the October Crisis were already in jail.

Section 4 of the regulations created an indictable offence punishable by up to 5 years imprisonment to be or profess to be a member of an unlawful association which was defined in s.3 as the FLQ or any group or association that advocates the use of force or the commission of crime as a means or aid of accomplishing governmental change in Canada. It was also illegal to contribute anything or solicit contributions for an unlawful association; interfere with the apprehension of a member or knowingly permit an unlawful association to use premises. Section 9 of the regulations provided for arrest on the basis of suspicion without warrant, bail or charge for up to 30 days. Section 10 provided for warrantless searches again on the basis of suspicion. The Canadian Bill of Rights did not apply to the invocation of the *War Measures Act.*

In December, 1970 these regulations were replaced by the *Public Order (Temporary Measures Act)* S.C.1970-71-72 c.2. The legislation included many of the same offences and arrest and search powers on suspicion as the previous regulations. It was enacted notwithstanding many rights in the Canadian Bill of Rights. Ibid s.12. It was also enacted with a sunset provision so that the legislation expired on April 30, 1971 ibid s.15 when it was not renewed. On the October crisis see generally John Saywell *Quebec 70* (Toronto: University of Toronto Press, 1971) at 86–93; Walter Tarnopolsky *The Canadian Bill of Rights* 2nd ed. supra at 331–348; Thomas Berger *Fragile Freedoms* (Toronto: Clarke Irwin, 1981) ch.7.

5 The American legislative response to terrorism, *The Patriot Act* H.R. 3162 was passed by a 98–1 vote in the Senate and a 356–66 vote in the House of Representatives. 'Antiterrorism bill becomes U.S. law' *Globe and Mail* October 27, 2001. The 1970 invocation of the *War Measures Act* was supported in Parliament by a vote of 190 to 16 while the subsequent *Public Order (Temporary Measures Act)* was passed 152 to 1 in Parliament. See Saywell *Quebec 70* supra at 106, 126.

At this time, the vote on Bill C-36 is not known. When it was introduced in Parliament, representatives of Her Majesty's Loyal Opposition, the Canadian Alliance, argued that Bill C-36 should be toughened to require extradition of suspected terrorists without assurances that the death penalty would not be applied and raised concerns that the due process protections in the investigative hearings might prevent timely disclosure of pending terrorism. Hansard October 16, 2001 per Vic Toews. Other opposition parties raised some concerns that some aspects of Bill C-36 may be overbroad.

6 The American constitutional law scholar James Bradley Thayer made a similar point close to a hundred years ago when he warned of the danger of turning 'subjects over to courts' and falling into 'a habit of assuming that whatever' legislatures 'could constitutionally do they may do ...' He feared that this would 'dwarf the political capacity of the people' and 'deaden its sense of moral responsibility.' As quoted in Alexander Bickel *The Least Dangerous Branch: The Supreme Court at the Bar of Politics* 2nd ed (New Haven: Yale University Press, 1986) at 21–22.

7 For example, the Quebec Court of Appeal rejected Professor Noel Lyon's arguments that by declaring the FLQ to be an unlawful association, 'the Public Orders Regulations, 1970 substituted executive judgment for judicial decision in areas so

basic to judicial duty as to threaten the integrity of our constitution.' Noel Lyon 'Constitutional Validity of Sections 3 and 4 of the Public Order Regulations, 1970' (1971) 18 McGill L.J. 136 at 138. Brossard J.A. indicated that Parliament could enact a retroactive criminal law, stating that as 'between commentators on the law and the judges charged with applying it, there is often a lack of pragmatism and realism distinguishing theoreticians and practioners.' *Gagnon* v. *Vallieres* (1971) 14 C.R.N.S. at 350.

8 Again, it should be remembered that the sweeping powers of the *War Measures Act* did not prevent the murder of Pierre Laporte and that subsequent convictions were entered not on the new offences created in October, 1970 but on charges of murder, kidnapping and being an accessory after the fact to kidnapping.

9 Anne McLellan Letter to the editor *Globe and Mail* October 25, 2001. See also the Minister's statements in Parliament that 'Charter rights have been considered and preserved against the objectives of fighting terrorism and protecting national security. I assure everyone in the House and all Canadians that we have kept the individual rights and freedoms of Canadians directly in mind in developing these proposals.' Hansard Oct 16, 2001.

10 'Anti terrorism law complies with the Charter of Rights, McLellan says' *Toronto Star* October 17, 2001. The Minister of Justice may herself be having some second thoughts given her indication that she would consider altering the definition of terrorist activity to exclude unlawful protests, strikes and advocacy. 'Terror bill worries Dhaliwal' *Globe and Mail* October 30, 2001.

11 A senior official involved in drafting the Charter has explained 'we built in the fundamental principles of justice and Charter analysis into all of this ... We were constantly with our human rights lawyers ...' '30 drafters, many Charter experts later' National Post October 16, 2001.

12 *Hunter* v. *Southam* (1984) 14 C.C.C.(3d) 97 (S.C.C.).

13 Alexander Bickel *The Least Dangerous Branch* supra at 129. See also my *The Supreme Court on Trial* (Toronto: Irwin Law, 2001) at 282ff for further arguments that the upholding of dubious laws under the Charter may inhibit the criticism and reform of such laws.

14 Doreen McBarnet *Conviction: Law, the State and the Construction of Justice* (London: Macmillan, 1981); Michael Mandel *The Charter of Rights and the Legalization of Politics in Canada* rev ed. (Toronto: Thompson, 1994).

15 The United Kingdom's *Terrorism Act, 2000* c.11 does not contain sunset provisions. Its *Human Rights Act, 1998* c.42 s.16, however, provides a 5 year sunset for derogations from the European Convention including one first made in 1988 in response to a decision concerning the detention of suspected terrorists. See generally Susan Marks 'Civil Liberties at the Margins: the UK, Derogation and the European Court of Human Rights' (1995) 15 Oxford Journal of Legal Studies 69.

16 The Committee has recommended a five year expiration for those parts of Bill C-36 not necessary to implement international conventions in order to require 'Parliament to justify the continuance of the powers granted, assuring Canadians

that the tools are sufficient, yet not exorbitant, and they continue to be justifiable and necessary in the battle against terrorism.' Special Senate Committee on Bill C-36 *First Report* Nov 1, 2001.

17 Patrick Monahan and Marie Finkelstein 'The Charter of Rights and Public Policy in Canada' in Monahan and Finkelstein *The Impact of the Charter on Public Policy Process* (Toronto: York University, 1993); James Kelly 'Bureaucratic Activism and the Charter' (1999) 42 Canadian Public Administration 476.

18 The preamble to Bill C-36 for example outlines the compelling objective of the legislation by indicating that 'terrorism is a matter of national concern that affects the security of the nation' while indicating its concern to continue 'to respect and promote the values reflected in, and the rights and freedoms guaranteed by, the Canadian Charter of Rights and Freedoms.' See generally my 'The Uses and Audiences of Preambles in Legislation' (2001) McGill L.J. forthcoming.

19 Many of these examples of quick legislative responses to Charter decisions are described in my *Due Process and Victims' Rights* (Toronto: University of Toronto Press, 1999) chs. 2, 3, and 5.

20 *R. v. Mills* (2000) 139 C.C.C.(3d) 321 (S.C.C.).

21 Under the common law and constitutional conventions, there seemed to be a greater awareness that the legally permissible was not necessarily proper or desirable. For further elaboration see my 'The Attorney General and the Charter Re-Visited' (2000) 50 U.T.L.J.1 at 4–9,30–40.

22 A person who knows about terrorist activity may be liable to prosecution under many of the new offences created in Bill C-36 including participating in the activities of a terrorist group, facilitating a terrorist activity, providing property or services for terrorists and harbouring or concealing terrorists. See Bill C-36 ss 82.02-83.04,83.18-83.23.

23 As Lilburne accurately described it: 'I was condemned because I would not accuse myself.' Roger Salhany *The Origins of Rights* (Toronto: Carswell, 1986) at 95.

24 *Criminal Code* R.S.C. 1985 c.C-34, s.487.01.

25 *R. v. S (R.J.)* (1995) 96 C.C.C.(3d) 1 (S.C.C.). The general rule is that evidence can be compelled from a witness providing that the compelled statement and evidence derived from it not be used in subsequent proceedings. The witness may be able to claim protection against compulsion if the predominant purpose of the investigative hearing is to incriminate the witness. See *British Columbia (Securities Commission) v. Branch* (1995) 97 C.C.C.(3d) 505 (S.C.C.). In many investigative hearings under Bill C-36, however, the government would argue that its predominant purpose was to discover information about terrorist activity, not incriminate the witness compelled to answer questions and produce documents.

26 Alexander A. Molina 'California's Anti-Gang Street Terrorism Enforcement and Prevention Act: one step forward, two steps back?' (1993) 22 Southwestern University Law Review 457. See also Oren Gross 'Cutting Down Trees' in this volume.

27 The *Patriot Act* H.R. 3162 s. 802 has added the term 'mass destruction' to its

definition of terrorism and this seems better designed to target the particular evil of the September 11 terrorists. Oklahoma City bomber Timothy McVeigh was convicted of using a weapon of mass destruction. *United States* v. *McVeigh* 153 F.3d. 1116 (10th Cir.).

28 For further discussion see my 'Terrorism and the Criminal Law' in this volume.

29 Within eight days of IRA bombings in Birmingham that killed 21 people, the United Kingdom had enacted new antiterrorism legislation. The subsequent wrongful convictions in these cases underline the dangers of seeing terrorist cases as an exception to the rule in the *United States of American* v. *Burns and Rafay* (2001) 151 C.C.C.(3d) 97 (S.C.C.) and of extraditing terrorist suspects without assurances that the death penalty would not be applied. See my 'Responding to Terrorism' (2001) 45 C.L.Q. 249.

30 American antiterrorism legislation was started in the wake of the 1993 World Trade Centre bombings and then enacted shortly after the 1995 Oklahoma City bombing. See Laurie M. McQuade 'Tragedy as a catalyst for reform: the American way?' (1996) 11 Connecticut Journal of International Law 325 at 359ff.; Blown Away? The Bill of Rights after Oklahoma City' (1996) 109 Harv.L.Rev. 2074.

31 First Session Thirty-seventh Parliament 49–50 Elizabeth II, 2001 as passed by House of Commons June 13, 2001. See my 'Panicking over Criminal Organizations: We Don't Need Another Offence' (2000) 44 C.L.Q. 1.

32 On these amendments see Don Stuart 'Politically Expedient but Potentially Unjust Legislation Against Gangs' (1997) 2 Can. Crim. L. Rev. 207 and (1998) 69 Int Rev of Penal Law 245.

33 Sections 83.26–83.27 of Bill C-36 increase punishment by enhancing the maximum penalty for offences that constitute terrorist activities to life imprisonment and by providing that sentences for the numerous new and overlapping offences it introduces be served consecutively. Gun control reforms in the wake of the massacre of 14 women on Dec 6, 1989 at Ecole Polytechnique in Montreal included not only provisions for gun control, but ten new mandatory minimum sentences of 4 years imprisonment for crimes committed with firearms. The Supreme Court has subsequently upheld this potentially harsh mandatory minimum in a case in which a distraught person unintentionally killed his friend with a firearm. *R.* v. *Morrisey* (2000) 148 C.C.C.(3d) 1 (S.C.C.)

34 Neo-liberal reforms in Canada and elsewhere have in many sectors shrunken the state. For example between 1992 and 1997, there was a 26% reduction in the staff of the Canadian Security Intelligence Service (CSIS) mandated with collecting intelligence to prevent terrorism. This amounted to a loss of 730 positions and saw staffing levels fall from 2760 people in 1992–1993 to 2030 in 1997–98. Canadian Security Intelligence Report, Annual Report 2000 Tables 1 and 2. This particular retraction of the state is likely to be reversed in the wake of September 11, but not in a manner that addresses the criminalization of politics.

35 See A. Alan Borovoy *The New Anti-Liberals* (Toronto: Canadian Scholar's Press, 1999).

36 See generally my *Due Process and Victims' Rights* (Toronto: University of Toronto Press, 1999) for an articulation of this argument.

37 Irwin Cotler 'Towards a Counter-Terrorism Law and Policy' (1998) 10 Terrorism and Political Violence 1 at 5. Professor Cotler argues that terrorism must be seen 'as the ultimate existential assault on human rights and human dignity and that the struggle against terrorism, therefore, must be seen as part of the longer struggle for human rights and human dignity' ibid at 3.

38 She added that it was helpful in 'helping people understand that what we are doing in the legislation is in no way in opposition to the protection and validation of people's fundamental rights.' 'Human rights lawyer unlikely ally of terror bill' National Post October 25, 2001.

39 Per the Minister of Justice Hansard October 16, 2001 describing Bill C-36 s.12 and proposed Criminal Code amendment s.430(4.1). American law already has various hate crime provisions. The *Patriot Act* H.R. 3162 s.102 does not contain new hate crimes, but a provision condemning discrimination against Arab and Muslim Americans. For arguments in favour of separate hate crimes, but also recognizing their limitations see Martha Shaffer 'Criminal Responses to Hate-Motivated Violence: Is Bill C-41 Tough Enough?' (1995) 41 McGill L.J. 199.

40 Bill C-35 s.9 proposed Criminal Code s.231(6.01).

41 Alaweed bin Talal, was reported to have stated: 'Our Palestinian brethren continue to be slaughtered at the hands of Israelis while the world turns the other check.' Mayor Giuliani responded that there was no 'moral equivalent' for September 11 or 'justification for slaughtering 5000–6000 innocent people.' 'Giuliani Nixes Saudi's 10M Gift' *New York Daily News* Oct 12, 2001. Professor Cotler argues against 'the moral and legal shibboleth that "one's person's terrorist is another person's freedom fighter" or that "the right to self-determination legitimates the use of armed struggle"; credos invoked by the terrorist themselves as covers for the commission of acts of international terrorism.' Irwin Cotler 'Towards a Counter-Terrorism Law and Policy' supra at 3. These arguments seem quite right when applied to individual acts of terrorism. Nevertheless, they also may make it difficult and even illegitimate to link terrorism with broader issues of foreign policy.

42 Thomas Homer-Dixon 'We Ignore Misery at our Peril' *Globe and Mail* Sept 26, 2001. But see Marcus Gee 'Stop Making Excuses for Terrorism' *Globe and Mail* Sept 15, 2001.

43 'Canada's bill for terrorism $1–billion' *Globe and Mail* October 27, 2001; 'Martin makes security first budget priority' National Post, November 5, 2001.

44 'Never mix security and profit' *Globe and Mail* November 3, 2001.

Criminalizing Terrorism

The New Terrorism Offences and the Criminal Law

KENT ROACH
Faculty of Law
University of Toronto

What the September 11 terrorists did was a crime long before they boarded the doomed aircraft. The existing criminal law relating to assisting, attempting, counselling and conspiring to commit criminal offences is very broad. Moreover, there is no reason to believe that weaknesses in the substantive criminal law, as opposed to weaknesses in law enforcement and intelligence gathering, contributed to the tragedy of September 11. Nevertheless, Bill C-36[1] proposes to respond to September 11 in part by adding new offences to the *Criminal Code* that would make it a serious crime punishable by between 10 years and life imprisonment to participate in a terrorist group; to facilitate terrorist activity; to instruct either the carrying out of terrorist activities or any other activity that would enhance the ability of terrorist groups to carry out terrorist activities; and to harbour or conceal those who have or are likely to carry out terrorist activities.

Some may be comforted by the fact that the new offences generally contain fault elements, often elements requiring knowledge and/or the purpose of enhancing the ability of a terrorist group to commit terrorist activities. They may also be comforted by the fact that, unlike anti-terrorism legislation in the United Kingdom,[2] the accused under Bill C-36 is not required to discharge reverse onuses or evidential burdens. Finally, some may be comforted by the fact that the consent of the Attorney General is necessary to commence prosecutions under these new offences. The most charitable reading of Bill C-36 suggests that the new offences add little to the existing law and are more about making a strong symbolic statement against terrorism than providing police and prosecutors with genuinely new tools to combat terrorism.

The above reading, however, discounts the manner in which Bill C-36 expands the criminal law. Making participation in a terrorist organization a crime strains traditional criminal law principles and comes uncomfortably close to making membership in or association with an unlawful organization a crime. This was, of course, done under the temporary regulations and legislation enacted as a response to the October crisis in 1970. There is indeed some uncomfortable similarities between the breadth of the offences proclaimed in force in the early morning hours of October 16, 1970 and those proposed in Bill C-36.[3] At present, Canadian criminal law has only made participation in an organization a crime with respect to criminal organizations.[4] Bill C-36 goes farther than these controversial provisions by basing liability not on the commission of offences already found in the criminal law, but on the contentious definition of terrorist activity found in s.83.01 of Bill C-36. At present, this definition includes not only politically, religiously or ideologically motivated violence and endangerment of life, health and safety, but also illegal acts and substantial property damage that would cause serious interference or disruption of essential public or private services. The definition of terrorist activities in Bill C-36 goes beyond American and British anti-terrorism legislation. It is overbroad and dangerous because it could catch young people engaged in illegal environmental, land claims or anti-globalization protests within the bill's web of unprecedented investigative powers, broad offences and harsh punishment.

The Existing Criminal Law

There are numerous offences already in the *Criminal Code* that make the activities of terrorists illegal. They include murder (s.230), hijacking, endangering or having offensive weapons on aircraft (ss.76–78), administering poisons or noxious substances (s.245), offences in relation to explosives (ss.81 and 82), offences in relation to nuclear materials (ss.7(3.2–3.6)), treason and sedition (ss.46,61), sabotage (s.52), intimidation of legislatures or people (ss. 51 and 423), uttering threats (s.264.1), unlawfully causing bodily harm or death (ss.269 and s.222), kidnapping and hostage taking (ss.279 and 279.1), conveying false messages to alarm (s.372) and various offences relating to forged passports, citizenship and naturalization certifications and other false documents (ss. 57–58, 366–369). In addition, there are offences relating to threatening internationally protected persons or their residences (ss.423.1, 424, 431), impersonation (s.403), and mischief to property (s.430). The criminal organization provisions in the Code (ss.467.1,467.11–467.13) may also apply to terrorist groups. In short, the existing criminal law already provides a wide array of offences that prohibit most terrorist acts.

The criminal law would, however, be inadequate if it only applied to completed crimes. For this reason, it applies to a wide range of inchoate crimes. Agreements between two or more people to commit a crime have been seen as a particular menace to society and for this reason, conspiracies to commit crimes are separate offences, generally punishable with the same maximum penalty as the completed offence. (s.465) The agreement necessary for a conspiracy conviction can be implicit or trans-national and 'there may be changes in methods of operation, personnel, or victims without bringing the conspiracy to an end.'[5] Terrorists can be guilty of conspiracy or agreement to commit a crime before they even prepare to commit the offence.[6]

Another important resource to combat terrorism in the existing criminal law is the broad Canadian law of attempts. (s.24) An attempt occurs when a person with the intent to commit the completed offence does any act beyond mere preparation to commit the crime. The act for an attempt need not be a crime, tort, moral wrong or even a social mischief.[7] Although proximity to the completed offence is an important consideration, the Supreme Court has indicated that an attempt can occur even though there might be a 'considerable period of time'[8] between the act that the person is charged with and the completed offence. For example, taking flying lessons with the intent to crash a commercial airliner could be sufficient to form the basis for a charge of attempted hi-jacking or attempted murder. The fact that it is impossible to commit the completed offence (for example, because the terrorists are being caught in a government sting operation) is not a defence.

In addition to attempts and conspiracies, the existing criminal law extends a wide net of liability around those who would assist or counsel terrorism. A person who counsels, solicits, incites or instructs another person to commit a crime is guilty of the crime of counselling a crime that is not committed, even if the person counselled immediately rejects the idea. (s.464) If the person counselled goes on to commit a crime, the counsellor can be guilty as a party to that crime even though the crime is committed in a different manner than was counselled. (s.22(1)) The counsellor is also guilty of any offences that he or she knew or ought to know were likely to be committed in consequence of the counselling. (s.22(2)) A person who intentionally assists, aids or encourages the commission of a crime is guilty of that crime as a party who aids or abets the crime. (s.21(1)). Passive acquiescence is not enough to be a party to an offence, but a broad range of acts of encouragement and assistance will suffice. Once an unlawful purpose has been formed with another person, the accused is also guilty of crimes that he or she knew or ought to have known[9] would occur from carrying out the common unlawful purpose (s.21(2)) Finally a person who receives, comforts or assists a person for the purpose of enabling that person to escape is guilty of the separate offence of being an accessory after the fact (s.23)).

In summary, the existing criminal law is very broad. It applies to those who agree to commit crimes; those who go beyond mere preparation to commit crimes; those who counsel others to commit crimes; and those who knowingly assist in the commission of crimes or escape from crimes. I can only echo the words of Professor Douglas Schmeiser, who writing thirty years ago in the aftermath of the October Crisis, concluded that 'the ordinary criminal law adequately covers dangerous conduct by insurgents.'[10]

The Definition of Terrorist Activity

The definition of terrorist activity in s.83.01 of Bill C-36 is the most important provision in the bill. The ambit of the new offences, as well as the investigative powers, the enhanced punishment and the definition of terrorist groups all depend on this crucial provision.[11] As such, great care should have been taken in its drafting. Unfortunately, the definition of terrorist activity is not nearly as clear, careful or restrained as it should be. It is in some respects broader than the wide definition of terrorism in the United Kingdom's *Terrorism Act, 2000* after which it was modeled. Unlike Bill C-36, the British definition of terrorism does not create new crimes of terrorism and it does not define as terrorism disruptions of essential public and private services.[12] The American legislation is also less broad and more precise than Bill C-36 in its definitions of terrorism and federal crimes of terrorism, all of which, unlike Bill C-36, are based on the commission of predicate offences already in the criminal law.[13] In some respects, the definition of terrorism in Bill C-36 presents an even greater risk of catching illegal dissent than the oft-criticized definition of an unlawful organization that was enacted by the regulations of October, 1970. The single most important change that must be made to Bill C-36 is to narrow its overbroad definition of terrorist activities.

Section 83.01(1)(a)

The definition of terrorist activity in s.83.01(1)(a) starts by incorporating ten offences defined in ss.7(2)–7.(3.73) of the Criminal Code. These offences relate to the seizure of aircraft or interference with civil aviation and maritime navigation, threats against internationally protected persons, the taking of hostages, the taking of nuclear material and terrorist bombings and finance as required to implement various United Nations conventions. Terrorist activity outside Canada can generally be prosecuted on the basis of some nexus with Canada. This part of the definition of terrorist activity incorporates offences found elsewhere in the Code. Nevertheless, the reference to the incorporation of those part of the offences which implement various United Nations conventions make the section less clear and accessible than is desirable under a criminal code.

Section 83.01(b)

The next part of the definition of terrorist activity in s.83.01(1)(b) is not based on the incorporation of offences found elsewhere in the Code. When read in conjunction with the number of offences in Bill C-36 that incorporate references to terrorist activity,[14] the broad definition of terrorist activity in s.83.01 effectively creates many new crimes of terrorism. For that reason, great care and restraint should have been taken in the definition of terrorism in this section.

A Globalized Definition of Terrorism

The definition of terrorist activity in s.83.01(1)(b) includes acts in or outside Canada 'committed in whole or in part for a political, religious or ideological purpose, objective or cause' and intended to intimidate the public 'with regard to its security, including its economic security' or compelling people, governments or domestic or international organizations 'to do or to refrain from doing any act' whether those targets are in or outside of Canada.

This definition of terrorist activity recognizes the changing nature of terrorism by criminalizing attempts to compel people and organizations, not only governments, to do certain acts. It also recognizes the international dimensions of terrorism as it applies to acts both in and outside Canada and to attempts to influence governments and international organizations outside of Canada. In contrast, the regulations enacted in October, 1970 applied solely to advocating force or crime to accomplish governmental change within Canada.

Security is defined broadly in Bill C-36 to include not only traditional concepts of national security but economic security. The preamble of the legislation refers to the threat of terrorism to 'the stability of the economy and the general welfare of the country.' Under Bill C-36, terrorist acts may be directed at transnational corporations, not just governments. They may include disruption of essential private services and substantial damage to private property if that damage disrupts essential private services. Again, the contrast with the stated-based definition of harm in the October 1970 regulations is striking. Today we are concerned not only with protecting governments and public order from terrorism, but also corporations and economic security. The definition of terrorism in Bill C-36 reflects our globalized world by including threats outside of Canada, threats to Canada's economic security, and threats to corporations as part of its globalized definition of terrorism. A global human rights agenda has been linked to a more controversial agenda of economic globalization.

A Motive-Based Definition of Terrorism

Another striking feature of the definition of terrorist activities in Bill C-36 is its requirement for proof of political or religious motives. The reference in s.83.01 to a 'political, religious or ideological purpose' essentially describes motives for the prohibited activity. The criminal law has traditionally been based on the proposition that it is not necessary for the Crown to establish motive as an element of the offence. Motives do not excuse the commission of crime[15] or even mitigate its punishment.[16] Some motives such as hate bias are, however, deemed aggravating factors at sentencing. Bill C-36 would change this traditional approach by making motive an essential element of all offences that incorporate the definition of terrorist activity, as well as a factor that can enhance punishment. It might be argued that the criminalization of certain political, religious or ideological motives violates fundamental freedoms in the Charter such as freedom of expression and conscience or equality rights. Although the courts have defined expression widely as attempts to convey meaning and speech that would otherwise be criminal, they have generally excluded violence from expression. Even if acts of violence were included as fundamental freedoms, their prohibition under the criminal law could be fairly easily justified by the state under s.1 of the Charter. At the same time, the implications of prohibiting certain political or religious motives in our criminal law could be far-reaching.

Overbreadth in the Definition of Terrorism

The next part of the definition is crucial because it provides that to be a terrorist activity, politically, religiously and ideologically motivated attempts to intimidate the public with regard to its security or attempts to compel people or organizations to do certain things must also be intended:

(A) to cause death or serious bodily harm to a person by the use of violence,
(B) to endanger a person's life,
(C) to cause a serious risk to the health or safety of the public or any segment of the public,
(D) to cause substantial property damage, whether to public or private property, if causing such damage is likely to result in the conduct or harm referred to in any of clauses (A) to (C) and (E) or
(E) to cause serious interference with or serious disruption of an essential service, facility or system, whether public or private, other than as a result of lawful advocacy, protest, dissent or stoppage of work that does not involve an activity that is intended to result in the conduct or harm referred to in any of clauses (A) to (C).

Subsection A relating to the intent to cause death or serious bodily harm by violence and subsection C relating to the intent to cause serious risk to public health or safety are not particularly controversial. They would capture both the acts of September 11 and the subsequent mailings of anthrax provided that the political, religious or ideological motivation discussed above was established. It is unclear whether the reference to an intent to endanger life in subsection B requires knowledge or reckless advertence of a threat to life. It might, however, include a politically motivated suicide and the British legislation requires that the person's life that is endangered by someone other than the person committing the offence.

The British law is broader with respect to property damage than Bill C-36 because it applies to the use or threat of 'serious damage to property' for the purpose of advancing a political, religious or ideological cause and influencing the government or intimidating the public. In contrast, subsection D of Bill C-36 requires an intent to cause 'substantial property damage,' but only if the damage is likely to result in death or serious bodily harm, serious risk to health or safety, endangerment of a person's life or serious interference with essential public and private facilities. The intent requirement, however, only applies to causing substantial damage to public or private property and not to the consequences listed in subsections A to C and E. It would be more restrained to require the accused not only to intend to inflict substantial property damage for political or religious motives, but also to know that such damage could endanger life, cause death or serious bodily harm or threaten public health and safety. In any event, subsection D seems overbroad to the extent that it defines as terrorist activity an intent to cause substantial property damage that disrupts essential public or private services whether the fault requirement is extended to the prohibited consequences or not.

Disrupting Essential Public or Private Services

Subsection E is the most overbroad and flawed part of the definition of terrorism. The comparable provision in the British legislation is much more narrowly drawn to only target interference or disruption with 'an electronic system.'[17] It is unclear exactly what services will be deemed essential, but it can be assumed that blockades or obstructions of roads (including privately owned roads by resource development companies) or entrances to essential public or private buildings will fall within that definition. Indeed a blockade of a private corporation that delivers essential services could fall within the broad parameters of section E. The more limited reference to disruptions to electronic systems in the British legislation may be related to the concerns that were expressed that the anti-terrorism measures should not apply to economically motivated protests.

In Bill C-36, concerns about dissent have been addressed by exempting 'lawful advocacy, protest, dissent or stoppage of work' from the definition. This, however, should not satisfy those concerned about dissent being defined, stigmatized and targeted as terrorism. A major problem is that a significant number of protests and strikes that intentionally disrupt essential services are unlawful. By including illegal protests that seriously disrupt essential public and private services, Bill C-36 goes significantly beyond the temporary War Measures regulations of October 1970. Those regulations defined an unlawful association as one that advocated crime to achieve governmental change. Crime under those regulations was presumably limited to violations of the Criminal Code whereas subsection E of Bill C-36 would catch illegal protests and strikes that disrupt essential services that violate the trespass, labour relations and other laws of the provinces. The October regulations were rightly criticized by the late Walter Tarnopolsky on the basis that they could apply to any group 'that advocated non-violent civil disobedience (which could be the commission of a crime) in order to promote governmental change'[18] and were changed within months of their enactment. It is shocking that a potentially broader definition of terrorism has been offered in Bill C-36 as a key component of permanent legislation.

The fact that s.83.01 defines security to include economic security, something that the British bill does not, only adds fuel to the fears that subsection E could be applied to the disruptions of essential public and private services that have accompanied some recent anti-globalization protests at home and abroad. Yet another problem is that subsection E also includes a badly drafted subordinate clause that seems to exempt activities intended to result in the conduct or harm referred to in subsections A to C from the exemption of lawful protests and strikes. This confusing exemption of an exemption seems to suggest that even a lawful protest or strike could be a terrorist activity if it was intended to endanger a person's life or cause serious risk to health or safety.

Fortunately, the Minister of Justice has indicated some willingness to delete the reference to dissent and strikes having to be lawful. This deletion would mean that illegal politically motivated disruptions of essential public or private services would no longer automatically be defined as terrorist activities. Nevertheless such protests that were intended to result in the conduct or harm referred to in subsections A to C would still constitute terrorist activity. Intentional property damage that would cause a serious disruption to essential public and private services would also still fall within the definition of terrorist activity in subsection D. It is even possible that lawful (or if the word lawful is removed, unlawful) protests that were otherwise exempted from the definition of terrorist activities in Subsection E would nevertheless be caught under subsection D if they were caused by the intentional property damage targeted in subsection D.[19] It would be clearer, safer and simpler to delete subsection E altogether.[20] Hopefully amendments will be forthcoming, but it is unsettling that this ominous, repressive and badly-drafted subsection E was included in the bill in the first place.

Piling Inchoate Liability on Top of Inchoate Crimes

A final but important feature of the definition of terrorist activities in Bill C-36 is that it covers not only complete terrorist activities but 'a conspiracy, attempt or threat[21] to commit any such act or omission, or being an accessory after the fact or counseling in relation to any such act or omission ...' The problem here is that many of the terrorist activity offences in the bill are best seen as a species of inchoate crimes themselves because they prohibit activities such as financing, facilitating, and instructing that are done in preparation and sometimes rather advance preparation to the actual commission of any complete terrorist crime. In this way, Bill C-36 runs the risk of piling inchoate liability on top of inchoate crimes. The ability to prosecute inchoate forms of preparatory crimes presents a real danger of extending the criminal law to absurd lengths and diminishing the meaningfulness of the act requirement.[22]

Under the existing criminal law, courts have largely managed to avoid monstrosities such as attempting attempts , attempting conspiracies[23] or counseling counseling , but they may have difficulties doing so under Bill C-36. The reason is that s.83.01 clearly and unequivocally defines terrorist activities, themselves most often inchoate and preparatory to completed crimes, to also include conspiracies, attempts, threats, and counseling to commit terrorist activities. Following s.83.01, a person who urges another person to urge another person to counsel a terrorist activity or even an activity that would facilitate the ability of a terrorist group to commit a terrorist activity could be charged with counseling one of the new offences of instructing in Bill C-36. Bill C-36 allows prosecutors and judges to pile inchoate liability on top of crimes that are already designed to criminalize activities in advance preparation for terrorist activities. The result of all these combinations is difficult to anticipate but it could extend the chain of criminal liability to an unprecedented degree. It could also result in convoluted and complex charges that will confuse judges, let alone juries. The reference to inchoate forms of terrorist activities in crimes that are themselves inchoate expands the net of criminal liability in unforeseen, complex and undesirable ways.

The New Criminal Offences

Leaving aside the numerous offences relating to property and financing which also incorporate the problematic definition of terrorist activities,[24] and new offences expanding first degree murder and creating a new hate crime of mischief to religious property,[25] five new indictable offences are added to the Code, punishable by maximum terms of 10 years to life imprisonment.[26]

Participating in the Activities of a Terrorist Group

The offence in s.83.18 relating to participation in a terrorist group applies to everyone who:

knowingly participates in or contributes to, directly or indirectly, any activity of a terrorist group[27] for the purpose of enhancing the ability of any terrorist group to facilitate or carry out a terrorist activity

This offence of participation in any activity of a terrorist group is inspired but goes beyond the recently broadened offence of participating in the activities of a criminal organization.[28] The prohibited act is very broad and may go beyond acts that would qualify as attempts to commit crimes or aiding and abetting crimes. Section 83.18(2) (b) makes clear that the offence applies even if the accused has not enhanced the ability of a terrorist group to facilitate or carry out a terrorist activity. Under s.83.18(3) (b), participation and contribution can include providing or offering to provide a skill or expertise for the benefit of a terrorist group. The Canadian Bar Association has expressed concerns that this could include lawyers representing terrorist groups and has asked for an exemption from this provision.[29] Such an amendment would not, however, preclude prosecutions of other service providers including perhaps doctors. Under s.83.18(3)(d), participating can also include entering or remaining in any country for the benefit of, at the direction of, or in association with a terrorist group. Thus a 'sleeper' who remains in a country but does nothing else for a terrorist group could be caught under this offence. The failure to act has been criminalized before, but only when the accused has a specific legal duty to act.

Both British and American anti-terrorism legislation more precisely enumerate the acts of assistance or participation in a terrorist activity that is prohibited. For example, the British legislation specifies weapons training, possession of articles giving rise to a reasonable suspicion that they are involved in terrorism and collection of useful information as separate offences.[30] The United States prohibits the provision of material support or resources for terrorists defined to include matters such as training, lodging, financial services, weapons, transportation, physical assets (except medicine and religious materials). The provision of expert advice and assistance is only criminalized if the accused knows or intends it will be used for specific crimes.[31] It would have been better for Bill C-36 to have more precisely defined the types of participation and preparation for crimes that are prohibited instead of criminalizing the great range of conduct that it presently does.

Section 83.18 requires subjective fault in the form of knowingly participating in an activity of a terrorist group for the purpose of enhancing the ability of any terrorist group to facilitate or carry out a terrorist activity. It is not clear that the fault requirement of knowingly participating or contributing refers to knowledge that the group is a terrorist group. Although this is not a constitutional requirement, the general principle should be that the fault element extends to all elements of the prohibited act in which case proof of the accused's knowledge that the group was a terrorist group should be required. The requirement that the accused act for the purpose of enhancing the ability of any terrorist group to facilitate or carry out a terrorist activity is an important requirement of subjective fault. Nevertheless, it is diminished because the requirement of purpose is only directed towards the broad act of either facilitating or carrying out terrorist activities. Respect for the principles of subjective fault may not salvage an offence that has an overbroad or vague prohibited act.

Possible Charter Challenges on the Basis of Vagueness and Overbreadth

It is possible but fairly difficult to challenge an overbroad prohibited act under the Charter. The prohibited act may infringe freedom of expression and association under s.2 or equality rights under s .15 of the Charter. It will then have to be justified by the government under s.1 of the Charter. Vagueness in the definition of an offence could potentially render a limit it imposes on a right as no longer prescribed by law – a requirement that is a prerequisite for justification under s.1 of the Charter. Unfortunately, the Supreme Court has not been rigorous about this requirement and requires only that the legislation provide an intelligible standard for legal debate and interpretation.[32] Overbreadth in the law may also be relevant to whether the offence was justified.[33] An important component of vagueness and overbreadth analysis in the criminal law should be its relation to law enforcement discretion. The broader and vaguer the law, the more scope it gives to law enforcement officials to pick and chose. After the fact remedies for discriminatory policing and racial profiling are limited,[34] so it is important that officials are not given laws that allow them to target people in a discriminatory manner.[35]

Under s.7 of the Charter, laws can be struck down if they are so vague as not to give the accused fair notice or limit law enforcement discretion. The Court has not been receptive to such claims reasoning that the ability of courts to interpret statutes should be considered and that the court should not be overly concerned with reasonable hypotheticals.[36] If s.83.18 of Bill C-36 was challenged, the likely Charter question would be whether the reference to participating so as to facilitate the commission of terrorist acts is so vague as to provide no basis for judicial interpretation of the term. An alternative s.7 challenge could be made on the basis that the offence is overbroad to the objective of combating terrorism. The Supreme Court has struck down an offence of vagrancy under s.7 of the Charter on the basis that its application to all convicted sex offenders loitering in places where children were not reasonably present was overbroad, arbitrary and disproportionate in relation to the government's objective of preventing the sexual abuse of children.[37] This is a possible line of challenge, but courts may well defer to the government's argument that it is necessary to criminalize all forms of participation that could facilitate the ability of terrorist groups to commit terrorist activities. The government could argue that its offence is less drastic and better tailored than an offence that would make simple membership in a terrorist group illegal. Charter arguments can and should be made that the offence is vague and overbroad and does not place enough limits on law enforcement discretion, but I am not terribly optimistic that courts will accept them.

Facilitating a Terrorist Activity

Section 83.19 of Bill C-36 applies to everyone 'who knowingly facilitates a terrorist activity.' It is not clear the extent to which the prohibited act of facilitating expands the criminal law beyond the requirements of aiding and abetting (s.21). Facilitating may not necessarily be much broader than aiding and abetting which includes acts of encouragement, assistance or promotion. The high fault level of subjective knowledge is appropriate given the breadth of the prohibited act. At the same time the fault is not directed towards the commission of specific crimes, but rather the broad act of facilitating a terrorist activity. The fault requirement in s.83.19 should not be displaced by the definition of facilitation in s.83.01(2) of Bill C-36 which states that facilitation can occur even if the accused does not know and cannot foresee that a particular terrorist activity was facilitated.

Instructing the Carrying Out of a Terrorist Activity

Section 83.22 of Bill C-36 applies to every person 'who knowingly instructs, directly or indirectly, any person to carry out a terrorist activity' Subsection 2 of the offence provides that the offence of instructing the carrying out of a terrorist activity would apply whether or not the accused instructs a particular person or knows the identity of those who are instructed to carry out a terrorist activity. General instructions to political or religious groups or the public-at-large to commit a terrorist activity could fall under this new offence.[38] A protest leader that instructs people to illegally disrupt an essential public or private service could also fall within this proposed new offence of instructing people to carry out a terrorist activity. The overbreadth of this new instructing offence is particularly troublesome as it is treated as the most serious of the new offences and is punishable by up to life imprisonment.

Instructing Activities For Terrorist Groups To Enhance their Ability to Carry Out Terrorist Activities

Section 83.21 contains an even broader more anticipatory crime for everyone:

> who knowingly instructs, directly or indirectly, any person to carry out any activity for the benefit of, at the direction of or in association with a terrorist group, for the purpose of enhancing the ability of any terrorist group to facilitate or carry out a terrorist activity ...

This offence applies to direct or indirect instructions to carry out activities for the benefit of terrorist groups in order to enhance the ability of any terrorist group to facilitate or carry out a terrorist activity. This offence criminalizes conduct that is more remote and removed from terrorist activity than instructing a person to carry out a terrorist activity under s.83.22.[39]

As with the offence of participating in the activities of a terrorist group, the prohibited act of this offence is very broad. It applies to instructing people to carry out activities that themselves may be legal, but are for the benefit, at the direction of , or in association with a terrorist group. These activities in turn must be for the purpose of enhancing the ability of that terrorist group, or any other terrorist group, to facilitate or carry out terrorist activity. This could include acts such as setting up a bank account or supplying lodgings and food that would under the law of attempts be held to mere preparation for the commission of a crime. It might also include some activities that would be too peripheral to be classified as aiding, abetting or counseling a crime. The group whose ability to commit terrorism is enhanced might not necessarily be the same as the terrorist group that is benefited. Even without resort to the extension of liability by the incorporation of various forms of inchoate liability in s.83.01(1)(b), this offence significantly extends the chain of criminal liability.

The very broad prohibited act in this section is somewhat restrained by requirements of subjective fault. These requirements are that the accused have knowingly instructed carrying out activities for the purpose of enhancing the ability of terrorist groups to facilitate or commit terrorist activities. Again, however, it is not clear that the fault element of knowledge applies simply to the act of instruction or also to the identity of the group assisted as a terrorist group. The second fault requirement is that the accused must instruct an activity that is for the purpose of enhancing the ability of any terrorist group to facilitate or carry out a terrorist activity. Purpose is a high level of fault but once again, its value in restraining the criminal law is diminished by its connection to the very broad act of enhancing the ability of any terrorist group not only to carry out, but also to facilitate terrorist activities at home and abroad.

Harbouring or Concealing Terrorists

Section 83.23 of Bill C-36 applies to:

> Every one who knowingly harbours or conceals any person whom he or she knows to be a person who has carried out or is likely to carry out a terrorist activity, for the purpose of enabling the person to facilitate or carry out any terrorist activity.

This offence covers conduct that otherwise might be prosecuted as constituting being an accessory after the fact or aiding and abetting in the commission of a crime.(ss.21 and 23) Like the existing Criminal Code sections, s.83.23 requires a high level of subjective fault, namely knowledge with respect to both the act of harbouring and concealing and knowledge that the person assisted has or will commit an offence. The difference, however, is that the knowledge requirement in s.83.23 is only directed to the overbroad concept of a terrorist activity. Again a high level of subjective fault only partially mitigates the potential unfairness of an offence with an overbroad prohibited act.

The requirement for subjective fault in s.83.23 differs from the comparable provision in the American legislation which applies to 'whoever harbors or conceals any person that he knows or has reasonable grounds to believe has committed, or is about to commit'[40] a long list of offences or the requirement under ss.5 of the October, 1970 regulations and legislation which made it a crime to assist a person 'knowing or have reasonable cause to believe' that they were guilty of an offence. The requirement of subjective fault in Bill C-36 is much more appropriate. It seems overly harsh to impose a maximum of 10 years imprisonment as does both the American and Canadian harbouring offences for someone who did not know but ought to have known that he or she was harbouring or concealing a terrorist.

Consent to Prosecute

The new offences require the consent of either the federal or provincial Attorney General before prosecution. This is intended as a safeguard on abuse of these sections by citizens who might otherwise be able to commence private prosecutions without the Attorney General's consent. In *R. v. Keegstra*,[41] the Supreme Court looked upon the requirements that the Attorney General consent to hate propaganda prosecutions as a restraint that helped to justify the limits placed on freedom of expression. Nevertheless, the consent to prosecute can take a more ominous meaning with respect to crimes that are based on political motivation. Even though Attorneys General should make prosecutorial decisions independently from Cabinet and in the public interest, they may be perceived as prosecuting those terrorists who are a particular concern to their governments. This may particularly be the case if the federal Attorney General prosecutes a group that the federal Solicitor General has already designated as a terrorist group or if a provincial Attorney General prosecutes a protest or strike that disrupts essential public or private services.

Punishment

Section 83.27 contemplates a general enhancement of maximum penalties of up to life imprisonment for all existing indictable offences 'where the offence also constitutes a terrorist activity' and the offender is given notice. Whether an offence constitutes a terrorist activity should depend on the definition of terrorist activity discussed above which includes factors of motivation and intent. Section 83.20 of Bill C-36 (misnumbered s.83.2 in the bill as originally printed) provides that everyone who commits an indictable offence 'for the benefit of, at the direction of or in association with a terrorist group' is guilty of an indictable offence and liable to life imprisonment. This provision is potentially broader than s.83.27 because it does not require that the indictable offence itself meet the requirements of a terrorist activity. Moreover an offence could be committed in association with a terrorist group without additional fault such as knowledge or intent to assist the terrorist group. It should be made clear that the enhanced penalties in s.83.20 only apply for those who commit indictable offences knowing or intending that they will benefit a terrorist group or following the directions or associating with a group known by the accused to be a terrorist group.

Section 83.26 of Bill C-36 follows the organized crime provisions by providing that a sentence other than life imprisonment imposed upon a person for any of the offences discussed above, as well as offences relating to providing property or services to terrorists, shall be served consecutively. This takes away from judicial discretion to determine that serving the penalties concurrently will result in a total sentence that is appropriate and fit. Although the Minister of Justice has stressed the need for tough penalties to deter terrorism, the result of this provision may well be disproportionate punishment. For example, a young protestor could be convicted of (1) participating in an activity of a group for the purpose of enhancing its ability to engage in illegal disruptions of essential services under s.83.18 , (2) of helping to finance such activities under s.83.02 , (3) of making available property for such activity under s.83.03 and (4) of using property for such activities under s.83.04. All four offences carry maximum penalties of 10 years imprisonment. The rule against multiple punishment for the same delict and double jeopardy under s.11(h) of the Charter may not protect the accused from being sentenced consecutively for these overlapping but legally distinct crimes[42] Thus, subject to rules about parole eligibility, one young person involved in illegal protests to disrupt an essential service could in theory be sentenced to a maximum of 40 years imprisonment! This should constitute grossly disproportionate punishment that violates the right against cruel and unusual punishment in s.12 of the Charter. Nevertheless, courts may defer to the legislative imposition of mandatory consecutive penalties on the basis that Parliament is entitled to stress the denunciation and deterrence of terrorism over what is necessary to deter, rehabilitate or punish a particular offender who may have only been peripherally involved in terrorism.

Conclusion

The temptation to view Bill C-36 as a benign and largely symbolic addition to the criminal law should be resisted. Although the existing criminal law already prohibits a broad range of terrorist activities, including agreements, attempts, assistance and counselling of crimes, Bill C-36 goes much farther. It goes beyond British and American legislation by defining terrorist activities to include illegal political, religious and ideological protests that intentionally disrupt essential services. The overbroad definition of terrorist activities is then incorporated in new offences such as facilitating and instructing terrorist activities and participating in the activities of or harbouring those who commit terrorist activities. These broad offences, which target activities well in advance of actual terrorism, are in turn expanded by the incorporation of inchoate liability such as conspiracies, attempts, counseling or threats, into the definition of terrorist activities. The overall effect is to lengthen the long reach of the criminal law in a manner that is complex, unclear and unrestrained. Although the government has generally required proof of knowledge or purpose in the new offences, the value of such fault requirements in ensuring restraint in the use of the criminal law are mitigated by the very broad act requirements in the new offences. It is possible, but difficult, to challenge the extended criminal acts in Bill C-36 under the Charter as overbroad and vague. They place few limits on law enforcement discretion and do not provide certainty about the ambit of criminal liability at the extreme periphery of activities defined as terrorism. Finally, the harsh punishment contemplated in Bill C-36 may be disproportionate as applied to those on the outer peripheries of terrorist activities who may be caught by the very wide net of criminal liability set by Bill C-36

Notes

1 First Session Thirty-seventh Parliament 49–50 Elizabeth II, 2001. (henceforth Bill C-36)

2 In light of the House of Lords decision in *R. v. DPP, ex parte Kebilene* [1999] 3 W.L.R. 972, s.118(2) of the *Terrorism Act, 2000* c.11 reduces many of the reverse onuses to evidential burdens.

3 Section 3 of the *Public Order Regulations, 1970* SOR/70-444 declared the FLQ to be an unlawful association as well as 'any group of persons or association that advocates the use of force or the commission of crime as a means of or as an aid in accomplishing governmental change within Canada.' As will be seen, the definition of terrorist activities in Bill C-36 is in some respects narrower and in some respects broader than this definition.

   The October 1970 regulations and the subsequent *Public Order (Temporary Measures) Act, 1970* S.C. 70-71-72 c.2, like Bill C-36, provided new and extremely broad criminal offences in an attempt to combat those who acted on behalf of or in association with terrorist organizations and those who provided financial and other benefits to such organizations. Section 4 of the regulations and the legislation made it an indictable offence punishable by up to 5 years imprisonment to be or profess to be a member of an unlawful association; to act or profess to act as an officer of an unlawful association; to communicate statements on behalf of an unlawful association; to advocate or promote unlawful acts or means to accomplish the association's aims, principles or policies; to contribute anything to the unlawful association or to anyone for the benefit of the unlawful association; or to solicit contributions for the benefit of the unlawful association. Section 5 made it a similar crime for a person 'knowing or having reasonable cause to believe' that another person is guilty of an offence to assist that person 'with intent thereby to prevent, hinder or interfere' with the person's apprehension, trial or punishment. Section 6 made it an offence to knowingly permit premises to be used for any meeting of an unlawful association. Section 8 provided that evidence that a person attended meetings of an unlawful association; spoke publicly in advocacy for the unlawful association or communicated statements as a representative or professed representative of an unlawful association was 'in the absence of evidence to the contrary, proof that he is a member of the unlawful association.' For further analysis of these provisions see Herbert Marx 'The Apprehended Insurrection of October 1970 and the Judicial Function' (1972) 7 U.B.C.L.Rev. 55; Noel Lyon 'Constitutional Validity of Public Order Regulations' (1971) 18 McGill L.J. 136; Walter Tarnopolsky *The Canadian Bill of Rights* 2nd ed (Toronto: McClelland and Stewart, 1975) at pp. 342–346.

4 *Criminal Code* R.S.C. 1985 c.C-34 s.467.1 making participating in the activities of a criminal organization knowing that any members of the organization engaged or have engaged in indictable offences and being a party to the commission of an indictable offence for the benefit or at the direction of a criminal organization a separate offence. For criticism of this offence enacted in 1997 see Don Stuart 'Politically Expedient but Potentially Unjust Legislation Against Gangs' (1997) 2 Can. Crim. L. Rev. 207 and (1998) 69 Int Rev of Penal Law 245. Sections 467.11-467.13 passed by the House of Commons in June 2001 as part of Bill C-24 further expands participation based offence with new offences of participation, commission of offences for and instructing the commission of offences for criminal organizations. For criticisms see Don Stuart 'Time to Recodify Criminal Law and Rise Above Law and Order Expediency: Lessons from the Manitoba Warriors Prosecutions' (2001) 28 Man.L.J. 89 and my 'Panicking over Criminal Organizations: We Don't Need Another Offence' (2000) 44 C.L.Q. 1.

5 *R. v. Cotroni* (1979) 45 C.C.C.(3d) 1 at 17 (S.C.C.).

6 The Supreme Court has recognized that conspiracy is 'a more "preliminary" crime that attempt' because it criminalizes an agreement to commit an offence and not any acts that go beyond mere preparation to commit the crime. *U.S.A.* v. *Dynar* (1997) 115 C.C.C.(3d) 481 at 512 (S.C.C.).

7 *R. v. Cline* (1956) 115 C.C.C. 18 at 28 (Ont.C.A.).

8 *R. v. Deutsch* (1986) 27 C.C.C.(3d) 385 at 401 (S.C.C.)

9 To be guilty of murder or attempted murder , the murder must have been actually

foreseen by the accused who assisted or counseled the crime. *R.* v. *Logan* (1990) 58 C.C.C.(3d) 391 (S.C.C.).

10 Douglas Schmeiser 'Control of Apprehended Insurrection: Emergency Measures vs. The Criminal Code' (1971) 4 Man.L.J. 359 at 365.

11 The definition of terrorist activity is effectively incorporated within many offences. This makes working with the bill awkward and confusing as constant reference must be made back to s.83.01 in order to understand the full ambit of many offences found in other parts of the bill.

12 Concerns were expressed in the drafting of the British bill that 'the definitions in the Bill should not catch actions in connection with industrial disputes, large demonstrations or even politically motivated mass boycotts of major oil companies' as quoted in J.J.Rowe Q.C. 'The Terrorism Act 2000' [2001] Crim.L.Rev. 527 at 532.

13 The *Patriot Act* H.R. 3162 targets as domestic terrorism 'acts dangerous to human life that are a violation of the criminal laws of the United States or any State' that 'appear to be intended 1) to intimidate or coerce a civilian population; 2) to influence the policy of a government by intimidation or coercion; or 3) to affect the conduct of a government by mass destruction, assassination or kidnapping ...' 18 USC s. 2331(1) as amended s.802 of the Patriot Act. Federal crimes of terrorism are also defined more precisely as an offence that 'is calculated to influence or affect the conduct of government by intimidation or coercion, or to retaliate against government conduct' and violates a long list of specific offences relating to aircraft, chemical weapons, nuclear material, explosives, assassination and kidnapping of governmental officials, arson and bombing, damage to computers, hostage taking, destruction of communication line, federal facilities, wrecking trains, weapons of mass destruction, and providing material support to terrorists and terrorist organizations, and harbouring terrorists. 18 USC s.2332b as amended s.808 of the Patriot Act.

14 These include ss.83.02-83.04 and ss.83.18-83.19 and 83.21-83.23.

15 *R.* v. *Lewis* (1979) 47 C.C.C.(2d) 24 at 33 (S.C.C.); *U.S.A.* v. *Dynar* (1997) 115 C.C.C.(3d) 481 at 509 (S.C.C.).

16 *R.* v. *Latimer* (2001) 150 C.C.C.(3d) 129 (S.C.C.).

17 *Terrorism Act, 2000* c.11, s.1(2)(e).

18 SOR/70-444 s.3. Walter Tarnopolsky *The Canadian Bill of Rights* 2nd ed. (Toronto: McClelland and Stewart, 1975) at 343. The replacement legislation enacted later in 1970 narrowed the definition of unlawful association to any group or association that 'advocates the use of force or the commission of crime as an aid in accomplishing the same or substantially the same governmental change within Canada with respect to the Province of Quebec or its relationship to Canada as that advocated by the said Le Front de Liberation du Quebec.' *Public Order (Temporary Measures) Act, 1970* S.C. 1970-71-72 c.2, s.3.

19 I thank my colleague David Schneiderman for bringing this point to my attention.

20 If concerns still remained, the British example could be followed by spelling out precisely the type of disruptions (ie of electronic systems and perhaps other systems) that should fall within the definition.

21 The effect of this reference to 'threats' is not clear and seems to have been taken from the British legislation in which threats are more widely punished in the criminal law. Certain threats are punished in the Criminal Code but unlike the other species of inchoate crimes listed in the quote, there is no generic provision in the Code which makes threats to commit any crime, a crime in itself.

22 Don Stuart persuasively argues: 'It is logically possible to arrive at preposterously wide definitions of offences by combining the present incomplete offences. Why not attempting to attempt, a conspiracy to attempt, counselling an attempt and so on? That the general principles of defining each incomplete offence would be applied to situations surely never imagined, suggests that the criminal sanction should not be extended at all to combinations of incomplete offences. The nature of criminal responsibility not yet committed is already wide enough.' Don Stuart *Canadian Criminal Law* 4th ed (Toronto: Carswell, 2001) at 704.

23 The Ontario Court of Appeal has rejected an attempt to create an offence of attempted conspiracy in *R. v. Dungey* (1979) 51 C.C.C.(3d) 86 (Ont.C.A.) The Ontario Court of Appeal has also interpreted complete offences, which like the offences in Bill C-36 are designed to criminalize preparations to commit crimes, in a manner that preserves the need for some meaningful prohibited act. *R. v. Mac* (2000) 152 C.C.C.(3d) 1 at para 20 leave to SCC granted. See also Hamish Stewart 'The Centrality of the Act Requirement for Criminal Attempts' (2001) 51 U.T.L.J. 399.

24 See Kevin Davis 'Cutting Off the flows of funds to Terrorists: Whose Funds? Which Funds?' in this volume.

25 These are briefly discussed in my 'The Dangers of a Charter-Proof and Crime-Based Response to Terrorism' in this volume.

26 The new offences of participating in the activity of a terrorist group or harbouring or concealing a terrorist carry the 10 year maximum while the offence of facilitating carries a 14 year maximum with the offences of instructing terrorism carry the harshest penalties of a maximum of life imprisonment.

27 A terrorist group is defined in s.83.01 to include an entity listed by the Solicitor General as a terrorist group or 'an entity that has as one of its purposes or activities facilitating or carrying out any terrorist activity.'

28 Bill C-24 s.27 adding s.467.11 to the Criminal Code.

29 Canadian Bar Association Submission on Bill C-36 at p.26.

30 *Anit-terrorism Act, 2000* c.11 ss.54, 57, 58.

31 18 U.S.C. s.2339A as amended by the *Patriot Act* s.805

32 *Irwin Toy* v. *Quebec* [1989] 1 S.C.R. 927 at 983. For a case under the European Convention requiring that laws be precise and foreseeable to constitute limits on rights that are prescribed by law see *Harrup* v. *United Kingdom* (2000) 30 E.H.R.R. 241 at para 31.

33 *Osborne* v. *Canada* [1991] 2 S.C.R.69; *R. v. Nova Scotia Pharamaceutical Society* (1992) 74 C.C.C.(3d) 289 (S.C.C.).

34 See generally my *Due Process and Victims' Rights* at pp. 222–225, 256–258 and Sujit Choudhry 'Racial and Ethnic Profiling and the Charter' in this volume.

35 See the daunting list of possible targets of the new offences in Don Stuart 'The Dangers of Quick Fix Legislation in the Criminal Law: The Anti-terrorism Bill C-36 Bill Should Be Withdrawn' in this volume.

36 *R. v. Nova Scotia Pharmaceutical Society* (1992) 74 C.C.C.(3d) 289; *R. v. Canadian Pacific* (1995) 99 C.C.C.(3d) 97 (S.C.C.)

37 *R. v. Heywood* (1994) 94 C.C.C.(3d) 481 (S.C.C.). See also s.161 of the Criminal Code enacted in reply.

38 Instructions to commit a crime as opposed to the actual commission of a violent crime may well qualify as expression protected under s.2 of the Charter in which case the government would have to demonstrate that the new broadly worded offence was a reasonable limit under s .1 of the Charter.

39 The marginal note to s.83.21 is inaccurate in stating that it applies to 'instructing commission of offence for a terrorist group.' In fact it criminalizes instructions of any activity that can benefit and enhance the ability of any terrorist group to facilitate or carry out a terrorist activity.

40 H.R. 3162 s.803 amending s.2339 of United States Code.

41 (1990) 61 C.C.C(3d) 1 (S.C.C.)

42 Courts have allowed people to be convicted of both conspiracy and the completed crime and of participation in a criminal organization and a completed crime. *R. v. Sheppe* [1980] 2 S.C.R. 22; *R. v. Leclerc* (2001)R.J.Q. 747 (Q.C.).

Political Association and
the Anti-terrorism Bill

DAVID SCHNEIDERMAN* AND BRENDA COSSMAN†
Faculty of Law
University of Toronto

After September 11th, it is said, the world changed forever. Public opinion polling data demonstrates that Canadians view the protection of civil liberties differently after the World Trade Centre disaster than before. Canadians now are prepared to sacrifice their liberties in order to enhance their security and safety. What specific liberties are we prepared to sacrifice, however, and to what degree? For many, this loss of liberty will entail only searches of bags and purses before embarking on a plane, or longer lines and more inquiries at border crossings. These are minor inconveniences, additional conditions imposed on what are privileges, not rights. In addressing the question of the appropriate balance between liberty and security in the aftermath of this new phase of terrorism, we should probe deeper into the civil rights that are precisely at stake at this critical juncture.

Canadians need to take more careful stock of Bill C-36, the *Anti-Terrorism Act*.[1] It poses a serious threat to the rights and freedoms of Canadians. The definition of 'terrorist activity' (s. 83.01) catches a potentially wide sphere of human activity, much of it done in combination with others. Many of the concerns we have with the Bill flow from the wide net cast by this definition section. Our discomfort is fuelled by that fact that many of the new offences that originate in the Bill turn on this particular definition. Not all of our concerns would be solved, however, were some of the offending language excised from the definition (though the Bill undoubtedly would be improved by it). The new offences of 'participating in' (s. 83.12) and 'facilitating' (s. 83.19) a terrorist activity aggravate our concern that Canadians are willing to give up too much in order to secure heightened feelings of safety. These provisions of the Bill potentially undermine, and cast a chill over, political, ethnic, and religious associations in Canada. In our view, Bill C-36 fails to take into account the complexities and capacious nature of associational life in a multicultural society.

Canadian's conceive of themselves as living in a tolerant and multicultural 'peaceable kingdom.' Organized constitutionally around the recognition and respect of difference – as between Anglophone and Francophone, for instance – Canadians have generalized from this experience by providing a safe and prosperous haven for people from many different lands.[2] With an official state policy that fosters affiliations based on ethnicity, nationality, country of origin or religion, this is a country presumably where associational life will flourish. One would expect this kind of pluralism in most democratic societies around the world, where the national make-up of populations are disparate and transnational in scope.[3] Recent studies in the United States, however, point to a decline in associational life.[4] Looking beyond these trends, there is value in promoting freedom of association in liberal democratic societies, for as Nancy Rosenblum argues, associational pluralism promotes the moral disposition requisite for democracy to thrive. Associations cultivate the 'disposition to cooperate' (though the moral value of any single association itself often is difficult to assess).[5] Associations are 'hybrid' and 'dynamic' movements, with shifting aims and objectives; members may join in the pursuit of these goals just as they may easily leave them.[6] In the language of the British political pluralists writing in the early part of the twentieth century, association's give expression to one's 'gregarious impulse' as 'a centre of diverse and possibly conflicting loyalties.'[7] It will be the case that some associations simply are so destructive of the aims and objectives of the larger association – the liberal democratic state – that these groups simply cannot be tolerated. It might be said that Bill C-36 targets just these kinds of groups. The breadth of the language used, however, belies this stated objective.

It also is the case that the places and spaces for the practice of associational life are shrinking. If groups, in the past, made their presence known by taking to the public square, those squares are turning increasingly private. Privately-owned shopping malls have replaced public streets as places to congregate in order to make one's voice heard. Increasing media concentration means that there are fewer outlets through which to get noticed. Even then, the costs of an ad in one of Canada's national newspapers usually will be beyond the means of most groups. The web enables these groups to send their messages out to the wide world, but it often will be the case that no one will notice. Voices on the web are proliferating daily, and it is difficult to sort out the significant from the trivial message. In order to control information input, users of the web filter their sources of information and so become fragmented from a larger public discourse.[8]

In this essay, we examine the impact of Bill C-36 on associational life in Canada, with a particular focus on the definition section and the offences of 'participating' and 'facilitating.' These provisions are not the only ones that may have a negative impact on associative activity (the provisions concerning charitable status or financing of terrorism also are important in this regard).[9] These aspects of the Bill are instructive, however, about its wide sweep and its potential impact on rights and freedoms.

A word should be said here about the *Canadian Charter of Rights and Freedoms*. When we talk of associational life, we do not intend to refer exclusively to the 'freedom of association' in the Charter as defined by Supreme Court of Canada. This is due, in part, to the fact that the Court has rendered this Charter right virtually meaningless. The right of association as defined by our Court encompasses only the right to organize into associations; it does not include the right to pursue any activity or goal for which a group may have been constituted.[10] Only the collective exercise of constitutional rights or of the lawful rights of individuals are protected by the scope of the guarantee. Fearing (perhaps rightly) that the Charter would upset the law of labour relations in Canada, the Court has steered clear of allowing any meaningful use of Charter rights in this and any other areas where collective action could threaten established expectations.[11] Whatever associational rights usually exist in this realm – the right of a union to conduct an information boycott, for instance[12] (K Mart) – are protected instead by the Charter's guarantee of freedom of expression. Bill C-36 may very well infringe even the limited definition of freedom of association by prohibiting associational activities in the pursuit of what the bill defines as 'terrorist activities' by 'terrorist groups.' We will have occasion to refer to these guarantees, but our analysis does not rely on arguments about the constitutional validity of the scheme *per se*. Rather, we are concerned with what should be acceptable limitations on Canadians' rights and freedoms in the wake of the September 11th attacks.

Definition of Terrorist Activity

The definition of terrorist activity in section 83.01 of Bill C-36 sets out the scope of new offences and investigative powers. The definition is a broad one, broader in scope than either the United Kingdom's *Terrorism Act*, 2000[13] or the *USA Patriot Act* of 2001.[14] The definition of terrorist activity begins by incorporating a range of offences, many already included in the Criminal Code, such as the seizure of aircraft and the taking of hostages, as set out in ten international United Nations Conventions.[15]

The second part of the definition, which is the focus of our critique, includes offences that go beyond the existing criminal law. Section 83.01(1)(b) in Part II.1 defines 'terrorist activity' as including an act or omission, in or outside of Canada 'committed in whole or in part for a political, religious or ideological purpose, objective or cause' and 'with the intention of intimidating the public, or a segment of the public, with regard to its security, including its economic security, or compelling a person, a government or a domestic or an international organization to do or to refrain from doing any act, whether the person, government or organization is inside or outside Canada.'[16] The act must also be intended:

(A) to cause death or serious bodily harm to a person by the use of violence,
(B) to endanger a person's life,
(C) to cause a serious risk to the health or safety of the public or any segment of the public,
(D) to cause substantial property damage, whether public or private, if causing such damage is likely to result in the conduct or harm referred to in any of clauses (A) to (C) and (E), or
(E) to cause serious interference with or serious disruption of an essential service, facility or system, whether public or private, other than as a result of lawful advocacy, protest, dissent or stoppage of work that does not involve an activity that is intended to result in the conduct or harm referred to in any of clauses (A) to (C).[17]

A terrorist group is, in turn defined as including 'an entity that has as one of its purposes or activities facilitating or carrying out any terrorist activity' or 'an entity' listed by the Solicitor General.

There are a number of new criminal code offences connected to the activities of terrorist groups. They include the offence of participating in a 'terrorist' activity.[18] An offence may be committed whether or not any activity actually is carried out, whether or not the participation actually enhances the group's ability to carry out a terrorist activity, and whether or not the accused has any specific knowledge about that activity.[19] The

Bill outlines a number of factors a court may consider in order to determine whether an accused participated or contributed to the activity of a terrorist group, including, whether the accused uses a name, word, symbol, or other representation that is associated with the group; frequently associates with its members; receives any benefit for the group; or 'repeatedly engages in activities at the instruction of any of the persons who constitute the terrorist group' (s. 83.18[4]). The Bill also makes it an offence to knowingly 'facilitate' a terrorist activity (s. 83.19) or to finance its activities (ss. 83.02.03). For these offences one is liable to term of imprisonment of up to 10 or 14 years. These offences all turn on the definition of terrorist activity as defined in the Bill.

The scope of the second part of the definition is, as many have been arguing, extremely broad. Our concern lies with the implications of the definition for political life in Canada, particularly for participation in political protest and dissent. Political association, the right to express oneself in concert with like-minded persons, seems to us a cornerstone of democratic society. Admittedly, people gather together in associations for all variety of purposes, but they often do so to take a stand publicly with others. This is the contribution of associational life to democratic politics. Here, we turn to a discussion of the kinds of activities that could be caught by the definition, though these are activities which we should be loathe to characterize as 'terrorist.'

The definition could capture individuals and groups engaged in a broad range of political activities. Of particular concern is clause (E), which catches any organization engaged in political activity that is intended to compel government to do or refrain from doing something by seriously disrupting 'essential services.' The government has attempted to clarify the scope of the definition, by providing that the definition does not include 'lawful advocacy, protest, dissent or stoppage of work.' The use of the word 'lawful' suggests that the definition could capture individuals and groups engaged in activity that, although perhaps not popular, is certainly a far cry from the terrorist activity that the *Anti-Terrorism Act* is intended to target. The use of the word 'lawful' means that individuals and groups engaged in unlawful advocacy, protest, dissent or stoppage of work could be cast as terrorists, and included within the ambit of the new anti-terrorist laws.

Though we do not mean to condone unlawful activity, this could include individuals and groups engaged in civil disobedience – that is, protestors who consciously choose to violate the law in order to advance their political cause.[20] Environmental activists such as Greenpeace, or the protestors at Tamagami who chain themselves to trees to prevent logging, are individuals who have chosen to violate the law in an attempt to advance their political causes. Blockades sets up by First Nations protesting governmental policies and intended to compel a change in government policy, similarly involve individuals who are motivated by a political commitment to self government and the illegitimacy of federal and provincial governmental authority to consciously break the law. The Ontario Coalition Against Poverty (OCAP) includes individuals who have chosen to engage in civil disobedience to focus attention on the conditions of Ontario's poor and marginalized communities. Though hardly an effective strategy, OCAP has elected to promote their cause through illegal activity.

The Anti-Globalization Movement

Peaceful anti-globalization protestors in Vancouver, Windsor or Quebec City could be captured by the proposed bill should they take to the streets without permits, or peacefully resist arrest when confronted by undercover police officers. Consider, for example, the case of Jaggi Singh, an anti-globalization organizer, who was arrested at the APEC summit in Vancouver for assaulting a police officer for having spoken loudly through a megaphone.[21] He was arrested again at the Summit of the Americas meeting in Quebec City for participating in a riot, violating bail conditions, and for possession of a weapon. The weapon, which never was in Singh's control or under his direction, was a catapult deployed to throw teddy bears over a fence surrounding the old city. Mr. Singh was arrested and detained for 17 days primarily on the ground that he had violated bail conditions arising from his involvement in a similar protest against the G-20 in Montreal.[22] Everyone admitted – everyone, that is, but the Quebec City Police, the Sureté du Quebec and the RCMP – that Jaggi Singh was not an individual who presented any sort of violent threat. He was involved in a peaceful protest, some 15–20,000 people strong. As for the catapult, it was a theatrical form of civil disobedience, one that sought media attention to illustrate what the protestors believed to be the absurdity of the fortress that had been erected around the meetings in Quebec City. Absurd as it may seem, the act of catapulting stuffed animals over police lines could be cast as intending to cause serious disruption to an essential service, namely, the protection of international dignitaries in attendance at the Summit.[23]

There is a marked difference, often lost in media representations of the anti-globalization protesters, between those who choose consciously to engage in violent protest (like members of the 'Black Bloc'), and the many thousands of peaceful protestors who choose consciously to do little more than march without permits. There similarly is a marked difference between those with violent intentions, and those peaceful protestors who may, in the heat of what many would consider an unjustified police response, lose their tempers. Indeed, it will be expected to be the case that people involved in some associational activity, like those protesting against the institutions of globalization – the IMF, World Bank, G-8 or World Trade Organization Meetings – will lose their tempers. It will be the case that civil society becomes uncivil.

Consider the events of December 1999 in Seattle – the 'Battle in Seattle' – a watershed moment for the anti-globalization movement. Some 30,000 peaceful protestors – environmental groups, trade unions, student groups – took to the streets to voice their protest at the meeting of the World Trade Organization. Starbucks windows were smashed, violence erupted, and the streets were choked not only with protestors but tear gas. Much of the destruction was carried out by 'a small gang of self-proclaimed anarchists' while the tear gas and rubber bullets was directed at containing the peaceful protesters.[24] The 'thin line' separating peaceful from violent protest was broken. Bill C-36 could catch both the anarchists and those protestors caught up in the riot, whether the events occurred 'in or outside of Canada.' What about the ensuing property damage? This could be caught by clause (D), where an intention to provoke political change by causing substantial property damage, whether public or private, is caught by the proposed definition. Property damage, however, must likely result in the conduct or harm identified in clauses (A) to (C) and (E), which includes harms like a serious risk to public safety or disruption of essential services. The 'lawful advocacy' exemption arguably is not even available in the case of property damage, as this usually is characterized as illegal activity. Due to the poor drafting of the definition section, it is not even clear that the exemption is available in the case of clause (D), as it is not mentioned in clause (E) as one of the activities to which the exemption applies.

If anti-globalization organizations could be considered to fall within clause (D) or (E) of the definition of terrorist activity, it then would be possible to catch anti-globalization protestors within the offence of participating in a 'terrorist' activity.[25] The factors to consider in determining whether a person participated in the activity of a terrorist group include whether the person uses words of symbols associated with the group (carrying a banner?), whether they frequently associate with persons who constitute the group (attending meetings or protests?), or repeatedly engages in activities at the instruction of any person in the terrorist group (assisting in the organization of protests or assisting in the internal affairs of the organization?). Once captured within the definition of terrorist activity, it would not be difficult to find ways in which individuals involved in these organizations would be considered to be participating, contrary to section 83.18(1).

Labour Disputes

The definition of terrorist activity also excludes 'lawful ... stoppages of work,' which suggests that the definition could include individuals engaged in unlawful work stoppages, if they otherwise fit the definition, that is, are motivated by a political cause and seek to disrupt an essential service. This means that individuals engaged in illegal strikes (that is, strikes that violate provincial or federal labour laws) could potentially be captured by the definition of terrorist. Unions occasionally choose to engage in illegal strikes. The membership of the union may decide that they have no other recourse but to face the potential consequences of an illegal strike.

Consider the recent labour struggles of the nurses in Nova Scotia. In June 2001, the Nova Scotia Conservative government introduced legislation taking the right to strike away from the province's health care workers. Bill 68, the *Health Care Services Continuation Act*, prohibited strikes by nurses and other employees of district health authorities for three years, and empowered the government to impose the workers' conditions of employment, including wages, by cabinet order. The Bill was rushed through the legislature to become law before the nurses were in a legal strike position. The nurses subsequently threatened a massive walk-out, as they individually signed resignation forms at their union halls. Under pressure of the massive walk-out, the government agreed to repeal Bill 68.[26] While what would have effectively been an illegal strike was averted, the nurses were of the view that this action was necessary. They were prepared to engage in a massive walkout to protest the draconian nature of the legislation that had been rammed through the legislature, and which took away not only their right to strike, but their right to have unresolved disputes sent to binding arbitration. The action was expressly political – to force the government to repeal legislation. And public opinion polls suggested that there was considerable sympathy for the nurses. Sixty three per cent of Nova Scotians indicated that they would be less likely to vote for provincial politician who had voted to impose a settlement on the nurses.[27] Many other health care workers have also engaged, or have threatened to engage in illegal work stoppages. Nurses in Saskatchewan and Quebec, paramedics in Edmonton, medical lab technologists in Regina are among those who have chosen to engage in illegal strikes in the past few years, to protest what they believed to be the unfair bargaining practices of governments.

Under the new terrorist bill, any such illegal walk out by nurses could fall within the definition of terrorist activity. It could be cast as politically or ideologically motivated – as opposing government health care policies and/or bargaining practices, and as seriously disrupting essential services, as set out in clause (E) of the definition. Further, it might be possible to cast the action intending to result in the conduct or harm referred to in either of clauses (B) or (C). More specifically, it might be cast as intending to endanger a person's life, as per clause (B) or more likely, to cause a serious risk to the health or safety of the public or any segment of the public, as per clause (C).

Moreover, as Kent Roach has pointed out, the poor drafting of clause E seems to exempt an exemption. Clause (E) seems to suggest that lawful protests or strikes will not be exempt from the definition of terrorist activity so long as the activity is intended to endanger a person's life or cause serious risk to health or public safety.[28] As a result, even a *legal* strike by health care workers could be cast as a terrorist activity if it both seriously disrupted essential services and caused a serious risk to health or safety of the public.[29]

Finally, it is possible to imagine the definition capturing individuals who engage in protest that does no more than violate provincial trespass laws or municipal bylaws. Individuals who organize a march without a permit, or who try to organize a protest in a shopping mall that constitutes private property, could be cast as engaging in unlawful activity and therefore, not included in the defense of lawful protest. While it might be more challenging to cast these protests as resulting in a disruption of an essential service – the activities must rise to some level of 'seriousness' – the ability to do so would no doubt depend on the particular nature of the protest.

The International Dimension

There is another dimension to the Anti-Terrorism Act which also causes us some concern. The Bill is intended to catch terrorist activities whether committed 'in or outside of Canada.' This suggests that support for political movements abroad that threaten property, persons, or essential services could be caught by the Bill.

It will be the case that in a country such as Canada, conflicts occurring abroad will arouse the interests and passions of many, particularly if one's country of origin or ancestry lies within a conflict zone. The terms of political engagement within these countries will resonate within the diasporic communities abroad. It will be the case, then, that many of the conflicts occurring elsewhere in the world will come home to Canada in one form or another. A vital and vibrant associational life speaks to the interest that many ethnic, religious, and cultural groups have in these disputes abroad.

Too often these disputes concern violence against military, political, and even civilian targets. It may be that we should expect both new and old citizens to abandon these political fights. Once one elects to commit to Canadian residency, it is argued, one must abandon any advocacy of violence abroad. Michael Ignatieff spoke to this issue recently in the *Globe & Mail*, expressing the anxiety that 'diasporic nationalism is a dangerous phenomenon because it is easier to hate from a distance: You don't have to live with the consequences – or the reprisals.'[30] It seems reasonable, Ignatieff maintains, in a political community that has renounced violence at home, that it require the renunciation of violence abroad.

Should Canada adopt a policy which requires citizens to renounce the support of any activities abroad falling within the definition of terrorism? Recall that these activities need not be violent and that they could include substantial damage to public or private property or serious disruptions in essential services.[31] It is unfortunate that this question has not been prominent in discussions around the Bill, as the stakes for associational rights quite high. Consider the many conflicts abroad that could have been caught by the Bill. Would Canadians have been able to support the anti-apartheid struggle in South Africa, so long as the ANC was engaged in violent resistance? Would it have been a criminal offence to support the Sandanistas in Nicaragua, or their enemies the Contras, operating out of El Salvador? What about engaging in activities that aimed to undermine or overthrow the Pinochet regime in Chile or Suharto in Indonesia that fell within the definition of terrorist activity? Could Canadians have taken measures to support republicanist forces during the Spanish Civil

War?[32] On these occasions, Canadians have been asked to take sides in sometimes violent conflict abroad and which also may have been inconsistent with official Canadian foreign policy. It is unrealistic, in our view, to believe that moral conflicts of these sorts are not presently before us – such as in Tibet or East Timor – or will not arise in the future.

The Bill inadequately accounts for these facts nor does it make any finer distinctions. Associations are formed for all variety of purposes, whether they be for moral, religious, cultural or political ends. Often these purposes are mixed, and so membership in groups brings with it multiple and shifting associations.[33] Associational life is fluid – people join and leave groups for all variety of reasons. They may support one aspect of a group cause but not others. They may find that there is only one viable opposition group, in which case support for a political movement may be expressed only through support of that one association. Associational life, then, is more complex than the drafters of the anti-terrorism bill will admit.

Some forms of international conflict, such as armed conflict conducted in accordance with international law or the use of military force by a state in the exercise of 'official duties,' are exempt from the definition of terrorist activity. It will be difficult, then, to justify prosecution against state officials and non-state actors engaged in conventional war. The fear is that many of the conflicts mentioned above would not fall within a conventional definition of war, nor could they be considered state-sponsored military actions.

It is disconcerting that we have not yet debated publicly the merits of criminalizing activities in support of one side or another in a conflict zone. Is it desirable to accord the state a monopoly over these foreign policy positions, or is it preferable that individuals and associations take sides by actively providing support? Short of an improved definition of 'terrorist activity,' it might be preferable if the Bill more clearly distinguished between support for a political movement abroad which employs tactics that fall within the scope of the definition of terrorism, and support for specific terrorist activities directed at innocent and unarmed civilian populations (as s. 83.02 suggests). The former should be immune from legal censure in Canada, while the latter more reasonably could be the subject of the criminal law. Ignatieff, for instance, acknowledges that there will be some political causes which justify armed resistance, but none that justify murdering civilians. The distinction may be hard to apply in practice, but would move the law in a more sensible direction.

The Shrinking Public Sphere

The definition of terrorist activity in the anti-terrorism bill, as it is currently drafted, represents a serious threat to an already beleaguered public sphere. The public sphere, as described by Jürgen Habermas, is a space of political opinion formation and participation.[34] The public sphere contracted during the Keynesian welfare state (KWS), as the political relationship of citizens was increasingly channeled through the state, and the state became the major site of political contestation. With the demise of the KWS, and the rise of the neo-liberal state, and its concomitant strategies of depoliticization,[35] the public sphere is further contracting, making it harder and harder to find spaces of legitimate political participation and protest. Simultaneously, equality seeking groups, and others with voices of political opposition and dissent are increasingly cast as special interest groups, no longer representative of legitimate political positions in a pluralist polity.[36]

In this context of an ever-shrinking public sphere, the broad definition of terrorist activity will have the effect of further restricting the space and legitimacy of political protest and dissent. The definition needs to be placed within the context of a political environment that is increasingly hostile to protest and dissent, in which we have witnessed a crack down on the public expression of political dissatisfaction and disenfranchisement. The processes of depoliticization and the privatization of public space makes it harder for individuals and organizations to express their political dissatisfaction in legitimate public arenas. And those who then seek to take their messages to once public and lawful arenas – the streets, the public agora, even the legislatures – find their protests cast as illegal. They are protesting without permits, they are protesting on private property, and finally they are protesting violently when they resist police efforts to dissipate the protest.

Legally, the definition of terrorist activity has the potential of criminalizing what is otherwise a fairly minor infraction of the law, and sweeps a range of political protestors into the ambit of the intensified criminal powers and sanctions of the *Anti-terrorist Act*. Discursively, the inclusion of unlawful political protest within a definition of terrorism has the potential to further delegitimatize and marginalize those on the political margins. It further casts these messengers of dissent as outlaws, as threats to law and order, as unworthy of the basic rights of freedom of expression and association.

Enforcement

Individuals participating in any of these organizations, protests and/or strikes could potentially be cast as terrorists, captured within the meaning of the definition, and thereby subject to the highly invasive powers accorded to the police and law enforcement authorities under Bill C-36. Some may be comforted by the comments of the Minister of Justice before the House and Senate Committees, indicating that it is not the government's intention to capture these kinds of protests within the law. She has even indicated some willingness to remove the word 'lawful' from the definition. Others may be comforted by the fact that a prosecution under the new offences requires the consent of the Attorney General, therefore, perhaps limiting the discretion of police and prosecutors from enforcing the law more broadly. And many others may have little sympathy for the plight of those who engage in unlawful protest. Many of these political organizations and protests are unpopular, and no doubt, many Canadians feel that protestors who choose to violate the law – or associate themselves with those who do – must be prepared to face the consequences of their illegal actions.

We, however, remain resolutely uncomforted. The government's mere assertion that it was not their intention to capture these kinds of protests rings hollow if the definition remains unchanged. And while the consent of the Attorney General may limit some of the potential abuses, the law continues to confer an enormous amount of discretion on police and other law enforcement agencies for investigation and surveillance. The case of Jaggi Singh reveals that it is not only the charges brought but the individuals detained and the protests stifled that are cause for concern. As civil libertarians argue, broad discretion almost inevitably leads to abuse. Further, legislation that confers such broad discretion on government authorities is increasingly difficult to challenge.[37]

Finally, the relative popularity of the political dissent must not be the yardstick for evaluating the acceptability of the Anti-terrorism bill. While Canadians may not sympathize with those who break the law, the distinction between these individuals and the international terrorist networks implicated in the September 11th attacks hardly needs to be argued. These simply are not and should not be the targets of an anti-terrorist law.

Nor are we confident that the judiciary can be relied upon to carefully scrutinize the application of the law. We have seen the Supreme Court of

Canada on more than one occasion evade the textual problems that arise by virtue of overbreadth and focus solely on the application of the law.[38] Any *Charter* problems that arise, such as overbreadth and consequent chilling effects, are viewed as the result of overzealous and overburdened administration. It is not a question of poor legislative drafting or debatable legislative ends. The 'legislative core' in these kinds of cases are unassailable, rather it is administrative problems that give rise to *Charter* problems.

In the *Little Sisters* case there was a voluminous 12–year record of harassment of the Vancouver gay and lesbian book sellers by Customs Canada. Yet the Supreme Court of Canada concluded there was nothing 'on the face of the Customs legislation, or in its necessary effects' that gave rise to Charter problems.[39] Rather, it was 'human, erroneous determinations'[40] at the 'administrative level'[41] that gave rise to problems. Justice Binnie writing for the Court was of the view that any Charter violation could easily be repaired: 'Customs legislation is quite capable of being applied in a manner consistent with respect for Charter rights.'[42] The majority saw no need to issue any meaningful remedy, despite the 'evidence of actual abuse' for 'there is a potential abuse in many areas, and a rule requiring Parliament to enact in each case special procedures for the protection of Charter rights would be unnecessarily rigid.'[43] The majority's ruling amounted to little more than a plea to continue to place confidence in customs officials, who time and again showed how ill-suited they were to perform the role of arbiter of sexual tastes.

The minority of opinion of Justice Iacobucci, with Arbour and Lebel JJ. concurring, was more attuned to the free speech and associational problems associated with the customs regime, where imprecise standards and ill-informed discretion are the manner of front-line enforcement. They rejected the majority's approach and admitted that where legislation 'lends itself to repeated violations of Charter rights, as does the legislative scheme here, the legislation itself is partially responsible and must be remedied.'[44]

Conclusion

Bill C-36 is still, at the time of writing, in draft form, and the Minister of Justice is expected to come back with at least some minor changes to the Bill before the end of November 2001. At the time of writing, the Special Senate Committee on the Subject Matter of Bill C-36 has delivered its First Report, with its recommendations for changes to the Act. In terms of the definition, the Senate Committee has recommended that the word 'lawful' be dropped from section 83.01(1)(b)(E). The Senate Committee observed and recommended:

> There were also concerns expressed that the definition of terrorist activity as it appears in Bill C-36 might encompass illegal strikes and other actions of civil disobedience that bear no relation to terrorism.

> The Minister of Justice made it clear to the Committee that this is not the intent of the bill. **To clarify that these types of unlawful acts are not terrorist activities, the Committee recommends deleting the word 'lawful' from proposed subsection 83.01(1)(b)(ii)(E).** (emphasis in original)

While removing the word 'lawful' will mitigate some of our criticisms, it will not resolve all of the potential problems that we have outlined. Removing the word lawful would mean that both lawful and unlawful activity could fit within the exemption, provided that the activity was not intended to bring about the kinds of harm set out in clauses (A) to (C). However, any advocacy, protest, dissent, or work stoppage – lawful or otherwise – that could be seen as intending to (A) cause death or serious bodily harm to a person by the use of violence, (B) endanger a person's life, or (C) cause a serious risk to the health or safety of the public or any segment of the public, could still be cast as terrorist activity. Many of our examples above – of nurses strikes or anti-globalization protests – could still be captured within the definition.

In our view, a better option would be to remove clause (E) from the definition altogether. If there are particular concerns regarding essential services that the government would like to see addressed, it could do so more precisely. The United Kingdom's *Terrorism Act, 2000*, on which Bill C-36 is modeled, does not contain such a broad clause dealing with disruption of essential services but, rather, a more specific clause dealing with the serious interference or disruption of an electronic system. The European Commission has proposed a narrower range of facilities, such as 'water, power or other fundamental resource' and 'information system.'[45]

Removing clause (E) from s. 83.01(1)(b)(ii) would not, however, resolve all of the problems that we have identified. There remain the potential problems associated with clause (D). As we discussed above, clause (D) – causing substantial property damage (which will likely result in the harms identified in the other sub-clauses including serious risk to public safety or disruption of essential services) – does not appear to include an exemption for lawful advocacy or protest. Therefore individuals involved in lawful protest that results in substantial property damage that presents a serious risk to public safety or disruption of essential services could be caught within the definition of terrorist activity. Without condoning property damage, in our view, this remains too broad a definition of terrorist activity.

It should be noted that the Senate Committee also recommended that the Act be amended so as to include an anti-discrimination clause.

> The Committee is aware of concerns that the definition of terrorist activity could be used to target ethnic or cultural communities in Canada. **The Committee therefore recommends that a non-discrimination clause be added to Bill C-36.**

While laudable in its intentions, adding a non-discrimination clause to Bill C-36 would have little legal value. There is nothing in the current draft of the Bill that would condone a discriminatory application of the law. Rather, the enforcement of the *Criminal Code* must already be enforced in accordance with the *Canadian Charter of Rights and Freedoms*. It must therefore be enforced in a manner that does not violate the equality rights in section 15. The problems that we have outlined, as well as those outlined by Sujit Choudhry of the potential for discriminatory enforcement of these laws through racial profiling, are created not by the absence of a non-discrimination provision, but rather, by the broad definitions and discretionary power conferred by the Bill on law enforcement authorities.

Some will no doubt suggest that we are fear mongering; that we are creating fantastical hypotheticals that will simply never come to pass. We do not believe that we are being unduly paranoid, or at least, that our paranoia is unjustified. Law enforcement authorities have been heard muttering the words 'domestic terrorists' in relation to protestors like OCAP. And there is more than one voice in the public sphere connecting anti-globalization protestors with the enemies of America. Consider the commentary by Aaron Lukas in the National Post, in which anti-globalization protestors are described as the 'enemies of capitalism and modernity'[46] Lukas not only compares the anti-globalization movement to terrorists ('Like terrorists, the anti-globalization movement is disdainful of democratic institutions'), but actually describes their activity as terrorism ('Terrorism, if not so heinous as what we witnessed last week, has always been part of the protestors' game plan'). This kind of demonization of the anti-globalization movement is part of the public discourse and hints at precisely the sort of thing that might trigger the ire of authorities.

Government and its supporters will no doubt counter that Canadians need to place their trust in the law enforcement authorities, who will be able to distinguish between the 'real' targets of the anti-terrorism legislation and legitimate forms of political protest. But, moments of fear and anxiety are precisely when that trust should be most suspect. Recent history is replete with examples of governments unduly sacrificing liberties in the name of security – from the internment of the Japanese in the Second World War to the invocation of the *War Measures Act* in 1970. In times of insecurity, both dissent and difference become suspect, and the lines between real threats to our security and unpopular opinions become blurred.

In conclusion, we return to the question with which we began this essay: what liberties are we prepared to sacrifice, however, and to what degree in the wake of the September 11th attacks? Nothing that we have argued is intended to in any way minimize the threat of terrorism, and the need for governments to find new ways to combat a globalized yet invisible enemy. But, we do believe that as Canadians, we have the right to demand that our governments draft our laws in careful and considered manner, and that they do so in a manner that minimally impairs the rights and freedoms of Canadians. We do not believe that the government has discharged this burden in the drafting of Bill C-36. The definition of terrorist is much too far reaching, and represents, in our view, a significant infringement on the right to political association and protest.

Notes

* Faculty of Law, University of Toronto.
† Faculty of Law, University of Toronto. We are grateful to Trish McMahon for research assistance and to Sharryn Aiken, Kevin Davis, Ed Morgan and Kent Roach for helpful conversations.
1 First Session Thirty-seventh Parliament 49–50 Elizabeth II, 2001.
2 Will Kymlicka, *Finding Our Way: Rethinking Ethnocultural Relations in Canada* (Don Mills: Oxford University Press, 1998) at 57.
3 Will Kymlicka, *Multicultural Citizenship* (Oxford: Oxford University Press, 1995).
4 Robert D. Putnam, *Bowling Alone: The Collapse and Revival of American Community* (New York: Simon and Shuster, 2000).

5 Nancy L. Rosenblum, *Membership and Morals: The Personal Uses of Pluralism in America* (Princeton: Princeton University Press, 1998) at 59.

6 Rosenblum, *ibid.* at 17.

7 Harold J. Laski, *A Grammar of Politics* (London: George Allen & Unwin Ltd, 1948) at 97, 81.

8 Cass Sunstein, *Republic.com* (Princeton: Princeton University Press, 2001).

9 See Kevin Davis, 'Cutting Off the Flow of Funds to Terrorists: Whose Funds? Which Funds? Who Decides?' and David Duff 'Charitable Status and Terrorist Financing' in this volume.

10 *Professional Institute of the Public Service of Canada* v. *Northwest Territories* [1990] 2 SCR 367.

11 See Patrick Macklem, 'Developments in Employment Law: The 1990–91 Term' *The Supreme Court Law Review* (2d) 3: 227 at 239–41.

12 *UFCW, Local 1518* v. *K Mart Canada Ltd.* [1999] 2 SCR1083.

13 Chapter 11. The *Terrorism Act 2000* defines 'terrorism' expansively:

> (1) In this Act 'terrorism' means the use or threat of action where – the action falls within subsection (2)
>
> the use or threat is designed to influence the government or to intimidate the public or a section of the public, and
>
> the use or threat is made for the purpose of advance a political, religious or ideological cause.
>
> (2) Action falls within this subsection if it –
> involves serious violence against a person,
> involves serious damage to property,
> endangers a person's life, other than that of the person committing the action,
> creates a serious risk to the health or safety of the public or a section of the public, or
> is designed seriously to interfere with or seriously to disrupt an electronic system.
>
> (3) the use or threat of action falling within subsection (2) which involves the use of firearms or explosives is terrorism whether or not subsection (1)(b) is satisfied.

14 P.L. 107–56, formerly H.R. 3162, *Uniting and Strengthening America by Providing Appropriate Tools Required to Intercept and Obstruct Terrorism Bill*. Section 802 of the *USA Patriot Act* expands the existing definition of terrorism set out in Section 2331, Title 18, United States Code to include domestic terrorism in addition to international terrorism:

> the term 'international terrorism' means activities that –
>
> (A) involve violent acts or acts dangerous to human life that are a violation of the criminal laws of the United States or of any State, or that would be a

criminal violation if committed within the jurisdiction of the United States or of any State;

(B) appear to be intended -
    (i)   to intimidate or coerce a civilian population;
    (ii) to influence the policy of a government by intimidation or coercion; or
    (iii) to affect the conduct of a government by mass destruction, assassination or kidnapping; and

(C) occur primarily outside the territorial jurisdiction of the United States, or transcend national boundaries in terms of the means by which they are accomplished, the persons they appear intended to intimidate or coerce, or the locale in which their perpetrators operate or seek asylum; ...

(5) the term 'domestic terrorism' means activities that –

(A) involve acts dangerous to human life that are a violation of the criminal laws of the United States or of any State;

(B) appear to be intended –
    (i)   to intimidate or coerce a civilian population;
    (ii) to influence the policy of a government by intimidation or coercion; or
    (iii) to affect the conduct of a government by mass destruction, assassination, or kidnapping; and

(C) occur primarily within the territorial jurisdiction of the United States.

15 S.83.01(1)(a). For a more general discussion of the definition, see Kent Roach 'The New Terrorism Offences and the Criminal Law,' in this volume.

16 S. 83.01(1)(b)(i).

17 S.83.01(1)(b)(ii)

18 Section 83.18 (1): 'every one who knowingly participates in or contributes to, directly or indirectly, any activity of a terrorist group for the purpose of enhancing the ability of any terrorist group to facilitate or carry out a terrorist activity is guilty of an indictable offence and liable to imprisonment for a term no exceeding ten years.'

19 Section 83.18 (2): '(a) a terrorist group actually facilitates or carries out a terrorist activity; (b) 'the participation of the accused actually enhances the ability of a terrorist group to facilitate or carry out a terrorist activity,' or (c) the accused knows the specific nature of any terrorist activity that may be facilitated or carried out by a terrorist group.' Participating in or contributing to an activity of a terrorist group includes 'receiving or recruiting' a person for 'training,' offering any 'skill' or 'expertise,' 'entering or remaining in any country for the benefit of, or at the direction of or in association with a terrorist group,' 'recruiting' someone, or making oneself 'available' in 'response to instructions' from any persons who

constitute a terrorist group, to 'facilitate or commit' a terrorism offence or an act or omission outside of Canada that, if committed in Canada, would be a terrorism offence (s. 83.18[3]).

20 Civil disobedience has a long and significant legacy in the struggles in and for liberal democracies. Civil disobedience has been generally defined as an act that 'must be illegal, predominantly nonviolent, intended to rouse the notice of the community to the illegal action, and for which those engaged are willing to accept punishment' (Mark E. DeForrest, 'Civil Disobedience: Its Nature and Role in the American Landscape' (1997–1998) 33 Gonzaga Law Review 653, 654). It has an extraordinarily distinguished list of advocates and practitioners. From Mohatma Gandhi to Nelson Mandela, the leaders of liberation struggles have consciously chosen to violate what they believed to be the fundamentally unjust laws of a colonizing power. The New England abolitionist Henry David Thoreau, the women's suffragist leader Susan B. Anthony and the civil rights leader Martin Luther King, Jr. have been amongst the most eloquent defenders of civil disobedience. See Henry David Thoreau, 'Civil Disobedience,' in *Walden and Other Writings*; Susan B. Anthony 'Statement to the Court (1873), reprinted in David R. Weber, Civil Disobedience in America (1978); Martin Luther King, J.r 'Letter from a Birmingham Jail' (1958) reprinted in Dyzenhaus and Ripstein, eds., *Law and Morality: Readings in Legal Philosophy* 453. King, for example, wrote at 459, 'I submit that an individual who breaks a law that conscience tells him is unjust and willingly accepts the penalty ... is in reality expressing the very highest respect for the law.'

21 See E.N. Hughes, RCMP Public Complaints Commission.

22 See Rheál Seguin, 'Jaggi Singh Freed After 17 Days in Jail' *The Globe and Mail* (8 May 2001) A7.

23 Canadian police have a duty to protect international dignitaries, like heads of states and diplomats, under the 1973 'Convention on the Prevention and Punishment of Crimes Against Internationally Protected Persons, Including Diplomatic Agents.' See Obiora Chinedu Okafor, 'The 1997 APEC Summit and the Security of Internationally Protected Persons: Did Someone Say 'Suharto?' in W. Wesley Pue, ed., *Pepper in Our Eyes: The APEC Affair* (Vancouver: UBC Press, 1999) 185–96.

24 Sam How Verhovek, ASeattle is Stung, Angry and Chagrined as Opportunity Turns to Chaos@ *The New York Times* (2 December 1999) A16.

25 Section 83.18 (1), supra note 18.

26 The Nova Scotia government has continued to indicate that it will reintroduce legislation banning the right to strike in essential health care services. However, the new bill will include provisions allowing unresolved disputes to go to binding arbitration, instead of being settled unilaterally by cabinet.

27 'Nova Scotia Enacts anti-right to strike bill' June 28, 2001, *Nurses Voice*.

28 Roach, supra note 15.

29 As with the anti-globalization protests, if it was found that the nurses strike consti-

tuted a terrorist activity, it would not be at all difficult finding individuals involved in the strike as violating the new participating offence contrary to section 83.18(1).

30 Michael Ignatieff, 'The Hate Stops Here' *The Globe and Mail* (2 October 2001) A17.

31 If 'lawful protest' is exempt, the law of which jurisdiction applies? Note that the relevant part of the definition of 'terrorist activity' (b) applies to acts committed in or outside of Canada. In the case of offences listed in (a), offences committed outside of Canada would have to be an offence within Canada. It also is a requirement that, in the case of acts or omissions committed outside of Canada, that are deemed offences under (b) (i.e. s. 7[3.75]), they must be an offence within Canada.

32 Nevertheless, the 1200 Canadians who fought in the Spanish Civil War were threatened with two- year jail terms. See Desmond Morton, *A Short History of Canada* (Edmonton: Hurtig Publishers, 1983) at 190.

33 Rosenblum, supra note 5 at 7.

34 See Jurgen Habermas, *The Structural Transformation of the Public Sphere: An Inquiry into a Category of Bourgeois Society*, trans. T. Burger (Cambridge: The MIT Press, 1991). Nancy Fraser, in *Justice Interruptus: Critical Reflections on the Postsocialist Condition* (Routledge: New York, 1997) at 70–71 describes and defends the idea of the 'public sphere' as 'a theater in modern societies in which political participation is enacted through the medium of talk ... [as] the space in which citizens deliberate about their common affairs, and hence, an institutionalized arena of discursive interaction ... (as) indispensable to critical social theory and democratic political practice.'

35 See Judy Fudge and Brenda Cossman, 'Introduction,' *Privatization, Law and the Challenge of Privatization* (Toronto: University of Toronto Press, forthcoming 2002) where we define depoliticization as a key of strategy of privatization referring 'to the ways in which reprivatisation involves removing a range of goods and service from political contestation. Encoding a particular good as 'naturally' located within the market or the family is to remove it from the realm of politics and political contestation. (Janine Brodie, 1995.) Normative claims about the natural superiority of the market and the family thereby come to trumph any and all political claims to the contrary. (Yeatman, 1990, 173)' (citing Janine Brodie *Politics on the Margins* (Halifax: Fernwood Publishing, 1985) and Anna Yeatman, *Bureaucrats, technocrats, femocrats: Essays on the Contemporary Australian State* (Sydney: Allen and Unwin, 1990).

36 Brodie , supra note 35.

37 See *Little Sister's Book and Art Emporium. v. Canada (Minister of Justice)*. 2000 2 SCR 1120.

38 *R. v. Keegstra* [1990] 3 SCR 697.

39 *Little Sister's* at para. 125.

40 *Little Sister's* at para. 77.

41 *Little Sister's* at para. 125.

42 *Little Sister's* at para. 133.
43 *Little Sister's* at para. 137.
44 *Little Sister's* at para. 205.
45 Commission of the European Communities, Proposal for a Council Framework Decision on Combatting Terrorism, Brussels, 19 September 2001.
46 Aaron Lukas 'America Still the Villain' *National Post* 18 September 2001).

Effectiveness of Anti-Terrorism Legislation: Does Bill C-36 Give Us What We Need?

MARTHA SHAFFER*
Faculty of Law
University of Toronto

The tragic events of September 11, 2001 have left most of us wondering how such a horrific thing could happen. How is it that terrorists managed to attack the World Trade Center and the Pentagon, bastions of U.S. financial and military might? How is it that the activity involved in planning the attacks escaped the notice of U.S. intelligence gathering agencies, as well as those of other countries? Why is it that this activity went undetected by law enforcement officials? Would an anti-terrorism law, such as Bill C-36, have made a difference?

In this paper I seek to raise concerns about the ability of legislation such as Bill C-36 to prevent events like those of September 11. Bill C-36 is sweeping legislation that expands the criminal law in significant and disturbing ways. The complexity of the legislation, as well as the somewhat clumsy drafting of many of its provisions, make the full impact of the Bill hard to predict. It is clear, however, that the Bill creates new offences that greatly expand the scope of criminal liability and abrogates some of the procedural protections we have come to view as central to criminal justice in a free and democratic society.

I argue that despite the horror aroused by the events of September 11 and our desire to ensure that such events not be repeated in Canada or elsewhere, it is dangerous to enact legislation that so drastically changes our legal norms without a clear sense that these changes will in fact effectively combat the perceived threat. In my view, if Parliament enacts Bill C-36, this is precisely what Parliament will be doing. As Kent Roach has pointed out, what the 'September 11 terrorists did was a crime long before they boarded the doomed aircraft.'[1] This suggests that the 'solution' – if there is one – to preventing terrorist attacks lies not in expanding the scope of criminal liability but in better enforcement of the laws we already have.[2] An additional danger of enacting legislation like Bill C-36 is that its provisions come at a high cost to individual liberty generally, but specifically to groups within Canada, such as Muslim Canadians, whose actions are currently viewed with suspicion, as well as other groups that voice political dissent.

What do the 'Criminal' Anti-Terrorism Provisions Do?

In thinking about whether Bill C-36 makes a meaningful contribution to the prevention of global terrorism, an important first step is to explore what these new provisions actually do. This requires an examination not only of the Bill's legal significance, but also of its political ramifications.

Politically, Bill C-36 attempts to show Canadians – and the international community – that the government is taking a strong stance against terrorism and will not allow terrorists to operate within its borders. Domestically, this is designed to make Canadians feel safe on the basis that their government is taking decisive action to avoid a repetition of the events of September 11th by rooting out terrorists operating here, punishing them severely, and deterring others from involving Canada in a network of terror. Internationally, Bill C-36 attempts to show the U.S. and other western nations that Canada will not be the weak link in an international effort to stop global terrorism (the war against terror) and will not allow Canada to become a 'haven' for terrorist activities.

Legally, Bill C-36 makes three significant changes to existing criminal law. First, the Bill expands the scope of criminal liability by creating new terrorism offences, tied in to its very broad definition of terrorist activity. As Kent Roach has pointed out, many of these offences are problematic because they appear to create liability by combining one inchoate offence with another.[3] In addition, as Don Stuart and others have pointed out, the definition of terrorist activity that would be contained in s. 83.01 of the *Criminal Code* is disturbingly broad. This is particularly true of s. 83.01(1)(b)(i)(E) which defines an act or omission intended to:

> cause serious interference with or serious disruption of an essential service, facility or system, whether public or private, other than as a result of lawful advocacy, protest, dissent or stoppage of work that does not involve an activity that is intended to result in the conduct or harm referred to in any of clauses (A) to (C)

as terrorist activity, provided it is committed in whole or in part for a 'political, religious or ideological purpose, objective or cause'[4] and in whole or in part with the intention of intimidating the public or a segment of the public with regard to its security or compelling a person, government or organization to do or refrain from doing an act.[5] This provision might potentially sweep within its grasp the actions of many political protestors, including many Aboriginal groups, anti-globalization protestors, and labour unions.[6] Protestors such as these are expressing the kind of political dissent that one expects in a democratic state. Even where they engage in actions that violate the law, it is problematic for a democratic state to label them as terrorists.

Second, the Bill gives the state new powers of investigation and detention once a person is believed to be involved in terrorist activity or a terrorism offence. The largest and most problematic of the changes here is the power under the proposed s. 83.28 to order 'investigative hearings' in which people can be compelled to assist in police investigations by appearing before a judge and answer questions or 'produce any thing in his [or her] possession.'[7] A person subjected to such an order must 'remain in attendance until excused by the presiding judge'[8] and 'shall answer questions put to the person by or on behalf of the police officer who applied for the order' unless the answer 'would disclose information that is protected by any law relating to non-disclosure of information or privilege.'[9] The wording of s. 83.28(4) suggests that the state's power to order participation in an investigative hearing is not limited to those suspected of having participated in a terrorism offence, but extends to *any* person who, in the case where there are reasonable grounds to believe a terrorism offence has been committed, may have information concerning the offence or the whereabouts of those suspected of perpetrating the offence. Where there are reasonable grounds to believe that a terrorism offence *will be* committed persons who may have 'material information' or who may reveal the whereabouts of individuals whom the peace officer suspects may commit the offence may be ordered to appear. This would include friends, relatives or acquaintances of a suspect, many of whom will be completely innocent of any involvement with terrorist activity. At present, there is no requirement under Canadian law that ordinary citizens assist police officers in their investigations, and certainly no power that would permit a person to effectively be detained, compelled to attend a hearing, and to answer questions for this purpose.

The other provision that extends the state's power of investigation is section 83.3 which allows a court to order a person to enter into a recognizance for up to 12 months and extends the power of warrantless arrest. Section 83.3(2) provides that a peace officer may lay an information before a provincial court judge if he believes on reasonable grounds that terrorist activity will be carried out and *suspects* on reasonable grounds that the imposition of a recognizance with conditions on a person, or the arrest of a person, is necessary to prevent the carrying out of terrorist activity. If the court is satisfied that there are reasonable grounds for the officer's suspicion, the court may order the person to enter into a recognizance. Section 83.3(4) extends the *Criminal Code's* existing power of warrantless arrest by removing the requirement that a peace officer believe that the commission of an offence be imminent, providing instead that warrantless arrest is permissible where 'the peace officer suspects on reasonable grounds that the detention of the person in custody is necessary to prevent the commission of an indictable offence, where the act or omission constituting the offence also constitutes a terrorist activity.'[10] Again, these provisions appear to be drafted in such a way that those subjected to these powers will not merely be those suspected of involvement in terrorist activity or terrorism offences, but anyone whose arrest or restriction of liberty is deemed necessary to prevent the carrying out of terrorist activity.[11] This could include innocent people who unwittingly convey messages to people involved in terrorist activities.

The third major change to the criminal law contained in Bill C-36 is the enhancement of penalties for conduct falling within the newly created terrorism offences. The terrorism offences created by the Bill, found in s. 83.02–83.04 and 83.18–83.23, bring with them steep maximum sentences, ranging from imprisonment for 10 years all the way to life imprisonment. Except where a person is sentenced to life imprisonment, these sentences are to be served *consecutively* to 'any other punishment imposed on the person, other than a sentence of life imprisonment, for an offence arising out of the same event or series of events' and 'any other sentence, other than one of life imprisonment, to which the person is subject at the time the sentence is imposed on the person for an offence under any of those sections.'[12] In addition, section 83.27 provides that a person convicted of an indictable offence, other than an offence for which a sentence of life imprisonment is imposed as a minimum punishment, is liable to imprisonment for life, where the act or omission constituting the offence also constitutes terrorist activity.[13] Section 231 would also be amended to add subsection (6.01) which would classify murder committed during the commission of an offence that also involved terrorist activity as first degree murder.[14]

These three changes – expanding the scope of criminal liability, expanding state power of investigation and elevating sentences – can be seen as an attempt to accomplish three objectives: (1) To denounce and punish terrorism through the imposition of higher penalties and the expansion of criminal liability for terrorist activity; (2) to deter terrorism through the imposition of higher penalties; and (3) to prevent terrorism and to facilitate the detection and prosecution of persons suspected of carrying out terrorist offences through the expansion of investigatory powers and the expansion of inchoate liability.

Will Bill C-36 Be An Effective Tool Against Terrorism?

To determine whether Bill C-36 will be an effective weapon in the quest to fight terrorism requires a two pronged analysis. First, there must be an examination of the extent to which the new provisions succeed in accomplishing their underlying objectives of denouncing, deterring, investigating and preventing terrorism. Second, there must be an assessment of whether they meet their objectives in a way that improves upon existing criminal law. If existing criminal provisions can provide a similar measure of protection against terrorist activities as the proposed Bill, there is no reason to enact legislation that dramatically alters the criminal law in uncharted and potentially problematic ways. If the Bill can be said to offer some additional protections, it is important to ask whether those protections come at too high a cost such that they do not constitute an improvement over existing criminal law provisions.

How successful, then, is Bill C-36 in meeting its objectives? Bill C-36 is certainly successful in denouncing terrorism by pronouncing that terrorist activities/offences will be subject to harsh punishment, harsher punishment than might be meted out under existing provisions. However, denunciation alone cannot be a sufficient reason for introducing in measures of such sweeping magnitude into the criminal law. Will Bill C-36 deter terrorists from operating in this country? The answer to this question is probably not. The people who perpetrated the atrocity of September 11 were not deterred by the fact that their activities were already criminal offences. They, of course, were prepared to die for their cause. It is highly unlikely that they – or many others committed to terrorist action – would have been deterred by the prospect of higher penalties, had they been caught prior to carrying out their mission. In terms of deterrence, it is certainly far from clear that Bill C-36 offers any improvement over the deterrence potential of the existing criminal law.

What about the objective of increased detection to preempt terrorist actions and to successfully prosecute perpetrators of terrorist action when preemption fails? Does Bill C-36 enhance our ability to meet this objective? On one level the answer to this question might be yes. The use of investigatory hearings may yield information that could permit the earlier detection of people involved in terrorist activities, and the expanded power of warrantless arrest may afford police officers a heightened ability to incapacitate these people before they can put their plan into action. The potential benefit of the recognizance power in this respect is less clear. Certainly it is unlikely that requiring a person committed to terrorist activity to enter into a recognizance with conditions will actually stop that person from carrying out the activity. It would therefore appear that the benefits of this provision, if there will be any, will come from its effect on people who are associates of persons suspected of terrorist action or are only peripherally involved in terrorist activity. By compelling persons to assist police investigations, investigatory hearings might also assist the goal of successfully prosecuting those who have managed to carry out terrorism offences.

It is, however, important to recognize that any increased ability to detect and prosecute terrorist activity these provisions create will come at a cost. They come at the expense of civil liberties generally by enhancing the investigatory powers of the state. The provisions allowing investigatory hearings are particularly disturbing in this regard as they completely derogate from the longstanding principle that citizens are under no legal obligation to assist the state in criminal investigations. Despite arguments that these measures are carefully limited to the terrorism context and require the prior consent of the Attorney-General, even allowing them at all creates the risk that these procedures will become normalized and will be extended to other areas of criminal liability. In addition, the possible discriminatory use of these provisions against members of racial or religious groups viewed as linked to terrorism as well as the disproportionate use of these provisions against politically unpopular groups should not be underestimated. Racial profiling is already a problem within the criminal law, but these expanded investigatory provisions have the potential to greatly exacerbate it. Use of investigatory hearings on members of unpopular political groups may have a chilling effect on political dissent. That there are significant costs to these provisions suggests that they do not constitute an improvement upon existing criminal law, even if they do afford more effective powers of detection.

On another level, however, the answer to whether Bill C-36 enhances the criminal law's ability to detect and prevent terrorist attacks might be a qualified no. The experience of other countries which have had a history of terrorist groups operating within their borders suggests that even draconian anti-terrorism measures do not prevent terrorist attacks. If there is a solution to the problem of terrorism it lies not in enacting stiff criminal laws against terrorism, but in trying to deal with the conditions that produce people who are willing to perpetrate terrorist acts in the first place. So long as those conditions exist, people will find a way to commit terrorist actions, notwithstanding harsh punishments or more invasive investigative techniques.

This analysis suggests that it is far from obvious that Bill C-36 will make much more of an effective contribution to the fight against terrorism beyond that already offered by the existing criminal law. To the extent that extended police powers might permit greater detection, apprehension and prosecution of people involved in terrorist activities, these potential gains will come at a cost, as do the provisions extending the scope of criminal liability. Legislation like Bill C-36 should not be enacted without a decision, based on clear and sober reflection, that the existing criminal law is inadequate and that any measures to increase public protection outweigh their costs.

Are The Proposed Criminal Law Provisions Constitutional?

One reason to be concerned about Bill C-36 is that it is not clear that it offers greater protection against terrorist action than the existing criminal law and it may introduce damaging changes. As others have pointed out, another reason for concern is that some of its provisions may be constitutionally suspect. In particular, some of the provisions, including the definition of terrorist activity in s. 83.01 may be subject to overbreadth concerns. The creation of nebulous, grossly inchoate offences may be subject to the challenge that these offences violate the principles of fundamental justice in s. 7 of the *Charter*. In my view, these concerns are serious enough that they should not be left to a court to decide following Bill C-36's enactment, but raise important issues that should factor into the discussion as to whether the Bill should become law in the first place.

Some of these issues become clear when one considers a possible challenge to the legislation based on the principle of overbreadth. As the Supreme Court of Canada explained in *R. v. Heywood*,[15] overbreadth examines the relationship between the objectives underlying a law and the measures used to attain those objectives:

Overbreadth analysis looks at the means chosen by the state in relation to its purpose. In considering whether a legislative provision is overbroad, a court must ask the question: Are those means necessary to achieve the state objective? If the state, in pursuing a legitimate objective, uses means which are broader than is necessary to accomplish that objective, the principles of fundamental justice will be violated because the individual's rights will have been limited for no reason.

To put this another way, the essence of an overbreadth argument is an evaluation of whether the means chosen outstrip the legislative objectives or whether the objectives could reasonably be met in less drastic ways.

How does an overbreadth analysis play out when applied to Bill C-36? To a certain degree, it is difficult to say. It is difficult because, although we know the objective is to fight terrorism, it is not clear that all of the measures the Bill proposes are actually needed for that fight. If, as I've argued earlier, the existing criminal law is up to the task of combating terrorist activities, then there is a strong argument that Bill C-36 is overly broad absent some evidence on the part of the government that the magnitude of the terrorist threat Canada and its allies are facing is so great that the law as it exists is not up to the task. The problem is that there is no real evidence of this, aside from claims by the Justice Minister that the existing criminal provisions are inadequate.

The absence of a real sense of the threat Canada is facing leaves courts performing an overbreadth analysis with two options. One option is to defer to Parliament's view of the threat and to uphold the legislation on the basis that the criminal law as it stands might not make us safe enough. In my view, this might be the option chosen by the courts were this Bill to be challenged in today's political climate. The danger in this approach, however, is that these measures may turn out to have been unwarranted but their enactment will have led to an unhealthy curtailment of civil rights and suppression of political dissent. An example of this problem can be drawn from Canada's own past. The bombing of Pearl Harbour during the Second World War created a fear that Canada was facing a threat from the people of Japanese origin living on the west coast, much like the events of September 11th have given rise to a fear about Muslim Canadians today. The solution to the potential threat posed by these people was to remove them from coastal areas, confiscating their property, and to place many of them in internment camps. At the time, this might have seemed like the safest and most prudent solution to a rather chilling but diffuse threat. While there are clear differences between Bill

C-36 and the internment of Japanese Canadians, I want to suggest that we are in danger now of enacting legislation that subsequently proves unwarranted and unwise in a similar way.

The other option available to the court would be to have a good hard look at the existing criminal law and its potential for fighting a vague and unknown terrorist threat. In other words, rather than simply deferring to Parliament's view that the threat requires drastic measures, courts should consider the extent to which the existing law protects against terrorism without departing from norms of procedural and substantive fairness that we have considered essential to a democratic state. As I have already argued, given the many provisions within existing law that already capture terrorist activities, I believe a strong case can be made that the provisions in Bill C-36 go beyond what is necessary to protect Canadians and others from terrorist acts. In my view, as unspeakable as the events of September 11th were, they are not hard evidence of the inadequacy of the criminal law as it exists to provide us with the protection we require.

I want to make one final point in this regard which has to do with the potential of these provisions to protect against the threat of terrorism. The point is a trite one, but trite as it is I believe it is an important one to make. The provisions contained within Bill C-36 on their own do absolutely nothing to fight terrorism. To the degree that they will be effective at all, they will only be effective when they are combined with the financial resources to enforce them. The same is true of the existing *Criminal Code* provisions. In my view, rather than creating new provisions that are broad, abrogate from longstanding legal principles and are potentially susceptible to misuse, we would be better to focus our energies on ensuring that we have the resources to enforce the laws we *already* have on the books to ensure that terrorist networks such as the ones involved in September 11th are not operating within our borders. Which gets us back to the question of whether the provisions contained in Bill C-36 are a proportional response to the amorphous threat we are facing. In my view, a proportional and effective response would be to ensure the ability to enforce the provisions we already have to detect and punish terrorist activities.

Conclusion

It would be a mistake to believe that Bill C-36 or similar anti-terrorist legislation will keep us safe from events like those of September 11. Passing legislation is, however, an easy way of appearing to take action, an easy way of making us believe that the world is a safer place than it was before that fateful date. The provisions contained within Bill C-36 are unwarranted and potentially dangerous. Our legitimate fear and revulsion at the events of September 11th and our desire to prevent them from ever happening again should not lull us into adopting an unwise and potentially dangerous law.

Notes

* Thanks to Shaun Nakatsuru for sharing ideas and to Scot Patriquin for extremely able and efficient research assistance.
1 Kent Roach, 'The New Terrorism Offences and the Criminal Law', in this volume.
2 A better solution would, of course, be to attempt to confront the social and political problems that foster terrorism.
3 Roach, supra note 1.
4 Section 83.01(1)(b)(i)(A).
5 Section 83.01(1)(b)(i)(B).
6 See Don Stuart, The Dangers of Quick Fix Legislation' in this volume for additional examples of conduct that could fall within terrorist activity.
7 Section 83.28(5)(c).
8 Ibid,
9 Section 83.28(8).
10 Sction 83.3(4)(b).
11 Contrast the wording of the powers to order recognizances in other contexts, found in s. 810 of the *Criminal Code*.
12 Section 83.26.
13 This provision cannot be used unless the prosecutor satisfies the court that the offender was notified, before making his or her plea, that the application of this provision would be sought.
14 Bill C-36, section 9.
15 [1994] 3 S.C.R. 761.

The Dangers of Quick Fix Legislation in the Criminal Law: The Anti-Terrorism Bill C-36 should be Withdrawn

DON STUART
Faculty of Law
Queen's University

Need for New Investigative Resources but not New State Powers

The horrifying events of September 11 make it easy to support the allocation of significant sums of Government money for preventive measures such as better airport security, medicine to counteract anthrax, more anti-terrorist police and C.S.I.S. personnel and perhaps even for our military assistance to the United State's uncomfortable war in Afghanistan. It is of interest considerable amounts of money are available although just short weeks ago we were being told there was no new money for health care and certainly not for day care.

What cannot be supported are the complex new criminal laws in Bill C-36. When the State turns to its power to punish and imprison the standard of justification should be high. Basic principles of a criminal justice system that deserves the name require the state to prove both that the individual acted and was at fault, that responsibility is fairly labelled and that any punishment is proportionate to the accused's actions. In my view the creation of new crimes in Bill C-36, in the manner well described by Kent Roach, cut across these principles and should be withdrawn. The new State power grab is unnecessary, will not make Canadians safer and will much more likely endanger the freedoms of the most vulnerable such as minority groups, immigrants and, especially, refugees.

Feeding Frenzy for Law and Order Quick Fixes

That our federal politicians would respond so quickly with a quick fix criminal law solution should come as no surprise. Although Parliament enacted our Charter of Rights and Freedoms in 1982, which set out new protection for those accused of crime, politicians of all stripes have been unable to resist the lure of courting votes by being seen to be tough on crime. In the last 20 years or so the Criminal Code is getting tougher and tougher and ever more complex. Successive Ministers of Justice have been largely content to listen and respond to *ad hoc* pleas of police and prosecutors, victims associations and womens' groups, that the Government counteract Supreme Court rulings, respond more punitively to particular problems and/or remedy various law enforcement concerns. Pleas[1] for a more restrained principled approach or to make the criminal law less complex and comprehensible have fallen on deaf ears. There are no votes there.

There has often been strong criticism of the activism of the Supreme Court. The activism of Parliament in its remorseless enactment of new state powers in the Criminal Code and other statutes has largely escaped critical review. The emerging public debate about the excesses of Bill C-36 may at least leave a legacy of healthy scepticism. We need a Minister of Justice with a better sense of balance and one who stands firm against the overuse of the blunt instrument of the criminal sanction. So too perhaps the Supreme Court which has bought into the dangerous notion of the need to dialogue with, and defer to, Parliament, may now be more prepared to submit these blunderbuss and hastily drafted laws to rigorous Charter review. Kent Roach has recently put this well:

> If ... the Court is too weak in protecting the rights of minorities and the unpopular, it is less likely that elected governments will do more. The result can be a complacent and majoritarian monologue that is less truly democratic.[2]

Lessons from Anti-gang Legislation

We should not be placated when the current Minister of Justice, Anne McLellan, petulantly asserts that Bill C-36 does not target minorities. The record of the enactment and subsequent application of the anti-gang measures is instructive and puts the lie to such Ministerial assurances.

In 1997 the Criminal Code was amended to include a wide variety of anti-gang measures. A crime of participation in a criminal organisation was created and already wide police powers, for example those authorising electronic surveillance, were extended even further. The immediate context was the eve of a federal election and the perceived need to respond to a plea by the Quebec Attorney General and Quebec mayors for measures to address a violent and protracted fight between two biker gangs: the Hell's Angels and the Rock Machine. We were told at the time that the bill was narrowly targeted.

That it was not is well demonstrated in the fiasco of the prosecution of the Manitoba Warriors in Winnipeg.[3] By laying extra charges of gangsterism a routine drug conspiracy case was conflated into a high security affair with a special new courthouse built at the cost of millions. Young aboriginal accused spent many extra months in high security pre-trial custody before the trial was aborted by a number of plea negotiations. Almost all the gangsterism charges were withdrawn. At best the new law had been applied in a counterproductive and unjust way, had made matters way too complicated and had wasted precious State resources.

On September 12, 2000, a Montreal crime reporter was shot several times the day after he had published an expose of organised crime. By September 14, 2000, a Quebec Minister, Serge Menard, usually moderate in his respected views about the criminal justice system, was calling for new and clearer organised crime laws to prohibit mere membership in criminal gangs like the Hell's Angels and the Rock Machine and the use of the notwithstanding clause to trump any Charter claim of freedom of association.

It is stunning that this initiative came from a province in which the invocation of the War Measures Act in 1970 and the banning of the F.L.Q. terrorist group lead to the arrests of hundreds of innocent Quebecois. Canada does not need laws of guilt by association or any overriding of Charter rights. Biker violence in Quebec and elsewhere may well require considerably more police investigative resources to gather evidence but no new laws were ever needed or likely to be effective.

On the eve of another Federal election a Parliamentary Sub-committee on Organised Crime held in camera hearings and released a hastily drafted report. I testified in an uncomfortable secret session about the outcome of Manitoba Warriors prosecution. Some M.P.'s seemed trouble by the account. But nobody subsequently saw this test case as pointing to the dangers of Parliament's overbroad anti-gang quick fix. During the 2000 federal election all politicians agreed that something more needed to be done about gangs. No politician dared to raise questions.

Bill C-24, which passed third reading in June, 2001, proceeded rapidly through a committee hearing and is before the Senate. The Department of Justice Backgrounder explained that a new and much broader definition of criminal organization was drafted to respond to concerns expressed by police and prosecutors that the current definition was 'too complex and too narrow in scope.' So once again the consultation was completely biased in favour of listening to those who enforce the law. By this time convictions had been registered in Quebec under the new gangsterism laws against members of the Hells Angels and Rock Machine. Parliament just pressed on. It also snuck in an unconscionable Ministerial power to designate police officers to break the law.

Now we have Bill C-36 which would piggy-back on the 'success' of the anti-gang initiative and go much, much further both in terms of State power and who is targeted.

Is There an Emergency?

We are being told that this is an emergency yet the Federal Government has not proclaimed a Public Order, International or War Emergency under the Emergencies Act.[4] Parliament passed this Act in 1988 as a late acknowledgement of the excesses of its invocation of the War Measures Act. If Bill C-36 passes it will, like the anti-gang laws, become part of our permanent legislation. A sunset clause or a Parliamentary review would be a weak compromise. The rights and freedoms of Canadians, especially those of minorities and other vulnerable groups, are too important to be brushed aside. This legislation is not needed and is dangerous. Of course the chances of stopping its passage are as good as holding up a hand to stop a freight train.

Excessive Width in Defining Terrorists

As Kent Roach points out the definition of 'terrorist activity' in s.83.01 is key. It decides who can be charged as a terrorist and against whom extensive new investigative powers can be exercised. In one respect the definition may be unduly narrow. There is no wisdom in requiring proof of a motive under (A) of 'a political, religious or ideological purpose, objective or cause.'

For years criminal law has sought to avoid proof of a bad motive as a requirement for criminal responsibility. It is too hard to prove and may, as here, lead to curious results. Why should a violent terrorist with unfathomable motives not be included?

A most pernicious aspect of the new definition is the wide extension in (E) to those who intend:

> to cause serious interference with or serious disruption of an essential service, facility or system, whether public or private, other than as a result of lawful advocacy, protest, dissent or stoppage of work that does not involve an activity that is intended to result in the conduct or harm referred to in any of clauses (A) to (C) [which include intending to cause a serious risk to the safety of the public]

The exemption of lawful protest is not worth the paper it is written on as most protesters in Canada have, if charged, been convicted of at least obstruction offences.

Equally disturbing is the alternative way the legislation would permit persons to be branded as terrorists. After the legislation becomes law the Governor in Council, on the recommendation of the Solicitor General, will be empowered to name by regulation a list of terrorist entities (s.83.05). This designation will be based on a determination by the Government, in private and without public debate and based merely on reasonable grounds rather than proof in a court of law. There are provisions for after the event review by a judge but there is unfettered power for Ministers not to disclose their sources for reasons of national security. Not even the Privacy Commissioner will get access for review of that determination. Expect Canada to embrace George Bush's most wanted list which excludes well established terrorist groups like the I.R.A. and those operating for Israeli and Palestine groups not because they don't fit violent terrorist criteria but for reasons of political comity and expediency.

Being branded as a terrorist in one of these ways is not an offence. Kent Roach has reviewed the new offences of Participating, Facilitating, Instructing and Harbouring. I will focus critical attention on the new offence of knowingly participating or contributing to terrorist activities. Similar criticism could be advanced against the other three offences. So what on earth, some might say, is wrong with creating a crime of knowingly participating in terrorist activity? The problem is that Parliament, just as it did in the case of the creation of a crime of knowingly participating in a criminal organisation, has cynically legislated out of existence any meaningful test of knowledge or meaningful test of participating or contributing.

The definition section is s.83.18(1):

> Every one who knowingly participates in or contributes to, directly or indirectly, any activity of a terrorist group for the purpose of enhancing the ability of any terrorist group to facilitate or carry out a terrorist activity is guilty of an indictable offence and liable to imprisonment for a term not exceeding ten years.

So there is here a fault requirement of knowledge plus a purpose of enhancing the terrorist group's ability to facilitate or carry out a terrorist activity. Yet consider the next subsection, which has a strange and revealing heading 'Prosecution':

(2) An offence may be committed under subsection (1) whether or not

  (a) a terrorist group actually facilitates or carries out a terrorist activity;
  (b) the participation or contribution of the accused actually enhances the ability of a terrorist group to facilitate or carry out a terrorist activity; or
  (c) the accused knows the specific nature of any terrorist activity that may be facilitated or carried out by a terrorist group.

Then we find a definition of participating or contributing which includes acts as vague as

(b) ... offering to provide a skill or an expertise for the benefit of, at the direction of or in association with a terrorist group and
(d) ... remaining in any country for the benefit of, at the direction of or in association with a terrorist group.

Clause (d) is particularly stunning. It creates guilt by association wherever you are and whatever you are doing. Finally the maximum sentence on conviction for such knowing participation in terrorism is 10 years (s.83.18). This must be served consecutive to a sentence for any other offence (s.83.26).

When such criminalisation is read in conjunction with the wide definitions of terrorism there would be good arguments that such provisions violate section 7 Charter protections requiring meaningful act and fault requirements. The Supreme Court has held that you cannot substitute elements to avoid fault standards[5] and that minimum standards established by the Court cannot be watered down[6]. Excluding a mistaken belief defence respecting an essential element of a crime has been held to be unconstitutional.[7] The Court has recently also re-asserted as a fundamental principle that the State prove a voluntary physical act.[8] In Bill C-36 there is often no real act requirement and there is no clear requirement that the accused knew that the group is involved in the acts which constitute terrorism. Other weaker Charter arguments would be vagueness and overbreadth and disproportionate punishment contrary to the cruel and unusual punishment protection of section 12.

Even if these new provisions are Charter-proof the larger issue is whether the new offences risk injustice in the former of unfair labelling and huge and dangerous overreaching of State power. I have suggested that they clearly do.

Potential Targets under Bill C-36

I invoke in aid a list of activities which, under Bill C-36, are in jeopardy of being investigated, charged and punished as terrorism:

1. Aboriginal groups' blockading of logger roads to assert aboriginal title.
2. Anti-globalisation protests such as those recently occurring in Quebec City.
3. Disruptive passive resistance actions inspired by Mahatma Gandhi.
4. Labour union stoppages of many types.
5. Sending aid to an Afghanistan refugee group later determined to be involved in terrorist activity.
6. Community group's sponsoring Muslim immigration into Canada where an immigrant is alleged involved in terrorist activities in the country of origin, even if this was some time in the past.
7. A person claiming refugee status in Canada has to establish fear of political persecution from his or her country of origin. It would not be difficult for opponents in that country to provide intelligence to Canada that the refugee had participated in terrorism. So now the risk for the refugee is not merely that of deportation but of being charged with a terrorist offence.
8. Gangs of bikers or even a couple of youths out to disrupt the town could certainly be charged. The anti-gang legislation may already be redundant.

Remember South Africa

Nelson Mandela and at least two thirds of the present South Africa Legislature were once branded and punished as terrorists. The line between a freedom fighter and terrorism often depends on your political allegiance. Apartheid South Africa had a well-documented record of torture and death at the hands of police interrogation of those detained without charge. Once a country embraces forms of preventive detention for interrogation history warns that the power will likely be extended and abused.

Repression is a matter of degree. In 1968 in South Africa there was a treason trial with accused in special cubicles. A large group of young black men had been recruited in what is now Namibia to rescue their brothers in South Africa. They set out on foot with guns and, many kilometers later, they were spotted by army helicopters as they crossed the border into South Africa. They were arrested and charged with terrorism. Since they are clearly intended the overthrow of the Government they were found guilty. All were convicted. Some were sentenced to death and executed.

Conclusion

Canada today is not South Africa in 1968. However Canada did proclaim the War Measures Act in 1970. The accompanying justification by Pierre Elliot Trudeau about suspending civil liberties to address terrorist threats was a speech about which any South African Minister of Justice of the day would have been proud. Many innocent people were arrested. We replaced that Act with the carefully drafted Emergency Act of 1988, which has detailed provisions to compensate those wrongly targeted. None of that care characterises Bill C-36. It confers permanent, unnecessary, dragnet and dangerous State powers. There is a serious risk that political dissenters and innocent vulnerable groups will be investigated, detained, interrogated, and prosecuted with broad offences which cut across normal Canadian criminal law protections. South African history warns against the risk of escalating oppression. Bill C-36 ought to be withdrawn.

Notes

1 See most recently, Stuart, Delisle and Manson (ed), *Towards a Clear and Just Criminal Law* (Carswell, 1999).

2 *The Supreme Court on Trial: Judicial Activism or Democratic Dialogue* (Irwin Law, 2001) p. 295.

3 For a fuller account see Stuart, 'Time to Recodify Criminal Law and Rise Above Law and Order Expediency: Lessons from the Manitoba Warriors Prosecution,' (2001) 28 *Manitoba L.J.* 89.

4 S.C. 1988, c.29

5 *Vaillancourt* [1987] 2 S.C.R. 636.

6 *Wholesale Travel Group Inc.* [1991] 3 S.C.R. 154.

7 *Hess and Nguyen* [1990] 2 S.C.R. 906.

8 *Ruzic* (2001) 41 C.R. (5th) 1 (S.C.C.). The Court also speaks of no criminal responsibility where there is 'moral involuntariness'.

Terrorism and Criminal Justice

Rule of Law or Executive Fiat?
Bill C-36 and Public Interest Immunity

HAMISH STEWART[1]
Faculty of Law
University of Toronto

'... when the President does it, that means that it is not illegal.'[2]

'Judicial control over the evidence in a case cannot be abdicated to the caprice of executive officers.'[3]

I. Introduction

Under the common law doctrine of public interest immunity and under ss. 37, 38, and 39 of the *Canada Evidence Act*,[4] a minister of the Crown and certain other persons may object to the disclosure of information in proceedings on grounds relating to the public interest or Cabinet secrecy. Typically, the validity of these objections is determined by a superior court or federal court judge, with appropriate procedural safeguards to prevent disclosure while the objection is being determined. The only information that is protected from disclosure without review by a judge is a Cabinet confidence.[5]

Bill C-36 repeals and replaces ss. 37 and 38 of the *CEA*.[6] The new provisions would give the Attorney General for Canada extraordinary powers over the disclosure of information relevant to a wide variety of proceedings. In particular, proposed s. 38.13 would give the Attorney General the power to 'prohibit the disclosure of information in connection with a proceeding for the purpose of protecting international relations or national defence or security.'[7] This power would be available regardless of the nature of the information, regardless of the outcome of any judicial determination of a claim of public interest immunity, and regardless of the effect of the prohibition on the proceeding to which it applies. Bill C-36 provides no mechanism for appeal from or review of the Attorney General's exercise of this power.

In this paper, I briefly review the existing law of public interest immunity (section II), and I describe the effect of Bill C-36 on that law (section III). I then analyze proposed s. 38.13 and argue that it is inconsistent with the rule of law values that underlie the Canadian constitution (section IV).

II. Public Interest Immunity: A Brief Review

A. *The Common Law*

On occasion, the state will possess confidential or secret information that is relevant to the resolution of a dispute, whether that dispute is between private parties or between an individual and the state. The doctrine of public interest immunity recognizes that sometimes the state's interest in protecting the information outweighs the individual and public interests in correctly determining a dispute. A claim of public interest immunity may therefore be made by an appropriate official in any litigation, whether or not the state is a party to that litigation, where disclosure of the information in question is sought. It is for the court to determine whether the claim is valid. If the claim is rejected, in private litigation, the state must disclose, while in public litigation, the state has other choices. In a civil claim against the government, refusal to disclose may result in consequences such as adverse inferences concerning the information concealed. In a criminal proceeding, the Attorney General may choose to stay the proceedings rather than disclose, and may reinstate the proceedings before a different judge.[8] But if the claim continues to be rejected, the prosecution may ultimately have to choose between disclosure and letting the accused go free.

Although it is for the court and not the state to determine the validity of a claim of public interest immunity, in assessing the claim the court may take a more or less deferential stance to the executive. In *Duncan*, a private action for negligence arising out of the loss of a submarine, the House of Lords stated that an affidavit from the First Lord of the Admiralty in the proper form stating proper grounds for non-disclosure of documents relating to the design of the submarine was conclusive of the claim:[9] the court did not examine the documents in question or assess the claim in any other way. Similarly, in *Reynolds*,[10] a tort claim against the government arising from a crash during a flight to test secret electronic equipment, the United States Supreme Court refused to go behind a claim by the Secretary of the Air Force that it was not in the public interest for the government to disclose an accident investigation report.[11] But over the past 60 years, the common law has become less deferential towards executive claims that the public interest requires non-disclosure of information. In *Conway*, an action for malicious prosecution, the House of Lords would *not* accept as conclusive the Home Secretary's affidavit that disclosure of reports concerning the plaintiff would be injurious to the public interest, and not only examined the reports but ordered their disclosure.[12] While it might be possible to distinguish *Duncan* from *Conway* and *Reynolds* in terms of the importance of the interests that were balanced against each other, the House's refusal to accept the affidavit on its face was clearly inconsistent with *Duncan*.[13] In Canada, the less deferential attitude was manifested in *Carey*,[14] which held that at common law, even Cabinet confidences were not absolutely or invariably protected. Again, while it was perhaps significant that the facts of the case concerned the government's involvement in a commercial transaction rather than a matter of state security, the court was clearly not prepared to accept the government's claim of public interest immunity at face value.

B. *The Existing Statutory Regime*

The law relating to public interest immunity in matters under federal jurisdiction is currently governed by ss. 37, 38, and 39 of the *CEA*.

Section 37 provides that an appropriate official 'may object to the disclosure of information on the grounds of a specified public interest before a court or, person or body with jurisdiction to compel the production of information ...' Where the objection is made before a superior court, 'that court may examine or hear the information ...' The test for disclosure is simply whether 'the public interest in disclosure outweighs in importance the specified public interest'; if so, the court 'may ... order its disclosure, subject to such restrictions or conditions as it deems appropriate ...' (s. 37(2)). The section goes on to provide for the objection to be determined by a provincial superior court judge or by a judge of the Federal Court, Trial Division, and for appeals from that determination (ss. 37(3), (4), (5), and (6)).

Section 38 concerns objections under s. 37(1) where the ground of the objection is that 'the disclosure would be injurious to international relations or national defence or security.' In such a case, 'the objection may be determined, on application, in accordance with subsection 37(2) only by the Chief Justice of the Federal Court, or such other judge of that court as the Chief Justice may designate ...' The procedural provisions of s. 37 are generally applicable to objections under s. 38 as well (see ss. 38(2), (3), (4)).

The first case decided under s. 38 was *Re Gougen*.[15] Two R.C.M.P. officers charged with criminal offences resulting from the theft of Parti Québecois membership lists sought disclosure of some 8200 pages of material. They submitted that examination of this material would reveal relevant and probative evidence relating to their defence of colour of right. A judge of the Federal Court, Trial Division, had accepted the Deputy Solicitor-General's certificate objecting to disclosure without inspecting the material in question, and the Federal Court of Appeal upheld this decision. But the Court did indicate that the judge hearing the application had a discretion to decide whether to examine the material, and noted that 'a possible danger to international relations or national security is not so easily capable of being recognized [as a "specified public interest" under s. 37] and, as a result, may be feared and evoked somewhat too quickly, albeit in perfectly good faith.'[16]

Section 39 provides extraordinary protection for the proceedings of the federal cabinet: where a minister or the Clerk of the Privy Council 'certifies in writing that ... information constitutes a confidence of the Queen's Privy Council for Canada, disclosure of the information shall be refused without examination or hearing of the information by the court ... .' This protection is significantly stronger than the common law rule enunciated in *Carey*, the executive privilege recognized in *Nixon*,[17] or the regime for other information established by ss. 37 and 38. The Federal Court of Appeal recently rejected a broad constitutional challenge to s. 39, on grounds to which I shall return below.[18]

III. The Effect of Bill C-36

Bill C-36 would repeal ss. 37 and 38 of the *CEA* and replace them with a regime that provides the federal executive with significantly more control over the disclosure of information. The most remarkable feature of this new regime would be the Attorney General's power to prevent disclosure of information in proceedings, apart from the outcome of any judicial determination of public interest immunity.

A. *Replacing Section 37*

Proposed ss. 37 through 37.3 are similar to existing s. 37: they contemplate claims of public interest immunity and judicial determination of those claims. But the proposed sections have three new features that are worth noting.

First, while the test for disclosure remains whether 'the public interest in disclosure outweighs in importance the specified public interest,' the court determining the question may attach 'conditions to disclosure that are most likely to limit any encroachment upon the specified public interest' (proposed s. 37(5)).

Second, proposed s. 37.3 expressly provides for a jurisdiction to protect the right to a fair trial: 'A judge presiding at a criminal trial or other criminal proceeding may make any order that he or she considers appropriate in the circumstances to protect the right of the accused to a fair trial, *as long as that order complies with the terms of any order made under any of subsections 37(4.1) to (6)* ...' (emphasis added). An accused person has a right to a fair trial at common law and under ss. 7 and 11(d) of the Canadian Charter of Rights and Freedoms. There is little doubt that the jurisdiction proposed s. 37.3 would grant is already available to trial courts under s. 24(1) of the Charter, which gives the court a broad power to remedy breaches of the Charter. But there is considerable doubt as to whether proposed s. 37.3 goes far enough to satisfy the fair trial right protected by s. 7 of the Charter, in that it subordinates the accused's right to a fair trial to the disclosure regime contemplated by proposed s. 37.

Third, and most important for the purposes of this paper, proposed s. 37 is 'Subject to sections 38 to 38.16 ...' As we shall see, those provisions would give the federal Attorney General a surprising degree of control over the disclosure of information: if the Attorney General is unhappy with a decision made pursuant to proposed s. 37, she will be able to ignore it.

B. *Replacing Section 38*

As it currently stands, s. 38 is not significantly different in substance from s. 37. It does name particular grounds on which public interest immunity might be sought, and it does channel determination of those questions to a particular court; but at least in principle, determinations under s. 38 are to be made on the same standard, and are subject to the same rights of appeal, as determinations under s. 37. The proposed replacements for s. 38 are substantially different from s. 37 in either its existing or proposed form. Five features of the proposed new regime are particularly noteworthy.

1. The Information Protected

Section 38 of the *CEA* concerns 'an objection ... on grounds that ... disclosure would be injurious to international relations or national defence or security.' Proposed s. 38 has a much wider ambit. It defines 'potentially injurious information' as 'information of a type that, if it were disclosed to the public, could injure international relations or national defence or security' and 'sensitive information' as 'information relating to international relations or national defence or security that is in the possession of the Government of Canada, whether originating from inside or outside Canada, and is of a type that the Government of Canada is taking measures to safeguard.'

The definition of 'sensitive information,' in contrast with 'potentially injurious information,' does not require any detrimental consequences to any specified public interest to flow from disclosure: 'sensitive information' is just information on certain topics that the government has decided to 'safeguard,' whether or not its disclosure would be harmful to international relations, defence, security, or any other public interest. The regime that would be created by Bill C-36 would therefore be much broader than public interest immunity as traditionally conceived.

The test for disclosure in proposed s. 38.06(1) is the same as in proposed s. 37(5), and the trial judge's power to protect an accused's right to a fair trial in proposed s. 38.14 is the same as in proposed s. 37.3.

2. The Relevant 'Proceedings'

Proposed s. 38 defines 'proceedings' with reference to the definition of 'judicial proceeding' in s. 118 of the *Criminal Code*:[19]

'judicial proceeding' means a proceeding

(a) in or under the authority of a court of justice
(b) before the Senate or House of Commons or a committee of the Senate or House of Commons, or before a legislative council, legislative assembly or house of assembly or a committee thereof that is authorized by law to administer an oath,

(c) before a court, judge, justice, provincial court judge or coroner,

(d) before an arbitrator or umpire, or a person or body of persons authorized by law to make an inquiry and take evidence therein under oath, or

(e) before a tribunal by which a legal right or legal liability may be established, whether or not the proceeding is invalid for want of jurisdiction or for any other reason ...

This definition has been held to cover a very wide range of proceedings, including examinations for discovery[20] and proceedings before administrative tribunals.[21]

3. New Obligations on 'Participants'

Under existing ss. 37 and 38, the responsibility to make an objection to disclosure on a ground of public interest immunity rests with an appropriate official. Bill C-36 would impose new obligations on participants in proceedings to bring potential disclosures to the attention of an appropriate official. Proposed s. 38 defines 'participant' as 'a person who, in connection with a proceeding, is required to disclose, or expects to disclose, or expects to disclose or cause the disclosure of, information.' Proposed s. 38.01(1) and (2) impose on 'participants' an obligation to 'notify the Attorney General of Canada in writing' of the possibility that he or she, or anyone else, may disclose sensitive or potentially injurious information; proposed s. 38.02(1) then prohibits disclosure *by anyone* of that information. Exceptions are available under proposed ss. 38.01(6) and (7), and disclosure may be authorized by the Attorney General subject to conditions (s. 38.03(1)) or pursuant to an agreement with a participant (s. 38.031).

This proposed obligation on participants is remarkable. The definition of 'participant' plainly includes parties, witnesses, and counsel in any 'proceeding' as defined in s. 118 of the *Code*. If Bill C-36 is enacted, virtually everyone connected with a proceeding would have a positive obligation to be aware of the nature of the information he or she might disclose and to notify the Attorney General of Canada of any possible disclosure. It is unclear how 'participants' are to be made aware of their obligations; whether there is any sanction for failure to discharge the obligation; and how the obligation relates to other obligations in the trial process, such as the Crown's constitutional duty of disclosure in criminal prosecutions,[22] or the accused's constitutional right to solicitor-client privilege.[23]

4. Secrecy

Under existing s. 38(5), applications and appeals of determinations under s. 38(1) are to be held in camera. This is a sensible precaution, given that the point of the proceeding is to determine whether the information in question is to be disclosed. Proposed s. 38.02 goes well beyond this rule: it prohibits disclosure not only of the information in question but also of the mere fact of the proceedings or any agreement with the Attorney General. This level of secrecy goes well beyond what is necessary to protect the information in question.

5. The Attorney General's Fiat

Historically, the prosecution of *Code* offences has been the responsibility of the provincial Attorneys General, and the prosecution of offences created by other federal statutes has been the responsibility of the federal Attorney General. In addition, private prosecutions may still be conducted under the *Code*. Proposed s. 38.15(1) provides:

> If sensitive information or potentially injurious information may be disclosed in connection with a prosecution that is not instituted by the Attorney General of Canada or on his or her behalf, the Attorney General of Canada may issue a fiat and serve the fiat on the prosecutor.

This provision permits the federal Attorney General to assume control of any prosecution under any federal statute where that prosecution was commenced by a provincial Attorney General or by a private prosecutor. This provision is probably constitutionally valid, in light of a series of cases holding that the federal Attorney General has at least concurrent jurisdiction over the prosecution of offences created pursuant to the federal criminal law power.[24] But it does permit a significant encroachment on the traditional role of the provincial Attorneys General.

IV. Proposed s. 38.13: The Minister's New Power

Proposed s. 38.13 would give the federal Attorney General a remarkable and unprecedented power to prevent disclosure of information in proceedings. It reads as follows:

38.13 (1) The Attorney General of Canada may at any time personally issue a certificate that prohibits the disclosure of information in connection with a proceeding for the purpose of protecting international relations or national defence or security.

(2) In the case of a proceeding under Part III of the *National Defence Act*, the Attorney General of Canada may issue the certificate only with the agreement, given personally, of the Minister of National Defence.

(3) The Attorney General of Canada shall cause a copy of the certificate to be served on

(a) the person presiding or designated to preside at the proceeding to which the information relates or, if no person is designated, the person who has the authority to designate a person to preside;

(b) every party to the proceeding;

(c) every person who gives notice under section 38.01 in connection with the proceeding;

(d) every person who, in connection with the proceeding, may disclose, is required to disclose, or may cause the disclosure of, the information about which the Attorney General of Canada has received notice under section 38.01;

(e) every party to a hearing under subsection 38.04(5) or to an appeal of an order made under any of subsections 38.06(1) to (3) in relation to the information;

(f) the judge who conducts a hearing under subsection 38.04(5) and any court that hears an appeal from, or review of, an order made under any of subsections 38.06(1) to (3) in relation to the information; and

(g) any other person who, in the opinion of the Attorney General of Canada, should be served.

(4) The Attorney General of Canada shall cause a copy of the certificate to be filed

(a) with the person responsible for the records of the proceeding to which the information relates; and

(b) in the Registry of the Federal Court and the registry of any court that hears an appeal from, or review of, an order made under any of subsections 38.06(1) to (3).

(5) If the Attorney General of Canada issues a certificate, then, notwithstanding any other provision of this Act, disclosure of the

> information shall be prohibited in accordance with the terms of the certificate.
>
> (6) The *Statutory Instruments Act* does not apply to a certificate made under subsection (1).

Quite apart from the breadth of its application to 'proceedings' as defined above, there are three remarkable features of this proposed new power.

First, the power applies to all information, not just to 'sensitive' or 'potentially injurious' information as defined in proposed s. 37. Nor does the section expressly state that the information itself must relate to state secrets, security, defence, or international relations.[25] The power is limited only by its purpose, 'protecting international relations or national defence or security,' not by the nature of the information.

Second, the power applies regardless of any proceedings taken or agreement made pursuant to the proposed replacements for ss. 37 and 38. If the Attorney General were unsatisfied with the outcome of the proceedings or with an agreement she or her delegates made, she could issue a certificate under proposed s. 38.13 to prevent disclosure.

Third, Bill C-36 provides no mechanism for judicial review of or appeal from the Attorney General's certificate. While the decision to issue a certificate under proposed s. 38.13 is undoubtedly amenable to judicial review, the absence of any explicit mechanism for review is troubling because, as I indicate below, there are likely to be serious obstacles to such judicial review.

A. *Proposed s. 38.13 and The Rule of Law*

Throughout the common law world, the traditional doctrine requires the judge (or other person presiding over a proceeding), and not the executive, to determine a claim of public interest immunity. As Wigmore put it,

> A court which abdicates its inherent function of determining the facts upon which the admissibility of evidence depends will furnish to bureaucratic officials too ample opportunities for abusing the privilege. The lawful limits of the privilege are extensible beyond any control if its applicability is left to the determination of the very official whose interest it may be to shield a wrongdoing under the privilege. Both principle and policy demand that the determination of privilege shall be for the court.[26]

This traditional doctrine expresses an important rule of law value: that an exercise of executive power, even a discretionary power, must be subject to some standard of accountability. Proposed s. 38.13 poses a serious threat to the rule of law in that it grants the executive sweeping and apparently unreviewable control over the disclosure of information in proceedings.

As a backdrop to these arguments, consider the facts and reasoning in *Westergard-Thorpe*. Following the 1997 meeting of the Asian Pacific Economic Cooperation Conference in Vancouver, more than 50 complaints were filed with the R.C.M.P. Complaints Commissioner, alleging that R.C.M.P. officers providing security at the conference had violated the constitutional rights of certain demonstrators and had otherwise misconducted themselves. A Commissioner was appointed to hear the complaints. It was suggested that 'there was direction and interference from political sources which had the effect of causing the RCMP to infringe [the complainants'] Charter rights.'[27] There was no question that officials in the Prime Minister's Office had discussed security arrangements with RCMP officials. So Commission counsel sought disclosure from the government of records relevant to the hearing of the complaints. Pursuant to s. 39 of the *CEA*, the Clerk of the Privy Council certified that the information constituted a Cabinet confidence; the records in question could therefore neither be disclosed nor examined to determine whether the refusal to disclose was warranted. Some of the complainants sought a declaration in the Federal Court that s. 39 was unconstitutional in that it was contrary to the basic principles of the Canadian constitution. McKeown J. dismissed the action, and the complainants' appeal was also dismissed (per Strayer J.A., Robertson and McDonald JJ.A. concurring). Strayer J.A. agreed that s. 39 was more restrictive than the common law position enunciated in *Carey*,[28] but noted that a validly enacted statute could override the common law. As for the argument from the rule of law, Strayer J.A. said:

... the elements of the rule of law [are]: that the law is supreme over the acts of both government and private persons ('one law for all'); that an actual order of positive laws be created and maintained to preserve 'normative order'; and that 'the exercise of all public power must find its ultimate source in the legal rule.' ... put another way, 'the relationship between the state and the individual must be regulated by law.'

... this is precisely the situation where section 39 of the *Canada Evidence Act* is applied to preserve the immunity from disclosure of Cabinet documents. The situation is clearly regulated by law, namely section 39, being an Act of Parliament operating in what has been held to be its field of legislative authority. The rule of law is not the equivalent of a guarantee of the paramountcy of the common law (which itself has mutated on this subject of immunity in recent decades). In fact the 'actual order of positive laws' in our system makes valid legislation paramount over the common law. That the government is bound by the law, just as are private citizens, is not in dispute here.[29]

In short, the rule of law did *not* require a mechanism for ensuring that someone other than an executive officer could judge the executive's own assessment of the proper balance between Cabinet secrecy and other matters.[30] Strayer J.A. added that the proper forum to question this balance would be in an application for judicial review of the Clerk's decision to issue the certificate, but he added: 'The reviewing court would of course be working under some difficulty in that it would be barred from examining the documents so certified by subsection 39(1).'[31]

Westergard-Thorpe is troubling because it holds that there is no effective way of testing the validity of the Clerk's certificate. We know that there is a serious issue about the propriety of the R.C.M.P.'s conduct at the APEC conference; and we know that the Prime Minister's Office discussed security with the R.C.M.P. We hope that the Clerk chose to protect the information in question because it was irrelevant to the Commission's task; but under Strayer J.A.'s understanding of the rule of law as applied to s. 39, not even a judge can do more than hope until 2017.[32]

The same problem will arise under proposed s. 38.13: will a judge considering an issue arising under s. 38.13 be able to review the information to determine whether the Minister's decision is proper? There are two possible interpretations. On the one hand, proposed ss. 38.13 might be interpreted as permitting this review: unlike *CEA* s. 39, proposed s. 38.13 does not expressly prevent the judge from reviewing the information, and the case law on public interest immunity indicates that at common law and under *CEA* s. 38, a judge does have a discretion to do so. On the other hand, proposed s. 38.13(5) states: 'If the Attorney General issues a certificate, then, notwithstanding any other provision of this Act, disclosure of the information shall be prohibited.' This wording indicates that s. 38.13 is intended to enable the Attorney General to ignore the outcome of any judicial determination of public interest immunity, and so suggests that Parliament intends to oust judicial discretion to examine the material. In the absence of extrinsic evidence of improper motivation, it is hard to see how a judge could have enough information to properly decide an application for judicial review of a Minister's certificate under proposed s. 38.13.

B. *Judicial Review of the Attorney General's Decisions*

There is no doubt that a decision taken by the Attorney General under proposed s. 38.13 would be, in principle, subject to judicial review.[33] The clear trend in administrative law, particularly in light of *Baker*, is to require a discretion delegated by the legislature to the executive to be exercised fairly;[34] an executive decision that affects constitutionally protected interests must be exercised in accordance with the Charter;[35] and even an exercise of a non-statutory executive prerogative is reviewable if it has the right sort of impact on a person's interests.[36] The primary ground for judicial review of a certificate would be that the Attorney General's discretion had not been exercised for the purpose granted, i.e., to protect 'international relations or national defence or security.' A secondary ground, which might be harder to persuade a court to accept, would be that the Attorney General had misjudged the balance between the public interest and the proper resolution of the dispute at hand.

But there are at least two obstacles to effective judicial review of a decision under s. 38.13. First, it is likely that a court will adopt a highly deferential standard of review. The four factors relevant to the 'pragmatic and functional' approach to judicial review are 'the presence or absence of a privative clause,' 'the expertise of the decision-maker,' the purpose of the provision in particular, and of the 'Act as a whole,' and 'the nature of the problem in question.'[37] While there is no privative clause applicable to proposed s. 38.13, the other factors will push towards deference. Courts are likely to regard the executive as experts on matters of national defence and security, and the decision in question is 'discretionary and fact-based' rather than legal, particularly on the secondary ground suggested above. Furthermore, it is plain from the scheme of Bill C-36 that the purpose of proposed s. 38.13 is precisely to enable the Attorney General to avoid the judicial procedure for determining a claim of public interest immunity. She will likely be accorded the highest degree of deference.

Second and more fundamental is the problem of statutory interpretation noted above. Judicial review will be effective only if the first interpretation of s. 38.13 is adopted. If the second interpretation is adopted, the presiding judge would not be allowed to look at the information in question to determine whether the Minister has exercised her power under proposed s. 38.13 for the proper reasons and on the proper grounds, then regardless of the standard of review, an application for judicial review will be ineffective.

C. *Charter Review of the Proposed Changes*

Some of Bill C-36's amendments to the *CEA* may be vulnerable to constitutional challenge on Charter grounds. The most obvious challenge would arise from the conflict between Bill C-36 and the Crown's disclosure obligations. According to *Stinchcombe*, the Crown has an obligation to disclose to the accused all relevant and non-privileged evidence. This right to disclosure flows from the more basic right to a fair trial, which is one of the 'principles of fundamental justice' which, under s. 7 of the Charter, limit the state's power to affect a person's rights to 'life, liberty, and security of the person.'[38] The new regime enables the Attorney General of Canada to prevent disclosure of information in criminal proceedings, regardless of whether those proceedings are in the first instance conducted by the federal or provincial Crown, and regardless of the Crown's disclosure obligations. Bill C-36 therefore subordinates the accused's right to a fair trial to the government's interest in protecting information. Proposed s. 38.13 obviously has this effect, but so do proposed ss. 38.031 and 38.04(6) and (7), ousting the court's jurisdiction to determine a claim of public interest immunity where the Attorney General has entered into an 'agreement' with a participant concerning disclosure. This participant need not, of course, be the accused but might well be a Crown attorney or a witness who would otherwise provide relevant and probative evidence.

Again, the seriousness of this problem would be mitigated (though not completely eliminated) if the presiding judge were able to examine the information in question. But if Bill C-36 is interpreted as preventing the judge presiding at the trial from assessing the merits of the government's claim of public interest immunity, then the changes to the *CEA* contemplated by Bill C-36 are inconsistent with the Crown's constitutional disclosure obligations.

D. *The Rule of Law as a Constitutional Value*

According to the *Secession Reference*,[39] 'constitutionalism and the rule of law' is one of the four unwritten principles on which the Canadian Constitution is founded.[40] But the meaning and content of the rule of law is itself contested. For some (the positivists), the rule of law is satisfied as long as an official decision is taken in accordance with a validly-enacted law;[41] for others, the rule of law requires a high degree of congruence between positive law and the demands of justice.[42] An intermediate position, put forward by David Dyzenhaus, proposes that the rule of law commits us not to any particular substantive outcome but to 'the idea of law as a culture of justification,' or to the idea that respect for the rule of law requires the exercise of public power to be subject to some standard of rational accountability.[43]

I do not propose to resolve this debate here; instead, I want to argue that it would be very dangerous to apply the positivist understanding of the rule of law to Bill C-36's proposed changes to the law of public interest immunity. Must a person presiding over a proceeding accept at face value an appropriate official's certification that information should be protected from disclosure on public interest grounds? As we have seen, at common law and under ss. 37 and 38 of the *CEA*, the answer is 'no'; while under s. 39, according to Strayer J.A., the answer is 'yes.' Recall that Strayer J.A.'s reasoning on this point was a typical instance of a positivist understanding of the rule of law. But if that understanding were correct, the rule of law would not be a *constitutional* value because it could never be invoked to question state action authorized by law. The Supreme Court's decision to link 'constitutionalism' with 'the rule of law' and treat the two together as a fundamental value indicates that, even for the purposes of describing Canadian constitutional law, our understanding of the rule of law should not be so limited.

More fundamentally, the rule of law ought to be hostile to an interpretation of a statute that permits the executive to prevent disclosure of information on the mere word of a member of the executive. In this connection, it is important to remember that the broad definition of 'proceedings' in proposed s. 38 includes not only criminal and civil trials but also proceedings before Parliamentary committees and judicial inquiries. Proposed s. 38.13 could therefore be used (or abused) to make legislative or judicial inquiry into executive wrong-doing completely ineffective. The danger of adopting the positivist understanding of the rule of law in this context is that the executive will be granted the discretion to control information, without any requirement that the exercise of that discretion be justified.

Ideally, respect for the rule of law would not be confined to judicial decisions or legal theory, but would infuse legislative debate and the

Attorney General's conduct as well.[44] The government's effort to 'Charter-proof' Bill C-36 and the debate about its wisdom in the Senate justice committee indicates that this value is not completely lost on our parliamentarians. But, as Kent Roach points out in his contribution to this conference, a law can comply with the Charter and still be a very bad and undesirable law; indeed, a law might comply with the Charter while offending fundamental rule of law values. It may well be that proposed s. 38.13 does not offend the Charter, particularly since a judicial stay of proceedings would undoubtedly be available under s. 24(1) for any criminal trial that was rendered unfair when s. 38.13 was invoked. The section nonetheless offends the rule of law in that it permits the Attorney General to prevent disclosure unilaterally and without justification.

In my view, a court committed to the rule of law ought to interpret proposed s. 38.13 as preserving the judge's power to examine the information to determine whether the Attorney General properly exercised her discretion. If this interpretation is not plausible, then in my view s. 38.13 is constitutionally invalid, and a court ought to read in the judge's power to examine the information s. 38.13.

E. *Is the New Regime Necessary?*

It has often been said that 'everything changed' on September 11, 2001. In this vein it might be said that the control over disclosure granted by Bill C-36 is a necessary response to terrorism, an extraordinary weapon for an extraordinary time. There is little evidence to support this claim of necessity. In particular, there is no evidence to suggest that the horrendous events of September 11 were in any way caused by the dissemination of information through proceedings; there is no evidence to suggest that *CEA* ss. 37 and 38 as they stand are inadequate to protect the public interest in non-disclosure; and there is nothing to suggest that judges have been irresponsible in exercising their discretion to examine information in assessing public interest immunity claims.[45] So it is unclear why this extraordinary power, so easily susceptible of abuse, is required.

V. Conclusion

During the first term of the Nixon Administration, 'an unauthorized, unknown intelligence-gathering and covert-operation unit operat[ed] from within the While House.'[46] The most notorious covert operation carried out on Nixon's behalf was the Watergate break-in, and it was his attempt to cover up his staff's role in that operation that led to his downfall. Central to the Justice Department and Congressional inquiries into the cover-up were the tapes of conversations in the White House that Nixon had secretly recorded. He claimed that the tapes were absolutely protected by Executive privilege. The Supreme Court rejected that claim:[47] the consequent release of the tapes showed that Nixon had lied to the American people and led directly to his resignation.

The Watergate operation was obviously motivated by partisan political considerations. But the motivation for an earlier covert operation was more complex. In June 1971, Daniel Ellsberg had leaked the Pentagon Papers to the press, and the Supreme Court had rejected the Administration's effort to enjoin their publication.[48] Nixon and his staff were furiously angry with Ellsberg. In September 1971, five burglars acting under the direction of Nixon's staff broke into the office of Ellsberg's psychiatrist, seeking information that would discredit Ellsberg. No doubt such information would have been used to Nixon's political advantage, but Nixon's staff suggested more than once that the operation was justified by national security.[49] The judge presiding over the trial of two of Nixon's staff rejected that suggestion, and ultimately the facts surrounding the administration's campaign against Ellsberg worked to his benefit: the charges against him arising from the alleged theft of the Pentagon Papers were dismissed because, in the trial judge's words, 'Bizarre events have incurably infected the prosecution of this case.'[50]

If in the early 1970s the Attorney General of the United States had had a power equivalent to that granted by *CEA* s. 39 and by proposed s. 38.13, and if that power had been interpreted to require a court or a legislative committee to accept a certificate at face value, all of this history would have unfolded quite differently. Invoking national security, the Attorney General would have been able to prevent disclosure of any information concerning the Ellsberg break-in; the judge at Ellsberg's trial would therefore not have found the prosecution to be 'infected'; and the Watergate break-in would more plausibly have been construed as an isolated incident than as part of a pattern of conduct. The Nixon administration did not assert that the White House tapes, as they related to the Watergate cover-up, were privileged on national security grounds; but if the administration had been able to invoke a privilege as strong as *CEA* s. 39, it could have concealed both the tapes and the testimony that revealed their existence.[51]

At common law, claims of public interest immunity are to be determined by a court. A statute can of course override the common law, but sometimes a common law rule or principle takes on a constitutional dimension, so that a statute inconsistent with the common law rule or principle is unconstitutional.[52] In *Carey*, emphasizing the court's role in determining a claim of public interest immunity at common law, La Forest J said:

> In the end, it is for the court and not the Crown to determine the issue ... The opposite view would go against the spirit of the legislation enacted in every jurisdiction in Canada that the Crown may be sued like any other person. *More fundamentally, it would be contrary to the constitutional relationship that ought to prevail between the executive and the courts in this country.*[53]

Carey was not a constitutional case, and the underlying factual issues did not involve national security. But La Forest J.'s point is applicable to the changes to the *CEA* contemplated by Bill C-36. The rule of law values embodied in the Constitution no doubt permit some changes to the doctrine of public interest immunity in response to terrorism, but they surely cannot permit an executive fiat to substitute for a proper determination of a claim that secrecy is required. The danger of that fiat being abused is too great.

Notes

1 Associate Professor of Law, University of Toronto. I am very grateful to Kent Roach for several useful suggestions, which I have incorporated into this paper, and to Lisa Austin and David Dyzenhaus for helpful discussions.
2 Richard Nixon, March 1977. See Stephen E. Ambrose, *Nixon: Ruin and Recovery 1973–1990* (New York: Simon and Schuster, 1991) at 508.
3 *United States* v. *Reynolds*, 345 U.S. 1 at 8 (1953).
4 R.S.C. 1985, c. C-5 [hereinafter *CEA*], ss. 37, 38, 39. For an overview of public interest immunity, see Alan W. Mewett, 'State Secrets in Canada' (1985) 63 Can. Bar Rev. 358.
5 *CEA*, s. 39; see also *Westergard-Thorpe* v. *Canada (Attorney General)* (2000), 183 D.L.R. (4th) 458 (F.C.A.), leave to appeal refused, 188 D.L.R. (4th) vii. Section 39 does not apply to confidences that are more than 20 years old and to certain discussion papers. The statutory protection for Cabinet confidences is significantly more restrictive than the common law position outlined in *Carey* v. *The Queen* (1986), 30 C.C.C. (3d) 498 (S.C.C.).
6 Bill C-36, *An Act to amend the Criminal Code, the Official Secrets Act, the Canada*

Evidence Act, the Proceeds of Crime (Money Laundering) Act and other Acts, and to enact measures respecting the registration of charities, in order to combat terrorism, 1st Sess., 37th Parl., 2001 (2d reading 18 October 2001). The proposed amendments I am concerned with are found in cls. 43–44 of Bill C-36; for convenience I will cite them as 'proposed s. 37' etc.

7 Proposed s. 38.13(1); compare Bill C-36, cls. 87, 103, and 104 (making the *Access to Information Act,* R.S.C. 1985, c. A-1, the *Personal Information Protection and Electronic Documents Act,* S.C. 2000, c. 5, and the *Privacy Act,* R.S.C. 1985, c. P-21, inapplicable where the Minister issues 'a certificate that prohibits the disclosure of information for the purpose of protecting international relations or national defence or security').

8 As in *R.* v. *Scott* (1990), 61 C.C.C. (3d) 300 (S.C.C.); see also *R.* v. *Meuckon* (1990), 57 C.C.C. (3d) 193 at 200 (B.C. C.A.).

9 *Duncan* v. *Cammell, Laird & Co.* [1942] 1 All E.R. 587 at 593–95 (H.L.). The House accepted the affidavit of the First Lord of the Admiralty that disclosure of information concerning the design of a submarine would be contrary to the public interest.

10 *Reynolds, supra* note 3.

11 But the court did not say that a judge should never examine the information in question: *ibid.* at 11.

12 *Conway* v. *Rimmer,* [1968] 1 All E.R. 874.

13 See *ibid.* at 892 per Lord Morris.

14 *Carey, supra* note 5; see also *United States* v. *Nixon,* 418 U.S. 683 (1974) (recognizing executive privilege, but rejecting the claim that it was absolute); Mewett, *supra* note 4, at 370.

15 *Re Goguen and Albert and Gibson* (1984), 10 C.C.C. (3d) 492 (F.C.A.)

16 *Goguen, supra* note 15, at at 504 per Marceau J. concurring.

17 *Supra* note 14.

18 *Westergard-Thorpe, supra* note 5. Mewett was 'disturbed' by s. 39 and noted that it was inconsistent with the approach taken in other common law countries: Mewett, *supra* note 4, at 375–6.

19 *Criminal Code,* R.S.C. 1985, c. C-46 [hereinafter *Code*].

20 *Foster* v. *The Queen* (1982), 69 C.C.C. (2d) 484 (Sask. C.A.).

21 *R.* v. *Wijesinha* (1995), 100 C.C.C. (3d) 410 (S.C.C.) at paras. 38–40 (Law Society disciplinary proceedings).

22 *R.* v. *Stinchcombe* (1991), 68 C.C.C. (3d) 1 (S.C.C.).

23 Despite certain recent inroads, there is no doubt that solicitor-client privilege remains a constitutionally protected pillar of the Canadian justice system. Recent judicial discussions of the privilege and its relationship to other privileges and principles include *Smith* v. *Jones* (1999), 169 D.L.R. (4th) 385 (S.C.C.); *R.* v. *McClure* (2001), 151 C.C.C. (3d) 321 (S.C.C.); *General Accident Assurance Co.* v. *Chrusz* (1999), 180 D.L.R. (4th) 241 (Ont. C.A.).

24 *Attorney General of Canada* v. *C.N. Transportation,* [1983] 2 S.C.R. 206; *R.* v.

Wetmore, [1983] 2 S.C.R. 284. For a recent application, see *R. v. Trang* (2001), 198 D.L.R. (4th) 362 (Alta.Q.B.).

25 Such a limitation might be inferred as a matter of statutory interpretation, so that use of the section to protect other kinds of information might be improper.

26 J.H. Wigmore, *Evidence*, vol. 8, ed. by John T. McNaughton (Boston: Little, Brown, 1961) at §2379.

27 *Westergard-Thorpe, supra* note 5, at para. 5.

28 *Supra* note 5.

29 *Westergard-Thorpe, supra* note 5, at paras. 33–34.

30 Contrast *Nixon, supra* note 14, at 706: 'Absent a claim of need to protect military, diplomatic, or sensitive national security secrets, we find it difficult to accept the argument that even the very important interest in confidentiality of Presidential communications is significantly diminished by production of such material for *in camera* inspection, with all the protection that a district court will be obliged to provide.' See also Mewett, *supra* note 4, at 374.

31 *Ibid.* at para. 50.

32 See *CEA* s. 39(4)(a).

33 Proposed s. 38.01(6)(b) mentions, in passing, judicial review of decisions taken under s. 38.13.

34 *Baker v. Canada (Minister of Citizenship and Immigration)* (1999), 174 D.L.R. (4th) 193 (S.C.C.); see also David Dyzenhaus and Evan Fox-Decent, 'Rethinking the Process/Substance Distinction: *Baker v. Canada*' (2001) 51 U.T.L.J. 193.

35 *Operation Dismantle Inc. v. The Queen*, [1985] 1 S.C.R. 441 at 455; *United States of America v. Burns* (2001), 195 D.L.R. (4th) 1 (S.C.C.).

36 *Black v. Canada (Prime Minister) (2001)*, 199 D.L.R. (4th) 228 (Ont. C.A.) at paras. 46–51.

37 *Baker, supra* note 34, at paras. 57–61, referring to *Pushpanathan v. Canada (Minister of Citizenship and Immigration)* (1998), 160 D.L.R. (4th) 193 (S.C.C.).

38 Even before *Stinchcombe*, several courts stated, in *obiter dicta*, that the balance between the state's interest in secrecy and the public's interest in disclosure might be struck differently in criminal than in civil proceedings: see *Gold v. Canada*, [1985] 1 F.C. 642 (T.D.) (applicant's interest was in a civil action against the Crown in right of Canada); *Henrie v. Canada (Security Intelligence Review Committee)* (1988), 53 D.L.R. (4th) 568 (F.C.T.D), aff'd 88 D.L.R. (4th) 575 (F.C.A.) (applicant's interest was in the upgrade of his security classification). In both cases, court affirmed the certificate because the state's interest outweighed the applicant's, but said that where the applicant's liberty was at stake, as in a criminal prosecution, the balance might be different. This distinction was alluded to even in *Duncan, supra* note 9, at 591, and in *Reynolds, supra* note 10, at 12.

39 *Reference re: Secession of Quebec* (1998), 161 D.L.R. (4th) 385 (S.C.C.) at paras. 70–78.

40 *Ibid.* at paras. 70–78. The other three are federalism, democracy, and respect for minorities. The Court noted that this list was not exhaustive: *ibid.* at para. 32.

These four unwritten principles are not merely theoretical or relevant only to exceptional situations but can affect the obligations of government in quite ordinary policy-making: see *Lalonde* v. *Commission de restructuration des services de santé* (1999), 181 D.L.R. (4th) 263 (Ont.Div.Ct.).

41 *Westergard-Thorpe, supra* note 5, at para. 34.

42 Dworkin's jurisprudence might be read this way: see, for instance, Ronald Dworkin, *Law's Empire* (Cambridge, Mass.: Harvard University Press, 1986) at 90–113. See also David Dyzenhaus, 'Form and Substance in the Rule of Law: A Democratic Justification for Judicial Review?' in *Judicial Review and the Constitution*, ed. by Christopher Forsythe (Oxford: Hart, 2000) 141 at 161–166.

43 Dyzenhaus, 'Form and Substance,' *supra* note 42, at 170–2; see also David Dyzenhaus, 'The Legitimacy of Legality' (1996) 46 U.T.L.J. 129.

44 See Kent Roach, 'The Attorney General and the Charter Revisited' (2000) 50 U.T.L.J. 1.

45 See *Carey, supra* note 5; *Meuckon, supra* note 8; *Gold, supra* note 38; *Henrie, supra* note 38.

46 Stephen E. Ambrose, *Nixon: The Triumph of a Politician 1962–1972* (New York: Simon and Schuster, 1989) at 660.

47 *Nixon, supra* note 14.

48 *New York Times Co.* v. *United States*, 403 U.S. 713 (1971).

49 Ambrose, *Nixon 1973–1990, supra* note 2, at 90 and at 343.

50 *Ibid.* at 144.

51 The Congressional investigation was well under way when Nixon aide Alexander Butterfield testified, to everyone's surprise, that Nixon had installed a recording system in the White House. *Ibid.* at 194.

52 This mode of argument is extremely significant in criminal cases, particularly those involving deep-seated procedural and evidentiary rules. Cases in which the argument has succeeded include *R.* v. *Oakes*, [1986] 1 S.C.R. 103 (common law rule requiring proof of elements beyond a reasonable doubt incorporated into s. 11(d) of Charter); *R.* v. *Seaboyer*, [1991] 2 S.C.R. 577 (common law rule requiring admission of defence evidence unless prejudicial effect significantly outweighs probative value a principle of fundamental justice); cases where the argument has failed include *R.* v. *L.(D.O.)* (1993), 85 C.C.C. (3d) 289 (S.C.C.) (statutory change to common law rule against hearsay did not offend principles of fundamental justice).

53 *Carey, supra* note 5, at 511, emphasis added.

The Anti-Terrorism Bill and Preventative Restraints on Liberty

GARY T. TROTTER
Faculty of Law
Queen's University

Few things would provide a more gratifying victory to the terrorist than for this country to undermine its traditional freedoms, in the very process of countering the enemies of those freedoms.[1]

I. Introduction

The unspeakable magnitude of the September 11, 2001 terrorist attacks in the United States casts the critic of anti-terrorist measures in an uncomfortable role. In the din of the painful aftermath, will a meaningful voice be given to those who wish to apply the brakes to a legislative program on an unremitting course? Suggestions for improvement and restraint cannot realistically expect to elude allegations of being naïve, insensitive to recent victims, disloyal or even worse. But this is precisely the climate in which the government's new *Anti-Terrorism Bill*[2] has been introduced. While no one can quibble with the timing of the Bill's introduction, concerns may be made about exploiting public panic to enact unduly broad measures with the expectation of little or no articulated dissent. This atmosphere no doubt inspired the present Justice Minister to proudly declare the new provisions '*Charter*-proof,' as if it were an admirable legislative goal to usurp as much individual freedom as possible, short of infringing the *Charter*. As Professor Roach observes,[3] the true measure should be whether the Bill is good law, including whether its components are reasonably necessary to achieve its objectives. It is this gap – the space between what is truly necessary and the *Charter* precipice – that is the focus of this paper. This analysis is undertaken with emphasis on the myriad ways that the Bill impacts on individual liberty, which has the potential to affect all individuals in Canada.

II. Terrorism and Criminal Legislation

Legislation focused on combating terrorism is not 'typical' criminal legislation. While clearly concerned with preserving (or re-establishing) order, anti-terrorism provisions are enacted in times of public panic or emergency situations. While not necessarily out-out-place in a *Criminal Code*, anti-terrorist provisions have military and national security aspects. Anti-terrorist provisions engage a broadening of the criminal law and ought to be considered carefully for that reason. British terrorism expert, Clive Walker, reminds us that 'there must be adherence to limiting principles which reflect the values of constitutionalism and democratic accountability, which can be considered as universal moral goods and not simply autopoietic features' of a justice system.[4] Walker identifies five principles or prescriptions:

1. Respect for national traditions, including agreements or documents protecting human rights;
2. Anti-terrorist laws should derogate as little as possible from 'normal' measures;
3. Special measures should be clear and precise and safeguards should be provided to prevent their improper introduction or exercise;
4. The application of anti-terrorism laws should be considered necessary by an objective and impartial arbiter and should be accompanied by remedies against unreasonable use; and
5. Special laws should be distinguished from ordinary powers because the assimilation of the two may damage in confidence in existing law, may hamper scrutiny of the impact of special laws and may retard their expiration.[5]

A number of the provisions of Bill C 36 discussed in this paper run afoul of these principles, particularly the last one. A review of the Act as a whole demonstrates that drafters combed through the *Criminal Code*, looking for opportunities to insert the words 'terrorist group, ' 'terrorist activity' or 'terrorist offence.'[6] While certain, discrete parts of the Act are susceptible to being repealed, the manner in which the terrorist theme has been woven into the fabric of our criminal law will ensure the permanence of most of these provisions.

Kent Roach observes that many aspects of the Bill are addressed by existing provisions of the *Criminal Code*.[7] The same may be said of some of the procedural provisions discussed below. The repetition involved in this strategy has a cluttering effect on an already unwieldy document. If amendments are truly duplicative, they are nothing more than window-dressing. However, window-dressing can be dangerous, especially in this context, because it creates a false sense of security in the public, all at a cost of lessening restraint in the criminal law.

III. Peace Bonds for Terrorists

The police and state powers created by the new Bill must be considered in the light of the substantive measures introduced by the Bill. The breadth of the offence-creating and definitional provisions of the Bill filter down and broaden some of the new procedural provisions and powers.

The Bill makes adjustments to the preventative provisions dealing with recognizances to keep the peace (or peace bonds). Over the last number of years, Parliament has tinkered with these provisions, gradually expanding the ambit of this preventative measure, by adding new provisions that address different perceived risks. In 1993, section 810.1 was created to deal with fear that a sexual offence might be committed.[8] In 1997, s.810.01 was added to the Code to create a special recognizance aimed at criminal organizations and section 810.2 to deal with fear of a 'serious personal injury offence.' Sections 810.01 and 810.1 are different from the main peace bond provision, s.810, because they do not require the information to be laid by the person who is in fear of apprehended harm. These various additional provisions were added to achieve different legislative objectives.[9] Some relate to the hysteria around criminal organizations (s.810.01), while others attempt to address post-sentence detention issues for dangerous offenders (s.810.02). Some require the consent of the Attorney General before they are triggered (ss.810.01 and 810.02, but not 810 or 810.1). The provisions are an incoherent collection.

Bill C-36 tinkers with these provisions in two ways. First, s.810.01 is amended to provide that an information may be laid where 'a person who fears on reasonable grounds that another person will commit a criminal organization offence or a terrorism offence.' As absurd as it is to think that a recognizance could be efficacious in the circumstances, beyond adding to the clutter, this amendment is unobjectionable.

More interesting is the proposed section 83.3 of the *Code*, which creates a new type of peace bond or recognizance. The heading preceding the section reads 'Recognizance with Conditions.' However, the heading is a Trojan horse, because the section is more concerned with arrest and detention, than with recognizances or conditions. With the consent of the Attorney General, an information may be laid if a peace officers:

(a) *believes* on reasonable grounds that a *terrorist activity* will be carried out; and

(b) *suspects* on reasonable grounds that the imposition of a recognizance with conditions on a person, *or the arrest* of a person, is necessary to prevent the carrying out of a *terrorist activity*. [emphasis added]

Unlike the amendment to s.810.01, this section purports to be focused, not on 'terrorism offences,' but on 'terrorist activities,' at least at the arrest stage.[10] This is one of the features of the Bill that requires close attention. This distinction appears again in the sentencing context, discussed below. The distinction is curious because the definition of a 'terrorism offence' includes indictable offences 'where the act or omission constituting the offence also constitutes a terrorist activity.'[11] Thus, because 'terrorist activity' only becomes a 'terrorism offence' when it accompanies an indictable offence, Parliament appears to give 'terrorist activity' a broader compass.

The differential criteria found in s.83.3 is beguiling. A peace officer must have reasonable grounds to believe that a 'terrorist activity' may be carried out. However, the officer need only 'suspect' on reasonable and probable grounds that the arrest of the individual or the imposition of a recognizance is necessary to prevent 'terrorist activity.' The normal course reflected in s.83.3(3) is for a provincial court judge to issue process (a summons or a warrant) to compel the person's appearance in court. Under ss.(4)(b), an individual can be arrested before an information is laid and/or after a summons has been issued if the officer believes on reasonable grounds that the 'detention of the person in custody is necessary in order to prevent the commission of an indictable offence, where the act or omission constituting the offence also constitutes terrorist activity.' The circumstances contemplated by these circumstances point to an arrest under s.495 of the *Criminal Code*, which permits a warrantless arrest of someone who the officer believes is 'about to commit an indictable offence.' However, under s.83.3, the apprehended 'terrorist activity' need not be imminent. Thus, subsections 83.3(3) and (4) broaden the scope of arrests to prevent the commission of offences which are not imminent. The section seems aimed at taking individuals out of circulation in the hopes of preventing terrorist activities.

This section also permits extended periods of detention. When an arrest is made without a warrant, s.83.3(6) of the *Code* provides that the individual should be brought before a provincial court judge without unreasonable delay and in any event within 24 hours. If a provincial judge is not available within that time period, the accused must be brought before a judge 'as soon as possible.' This is uncontroversial and basically tracks the typical temporal criteria for bringing an accused charged with an offence before a justice of the peace.[12] Subsection (8) provides that, once the individual has been brought before a provincial court judge, and an information has been laid, the accused is to be dealt with in accordance with the bail provisions in ss.515 to 524 of the *Criminal Code*, with proper modifications. The most serious modification is contained in paragraph (8)(iii), which requires that the person not be detained in custody, 'by virtue of this section for longer than forty-eight hours following the appearance before the provincial court judge.'

This is the most problematic aspect of the section. Performing the calculations that this elusive section requires, it permits a total period of at least 72 hours detention prior to a bail hearing. This applies to a person who has yet to be charged with an offence (although it would appear that the idea of the provision is to provide the police with time to develop a case against an individual to the point where a charge can be laid). Where will the individual be detained during this period of time? In the bail context, it is understood that, once an individual has been brought before a justice of the peace under s.503, the individual should not be returned to the local police lock-up for further interrogation. Section 503 contemplates that following the appearance before a justice of the peace, the individual will be taken to a detention center.[13] Bill C-36 should address this issue directly.

Compared to the manner in which other countries have dealt with terrorism, detention in custody for 72 hours is not unreasonable, especially when the individual is taken before a judge at an early stage.[14] However, this type of provision is vulnerable to expansion in the right political climate.[15] Parliament should be more forthright about the purpose and impact of this section so that its true effect can be evaluated and attempts at expansion properly monitored.

If it is determined that the arrest truly was for the purpose of having an accused enter into a recognizance with conditions, under ss.83.3(8), the provincial court judge will determine whether a recognizance with conditions is necessary to prevent the commission of a 'terrorism offence.' Thus, at the end of this process, 'terrorism offence' becomes the marker, even though the arrest was inspired by fear of 'terrorism activity.' It is unclear whether this is a mistake or whether the distinction is intentional. If it is intentional, the significance behind the distinction is not apparent. Given that s.83.3 reverts to a focus on preventing a 'terrorism offence,' it seems that the only value-added to using this provision over the amended peace bond provision in s.810.01 (discussed above) is the more generous detention provisions associated with s.83.3. As with other recognizances, like s.810.01, failure to enter into the recognizance may result in detention in custody for a year.[16]

In a climate where Parliament purports to legislate in order to save lives by fighting terrorism, the extended period of detention reflected in s.83.3 is not particularly offensive. However, the confusion engendered by the provision, the work that it takes to get at its true meaning and the use of deceptive language flouts the need to be clear and open about extending state powers in emergency situations.[17] Beyond being *Charter*-proof, there also appeared to be an attempt to make this provision *Charter*-elusive. Lastly, given the psychology of the 'new terrorism,' in which individuals are prepared to sacrifice their own lives for the cause, the predicted efficacy of a recognizance in these circumstances ought to be seriously considered.

IV. Stricter Bail Laws

Tightening the bail provisions of the *Criminal Code* is another crowd pleaser in terms of making the criminal law responsive to public concern about crime on the rise. Parliament resorted to this device in Bill C-36, but not in a dramatic way. Section 515(4.1), concerning firearms and weapons prohibitions, will be reconfigured to require judges to consider imposing this type of condition when the accused is charged with a terrorism offence (*a.1*) and offences under the *Security of Information Act* (*e*). Section 515(4.2) is amended (and augmented by new (4.3)) to bring to the attention of justices of the peace that, where an accused is charged with a terrorism offence or an offence under the *Security of Information Act*, it is necessary to consider whether it is desirable to impose a condition on the accused person to prohibit or limit communication with others, or to refrain from going to any specified place. The necessity of including each of these types of terms when dealing with a terrorist would strike most judges as obvious. Long before

Parliament started tinkering with ss.515(4) of the Code a number of years ago, the power to impose these types of conditions was available. In this respect, the new provisions are superfluous and do not realistically toughen the bail provisions, although they may have some negligible symbolic value. They do make a complicated section of the Code even less accessible.

The last change to the bail provisions concerns reverse-onus clauses. Parliament again steps away from the vision of the *Bail Reform Act* of 1972[18] by enacting another exception to the general rule that the onus to establish that pre-trial detention is necessary lies with the state. Recently, s.515(6)(a) was amended to include offences relating to criminal organizations as situations in which a reverse-onus provision was warranted. Following on this theme, Bill C-36 adds three paragraphs ((iii) to (v)) to include terrorism offences and offences under the *Security of Information Act* to the roster of reverse-onus offences. If a revere-onus provision is constitutional with respect to drug trafficking,[19] a provision focused on terrorism is sure to be upheld. Whether a reverse-onus provision is necessary in this context (or any context, for that matter) is another question. The same features of terrorism that inspired Parliament to create a reverse-onus provision would also make it difficult for an individual to get bail on a straight application of the criteria for detention in s.515(10) of the *Criminal Code*.

V. Harsher Sentences

As pointed out in Professor Roach's paper, Bill C-36 creates new substantive offences, terrorism offences (ss.83.02 to 83.04 and 83.18 to 83.23), with serious statutory sentencing maxima of 10, 14 years and life imprisonment. Moreover, Bill-36 provides that sentences for these types of offences shall be made consecutive to other offences (with exception of life imprisonment).[20] This legislative strategy, which is popular with Parliament, may lead to injustice through disproportionate punishment.

Another, more far-reaching provision in Bill C-36 is s.86.27 (1). Again, riding the distinction between 'terrorism offences' and 'terrorist activity,' this section provides:

s.83.27(1) Notwithstanding anything in this Act, a person convicted of an indictable offence, other than an offence for which a sentence of life imprisonment is imposed as a minimum punishment, where the act or omission constituting the offence also constitutes a terrorist activity, is liable to imprisonment for life.[21]

The prosecutor is required to give notice of its intention to seek this enhanced penalty prior to a plea being entered. This sentence is as dramatic as the definition of 'terrorist activity' is wide. Building on the nebulous definition of 'terrorist activity' in s.83.01, the provision has the effect of increasing sentencing maxima to life, if committed in a particular setting, for a particular purpose. Much of the more egregious offences captured in this definition carry the possibility of life imprisonment in any event. Those that do not, and cause serious bodily harm or endanger life, are unobjectionable inclusions. However, life imprisonment for some of the lower level offences caught in the web of s.83.01 may be excessive.

There are two further, tinkering amendments to the sentencing provisions found in Bill C-36. Section 231 is amended to add ss.(6.01), which makes murder first-degree murder where death is caused 'while committing or attempting to commit an indictable offence that also constitutes terrorist activity.' This too follows the recent legislative trend of expanding the categories of first-degree murder. In 1997, Parliament created ss.231(6) and (6.1) to include as first-degree murder killings committed in circumstances involving criminal harassment (ss.(6)) and in respect of a criminal organization (ss.6.1)).[22] The anti-terrorism and criminal organizations amendments to s.231 cast doubt on whether the organizing principle behind these instances of first-degree murder is the domination of one person over another when the murder is committed.[23] The current legislative approach to constructive first-degree murder seems much more political and pragmatic.

Lastly, s.718.2(a) is amended to include ss.(v), which makes it an aggravating factor if there is evidence that the offence was a terrorism offence. The terrorist context is rather obvious candidate for enhanced sentences and was already recognized by the courts.[24] Thus, s.718.2(a)(v) is symbolic.[25]

VI. Conclusions

The most dramatic impact of the Bill C-36 is the creation of the sweeping substantive provisions designed to combat terrorism. Augmenting these substantive powers are myriad small changes that directly impact on liberty through detention or conditional restraint. Individually, most of these changes are small. Cumulatively, they claim significant liberty, in an insidious way. The legislative style of Bill C-36, apparently fashionable these days, is to graft onto existing provisions terminology, nuances and new categories, designed to cover the latest emergency situation. This triage style of legislation creates for law that is confusing and unwieldy.

Many of these provisions are unnecessary because the issues they confront are addressed in existing law. Thus, they are mere window-dressing. Nothing has changed, except in word alone. This contributes to a false sense of security that we are now somehow safer because of the new law. In many ways, we are not. Peace bonds, stricter bail conditions and consecutive sentences will not make us safe from terrorists. In terms of its impact on individual liberty, Bill C-36 merely makes the criminal law more labyrinthine and more invasive. Moreover, these expanded powers are here to stay. It would take a massive legislative undertaking, almost as ambitious as Bill C 36 itself, to roll-back many of these newly-created powers. It is not realistic to think that this will happen anytime soon.

Notes

1 British M.P. A Jenkins (Nov. 29, 1974), H.C. Debs. Vol. 833, debating the *Prevention of Terrorism (Temporary Provisions) Act, 1974*, following the bombing of two public houses in Birmingham. Clive Walker, *The Prevention of Terrorism in British Law*, 2nd ed. (Manchester: Manchester University Press, 1992), at p. 11.

2 Bill C-36, 2001.

3 Kent Roach, 'The Dangers of a Charter-Proof and Crime-Based Response to Terrorism,' in this volume.

4 Clive Walker, 'Anti-Terrorism Laws for the Future' (1996), 146 New Law Journal 586, at p. 587.

5 Ibid., p. 587. See also Clive Walker, *The Prevention of Terrorism in British Law*, 2nd ed., *supra*, note 1, at pp. 11–12.

6 Bill C-36, sections 2 and 83.01.

7 Kent Roach, 'The New Terrorism Offences and the Criminal Law,' in this volume.

8 S.C. 1993, c.45, s.11.

9 See generally Allan Manson, *The Law of Sentencing* (Toronto: Irwin Law, 2001), at pp. 344–353. See also *R. v. Budreo* (2000), 32 C.R. (5th) 127 (Ont. C.A.).

10 Note that, further into the section, in ss.83.3(8), which specifies the contours of the hearing as to whether a recognizance should be ordered, the judge must determine whether the imposition of certain conditions are desirable for the purposes of preventing the commission of 'a terrorism offence.'

11 S.2.

12 See s.503 of the *Criminal Code*, as interpreted in *R. v. Storrey* (1990), 53 C.C.C. (3d) 316 (S.C.C.).

13 See *R v. Koszulap* (1974), 27 C.R.N.S. 226 (Ont. C.A.) and *R. v. Precourt* (1976), 39 C.C.C. (2d) 31 (Ont. C.A.).

14 See J.J. Rowe, 'The Terrorism Act 2000,' [2001] Crim. L.R. 527, at p. 533. Under s.41 of that Act, detention may be for a maximum period of seven days, with the authorization of a judge. Previous legislation that permitted detention up to seven days was found to contravene Art.5(3) of the *European Convention on Human Rights* because further detention was not authorized by a judge: see *Brogan et. al.* v. *U.K.* (1989), 11 E.H.R.R. 539. The British Government entered a derogation from Article 5(3) on the grounds of a public emergency, pursuant to Article 15 of the *Convention*. Since the passage of The Terrorism Act 2000, the derogation was removed. See also Clive Walker, 'The Bombs in Omagh and Their Aftermath: The Criminal Justice (Terrorism and Conspiracy) Act 1998' (1999), 62 Mod. L. Rev. 879, at p.891.

15 See Don Stuart, 'The Dangers of Quick Fix Legislation in the Criminal Law: The Anti-Terrorism Bill C-36 Should Be Withdrawn,' in this volume.

16 Ss.83.3(9). The decision in *R. v. Ferrier* (2001), 155 C.C.C. (3d) 521 (Ont. S.C.J.) demonstrates how onerous this regime can be.

17 See the third principle articulated by Clive Walker, *supra* note 5

18 S.C. 1971–72–73, c.37.

19 *R. v. Pearson* (1992), 17 C.R. (4th) 1 (S.C.C.).

20 s.83.26.

21 The reference to life as a minimum penalty points to the sentence for murder.

22 S.C. 1997, c.16, s.3 and c.23, s.8, respectively.

23 See *R. v. Pare* (1987), 38 C.C.C. (3d) 97 (S.C.C.) and *R. v. Harbottle* (1993), 84 C.C.C. (3d) 1 (S.C.C.).

24 See *R. v. Atwal* (1990), 57 C.C.C. (3d) 143 (B.C.C.A.) and *R. v. Balian* (1988), 29 O.A.C. 387 (C.A.).

25 Again, it tracks the inclusion of offences committed for the benefit of, at the direction of or in association with a criminal organization in s.718.2(iv): S.C. 1997, c.23, s.17.

Information Gathering

Is Privacy a Casualty of the War on Terrorism?

LISA AUSTIN
Faculty of Law
University of Toronto

Introduction[1]

Prior to September 11, many airlines in the United States were already using a Computer Assisted Passenger Screening system (CAPS).[2] The system collects information about passengers and then screens individuals who are checking baggage according to ticket-purchase methods and travel patterns. The point of the system is to flag 'suspicious' behaviour, such as purchasing a one-way ticket with cash, as well as to periodically select travelers at random. If selected by the system, the passenger, along with her baggage, is taken aside for further investigation. Currently there are proposals to expand the use of CAPS and to integrate it with law enforcement and national security intelligence data.[3] Canada may soon follow suit. Transport Minister David Collenette recently announced that Canada will amend the *Aeronautics Act* in order to allow airlines to share information about their passengers with U.S. authorities.[4] Moreover, this is likely to be part of a much larger security effort for which collecting, storing, aggregating, sharing, and linking information will play a key role. For example, the American anti-terrorism bill recently signed into law by President Bush contained provisions to allow the American Attorney General to implement an identification-card system for foreigners entering the United States.[5] Such a system would not only allow the tracking of individuals crossing the border, but when combined with other databases would allow for better screening at borders.

It seems clear, therefore, that the post-September 11 world is one of increased surveillance. Is this a concern? After all, as the popular refrain goes, if you have nothing to hide then you have nothing to worry about. And in fact we have long accepted the need for a level of surveillance at borders that we would never agree to in our daily lives.[6] The concern, however, is not so much with specific searches that occur at the border as it is with the screening that allows individuals to be singled out as suspicious and then searched. What is being implemented is a new type of surveillance, one that depends on collecting, storing, aggregating, sharing and linking vast amounts of information about people and then using this information for screening purposes. This kind of surveillance shifts the focus away from the border to the many non-border areas where that information will be collected. By doing so, such surveillance potentially intrudes on the privacy of individuals who may never become the target of more specific searches at the border. Moreover, this new surveillance will involve the cooperation of the private sector, such as airlines. Personal information that you might think appropriate for an airline to collect could be shared with law enforcement agencies and used in ways you never anticipated. Combined with further worries about function creep – that these surveillance systems will be used for an ever-widening set of applications – as well as concerns about their abuse, and we may well conclude that privacy will be a casualty of the war on terrorism.

This should concern us deeply. Privacy is recognized as a fundamental right in a free and democratic society. This finds constitutional expression in s. 8 of the *Charter of Rights and Freedoms*, which guarantees the right to be secure against unreasonable search and seizure, and also in s. 7 of the *Charter*, which guarantees the right to life, liberty and security of the person.[7] As the Supreme Court of Canada has stated, 'privacy is at the heart of liberty in a modern state.'[8]

I will argue that many elements of the Canadian government's proposed anti-terrorism package undermine privacy by allowing for these very activities: increased collection, storage, aggregation, sharing and linking of information sometimes with few accountability mechanisms attached. The question is then whether the new balance between privacy and security announced in these measures, and our move towards increasing surveillance, is consistent with the constitutional values of a free and democratic society as enshrined in the *Charter*. As I will outline, it is clear that the *Charter* allows for a lower level of privacy protection when state security is at stake rather than law enforcement more generally. But this still raises the question of exactly what kind of new balance is permissible and desirable.

My argument is that the proposed amendments to the *Privacy Act*, the

Personal Information Protection and Electronic Documents Act and the *Access to Information Act* are not consistent with the principles of a free and democratic society. However, for most of the other provisions that affect privacy I think that it is difficult to give and an adequate answer to this question. This is because our current constitutional thinking regarding privacy is not able to articulate the nature of an individual's privacy interest in the face of widespread, expected surveillance. Moreover, new technologies facilitate the erosion of privacy through the cumulative effect of what are often minor privacy infractions. Assessing these technologies, and the provisions that facilitate and authorize their use, therefore requires attention to the collective effect of surveillance in the post-September 11 world. We therefore need new tools of analysis to deal with this context and such a complex assessment requires more than the current time frame for debate regarding the proposed legislation.

Given these concerns, the government should do several things. First, it should not enact the proposed changes to the *Privacy Act*, the *Personal Information Protection and Electronic Documents Act* and the *Access to Information Act*. Second, it must justify why the remaining proposed provisions will be more effective in attaining their stated goals than the existing legal regime. Third, if it meets this burden of justification then it should add a sunset-clause to the legislation. This would recognize that we are unable to properly assess and debate its impact on our society in the short timeframe that has been allotted for passage of this bill. Until we are able to do so, it should remain a set of temporary measures.

Tipping the Balance: The Security of Surveillance

(a) *Information gathering*

Bill C-36[9] introduces a number of reforms that facilitate information gathering on the part of law enforcement agencies in the context of terrorist crimes. For example, the electronic surveillance provisions of the *Criminal Code* will no longer require, when investigating terrorist crimes, that such surveillance be used only as a last resort when other investigative techniques have proved inadequate.[10] As well, *Bill C-36* amends the *National Defence Act*[11] by codifying the mandate of the Communications Security Establishment (CSE), the branch of the Ministry of National Defence responsible for collecting foreign intelligence.[12] Although under this new mandate the CSE is prohibited from directing their activities toward Canadians, there is a concern that there is little to preclude the CSE from nonetheless intercepting the communications involving Canadians.[13] *Bill C-36* also amends the *Proceeds of Crime (Money Laundering) Act* to apply to terrorist activities, facilitating the investigation of terrorist financing.[14] These reforms would include record keeping and disclosure obligations that could have an impact on privacy.

These are not the only provisions to affect state information-gathering. Canada has announced, as part of its anti-terrorism package, that it will sign the Council of Europe's *Convention on Cyber-Crime*.[15] Apart from calling for the establishment of a number of criminal offences relating to computers,[16] the *Convention* also calls for the establishment of procedures with respect to criminal investigations and proceedings. These procedures are to apply to these new offences but, importantly, also to any criminal offence committed by means of a computer system, and to the collection of electronic evidence with respect to any criminal offence. It is open to signatories to restrict the number of offences that such procedures apply to, and they are required to put into place procedural safeguards to protect fundamental human rights.

Prior to September 11, the *Convention* received a great deal of attention among privacy advocates, who criticized it on several grounds.[17] The overarching concern is that it does not provide enough protection for civil liberties, leaving these safeguards to domestic definition rather than outlining minimum standards in the *Convention* itself.[18] This exacerbates concerns regarding provisions that could be interpreted to require laws that would force users to provide the government with their encryption keys, raising issues regarding both privacy and self-incrimination.[19] Other provisions of the *Convention* require the establishment of laws that would allow authorities to collect and record traffic data and content data on the internet – both with and without the cooperation of service providers.[20] This would facilitate the use of systems like the U.S. Carnivore technology.[21] Concerns about Carnivore include that it will collect more information than permitted, collect it about individuals not under specific investigation, and easily shift from collecting traffic data to collecting content data. If Canada implements the *Convention* in the current context of the fight against terrorism then there is a worry that protections for civil liberties will be diluted and the balance will shift even further away from privacy in favour of security.

(b) *Information preservation and retention*

The *Convention* also has provisions requiring the preservation of data required for a criminal investigation.[22] Again, there are concerns that this be implemented in a manner that protects civil liberties and does not put too onerous a burden on internet service providers. However, there are also concerns that states will move beyond data preservation and require data *retention*. Already, in Europe, there is a proposal before the EU that, if adopted, could effectively require service providers to retain communications data for law enforcement purposes for up to seven years.[23] Indeed, following the September 11 attacks, the UK government lost no time in requesting that all communications service providers retain and preserve existing communications data, including logs of emails, internet usage and telephone calls indefinately.[24] The obvious concern with such data warehousing is that it leads to the creation of immense searchable databases of personal information. This in turn raises concerns about security of information, and more broadly, the privacy of the individuals whose information is retained.

Bill C-36 alters a data retention scheme of a different sort: our national DNA data bank.[25] Under our current *DNA Identification Act*, the DNA profiles of convicted offenders obtained through the DNA warrant scheme in the *Criminal Code* form a 'convicted offender's index,' which is one part of a national DNA data bank (the other part is a crime scene index). This DNA databank is meant to facilitate the identification of individuals who have committed crimes. The information contained in it is kept indefinitely, with exceptions for Young Offenders and convicted individuals who have had their conviction quashed or who have been discharged.[26]

What *Bill C-36* does is make many of the new terrorist offences, and a number of existing terrorist-related offences, primary designated offences under the DNA warrant scheme. A primary designated offence is one for which an order *shall* be made to obtain a DNA sample for forensic analysis rather than, as in the case of a secondary designated offence, an order *may* be made 'if the court is satisfied that it is in the best interests of the administration of justice to do so.'[27] So, for example, new offences such as participation in the activity of a terrorist group (proposed s. 83.18), facilitating terrorist activity (proposed 83.19) and existing offences such as endangering the safety of aircraft or airport (s. 77) are now primary designated offences: convictions will result in the offender's inclusion in the DNA databank. Proposed ss. 83.2-83.23 are also included, but the financing offences (83.02-83.04) are excluded.

Like the electronic surveillance provisions, these changes to the DNA databank regime underscore the issue of the overbreadth of the new terrorisms offences; if the definitions of the new offences are too broad, then this will lead to unnecessary privacy violations of those convicted of these offences. Even if there are no definitional difficulties with the new offences, their inclusion as primary designated offences for the purpose of the DNA warrant scheme signals that security concerns are taken to justify a departure from the past balance between safety and privacy. The existing primary designated offences share the common feature of being violent or sexual offences – offences regarding which the government has argued DNA evidence will be of the most assistance in solving crimes because biological material is likely to be left at the crime site.[28] It is not at all clear that all of the new terrorist offences fall within this rationale. Instead, it appears that the government is lowering the threshold for inclusion in the name of national security.

(c) *Secrets and accountability*

Section 104 of *Bill C-36* amends the *Privacy Act* to allow the Attorney General to prohibit the disclosure of information 'for the purpose of protecting international relations or national defence or security.' This specially designated information would then not be subject to the *Privacy Act* at all. *Bill C-36* amends the *Personal Information Protection and Electronic Documents Act (PIPEDA)* and the *Access to Information Act* in a similar manner.[29]

What is the effect of this? I will outline here only some of the concerns with respect to the *Privacy Act*, although it is my view that the major implications of these amendments to *PIPEDA* and the *Access to Information Act* are similar. The general purpose of the *Privacy Act* is to 'protect the privacy of individuals with respect to personal information about themselves held by a government institution and ...[to] provide individuals with a right of access to that information.'[30] Generally, then, the government can only disclose personal information under certain circumstances outlined by the *Privacy Act*, which is meant to protect the privacy of Canadians. Citizen privacy is not apparently compromised by a provision that prevents disclosure.

However, it is not clear just what this disclosure might include. For example, it appears the Attorney General could issue a certificate regarding a personal information bank and thereby prevent the publication of information regarding this bank under s. 11 of the *Act* – publication that is crucial for citizens to know what information is being collected about them. Would the Attorney General also be able to prevent an individual from gaining access to the information held about them, as s. 12 of the *Privacy Act* currently allows? This concern is particularly acute if the information being gathered is used for profiling purposes. If the information is inaccurate then the individual concerned could face repeated unwelcome intrusions and not be able to gain access to and correct that information.

Sections 18-25 of the *Privacy Act* already contain provisions that allow the government to exempt information from the disclosure requirements if disclosure would compromise international relations and security concerns. For example, s.19(1) provides that the government 'shall refuse to disclose any personal information requested ... that was obtained in confidence' from a foreign government or international organization. Section 21 gives the government the discretion to prevent the disclosure of information 'the disclosure of which could reasonably be expected to be injurious to the conduct of international affairs, the defence of Canada or any state allied or associated with Canada ... or the efforts of Canada toward detecting, preventing or suppressing subversive or hostile activities.'

Bill C-36 is therefore not necessary if the government is merely seeking to prevent the disclosure of information in certain circumstances. What the new provisions accomplish is several things. First, *Bill C-36* lowers the threshold for preventing disclosure in a number of cases. Instead of requiring a test like 'could reasonably be expected to be injurious to the conduct of international affairs,' as in s. 21 of the *Privacy Act*, it only requires a 'purpose of protecting international relations or national defence or security.' Second, *Bill C-36* removes the power of the Privacy Commissioner to investigate complaints regarding disclosure, which includes the power to examine the information in question and, could lead potentially to judicial review of the decision under the Act. By way of contrast, the only exemption to the Privacy Commissioner's investigatory power to examine information that is under the control of the government pertains to confidences of the Queen's Privy Council for Canada as provided in s. 70 (1). However, even these confidences are only protected for a period of 20 years. Furthermore, under s.36 of the *Privacy Act*, the Privacy Commissioner may review information banks that are exempt from the disclosure requirements and request that a file held inappropriately in such a bank be removed. The government's response to such a request is also reviewable by the courts under s. 43. In reviewing such decisions, the court is also to be given access to the information in question, and there are special provisions for court proceedings regarding information that is exempt for reasons of international affairs and defence that address the particular challenges of balancing privacy with security and other interests in these areas. Third, *Bill C-36* exempts any certificate issued to prohibit the disclosure of information from the application of the *Statutory Instruments Act*. The effect of this is that even the fact that the Attorney General has issued a certificate under this new authorization will not be made public.

While these provisions of *Bill C-36* target the disclosure of information, the effect of the Attorney General issuing a certificate prohibiting the disclosure of information is that this designated information is then entirely exempt from any application of the *Privacy Act, Access to Information Act*, or *PIPEDA*. And this leaves this power of issuing a certificate open to abuse much broader than that with respect to prohibiting disclosure alone. These three pieces of legislation together provide many safeguards regarding the collection, retention, use and access to personal information as well as its disclosure. The government could violate these other safeguards with impunity if they are veiled by the level of secrecy and lack of review mechanisms contemplated by *Bill C-36*.

Is This New Balance Consistent with *Charter* Values?

If we want to ensure the most efficient system possible for the detection and apprehension of terrorists, then we should seek at least two things: the secrecy of state actions and the absence of secrecy for citizens. The problem, of course, is that this describes a police state, and not a liberal democracy. Secrecy for the state entails a lack of accountability to its citizens. The absence of secrecy for citizens entails a lack of individual privacy. And a liberal democracy governed by the rule of law demands both state accountability and the protection of individual civil liberties such as privacy. As a result, a liberal democracy can never have the most efficient system possible for the apprehension of criminals. A balance must be struck between safety and security on the one hand, and privacy and accountability on the other.

The federal government's proposed anti-terrorism legislation diminishes the existing level of privacy protection in the name of security. And there is no reason to believe that the erosion of privacy protection will stop with *Bill C-36*. The announcements that Canada will sign the *Convention on Cyber-Crime*, as well as amend the *Aeronautics Act* to allow data sharing, indicate that we will face further reforms that may compromise privacy. The government is proposing that a new balance between privacy and security be struck. This new balance raises the question of justification.

The first question we should have about these proposed measures is whether they will actually meet their goal of increasing security. We can see that they come at a price, that price being the diminishment of privacy protection. This is a price that the government should not ask us to pay needlessly. Therefore the government must meet its burden in justifying that these provisions will provide us with more actual security than our existing legal regime.

The second question we need to ask is whether this new balance between privacy and security remains consistent with the principles of a free and democratic society, as enshrined in our *Charter*. Here I want to comment on *Charter* values generally as they apply to this package of provisions and not make specific *Charter* arguments about individual provisions.

Privacy has had its most sustained treatment in discussions of s.8 of the *Charter* which guarantees the right 'to be secure against unreasonable search or seizure.' Ever since *Hunter* v. *Southam*, this provision has been interpreted to protect a 'reasonable expectation of privacy.' In that case, Dickson C.J. held that s.8,

> whether it is expressed negatively as freedom from 'unreasonable' search and seizure, or positively as an entitlement to a 'reasonable'" expectation of privacy, indicates that an assessment must be made as to whether in a particular situation the public's interest in being left alone by government must give way to the government's interest in intruding on the individual's privacy in order to advance its goals, notably those of law enforcement.

Dickson C.J. argued that the point at which state interests prevail over individual interests is when 'credibly-based probability replaces suspicion,' although he noted that this threshold might be lower when state security and not simply law enforcement was at stake. Therefore the *Charter* allows state interests to be balanced against individual privacy interests. Furthermore, it allows a lower level of privacy protection when state security is at stake rather than law enforcement more generally. The question then is, even if we are permitted to strike a different balance when state security is at issue, exactly what balance is constitutionally permissible?

I believe that a number of the provisions of *Bill C-36* in fact subvert privacy in the name of security rather than balance these interests. Sections 87, 103 and 104 of *Bill C-36*, which amend the *Access to Information Act*, *PIPEDA* and the *Privacy Act* in the manner outlined above, indicate that domestic privacy protections could be completely waived in the name of international relations and national security. Or, at least, it will be impossible to determine whether privacy has been waived because practices with regard to information designated under these provisions will be unreviewable. If unreviewable, then there is no effective remedy for abuse. As lawyers would say, a right without a remedy is no right. Therefore, in the absence of mechanisms to ensure accountability, important aspects of our rights to privacy are subverted by *Bill C-36*. While these provisions may not engage s.8 directly – one would have to argue that the issuing of a certificate prohibiting disclosure constituted a search or seizure – nonetheless they violate *Charter* values regarding privacy and the balance that should be struck between privacy and state interests. In doing so, these provisions appear inconsistent with the values of a free and democratic society.

The question of the justification of the provisions regarding information gathering, preservation and retention is less clear. But here I think the dilemma lies in our current constitutional thinking about privacy. The anti-terrorism legislation, and other impending reforms, increases the level of surveillance in our society. And it is in just this kind of context of widespread surveillance that our current constitutional test regarding a 'reasonable expectation of privacy' is inadequate. Because of this it is very difficult for us to say whether this increased surveillance is consistent with a free and democratic society; we simply have not developed an adequate language regarding privacy and so are ill-equipped to balance privacy against state security.

The Supreme Court of Canada has generally taken two approaches to determining a 'reasonable expectation of privacy.' One approach involves a descriptive appeal to social conventions to determine an individual's privacy interest and the other involves reference to an independent normative account of privacy. Both of these approaches are illustrated in a trilogy of Supreme Court of Canada cases dealing with electronic surveillance: *R. v. Duarte*, *R. v. Wong*, and *R. v. Wise*. *Duarte* concerned the constitutionality of participant surveillance whereby one party consents to the surreptitious recording of a conversation. The argument put to the Court was that when an individual chooses to divulge a confidence to another, there is always the risk that that person will betray the confidence. Surveillance, where one participant consents, does not alter this risk of disclosure. La Forest J., writing for the majority, disagreed, arguing that the risk that someone may divulge our confidence and the risk that the state may electronically record and transmit that confidence are 'of a different order.'

However, La Forest J. had two different rationales for why this risk is 'of a different order.' One is that what is wrong is the *surreptitious* nature of the surveillance and the fact that it alters our reasonable assessment of the situation. An individual, when having a private conversation, expects that 'his or her words would only be heard by the persons he or she [is] addressing.' The fact that the person an individual talks to may divulge the confidence does not alter the expectation that at the time of the conversation there was no third party present.

A different way to assess why the risk of electronic surveillance is 'of a different order' is not to look at the reasonable assessment an individual makes according to the conventional understanding of a situation but to an independent justification for privacy. This approach is also present in La Forest J.'s reasons, for he argued that we 'need to strike a fair balance between the right of the state to intrude on the private lives of its citizens and the right of those citizens to be left alone.' This rationale does not depend on conventional expectations, but the norms of a free and democratic society, norms that dictate a certain amount of privacy. 'Reasonable' therefore takes its content from 'free and democratic society.'

In *R. v. Wong*, the Court endorsed this latter approach. At issue in *Wong* was the video surveillance of a hotel room gambling operation. La Forest J., writing for the majority, argued that 'there is an important difference between the risk that our activities may be observed by other persons, and the risk that agents of the state, in the absence of prior authorization, will permanently record those activities on videotape.' This difference is not simply the difference between the presence of an officer in the room and the presence of a video camera, a difference that is captured by a concern about the surreptitious nature of the surveillance. Indeed, La Forest J. invoked George Orwell's *1984*, which 'paints a grim picture of a society whose citizens *had every reason to expect* that their every movement was subject to electronic video surveillance.' The question therefore is not whether it is likely true that an individual is under observation of some kind, but whether a particular kind of surveillance is consistent with the values of a free and democratic society. As La Forest J. argued, the 'adoption of this standard invites the courts to assess whether giving their sanction to the particular form of unauthorized surveillance in question would see the amount of privacy and freedom remaining to citizens diminished to a compass inconsistent with the aims of a free and open society.'

Unfortunately, *Duarte* and *Wong* represent the high water mark for interpreting a reasonable expectation of privacy in light of the values of a free and democratic society rather than according to a description of social conventions regarding privacy. For example, in *Wise*, decided just two years after *Duarte* and *Wong*, the Court retreated from this normative approach. The case dealt with the use of an electronic tracking device in a car. Writing for the majority, Cory J. held that an individual has a reduced privacy interest in his or her car. He argued that '[s]ociety ... requires and expects protection from drunken drivers, speeding drivers and dangerous drivers. A reasonable level of surveillance of each and every motor vehicle is readily accepted, indeed demanded, by society to obtain this protection.' Not only do we expect surveillance of our cars, but we *accept* this surveillance and because of this we have a lesser expectation of privacy in our cars. In dissent, La Forest J. warned that finding such a thin privacy interest would open the door for the use of surveillance at the whim of law enforcement agents with no requirement of prior authorization.

The concern about an approach like that endorsed in *Wise* is that in the face of known widespread surveillance, the response to a complaint about privacy is that in such circumstances it is unreasonable to expect privacy – you should expect to be watched. The constitutional cousin of 'If you aren't doing anything wrong then what do you have to hide?' is 'What did you expect?' If we expect surveillance, then on this test it is difficult to argue that this expected surveillance nonetheless violates our privacy.

We therefore cannot properly assess the threats to our privacy brought about by the widespread expected and accepted surveillance that will be part of the post-September 11 reality unless we adopt a more normative analysis of privacy than the one that currently dominates *Charter* jurisprudence. And this raises a dilemma for anyone seeking to claim that the government's proposals are consistent with *Charter* values: they may be consistent with current *Charter* thinking but that thinking may be inadequate to deal with the challenges posed by the present context.

This dilemma is exacerbated by the kind of surveillance systems that will be put into place. These depend upon the collection and aggregation of personal information. The collection of any one piece of information may not be problematic, especially if this information is not particularly sensitive when considered in isolation. However, when this information is aggregated with other pieces of information into a fairly revealing profile you may consider your privacy violated. Who collects this, what it gets matched with and who has access to it are all important questions. And this concern that privacy will bleed away through a thousand minor, almost unnoticeable, cuts makes the constitutional dilemma even more striking. If we assess any particular proposal then the infringement of privacy to further the interest of national security may seem slight and justifiable. If we assess the proposals together, in order to understand their collective effect on privacy, and do so alongside other related proposals such as the announced changes to the *Aeronautics Act* and Canada's signing of the *Convention*, then the results do appear so benign.

The dilemma of justification therefore has many aspects: the need for an adequate constitutional test regarding privacy, the need to understand the ways in which new technologies facilitate the erosion of privacy in unprecedented ways and often through the cumulative effect of minor privacy infractions, and the need for an assessment mechanism that can take into account the collective effect of any proposed surveillance measures and not scrutinize them piecemeal. This is not a dilemma that can be resolved within the current time frame for debate regarding *Bill C-36*.

In conclusion, while a diminishment in privacy protection when state security is at stake is consistent with the values of a free an democratic society, this does not mean that the government is at liberty to completely undermine privacy rights. Because of this, I argue that the proposed amendments to the *Privacy Act*, *PIPEDA*, and the *Access to Information Act* violate *Charter* values. The question then is whether the remaining provisions strike a balance that is consistent with *Charter* values. What I have called the dilemma of justification indicates that it very difficult to answer this question. However, I think that this dilemma highlights the need for two things. First, the government must at least meet its burden of justifying that these measures will be effective in meeting their objectives and, indeed, more effective than our existing regime. Second, if the government meets this burden then it must nonetheless include a sunset-clause in the proposed legislation to ensure that it is a temporary measure that only becomes a part of our permanent legal landscape after due reflection and debate.

Notes

1 I would like to thank Kevin Davis, David Dyzenhaus, Kent Roach, Joe Murray, Martha Shaffer and Hamish Stewart for their helpful comments on earlier drafts of this paper. Above all, I would like to thank Karen Park for the superb research assistance she provided me with in the course of writing this paper.

2 'Database May Screen More Travelers' *Tech Live* (04 October 2001), online:

TechTV <http://www.techtv.com/news/culture/story/0,24195,3351689,00.html> (date last accessed: 07 November 2001)

3 J. Hilkevitch & R. Worthington, *Chicago Tribune* 'Task Forces Urge Arming Crews, Protecting Pilots' (03 October 3 2001), online: Chicago Tribune <http://chicagotribune.com/news/nationworld/chi-0110030484oct03.story?coll=chi-newsnationworld-hed> (date last accessed: 07 November 2001)

4 C. Clark, 'Privacy Restrictions in Air Travel To Be Eased' *The Globe and Mail* (03 November 2001) A8

5 D. Boyer, 'New Law Contains ID-Card Proposal' *The Washington Times* (01 November 2001), online: http://www.washingtontimes.com/national/20011031-576161.htm (date last accessed: 07 November 2001)

6 See *R. v. Monney*, [1999] 1 S.C.R. 652 and *R. v. Simmons*, [1988] 2 S.C.R. 495

7 See, for e.g., *R. v. O'Connor*, [1995] 4 S.C.R. 411, at paras. 110-119, per L'Heureux-Dubé J. The other members of the Court indicated that they were in general agreement with her analysis of privacy. See also *R. v. Beare*, [1988] 2 S.C.R. 387 at p. 412 and *B. (R.) v. Children's Aid Society of Metropolitan Toronto*, [1995] 1 S.C.R. 315, at p. 369, per La Forest J.

8 *R.. v. Dyment*, [1988] 2 S.C.R. 417 at p. 427, per La Forest J. This was cited with approval by McLachlin and Iacobucci JJ. in *R. v. Mills*, [1999] 3 S.C.R. 668 at para. 79

9 Bill C-36, *An Act to amend the Criminal Code, the Official Secrets Act, the Canada Evidence Act, the Proceeds of Crime (Money Laundering) Act and other Acts, and to enact measures respecting the registration of charities, in order to combat terrorism*, 1st Sess., 37th Parl., 2001 (1st reading 15 October 2001) [hereinafter *Bill C-36*]

10 *Bill C-36* s. 6, amending s. 185(1.1)(a) of the *Criminal Code*. Note that *Bill C-36* has a drafting error and should also amend s. 186(1)(b) of the *Criminal Code*

11 R.S.C. 1985, c. N-5

12 *Bill C-36*, s. 102

13 The proposed amendments require that the Minister of National Defence must be satisfied that 'satisfactory measures are in place to protect the privacy of Canadians' before he or she issues an authorization to intercept private communications. It is not clear what 'satisfactory' means. Moreover, while the Commissioner of the Communications Security Establishment has the power to review activities carried out under a particular authorization, he or she does not appear to have the power to review the authorization itself.

14 *Ibid.*, Part 4

15 Government of Canada, News Release, 'Government of Canada Introduces Anti-terrorism Act' (15 October 2001), online: Government of Canada < http://www.sgc.gc.ca/Releases/e20011015.htm> (date last accessed: 07 November 2001); Council of Europe, *Draft Convention on Cybercrime*, online: Council of Europe <http://conventions.coe.int/Treaty/EN/cadreprojets.htm> (date last accessed 07 November 2001) [hereinafter *Convention*]. On September 19, 2001, the Council of Europe's Ministers' Deputies approved the final draft of the *Convention* and will

be presenting it to the Committee of Ministers for formal adoption, which is expected to take place on November 8.

16 There is wide acceptance of some of these offences, such as illegal access. Other offences that are more contentious include offences relating to child pornography and copyright violations.

17 D. Banisar, G. Hosein, B. Steinhardt & D. Sobel, 'Comments of the American Civil Liberties Union, the Electronic Privacy Information Center and Privacy International on Draft 27 of the Proposed CoE Convention on Cybercrime' (07 June 2001), online: Privacy International <http://www.privacyinternational.org/issues/cybercrime/coe/ngo_letter_601.htm> (date last accessed: 07 November 2001); 'Global Internet Liberty Campaign Member Letter on Council of Europe Convnetion on Cyber-Crime Version 24.2' (12 December 2000), online: GILC <http://www.gilc.org/privacy/coe-letter-1200.html> (date last accessed: 07 November 2001).

18 *Convention, supra* note , Art. 15

19 *Ibid.*, Art. 1

20 *Ibid.*, Arts. 20-21

21 Created by the Federal Bureau of Investigation (FBI), Carnivore is a powerful network diagnostic tool that operates much like commercially available 'sniffers.' When the FBI installs Carnivore on an ISP server, it 'snoops' (i.e. monitors and examines without altering) the data flowing through the server and saves the portions that conform to a previously-specified profile, like email sent or received by a particular user under investigation. The saved portions can then analyzed further by investigators. See 'Carnivore Diagnostic Tool,' online: FBI <www.fbi.gov/hq/lab/carnivore/carnivore2.htm> (date last accessed: 07 November 2001)

22 *Convention, supra* note , Arts. 16 and 17.

23 Statewatch, 'Data Surveillance Introduced in UK and USA,' online: Statewatch <www.statewatch.org/news/2001/sep/11retorder.htm> (date last accessed: 07 November 2001). Although this request came in the form of an open letter and not legislative action thereby lacking the force of law, it nonetheless signalled a state-level movement toward increased data retention

24 Statewatch, 'EU Governments to Decide on Retention of Telecommunications Data (Including Internet Usage) by Law Enforcement Agencies,' online: Statewatch <www.statewatch.org/news/2001/jun/07retention.htm> (date last accessed: 07 November 2001). The Guardian has recently reported that access to this information will not be restricted to investigations of terrorist activity. Stuart Millar, 'Police get sweeping access to net data; Blunkett will not limit scope of measure to terrorist cases' *The Guardian (UK)*, (07 November 2001)

25 The national DNA data bank officially opened on June 30, 2000. See Solicitor General Canada, News Release, 'National DNA Data Bank Already Linking Crime Scenes and Offenders, Says Federal Solicitor General Lawrence Macaulay' (02 February 2001), online: Solicitor General Canada <http://www.sgc.gc.ca/releases/e20010202.htm> (date last accessed: 07 November 2001).

26 *DNA Identification Act*, S.C. 1998, c. 37, ss. 9-9.1.

27 *Criminal Code*, R.S.C. 1985, c. C-46, s. 487.051.

28 Department of Justice Canada, News Release, 'Highlights of Bill C-3: A National DNA Data Bank,' online: Department of Justice Canada <http:// canada.justice.gc.ca/en/news/nr/1998/highligh.html> (last modified: 05 January 1998)

29 Section 103 of *Bill C-36* amends the *Personal Information Protection and Electronic Documents Act*, S.C. 2000, c.5 [hereinafter *PIPEDA*]; section 87 of *Bill C-36* amends the *Access to Information Act*, R.S. 1985, c. A-1. The proposed amendments to the *Canada Evidence Act* raise similar concerns. See Hamish Stewart's analysis in this volume.

30 *Privacy Act*, R.S. 1985, c. P-21, s. 2

31 *Ibid.*, s.45

32 *Ibid.*, s.51

33 For similar criticisms, see the Canadian Bar Association *Submission on Bill C-36, Anti-terrorism Act*, October 2001, Available at http://www.cba.org. and G. Radwanski 'Testimony Regarding bill c-36, the *Anti-Terrorism Act*, to the House of commons Standing Committee on Justice and Human Rights' (23 October 2001), online: Privacy Commissioner of Canada <http://www.privcom.gc.ca/speech/ 02_of_a_01124_e.asp> (date last accessed: 07 November 2001).

34 *Hunter v. Southam*, [1984] 2 S.C.R. 145.

35 *Ibid.*, at 159–60. Generally this assessment must be made prior to a search or seizure in order to prevent unjustified searches.

36 *Ibid.*, at 167.

37 They might violate s.7. See *supra* note 7 and accompanying text.

38 For a more sustained discussion about privacy and the challenges posed to it by new technologies, see Lisa Austin, 'Privacy and the Question of Technology' (University of Toronto, 2001) [unpublished].

39 *R. v. Duarte*, [1990] 1 S.C.R. 30; *R. v. Wong*, [1990] 3 S.C.R. 36; *R. v. Wise*, [1992] 1 S.C.R. 527.

40 S. 178.11(2)(a) of the *Criminal Code* excepted the interception of conversations to which one of the parties consents from the prohibition of unauthorized electronic surveillance. This was challenged as violating s. 8 of the *Charter*.

41 *R. v. Duarte*, *supra* note 39 at 44.

42 *Ibid.*, at 47.

43 *ibid.*, at 49.

44 *R. v. Wong*, *supra* note 39 at 48.

45 *Ibid.* at 47 [emphasis added].

46 *Ibid.* at 46.

47 Compare *Duarte*, *supra* note 39, for example, with *R. v. Edwards*, [1996] 1 S.C.R. 128 and *R. v. Belnavis*, [1997] 3 S.C.R. 341. But the recent case of *R. v. Mills*, [1999] 3 S.C.R. 668 might be signalling a return towards a normative account of privacy by listing the values protected by privacy. It remains to be seen whether this will inform the content of 'reasonable expectation of privacy.'

48 *R.* v. *Wise, supra* note 39 at para. 6. Cory J. makes a very similar argument in the context of school searches in the more recent case *R.* v. *M.R.M.*, [1998] 3 S.C.R. 393.
49 *Ibid.* at para 73.

Police Powers in Bill C-36

MARTIN L. FRIEDLAND*
Faculty of Law
University of Toronto

There are a series of interrelated questions one must ask before it is possible properly to evaluate whether the police powers in Bill C-36[1] are desirable.

What is the threat posed by terrorism? What are the new powers given to the police? How are the offences that are the subject of these powers defined? Who exercises the new powers? And finally, who reviews the exercise of the powers?

What is the threat posed by terrorism?

The threat is clearly a serious one. The threat was well known to the Canadian government long before the tragic events of September 11th. Report after report produced by the Canadian Security Intelligence Service (CSIS) detailed the concern over terrorist attacks.[2] There was, for example, a public report in May 2000 on 'International Terrorism: the Threat to Canada,'[3] and another in December 1999 on 'Chemical, Biological, Radiological and Nuclear Terrorism,'[4] as well as one the same month on 'Trends in Terrorism.'[5] There were, of course, other reports and studies that were not made public.

In one unclassified CSIS paper from 1995, an internationally-recognized authority on terrorism, Paul Wilkinson, stated in his paper, 'Terrorism: Motivations and Causes': 'In view of the fact that attacks by terrorist groups have become increasingly lethal over recent years, it is wise to plan for a continuing trend towards massive car and truck bombings in crowded city areas, and "spectacular" terrorist attacks ... designed to capture maximum attention from the mass media, to cause maximum shock and outrage.'[6] I will leave it to others to analyze the continuing concern over terrorism. The threat is not likely to disappear quickly.

What are the new powers given to the police and others?

I will be examining four new powers in the bill: changes to the wiretapping laws; the recognition and enlargement of the surveillance powers of the highly secret Communications Security Establishment (CSE); the formation of a new power called 'investigative hearings'; and the creation of what has been euphemistically labelled in the Act as 'recognizance with conditions.' In addition, I will say something about undercover agents, who are not mentioned in the bill and yet are an important potential source of information on threats to the security of Canada.

How are the offences that are the subject of the investigation defined?

As others have and will observe at this conference, this is a crucial question. It is particularly important to get the definition of 'terrorist activity'[7] right. It is now too broad. Clause (E), which refers to causing 'serious interference with or serious disruption of an essential service, facility or system,' should be dropped. What can it refer to except an electronic system? Other threats – such as poisoning the water supply or blowing up a bridge – can be handled under the earlier sub clauses. Why not do what the UK terrorism legislation does and just include the clause: 'is designed seriously to interfere with or seriously to disrupt an electronic system?'[8] If there is another 'essential service, facility or system' that is not covered in (A) to (D) then it can be specifically added. An alternative – and perhaps preferable – way of drafting the provision is to add 'or seriously interferes with or seriously disrupts an electronic system' after the words 'substantial property damage' in clause (D). This would ensure that the disruption would only be caught by the section if it was 'likely to result in the conduct or harm' referred to in the previous sections.

Who exercises the new powers?

In my view the major fault with the bill is that the new powers are given to every police force in Canada, including the RCMP. The use of these powers should be subject to the control of CSIS, with all the review and supervision built into the CSIS Act.[9] Let me provide some background to this statement.

Prior to 1984, it was the RCMP that handled threats to the security of Canada. The McDonald Commission on the RCMP that reported in 1981 criticized the excessive zeal of RCMP activities.[10] The commission was set up because it had been revealed, for example, that in Quebec in the early 1970s the Mounties had, without a warrant, entered and removed documents from the premises of a press agency; had similarly removed from private premises computer tapes containing membership lists of the Parti Québecois; had issued a fake communiqué urging FLQ extremists to continue on a course of revolutionary action; had burned down a barn to prevent a meeting taking place; and had engaged in many more questionable activities.[11]

The McDonald Commission recommended that national security matters be taken over by a civilian agency. A similar recommendation had been made in 1969 by an earlier committee, the Mackenzie Committee.[12] The recommendations were adopted by the government after a thorough examination of the bill setting up CSIS by the Senate's Pitfield Committee.[13] The Canadian Security Intelligence Service Act was brought into force in 1984.

A similar tightening of control occurred about the same time in the United States – after President Nixon tried to use national security to justify the Watergate break-in, and after it was revealed by the Church Commission[14] that the FBI was targeting such groups as labour unions, universities, and civil rights organizations. Martin Luther King, Jr., for example, was one of the FBI's targets.

Terrorism was and is part of the CSIS mandate. Although not specifically called terrorism in the act, it is covered under sub clause C of the definition of threats to the security of Canada in the CSIS Act: 'activities ... directed toward or in support of the threat or use of acts of serious violence against persons or property for the purpose of achieving a political objective within Canada or a foreign state.' This is to be amended by Bill C-36 by adding 'religious or ideological objectives' so that it will read, 'a political, religious or ideological objective.'[15] There are over 2,000 employees in CSIS[16] with a budget in the year 2000 of about $200 million.[17] An increasing amount of attention and resources has been devoted to terrorism.[18] The CSIS 2000 Public Report lists 'public safety from the effects of terrorism' at the top of its list of intelligence interests.[19]

A number of important safeguards were put into place, the most important being the Security Intelligence Review Committee that reviews the operations of CSIS.[20] SIRC is composed of five privy councillors who produce impressive public annual reports and a large number of primarily classified reports and studies.[21] The chair of the committee is Paule Gauthier, a former president of the Canadian Bar Association, and the members include former premiers Bob Rae and Frank McKenna.[22] SIRC, for example, carefully examines the warrant procedures and a sample of warrants that have been used by CSIS.[23]'This kind of review,' stated CSIS director Ward Elcock in his recent appearance before the Special Senate Committee, 'makes for a very disciplined organization. That is a good thing in this kind of business ... SIRC and CSIS were not meant to be close friends. We are mutually respectful professionals, but the relationship is not always friendly.' Elcock then observed that, 'By far and away the most rigorous review process in the world is in Canada.'[24]

The powers given to the police under Bill C-36 are not subject to the review of SIRC. They are subject to the supervision of the attorney general of the province, if the powers are exercised by a municipal or provincial force.[25] Arresting a person on suspicion of terrorism – to give only one example – may seem like a good idea to a municipal force and even to an attorney general, but it may interfere with CSIS' surveillance of that person. Similarly, it would be like a farcical old movie to have an application for a provincial wiretap when there is already one in place through an authorization by the Federal Court of Canada. In most cases, no doubt, there will be consultation between the provincial attorney general and CSIS, but there is no assurance of that. The federal government can by fiat under the Security Offences Act take over prosecutions,[26] but this has only happened on one occasion.[27]

Surely, the exercise of special powers relating to terrorism should require the consent of CSIS. Indeed, I would go further and not place these special powers in the Criminal Code but rather put them in the CSIS Act. The offences, however, should remain in the Criminal Code. CSIS would, of course, work with the RCMP and other police forces in exercising these powers, but at least the control would be centralized and would be subject to review by SIRC. Moreover, by taking the powers out of the Criminal Code there is less danger – as Kent Roach warns in his paper – that the powers will become an established part of the criminal law.[28]

Bill C-36 gives too much emphasis to prosecution and punishment. We are not going to feel or be much safer if half a dozen terrorists are prosecuted and punished after terrorist attacks. Our emphasis should be on discovering and thwarting terrorist activities before they occur. It is obviously far better to prevent destructive action before it occurs than it is to prosecute and punish persons afterwards.

The report of the Pitfield Committee in 1983 put the difference well when it stated: 'Law enforcement is essentially reactive. While there is an element of information-gathering and prevention in law enforcement, on the whole it takes place after the commission of a distinct criminal offence. The protection of security relies less on reaction to events; it seeks advance warning of security threats, and is not necessarily concerned with breaches of the law.'[29]

The proposed bill reverses much of what was accomplished in the 1980s, that is, controlling excess zeal by the police in the area of national security.

It could be argued that the Canadian bill follows the approach in the United States and the UK in giving these wider powers to police officers. But there are important differences between Canada and the other two countries. In the United States, domestic security is handled by the FBI. (The CIA handles foreign threats and the FBI domestic threats to the security of the United States.) The FBI therefore handles the terrorism matters that in Canada are within the responsibility of CSIS. The special powers given to the police in the proposed US legislation on terrorism are given to the FBI, not to every peace officer in the United States.[30] The UK agency comparable to CSIS is MI5. It works very closely with the 'Special Branch' of the Metropolitan Police (Scotland Yard). Although the UK legislation gives wide powers under its recent terrorism legislation to peace officers, policing in the UK is much more centralized and controlled than in Canada. The Home Office has overall responsibility for policing. So, to apply the UK or US legislation to Canada and to give every municipal or provincial police force these special powers goes much further than is desirable.

CSIS may not now have the resources needed to handle the present crisis. The most recent report by CSIS shows that the number of employees went down to about 2,000 persons from over 2,700 in the early 1990s.[31] More funds are to be given to CSIS, but it takes time to build up the necessary personnel. Giving the powers exclusively to CSIS now may not be practical. The proposed review of the Act[32] should determine whether the special powers should be included in the CSIS Act, where I believe they belong, or be kept in the Criminal Code, or not be renewed.

In the meantime, the use of the special powers should, by legislation, require the consent of CSIS and should be subject to review by the Security Intelligence Review Committee.

Who reviews the exercise of the powers?

It is clear from what I have said above that I would like SIRC to be the principal body to review the exercise of the powers. The recent interim report of the Senate Committee on Bill C-36 recommended the appointment of an 'Officer of Parliament to monitor, as appropriate, the exercise of powers provided in the bill.' The officer would table a report annually, or more frequently, as appropriate, in both Houses.[33] It is not clear, however, why the committee did not recommend that SIRC perform this function.

Another safeguard that should be introduced is to ensure that the Federal Court of Canada has the exclusive jurisdiction to grant wiretapping warrants based on the new terrorism legislation. The Federal Court now handles warrants under the CSIS Act[34] and has built up expertise in the national security area. Moreover, as in the United States,[35] there can be the assurance of a greater degree of secrecy and consistency than if every superior court judge in Canada could grant a warrant.

Let us turn to an analysis of the specific powers.

Wiretapping

Bill C-36 introduces three specific and reasonable changes in the law relating to wiretapping. They are already in the Criminal Code for offences involving criminal organizations.[36] If they are warranted for such offences, they are even more acceptable for terrorism offences – on a permanent basis.

Eliminating the requirement of a finding that 'other investigative procedures have been tried and have failed' or are 'unlikely to succeed' in Bill C-36[37] means that such a factor will no longer be necessary for terrorism offences, just as it is not now necessary for criminal organization offences.[38] The requirement should not have been in the CSIS Act to start with. One would have thought that where there is a serious threat to national security, wiretapping with a judicial authorization should be at or near the top of the list of techniques that could be used.

Another change is to provide for wiretaps with judicial approval for up to a year for terrorist offences, rather than the normal 60–day limit.

Again, this is sensible and is in line with the extended period with respect to participation in a criminal organization.[39] Similarly, it makes sense to allow the judge to extend the period before notice of wiretapping has to be given to up to three years. Again, this is in line with the provision with respect to criminal organizations.[40]

I see no need for a sunset clause for these particular changes. My preference, however, is for the Solicitor General of Canada and the Federal Court of Canada to have exclusive jurisdiction over these extended powers and for them to be in the CSIS Act. Strangely, the CSIS Act was not changed by Bill C-36 to incorporate the provision that no longer would require that 'other investigative procedures have been tried and have failed.' This, therefore, is still a requirement if a wiretap is done under the CSIS Act.[41] The other two changes are already covered in the CSIS Act.

Another change which should be considered is to introduce legislation similar to the UK's Regulation of Investigatory Powers Act 2000 which provides procedures for obtaining keys for encrypted communications.[42]

The Communications Security Establishment

It is good to have the existence of the Communications Security Establishment (CSE) spelled out in legislation.[43] The CSE, which 'provides the Government of Canada with foreign signals intelligence ... which it obtains by gathering and analyzing foreign radio, radar and other electronic emissions,'[44] is a very large establishment, employing about 1,000 persons.[45] At the present time, the Criminal Code prevents the CSE from collecting communications that originate or terminate in Canada.[46] Under C-36, the Minister of National Defence will be able to authorize interceptions involving persons in Canada 'if the interception will be directed at foreign entities located outside Canada.'[47] Formerly, such interceptions were not permitted.

The review of the agency is now done by a retired or supernumerary judge, not by SIRC.[48] Would it not be better to have SIRC review the work of the CSE? How can SIRC effectively do its job unless it knows what the CSE is doing? Note that the UK Intelligence Services Act 1994, which officially recognizes the formerly secret Government Communications Headquarters (GCHQ), a comparable body to the CSE, gives supervisory powers to a judge who holds or has held high judicial office.[49] But the UK Act also gives a group of parliamentarians drawn from the Commons and the Lords the power to examine the expenditure, administration, and policy of the GCHQ, as well as the Security Service and the Intelligence Service.[50]

The extension of CSE's activities to persons in Canada – even though the communication is to or from abroad – is a troubling aspect of the bill. The information can be passed on to law enforcement agencies. In the recent American legislation, the USA PATRIOT Act, it is only the wiretapping provisions – and only some of them – that are subject to a sunset clause.[51] Why is the Federal Court of Canada not approving electronic surveillance involving persons in Canada?[52] The court could use the same standard for getting a warrant as is now provided in the CSIS Act. I do not, of course, know the technicalities of how the CSE presently identifies the place that a telephone, radio, or internet signal originates or ends up. I presume that they may discover this while they are recording something. They should be permitted to preserve the material, with the Minister of National Defence's approval, until an application can be made to the Federal Court. If the Federal Court of Canada does not presently have the capacity to deal with these matters, then the proposed extension giving the power of approval to the minister should be limited to a fixed period until the necessary additional resources are given to the Federal Court.

Investigative Hearings

There is nothing exactly comparable to the proposed section 83.28 in the Criminal Code. An investigative hearing allows a person to be ordered to appear before a judge to give evidence[53] – and arrested with a warrant if he or she fails to appear.[54] The judge has to be satisfied that there are 'reasonable grounds to believe' that a terrorism offence has been committed or will be committed and that the person summoned has 'information that may reveal the whereabouts' of the perpetrator or of a person who 'may commit a terrorism offence,' as the case may be.[55] Failure to comply will result in committal to jail for contempt of court. So the section covers cases where the offence has been committed as well as cases where the terrorism act may be committed.

There are many cases where persons are compelled to give evidence under oath. This occurs under various inquiries, fire marshals, and securities Acts.[56] Compelling testimony happens, of course, under the Criminal Code. Persons who have knowledge of an offence can be called at a preliminary hearing and if they refuse to answer can be jailed for successive eight day periods.[57] Persons who are subpoenaed for a trial and refuse to give evidence can be held in contempt of court. The investigative hearing is different in two respects. It will apply to an offence that has been committed but before proceedings have been commenced and it applies to offences that have not yet been committed.

Under Canadian law, proceedings have not commenced until the accused appears before the court. We do not permit trials in absentia. Nor does Canadian law permit a person to be held in custody as a material witness before a charge has been laid, as has been happening in the United States.[58] The Canadian Criminal Code permits a person who 'is likely to give material evidence' to be arrested if the person fails to obey a subpoena, but proceedings first have to be commenced against some one by bringing that person before the court.[59] In many of the terrorism cases, the perpetrator of an offence cannot be found and so no proceedings have been commenced.

The provision also applies before an offence has been committed. Again, there is nothing like this in the Criminal Code. But there are sections that make it an offence to fail to disclose information to the police. The prime example is treason. Under the law of treason a person commits an offence who 'knowing that a person is about to commit high treason or treason does not, with all reasonable dispatch, inform a justice of the peace or other peace officer thereof or make other reasonable efforts to prevent that person from committing high treason or treason.'[60] The penalty is up to fourteen years imprisonment.

Terrorism, like treason, is a threat to the security of the state. Another provision relating to a duty to tell the authorities found in the Criminal Code is section 418(2). It makes it an offence for a person in a corporation that commits fraud by 'selling defective stores' to the government not to 'inform the responsible government, or a department thereof' if the person 'knows or has reason to suspect that the fraud is being committed or has been or is about to be committed.'[61]

The investigative hearing procedure is therefore far less invasive than provisions that create criminal penalties. The UK Terrorist Act 2000, for example, makes it an offence, in certain circumstances, to fail to disclose information if the person 'believes or suspects that another person has committed' certain offences.[62] Investigative hearings are therefore not necessary in the UK. The person can be arrested and questioned for failure to disclose information. I am not suggesting that Canada take this route. I am arguing, however, that the investigative hearing is far less coercive than making it an offence to fail to disclose information. Moreover, it is far preferable than the US material witness route where witnesses are being held in custody for lengthy periods of time.

There is, of course, a danger that the hearing will be used against a prime suspect. The witness is, however, given the right to counsel 'at any stage of the proceedings.'[63] If the proceedings are being used to compel testimony from a prime suspect, then the proceedings can be challenged under the existing law.[64] Moreover, the statements and any evidence derived from the evidence obtained cannot be used against the person in subsequent proceedings, except perjury or giving contradictory evidence.[65]

So I do not find the procedure particularly troubling. I do wonder, however, what the provision will actually accomplish. Is it worth including in the bill? If the person has relevant information, he or she will have an incentive to co-operate with the police to avoid the possibility of being charged with a substantive offence, and as we will hear tomorrow when discussing the substantive offences, there are many offences and many different ways of committing them. These range from conspiracy and attempts,[66] through facilitating[67] and aiding and abetting, to harbouring or concealing.[68] In addition, there are offences for failure to disclose information.[69]

In any event, as with other special police powers in C-36, the exercise of this power, which can be subject to abuse, should require the consent of the federal authorities.

Recognizance with conditions

This provision (83.3) will, I understand, be discussed in detail by Gary Trotter in one of the sessions tomorrow. The provision has three aspects. One is requiring the person to enter into a recognizance with conditions[70] – more or less a peace bond. Another is to allow the police to arrest the person without a warrant on the basis of 'reasonable suspicion' that he or she will commit a terrorist offence – rather than on the basis of 'reasonable belief.'[71] Thirdly, the person can be held beyond the 24-hour maximum period normally allowed under the Criminal Code.[72]

The peace bond provision requirement is not very different from other cases in the Criminal Code requiring a peace bond 'to keep the peace and be of good behaviour.'[73] A peace bond can now be required where a person has reasonable grounds for his or her fears that injury or damage will be caused, or a sexual assault or serious personal injury offence or criminal organization offence will be committed. Whatever one may think of these provisions, which permit the judge to impose conditions for a 12–month period if there are 'reasonable grounds' for the fear of the named harm, it is not a great stretch to carry the technique over to fear of a terrorist offence. The recognizance under the proposed 83.3 of Bill C-36 is similar to those under section 810 of the Criminal Code. It can be for up to 12 months, firearms can be prohibited, and the person can be committed to prison for up to twelve months for refusing to enter into the recognizance.

The other two aspects of the section are more difficult.

A person can be arrested if the peace officer 'suspects on reasonable grounds that the detention of the person in custody is necessary in order to prevent the commission of an indictable offence, where the act or omission constituting the offence also constitutes a terrorist activity.'[74] This is arrest on reasonable suspicion, not on reasonable belief. Is this acceptable? The Criminal Code at present allows a person to be arrested on the basis that the person is 'about to commit' an indictable offence.[75] It is not clear what is meant by 'about to commit,' but it must be earlier in the range of preparatory offences than an attempt, otherwise the words 'about to commit' would be unnecessary. But it would still require a 'reasonable belief.' The present Canadian Official Secrets Act,[76] however, permits arrest on reasonable suspicion in certain cases. Section 10 of the Act provides: 'Every person who is found committing an offence under this Act, or who is reasonably suspected of having committed, having attempted to commit or being about to commit an offence under this Act, may be arrested without a warrant and detained by any constable or police officer.' Such a provision has been in the Official Secrets Act since it was first enacted in the UK in 1911.[77] The UK Terrorism Act also permits the police to arrest on reasonable suspicion.[78]

The Supreme Court of Canada has indicated that in matters involving national security a lower burden may be acceptable under the Charter.[79] The Supreme Court of the United States has taken the same position.[80] Is a lower standard of proof acceptable to arrest a person who is suspected of being about to commit a terrorist offence? That depends on the threat. My own view is that it is clearly acceptable for terrorist offences under a restricted definition of terrorism.

Further, the extension beyond 24 hours is not out of line with the Terrorism Act in the UK, passed in 2000, which allows detention in certain circumstances of up to 7 days.[81] The UK legislation goes further than Bill C-36 in another respect, that is, permitting stops and searches[82] and entering premises[83] on reasonable suspicion. It also gives the military the power to arrest without a warrant on suspicion of terrorism and the right to detain the person for up to four hours.[84] In many respects, therefore, the UK legislation is much wider than Bill C-36.

As with the other sections dealing with special police powers, I would require the consent of CSIS before the application is made to request detention beyond the normal 24 hours.

Undercover Agents

Bill C-36 does not deal with undercover agents. They are important in national security matters to find out what terrorist groups are planning. As the McDonald Commission stated: 'The use of undercover operatives is at once one of the R.C.M.P.'s most effective investigative techniques ... An undercover operative can gather more important information than any technical or mechanical source.'[85] Both in the United States and Canada serious limitations were placed on their effectiveness. The McDonald Commission took the position that undercover agents could never break the law – even provincial driving laws. Persons would not last long as undercover agents, however, if they refused to go through stop signs or insisted upon using their right names and occupations on their personal documents. Moreover, illegal organizations often test the bona fides of their members by making them engage in illegal activity. The McDonald Commission argued that the security service should lobby for legislative changes.[86]

The government did not at first accept the view of the McDonald Commission. The original draft of the CSIS bill in 1983 would have given undercover operatives some leeway to engage in illegal conduct. The bill provided that a CSIS employee would be 'justified in taking such reasonable actions as are reasonably necessary to enable them to perform the duties and functions of the Service under this Act.'[87] The Senate's Pitfield Committee held hearings on the bill and concluded that the proposed provision was too broad, and recommended that agents have 'the same protection under the law as peace officers have in performing their duties and functions as peace officers.[88] This was accepted by the government and is still the law.[89] It was hoped that the courts would develop guidelines on how far the police could go.

Canadian courts, unlike the American courts,[90] have, however, refused to allow peace officers to break the law. They have not recognized any possible justification for such actions and instead, have tossed the issue back to the legislature by demanding specific legislation. The Ontario Court of Appeal held, for example, in a 1989 case (*Regina* v. *Brennan*)[91] that a police officer could not go through a stop sign without specific legislative authorization. And in 1999 the Supreme Court of Canada held (*Regina* v. *Shirose*)[92] that an undercover police officer could not offer to sell drugs to a dealer in a so-called reverse sting operation, although undercover officers could buy drugs because specific legislation allowed such purchases. The Security Intelligence Review Committee (SIRC) noted in its 1999–2000 annual report that 'none of the human sources' used by CSIS 'engaged in illegal ... activities.'[93]

A bill that passed through the House of Commons last June dealing with organized crime and law enforcement (Bill C-24) and that is now before the Senate, permits a measure of lawbreaking by peace officers who are undercover operatives in dealing with those offences. The bill is, apparently, not designed to cover CSIS officers, who, in any event, are not 'peace officers.' There are a number of safeguards in the legislation, such as requiring the personal consent of the Solicitor General of Canada, in the case of the RCMP, and there are some actions, such as causing 'death or bodily harm,' which can never be justified.[94] Similar legislation should be considered for the equally if not more important area of national security and terrorism.

Conclusion

This review of special police powers has argued that some additional police powers should be added, such as the power to deal with encryption and to make undercover operatives more effective by permitting some illegality. Other powers, such as investigative hearings, are probably unnecessary. Still others, such as wiretapping and arrest on suspicion, are justified to deal with the very serious problem of terrorism. In all these cases, however, the definition of terrorism should be more limited, the consent of CSIS or the Solicitor General of Canada should be required, and the Security Intelligence Review Committee should play a greater role in reviewing any actions taken.

Notes

* University Professor and Professor of Law Emeritus, University of Toronto. Some of the material in this paper is drawn from a talk given at a Constitutional Round-table at the Faculty of Law on October 3, 2001 as well as from a memo on Bill C-36 dated October 26, 2001 that I prepared after the introduction of Bill C-36 at

the request of Richard Mosley, assistant deputy minister, Department of Justice, Ottawa. I am grateful to Jeremy Millard, now in his third year in the faculty of law, for his research assistance. I would also like to thank Kent Roach, Colin Grey, and Katrina Wyman for their comments on an earlier draft of this paper.

1 Bill C-36, given first reading by the House of Commons, October 15, 2001. The bill is at present being studied by a Commons committee and has been given a pre-study by a Special Senate committee. See the Special Senate Committee's First Report, November 1, 2001.

2 See the CSIS website www.csis-scrs.gc.ca.

3 Report # 2000/04, 'International Terrorism: the Threat to Canada,' May 3, 2000.

4 Report # 2000/02, 'Chemical, Biological, Radiological and Nuclear (CBRN) Terrorism,' December 18, 1999.

5 Report # 2000/01, 'Trends in Terrorism,' December 18, 1999.

6 Paul Wilkinson, 'Terrorism: Motivations and Causes,' January 1995, Commentary No. 53.

7 See the proposed 83.01(2) in the bill defining 'terrorist activity.'

8 Terrorism Act 2000, 2000 Chapter 11, section 1(2)(e). See generally, J.J. Rowe, 'The Terrorism Act 2000,' [2001] *Criminal Law Review* 527.

9 Canadian Security Intelligence Service Act, Chapter C-23.

10 Second Report, volumes 1 and 2, *Freedom and Security under the Law*; Third Report, *Certain R.C.M.P. Activities and the Question of Governmental Knowledge* (Ottawa: 1981). The author prepared a report for the commission, *National Security: The Legal Dimensions* (Ottawa: 1980).

11 See the document dated October, 1978, 'Freedom and Security: An Analysis of the Policy Issues before the Commission of Inquiry.' See also M.L. Friedland, 'National Security: Some Canadian Legal Perspectives' in Friedland, *A Century of Criminal Justice* (Toronto: Carswell, 1984) at 141.

12 *Report of the Royal Commission on Security* (abridged) (Ottawa: June 1969) (the Mackenzie Report).

13 Report of the Special Committee of the Senate on the Canadian Security Intelligence Service, *Delicate Balance: A Security Intelligence Service in a Democratic Society*, (Ottawa: November 1983).

14 Final Report of the US Senate Select Committee to Study Governmental Operations with respect to Intelligence Activities, set up in January 1975.

15 Bill C-34, section 89.

16 *Canadian Intelligence Service 2000 Public Report*, part VI.

17 Ibid.

18 SIRC Report 2000–2001, Statement from the Committee.

19 Ibid, part I.

20 Canadian Security Intelligence Service Act, Chapter C-23, sections 34–55. See also the CSIS Act, sections 30–33 concerning the office of the Inspector General.

21 See www.sirc-csars.gc.ca.

22 SIRC Report 2000–2001

23 See, e.g., ibid., 1(C).

24 Special Senate Committee on Bill C-36, October 22, 2001.

25 See, e.g., the proposed sections 83.28 and 83.3 of the Criminal Code.

26 Security Offences Act, Chapter S-7, section 5.

27 According to officials in the Department of Justice, Ottawa.

28 See Kent Roach, 'The Dangers of a Charter-Proof and Crime-Based Response to Terrorism.'

29 *Delicate Balance* at 6.

30 See the Foreign Intelligence Surveillance Act of 1978, 50 USC, sections 1801 et seq.

31 *Canadian Intelligence Service 2000 Public Report*, part VI.

32 Bill C-36, section 145.

33 First Report of the Special Senate Committee, November 1, 2001, B(III).

34 CSIS Act, section 21.

35 See Friedland, *National Security: The Legal Dimensions* at 90.

36 See Criminal Code, sections 185(1.1), 186(1.1), 186.1, and 196(5).

37 Bill C-36, section 6. A necessary amendment to 186 (1.1) was inadvertently left out of C-36.

38 Criminal Code, sections 184.6(1.1) and 186(1.1).

39 Ibid., section 186.1.

40 Ibid., section 196(5).

41 Canadian Security Intelligence Service Act, section 21(2)(b). In addition, section 21(5) still limits wiretapping with respect to insurrection under clause (d) of the definition of 'threats to the security of Canada' in section 2.

42 Regulation of Investigatory Powers Act 2000, 2000 Chapter 23, sections 49–51. See also the Report of the Special Senate Committee on Security and Intelligence (William Kelly, chair) January, 1999, chapter III, 'Encryption.'

43 Bill C-36, section 102, amending the National Defence Act.

44 SIRC Report 1999–2000, footnote 19.

45 Report of the Special Senate Committee on Security and Intelligence (William Kelly, chair) January 1999, chapter I. See the evidence of Arthur Eggleton, minister of national defence, to the Special Senate Committee on October 24, 2001.

46 See the evidence of the minister of national defence, Arthur Eggleton, to the Special Senate Committee on October 24, 2001.

47 See the proposed 273.65, which overrides 273.64(2), which provides that the operations 'shall not be directed at Canadians or any person in Canada.' Under 273.65(2) the Minister must be satisfied, *inter alia*, that 'the interception will be directed at foreign entities located outside Canada' and that 'satisfactory measure are in place to protect the privacy of Canadians and to ensure that private communications will only be used or retained if they are essential to international affairs, defence or security.'

48 Section 273.63 of the National Defence Act, introduced by C-36, will put the position on a statutory basis. See the evidence of Claude Bisson, the commissioner of the CSE, before the Special Senate Committee on October 22, 2001.

49 Intelligence Services Act 1994, 1994 Chapter c.13, section 8.

50 Ibid., section 10.

51 USA PATRIOT Act, section 224. See the *Washington Post*, October 25, 2001.The money-laundering provisions require a positive vote of Congress after 4 years for them to terminate – see section 303. For an analysis of the wiretapping provisions in the USA PATRIOT Act, see the American Civil Liberties website www.aclu.org/congress

52 Arthur Eggleton stated before the Special Senate Committee on October 24, 2001 that 'the judicial system has no authority in terms of collecting information internationally.' This may be true under the current legislation, but the legislation can, of course, be amended.

53 Proposed section 83.28(5).

54 Ibid., section 83.29.

55 Ibid., section 83.28(4).

56 See, e.g., in Ontario, the Public Inquiries Act, RSO 1990, c. P-41, the Fire Protection and Prevention Act, 1997, Stat. Ont. 1997, c. 4, and the Securities Act, RSO 1990, c. S-5.

57 Criminal Code, section 545.

58 See *Globe and Mail*, November 5, 2001, 'Detentions cloaked in secrecy.' For a discussion of the US law on material witnesses, see Laurie L. Levenson, 'Material Witnesses,' *The National Law Journal*, October 31, 2001. See section, 3144 of the U.S. Code.

59 Criminal Code, section 698(2). But see the Mutual Legal Assistance in Criminal Matters Act, which allows a Canadian judge to obtain testimony and other evidence for use by a foreign criminal court, including an international tribunal. It is not limited to cases where an accused has already been charged and arrested in the foreign country. The Canadian court has the power to arrest the witness and can use the contempt power if the witness refuses to give evidence. See Mutual Legal Assistance in Criminal Matters Act, RSC 1985, c. 30 (4th Supp.), sections 18, 22, and 23.

60 Criminal Code, section 50(1)(b); see Friedland, *National Security: The Legal Dimensions* at 11.

61 See also the proposed 83.1 in C-36 which imposes a duty to disclose to the authorities property relating to terrorism.

62 Terrorist Act 2000, section 19.

63 Proposed 83.28(11).

64 *British Columbia Securities Commission* v. *Branch* (1995), 97 CCC (3d) 505 (SCC); *R.J.S.* v. *The Queen* (1995), 96 CCC (3d) 1 (SCC).

65 Proposed 83.28(10).

66 See the definition of 'terrorist activity' in the proposed 83.01.

67 Proposed 83.19.

68 Proposed 83.23.

69 See, e.g., the proposed 83.1. See also section 8 of the Official Secrets Act, chapter

O-5 which makes it an offence not to disclose information to a senior police officer if the person has harboured a person who is about to commit or has committed an offence under the Act.

70 Proposed 83.3(8).
71 Proposed 83.3(2)(b). The exact words in 83.3 are 'suspects on reasonable grounds.'
72 Proposed 83.3(7).
73 Criminal Code, sections 810 and 811.
74 Proposed 83.3(4)(b).
75 Criminal Code, section 495(1)(a).
76 Official Secrets Act, chapter O-5.
77 Official Secrets Act, 1911, 1 & 2 Geo. 5, c. 28, section 6.
78 Terrorism Act 2000, 2000 Chapter 11, section 41(1) and 83.
79 *Hunter* v. *Southam* (1984), 14 CCC (3d) 97 (SCC).
80 *United States* v. *United States District Court* (1972), 407 U.S. 297.
81 Section 41 and Schedule 8.
82 Sections 43–47.
83 Section 81.
84 Section 83.
85 McDonald Commission Second Report, volume 1, at 295 (August 1981).
86 Second Report, volume 2, at 1030 et seq.
87 See M.L. Friedland, 'Controlling Entrapment,' in Friedland, *A Century of Criminal Justice* (Toronto: Carswell, 1984) 171 at 202, referring to section 21(1) of Bill C-157. See also Reg Whitaker, 'Designing a Balance between Freedom and Security' in Joseph F. Fletcher, *Ideas in Action: Essays on Politics and Law in Honour of Peter Russell* (Toronto: U of T Press, 1999) 126 at 135–36.
88 *Delicate Balance* at 24–25.
89 CSIS Act, section 20.
90 See Wayne R. LaFave and Austin W. Scott, *Criminal Law*, 2nd ed. (St. Paul, Minn.: West, 1986) 5.11(d) at 476 et seq.; Wayne La Fave, Jerold H. Israel, and Nancy J. King, *Criminal Procedure* (St. Paul, Minn.: West) section 5.4; *Hampton* v. *United States* (1976), 425 U.S. 484.
91 (1989), 52 CCC (3d) 366.
92 (1999), 133 CCC (3d) 257. See Peter M. Brauti and Candice Welsch, 'Illegal Police Conduct in the Course of a Bona Fide Investigation; (1999–2000) 43 *Criminal Law Quarterly* 64.
93 1999–2000 Annual Report at 16.
94 Bill C-24, section 2, adding section 25.1 to the Criminal Code. Note that the recent UK Regulation of Investigatory Powers Act 2000, part II, provides a desirable statutory framework for controlling covert human intelligence sources. There has to be an authorisation by the Home Secretary or certain other persons and the agent's conduct has to be in accordance with the authorisation. See also M.L. Friedland, 'Controlling the Administrators of Criminal Justice,' (1988–89) 31 *Criminal Law Quarterly* 280 at 290.

Intelligence Requirements and Anti-Terrorism Legislation

WESLEY K. WARK
University of Toronto
Munk Centre for International Studies

Montesquieu's famous *Persian Letters*, once on the Vatican Index, reminds us of an important facet of all law. This is what he wrote:

> I have often tried to decide which government was most in conformity
> with reason. I have come to think that the most perfect is the one which
> attains its purpose with the least trouble, so that the one which controls
> men in the manner best adapted to their inclinations and desires is the most
> perfect.[1]

To view Bill C-36 in the light of this maxim would be an interesting exercise, for it would force us to examine, as a society, what it is that our 'inclinations and desires' require in the way of anti-terrorism legislation.

My purpose in this paper will be less ambitious than that framed by Montesquieu, but conducted in the spirit of his inquiry. One question that needs to be asked of Bill C-36 is the extent to which it satisfies legitimate intelligence-gathering and information-security requirements.

To begin, it might be useful to pose a checklist of ingredients that make for the effective and democratic functioning of security and intelligence institutions in Canada in response to terrorist and other threats. I would include, in such a checklist, the following:

1. good laws
2. a coherent government organization for intelligence policy, the collection and analysis of intelligence, and for the dissemination of intelligence to decision-makers at all levels.

3. sufficient resources for the intelligence community
4. talent
5. ally-worthiness
6. public legitimacy

The elements of this checklist are, or course, deeply intertwined. Each is necessary, none is sufficient unto itself. Good laws alone do not make for effective and democratic intelligence services. Nor is it the purpose of good laws to do so. But laws which serve to hinder, or fail to advance, the effective functioning of intelligence and security agencies need special scrutiny in order to ensure that a proper balance is ultimately being established between public safety and other societal demands. The connections are especially strong between good laws and public legitimacy. It needs to be recognised, as well, that good laws can assist in establishing and maintaining ally-worthiness and that good laws help frame coherent organizational structures. The question to be addressed here is the extent to which the provisions of Bill C-36 are conducive to effective and democratic intelligence practices.

One of the most controversial elements of Bill C-36 is the definition it provides of terrorism. This definition is tacked on to a series of United Nations resolutions and international law conventions dating back to the 1970s now to be incorporated directly in Canadian law. The definition addresses, very broadly, violent acts undertaken for 'political, religious or ideological' purposes designed to cause serious harm to Canadians persons and property, or to interfere with an essential service. Definitions of terrorism are a tricky business, but clearly necessary, at least under the law. From the perspective of intelligence and security requirements, perhaps the most striking aspect of Bill C-36's definition of terrorism is the very broad meaning given to the 'facilitation' of terrorist offences, including financing of terrorist operations. In effect, a person can be charged with facilitation of terrorism without having direct knowledge of the operation being planned. At first glance, this seems draconian and open to all kinds of abuse.

But it needs to be admitted that this definition in fact matches our general understanding of the terrorist *modus operandi*. Terrorism functions clandestinely. It depends for operational success on secrecy and surprise. Terrorism has, in one of the terrible ironies of history, borrowed its operational security practises from its opponents – security and intelligence services. This is a long-standing reality, that probably dates back at least to the underground contest between the clandestine Bolshevik party in pre-revolutionary Russia and the secret police of the Tsarist regime. In modern times, we see terrorist operations placing stress on compartmentalisation of operations, the 'need to know' principle, the use of operational cut-outs to shield different components of a terrorist mission, and the employment of 'deep cover' or 'sleeper' agents. In so far as we have any reliable picture, as yet, of the operational planning behind the September 11 attacks, all of these practices seem to have been very effectively utilised.

The lessons of past terrorist operations indicate that facilitation can and will occur without the full knowledge of those who are contributing to the fulfillment of terrorist plans. Any legislation that did not take this reality into account would be inadequate.

As part of the functional definition of terrorism, and in order to provide the government with tools to take action against terrorist fundraising, Bill C-36 provides a legal mechanism for the listing of proscribed terrorist entities. There are safeguards built into the legislation to allow for challenges to the government list. The dilemma underlying this part of the Bill lies less in the fact of a list itself, which has long been a practice among such major allies as the United Kingdom and the United States, than in exercising good judgement regarding organizations to be proscribed. Such good judgement, which will have to be capable of distinguishing between terrorist organizations, and those engaged in legitimate domestic and international work in such areas as charitable relief and humanitarian aid, will ultimately depend on high-quality intelligence work. It might be asked in this connection whether having a public list of proscribed organizations makes any sense, if it simply represents a public dimension to available intelligence knowledge. The answer, in my view, is that it does, for a number of reasons. A public list of proscribed organizations, as opposed to a tightly held and undisclosed list generated by intelligence agencies, serves the following objects:

1. to send a warning to individuals involved in proscribed organizations
2. to deter
3. to provide for public education
4. to assist in sustaining Canada's ally-worthiness

These objects themselves need to be balanced against the fact that a public list of proscribed terrorist organizations will have the inevitable effect of either driving open activity underground, or causing terrorists to seek camouflage for illegal activity behind the screen of 'front' organizations.

Alas, we seem to be heading back to some of the lexicography of the Cold War. On balance, and despite the legal and practical objections to a list, it seems better to have one, than not. A public list better serves public education and the maintenance of Canada's reputation as an ally.

Two further aspects of Bill C-36 have behind them the hot breath of emergency. The provisions for investigative hearings and preventative detention (in legal terms 'laying an information') are measures best left to a country at war. But then we are at war, or at least in a war. Our problem is that we don't yet understand the nature of this war on terrorism, or its future. We have not been directly targeted, although Canadian lives were lost in the World Trade Center towers and the Canadian economy has suffered significantly in the aftermath of the attack. No direct Canadian 'connection' has yet been established to the perpetrators of the September 11 attack, though it is still, in the context of the security investigation, early days and we may learn some disagreeable facts. We are making legislation for a war we don't yet understand, and for a future which we cannot discern.

On the face of it, investigative hearings and preventative detentions are repugnant measures, which clearly strike at basic notions of habeas corpus. From the perspective, again, of intelligence requirements and with one eye on terrorist methodology, we need to ask whether there is anything to be gained by such legal powers, given the obvious costs? Such measures, of course, might prevent catastrophes by warding off terrorist attacks, assuming that good fortune and good intelligence, or both, were on our side. But there is more to consider. Investigative hearings might in fact serve to prevent any temptation on the part of law enforcement and intelligence agencies to consider illegal means to collect information, including, *in extremis*, torture.

Investigative hearings and preventative detention might also have the effect of usefully focussing urgent investigations on genuine threats, by reducing the scope for mysteries and security paranoia. Counter-terrorist investigations are, by nature, extremely difficult and the costs of failure are potentially high. Given the pressures that such investigations inevitably generate, pursuing false trails is an ever-present danger. Their pursuit itself can do grave damage to civil liberties. It is an admittedly heretical thought, but some of the powers of Bill C-36 might have proved useful in an earlier era in Canadian history. They might have made a useful contribution back in 1946 when the Canadian government floundered its way through a Royal Commission on Espionage which ultimately failed to distinguish between two very different threats – espionage and subversion. The result was a decades long, oppressive, and misguided hunt for Communist front organizations, whose 'front' connections were often the product of nothing more than the over-heated imagination of the RCMP Security Service.

Investigative hearings and preventative detention are emergency measures, serious and ugly. But they have a practical role in preventing catastrophes, and focussing the minds of the security and intelligence community. They also send a signal to both the Canadian public and to our coalition allies in the war on terrorism. The signal is simple: Canada is serious.

Behind the front-line legislative aspects of Bill C-36, mostly justified in my view, lie some rear area measures that we need to approach with caution. One of these concerns the Official Secrets Act (OSA), now renamed the 'Security of Information Act.' It is important that we have in Canada an act capable of being enforced. Canada does have secrets. Some of these secrets are made-in-Canada; many are supplied to the Canadian intelligence community by our allies. Ally-worthiness is one of the things at stake. The ability to protect intelligence sources and methods in counter-terrorist operations is another. Without the deterrence of an enforceable official secrets act, the possibilities of harmful leaks in the course of on-going intelligence operations is higher than is necessary or safe. The situation, prior to Bill C-36 was untenable. The old Official Secret Act had fallen into disuse, and was widely regarded as inoperable subsequent to the passage of the Canadian Charter of Rights. Successive efforts, prior to September 11, to introduce an amended OSA never got very far. The new sense of urgency in the aftermath of the terrorist attacks has forced action on a cob-webbed file. So far, so good.

But there are two aspects to the new Security of Information Act that need to be re-thought. One concerns the whistle-blowing, or public interest provisions of the Act. The whistle blowing protection provided for is, in my view, far too narrow. A greater capacity for legitimate whistle-blowing needs to be built into the system. This can be done either by loosening the law, perhaps the more difficult option, or by building into institutional structures a respected and powerful internal ombudsman to whom individuals in the security and intelligence community could turn to argue their case that disclosure of secret information was in the public interest, in order to prevent an act of terror or an illegal operation. A variety of pseudo-ombudsmen are provided for in the current bill, including deputy heads of departments, the CSE Commissioner and the Security and Intelligence Review Committee. It would be best to centralise this function in a single person and office.

The new Security of Information Act also makes provisions for what it calls 'persons permanently bound to secrecy.' The intent is clearly to provide security safeguards around particularly sensitive forms of intelligence, called in the Act 'special operational information.' Such information needs to be protected, but the idea of its being protected 'permanently' is a useless anachronism. It brings to mind the old security classification stamped on especially sensitive intelligence: 'never to be seen by unauthorised persons.' The government has no need, nor right, to permanently protect information. Such a measure serves only to cast a permanent and unhelpful veil of secrecy over security and intelligence institutions that have to function in public, supported by a reasonable degree of public knowledge and sure of some measure of public legitimacy. In the war on terrorism, publics will need to be told more, rather than less, about the actions and capabilities of Canadian security and intelligence institutions. It would be sufficient to bind persons to secrecy over a span of years that might be specified to match needed time horizons for material to be opened under the Access to Information Act, say 30 years. Currently, no such time horizons for the routine release of historic records exist.

In Bill C-36, measures for the monitoring and suppression of terrorist financing are to be added to the existing Proceeds of Crime (Money Laundering) Act. This may have been an administrative and legal convenience, but it raises a troubling issue of overlapping intelligence-gathering jurisdictions. When the government passed the Proceeds of Crime Act it also created a new organization called FINTRAC ('Financial Transactions and Activities Tracking Centre') under the Department of Finance. FINTRAC is referred to in Bill C-36, unhelpfully, by an abbreviation straight out of a Le Carre novel, 'The Centre.' FINTRAC, or The Centre, is the organization responsible for analysis of criminal and now terrorist money flows. But Bill C-36 also states that 'If the Centre ... has reasonable grounds to suspect that designated information would be relevant to threats to the security of Canada, the Centre shall disclose that information to the Canadian Security Intelligence Service.' Such an injunction is fine so far as it goes, but it begs two questions. One is where the best expertise lies in the Canadian government regarding terrorist financing activities. It is, in my view, unlikely to reside at FINTRAC, not least because FINTRAC is essentially a neophyte organizaton. The second question concerns the sport of turf warfare which is endemic in all government structures. Overlapping jurisdictions are the bane of security and intelligence communities and the potential for such overlap in relations between CSIS and FINTRAC need to be sorted out sooner rather than later.

One traditionally secret part of the Canadian intelligence community has come in from the cold in Bill C-36. The government has wisely taken advantage of the omnibus nature of the Bill to give the Canadian signals intelligence agency, the Communications Security Establishment, an explicit and public mandate. Prior to Bill C-36, CSE's legal standing rested on a succession of secret Order in Councils, dating back to 1946. Article 273.62 of the Bill allows that 'the part of the public service of Canada known as the Communications Security Establishment is hereby continued.' This is unremarkable, but there are other aspects of the Bill which deserve serious notice. One is that CSE has now been given the power, under written Ministerial directive, to intercept Canadian communications, when such communications are one end of a network located overseas. Thus, if a terrorist organization located in Afghanistan attempted to maintain communications with an individual in Canada, CSE would have the legal mandate to monitor both ends of the message traffic. This is a historic change to CSE's mandate, which since its birth at the dawn of the Cold War, has been exclusively targeted at foreign communications. The change is, in fact, long overdue, a simple recognition of the nature of global communications and the 'intermestic' reality of the terrorist threat. Terrorism respects no borders, and it would be absurd to hobble Canadian intelligence capabilities by restricting monitoring to foreign targets exclusively.

But the powers accorded to CSE in Bill C-36 also rest on an invisible division of responsibilities between the Communications Security Establishment and the Canadian Security Intelligence Service. CSE, even under Bill C-36, will be focussed on the collection of foreign intelligence; CSIS will continue to be responsible for domestic security intelligence. Thus we persist in maintaining an intelligence border between foreign and domestic information-gathering. CSIS will continue to have the responsibility for domestic monitoring of communications. How well this arrangement will work depends on the quality of cooperation between CSE and CSIS. But the division of responsibilities also raises questions about whether the extension of CSE's powers is a half-measure. There are efficacy issues. Which agency is, in fact, best equipped to deal with the challenges of signals intelligence in an age of public encryption and information overload? We might need to look, at some point in the future, at giving CSE complete jurisdiction over communications monitoring, both at home and abroad. Were this ever to happen, it would of course take CSE into the realm of judicial warrants for wiretaps and other forms of communications surveillance within Canada. This is an area that CSE, for historic reasons and due to the nature of its alliance relationships, would not be happy to venture.

In the section of Bill C-36 dealing with the Communications Security Establishment, there are some other noteworthy, but perhaps obscure, features. For one thing, the Bill would appear to extend the power of CSE to fulfill its defensive mandate for the protection of government communications networks. In the professional jargon, this mission is labeled COMSEC. Bill C-36 allows CSE, again under Ministerial directive, to target the message traffic of individuals suspected of 'mischief, unauthorized use or interference' with government computer systems or networks. This puts CSE squarely on the offensive against all manner of hackers and crackers, both domestic and foreign.

Finally, Bill C-36 hints at a shift in authority over the Communications Security Establishment that bears watching. The system in place prior to the Bill was somewhat odd. It provided for dual control of this sensitive and secretive agency. Logistical and financial matters were the purview of the Department of National Defence, and thus CSE was overseen in that field by the Deputy Minister for National Defence. Policy direction was provided by the senior intelligence official in the Privy Council Office, the Coordinator for Security and Intelligence. This dual authority is not specifically mandated under Bill C-36. It may continue. But the Bill does provide for much stronger control of CSE by the Minister of National Defence, specifically under the provision that 'The Minister may issue written directions to the Chief respecting the carrying out of the Chief's [of CSE] duties and functions.' Whether this is a good thing will depend on the quality of DND Ministers and on the attention that the Department is prepared to pay to CSE's broad mandate, which involves it in signals intelligence activities that range far beyond strictly military matters.

The presence of an explicit mandate for the Communications Security Establishment in Bill C-36 would appear to be a matter largely of opportunism for the government, a chance to take advantage of an omnibus bill and a sympathetic mood in Parliament and throughout the nation. The opportunism is noted, but not objectionable. The Communications Security establishment is one of the most important components of our intelligence system; it needs a clear mandate, some public exposure, and attendant public legitimacy.

Opportunism would also appear to lie behind another measure that makes a surprise appearance in the Bill. This concerns amendments to the Access to Information Act and the Privacy Act. In both cases, Bill C-36 authorizes the Attorney General to 'personally issue a certificate that prohibits the disclosure of information for the purpose of protecting international relations or national defence or security.' Both the Access Act and the Privacy Act, in unamended form, give the government extensive powers through the application of exemptions, to protect such categories of information from disclosure. Bill C-36 would, in effect, nullify a key provision of both Acts – the opportunity for individual challenges to the closure of information adjudicated by the offices of the Information and Privacy Commissioners. Government officials may see Bill C-36 as closing a loophole and as a weapon to swat at the pests of the Information and Privacy Commissioners. But in truth, these provisions of Bill C-36 are both unnecessary and unwise. Unnecessary because the government already possesses more than sufficient powers to protect information – a fact widely recognised within the intelligence community itself. Unwise, because the application of an Attorney general certificate would be like the waving of a red flag. For one thing, it might have the effect of encouraging undue skepticism about government motives in regard to the protection of information, and thereby undermine the public legitimacy of the keepers of the secrets, the agencies of the intelligence community. For another thing, an Attorney General certificate might well encourage overzealous efforts to root out secrets or motivate leakers with all manner of agendas. In short, it is bad policy to label hot intelligence, hot.

Bill C-36, like all omnibus legislation, is a mixed bag. In many of its general features it is responsive to the nature of terrorist operational methodology. It provides for increased powers for intelligence and law enforcement agencies. Such powers are, in the current environment, necessary. But it is worth remembering that increased powers do not guarantee skillful execution. Good laws are only part of the checklist of what makes for the effective and democratic functioning of a security and intelligence community.

Returning to the Montesquieu quote from the *Persian Letters*, we can probably agree that Bill C-36, in most particulars, is well adapted to our current 'inclinations and desires' as a society. We want protection and assurances of safety; we are awakening to the fact that proficient security and intelligence agencies are one guarantor of public safety. But our inclinations and desires may change in the future, as the war on terrorism progresses. For that reason, if for no other, the government should make one key amendment to Bill C-36 if it makes no other. A sunset clause, perhaps of four years, is the appropriate measure, in the spirit of Montesquieu. Our allies know this; it is time for our government to know it as well.

Note

1 Montesquieu, *Persian Letters*, trans. C.J. Betts (Penguin, 1973), Letter 80, Usbek to Rhedi, p. 158.

Financing Terrorism

Cutting off the Flow of Funds to Terrorists: Whose Funds? Which Funds? Who Decides?

KEVIN E. DAVIS[*]

University of Toronto
Faculty of Law

1. Introduction

One of the most important fronts in the newly declared war on terrorism is the financial one. The avowed aim of the United States and its allies is to cut off the flow of funds to terrorists.[1] This campaign involves a two-pronged attack: The first prong involves prosecuting the financiers, *i.e.* individuals or organizations that provide money or property to support terrorist activities. The second prong involves freezing, seizing and forfeiting property that has been or might be directed toward terrorist activities. This paper analyses the portions of the *Anti-terrorism Act*[2] that represent the federal government of Canada's first sortie on the financial front of the war against terrorism.

Although the government's two-pronged strategy is simple to describe, it is actually inherently difficult to implement through legislation. One reason is because legislation of this sort is designed to capture economic activity that only poses a *risk* of contributing to future terrorist activity. This forces lawmakers to decide how much risk must be posed by a given activity before it ought to be criminalized, recognizing that the lower the threshold they establish, the more likely it is that they will capture activity that would not, if events proceeded in due course, actually lead to harm. A second challenge associated with legislation of this sort is to determine how close the connection between economic activity and terrorist activity must be in order for the economic activity to warrant criminal sanction. At some point the connection may be so remote that many reasonable people would conclude – for example, on the basis of concerns about personal liberty – that the economic activity should not attract criminal liability.

My primary objective in this paper is a relatively modest one: I simply intend to describe how the drafters of the *Anti-Terrorism Act* have responded to the challenge of defining the relationship that must exist between individuals and property on the one hand, and terrorist activity on the other hand, in terms of both certainty and proximity, in order to trigger criminal penalties. Where appropriate I compare the approach taken in the new legislation to the approach that Canadian law has previously taken to similar issues, as well as to the approach adopted in the *International Convention for the Suppression of the Financing of Terrorism* (the '*Financing of Terrorism Convention*'), which Canada signed on February 10, 2000.[3] I do not attempt to assess directly whether the approach that the *Anti-terrorism Act* has taken is justifiable, since answering that question would involve canvassing a wide range of ethical, economic and political factors. However, towards the end of the paper, I do analyze the legislation in terms of the amount of power Parliament has given law enforcement officials, trial judges, juries and appellate courts respectively to determine which conduct should attract criminal sanction. I argue that some of the new provisions give law enforcement officials too much power and appellate courts too little.

2. Prosecuting financiers

2.1. *Overview*

The *Anti-terrorism Act* creates three new offences under the heading 'financing of terrorism' (the 'financing of terrorism offences').[4] Under these provisions it is an offence to provide, invite a person to provide, collect, make available, use or possess property intending that it be, or knowing that it will be, used for specified purposes. Depending on the provision in question, the proscribed purposes involve either facilitating or carrying out terrorist activity, or benefiting either a person facilitating or carrying out terrorist activity or a terrorist group.[5] The following sections of this paper provide a more detailed examination of the physical and mental elements of the financing of terrorism offences and examine the extent to which they overlap with other offences created by the *Anti-terrorism Act*.

2.2. Prosecuting financiers: physical elements of the offences

The physical elements of the provisions dealing with financing of terrorism are defined so as to capture a very broad range of dealings with terrorists. Some of those dealings will have only uncertain or tenuous connections to terrorist activity. Specifically, there are three aspects of the relevant provisions that serve to attenuate that connection.

First, mainly because they use the terms 'provides' and 'makes available' without qualification,[6] the financing of terrorism offences seem broad enough to apply to people who provide property for proscribed purposes on a purely commercial basis. In other words, they do not appear to apply only to people who donate property for use in connection with terrorism, but also to those who sell or lease property for use in connection with terrorism on commercially reasonable terms. Whether or not one believes that it is appropriate to proscribe the latter class of dealings, they are arguably more remotely connected to terrorism than the former. On the one hand, it does not seem so farfetched to target a person who sells a cropduster to a known terrorist. On the other hand, it does seem a bit farfetched to convict a restaurant owner simply for serving food and drink to known terrorists. Moreover, leaving aside the question of remoteness, it is reasonably clear that dealing with terrorists on commercially reasonable terms is somewhat removed from the ordinary meaning of 'financing of terrorism.' The man on the street may appreciate the fact that knowingly donating money, or even a carton of milk, to a member of a terrorist group might qualify as financing terrorism, but not that selling a carton of milk would also qualify.

A second noteworthy feature of the new legislation is section 83.04(b), which makes it an offence to possess property 'intending that it be used or knowing that it will be used, directly or indirectly, in whole or in part, for the purpose of facilitating or carrying out a terrorist activity.' This provision, which in this respect goes beyond the language used in the *Financing of Terrorism Convention*,[7] does not require the prosecution to show that any property has actually been provided to a person who is engaged in facilitating or carrying out a terrorist activity. Moreover, unlike sections 83.02 and 83.03, which refer to a person who 'collects' property for a similar purpose, section 83.04(b) does not require the prosecution to show that the accused has committed any overt act in order to give effect to their illicit intention. The prosecution need only show that the accused retained possession of, as opposed to providing, collecting or using, property, even if the accused possessed the property before forming the proscribed intention. Thus, in theory, the restaurant owner referred to above could attract criminal liability as soon as he accepted a reservation from known terrorists, intending or knowing that they would discuss terrorist activities in the course of their meal.

Section 83.04(b) comes perilously close to making it an offence merely to have a proscribed intention as opposed to committing an overt act. Some might object on philosophical grounds to allowing criminal liability to be imposed on the basis of such a minimal connection between the accused and harmful activity. The concern is essentially that such an offence unduly limits individuals' freedom of thought and expression, and in particular their freedom to form and express – but not act upon – illicit intentions. This kind of argument is typically used to justify the rule that criminal liability for an attempt cannot be imposed unless the accused has committed an overt act that goes beyond mere preparation.[8]

On the other hand, there are numerous instances in which Canadian law permits criminal liability to be imposed upon a person who has taken only the most minimal steps to give effect to a proscribed intention. For example, a person can be convicted of conspiracy to commit an offence without engaging in any overt act (beyond entering into an agreement) in furtherance of the conspiracy.[9] Similarly, in order for someone to be liable as a party to an offence, once the requisite mental element is present virtually any overt act or omission that goes beyond passive acquiescence, including mere encouragement, will be sufficient.[10] There are even offences where someone can be held liable as a principal (as opposed to a party) on the basis of wholly innocuous overt acts. For example, technically, a person can be convicted of possessing a weapon dangerous to the public peace by doing something as innocuous as holding a screwdriver.[11] It is also possible to be convicted of high treason simply for having formed an intention to do anything that   is high treason and manifesting that intention by any overt act.[12]

A third significant feature of the provisions dealing with financing of terrorism is the fact that one of them, section 83.03, makes it an offence not only to 'finance' terrorist activity,[13] but also to finance 'any person who is facilitating or carrying out such an activity' or 'a terrorist group.'[14] It may be reasonable to presume that financing a person who is participating in terrorist activity – keeping in mind that, for the reasons noted above, here 'financing' covers a very broad range of dealings – tends to play a causal role in subsequent terrorist activity. However, in some scenarios it will be clear that there is either no causal connection or that the connection is extremely remote. For example, suppose that the restaurant owner mentioned above serves a meal to a person knowing that they have, in other venues, participated in terrorist activity. In that case the restaurant owner could be liable for having 'provided property ... knowing that [it] will be used, in whole or in part ... for the purpose of benefiting any person who is facilitating or carrying out [terrorist] activity.'[15] However, the connection between the restaurant owner's actions and any subsequent terrorist activity will be uncertain and, if it exists at all, remote. This problem is exacerbated by the fact that, for the purposes of section 83.03, 'terrorist activity' appears to include acts that constitute certain financing of terrorism offences.[16] This implies that our restaurant owner could be held liable for serving customers who he knows are in the habit of making contributions to terrorist groups.[17]

It is also significant that section 83.03 captures both dealings with people who are participating in terrorist activity and dealings with a 'terrorist group.' The term 'terrorist group' is defined as follows:

(a) an entity that has as one of its purposes or activities facilitating or carrying out any terrorist activity, or
(b) a listed entity,
      and includes an association of such entities.[18]

The term 'entity' is also a defined term and includes a 'person.'[19] Consequently, it appears to be the case that a natural person who 'has as one of his or her purposes' facilitating or carrying out any terrorist activity qualifies as a terrorist group for the purpose of this legislation. In addition, given the broad definition of facilitation, an expression of intention to support terrorist activity in general, as opposed to any particular terrorist activity, could cause a person to qualify as a terrorist group. Section 83.03 appears to capture a broad range of dealings with such a person. So, for example, it appears that the restaurant owner referred to above (not to mention a waiter) could be liable for serving any person who he knows has previously expressed an intention to support terrorist activity. Again, this suggests that the new legislation permits criminal liability to be imposed upon people whose connection to actual terrorist activity is highly uncertain and remote.

The most striking feature of the provisions on financing of terrorism is the breadth of the range of activities to which they apply. In this context it is easy to overlook the curious fact that the provisions dealing with financing of terrorism also exclude a sizeable number of activities that are functionally quite similar to the ones that are included within their scope. Here I am referring to the fact that although the legislation captures virtually any effort to provide property for use in connection with terrorism, it does not capture all efforts to provide services for similar purposes. Instead, the legislation only captures the act of making 'financial or other related services' available for use in connection with terrorist activity.[20] Although the term 'other related services' is ambiguous, it probably excludes many types of services that terrorists might find just as valuable as any given type of property. Consider, for example, services such as legal advice (some of which may fall under the rubric of 'financial or other related services'),[21] medical care or education. The rationale for excluding provision of these services from the scope of the financing of terrorism offences is unclear.[22]

2.3. *Prosecuting financiers: mental elements of the offences*

Supporters of the new legislation are likely to argue that even if the physical elements of the financing of terrorism offences are broadly defined, concerns about abuse are unwarranted because the mental elements are defined so as to preclude convicting truly innocent individuals.[23] However, the mental elements of these offences are also broadly defined and it is not entirely clear what sort of evidence the courts will consider sufficient to establish their existence.[24]

As far as the breadth of the mental elements is concerned, two factors are worth noting. First, most of the provisions of the *Anti-terrorism Act* that proscribe financing of terrorism create offences whose mental element consists of either 'intending' or 'knowing.' This language allows a conviction to be obtained even in cases where the accused is uncertain whether his or her actions will ultimately be connected to terrorist activity. 'Intending' that an event occur does not necessarily imply that one believes that the event is certain to occur as a result of one's actions, it simply implies that one is aware that the event is a likely consequence of those actions.[25]

Second, the language of the new legislation also allows a person to be convicted even if they do not have any particular desire to facilitate terrorist activity, and are in fact indifferent or even averse to the prospect of terrorist activity. The degree of satisfaction that a person derives from an event is only relevant to their motive, and, possibly, to their intention or purpose,[26] but the term 'knowing' merely involves awareness of the likelihood of the event. To appreciate the distinction between knowledge and these other mental states, we can return to the case of a restaurant owner who knows that certain customers are using her restaurant to plot terrorist activity. The new legislation appears to make it possible for the restaurant owner to be held criminally liable as someone who 'provides or ... makes available property ... knowing that [it] will be used...in part ... for the purpose of facilitating ... terrorist activity.'[27] The owner probably cannot escape liability by arguing that her only objective was to earn a profit from her customers and that she did not have any particular desire to assist them in their criminal purpose. The court's response is likely to be that whatever her reasons for acting, the owner knew that her property would be used to facilitate terrorist activity. Like the other versions of this hypothetical discussed above, this example illustrates that the new legislation has the potential to expose people who are only remotely connected to terrorist activity to criminal liability.

Although the mental elements of the financing of terrorism offences are broadly defined there are at least two sources of uncertainty about what sorts of evidence the prosecution will have to adduce in order to prove their existence. First, evidence that an accused has committed the physical elements of an offence is sometimes treated as evidence that the requisite mental elements are present.[28] This procedure is commonly and necessarily allowed in criminal prosecutions because of the difficulty of obtaining direct evidence of an accused's mental state. But of course, to the extent that proof of the mental elements of an offence is provided by proof of the physical elements it becomes impossible to claim that the mental elements place an independent constraint on the prosecution's ability to obtain a conviction.

A second unresolved issue is the extent to which concerns about freedom of expression, religion and association will influence the types of evidence that courts consider admissible in proving that an individual possesses a culpable mental state. In the context of prosecutions for some terrorism offences the best evidence that an accused possesses a culpable mental state (e.g. intention) is likely to be the fact that he or she has expressed support for a political, religious or ideological purpose, objective or cause that others have attempted to further through violent means.[29] However, relying on this sort of evidence will expose people who express unpopular views to greater risk of prosecution than other members of society. This in turn implies that if the principal check on abusive prosecutions is the way in which the mental elements of the offences are defined, then people will have a strong incentive to refrain from expressing unpopular views. Some courts may conclude that these outcomes are objectionable on constitutional grounds and take steps to limit either the weight or the admissibility of such evidence.

2.4. Is financing of terrorism captured by other terrorism offences?

In some cases providing property or services to a terrorist group will trigger liability under the portion of the *Anti-terrorism Act* that creates offences relating to participating in, facilitating, instructing and harbouring terrorist activity (the 'participation offences').[30] Those provisions capture, among others, 'every one who knowingly participates in or contributes to, directly or indirectly, any activity of a terrorist group.'[31] This language, and in particular the phrase 'contributes to,' certainly seems broad enough to capture many forms of financing of terrorism.

On the other hand, notwithstanding the fact that the legislation provides an inclusive definition of the phrase 'participating in or contributing to the activity of a terrorist group,' it is unclear whether the participation offences extend as far along any of the three dimensions highlighted above as do the provisions that fall under the heading 'financing of terrorism.' First, the term 'participates in or contributes to' does not clearly capture dealing with terrorists on a purely commercial basis. Second, it is not clear that this term is broad enough to capture someone whose only overt act is to possess property. Third, the participation offences generally require the prosecution to establish that the purpose – though not, necessarily, the effect – of the accused's actions was to enhance the ability of the group to facilitate or carry out terrorist activity. By contrast, recall that at least one of the financing of terrorism offences permits liability to be imposed upon anyone who knowingly attempts to provide any sort of benefit to a terrorist group, whether or not it enhances the group's ability to carry out terrorist activity.[32]

It is also interesting that, in contradistinction to the financing of terrorism offences, the main participation offence appears to cover the provision of all sorts of services. In fact, the legislation explicitly lists several types of services whose provision might qualify as participating in or contributing to an activity of a terrorist group.[33] At first glance this feature of the participation offences makes the exclusion of a large class of non-financial services from the scope of the provisions on financing of terrorism even more puzzling. One possible explanation, however, is that the government only intends to sanction those who provide property or services that enhance a terrorist group's ability to carry out terrorist activity. There may be an assumption that providing property and 'financial or other related services' necessarily enhances a group's ability to carry out terrorist activity and so can be proscribed in unqualified terms, whereas providing other services does not.

3. *Freezing of property*

The provisions of the *Anti-terrorism Act* that deal with freezing of property can be distinguished from the ones dealing with financing of terrorism by the fact that they are concerned with property that is already owned or controlled by a terrorist group, as opposed to property that has yet to be made available to the group.[34] The way that the government has chosen to achieve the goal of freezing terrorists' property is by making it an offence to knowingly have virtually any sort of dealings with, including providing financial services 'or other related services' in respect of, property that is owned or controlled by or on behalf of a terrorist group.[35]

The breadth of this relatively simple provision flows from two features of the legislation. The first has already been discussed: The wide scope of the definition of a 'terrorist group.' By the terms of that definition an entity need not actually engage in terrorist activity in order to be characterized as a terrorist group. The second key feature of the legislation is that all property of a terrorist group is frozen, whether or not there is evidence that the property is or will be connected to terrorist activity. In this respect the provision goes beyond what is strictly required by the *Financing of Terrorism Convention*, which only refers to freezing of funds 'used or allocated for the purpose of committing' offences analogous to Canada's proposed financing of terrorism offences and 'the proceeds derived from such offences, for the purposes of possible forfeiture.'[36] Again, the overall effect is to capture dealings in property whose connection to terrorist activity is potentially uncertain and remote. Here it is important to recall that a natural person can qualify as a terrorist group. Consequently, if the provisions on financing of terrorism were not sufficient, the freezing provisions should serve to completely deter people from having any dealings whatsoever with individuals as well as groups who they believe intend to facilitate or carry out terrorist activities. When these provisions are compared to the provisions on financing of terrorism it becomes clear that it is an offence not only to give property to a terrorist, but also to receive money from one too.

One possible virtue of the freezing provisions is that they permit the Solicitor General to exempt certain people and classes of activity from their scope.[37] The grounds upon which such exemptions are to be granted are not specified and so there is risk of the Solicitor General's discretion being exercised in an arbitrary or abusive way. Nevertheless, Parliament may wish to consider providing a similar mechanism for granting exemptions from the financing of terrorism offences.

4. Forfeiture and seizure of property

4.1. *Overview*

In addition to providing for the prosecution of those who fund terrorists and for the freezing of terrorists' property, the *Anti-Terrorism Act* also provides for the seizure and forfeiture of property that is connected in various ways with terrorist activity. Since one of the most important categories of property that can be seized is property in respect of which an order of forfeiture might be made, it is convenient to begin by discussing the forfeiture provisions.

4.2. *Forfeiture*

The new legislation is easiest to understand against the backdrop provided by existing federal law governing criminal forfeiture. The *Criminal Code* currently provides, essentially, for the forfeiture of two broad classes of property: property that constitutes proceeds of what are currently known as 'enterprise crime offences,'[38] and property that is used to commit what are currently known as 'criminal organization offences.'[39] Under these provisions property cannot be forfeited unless it is either derived from or used in connection with an offence. Moreover, except in cases where a person has died or absconded, a forfeiture order can only be made once a person has been convicted of an offence, and a conviction will almost invariably be based on proof of many relevant facts beyond a reasonable doubt.[40] It is possible to make a forfeiture order in respect of property that is not related to the one for which the owner is convicted, however, in that case the Crown must establish beyond a reasonable doubt that the property is connected to another offence.[41]

The *Anti-terrorism Act* adds 'terrorism offences' to the list of predicate offences in respect of which a forfeiture order can be made under the current provisions of the *Criminal Code*.[42] Terrorism offences are defined to include the new offences concerning financing and participating in terrorism, as well as other offences that either constitute terrorist activity or are committed for the benefit or at the direction of, or in association with, a terrorist group.[43] This feature of the new legislation ensures that significant economic consequences can be visited upon anyone convicted of a terrorism offence. For example, if the restaurant owner referred to in any of the hypothetical cases presented above were to be convicted of a terrorism offence, his restaurant could be forfeited under the provisions permitting forfeiture of property used to commit a criminal organization offence.

The *Anti-terrorism Act* also contains a wholly new provision that requires a court, upon the application of the Attorney General, to order forfeiture of two main classes of property: (1) Property that is either owned or controlled by a terrorist group or, in the case of property that consists of currency and monetary instruments, an individual who has facilitated or carried out a terrorist activity or is planning to do so; and (2) property that will be used to facilitate or carry out a terrorist activity.[44]

The new forfeiture provision departs from prior law in at least three respects. The first is that it permits forfeiture of all of the property owned or controlled by a terrorist group, and all of the money owned by other types of 'terrorists.'[45] In many cases it will be reasonable to presume that all of the property owned or controlled by or on behalf of a terrorist group or an individual terrorist is available for use in connection with terrorist activities. However, the new legislation leaves no room for an individual or group to rebut that presumption. Therefore, in principle, the new legislation provides for forfeiture of property even where there is no reason to believe that it is derived from, or has been or will be used in connection with, any offence. In this respect the *Anti-terrorism Act* goes further than the *Financing of Terrorism Convention*, which only provides for the forfeiture of funds 'used or allocated for the purpose of [financing of terrorism offences] and the proceeds derived from such offences.'[46]

A second difference between the new forfeiture provision and prior federal law lies in the degree of certainty with which the prosecution must establish that the property in question deserves to be forfeited. The new legislation requires a forfeiture order to be made once a judge is satisfied on the balance of probabilities that the relevant conditions have been satisfied.[47] There is no requirement that anyone connected with the property be convicted of any offence. Consequently, whereas under current law much of the factual underpinning for a forfeiture order typically must be established beyond a reasonable doubt, the new legislation permits all of the analogous facts to be proven on the balance of probabilities. This feature of the new legislation, in combination with the broad definition of the classes of property that may be forfeited, permits property to be forfeited even in the face of a fair amount of uncertainty about whether it will actually be used to facilitate or carry out terrorist activity. Recall that, under this Act, once the Attorney General has satisfied a judge that, on the balance of probabilities, a person 'has as one of [his or her] purposes... facilitating...any terrorist activity,' that judge *must* (there is no discretion) order that all of the property owned by the person be forfeited to the Crown.[48]

A third set of differences between the *Anti-terrorism Act's* forfeiture provisions and other aspects of federal forfeiture law relate to the treatment of innocent third parties who happen to have an interest in property subject to forfeiture. Interestingly, some of the differences work in favour of innocent third parties. For instance, the new legislation requires a judge to declare that a forfeiture order does not affect the proprietary interest of any person who satisfies her (presumably on the balance of probabilities) that they are not a member of a terrorist group and have exercised reasonable care to ensure that the property would not be used to facilitate or carry out a terrorist activity.[49] This provision is much more straightforward than other comparable provisions of the *Criminal Code* which not only define an 'innocent third party' in more complicated terms, but also give the judge discretion over whether and to what extent to protect the interests of innocent third parties.[50] Elimination of judicial discretion in this area should provide a net benefit to third parties. In addition, one consequence of the relatively simplified approach to describing innocent third parties is that a person to whom property has been transferred for the purpose of avoiding forfeiture appears to be entitled to relief from forfeiture under the new legislation, whereas they would not be entitled to such relief under other forfeiture provisions. Thus, both these features of the new forfeiture power tilt the balance in favour of third parties.

On the other hand, from the perspective of third parties a major deficiency in the new legislation is that, unlike under other federal forfeiture legislation, they are not guaranteed the right to receive notice that an application has been made to forfeit property in which they have an interest. Instead the court appears to have a broad discretion to determine who is entitled to receive notice.[51] Moreover, parties who did not receive notice only have 60 days to bring a motion to vary or set aside a forfeiture order. The court is expressly barred from extending this 60 day period.[52]

4.3. *Seizure*

The reach of the *Anti-terrorism Act's* forfeiture provisions – including those that merely extend pre-existing forfeiture legislation to cover terrorism offences – is significantly extended by the fact that any property that is subject to forfeiture under those provisions may be made the subject of a restraint order or a warrant authorizing its seizure and the search of any place where it is located.[53] Unlike forfeiture orders, restraint orders and warrants are temporary.[54] On the other hand, these orders and warrants can be obtained even when there is very little certainty that the property in question is subject to forfeiture; typically the court need only be satisfied that there are reasonable grounds to believe that the property is subject to forfeiture.[55]

5. Enforcement and application

One of the most interesting features of the new legislation is the way in which it allocates the power to determine whose conduct should be sanctioned and which property should be subject to forfeiture and seizure among the various actors in the criminal justice system – i.e. police, Crown attorneys, the Attorney General, trial judges, juries and appellate courts.

Consider the provisions defining the physical elements of the financing of terrorism offences and the freezing offence. It is difficult to imagine that they could be defined to capture a broader range of conduct. This means that, effectively, the power to determine which physical acts will attract punishment under these provisions rests with the police, crown attorneys and, because his or her consent is required to initiate proceedings in respect of all of the offences discussed in this paper, the Attorney General.[56] Once those officials have (collectively) decided to initiate proceedings, the courts have little leeway to interpret the provisions in such a way as exclude any given type of conduct. In this respect the financing of terrorism offences can be contrasted with the proposed 'participating and contributing' offence,[57] which appears to leave the courts substantial room to determine the outer limits of liability. To illustrate this point, suppose that law enforcement officials decided to initiate proceedings against a hapless restaurant owner who served food to known terrorists. In my view, without resorting to the *Charter* it would be difficult for a court to reasonably interpret the physical elements of the financing of terrorism offences in such a way as to exclude this type of activity. However, if the restauranteur was prosecuted under the new participation offence, a court could reasonably hold that, properly interpreted, the statutory language is not broad enough to capture his conduct.

The situation is slightly different with respect to the mental elements of the financing of terrorism offences. The trier of fact, whether a judge or a jury, has a fair amount of discretion to determine what sort of evidence is sufficient to establish that an accused intended or knew that property would be used to facilitate or carry out a terrorist activity or to benefit terrorists. So for example, it is not too difficult to imagine a judge or jury acquitting the restaurant owner described above on the grounds that they were not satisfied of the existence of the requisite mental elements. It is important to note however, that an appellate court will typically have relatively little scope to overturn whatever decision is reached by the trier of fact on an issue of this sort. In technical terms, determinations of these types of issues are treated as questions of fact rather than questions of law and are generally insulated from scrutiny on the part of appellate courts.[58] The principal exception is that appellate courts will scrutinize a trial judge's decisions regarding what sort of evidence is admissible to establish the mental elements of an offence. Therefore, appellate courts will have some control over whether evidence of political, religious or ideological expression is admissible to determine knowledge and intent, even if they do not refer to the proposition that legislation ought to be interpreted in line with the *Charter*. Otherwise though, appellate courts appear to have very little opportunity to influence the application of the legislative provisions creating offences in respect of financing of terrorism and freezing of property.

The situation is different again with respect to forfeiture. As far as deciding which property is to be forfeited, power rests largely with the Attorney General, who, presumably with input from the police, decides whether to apply to the Federal Court for a forfeiture order and in respect of which property. The trial judge obviously has some power to decide whether to grant an order of forfeiture in respect of property selected by the Attorney General in the sense that he or she can always conclude that the evidence does not satisfy him or her that the preconditions to granting a forfeiture order have been met. However, since this decision is likely to be characterized as one of fact rather than law, it is largely insulated from appellate review. In this respect it is instructive to compare the federal forfeiture provisions with Ontario's recently proposed forfeiture legislation, which allows a judge to decline to make an order of forfeiture even where all the statutory pre-conditions have been satisfied 'where it would clearly not be in the interests of justice.'[59] The language of the Ontario provision confers substantially more power on trial courts, and perhaps even appellate courts, to decide whether or not to make a forfeiture order in respect of property identified by the Attorney General.

Finally, one of the most curious provisions of the new legislation is the one that gives the courts ultimate power to determine whether third parties receive notice of forfeiture proceedings.[60] This in turn determines the extent to which those third parties' interests in property are protected from forfeiture. Giving individual judges the power to make this determination rather than having Parliament clearly indicate what sort of notice is to be provided is highly unusual.

Taken as a whole, one of the most striking features of the new legislation is the fact that, in effect, it gives the police and the Attorney General the authority to decide whether a broad range of conduct will attract liability under the financing of terrorism offences, and whether a broad variety of property will be subject to forfeiture. The other striking feature of the legislation is how little authority the courts, and particularly the appellate courts, are given to make decisions on these matters.

The first aspect of the legislation may trouble some civil libertarians. However, it can be defended partially on the grounds that when facing poorly understood threats it would be unwise to decide precipitously that certain types of conduct are not subject to criminal sanction or that certain types of property are not subject to forfeiture. As a general principle, when it is difficult to foresee all of the circumstances in which legislation might be applied it is appropriate to leave room for decisions about the legislation's scope to be made at a later date when more information is available. This argument militates in favour of enacting legislation that is potentially applicable to a broad range of conduct and property and deciding on the actual scope of its application later on.[61]

The argument that legislators should proceed with caution in the face of uncertainty does not, however, support the conclusion that the courts should be excluded from the process of making future decisions about the circumstances in which legislation directed at financing of terrorism should be applied. In fact, I would argue that this is one of the major defects of the new legislation. Having the courts play a greater role in the process of determining the scope of the new legislation would be a virtue because they are independent of the government and so their views are less likely to be compromised by political considerations. Moreover, the courts obviously possess a certain amount of expertise in criminal justice matters and, because of the adversarial nature of the judicial process and the judicial practice of giving reasons for decisions, are likely to produce decisions of relatively high quality. It is also significant that, as has frequently been noted by constitutional scholars, having the courts participate in the process of assessing the merits of legislation does not detract from the legislature's power to ultimately determine the content of our laws. Parliament is always free to respond to a judicial decision with which it disagrees by enacting new legislation, resorting if necessary to the *Charter*'s notwithstanding clause.[62]

For all these reasons I would argue that the inclusion of most, if not all, of the financing of terrorism offences in the *Anti-terrorism Act* was unwise because they give the courts too little explicit authority to participate in the process of deciding on their effective scope. I believe that a preferable approach would have been to address the conduct at issue under the rubric of the offence dealing with participating in and contributing to the activity of a terrorist group. Since the scope of that offence is defined quite vaguely the courts will play a more significant role in defining its outer limits than they will in defining the scope of the financing of terrorism offences. As for the forfeiture provisions, for similar reasons I believe that it would have been preferable to build in some discretion on the part of the court to determine whether or not a forfeiture order should be made in cases where the statutory pre-conditions have been satisfied.[63]

Finally, although the *Anti-terrorism Act* does not explicitly give the courts a significant role to play in the process of determining the scope of the new financing of terrorism offences, freezing offences and forfeiture provisions, it is always possible for the courts to effectively seize this power by holding that in certain respects the legislation violates the *Charter*. Plausible arguments can be made to the effect that certain applications of this legislation will involve impermissible violations of rights to equality, liberty and freedom of conscience, religion, expression or association. I believe that if the new provisions are to be retained then the courts should pay close attention to those arguments. This in turn implies that in cases where they give effect to constitutional arguments the courts will have to search for creative methods of precluding inappropriate enforcement of the legislation without unduly limiting the scope of the legislation in future cases. I personally have little doubt that such remedial techniques can be found. For example, one can imagine a court concluding that as a matter a constitutional law proposed section 83.03(b) must be read to include a requirement that property or financial or other related services that are provided etc. to a terrorist group must not only benefit the group, but also enhance its ability to facilitate or carry out a terrorist activity, before liability may be imposed. This additional requirement might serve to allow a court to bar a conviction in an appropriate case while still leaving a great deal of flexibility for other courts to determine whether other transactions enhance a group's ability to facilitate or carry out terrorist activity.[64]

6. Conclusion

The proposed *Anti-terrorism Act* is broad enough to be used to force Canadians to sever all economic ties with known terrorists, regardless of how uncertain it is whether creating or maintaining those ties will serve to facilitate terrorist activity, or how remote the resulting connection to terrorist activity might be. Striving to achieve this objective may well further important national interests, but only at the expense of, among other things, certain civil liberties. Moreover, at least initially, the costs of this legislation are likely to fall disproportionately on members of specific ethnocultural groups as their ability to engage in ordinary commercial transactions – both inside and outside of those groups – is impaired. In my view, the power to decide upon the circumstances in which the benefits of targeting people and property associated with terrorists outweigh the costs should be made cautiously and is too important to be left almost entirely in the hands of law enforcement officials. Unfortunately, the present government appears to have different views.

Notes

* Faculty of Law, University of Toronto. I am grateful to Jane Bailey, Guy Laine Charles, Kent Roach, Julian Roy, David Schneiderman, Martha Shaffer, Hamish Stewart and participants in the 'Security of Freedom' conference for helpful comments and conversations. Scott Patriquin provided outstanding research assistance. All errors remain my own.
1 For example, U.S. President Bush has stated, 'we will starve the terrorists of funding.' See www.washingtonpost.com/wpsrv/nation/specials/attacked/transcripts/bush092401.html.
2 Bill C-36, First Session, 37th Parl., 49-50 Elizabeth II, 2001. First reading, October 15, 2001.
3 The Convention was adopted by the General Assembly of the United Nations on

December 9, 1999 but is not yet in force. Canada has signed but not yet ratified the Convention. The Justice Minister and her staff have suggested that many of the provisions of the *Anti-terrorism Act* were designed to implement Canada's obligations under the Convention. See testimony of Anne McLellan, Minister of Justice and Attorney General of Canada and Mr. Donald Piragoff, Senior General Counsel, Criminal Law and Policy Division, Department of Justice, before the Special Senate Committee on the Subject Matter of Bill C-36, Monday October 22, 2001.

4 Proposed sections 83.02-83.04 (The *Anti-terrorism Act* proposes that all of these sections be added to the *Criminal Code*).

5 *Ibid.* One of the financing of terrorism offences, the one set out in proposed section 83.02, applies to different types of 'terrorist activity' from the other provisions. Section 83.02 essentially adopts the definition of terrorist activity used in the *Financing of Terrorism Convention*, whereas the other two financing of terrorism offences simply use the general definition of 'terrorist activity' provided in proposed section 83.01. The rationale for this lack of uniformity is unclear. One of the potential consequences is discussed below in footnote 16.

6 Proposed section 83.03.

7 Article 2 of the Convention outlines principal offences that cover any person who 'provides' or 'collects' funds. It then goes on to embrace anyone who 'participates as an accomplice in,' 'organizes or directs others to commit' and 'contributes to the commission of [by a group of persons acting with a common purpose]' the principal offences.

8 See H. Stewart, 'The Centrality of the Act Requirement for Criminal Attempts,' (2001) 51 UTLJ 399 at 401 and sources cited therein.

9 *Belyea* v. *R.* (1932), 57 C.C.C. 318 (S.C.C.).

10 *R.* v. *Dunlop* [1979] 2 S.C.R. 88.

11 *Criminal Code* section 88(1). Typically, however, a person charged with this offence will have done much more than simply possess the weapon. See *e.g. R.* v. *Jess,* [2000] O.J. No. 365; and *R.* v. *Saunders*, [1996] O.J. No. 518.

12 *Criminal Code* section 46(2)(d); *R.v. Schaefer* (1918), 31 C.C.C. 22 (Que. C.A.), leave to appeal to the Supreme Court of Canada refused (1919), 31 C.C.C. 252.

13 Proposed sections 83.03 and 83.04 apply to acts that amount to 'facilitating or carrying out any terrorist activity.' The reference to financing of facilitation goes further than required by the relevant provisions of the *Financing of Terrorism Convention*, which are outlined in note 7 above.

14 Proposed section 83.03. This provision is slightly broader than the equivalent provisions of the *Financing of Terrorism Convention*. The Convention does not clearly cover the financing either of facilitation or of individual terrorists.

15 *Ibid.*

16 This section uses the general definition of 'terrorist activity' provided in proposed section 83.01. Paragraph (a) of that definition includes, 'an act or omission committed or threatened in or outside Canada that, if committed in Canada, is one of the

following offences ... (x) the offences referred to in subsection 7(3.73) that implement [the *Financing of Terrorism Convention*].' Proposed section 83.02 avoids this problem by excluding offences listed in sub-paragraph (a)(x) of the definition of 'terrorist activity.'

17 In principle, he could also be liable for serving customers who, to his knowledge, simply have ordinary commercial dealings with terrorists.

18 Proposed section 83.01(1)

19 *Ibid.*

20 Proposed section 83.03.

21 See Canadian Bar Association, Submission on Bill C-36 – Anti-Terrorism Act (Toronto: Canadian Bar Association, October 2001), at 24.

22 However, see section 2.4 below for a possible explanation based on an analysis of the other terrorism offences.

23 See, *e.g.*, the testimony of Mr. Yvan Roy, Assistant Deputy Minister, Counsel, Department of Finance, to the Special Senate Committee on the Subject matter of Bill C-36, Monday October 22, 2001.

24 The mental elements of the offence created by proposed section 83.02 are slightly different from those of the offences created by the other two provisions dealing with financing of terrorism: section 83.02 requires the accused's conduct to be 'willfully and without lawful justification.' Section 83.02 is similar in this (and other) respects to the *Financing of Terrorism Convention*. The reasons for and implications of the lack of uniformity between the various financing of terrorism offences are unclear.

25 A.W. Mewett and M. Manning, *Mewett & Manning on Criminal Law* (3rd ed.) (Toronto: Butterworths, 1994) at 173–4.

26 But see *R. v. Hibbert*, [1995] 2 S.C.R. 973, paras. 23–39 (holding that the term 'purpose' in subsection 21(1)(b) should not be equated with 'desire').

27 Proposed section 83.03. Because the physical element of this offence is broadly defined it appears that the owner could be held liable whether or not his premises are actually used to plan terrorist activity, so long as he knows that they are being used by people who intend to use other venues to facilitate or carry out terrorist activity.

28 See *e.g. R. v. Patrygura*, (1960), 129 C.C.C. 333 (Sask.C.A.).

29 All of the terrorism offences require the prosecution to establish the existence of some degree of awareness on the part of the accused of a connection between his or her actions and terrorist activity. One of the definitions of terrorist activity refers to acts that are committed 'in whole or in part for a political, religious or ideological purpose, objective or cause.' See proposed section 83.01(1).

30 Proposed sections 83.18–23.

31 Proposed section 83.18.

32 Proposed section 83.01(2).

33 Proposed section 83.18(3).

34 It is beyond the scope of this paper to discuss the reporting obligations that are

created by several of the provisions located under the heading 'Freezing of Property.'

35 Proposed section 83.08.

36 *Financing of Terrorism Convention, supra* note 3, Article 8(1).

37 Proposed sections 83.09.

38 Proposed sections 83.13-17, 462.3(a.01) and 490.1 (1.1).

39 *Criminal Code* section 462.37(1).

40 *Criminal Code* section, 490.1(1).

41 *Criminal Code* sections 462.37, 462.38, 490.1 and 490.2.

42 Proposed section 462.37(2).

43 Proposed sections 462.3(a.01) and 490.1 (1.1). These provisions will be repealed (on account of redundancy) once Bill C-24, *An Act to amend the Criminal Code (organized crime and law enforcement) and to make consequential amendments to other Acts*, 1st Session, 37th Parliament, 49-50 Elizabeth II, 2001, comes into force. That Bill provides the predicate offences upon which the *Criminal Code's* current forfeiture provisions are based include all but prescribed indictable offences. See *Anti-terrorism Act*, subsections 130(3), (4), (6) and (7).

44 Proposed sections 2 and 83.18

45 Proposed section 83.14(1).

46 Proposed section 83.14(1)(a).

47 *Financing of Terrorism Convention, supra* note 3, Article 8(2).

48 Proposed section 83.14(5).

49 Proposed section 83.14(5).

50 Proposed section 83.14(8).

51 See *e.g. Criminal Code* sections 462.42 and 490.5. For further discussion see K. Davis, 'The Effects of Forfeiture on the Property of Third Parties' (unpublished manuscript).

52 Proposed section 83.14(7) (using the word 'may' rather than 'shall').

53 Proposed sections 83.14(10) and (11).

54 See proposed section 83.13(1) and *Criminal Code* sections 462.32, 462.33, 487, 490.8.

55 See proposed section 83.15 and *Criminal Code* section 462.35.

56 Proposed section 83.13(1).

57 Proposed section 83.24.

58 Proposed section 83.18.

59 *Stein* v. *Kathy K (The)*, [1976] 2 S.C.R. 802; *Jaegli Enterprises Limited* v. *Taylor (Guardian ad litem of)*, [1981] 2. S.C.R. 2 (stating general principle and noting that an exception can be made in the case of a 'palpable and overriding error').

60 Bill 30, *Remedies for Organized Crime and Other Unlawful Activities Act, 2001*, 2d Session, 37th, Ont. 2001, S. 3(1) and (3), (1st reading, May 9, 2001).

61 Proposed section 83.14(7) (discussed in section 4.2 above).

62 This argument does not apply to legislation enacted in response to problems whose dimensions are well understood. Most criminal offences are designed to deal with

very familiar problems and so their scope should be defined clearly and narrowly. See K. Davis and J. Roy, 'Fraud in the Canadian Courts: An Unwarranted Expansion of the Scope of the Criminal Sanction' (1998) 30 *Can. Bus. L. J.* 210.

63 Some might go further and argue that Parliament should have left the financing of terrorism to be dealt with under existing law concerning liability of co-conspirators and parties in relation to offences committed by carrying out or attempting terrorist activity.

64 The most significant obstacle to a successful constitutional challenge would be the fact that section 1 of the *Charter* protects limitations on constitutional rights that are demonstrably justified in a free and democratic society. Here it is relevant that strong arguments can be made that the objective of the provisions in question is to encourage Canadians to sever all economic ties with terrorists and that this is a legitimate governmental objective. Virtually all of the provisions discussed in this paper appear to be rationally connected to achieving this objective and may even represent the most minimally intrusive means of doing so. In addition, as far as the forfeiture provisions are concerned, another obstacle to a successful constitutional challenge is likely to be the fact that the *Charter* does not explicitly protect rights to property.

Charitable Status and Terrorist Financing: Rethinking the Proposed *Charities Registration (Security Information) Act*

DAVID G. DUFF[*]

Faculty of Law
University of Toronto

I. Introduction

Among the many provisions of Bill C-36,[1] Part 6 contains the *Charities Registration (Security Information) Act* (CRSIA) and consequential amendments to the federal *Income Tax Act*,[2] which provide for the denial of charitable status to an applicant and revocation of charitable status of a registered charity where a Federal Court judge determines that there are reasonable grounds to believe that the applicant or registered charity has made, makes or will make available any resources directly or indirectly to an entity that engages or will engage in terrorist activities or activities in support of terrorist activities.

Unlike other Parts of Bill C-36, Part 6 was not drafted in response to the horrific events of 11 September 2001, but originates in former Bill C-16,[3] which was introduced on 15 March 2001 and withdrawn by unanimous consent with the introduction of Bill C-36 on 15 October 2001. While the introduction of Bill C-16 was obviously motivated by the same concerns about international terrorism that underlie Bill C-36, its direct antecedents are resolutions adopted by the G-7 and the United Nations in 1996,[4] and a specific recommendation by the Special Senate Committee on Security and Intelligence in January 1999.[5] According to CRSIA, subsection 2(1), moreover:

> The purpose of this Act is to demonstrate Canada's commitment to participating in concerted international efforts to deny support to those who engage in terrorism, to protect the integrity of the registration system for

charities under the *Income Tax Act* and to maintain the confidence of Canadian taxpayers that the benefits of charitable registration are made available only to organizations that operate exclusively for charitable purposes.

As a result, the purpose of Part 6 of Bill C-36 is not only to prevent fundraising for terrorist activities, but also to ensure that organizations obtaining charitable status under the ITA use their resources in a manner consistent with the purposes underlying the favourable tax treatment that they receive. Indeed, with the introduction in Bill C-36 of specific offences against funding terrorism and other provisions governing the freezing, seizure or forfeiture of property,[6] which address the first of these purposes much more effectively than denial of charitable status could ever hope to do, it is arguable that compliance with the goals of charitable status under the ITA should now be viewed as the primary purpose of the CRSIA. From this perspective, this paper will argue, Part 6 of Bill C-36 is deeply flawed.

In order to make this argument, the remainder of this paper is divided into three parts. Part II summarizes the implications of and criteria for determining charitable status under the ITA, reviewing statutory rules, judicial principles and administrative practices governing their registration and the revocation of charitable status. Part III describes the main features of the CRSIA and its implications for charitable status under the ITA. Part IV evaluates specific aspects of the new legislation, identifying a number of concerns with the proposed legislation as a sound method 'to protect the integrity of the registration system for charities under the *Income Tax Act* and to maintain the confidence of Canadian taxpayers that the benefits of charitable registration are made available only to organizations that operate exclusively for charitable purposes.'

II. Charitable Status and the Income Tax Act

Charitable status confers two benefits under the ITA. First, under paragraph 149(1)(f), registered charities are exempt from tax on their income. This benefit is also enjoyed by non-profit organizations, which are defined in paragraph 149(1)(l) of the ITA as clubs, societies or associations that, in the opinion of the Minister of National Revenue, were not charities and that were 'organized and operated exclusively for social welfare, civic improvement, pleasure or recreation or for any other purpose except profit, no part of the income of which was payable to, or was otherwise available for the personal benefit of, any proprietor, member or shareholder thereof ...'

Second, and more importantly, unlike non-profit organizations, registered charities may issue receipts for qualifying contributions that they receive, which entitle corporate donors to claim a deduction in computing their taxable income,[7] individual donors to claim a non-refundable credit in computing federal and provincial tax payable,[8] and both kinds of donors to obtain the benefit of a lower rate of capital gains tax than might otherwise be payable on gifts of publicly-traded securities or ecologically sensitive land where this property has appreciated in value prior to the making of the gift.[9] Although various rationales are often advanced in favour of these kinds of provisions,[10] they are best viewed as tax incentives or 'tax expenditures' that are designed to provide an indirect subsidy to registered charities and other 'qualified donees'[11] by encouraging individuals and corporations to make donations to these entities. A subsidy for these entities is generally justified on the grounds that they provide public benefits that would otherwise be undersupplied, and perform quasi-governmental functions that would otherwise have to be financed by tax revenues.[12] The indirect form of this subsidy in the form of a tax incentive is often favoured as a more pluralistic method of subsidizing these activities than direct subsidies – allowing donors to select the organizations and purposes to which they wish to direct public subsidies without having to obtain the agreement of a political majority.[13] Although there is considerable debate over the appropriate design of these tax incentives,[14] this issue is not the concern of this paper. The annual cost of these incentives in terms of foregone revenues was estimated to be approximately $1.36 billion in 1997.[15]

If the public benefits and quasi-governmental functions that are provided or carried on by specific kinds of organizations are the primary justification for public subsidies, one might reasonably expect that these characteristics would be the key criteria governing ITA status as a registered charity or other qualified donee.[16] In practice, however, while these considerations may explain the inclusion of qualified donees in addition to registered charities, an assessment of public benefits and quasi-governmental functions plays only a limited part in the determination of charitable status.

The starting point for this determination is ITA subsection 248(1), which defines a 'registered charity' as a charitable organization, private foundation or public foundation (or division thereof) that is resident in Canada and was either created or established in Canada, provided that it has 'applied to the Minister in prescribed form for registration, and is at that time registered as a charitable organization, private foundation or public foundation.' Pursuant to this provision, the Canada Customs and Revenue Agency (CCRA) supervises initial and continuing eligibility for charitable status, subject to a right of appeal on the part of an applicant or registered charity to the Federal Court of Appeal.[17]

The terms charitable organization, private foundation, and public foundation are defined in ITA section 149.1, which contains the statutory rules governing charitable status. According to subsection 149.1(1), a charitable organization means an organization, whether or not incorporated,

(a) all the resources of which are devoted to charitable activities carried on by the organization itself,
(b) no part of the income of which is payable to, or is otherwise available for, the personal benefit of any proprietor, member, shareholder, trustee or settlor thereof, [and]
(c) more than 50% of the directors, trustees, officers or like officials of which deal with each other and with each of the other directors, trustees, officers or officials at arm's length ...

while a 'charitable foundation' means

a corporation or trust that is constituted and operated exclusively for charitable purposes, no part of the income of which is payable to, or otherwise available for, the personal benefit of any proprietor, member, shareholder, trustee or settlor thereof, and that is not a charitable organization.

A charitable foundation is classified as a 'public foundation' where most of its officials deal with each other at arm's length and no more than 50% of the foundation's capital was contributed by a single person or by members of a group who do not deal with each other at arm's length.[18] Otherwise, the charitable foundation is classified as a 'private foundation.'

Whereas the distinction between a public and private foundation turns on the extent to which it is controlled by a single person or related group, the distinction between a charitable organization and a charitable foundation generally turns on the manner in which they engage in charitable pursuits. As a general rule, charitable organizations must devote their resources to 'charitable activities' that they themselves carry on, although ITA subsection 149.1(6) relaxes this requirement by considering a charitable organization to be devoting its resources to charitable activities carried on by it where it carries on a related business, disburses not more than 50% of its income to qualified donees, or disburses income to a registered charity with which it is 'associated.'[19] As an administrative practice, moreover, the CCRA recognizes as charitable activities carried on by a registered charity any charitable activity that is carried on outside Canada through an intermediary such as an agent, a contractor or other body.[20] In contrast to charitable organizations, charitable foundations are merely required to operate for 'charitable purposes' – a term which subsection 149.1(1) specifically defines to include 'the disbursement of funds to qualified donees.' In general, therefore, charitable organizations engage in charitable activities themselves or through intermediaries, while charitable foundations operate for charitable purposes by disbursing funds to charitable organizations and other qualified donees.

Notwithstanding these differences between charitable organizations and charitable foundations, the ITA requires both types of registered charity to be 'exclusively charitable' – devoting 'all' of their 'resources' to charitable activities in the case of charitable organizations, and operating 'exclusively' for charitable purposes in the case of charitable foundations. Where a charitable foundation or organization devotes 'substantially all of its resources' to charitable purposes (in the case of a charitable foundation) or charitable activities carried on by it (in the case of a charitable organization), however, ITA subsections 149.1(6.1) and (6.2) permit the charity to devote part of its resources to 'political activities,' provided that they are 'ancillary and incidental' to the foundation's charitable purposes or the organization's charitable activities and 'do not include the direct or indirect support of, or opposition to, any political party or candidate for public office.' More generally, judicial decisions have held that the pursuit of purposes that are not themselves charitable, but 'incidental to' or 'a means to the fulfillment of' other charitable purposes' will not deprive an organization or foundation of charitable status.[21]

Since the ITA does not, aside from these provisions, define the terms 'charitable activities' and 'charitable purposes,' Canadian courts have generally sought guidance in the common law of trusts, which admits charitable purpose trusts as an exception to the general rule that a purpose trust is invalid. Although the definition of a charitable organization mentions charitable activities, not purposes, the Supreme Court of Canada has downplayed the distinction, stating that 'it is really the purpose in furtherance of which an activity is carried out, and not the character of the activity, that determines whether or not it is of a charitable nature.'[22]

Where an organization is established for a charitable purpose, however, the Court has also emphasized that it is necessary to consider the activities carried on by the organization in order to ensure that they are 'in furtherance of' the charitable purpose.[23]

The traditional starting point for judicial interpretations of charitable purposes is Lord Macnaghton's statement in *Commissioners for Special Purposes of the Income Tax v. Pemsel*,[24] that:

> 'Charity' in its legal sense comprises four principal divisions: trusts for the relief of poverty; trusts for the advancement of education; trusts for the advancement of religion; and trusts for other purposes beneficial to the community, not falling under any of the preceding heads.

Superimposed on these categories, however, is a further requirement that the purpose of the trust must be '[f]or the benefit of the community or of an appreciably important class of the community.'[25] On the basis that judges cannot and/or should not determine whether a proposed change in the law is for the public benefit,[26] moreover, the courts and revenue authorities have traditionally denied charitable status where the activities or purposes of the organization or foundation advocate social change or promote a particular ideological outlook.[27]

Consistent with these judicial tests, registration as a charitable organization or foundation by the CCRA turns on the existence of a charitable purpose under one of the four *Pemsel* categories, the demonstration of a public benefit, an absence of political purposes or activities, and an indication of the manner in which the activities of a charitable organization will fulfill its charitable purpose or purposes.[28] Once registered, charitable organizations and foundations are subject to further requirements: (1) to maintain books and records containing sufficient information to permit the Minister to determine whether the charity is operating in accordance with the ITA;[29] (2) to file annual information and public information returns,[30] the latter of which is made available to the public;[31] (3) to refrain from various commercial activities;[32] and (4) to satisfy a 'disbursement quota' according to which the charity must generally expend 80% of the amount of receipted gifts from the previous year on charitable activities or gifts to qualified donees.[33] Where the registered charity ceases to comply with these requirements or with the initial statutory and judicial requirements for registration, the Minister may revoke this status,[34] subject to a right of appeal by the registered charity to the Federal Court of Appeal.[35] Where charitable status is revoked, the charity is given one year to distribute its assets to qualified donees or expend its resources on charitable activities, after which the value of any remaining assets is effectively forfeited to the Crown under the special tax for this purpose.[36]

III. The Proposed *Charities Registration (Security Information) Act*

Although formally distinct from the ITA, the proposed CRSIA in Part 6 of Bill C-36 is best understood as a series of amendments to the substantive and procedural rules governing charitable status under the ITA that were outlined in Part II of this paper. In order to accomplish this objective, Bill C-36 also contains consequential amendments to the ITA itself.

Substantively, the key provisions of the CRSIA are subsections 4(1) and 9(1). According to the first of these provisions, the Solicitor-General and Minister of National Revenue may sign a certificate expressing their opinion, based on security or criminal intelligence reports, that there are reasonable grounds to believe:

(a) that an applicant or registered charity has made, makes or will make available any resources directly or indirectly, to an entity that is a listed entity as defined in subsection 83.01(1) of the *Criminal Code*;

(b) that an applicant or registered charity made available any resources, directly or indirectly, to an entity as defined in subsection 83.01(1) of the *Criminal Code* and the entity was at that time, and continues to be, engaged in terrorist activities as defined in that subsection or activities in support of them; or

(c) that an applicant or registered charity makes or will make available any resources, directly or indirectly, to an entity as defined in subsection 83.01(1) of the *Criminal Code* and the entity engages or will engage in terrorist activities as defined in that subsection or activities in support of them.

According to subsection 9(1), a certificate that is determined to be reasonable under the process outlined below is 'conclusive proof, in the case of an applicant, that it is ineligible to become a registered charity or, in the case of a registered charity, that it does not comply with the requirements to continue to be a registered charity.' On this basis, therefore, the CCRA may deny charitable status to an applicant or revoke the charitable status of a registered charity where the applicant or registered charity is subject to a certificate that is determined to be reasonable under the CRSIA. For the latter purpose, moreover, section 114 of Bill C-36 proposes to amend the ITA by adding new subsection 168(3), providing for the immediate revocation of a registered charity's charitable status upon a determination that a certificate is reasonable under the CRSIA.

The process for determining whether a certificate issued under subsection 4(1) is reasonable is set out in CRSIA sections 5 to 8. According to subsection 5(1) of the proposed legislation, as soon as the Solicitor-General and the Minister of National Revenue have signed a certificate, the Solicitor-General or a person authorized by the Solicitor-General shall cause the applicant or registered charity to be served with a copy of the certificate and a notice informing it that 'the certificate will be referred to the Federal Court not earlier than seven days after service and that, if the certificate is determined to be reasonable, the applicant will be ineligible to become a registered charity or the registration of the registered charity will be revoked, as the case may be.' In addition, CRSIA subsection 5(5) stipulates that seven days after this service 'or as soon afterwards as is practicable,' the Solicitor-General or a person authorized by the Solicitor-General shall file a copy of the certificate with the Federal Court for it to make a determination under paragraph 6(1)(d) and cause the applicant or registered charity to be served with a notice informing it of the filing of the certificate.

Once the certificate is referred to the Federal Court, CRSIA subsection 6(1) provides that the Chief Justice of the Federal Court or a judge of the Trial Division designated by the Chief Justice shall, without delay:

(a) examine, in private, the security or criminal intelligence reports [on which the certificate is based] and hear any other evidence or information that may be presented by or on behalf of [the Solicitor-General or Minister of National Revenue] and may, on the request of [one of these Ministers], hear all or part of that evidence or information in the absence of the applicant or registered charity and any counsel representing it, if the judge is of the opinion that disclosure of the information would injure national security or endanger the safety of any person;

(b) provide the applicant or registered charity with a statement summarizing the information available to the judge so as to enable the applicant or registered charity to be reasonably informed of the circumstances giving rise to the certificate, without disclosing any information the disclosure of which would, in the judge's opinion, injure national security or endanger the safety of any person;

(c) provide the applicant or registered charity with a reasonable opportunity to be heard; and

(d) determine whether the certificate is reasonable on the basis of the information available to the judge and, if found not to be reasonable, quash it.

For the purpose of this process, moreover, section 7 waives the ordinary rules of evidence regarding the admissibility of information, and section 8 authorizes the judge to examine 'in private and in the absence of the applicant or registered charity or counsel representing it,' information provided by the Solicitor-General or Minister of National Revenue that was 'obtained in confidence from a government, an institution or an agency of a foreign state, from an international organization of states or from an institution or agency of an international organization of states' and base the determination under paragraph 6(1)(d) on this information without disclosing it in the statement mentioned in paragraph 6(1)(b) if the judge decides that 'the information is relevant but that its disclosure would injure national security or endanger the safety of any person.'

Although an applicant or registered charity may, upon receiving a notice of the certificate, apply to the Federal Court for an order prohibiting the publication or broadcast of the identity of the applicant or registered charity and treating all documents filed with the Court as confidential,[37] where a certificate is determined to be reasonable under CRSIA paragraph 6(1)(d), the Solicitor-General is required 'without delay' to cause the certificate to be published in the *Canada Gazette*,[38] thereby making the name of the applicant or registered charity public information. In addition, subsection 6(2) of the proposed legislation stipulates that a determination under paragraph 6(1)(d) is 'not subject to appeal or review by any court.' For this purpose, section 115 of Bill C-36 proposes to amend section 172 of the ITA to preclude the normal right of appeal by an applicant or registered charity to the Federal Court of Appeal where the applicant or registered charity is the subject of a certificate that has been determined to be reasonable under CRSIA paragraph 6(1)(d). Finally, where an applicant or former registered charity that was subject to a certificate that was determined to be reasonable under paragraph 6(1)(d) 'believes that there has been a material change in circumstances since that determination was made,' the applicant or former registered charity may request a review of the certificate by the Solicitor-General and the Minister of National Revenue, which may continue or cancel the certificate, subject to a further review by the Federal Court in accordance with the procedure established for the original determination regarding the certificate's reasonableness under CRSIA sections 6 to 8.[39] Where a certificate is not cancelled pursuant to this process, CRSIA section 13 provides that it is 'effective for a period of seven years beginning on the day it is first determined to be reasonable under paragraph 6(1)(d).' As a result, the effect of a determination that a certificate is reasonable is subject to its own 'sunset clause.'

IV. Evaluation

In order to evaluate the merits of the proposed CRSIA and consequential amendments to the ITA, it is useful to begin with ten general propositions that shape this evaluation.[40] Although my specific comments on the proposed legislation are directly mainly at the new substantive criteria for denying or revoking charitable status, these relate to a more general understanding of the relationship between this sanction and other measures directed at the suppression of terrorist financing.

First, although the concept of terrorism, like many concepts, may be contestable and difficult to define, it is sufficiently intelligible to permit meaningful legal regulation of individual or organizational conduct in respect of terrorist activities.[41] Second, as international conventions have emphasized,[42] it is imperative that governments take all necessary and reasonable measures to suppress the financing of these activities, whether this financial support is intentional or unintentional. Third, where fundraising for terrorist activities is intentional, this conduct is properly regarded as criminal, and appropriately addressed through criminal procedures incorporating well-established rights for the accused. Fourth, where organizations negligently permit the financing of terrorist activities, these organizations might reasonably be subject to lesser sanctions including, where applicable, the denial or revocation of charitable status. Indeed, as subsection 2(1) of the CRSIA explains, the rationale for the denial or revocation of charitable status in these circumstances is not only to discourage charitable fundraising for terrorist organizations, which is more appropriately and effectively addressed by criminal sanctions in any event, but also 'to protect the integrity of the registration system for charities under the *Income Tax Act* and to maintain the confidence of Canadian taxpayers that the benefits of charitable registration are made available only to organizations that operate exclusively for charitable purposes.' Fifth, in denying or revoking charitable status, the procedures and burden of proof involved need not be as rigorous as those involved in the application of criminal laws involving the liberty of individuals in a more substantial way.

Sixth, in addressing concerns about terrorist fundraising and the integrity of the tax regime for registered charities, it is also important to recognize the useful and important work that most of these organizations and foundations perform, both domestically and internationally, particularly in countries that have been devastated by the kinds of political, religious, ethnic and/or ideological conflicts which frequently foster the kinds of activities that are often regarded as terrorist. Indeed, the kinds of international charitable activities carried on by these organizations are properly regarded as crucial efforts in the current campaign against international terrorism. Seventh, regarding the pursuit of charitable activities outside Canada, it is important to appreciate the limitations under which many charitable organizations operate – limitations which the CCRA recognizes through its administrative practice of recognizing as charitable activities of the registered charity in Canada any charitable activity that is carried on outside Canada through an intermediary such as an agent, a contractor or other body.[43] As a result, as aerial drops of food aid in Afghanistan illustrate, in providing international aid in many countries it is often necessary to balance the benefits of this aid against the risk that some resources may end up in the hands of persons engaged in terrorist activities.

Eighth, given the important work that many charitable organizations and foundations carry out and the considerable difficulties carrying out charitable activities outside Canada and particularly in countries in the most desperate conditions, it would be inappropriate to assume bad faith on the part of a charitable organization or foundation some of the resources of which end up in the hands of persons engaged in terrorist activities, absent some indication that persons directing the organization or foundation actually intended to finance terrorist activities or were willfully blind regarding the activities carried on or the funds disbursed. As a result, absent some suspicion of criminal intent, any applicant or registered charity that is determined to have made or to be making available resources to a person or organization engaging in or likely to engage in terrorist activities should be given a reasonable opportunity to change its practicesprior to the denial or revocation of its charitable status. Likewise, where charitable status is ultimately denied or revoked, the applicant or registered charity should be given a reasonable opportunity to respond to the case against it in as open a process as possible.

Ninth, in evaluating the need for new measures like the CRSIA, it is important to acknowledge existing rules governing charitable status under the ITA, which would be unavailable in any event to any organization that does not devote 'all of its resources' to charitable activities (including limited disbursement of funds to qualified donees and 'ancillary and incidental' political activities) and to any foundation which does not operate 'exclusively' for charitable purposes (also including the disbursement of funds to qualified donees and 'ancillary and incidental' political activities).[44] Finally, to the extent that existing rules are considered inadequate to address concerns about terrorist financing, it is not clear that the optimal solution lies in further rules and more restrictive procedures than in administrative support to registered charities which are often lacking in the necessary staff and resources to properly monitor overseas activities and disbursements, as well as more effective administration and enforcement of existing rules through an increase in CCRA audits.

Turning to the proposed legislation itself, the last two comments might suggest that there is no pressing need for the CRSIA, the objectives of which could be achieved through a more rigorous supervisory role on the part of the CCRA. Indeed, with the introduction in Bill C-36 of specific offences against terrorist financing and other provisions governing the freezing, seizure or forfeiture of property, it is not clear that the CRSIA has an important role to play in the context of charitable status that cannot be fulfilled by the existing rules. For similar reasons, the Canadian Bar Association opposed the enactment of Bill C-16 last May and recommended in its submission on Bill C-36 that Part 6 should be deleted.

Notwithstanding this conclusion, it is arguable that something like the CRSIA may be useful as a supplement to the current rules governing charitable status and to the proposed criminal offences for terrorist financing – providing a process whereby security and intelligence information might be employed to warn applicants and registered charities that their activities or disbursements are supporting terrorism. From this perspective, however, the current legislation is draconian in the extreme – applying where 'any resources' are made available 'directly or indirectly' to one of the targeted entities, without defining the concept of 'indirect' availability; defining the targeted entities not only as listed entities and entities engaged in terrorist activities, but also entities that 'will engage' in terrorist activities, and entities that engage or will engage in 'activities in support of' terrorist activities, without providing any indication regarding the kinds of activities that might be considered to be 'in support of' terrorist activities; adopting an extremely low standard of reasonable belief for the issuance of a certificate under subsection 4(1), and a minimal standard of reasonableness for judicial review of the certificate under subsection 6(1); providing no opportunity for the applicant or registered charity to change its practices in response to the issuance of the certificate; applying on an absolute liability basis without any defence of due diligence; setting out a secretive process of judicial review that makes it difficult for the applicant or registered charity to know the case against it; and providing no right of appeal.[45]

Not surprisingly, organizations which have made representations to Parliamentary committees examining Bills C-16 and C-36 have suggested that the enactment of these measures will have a 'chilling effect' on charitable fundraising, particularly for international assistance in the most volatile and desperate countries in the world. While this result will undoubtedly deny some resources to terrorists and their supporters, as would happen if the U.S. ceased aerial drops of food aid to Afghanistan, the ultimate outcome may well produce more harm than good.

Notes

* Associate Professor, Faculty of Law, University of Toronto. I am indebted to Simon Proulx for research assistance in the preparation of this paper.
1 *An Act to amend the Criminal Code, the Official Secrets Act, the Canada Evidence Act, the Proceeds of Crime (Money Laundering) Act and other Acts, and to enact measures respecting the registration of charities, in order to combat terrorism,* First Session, Thirty-seventh Parliament, 49–50 Elizabeth II, 2001 (First Reading, 15 October 2001) (hereafter 'Bill C-36').
2 R.S.C. 1985, c.1 (5th Supp.) [as amended] (hereafter 'ITA').
3 *An Act respecting the registration of charities and security information and to amend the Income Tax Act,* First Session, Thirty-seventh Parliament, 49–50 Elizabeth II, 2001 (First Reading, 15 March 2001) (hereafter 'Bill C-16').
4 G-7 Ministerial Conference on Terrorism (Paris, 30 July 1996), 'Agreement on 25 Measures,' Resolution 19 (calling on all States to; '[p]revent and take steps to counteract, through appropriate domestic measures, the financing of terrorists and terrorist organizations, whether such financing is direct or indirect through organizations which also have, or claim to have charitable, social or cultural goals, or which are also engaged in unlawful activities such as illicit arms trafficking, drug dealing, and racketeering'); and General Assembly resolution 51/210 (17 December 1996), paragraph 3(f) (calling on all States to tax steps 'to prevent and counteract,

through appropriate domestic measures, the financing of terrorists and terrorist organizations, whether such financing is direct or indirect through organizations which also have or claim to have charitable, social or cultural goals or which are also engaged in unlawful activities such as illicit arms trafficking, drug dealing and racketeering, including the exploitation of persons for purposes of funding terrorist activities ...').

5 *The Report of the Special Senate Committee on Security and Intelligence*, Chair: Hon. William M. Kelly, (January 1999), Recommendation 13 ('that consideration be given to amending the *Income Tax Act* to allow Revenue Canada [now the Canada Customs and Revenue Agency] to deny charitable registration to any group on the basis of a certificate from the Canadian Security Intelligence Service that the group constitutes a threat to the security of Canada.').

6 See proposed *Criminal Code* sections 83.02, 83.04, and 83.08–83.17. For a review of these provisions, see Kevin Davis, 'Cutting Off the Flow of Funds to Terrorists – Whose Funds? Which Funds? Who Decides?' in this volume.

7 ITA, section 110.1.

8 ITA, section 118.1. At the federal level, this credit is computed at the lowest marginal rate of tax for the first $200 of total gifts claimed in the taxation year and the highest marginal rate for amounts exceeding $200. For the year 2001, the federal rate structure implies a credit of 16 percent on the first $200 claimed each year and 29 percent on amounts over $200. Most provinces adopt a similar two-tiered rate structure for their credits, which generally range from 6.2 to 11.5 percent on the first $200 and 16 to 18.2 percent on amounts above this threshold. In Alberta, which introduced a flat-rate income tax of 10% effective for 2001 and subsequent taxation years, the credit is computed at 10% for the first $200 and 12.75% on amounts over $200. In Quebec, the credit is computed at a rate of 22% on the first $2,000 claimed in the year, and 25% on amounts exceeding $2,000.

9 ITA, paragraphs 38(a.1) and (a.2) (reducing the capital gains 'inclusion rate' on gifts of these kinds of property to registered charities and other 'qualified donees' from one-half to one-quarter).

10 For a review and critical evaluation of alternative rationales for the tax recognition of charitable contributions, see David G. Duff, 'Charitable Contributions and the Personal Income Tax: Evaluating the Canadian Credit' in Jim Phillips, Bruce Chapman, and David Stevens, eds., *Between State and Market: Essays on Charities Law and Policy in Canada*, (Montreal and Kingston: McGill-Queen's University Press, 2001) 407 at 425–36.

11 In addition to registered charities, ITA sections 110.1 and 118.1 also permit donors to claim a deduction or non-refundable credit, as the case may be, for gifts to a registered Canadian amateur athletic association, a housing corporation that is resident in Canada and that was 'constituted exclusively for the purpose of providing low-cost housing accommodation for the aged, no part of the income of which was payable to, or was otherwise available for the personal benefit of, any proprietor, member or shareholder thereof,' a Canadian municipality, the United Nations

or an agency thereof, a university outside Canada that is prescribed to be a university the student body of which ordinarily includes students from Canada, a charitable organization outside Canada to which Her Majesty in right of Canada has made a gift in the year or in the 12–month period preceding the year, or Her Majesty in right of Canada or a province. ITA subsection 149.1(1) defines these entities as well as registered charities as 'qualified donees.'

12 See, e.g., Lester M. Salamon, 'Partners in Public Service: The Scope and Theory of Government-Non-profit Relations,' in Walter Powell, ed., *The Non-profit Sector: A Research Handbook* (New Haven, Conn.: Yale University Press, 1987) 99; and Rick Krever, 'Tax Deductions for Charitable Donations: A Tax Expenditure Analysis' in Richard Krever and Gretchen Kewley, eds., *Charities and Philanthropic Institutions: Reforming the Tax Subsidy and Regulatory Regimes*, (Melbourne: Australian Tax Research Foundation, 1991) 1 at 8–13.

13 See, e.g., Krever, 'Tax Deductions and Charitable Donations,' *supra* note 12 at 11–13; and Duff, 'Charitable Contributions and the Personal Income Tax,' *supra* note 10 at 433–36. For a more general discussion of the use of the tax system to vote on public spending decisions, see Saul Levmore, 'Taxes as Ballots' (1998), 65 *U. Chi. L. Rev.* 387. For a critical view of tax incentives for charitable giving, see Neil Brooks, 'The Tax Credit for Charitable Contributions: Giving Credit Where None is Due' in Phillips et. al., eds., *Between State and Market, supra* note 10, 457 (favouring direct subsidies over indirect subsidies delivered through the tax system).

14 See, e.g., David G. Duff, 'Tax Treatment of Charitable Contributions in Canada: Theory, Structure, and Reform,' Paper Delivered at the Thirteenth Annual Conference of the National Center on Philanthropy and the Law, (New York University School of Law, 25 October 2001) (advocating repeal of the corporate deduction, elimination of the lower capital gains inclusion rate on gifts of publicly-traded securities and ecologically sensitive land, and the conversion of the non-refundable tax credit for individuals into a refundable tax credit with a declining rate structure designed to provide a greater tax incentive for a large number of small gifts than for a small number of very large gifts).

15 Department of Finance, *Tax Expenditures and Evaluations*, (Ottawa: the department, 2001).

16 For an argument to this effect, see Duff, 'Tax Treatment of Charitable Contributions in Canada,' *supra* note 14.

17 ITA, subsections 172(3) and (4), and section 180.

18 For foundations registered before February 16, 1984, the limit on contributions of capital by a single person or group of persons not dealing with each other at arm's length is 75% rather than 50%.

19 According to ITA, subsection 149.1(7), the Minister may on application designate a registered charity as a charity associated with one or more registered charities where 'the Minister is satisfied that the charitable aim or activity of each of the registered charities is substantially the same ...'

20 CCRA, *Registered Charities: Operating Outside Canada*, RC4106(E), available

on the CCRA website: http://www.ccra-adrc.gc.ca. According to this document, '[t]hese arrangements can be an acceptable devotion of the charity's resources to its "own activities" providing: the charity has obtained reasonable assurance before entering into agreements with individuals or other organizations that they are able to deliver the services required by the charity (by virtue of their reputation, expertise, years of experience, etc.); all expenditures will further the Canadian charity's formal purposes and constitute charitable activities that the Canadian charity carries on itself; an adequate agreement is in place [as suggested in the document]; the charity provided periodic, specific instructions to individuals of organizations as and when appropriate; the charity regularly monitors the progress of the project or program and can provide satisfactory evidence of this ...; and, where appropriate, the charity makes periodic payments on the basis of this monitoring (as opposed to a single lump sum payment) and maintains the right to discontinue payments at any time if not satisfied.'

21 *British Launderers' Research Association* v. *Borough of Hendon Rating Authority*, [1949] 1 K.B. 462 (C.A.), cited with approval by the Supreme Court of Canada in *Guaranty Trust Co. of Canada* v. *MNR*, [1967] SCR 113 at 143 (hereafter *Guaranty Trust*).

22 *Vancouver Society of Immigrant and Visible Minority Women* v. *MNR*, [1999] 1 SCR 10 at para. 152.

23 *Ibid.* at para. 194.

24 [1891] A.C. 531 at 583 (hereafter *Pemsel*).

25 *Verge v. Somerville*, [1924] AC 496 at 499, cited with approval in *Guaranty Trust*, *supra* note 21 at 141.

26 See, e.g., *Bowman v. Secular Society, Ltd.*, [1917] AC 406 at 442 ('the Court has no means of judging whether a proposed change in the law will or will not be for the public benefit, and therefore cannot say that the gift to secure the change is a charitable gift'); and *Human Life International in Canada Inc. v. MNR*, [1998] 3 CTC 126, 98 DTC 6196 (FCA) ('Courts should not be called upon to make such decisions as it involves granting or denying legitimacy to what are essentially political views: namely what are the proper forms of conduct, though not mandated by present law, to be urged on other members of the community?'). For a conceptual discussion of the political purposes doctrine in the law of charities, see Abraham Drassinower, 'The Doctrine of Political Purposes in the Law of Charities: A Conceptual Analysis,' in Phillips et. al., eds., *Between State and Market*, *supra* note 10, 288.

27 See, e.g., *Challenge Team v. Revenue Canada*, [2000] 2 CTC 352, 2000 DTC 6242 (FCA). See also CCRA, *Registered Charities: Education, Advocacy, and Political Activities*, RC4107E Draft#2, available on the CCRA website.

28 CCRA, *Registering a Charity for Income Tax Purposes*, T4063(E), (21 January 2000).

29 ITA, section 230.

30 ITA, subsection 149.1(14).

31 ITA, subsection 149.1(15).

32 See ITA, paragraph 149.1(2)(a) (charitable organization cannot carry on an unrelated business), paragraphs 149.1(3)(a), (c) and (d) (public foundation cannot carry on an unrelated business, cannot acquire control of any corporation, and cannot incur debts other than those specified), and paragraphs 149.1(4)(a), (b) and (c) (private foundation cannot carry on any business, cannot acquire control of any corporation, and cannot incur debts other than those specified).

33 ITA, paragraphs 149.1(2)(b), 3(b), and 4(b).

34 ITA section 168.

35 ITA, subsection 172(3) and section 180.

36 ITA, section 188.

37 CRSIA, subsection 5(3). According to subsection 5(4) an order on this application is 'not subject to an appeal or review by any court at the instance of a party to the application.'

38 CRSIA, subsection 9(2).

39 CRSIA, sections 10 and 11.

40 In formulating my own views on the proposed CRSIA and consequential amendments to the ITA, I have benefited enormously from briefs presented by the Canadian Bar Association, the Canadian Islamic Congress and the Council on American-Islamic Relations (Canada) to the House of Commons Standing Committee on Finance, which examined Bill C-16 prior to its withdrawal on 15 October 2001, from Minutes of the Proceedings of this Committee on 16, 17 and 29 May 2001, and from the Canadian Bar Association's Submission on Bill C-36.

41 In this respect, I agree with what I take to be the main point of Patrick Macklem's contribution to this volume, 'Canada and its Obligations under International Criminal Law.' This is not intended as an endorsement of the definition of 'terrorist activities' in Bill C-36, which I have not examined in detail and cannot do in the context of this paper. For criticisms of the definition of terrorism in Bill C-36, see Brenda Cossman and David Schneiderman, 'Associational Life and the Anti-Terrorism Bill' and Kent Roach, 'The Intersection of the New Terrorism Offences and the Criminal Law' in this volume.

42 See, e.g., *International Convention for the Suppression of the Financing of Terrorism*, adopted by the General Assembly of the United Nations on 9 December 1999.

43 CCRA, *Registered Charities: Operating Outside Canada, supra* note 20.

44 For a similar point, see Lorne Sossin, 'The Intersection of Administrative Law and The Anti-Terrorism Bill' in this volume.

45 For a more detailed critique of the procedural aspects of the CRSIA, see *ibid.*

International Dimensions of the Response to Terrorism

Terrorism and Legal Change: An International Law Lesson

JUTTA BRUNNÉE*
Faculty of Law
University of Toronto

Introduction

Bill C-36, the proposed *Anti-Terrorism Act*,[1] is part of the crescendo of domestic and international anti-terrorism activities that we have witnessed since September 11. At an obvious level, Bill C-36 is intended to enable Canada to make its contribution to international anti-terrorism initiatives, including through the implementation of various conventions.[2] Indeed, the proposed *Anti-Terrorism Act* relates its sweeping definition of 'terrorist activity' to ten such conventions,[3] and extends Canada's criminal jurisdiction so as to capture acts within the scope of these conventions as comprehensively as possible, whether committed in or outside of Canada.[4] The proposed *Act* also contains provisions to implement the two most recent conventions, the 1997 *International Convention for the Suppression of Terrorist Bombings* and the 1999 *International Convention for the Suppression of Terrorist Financing*, both of which Canada has signed but not yet ratified.[5]

Bill C-36, then, must be appreciated not only in the context of domestic pressures to respond to the threat of terrorism but also against the background of international efforts to combat terrorism. However, I do not propose to examine whether Bill C-36 matches Canada's international obligations, or what anti-terrorism measures are required by international law. Rather, I want to pursue some perhaps less obvious parallels between the Bill and developments in international law since September 11. Observing both the domestic and international debates on responses to terrorism, it struck me that the proposed *Anti-Terrorism Act* may be but one facet of a larger pattern of legal moves that may end up facilitating, intentionally or not, the subordination of means to ends. To illustrate the point, I will examine some of the undertones of current international developments that may be drowned out in the rush to action but may have significant long-term implications for some of the cornerstones of the international legal system. Specifically, I will consider potential shifts in the world's collective security system and in the rules governing states' rights to use force.

Collective Security and the Use of Force by States – Shifting Patterns?

Art. 2(4) of the *Charter of the United Nations (UN Charter)*, requires states to 'refrain in their international relations from the threat or use of force against the territorial integrity or political independence of any state, or in any other manner inconsistent with the purposes of the United Nations.' The vision of the drafters of the *UN Charter* was to strictly limit the unilateral use of force by states and to establish a collective security system under the auspices of the UN Security Council. Accordingly, the *Charter* gives the Security Council a central role in the maintenance of peace and security (Chapter VI), and in dealing with threats to or breaches of peace and security (Chapter VII). Under Chapter VII, the Security Council may decide upon various measures to address such threats or breaches, including forcible measures to be taken under its authority.[6] The *Charter* text envisages that UN member states make available contingents of their armed forces for coordinated international enforcement actions.[7] No such international force has ever been assembled and it is common ground that the collective security system never operated as outlined in the *Charter*.[8] Yet, with the end of the Cold War, more room emerged for consensus between the five permanent members of the Security Council on collective security issues. Notably, during the 1990s, the Security Council moved in several cases captured by Chapter VII to approve – explicitly or implicitly – the use of force by member states.[9]

In the context of the recent attacks in New York and Washington it is relevant that, in several resolutions since 1998, the Security Council condemned Osama bin Laden's activities, and Afghanistan's Taliban regime for sheltering him and his organization. It repeatedly called upon the Taliban to surrender Bin Laden and imposed various non-military sanctions upon the regime.[10] In 1999, the Security Council first determined that the Taliban's failure to comply with its demands constituted a 'threat to international peace and security.'[11] In Resolution 1368 of September 12, 2001, and Resolution 1373 of September 28, 2001, the Council determined that the terrorist acts of September 11 themselves constituted a threat to international peace and security.[12]

In legal terms, these determinations are significant because they cleared the way for Security Council measures under Chapter VII of the *UN Charter*, including the delegation of enforcement measures to individual UN members. However, the Security Council arguably has not opted for the latter course.[13] Certainly, it has not explicitly authorized the use of force by member states. Instead, Resolution 1373 requires member states to take various measures directed at the suppression of the financing of terrorist acts, and at the suppression of terrorism as such. One can only speculate why the Council did not speak to the question of the use of force. Inability to secure agreement on forcible measures in Afghanistan may have been a factor or, perhaps more likely, the reluctance on the part of some states to subject their freedom of response action, and strategic information, to UN authority. It is also conceivable that the Council thought it politically wiser to wash its hands of the use of force in Afghanistan.

Be that as it may, Resolutions 1368 and 1373 take me to the heart of the matter – the apparent retreat of the Security Council from the question of forcible measures, and the possible parallel expansion of states' right to use force unilaterally (or in 'coalitions' of various shapes and sizes).

The charge that the Security Council is avoiding direct UN responsibility and accountability for forcible measures, and is yielding the terrain to unilateral determination and coordination of such measures by powerful states, is not new. This criticism has been voiced in the context of Security Council authorizations of the use of force by member states,[14] particularly where those authorizations were merely implicit,[15] or even occurred after forcible measures had already been taken.[16] However, in its Resolutions 1368 and 1373, the Security Council appears to retreat yet further.[17] With respect to the potential use of force, the resolutions would appear to limit themselves to affirming the 'inherent right of individual or collective self-defence in accordance with the Charter,' thereby leaving it to individual states to determine what actions to undertake.

Indeed, this is precisely what has unfolded. On October 8, 2001, the Security Council received notice from the United States and the United Kingdom that military action had been initiated by their armed forces in Afghanistan, with the contribution and support of other UN member states.[18] The Council was informed that the military action was 'taken in self-defence and directed at terrorists and those who harboured them.'[19]

Short of action authorized by the Security Council, an exception to the prohibition of the use of force in Article 2(4) of the *UN Charter* is provided in its Article 51: pursuant to their 'inherent right of individual or collective self-defense,' states may use force to respond to an 'armed attack.' A number of issues require attention in this context. For example, given that the military strikes in Afghanistan occurred in response to the terrorist acts of September 11, care must be taken to distinguish legitimate self-defence measures from retaliatory measures.[20] Retaliation, clearly, is not self-defence and any retaliation through forcible measures is quite simply unlawful.[21] Thus, unless authorized by the Security Council, all military action in Afghanistan must be undertaken as genuine 'anticipatory self-defence' against a concrete threat of further attacks, and must be necessary and proportionate. Although Art. 51 of the *UN Charter* does not envisage anticipatory self-defence, it is widely held that customary law, allowing for anticipatory self-defence in limited circumstances, has survived the adoption of the *Charter*.[22] In any case, after initial descents into the rhetoric of retaliation ('Wanted – Dead or Alive'),[23] the United States and its coalition partners have been careful to cast their actions in self-defence terms.

My concern here is not so much the question of whether or not the military actions in Afghanistan can be justified as anticipatory self-defense, although this question does merit continuing attention. Rather, my concern is that the framing of the self-defence action as directed at terrorists and those who harbour them is pushing the boundaries of what, up until this point, has been acceptable as self-defence. More specifically, I am concerned that this boundary shifting has been occurring without attracting much attention or debate. I will address each of these aspects in turn.

From the outset, the United States sought to pursue both the terrorists and those who harboured them.[24] As noted above, the military actions by the United States and coalition partners in Afghanistan are similarly cast as self-defence directed at terrorists and those who harbour them. At first glance, this focus of military action may seem sensible and legitimate, notably in light of the fact the Security Council has declared both the terrorist acts and the failure of the Taliban to surrender the terrorists to be threats to international peace and security. However, there is a fundamental difference between Security Council action under Chapter VII of the *Charter* and actions of individual states in self-defence. Article 39 of the *Charter* gives the Security Council broad discretion to determine the existence of threats to security, and to decide upon suitable response measures, including the use of necessary force. By contrast, a right of self-defence is triggered only by an armed attack by another state, or where an armed attack can be clearly attributed to a state.

To be sure, harbouring, or refusing to extradite, terrorists is offensive and arguably illegal. Apart from the duty of a UN member state to pay heed to Security Council resolutions, all states have a general 'obligation not to allow knowingly its territory to be used for acts contrary to the rights of other States.'[25] Thus, under the law of state responsibility, states may be responsible for failures to prevent unlawful acts by nationals, or aliens living within their territory, that cause harm in other states.[26] Similarly, it is conceivable that certain types of support for the acts of certain groups undertaken abroad violate the principle of non-intervention in another state. For example, the International Court of Justice (ICJ) held in the *Nicaragua* case that the support (financial, training, supply of weapons, logistics) given by the United States to the military and paramilitary activities of the *Contras* in Nicaragua amounted to unlawful intervention.[27] Both types of indirect responsibility for the acts of non-state actors may entitle the Security Council to step in to address attendant threats to peace, and may entitle the target state to take countermeasures against the responsible state. However, countermeasures by individual states may not involve the use of force.[28]

This takes me back to the requirement of an armed attack as a trigger for the right to self-defence by forcible measures. Prior to the events of September 11, restrictive interpretations of the term 'armed attack' prevailed. In the *Nicaragua* case, the ICJ held that 'the sending by a State of armed bands on to the territory of another State' would amount to an armed attack but that assistance in the form of money, weapons, training or other support does not.[29] The Court was criticized for what some perceived to be 'encouragement of low-grade terrorism because the [target] state ... cannot use force in self-defence.'[30] However, the Court was not alone in the conclusion that, under international law, the armed activities of non-state actors can be imputed to a state as an armed attack only when the actors operate *de facto* as agents of that state.[31] One may or may not agree with the ICJ that even supporting activities such as financing, training or provision of arms do not suffice to establish agency. But there can be little doubt that, until recently, mere harbouring of terrorists, albeit potentially illegal, did not suffice for purposes of imputability of an armed attack. The United States had employed 'harbouring' arguments on previous occasions to justify the use of force as (anticipatory) self-defence.[32] However, those attempts at justification generally met with the resistance of other states.[33]

From a legal standpoint, then, the issue of evidence of Osama bin Laden's responsibility for the September 11 attacks *and* of sufficient links to make these terrorist acts the Taliban's is crucial. NATO members' references to existing evidence have placed relatively less emphasis on the latter link. For example, the NATO Secretary General, Lord Robertson, stated on October 2, 2001:

> The facts are clear and compelling. The information presented points conclusively to an Al-Quaida role in the 11 September attacks.

> We know that the individuals who carried out these attacks were part of the world-wide terrorist network of Al-Quaida, headed by Osama bin Laden and his key lieutenants and protected by the Taleban.

> [...], it has now been determined that the attack against the United States on 11 September was directed from abroad and shall therefore be regarded as an action covered by Article 5 of the Washington Treaty, which states that an armed attack on one or more of the Allies in Europe or North America shall be considered an attack against them all.[34]

In other words, NATO states considered there was sufficient evidence to conclude that an armed attack justifying the use of force in Afghanistan had occurred. Yet, it remains unclear whether there is evidence that the Taliban have given shelter to bin Laden and his organization, or that they have supported *al-Quaeda* to a degree that gives rise to an agency relationship. Perhaps more disturbingly, it is unclear whether anyone really cares about the distinction. If not, have we arrived at a point where evidence of the responsibility of terrorists for violent acts, coupled with evidence of harbouring by a state, is sufficient to impute an armed attack to the latter?

Customary international law evolves largely through a process of claim and response. Claims are advanced and actions are taken that may be inconsistent with the existing normative framework. However, if such acts occur repeatedly and without resistance by, or even with the approval of other states, then a tipping point may reached at which the underlying norm itself is changed. In light of the 'harbouring' language employed by the US and endorsed or tolerated by other states, it must be asked whether we are witnessing a change in the rules governing the use of force by states. This question of normative shift is given further purchase by the Security Council's affirmation of the 'inherent right of individual or collective self-defence in accordance with the Charter.' While the clause does not state that the use of force by individual UN members is justified as self-defence,[35] just that conclusion can be – and has been – implied.[36] By permitting this implication, the Security Council not only allows itself to be seen as endorsing a significant broadening of the notion of armed attack. It also allows individual states to assert ground that previously only the Council, in response to a threat to international peace, could legally hold. As noted earlier, the Security Council may therefore be simultaneously retreating from the question of use of force and assisting in placing greater power to use force in the hands of states.

International Law Lessons

I have sought to trace out two related shifts in the approach of international law to the use of force. On the one hand, there appears to be a further retreat of the Security Council from its powers – and responsibilities – in the context of the *Charter*'s collective security regime. On the other hand, we may be in the midst of a significant expansion in the scope of states' right to resort to forcible self-defence, resulting from a considerable broadening of the previously narrow agency rules with respect to armed attacks.

Perhaps there is enough evidence to show that Osama bin Laden's organization and the Taliban are interwoven to such an extent that one is in fact an agent of the other. In that case, care should be taken to make the requisite argument, so as to avoid any unintended normative effects of the harbouring language. It may also be the case that the threat of terrorism and the difficulties involved in responding to threats posed by non-state actors do indeed require an expansion of the notion of armed attack to include harbouring of terrorists. Nonetheless, I am concerned that a potentially significant change in the rules governing the use of force by states may be brought about too swiftly, and without sufficient reflection on its longer-term consequences. At an obvious level, we should ask what the boundaries of 'harbouring' are. Does the expansion of the concept of armed attack entailed by the notion of 'harbouring' apply only to situations involving international terrorism? Is some measure of active support by the harbouring state required, such as the type of conduct previously rejected by the ICJ as sufficient for the imputation of non-state actors' use of force to states? Or is mere provision of 'shelter' sufficient? Could a state's regulatory or enforcement failure ever expose it to the charge that it is harbouring terrorists?

All of these questions – and many others – remain unanswered. This state of affairs introduces dangerous ambiguity into a system of rules that is to constrain state conduct in a context where this task is difficult at the best of times. Already, international law is exposed to the common charge that it has little influence on the conduct of states, or can be moulded to justify any chosen course of action. In my view, this assessment is correct only if one asks the impossible of international law: to provide black and white answers for all cases and to completely control state behaviour. As I have noted, law involves a process of claim and counterclaim. This does *not* mean that 'anything can be justified.' Arguments are persuasive when they are congruent with the existing framework of norms, values and expectations. The task of international lawyers is to make principled use of the existing norms on the use of force, so as to help identify, defend, and, if necessary, recast the boundaries of response action. It is through this process that international law influences states.[37]

That said, I am concerned that, since September 11, we have not been as diligent as we should be in the use of the existing normative framework and in the shaping of potential new norms. My concern is that the processes through which law exerts its influence are being undermined by a potentially rash change of rules, lack of attention to the normative parameters of the new rules, and the attendant creation – as David Dyzenhaus put it in his paper on Bill C-36 – of a 'legal vacuum.'[38] In the rush to respond to the threat of international terrorism, we are exposing ourselves to the risk that ends will enable uncritical justification of means. Suffice it to point again to the Bush Administration's initial Wild West rhetoric. This rhetoric did place ends above means and thereby appeared to downgrade law to mere ornament. It does seem that international law has played some role in shifting this rhetoric and in shaping the international response. However, to the extent that amorphous notions of harbouring or armed attack are implanted in international discourse, the ability of international law to constrain self-justification – and the use of force by states – will surely suffer.

The concerns I have raised with respect to recent developments in international law, needless to say, apply equally to changes that may be brought about by the proposed *Anti-Terrorism Act*. Some of these changes may be obvious and we may or may not consider them to be necessary or wise. Others, similar to the shifts I have suggested may be underway at the international level, may be less clearly visible. At least, in the context of Bill C-36, we have the opportunity for debate on its potentially sweeping implications. We should take this opportunity seriously and not allow the Bill to become part of what may well be a much larger pattern of emergency driven lawmaking with uncertain consequences.

At the risk of straying from the immediate purpose of this forum on Bill C-36, I will end by suggesting that our current preoccupation with the development of Canadian law should not distract our attention from potentially equally significant developments in international law. In the context of Bill C-36, we are at least debating a 'sunset clause' for the operation of the law. In the international arena, we do not have that luxury. Once a normative change has implanted itself it will require hard work to undo. We should pay much closer attention to current developments and ask whether the normative shifts they may entail are all for the better.

Notes

* Professor of Law, University of Toronto. My thanks go to Professor Stephen J. Toope for his very helpful comments on an earlier draft. I have also appreciated the research assistance of Johanna Myers.

1 Available at http://laws.justice.gc.ca/en/index.html.

2 *See id.*, Preamble.

3 *See id.*, s. 83.01 (1) (a) (i)–(x).

4 *See, e.g., id.*, ss. 3.72, 3.73, outlining a broad range of situations in which relevant acts or omissions are deemed to have been committed in Canada.

5 The text of both conventions is available at http://www.untreaty.un.org/English/ Terrorism.asp. While the former convention is in force as of May 23, 2001, the latter has yet to achieve the requisite number of ratifications. For the provisions designed to implement these conventions in Canada, *see* Bill C-36, *supra*, note 1, ss. 3.72, 83.01 (1) (a) (ix), 431.2 (regarding the *Terrorist Bombing Convention*), and ss. 3.73, 83.01 (1) (a) (x), 83.02 (regarding the *Terrorist Financing Convention*). Note that these examples are taken from Part 1 of the Bill, and thus relate only to amendments to the *Criminal Code*; other parts of the Bill contain implementing provisions relating to further statutes.

6 *UN Charter*, Articles 39–42.

7 *UN Charter*, Articles 43–47.

8 *See* Rosalyn Higgins, Problems and Process: International Law and How We Use It (1994), at 254–266.

9 Whether or not the *UN Charter* empowers the Security Council to delegate enforcement action to member states is a matter of debate. Nonetheless, in recent years Security Council resolutions have been employed to legitimize enforcement actions. For a detailed review, *see* Niels Blokker, *Is the Authorization Authorized? Powers and Practice of the UN Security Council to Authorize the Use of Force by 'Coalitions of the Able and Willing'* 11 Eur. J. Int'l L. 541 (2000) (citing isolated examples dating back to 1950; and an array of recent examples).

10 *See* UN SC Resolutions 1189, 1193 and 1214 (all 1998), all available at http://www.un.org/documents/scres.htm.

11 *See* UN SC Resolutions 1267 (1999), and 1333 (2000), both available at http://www.un.org/documents/scres.htm.

12 Both available at http://www.un.org/documents/scres.htm.

13 In my view, the resolutions cannot be interpreted to authorize the use of force by individual states. Notably, given the overall thrust of the decision paragraphs of Resolution 1373, such an authorization cannot be read into its paragraph 2(b), according to which states shall 'take the necessary steps to prevent the commission of terrorist acts, including by provision of early warning to other States by exchange of information.' Nor can it be read into decision paragraph 8, according to which the Council expresses '*its* determination to take all necessary steps in order to ensure the full implementation of this resolution' (emphasis added). *See also* Frederic Kirgis, *Addendum: Security Council Adopts Resolution on Combating International Terrorism*, ASIL Insights (October 1, 2001), available at http://www.asil.org/insights.htm. But see also Jordan Paust, *Addendum: Security Council Authorization to Combat Terrorism in Afghanistan* (October 28, 2001), available at http://www.asil.org/insights.htm (reaching the opposite conclusion). Even less convincing is the argument that any determination by the Security Council of a threat to international peace and security implies an authorization of force. This latter argument was advanced in the context of the interventions in Iraq and Kosovo. *See, e.g.*, Ruth Wedgwood, *NATO's Campaign in Yugoslavia*, 93 Am. J. Int'l L. 828, at 829–830 (1999).

14 *See* discussion in Blokker, *supra*, note 9, at note 6.

15 *See, e.g.*, UN SC Resolution 688 (1990) on Iraq, and UN SC Resolutions 1199 (1998) and 1203 (1998) on Kosovo, both available at http://www.un.org/documents/scres.htm.

16 UN SC Resolution 1203 (1998), *id.*

17 *See also*, Micaela Frulli, *Is there Still a Chance of Revitalizing the United Nations Security Council?*, 16 German L. J. (1 October 2001), available at http://www.germanlawjournal.com; Mark A. Drumbl, *Terrorist Crime, Taliban Guilt, Retaliatory Strikes and Western Innocence*, Washington & Lee Public Law and Legal Theory Research Paper Series, Working Paper No. 01–13 (September 2001), available at http://papers.ssrn.com/abstract=286637.

18 *See* Press Statement on Terrorist Threats by Security Council President, UN Doc.

AFG/152, SC/7167, 8 October 2001; available at http://www.un.org/News/Press/docs/2001/afg152.doc.htm.

19 *Id.* Art. 51 of the *UN Charter* requires states to immediately report any measures taken in exercise of the right of self-defense to the Security Council. On Art. 51, *see* further *infra*, text accompanying notes 20–23.

20 Although retaliatory measures have certainly been taken in the past. In the context of terrorism, consider the US bombings in Afghanistan and Sudan in 1998, in response to terrorist bombings of US embassies in Nairobi and Dar-es-Salaam earlier in the same year.

21 For a discussion, *see* Yoram Dinstein, War, Aggression and Self-Defence (1994), at 220–221; *and* Higgins, *supra*, note 8, at 241. *See also Declaration of Principles of International Law Concerning Friendly Relations and Co-operation Among States in Accordance with the Charter of the United Nations*, UN General Assembly, Resolution 2625 (XXV) 1970, UN Doc. A/8028 (1970) [hereinafter *Friendly Relations Declaration*].

22 *See, e.g.*, Higgins, *supra*, note 8, at 242; Stephen J. Toope, *Clothing the Emperor: Saving the Non-Use of Force from Jus Cogens*, forthcoming in James Crawford, ed., The Use of Force: Essays in Honour of Sir Derek Bowett (2001) (at 17–18; manuscript on file with author). Note also that the International Court of Justice (ICJ), although not speaking to the question of anticipatory self-defence, held in the *Nicaragua Case* that customary norms on the use of force are applicable notwithstanding the existence of parallel norms in the *Charter*. *See Case Concerning Military and Paramilitary Activities in and against Nicaragua (Nicaragua v. United States)* (Merits) (1986) ICJ Rep. 14, paras. 172–182.

23 And notwithstanding the practice, displayed in various newscasts, of 'dedicating' missiles to the revenge of those who perished in the New York and Washington attacks.

24 A Joint Resolution of both Houses of the US Congress authorizes President Bush to use 'All necessary an appropriate force against those nations, organizations, or persons he determines planned, authorized, committed, or aided the terrorist attacks ..., *or harbored such organizations or persons*, in order to prevent any future acts of international terrorism against the United States ...' Public Law 107–40– Sept. 18, 2001, 115 STAT. 224 (emphasis added).

25 *Corfu Channel* case (Merits), ICJ Rep. (1949) 4, at 22.

26 *See United States Diplomatic and Consular Staff in Tehran (United States v. Iran)*, ICJ Rep. (1980), 3. *See generally*, Ian Brownlie, Principles of Public International Law, 5th ed. (1998), at 449–450.

27 *Nicaragua* case, *supra*, note 22, at paras. 239–245.

28 *Id.*, at paras. 210–211, 246–249.

29 *Id.*, at paras. 187–201, 227–238.

30 *See* discussion in Higgins, *supra*, note 8, at 250–251.

31 The same is true also under the law of state responsibility. While, as noted earlier, a

state may be responsible for certain failures to prevent unlawful acts of individuals, these acts are deemed acts of the state itself only 'if the person or group of persons was in fact acting on the instructions of, or under the direction or control of, that State in carrying out the conduct.' *See* Article 8, Draft Articles on the Law of State Responsibility, in *Report of the International Law Commission on the Work of its Fifty-Third Session*, UN Doc. A/56/10 (2001).

32 *See, e.g.*, Peter Malanczuk, Akehurst's Modern Introduction to International Law, 7th ed (1997), at 316 (citing, *inter alia*, the 1986 US bombing of Libya in response to a terrorist attack against US Soldies in West Berlin).

33 *See, id.*; and *see* Gregory H. Fox, *Addendum to ASIL Insight on Terrorism* (September 2001), available at http://www.asil.org/insights.htm (discussing the Security Council response to the 1985 bombing by Israel of PLO headquarters in Tunisia).

34 Text available at http://www.nato.int/docu/speech/2001/s011002a.htm.

35 *See also* Kirgis, *supra*, note 13. But note that the UN continues to use enigmatic language in this regard. In a statement of November 6, 2001, entitled *Message to Warsaw Meeting Says Current Military Action in Afghanistan Fits Context of Security Council Resolutions, UN Charter of Self-Defence*, the UN Secretary General stated that the Security Council 'affirmed the inherent right of individual and collective self-defence ... The States concerned have set their military action in Afghanistan in that context.' Available at http://www.un.org/News/Press/docs/2001/sgsm8013.doc.htm.

36 *See, e.g.*, Said Mahmoudi, *Comment on Fox Addendum* (September 24, 2001), available at http://www.asil.org/insights.htm.

37 *See* Jutta Brunnée & Stephen J. Toope, *International Law and Constructivism: Elements of an Interactional Theory of International Law*, 39 Col. J. Trans. L. 19, at 20–25 (2000) [hereinafter *Elements*]; and *The Changing Nile Basin Regime: Does Law Matter?*, Harv. J. Int'l L. (forthcoming 2002).

38 David Dyzenhaus, *The Permanence of the Temporary: Can Emergency Powers be Normalized?*, in this volume.

Canada's Obligations at International Criminal Law

PATRICK MACKLEM*
Faculty of Law
University of Toronto

I have sent my Death's Head units to the East with the order to kill without mercy men, women and children of the Polish race or language.

Adolf Hitler, briefing his generals in 1939
on the eve of the Polish invasion.[1]

Perhaps 'the first and foremost requirement imposed by international law upon a State is that ... it may not exercise its power in any form in the territory of another state.'[2] But, in no small measure due to the atrocities committed by the Nazi forces in World War II, international law – specifically, international criminal law – also provides that a state has the jurisdiction to prosecute and punish the commission of certain crimes even if such crimes have no territorial link to the state or to the nationality of the offender or victim. Made famous in recent years by Spain's attempt to prosecute and punish former General Augusto Pinochet for crimes allegedly committed during his reign in Chile,[3] the principle of universal jurisdiction authorizes – indeed requires – a state to prosecute and punish individuals for certain actions that amount to international criminal behaviour.

International crimes include actions that involve means or methods that transcend national boundaries and thus can be said to possess a transnational dimension. But a transnational dimension is not a necessary element of an international crime. International crimes also include certain actions that 'shock the conscience of mankind or ... threaten the peace and security of the world.'[4] Some of these crimes are said to attract international condemnation as a matter of international customary law and, as a result, international law obligates all states not to grant immunity to those who commit them.

A typical list of such crimes includes apartheid, genocide, crimes against humanity, 'grave breaches' of the Geneva Conventions, slavery and torture. These and additional crimes, such as acts of terrorism, unlawful use of the mail, and the taking of civilian hostages, have been codified by treaty as international crimes, thereby removing any doubt as to the obligations they impose on state parties. An international treaty typically defines the activity in question as a crime at international law, and imposes a range of duties on states party to its terms to prohibit, prevent, prosecute, punish, or extradite an individual who engages in such activity regardless of where it occurs and regardless of the nationality of the offender or victim.

Although it imposes obligations on states to prosecute and punish international crimes, international criminal law does not rely solely on domestic law for its enforcement. As is well known, the field has also experimented with international enforcement. By agreement in 1945, the Allied powers established an International Military Court to try and punish persons who, acting in the interests of the European Axis countries, committed crimes against peace, war crimes, or crimes against humanity. More recently, in the mid-1990s the U.N. Security Council created two *ad hoc* international criminal tribunals to prosecute and punish individuals for war crimes, genocide, and crimes against humanity committed in the former Yugoslavia and Rwanda. And in the summer of 1998, a diplomatic conference in Rome approved a statute establishing a permanent International Criminal Court with jurisdiction to prosecute and punish acts of genocide, crimes against humanity, war crimes, and crimes of aggression.[5] But, despite these developments, international criminal law is primarily enforced through the operation of domestic criminal law regimes.

Prior to September 11, Canada had asserted universal jurisdiction and implemented many of its international legal obligations concerning the prosecution and punishment of terrorist acts by amending the Criminal Code to render certain international crimes punishable in Canadian courts regardless of where or against whom they are committed. Section 7 of the Code prohibits airplane hijacking, certain acts against internationally protected persons or property, hostage taking, the unlawful use of nuclear material, and acts of piracy regardless of where they occur and regardless of the nationality of the offender or victim.[6]

The *Anti-terrorism Bill* (the 'Bill') adds two additional offences to s. 7 of the Code – offences involving explosives or other lethal devices and offences relating to financing of terrorism – and designates the commission of any of these existing or proposed offences as 'terrorist activity' for the purposes of the Bill.[7] It also provides a more general definition of terrorist activity as any other act or omission that is committed at home or abroad, under certain conditions, for a political, religious or ideological purpose, with the intention of intimidating the public and with the intention of causing death, serious bodily harm, a serious risk to public health or safety, or a serious interference with an essential service. In addition, the Bill proposes to make it an offence to knowingly participate in, contribute to or facilitate the activities of a terrorist group, to instruct anyone to carry out a terrorist activity, or to knowingly harbour a terrorist. Finally, the Bill proposes to provide law enforcement and national security agencies new investigative tools to gather information and prosecute terrorists.

A number of commentators have argued that the Criminal Code's existing prohibitions, such as those relating to offences against the person as well as those contained in s. 7, are sufficient to address terrorist activity, and that the Bill's definition of 'terrorist activity' gives rise to more questions than it answers. The Bill's general definition of 'terrorist activity' appears to inappropriately sweep in legitimate but unlawful forms of political protest – a concern that Parliament should address by clarifying the definition prior to enactment. But a general definition of 'terrorist activity' – redrafted to ensure that it does not apply to legitimate but unlawful forms of political protest – is a valuable legislative contribution to domestic and international assertions of universal jurisdiction.

With respect to domestic assertions of universal jurisdiction, the significance of the Bill lies in the fact that it represents an effort to identify what distinguishes terrorist activity – activity that amounts to an international as well as domestic crime – from criminal behaviour that merits domestic condemnation but which does not possess international criminal significance. The Bill reclassifies existing offences – airplane hijacking, certain acts against internationally protected persons or property, hostage taking, the unlawful use of nuclear material, and acts of piracy – as terrorist activity and seeks as well, through its general definition, to identify unique attributes of terrorist activity that distinguish it from domestic crimes. To reiterate, international crimes typically possess but do not require a transnational element. Their significance lies instead in the fact that they involve actions that 'shock the conscience of mankind or ... threaten the peace and security of the world.'[8] Given that international law regards certain crimes as international in nature, a crucial domestic task is to identify their unique attributes with sufficient specificity in order to legitimately claim universal jurisdiction in domestic settings.

Canadian courts have had limited experience with this task. In *R. v. Finta*,[9] at issue were other provisions contained in s. 7 of the Criminal Code, which, at the relevant time, prohibited crimes against humanity and war crimes committed outside Canada if such acts constituted an criminal offence if committed in Canada. Finta had been tried and convicted in abstentia in Hungary after the Second World War for his actions as the commander of an investigative unit in Hungary where over 8000 Jewish people were detained in a brickyard, forcibly stripped of their valuables and departed to concentration camps. His conviction was eventually statute barred and he later benefited from a general amnesty. He ended up a Canadian citizen living in Ontario. He was charged, tried but acquitted of unlawful confinement, robbery, kidnapping and manslaughter in Canada. These charges were four pairs of alternate counts – one series as crimes against humanity and the other as war crimes. At issue before the Supreme Court of Canada was whether the accused could rely on a defence that he was following military orders. The Court held the defence to be available except where the orders were manifestly unlawful or where, by virtue of an air of compulsion and threat to the accused, the accused had no moral choice as to whether to obey the orders.

Also at issue in *Finta* was whether the Criminal Code offences of war crimes and crimes against humanity are merely jurisdictional in nature or whether they create new categories of criminal behaviour. If the former, then the Crown merely had to prove that Finta committed certain Code offences such as manslaughter and robbery. If the latter, the Crown would have to prove elements specific to the new crimes in question. A majority of the Court held that war crimes and crimes against humanity possess features that distinguish them from domestic criminal offences. According to the Court, one difference is that such crimes are committed by those 'who inflict immense suffering with foresight and calculated malevolence.'[10] As such they include a *mens rea* requirement that the accused know his acts constitute war crimes or crimes against humanity or be willfully blind to facts of circumstances that would bring his actions within the definition of these crimes. Another difference is in the *actus reus* of the crimes. Such crimes possess an element of 'inhumanity,' and involve acts that 'shock the conscience of all right-thinking people.'[11] For crimes against humanity, the inhumane acts must be based on discrimination against or the persecution of an identifiable group of people. For war crimes, the additional element is that the actions constitute a violation of the laws of armed conflict.

When the Bill becomes law, the judiciary will face a similar challenge in the context of a prosecution of an individual charged with committing terrorist acts. What distinguishes terrorist activity from other forms of criminal behaviour? As the debates surrounding the Bill reveal, answering this question is no easy matter. But it is a task that needs to be undertaken. The gross human rights violations committed on September 11 demonstrate that at least some terrorist activity merits international legal condemnation in addition to domestic prosecution and punishment of its constituent elements. As with the case of crimes against humanity, domestic law must be able to articulate with sufficient precision what distinguishes terrorist acts from other criminal acts to justify the assertion of universal jurisdiction that such international condemnation confers. Precision is a function of experience, and neither legislatures nor courts have had much experience defining the term. In this light, the Bill – however flawed in this and other respects – is an important contribution in ongoing efforts to comprehend the international legal significance of terrorist activity. Some of the language contained in the Bill may well – and should – be revised before it becomes law. But statutory text – however precise – will not eliminate interpretive ambiguities, and the judiciary too will be called on to assume the task of defining terrorism by refining the nature and scope of the legislation.

The legal challenge of defining terrorism is doubly difficult at the international level. Coupled with domestic fears that a definition will sweep in legitimate but unlawful forms of political protest, is the oft-heard remark that, internationally, 'one person's terrorist is another's freedom fighter.' The United Nations has been debating its meaning for several decades and has achieved some progress in delineating its constituent elements as well as an appropriate institutional response.[12] But a 1996 proposal by India to establish a comprehensive treaty on terrorism was met with a distinct lack of political will in the General Assembly. And uncertainties continue to thwart the elevation of terrorism to the status of an international crime in the absence of a treaty or treaties on the topic.[13] Ambiguities surrounding its precise meaning also led to the rejection of proposals that terrorism be considered as one of the international crimes subject to the jurisdiction of the International Criminal Court.[14]

As a result, international efforts to stem terrorism thus far tend to disaggregate the phenomenon into a number of relatively discrete forms of terrorist activity regulated by an international instrument specific to each form, such as the *Convention for the Suppression of Unlawful Seizure of Aircraft*. Whether, at the international level, terrorism can be defined in all of its manifestations with sufficient specificity to enable an integrated international response is still an open question. But as domestic legislatures and courts here and elsewhere increasingly turn their attention to these questions, their iterative efforts may eventually assist in promoting sufficient consensus at the international level to warrant a more integrated international approach coupled with international enforcement mechanisms.

The Bill's proposed amendments to s. 7 of the Criminal Code are only one half of the story of Canada's obligations at international criminal law. The other half is less well known but equally significant. In 2000, Parliament, with little fanfare, enacted another piece of legislation – one that incidentally receives no mention in the Bill. The *Crimes Against Humanity Act*[15] implements international obligations Canada assumed by ratifying the Statute of Rome, which establishes the International Criminal Court (the 'ICC'). When the ICC comes into effect,[16] it will operate as 'a permanent institution and shall have the power to exercise its jurisdiction over persons for the most serious crimes.'[17]

Specifically, the ICC will have jurisdiction to prosecute and punish genocide, crimes against humanity, war crimes, and the crime of aggression. A charge of *genocide* must relate to specified crimes committed 'with intent to destroy, in whole or part, a national, ethnic, racial or religious group.'[18] *Crimes against humanity* are defined as specified crimes 'committed as part of a widespread or systematic attack directed against any civilian population, with knowledge of the attack,' and an 'attack directed against any civilian population' is defined as 'a course of conduct involving the multiple commission of specified acts ... against any civilian population, pursuant to or in furtherance of a State or organizational policy to commit such attack.'[19] *War crimes* are defined as 'grave breaches of the Geneva Conventions' as well as other offences, such as hostage taking, murder, and mutilation, committed 'during an armed conflict not of an international character.'[20] The crime of aggression is to be defined at some point in the future.

The ICC will possess jurisdiction to prosecute and punish an individual or individuals for the commission of such crimes if the state in which the crime occurred is a party to the Rome Statute or if the person accused is a national of a party state. It cannot assume jurisdiction simply on the basis that the state of the victim's nationality has ratified the treaty or on the basis that the state which gained custody of the suspect has ratified the treaty. Despite these restrictions, the UN Security Council possesses the authority to refer to the ICC any matter prohibited by the Rome Statute regardless of where it occurs and regardless of the nationality of the offender or victim.[21] In all cases, the ICC has jurisdiction over persons regardless of their official capacity as a head of state, member of the government, or military commander.[22] And the ICC's jurisdiction is not affected if the person accused of a crime acted under superior orders whether these orders were military or civilian.[23]

The ICC will complement, not supplant, domestic criminal law enforcement. Unlike procedures governing the *ad hoc* tribunals established in relation to the former Yugoslavia and Rwanda, a case before the ICC is inadmissible when it is being investigated or prosecuted by a state that has jurisdiction over it, and a case is inadmissible when a state has investigated the matter and chosen not to prosecute.[24] Only when the state is 'unwilling or unable genuinely to carry out the investigation or prosecution' can the ICC assume jurisdiction. In determining unwillingness, the ICC will examine such factors as whether the state is merely trying to shield the person in question from criminal responsibility; whether an unjustified delay in the proceedings is consonant with an intent to bring the person to justice; and whether the proceedings are being conducted impartially or independently.[25] In determining inability, the ICC must look at such factors as whether there is total disintegration or unavailability of the state's judicial system; and whether the state is unable to obtain either the accused person or evidence needed to prosecute.[26]

The ICC will not possess the jurisdiction to prosecute or punish individuals for participating in the atrocities committed on September 11, 2001. It only has jurisdiction with respect to crimes committed after the Statute comes into force or after the state in question has ratified the Statute, whichever is later.[27] But, as stated, Canada has introduced legislation to implement the Rome Statute in Canadian law. The *Crimes Against Humanity Act* enables domestic prosecution and punishment for acts committed at home or abroad that amount to crimes against humanity, war grimes and genocide. As illustrated in *R. v. Finta*, Canadian law prohibited crimes against humanity and war crimes prior to the enactment of the Act, and the Act's definitions of 'crime against humanity' and 'war crime,' generally speaking, are similar to those at issue in *Finta*. [28]

The Act defines a *crime against humanity* as:

> murder, extermination, enslavement, deportation, imprisonment, torture, sexual violence, persecution or any other inhumane act or omission that is committed against any civilian population or any identifiable group and that, at the time and in the place of its commission, constitutes a crime against humanity according to customary international law or conventional international law or by virtue of its being criminal according to the general principles of law recognized by the community of nations, whether or not it constitutes a contravention of the law in force at the time and in the place of its commission.

The new definition of 'crime against humanity' adds express references to 'imprisonment,' 'torture,' and 'sexual violence' as examples of 'inhumane acts' that qualify as crimes against humanity.

The Act defines *war crimes* as:

> acts or omissions committed during an armed conflict that, at the time and in the place of its commission, constitutes a war crime according to customary international law or conventional international law applicable to armed conflicts, whether or not it constitutes a contravention of the law in force at the time and in the place of its commission.

The new definition of 'war crime' applies to internal, as well as international, armed conflicts.

The Act also creates a new crime of *genocide*, and defines genocide as:

> an act or omission committed with intent to destroy, in whole or in part, an identifiable group of persons, as such, that, at the time and in the place of its commission, constitutes genocide according to customary international law or conventional international law or by virtue of its being criminal according to the general principles of law recognized by the community of nations, whether or not it constitutes a contravention of the law in force at the time and in the place of its commission.

Together, these provisions enable Canada to prosecute persons directly for committing crimes against humanity, war crimes and genocide without requiring proof that the acts in question would also constitute an criminal offence if committed in Canada.

In at least two respects, Canada's *Crimes Against Humanity Act* reaches further than the Rome Statute. First, the Act authorizes prosecution and punishment of an individual regardless of his or nationality and regardless of the nationality of the victims. Unlike the Rome Statute, the Act does not require that the state in which the crime occurred be a party to the Rome Statute or the person accused to be a national of a party state. While the Rome Statute allows individuals who are not nationals of a party state suspected of committing an international crime in a non-party state to travel relatively freely throughout the world, Canada has assumed the authority to prosecute and punish such individuals if they are present on Canadian soil. Second, the Act authorizes the prosecution and punishment of an individual who commits a crime against humanity, a war crime, or genocide outside Canada regardless of when the act occurs. In other words, unlike the Rome Statute – and unlike the *Anti-terrorism Bill*, the Act has retroactive application.

Moreover, the Act significantly broadens domestic criminal law in its application to acts of terrorism at home and abroad. This is because ambiguities surrounding the legal definition of terrorism spill over into ambiguities surrounding the legal definition of a crime against humanity. Atrocities such as those committed on September 11 cannot be neatly characterized as acts of terrorism as opposed to crimes against humanity. Both U.N. Secretary-General Kofi Annan and U.N. High Commissioner for Human Rights, Mary Robinson, have characterized those atrocities as crimes against humanity, and for good reason. Their magnitude, gravity, as well as the deliberate and systematic targeting of civilians render those actions crimes committed not only against the victims but against all of us.[29]

The United States has stated that it will 'bring to justice' those responsible for the atrocities of September 11. But it is not at all clear what type of trial justice would require in these circumstances. The U.N. Security Council could establish an ad hoc international tribunal for this purpose similar to the International Criminal Tribunal for the Former Yugoslavia. Another possibility is an international military tribunal established by the United States and its current allies similar to the International Military Court established after World War II. A third possibility is that those responsible be tried in the domestic courts of the United States or another country. Because of its retrospective application, the Act enables Canada to offer to prosecute and punish acts of terrorism associated with September 11 as crimes against humanity or genocide.

In combination, the *Anti-terrorism Bill* and the *Crimes Against Hu-*

manity Act appear to allow for alternative domestic prosecutions of wrongdoing. In at least some circumstances, acts of terrorism prohibited by the Bill might also amount to crimes against humanity, genocide or war crimes.[30] Alternative prosecutions of international crimes serve to highlight their differences and similarities and profoundly affect domestic and international understandings of the contours of such crimes. When crimes of sexual violence against women, for example, are classified as a war crime, the offence constitutes a limit on the waging of war. When classified as a crime against humanity, the offence emphasizes that, at war or peace, women are part of humanity. When categorized as genocide, the offence emphasizes the intersection of gender and ethnic violence and shows how violence against women can serve as an instrument of ethnic destruction.[31] Classifying actions as terrorism emphasizes the heightened sense of individual and collective insecurity produced by such actions. Classifying terrorist actions as crimes against humanity emphasizes the universal harm that flows from terrorist activity. As states come to comprehend terrorist activity as not only a crime unto itself but also as a crime against humanity, the ICC may be able eventually to include terrorism within its international jurisdiction.[32]

Winston Churchill famously remarked that genocide is a 'crime without a name.'[33] This, of course, is no longer the case. Numerous international instruments and domestic laws offer detailed definitions of genocide and legal provisions designed to prosecute and punish its commission. They signify that Hitler, in 1939, instructed his Death's Head units to commit genocide. Terrorism, however, remains a crime without a name. International and domestic law criminalizes certain discrete elements of terrorist activity but neither international nor domestic law has yet to fully comprehend terrorism as an activity unto itself – let alone as a crime against humanity – that merits international condemnation and universal prosecution and punishment. For too long, international law has not had the fortitude to address the distinction between the justified use of force and terrorist activity. Canada has been blessed by the fact that it has not felt the need to assume this task in the past. After September 11, it's time to give terrorism a name. For all of its flaws, the *Anti-terrorism Bill* merits praise for asserting universal jurisdiction to declare terrorism to be an international crime. Its revision and enactment hopefully mark the beginning of a process whereby Canadian and international political and legal institutions grapple with fundamental questions surrounding the nature of terrorism and its relationship to civil disobedience, human security, and national liberation.

Notes

* Professor of Law, University of Toronto. Research assistance by Justin Bates (LL.M. candidate, University of Toronto) and comments on a previous draft by Sonia Lawrence and David Schneiderman are greatly appreciated.

1 Quoted in Norman Davies, *Europe: A History* (London: Pimlico, 1997), at 909.

2 *The Case of the S.S. Lotus* (1927), P.C.I.J. Ser. A, No. 10, at p. 18 (Permanent Court of International Justice).

3 Seee *R.* v. *Bartle*, [1999] 2 All E.R. 97 (H.L.).

4 M. Cherif Bassiouni, *International Criminal Law: A Draft International Criminal Code* (Alphen aan den Rijn: Sijthoff & Noordhoff, 1980).

5 See *Rome Statute of the International Criminal Court*, 17 July 1998.

6 These prohibitions implement Canada's international obligations under the *Convention for the Suppression of Unlawful Seizure of Aircraft*; the *Convention for the Suppression of Unlawful Acts against the Safety of Civil Aviation*; the *Convention on the Prevention and Punishment of Crimes against Internationally Protected Persons, including Diplomatic Agents*; the *International Convention against the Taking of Hostages*; the *Convention on the Physical Protection of Nuclear Material*; the *Protocol for the Suppression of Unlawful Acts of Violence at Airports Serving International Civil Aviation*; and the *Convention for the Suppression of Unlawful Acts against the Safety of Fixed Platforms Located on the Continental Shelf*.

7 These prohibitions will implement Canada's international obligations under the *International Convention for the Suppression of Terrorist Bombings*; and the *International Convention for the Suppression of Terrorist Financing*.

8 Bassiouni, *supra* note 4.

9 [1994] 1 S.C.R. 701.

10 *Ibid.*, at 817.

11 *Ibid.*, at 812.

12 See U.N. *Declaration on Measures to Eliminate International Terrorism.*

13 See, for example, *Tel-Oren* v. *Libyan Arab Republic*, 726 F.2d 774 (D.C. Cir. 1984) (because of a lack of agreement on its definition, terrorism does not attract universal jurisdiction as an international crime under customary international law); *Bulletin des arrêt de la Cour de Cassation, Chambre criminelle*, March 2001, no. 64, at 2180-9 (terrorism is not an international crime that authorizes the lifting of immunity for heads of state). For commentary, see Salvatore Zappalà, 'Do Heads of State in Office Enjoy Immunity from Jurisdiction for International Crimes? The Ghaddafi Case Before the French Cour de Cassation,' 12 Eur. J. Int'l L. 595 (2001).

14 Algeria, India, Sri Lanka and Turkey made proposals along these lines. See A/CONF.183/C.1L 27.

15 S.C. 2000, c. 24.

16 The ICC will come into effect when the Rome Statute receives 60 ratifications. As of 07 November 2001, the following 43 states have ratified the Statute: Andorra, Antigua and Barbuda, Argentina, Austria, Belgium, Belize, Botswana, Canada,

Central African Republic, Costa Rica, Croatia, Denmark, Dominica, Fiji, Finland, France, Gabon, Germany, Ghana, Iceland, Italy, Lesotho, Liechtenstein, Luxembourg, Mali, Marshall Islands, Netherlands, New Zealand, Nigeria, Norway, Paraguay, San Marino, Senegal, Sierra Leone, South Africa, Spain, Sweden, Switzerland, Tajikistan, Trinidad and Tobago, United Kingdom of Great Britain and Northern Ireland, Venezuela, and Yugoslavia.

17 Preeamble.

18 Art. 6. This definition mirrors that found in the *Convention on the Prevention and Punishment of the Crime of Genocide.*

19 Arts. 7(1), 7(2), respectively. This definition is broader than previous definitions at international law, which required that such serious crimes be committed as part of an international or internal armed attack.

20 Arts. 8(2)(c) and (e).

21 Art. 13(b).

22 Arts. 27, 28. But see Art. 98, which provides that a state is not required to surrender an accused if to do so would violate its obligations under international law with respect to state or diplomatic immunity.

23 Art. 33.

24 Art. 17(1)(a).

25 Art. 17(2)(a)–(c).

26 Art. 7(3).

27 This is not to say that an international court could not be established to prosecute and punish individuals and groups associated with the September 11 atrocities. As was the case with the former Yugoslavia and Rwanda, the U.N. Security Council could establish an *ad hoc* tribunal for this purpose.

28 The Act rules out a defence of obedience to superior orders accepted in *Finta* where the order is manifestly unlawful and the defendant's belief in its lawfulness was based on hate propaganda, and deems orders to commit genocide or crimes against humanity to be manifestly unlawful.

29 On this point, see Antonio Cassese, 'Terrorism is Also Disrupting Some Crucial Legal Categories of International Law' (www.ejil.org/forum_WTC/ny-cassese.html).

30 The Bill excludes from its definition of 'terrorist activity' acts committed during an armed conflict that are authorized by international law, thereby implicitly including acts that amount to war crimes.

31 This point borrows from Ruti Teitel, 'The Universal and the Particular in International Criminal Justice,' 30 Col. H.R. L. Rev. 286 (1999), at 301, and sources therein

32 See Cassese, *supra* note 29.

33 Quoted in Leo Kuper, *Genocide: Its Political Use in the Twentieth Century* (New Haven: Yale University Press, 1981), at 12.

Administering Security in a Multicultural Society

Protecting Equality in the Face of Terror: Ethnic and Racial Profiling and s. 15 of the *Charter*

SUJIT CHOUDHRY*
Faculty of Law
University of Toronto

A. Introduction

The anti-terrorism omnibus bill currently before Parliament is a lengthy and complex statute whose provisions, taken together, have the twin goals of enhancing the effectiveness of existing instruments, and creating new instruments, for law enforcement officials to prevent terror both in Canada and abroad. What is striking about the legislation is its silence on one of the central issues in the public debate over how Canada and other liberal democracies should respond to September 11: ethnic and racial profiling (which I shall refer to simply as profiling in this paper).

Profiling has burst onto the national agenda in the wake of the horrific events of September 11. Long criticized by academics and public interest organizations examining the workings of the criminal justice and immigration systems, profiling has now, as a result of September 11, attained renewed prominence. The reason is clear – the hijackers identified by American law enforcement officials all appear to have been Arab, and the argument made by proponents of ethnic and racial profiling is that had airport security officials engaged in profiling, the terrorist acts of September 11 could have been prevented. It was no doubt this sort of reasoning that led retired Major-General Lewis MacKenzie, now security advisor to Premier Mike Harris, to suggest that profiling would be an acceptable law enforcement strategy to fight terror.[1] Indeed, an editorial in the *National Post* went so far as to state that 'it would be criminally negligent if Air Canada did not engage in racial profiling.'[2] Advocates of profiling have not made clear who it is who would be profiled – Arabs, persons of

Middle Eastern appearance, or Muslims, three groups whose member-ship overlaps, but is not at all identical. I will assume that it is the first group which is at issue.

Despite the lack of clarity over who would be profiled, the mere prospect of profiling has met with a chorus of disapproval. Federal Fisheries Minister Herb Dhaliwal has denounced the practice, having once been profiled himself,[3] as have organizations such as the Canadian Arab Federation, the National Council on Canadian Arab Relations, and the Canadian Muslim Civil Liberties Association. And a controversial directive issued to port-of-entry immigration and customs officers, pub-lished in the *Globe and Mail*,[4] prompted federal Immigration Minister Elinor Caplan to state '[t]here is no racial profiling, not by gender or religion.'[5]

What is extraordinary about the debate over profiling is the absence, for the most part, of any analysis of whether it would be constitutional. This is all the more extraordinary, since the constitutional concerns raised by the omnibus bill have already generated considerable interest in the legal community, and will propel various provisions of the statute to court in the weeks, months, and years to follow. In my view, the rather minimal public attention devoted to the constitutional challenges raised by profiling is a direct function of the form that such a policy would likely take. If immigration and law enforcement agencies begin to engage in the profiling of persons of Arab background or appearance, they will do so through means – ranging from internally distributed departmental memoranda, to informal word-of-mouth directives issued by superior officers – which are less visible and hence less susceptible to public scrutiny and democratic debate than publicly promulgated legal texts such as statutes and regulations. Civil libertarians must therefore ensure that in focusing so closely on the text of the omnibus bill, they do not overlook the threat posed by other components of the war against terror-ism to the very values that that war seeks to defend. This is particularly true in a multiracial and multiethnic democracy such as Canada, which is constitutionally committed to equality and non-discrimination.

B. What is Racial and Ethnic Profiling?

What is racial and ethnic profiling? It is important to be absolutely clear here, because the debate over profiling has not yielded a precise defini-tion of what that practice is. As Randall Kennedy of the Harvard Law

School has suggested, there seem to be two definitions of profiling.[6] The broad definition holds that profiling consists of a decision to detain or arrest an individual, or to subject an individual to further investigation, '*solely* on the basis of his or her' race or ethnicity.[7] The narrow definition is that profiling consists of the use of race or ethnicity *along with other factors*, such as suspicious behaviour. The narrow definition has been seized upon by advocates of profiling, not only because it may better fit the actual practice of law enforcement (a disputed point), but also because it appears to dilute the importance of race and ethnicity, and hence gives the impression that race or ethnicity would not drive law enforcement decisions. However, Kennedy correctly argues that this inference is based on faulty reasoning, because allowing the use of race or ethnicity even as one factor must mean that it can play a 'decisive' role in whether to subject an individual to further investigation.[8] That is, any use of race and ethnicity may serve to distinguish two individuals who otherwise manifest identical suspect behaviour, subjecting one to heightened scrutiny, while letting the other walk free. And if this is true, then decisions to target law enforcement will still be made on the basis of race or ethnicity, even if that factor is one among many.

There are two additional points to note here. First, to the best of my knowledge, profiling has been advocated in order to target investigative efforts, but not as a reason for final decisions, such as to prove guilt in a criminal proceeding, or to deny persons admission to Canada. This is important, because at times, profiling has played this role. During the Second World War, for example, the internment of Japanese Canadians amounted to the use of profiling to conclusively deprive persons of their liberty without due process of law, not merely to subject them to more probing investigation.

Second, Kennedy's definitions are very much framed in the context of the United States, where a significant body of evidence documents the use of profiling in law enforcement against African Americans and Latinos. In recent years, the tool of choice for law enforcement has been the pretext stop, in which a police officer stops a driver, ostensibly because of a traffic violation, for the purpose of searching his vehicle and its passengers in connection with non-traffic related offences, usually related to drugs.[9] The evidence suggests that pretext stops have been employed disproportionately against African Americans and Latinos, because law enforcement officials believe those groups are more likely to commit drug-related offences. Many will be familiar with the recent controversy surrounding racial profiling in New Jersey, where state troopers had a policy of pulling over African American and Latino drivers, while the state governor denied the very existence of that policy for over a decade.[10] What is striking about the American experience is that prior to Sept. 11, a broad consensus had emerged that racial profiling in policing was unacceptable and should be banned. According to a Gallup poll taken in 1999, 81% of respondents, including 80% of white respondents, opposed racial profiling in policing.[11] During the 2000 presidential campaign, both candidates pledged to ban racial profiling in policing, and President Bush reiterated his position as late as July, 2001.[12] Indeed, a bill that would ban profiling – the *End Racial Profiling Act* – was introduced in the United States Senate in June, 2001.[13]

The dominance of the American experience should not lull Canadians into thinking that racial and ethnic profiling is not a problem that we face. It most certainly is. Let me cite two pieces of evidence. The first is a study initially prepared by Scot Wortley of the University of Toronto's Centre for Criminology for the Commission on Systemic Racism in the Ontario Criminal Justice System.[14] The study surveyed Torontonians to establish whether the likelihood of people being stopped and searched by police officers differed on the basis of race. The study found that African Canadians were twice as likely as whites to be stopped once, and four times as likely to be stopped more than once. In particular, African Canadian men seem to be the targets of policing activity. The second piece of evidence is an analysis by Wortley of data collected by the African Canadian Legal Clinic that strongly suggests that African Canadians are subject to higher levels of scrutiny than white individuals by customs and immigration officers at Pearson International Airport.[15]

For the sake of simplicity, when I talk about profiling in Canada, I would like to focus on two situations that involve profiling by the state or its agents, and hence that engage the *Charter*. First, there is the use of profiling at the border, with respect to the degree of scrutiny that travellers – be they citizens, permanent residents, or visitors – receive by customs and immigration officers as they enter Canada. Second, there is the use of profiling by airport security, prior to boarding, on both domestic and international flights. Needless to say, there are other examples I could use – such as the profiling of applicants for immigration, or of candidates for civil service jobs – both of which have been suggested in the wake of September 11, and both of which are extremely problematic from a constitutional perspective. But I have chosen these two examples because they are at the forefront of public debate.

C. The Constitutionality of Racial and Ethnic Profiling under s. 15 of the *Charter*

Is profiling constitutional? I will confine my constitutional analysis to the *Charter*'s equality rights provision, s. 15, and its reasonable limits clause, s. 1. For this reason, I will not be touching upon ss. 7 through 10, which confer procedural rights on persons who come into contact with the criminal justice system. However, as I will show, there is some cross-over between the procedural fairness and equality arguments.

The test for determining whether there has been a s. 15 violation was recently rearticulated by the Supreme Court in *Law* v. *Canada*,[16] and has three parts: (a) that a distinction be drawn, (b) that it be drawn on the basis of a prohibited ground, and (c) that it be a discriminatory distinction. The first two steps would be easily met by a policy of profiling, because the whole point of profiling would be to target individuals for heightened scrutiny on the basis of their race and ethnicity, both of which are enumerated in s. 15 as prohibited grounds of discrimination. The heart of the analysis, as in all recent s. 15 cases, would be whether this differential treatment is discriminatory. To answer this question, *Law* states that we must ask whether the distinction demeans the dignity of the rights-claimant, where dignity 'means that an individual or group feels self-respect and self-worth,' understood in terms of both 'physical and psychological integrity and empowerment.'[17]

Several strands of the Court's equality jurisprudence suggest that profiling would be found to be discriminatory under s. 15. One of these is the centrality of stereotyping to a finding of discrimination. In the context of s. 15, *Law* explained that a stereotype can mean one of two different things. It can mean that a distinction drawn on the basis of a prohibited ground reflects the view that all members of a group who share that characteristic – race, religion, gender, and so on – possess certain undesirable traits that in fact none of them do. The most virulent forms of anti-Semitism, for example, rely on stereotypes of this sort. Far more common, though, is a stereotype that is an over-generalization – that is, an assumption that all members of a group possess certain undesirable traits that some members of those groups possess, when in fact some, or many, do not. The harm to human dignity – what transforms the use of stereotypes into discrimination – is that doing so has the effect of stigmatizing all members of that group, by promoting the view that they are somehow less worthy of respect and consideration, because they all possess the undesirable trait in question. The Court suggested that these claims would be easiest made out if the group at issue experienced pre-existing prejudice, because the use of stereotypes in framing government action can interact with and reinforce that existing disadvantage. Finally, the perspective to be adopted in this inquiry is subjective and objective: 'that of the reasonable person, dispassionate and fully apprised of the circumstances, possessed of similar attributes to, and under similar circumstances as, the claimant.'[18]

Front and center in *Law*, then, are the *social meaning* of government practices and the *social context* within which those practices occur. In *M. v. H.*, for example, the Court found that the exclusion of same sex couples from the spousal support provisions of the Ontario *Family Law Act*, in the context of widespread prejudice against same sex couples, meant that that exclusion promoted the view that same sex relationships were 'less worthy of recognition and protection.'[19] In the context of September 11, profiling would take the fact that some Arabs committed terrorist acts as a reason to subject *all* Arabs to heightened scrutiny. In other words, profiling employs race and ethnicity as a *proxy* for the risk of committing terrorist or criminal acts. But to profile in this way raises the serious danger of tarring an entire group with the crimes of the few, by giving rise to the myth that being an Arab reflects a propensity to engage in terrorist activity.

An aid to the success of this argument would be the demonstration of pre-existing disadvantage faced by Arabs. But the Court also made it very clear in *Law* that proof of pre-existing social disadvantage was not a *sine qua non*. What would be very significant to the s. 15 inquiry, in my view, is the kind of treatment that profiling entails. In both of my examples, profiling would involve the differential imposition of the burden of law enforcement on Arab travellers by agents of the state, in public and in full view of other passengers. The image here is stark: persons of Arab appearance being taken aside before boarding for more intensive questioning, or being steered at customs and immigration for secondary questioning, not because of any evidence that could reasonably give rise to suspicion of their links to terrorist organizations, but rather because of their physical appearance. It would also be significant that profiling would occur in the context of law enforcement, where the goal is to identify those who pose a threat of engaging in criminal activity. The mere fact of being subject to heightened scrutiny in the criminal context carries with it a stigma. Subjecting members of a racial or ethnic group to more probing investigation threatens to stigmatize an entire community.

To be sure, this kind of targeting would be rightly viewed as revolting by many Canadians. Indeed, images of the coercive power of the state directed at visible minorities in a public manner – at blacks in South Africa or in the American South, at Muslims in Bosnia – stand for many Canadians as paradigmatic examples of the grossest violations of human rights. In all of these cases, what was often involved was the selective enforcement of laws that themselves did not distinguish upon the basis of race or ethnicity. And that same history has taught us the chilling lesson that the targeting of state power on minorities can socially label those persons as deviant or inferior. It can lead otherwise reasonable and fair-minded people to rationalize or explain away the discriminatory application of state power, and even to engage in discrimination themselves. This prospect is all the more likely in a climate of fear.

Defenders of profiling might counter that the extent to which profiling stigmatizes turns on *how* profiling is handled in practice. The frame of reference here is the use of pretext stops in the United States, where what is objectionable is not simply the use of racial profiling, but the way in which those stops and the subsequent searches have not infrequently been conducted – with guns drawn, with verbal abuse, with no explanation as to why individuals have been stopped, and with no apology afterward.[20] A defender of profiling would argue that if handled professionally and politely, the more intrusive investigation of Arabs by airport security and immigration officials would minimize the indignity and stigmatization experienced by those passengers.

However, I reiterate that the relevant perspective under s. 15 is that of the reasonable person in the position of the rights-claimant. Even if the heightened scrutiny is handled professionally and politely, for the persons who are subject to profiling, the indignity is real. Those travellers would essentially be asked to establish their legitimacy; they would be placed in the position of having to state and justify their reasons for travelling, an entirely legal activity, while other travellers would face no such burden. They would faced this burden of persuasion every time they fly, or pass through customs and immigration. The cumulative effect on individuals of bearing this burden, simply because of one's looks, in a historical and social context where the differential imposition of the burden of law enforcement on the basis of race and ethnicity have been identified with the most odious forms of discrimination, would be enormously damaging on their self-respect and self-worth. And it is a cost that advocates of profiling altogether ignore.

Another factor identified by *Law* as relevant to a finding of discrimination is the nature of the interest at stake, the idea being that the more important the interest, the more likely a finding of discrimination. In the two examples I have chosen, the interests at stake are nothing less than physical liberty and privacy. It is important to be absolutely clear on how physical liberty and privacy are implicated in these two situations. I am not suggesting that anyone has a constitutional right to travel by air, or that non-citizens have a constitutional right to enter the country. However, in both of these cases, profiling would entail additional questioning by agents of the state regarding a variety of personal matters. It might also entail the involuntary, physical redirection of travellers to areas where they can be questioned further. The significant point here is that both privacy and physical liberty attract the protection of several rights in the *Charter*, unlike many of the interests which the court has found sufficiently important to count as reasons in favour of finding distinctions discriminatory – e.g., the protection of a human rights code,[21] or the right to seek spousal support payments.[22] The constitutional status of these interests should count as a reason to view with deep suspicion distinctions drawn with respect to their enjoyment.

Although *Law* strongly suggests that racial profiling would be found to violate s. 15, it contains one significant holding that cuts the other way. The Court in *Law* stated that a distinction is not discriminatory if it treats a rights-claimant 'differently on the basis of actual personal differences between individuals.'[23] The Court made this point by reference to an earlier decision upholding the separate placement of a child with a learning disability, which, the Court held, did not discriminate against her because it was made in her best interests.[24] This argument, if anything, could cut against profiling, because profiling treats people differently regardless of anything about them *per se*, but rather because of behavioural inferences drawn from their race and ethnicity. However, the Court in *Law* then went on to say that distinctions made on the basis of 'informed statistical generalizations' would not be discriminatory, because they corresponded closely enough with actual need.[25] What does this statement mean? Look at the holding of *Law* itself – the Court upheld age-based restrictions on survivors' benefits under the Canada Pension Plan on the ground that younger individuals were more likely to be able to re-enter the workforce than older persons – using 'age as a proxy for long-term need'[26] – knowing full well that this generalization did not hold true for many individuals. What the Court seemed to be saying is that relying on generalizations is acceptable in some circumstances, even if those generalizations are stereotypes. This is an apparent contradiction to what the Court said a few paragraphs earlier in its judgment.

The implications of permitting statistical generalizations for the constitutionality of profiling under s. 15 are clear and dramatic. But *Law* contained narrowing language, suggesting that this derogation from equality principles was only permissible in the context of remedial social benefits legislation which is under-inclusive, and stating that generalizations would be impermissible 'where the individual or group which is excluded by the legislation is already disadvantaged or vulnerable within Canadian society.'[27] These caveats should have been enough to put to rest any suggestion that the use of statistical generalizations would be acceptable in applying the burden of law enforcement upon a racial and ethnic minority.

What gives me pause for thought, though, is the majority judgment of the Supreme Court in *Little Sisters* v. *Canada*.[28] In that case, the Court held that Customs agents had discriminated on the basis of sexual orientation by targeting their enforcement efforts at homosexual erotic materials being imported by a lesbian bookshop, while adopting a relatively lax attitude to the importation of heterosexual materials by mainstream booksellers. *Little Sisters*, on its face, would thus seem to set a helpful precedent, because it found profiling based on sexual orientation to be discriminatory under s. 15. But the majority went on to say that the targeting would have been constitutional had it been based on 'evidence that homosexual erotica is proportionately more likely to be obscene than heterosexual erotica,' because in those circumstances, there would be a 'legitimate correspondence between the ground of alleged discrimination (sexual orientation) and the reality of the appellant's circumstances (importers of books and other publications including, but by no means limited to, gay and lesbian erotica).'[29] So even in a law enforcement context involving the differential application of burdens on a vulnerable minority, *Little Sisters* suggests that an informed statistical generalization would count as a reason for holding that profiling is not discriminatory, despite what was said in *Law*.

Little Sisters forces us to consider the rationale behind the use of, and the constitutional discipline to be imposed on, informed statistical generalizations. Amazingly, both *Law* and *Little Sisters* say little to nothing about either of these issues. This is a glaring oversight, given the obvious tension between permitting statistical generalizations and the Court's own emphasis in *Law* on the harm to equality caused by over-generalization. What are likely at work here are efficiency concerns of different sorts. In the social benefits context, the alternative to rules determining eligibility on the basis of personal characteristics such as age is a process of case-by-case decision-making that directly assesses need. Such a situation would be time-consuming, expensive, and potentially open to abuse because it would require that individual decision-makers be vested with considerable discretion. In the law enforcement context, the Court in *Little Sisters* suggested that targeting is permissible because Customs 'is obliged to use its limited resources in the most cost-effective way,' an explicitly utilitarian line of argument that gives priority to maximizing the yield of finite law enforcement activities.[30] Proponents of profiling at airports and at immigration will no doubt point to this latter comment in *Little Sisters* in defence of the constitutionality of such policies.

However, there are three large problems with permitting informed statistical generalizations to defeat claims of discrimination. First, statistical generalizations may often be unreliable, or, even worse, reflective of discrimination themselves. To permit governments to rely on them as justification for differential treatment may do no more than to revictimize the victims of discrimination. This is a well-known argument in the context of racial crime statistics, which are notoriously unreliable because they may reflect discriminatory policing practices in the process of investigation. A proponent of profiling would respond that the events of September 11 are different, because the perpetrators of those terrorist acts are clearly drawn from one ethnic group. But here we encounter the second problem – the question of fit. The justification for using personal characteristics such as race or ethnicity as proxies for risk is that they have some sort of predictive value. *Law* says nothing, though, about *how much* predictive value they must have to suffice for the purposes of s. 15. More precisely, profiling generates both false positives and false negatives, because they subject to scrutiny people who pose no risk whatsoever, and omit from scrutiny people who do in fact pose some risk. *Law*'s silence on this issue is deeply problematic, because both false positives and false negatives generate equality concerns. For the former, innocent persons are subject to the unequal burden of law enforcement because of their race and ethnicity, and for the latter, the law is enforced unequally against persons who pose a risk because of their race and ethnicity.

This leads me to the final and most important point: that statistical generalizations cut against the grain of a conception of equality itself – that is, that individuals not be judged on the basis of presumed group characteristics, but rather on the basis of their individual traits.[31] This theme has been very important in the Court's equality jurisprudence, and comes from its case-law interpreting human rights codes. That jurisprudence has been shaped by the impulse that access to the goods whose distribution is regulated by those statutes – principally employment, but also housing and services – should not be governed by criteria that erect arbitrary and irrational barriers, but instead by criteria that are relevant, such as talent, ability to pay, and need. The difficulty with profiling is that it subjects persons to heightened scrutiny not on the basis of criteria that are tied to their conduct, which is the legitimate concern of law enforcement, but instead to the colour of their skin or appearance, which is not.

What is the way forward? As constitutional lawyers know, concerns regarding administrability are classically considered under s. 1, where the burden of proof is on the governments who possess the relevant information, not rights-claimants, who do not. Because they are motivated by efficiency concerns, the justification of statistical generalizations should therefore be relegated to s. 1. But even there the Court must soon develop an account of the legitimate and illegitimate use of statistical generalizations in equality rights cases. Left unchecked, the combination of *Little Sisters* and *Law* is dangerous.

As a tentative suggestion, I would propose the courts distinguish on the basis of the nature of the policy at issue. In cases involving under-inclusive social benefits schemes, a good case can be made for the constitutionality of distinctions drawn on prohibited grounds of discrimination if the statistical generalizations meet some threshold level of fit. But with respect to the burden of law enforcement, which by necessity entails deprivations of liberty and privacy, generalizations of this sort are deeply problematic. It is here that procedural fairness concerns can inform the interpretation of s. 15. Section 8 of the Charter prohibits 'unreasonable' search and seizures, and s. 9 prohibits 'arbitrary' detention and arrest, which has been interpreted to impose a requirement of 'articulable cause.' Although a majority of the Supreme Court has not spoken to this issue directly, the dissenting judgments of Sopinka J. in *R. v. Ladouceur*,[32] and La Forest J. in *R. v. Belnavis*,[33] as well as the Ontario Court of Appeal's judgment in *R. v. Simpson*,[34] all indicate that detaining an individual simply because of her race constitutes an arbitrary detention or arrest under s. 9 (*Ladouceur, Simpson*) or makes a search unreasonable under s. 8 (*Belnavis*). In my view, the interpretation of 'arbitrary' under s. 9 and 'unreasonable' under s. 8 should inform the interpretation of 'discrimination' under s. 15, so as to render race and ethnic-based deprivations of liberty and privacy based on statistical generalizations *per se* discriminatory. What is required instead is a proces of individual decision-making on a case-by-case basis.

D. Conclusion: Section 1, Alternative Means and the Anti-Terrorism Bill

If a policy of profiling were found to violate s. 15, many difficult issues would arise under s. 1, such as whether that policy would be prescribed by law, the appropriate level of deference owed by the courts, and whether profiling minimally impairs the right to equality. By way of conclusion, I want to focus on the last of these three issues. The obvious alternative to race- or ethnic-conscious policies for airport security and immigration is the use of other criteria that are not prohibited grounds of discrimination, nor thinly veiled proxies for them. Indeed, I want to argue in favour of one provocative alternative to profiling, which is to subject *everyone* to intrusive investigation both by airport security personnel and immigration officers. This policy would be extremely effective, and would comport entirely with the equality guarantee. But amazingly, not a single proponent of profiling has even considered it, even if only to reject it.

If we were to take this proposal seriously, as we should, what would be the principal arguments against it? One argument is that it would be extremely costly, and that in a world of scarce resources, governments cannot be expected to adopt the absolutely least intrusive means for securing their public policies. However, we should be extremely sceptical of this claim. The same voices that are calling for racial and ethnic profiling also claim that in the war on terrorism, money is no object, and that significant resources should now be devoted to Canada's military, intelligence services, and law enforcement agencies. And the expectation is that significant resources will be made available. If this is true, the plea of poverty rings hollow. The true question is not whether moneys are available, but the relative priority to be attached to different kinds of expenditures prompted by September 11. At the very least, in tallying up the costs of the war on terror, the costs of complying with s. 15 must be taken into account. Indeed, I would go even further, and argue that in the allocation of scarce resources, compliance with the *Charter* should presumptively take priority.

The other argument against a policy of blanket scrutiny is that it would exact enormous costs in terms of liberty and privacy. No doubt, the infringements on liberty and privacy of a blanket policy would be severe, and would be a significant cost to be weighed. However, the policy would also have an enormous benefit, because it would eliminate one of the principal costs of profiling: the stigma born by those who are singled out for heightened investigation. What this means is that a blanket policy would *redistribute* the costs of the fight against terrorism, and ensure that they are borne by everyone, not just those who through no choice of their own share the race and ethnicity of those responsible for September 11. Indeed, distributing the costs in this way might lead to a better social valuation of the war on terror, because those who advocate racial and ethnic profiling are not the ones who will bear the costs of that policy. It is deeply ironic that the same voices who call for racial and ethnic profiling are precisely those who now call for solidarity across ethnic and racial lines, and proclaim that we should all be willing to surrender some freedom in favour of security. But if solidarity is truly their guiding principle, and their willingness to surrender freedom is genuine, then their policy proposals should match their rhetoric. Profiling does not.

Notes

* I would like to thank Ron Daniels for his invitation to speak at the conference, Rebecca Jones for excellent research assistance, Ira Parghi for perceptive comments on an earlier draft, and Kent Roach, Julian Roy and Scot Wortley for extremely helpful discussions and invaluable background material. None of them necessarily shares the views that I express here. I acknowledge the financial support of the Faculty of Law, University of Toronto, in preparing this manuscript.

1 S. Schmidt, 'Ontario denies anti-terror policy is racist: Retired general says checking Arabs "common sense"' *National Post* (5 October 2001) (available on-line at: http://www.nationalpost.com/search/story.html?f=/stories/20011005/721871.html&qs=MacKenzie%) (date accessed: 7 November 2001).

2 'Profiles in Prudence (editorial)' *National Post* (20 September 2001) A17.

3 D. Leblanc & S. McCarthy, 'The War on Terror: Terror bill worries Dhaliwal' *The Globe and Mail* (30 October 2001) A11.

4 E. Oziewicz, 'The Brink of War: Border alert targets pilots, Canadian guards told to watch for men with technical training and links to 16 "conflict" countries' *The Globe and Mail* (19 September 2001) A1.

5 S. McCarthy & E. Oziewicz, 'The Brink of War: CANADA'S RESPONSE – Ministers defend new border alert' *The Globe and Mail* (20 September 2001) A6.

6 R. Kennedy, 'Suspect policy: racial profiling usually isn't racist. It can help stop crime. And it should be abolished' (1999) 221:11 *New Republic* 31 (available on-line at: http://www.thenewrepublic.com/archive/0999/091399/coverstory 091399.html) (date accessed: 7 November 2001). Kennedy's definitions actually refer only to racial profiling, but in fact encompass profiling on the basis of both race and ethnicity.

7 *Ibid.* (emphasis mine).

8 R.L. Kennedy, *Race, Crime and the Law* (New York: Vintage Books, 1998) at 148.

9 The constitutionality of this practice was upheld by the United States Supreme Court in *Whren v. United States*, 116 S.Ct. 1769 (1996).

10 P. Verniero & P.H. Zoubek, *Interim Report of the State Police Review Team Regarding Allegations of Racial Profiling* (20 April 1999).

11 F. Newport, 'Racial Profiling is Seen as Widespread, Particularly Among Young Black Men' *Gallup News Service* (9 December 1999) (available on-line at: www.gallup.com/poll/releases/pr991209.asp) (date accessed: 7 November 2001).

12 'Remarks by the President to National Organization of Black Law Enforcement Executives' (30 July 2001) (available on-line at: http://www.whitehouse.gov/news/releases/2001/07/20010730-5.html) (date accessed: 7 November 2001).

13 S 989.

14 S. Wortley, 'The Usual Suspects: Race, Police Stops and Perceptions of Criminal Injustice,' *Criminology* (forthcoming); Commission on Systemic Racism in the Ontario Criminal Justice System, *Report of the Commission on Systemic Racism in the Ontario Criminal Justice System* (Toronto: Queen's Printer for Ontario, 1995) at 352 to 360.

15 R. James, 'Black Passengers Targeted in Pearson Searches? Lawyers plan court fight over "racial profiling" by customs officials at airport,' *The Toronto Star* (29 Sunday 1998) A1.

16 *Law v. Canada (Minister of Employment and Immigration)*, [1999] 1 S.C.R. 497 [hereinafter *Law*]

17 *Ibid.* at para. 53

18 *Ibid.* at para. 60

19 *M. v. H.*, [1999] 2 S.C.R. 3 at para. 73.

20 D.A. Harris, *Driving While Black: Racial Profiling On Our Nation's Highways* (American Civil Liberties Union, 1999) (available on-line at: http://www.aclu.org/profiling/report/index.html) (date accessed: 7 November 2001). For those who think that demeaning police conduct toward members of racial minorities is strictly an American problem, we need only remind ourselves of the public strip search conducted of Ian Vincent Golden, an African Canadian, the constitutionality of which is currently before the Supreme Court of Canada: *R. v. Golden*, [1999] S.C.C.A. No. 498 (hearing date: Feb. 15, 2001).

21 *Vriend v. Alberta*, [1998] 1 S.C.R. 493.

22 *M. v. H.*, supra note .

23 *Law, supra* note at para. 71.

24 *Eaton v. Brant (County) Board of Education*, [1997] 1 S.C.R. 241.

25 *Law, supra* note at para. 106.

26 *Ibid.* at para. 104.

27 *Ibid.* at para. 106.

28 *Little Sisters Book and Art Emporium v. Canada (Minister of Justice)*, [2000] 2 S.C.R. 1120 [hereinafter *Little Sisters*].

29 *Ibid.* at para. 121.

30 *Ibid.* at para. 120.
31 *Miron* v. *Trudel,* [1995] 2 S.C.R. 418 at para. 131.
32 [1990] 1 S.C.R. 1257 at 1267.
33 [1997] 3 S.C.R. 341 at 376-7.
34 (1993), 12 O.R. (3d) 182 (C.A.). Also see *Brown* v. *Durham Regional Police Force (1998),* 131 C.C.C. (3d) 1 at 17 (Ont. C.A.) (stating that detention under Ontario *Highway Traffic Act* for reasons of race would be illegal because of lack of articulable cause).

Borderline Security

AUDREY MACKLIN*
Faculty of Law
University of Toronto

Introduction

Geo-political borders serve many functions in public consciousness, both literal and symbolic: They demarcate the nation-state's essential territoriality; they assert and exert sovereignty; and finally, their selective permeability operates as a measure of the nation-state's security against external threat, whether characterized in physical, ideological or ethno-cultural terms. The events of September 11 elicited an almost reflexive public clamour throughout Canada and the US to tighten their respective borders, followed by promotion of a fuzzily-defined 'security perimeter' that would encompass Canada and the United States and, in some versions, Mexico.

It is unsurprising that many in the US, Canada and other Western nations would telescope their anguish, anger and apprehension into a demand to exclude foreigners – was it not, after all, foreigners who committed these heinous acts? Casting the current social climate in the language of moral panic strains against this brute fact.

Yet the media response has generally failed to distinguish between problems of policy on the one hand and failures of implementation, enforcement and intelligence on the other. For instance, there seems little doubt that the utter inadequacy of security checks in airports across North America contributed to the outcome of September 11, but this is not an immigration matter. Other major lapses include the ease with which false identity documents are obtained, the apparent lack of co-ordination and sharing of information among police, immigration, and intelligence agencies within and between states, and the inability to execute deportation orders. These are not matters of law, but of crime prevention, as well as implementation and enforcement of existing immigration powers. Nevertheless, systemic explanations cannot compete with the simplicity and emotive power of invoking the spectre of the foreigner as an intrinsic menace to national security.

By coincidence, the immigrant-as-security-threat leitmotif already figured prominently in Bill C-11, the *Immigration and Refugee Protection Act*.[1] The Bill was introduced in spring, 2001, but passed into law on November 1, 2001, in the wake of September 11. The *Immigration and Refugee Protection Act* casts a wide net over non-citizens rendered inadmissible on security grounds, expands the detention power over designated security risks, and reduces access to independent review of Ministerial security decisions.

Despite the focus on intensification of border control in light of September 11, I argue that both the event itself and Canada's legislative response, the proposed *Anti-Terrorism Act* (Bill C-36)[2] and the security provisions of the *Immigration and Refugee Protection Act*, reveal how the functionality of borders is simultaneously overdetermined and crucially destabilized by the quest for security. By this I mean that the only question asked about immigration policy at present is whether and how effectively it enhances the security of citizens. Yet this singular insistence upon what borders *must* do, namely, protect Us from Them, cannot but expose the limits on what borders *can* and *actually* do. This in turn returns us to the disjuncture between how we imagine the borders that circumscribe our national communities, and how we imagine those communities. By examining how the events of September 11 and the response to date complicate our tacit associations between borders and territoriality, sovereignty and security, I intend to reveal how the functionality of borders is being eroded even as – or perhaps because – the demand to fortify them is reaching new levels of fervour.

Territoriality

Every schoolchild in Canada is acquainted with the borders demarcating her country. Maps hang on classroom walls and their brightly coloured lines jauntily inform us of where our country begins and ends. The oft-repeated claim that the Canada-US border is the longest undefended border in the world only reifies the border's autonomous existence in the collective imagination, proving that no material effort is required to signify or maintain it.

How have recent events challenged assumptions about territoriality and borders? First, if one looks back from September 11 and considers other attacks on US interests, it becomes obvious that assaults on a given state do not actually require access to its territory. The United States has been attacked in its embassies in Kenya and Tanzania, in military operations in Somalia, at sea as well as on land.[3] The territoriality of borders is also challenged by tactics of terror that do not rely on the corporeal presence of the perpetrators: letters with anthrax powder can be mailed from anywhere, and internet viruses launched from abroad can wreak havoc in the time it takes us to open an e-mail message.

Enemies of a state exploit the discontinuity between territorial boundaries and the nation-state, but many states do as well. I am referring here not to the obvious military, diplomatic and economic presence of states outside their borders, but rather to increasing efforts to control access to territory through extraterritorial measures. Visa requirements are the oldest and most obvious example. A more recent illustration is the US immigration and customs pre-clearance point at Toronto's Pearson Airport. Rather than wait until landing on American soil, US-bound air travelers submit to 'border' inspection before departing Canada. Expedience and convenience explain this initiative, but less benign motives animate Canada's extensive interdiction strategy.[4] Canada routinely imposes visa requirements on countries that generate significant refugee flows in order to prevent refugee claimants from reaching the Canadian border.[5] Canada also penalizes private carriers who transport improperly documented passengers to Canada. One consequence of this policy is the tacit conscription of private airline, transport and shipping employees as amateur immigration officers, who attempt to avoid carrier sanctions by examining travel documents and rejecting passengers with documents deemed suspicious. Much publicity accompanied the Australian government's recent interdiction of a boat carrying asylum seekers (mainly Afghan and Iraqi) en route from Indonesia. But Canada set a precedent in 1998 with the interdiction of a boat of 192 Tamil asylum seekers off the coast of Africa. The ship was escorted back to Sri Lanka, where all passengers were detained and at least one was tortured by Sri Lankan authorities.[6]

All of these interdiction techniques represent extra-territorial assertions of state coercion to facilitate more effective border control. Canada boasts of deflecting 33,000 people from reaching Canada in the past five years, and Canada's interdiction practices have been invoked to assure Canadians that the government indeed takes decisive action to protect the integrity of the border by preventing the arrival of undocumented and improperly documented migrants.[7] Since these same strategies also render it virtually impossible for refugees to obtain legitimate travel documents for Canada, the number of refugees caught in the interdiction net can never be known.

Terrorism may not respect borders, but neither do states in pursuit of border control. The result is a trend toward the decline of geo-political borders as the limit of state jurisdiction or assertion of power over non-citizens.

I have watched with bemusement as public debate has erected the concept of a 'security perimeter' as a means of ensuring greater protection from external threat. My first response was to wonder exactly what was meant by 'security perimeter.' When I could not discern a consistent definition for the term, my next response was to wonder what work was being done by an expression so manifestly imprecise. I have since come to view the 'security perimeter' as a discursive security blanket, one that furnishes comfort by conjuring up a visual image around which people can deposit their anxieties. From a functional perspective, the vagueness of the term is one of its virtues, for it has the capacity to mutate into whatever is required to perform its task of reassurance.

A minimalist conception of a security perimeter denotes little more than improved co-ordination in the gathering and sharing of intelligence within and between Canadian and US state agencies, such as the FBI, CIA, CSIS, Citizenship and Immigration, Immigration and Naturalization Service, and municipal, state and provincial police.[8] Improved methods of gathering data, and technology that enables access to multiple databases of security related information play a central role in this conception of a security perimeter. Another version of the security perimeter consists of harmonization of examination and enforcement practices, including detention, border inspection, and removal.[9]

A stronger variant of a security perimeter more or less adopts the European Union as a precedent:[10] Standards of entry for third country nationals are harmonized between all Member states, and once an individual passes through the external border, internal borders within the Union are erased for purposes of travel. A common EU list of visa-exempt countries is a pre-requisite to the implementation of a single external border. Pursuant to the provisions of the *Dublin Convention*,[11] an asylum claim must be lodged in the first EU country to which a claimant arrives, and the result is binding upon all Member states. Preliminary discussions have also been conducted on the adoption of a common interpretation of the international refugee definition.[12]

The most ambitious version of a security perimeter purports to supplant the full range of national selection, admission and enforcement policies with a binational scheme, jointly administered by Canada and the US.[13] A momentary glance at Canada's new *Immigration and Refugee Protection Act* and its mammoth and byzantine US counterpart should satisfy any reasonable observer that such a prospect is hardly feasible. I leave for future discussion the myriad theoretical objections one might mount to a comprehensive immigration policy. However, it should be noted that consolidating criteria for immigration is not an issue in the EU because all member states understand themselves not to be countries of immigration. Therefore, none have developed schemes for the systematic, permanent admission of immigrants, apart from fam-ily reunification or asylum. There is nothing for EU Members to co-ordinate as individual states.

The idea of co-ordinating refugee admission (inspired by the European Union's Dublin Convention) was the subject of a Canada-US Memorandum in the 1990s.[14] The core of the proposal required refugee claimants to lodge their claim in the first country of arrival. An unsuccessful claimant would be prohibited from filing a second claim in the other country. Negotiations around the Memorandum of Understanding lost momentum and the agreement was never finalized. Among other things, the fact that most refugee claimants arrive in Canada by transiting through the US meant that the Agreement would redound primarily to Canada's benefit and leave the US processing the vast majority of North American claims. Despite this asymmetry, the idea of a common refugee admission scheme has been revived lately under the rubric of the security perimeter.[15]

To the extent that a security perimeter would involve a common, standardized set of procedures governing admission of third-country nationals (non-citizens of North America), it follows logically that the border between Canada and the US should be permitted to atrophy for purposes of cross border movement. For those who identify at the border as Canadian or US citizens, the change would hardly be noticeable – until September 11, border officials exerted only nominal control over cross-border movement of most citizens anyway.[16] It could, however, make a significant difference for third party nationals, since the external border examination would presumably obviate the need for a check at the Canada-US border.

The operative premise is that the security of the individual state (be it Canada or the US) would be better served through a supra-national mechanism that conjoins the territory of the two states into one administrative unit. The assumption hitherto has been that national security is best assured by fortifying the borders that define each country as a sovereign entity. The effect of adopting a security perimeter is to decouple national security from territoriality. A certain paradox lurks here, for the concept of a US–Canada security perimeter surely subverts the function of borders as the means of securing the territory contained within them.

Sovereignty

Like a deranged man who compulsively confesses to crimes he did not commit, a coterie of Canadian media commentators and right-wing politicians have tripped over each other in the rush to blame Canada's allegedly lax refugee policies for September 11 in particular and global terrorism in general.[17] Despite the dearth of evidence in support of this allegation, two cases are repeatedly cited as illustrative of the failings of Canadian refugee policy.[18] The first concerns Ahmed Ressam, an Algerian national caught by US authorities in December 1999 as he tried to cross into the US border from British Columbia with a trunk full of explosives. He was apparently headed for Los Angeles, where he intended to detonate a bomb at LA International Airport. Ressam had made a refugee claim in Canada a few years earlier.

So too had Nabil al-Marabh, a Syrian national born in Kuwait who is presently detained in the US on suspicion of links to Al-Qaeda. In fact, both Ressam's and al-Marabh's refugee claims were rejected. Al-Marabh left Canada in 1995, and re-entered the US, where he apparently resided and worked prior to making his refugee claim in Canada.

In July 2000, al-Marabh was caught trying to enter the US illegally from Canada. At the time, he was wanted in Massachusetts for violation of a probation order arising out of a conviction for stabbing his roommate. He was also under suspicion by US intelligence for security related reasons. Yet US border officials were ignorant of his chequered history in the US when he was caught at the border, and simply turned Al-Marabh back over to Canada.

Ressam was not deported from Canada, and there is some indication that one reason was that deportations to Algeria were suspended due to the massive human rights violations in that country, but another reason was that CSIS wanted to keep him under surveillance in Canada. Eventually, he fraudulently obtained a Canadian passport in the name of Benni Noris and left the country on his own initiative to pursue training at an

Al-Qaeda camp in Afghanistan. Ressam re-entered Canada on his Canadian passport and false identity, thereby eluding CSIS upon return.

While the respective cases of Ressam and el-Marabh case reveal egregious failures of Canadian and US intelligence and enforcement, both in terms of detection and of co-ordination, in neither case was the refugee determination system the weak link. Both men's refugee claims were rejected. Nor is there evidence that any of the actual perpetrators of the September 11 hijacking/bombing entered the US as refugee claimants, much less Canada. Each apparently arrived with fixed-term visitor or student visas and then overstayed their visas, thereby joining the ranks of an estimated 6 million other migrants residing in the US without legal status.[19] Despite its harsher detention policies, especially in relation to undocumented asylum seekers, the US is generally no more successful in Canada at monitoring the whereabouts, much less removing, migrants lacking legal status.[20] Indeed, about half of Canada-bound refugee claimants seek entry at the Canada-US border. The obvious inference is that it must be easier for many refugee claimants to enter the US than Canada.[21] None of these facts have dispelled the notion that refugee policies are somehow responsible for rendering Canada's border dangerously porous. Why?

I believe the answer lies in the popular belief that excluding non-citizens is the ultimate prerogative of sovereignty.[22] Canadians assume that the state has an unfettered right to admit or refuse any non-citizen in accordance with its own legal standards. The categories of prospective entrants (visitors, temporary workers, economic immigrants, and family class) and the criteria for entry are all creatures of Canadian immigration law. Their admission is governed by Canadian immigration law, and if Parliament wishes to change the rules, it can do so. The singular exception to this principle are refugee claimants who arrive at Canadian ports of entry seeking asylum. By virtue of Canada's international obligations under the 1951 UN *Convention Relating to the Status of Refugees*,[23] Canada is bound not to *refoule* (return)[24] a person who meets the international definition of a refugee. Refugee claimants are self-selected in the sense that they choose Canada; Canada does not choose them. If they reach the border and meet the refugee definition, Canada must accept them. Of course, as noted earlier, Canada expends considerable effort on preventing refugee claimants from reaching Canada. Part of that task is achieved through a chain of discursive links that discredit them upon arrival: Citizens of most countries require visas to enter Canada; Canada does not issue visas to persons deemed likely to make a refugee claim;

people without visas cannot lawfully enter Canada; Refugees often resort to smugglers who furnish false documents or otherwise circumvent border control; persons who enter Canada without the requisite documents are illegal immigrants, and illegal immigrants represent a breach of security for Canada. *Ergo*, refugees are a danger to the security of Canada.

If one takes the view that the refugee regime imperils Canadian sovereignty by foisting the uninvited upon us, how better to demonstrate the catastrophic consequences of 'losing control' than by linking the events of September 11 to refugee admission? I suggest that this visceral anxiety about sovereignty offers the best account for the demonization of refugees as the figurative culprits for September 11.

Having said that, I suggest that if there is a correlation between sovereignty, security and border control, the place to look is not the refugee regime, but to an array of neo-liberal shifts in governance. Free trade advocates often point to increased border traffic as an indicator of NAFTA's success. One need not hypothesize about the consequences of accelerated movement of capital and goods on the movement of labour to recognize that increased cross-border human movement (whether as business professionals, tourists, freight carriers, etc.) is an inevitable corollary of liberalized trade between contiguous states. A second dimension of neo-liberal governance is the downsizing of the public sector as part of an overall campaign to diminish the scale of government in absolute terms and in relation to the private sector. Budget cuts and staff reduction in the immigration bureaucracy played out in office closure, fewer resources to devote to investigation and enforcement, and overall demoralization and decline in service delivery.[25] A similar story could be told of CSIS and the RCMP.

Privatisation of airports relegated airport security to market discipline, where maximizing return on investment resulted in insufficient numbers of security personnel who were poorly paid, inadequately trained and unlikely to remain in the job. The tragic consequences of the privatization of airport security in the US are evident.[26]

The upshot of freer trade and less government is the quantitative and qualitative decline in resources allocated to vetting increased numbers of border-crossers. One concrete example concerns refugee claimants. Although border officials are legally authorized to commence security inquiries at the border, lack of resources meant that refugee claimants were routinely admitted and given forms to fill out and mail back. Although immigration officials are legally entitled to photograph, fingerprint and examine refugee claimants at the port of entry, lack of personnel made it impossible for immigration officers to conduct extensive interviews at the port of entry. I emphasize, however, that this laxity had nothing to do with refugee policy, or a dearth of state power, but was entirely attributable to lack of staff and resources to do the job. In the wake of September 11, Minister Caplan announced a resumption of 'front-end screening' of refugee claimants, and promised an additional $9 million for detention, screening and deportation, and $17.3 million to expedite development of a permanent resident card to replace the notoriously flimsy 'IMM1000'.[27]

By drawing connections between neo-liberal policies and systematic security lapses, I am not attempting to mount an anti-free trade argument based on security considerations. My claim is rather that the relationship between sovereignty, state policy, and the policing of borders cannot be reduced to a simplistic equation between a specific admission policy and security. It should not escape notice that the loudest voices expressing concern about intensified border inspection have not been refugee advocates or civil libertarians; the voices belong to owners, managers, and employees justifiably distressed about the detrimental commercial impact of increased delay at the US-Canada border.[28] Perhaps some Canadians would not agonize over perceived trade-offs between national security and our moral and legal obligations to refugees: They are all too willing to sacrifice the latter in the name of the former. Many Canadians would struggle, however, over actual trade-offs between security-related practices and trans-border economic activity. And that is where the real trade-offs will be.

It seems reasonable to assert that drawing a perimeter around two or more countries and erasing internal borders may confer efficiency benefits on a free trade regime by expediting cross-border movement. It is not at all apparent how it enhances security. After all, erasing the internal border only removes an additional check, and no matter how strict the scrutiny at the external border, no screen is infallible. In any event, voluntarily undertaking to provide refuge to persons fleeing persecution is no more or less a surrender of sovereignty than choosing to relinquish control over Canadian borders, whether in the name of free trade or in the name of security. Once this point is acknowledged, the talismanic power of borders as the sign of sovereignty is crucially disrupted.

Securing the Nation

Until Bill C-36, terrorism as a discrete legal category of conduct only existed within the confines of the immigration legislation. A non-citizen is inadmissible if, *inter alia*, reasonable grounds exist to believe that the person is, was, or will be[29] a member of an organization that there are reasonable grounds to believe is, was, or will be engaging in terrorism, acts of espionage or subversion against a democratic government, or acts of subversion against any government. A non-citizen may also be removed if there are reasonable grounds to believe the person is, was or will be a danger to the security of Canada.

Locating terrorism exclusively in immigration legislation institutionalized in law the figure of the immigrant as archetypal menace to the cultural, social, and political vitality of the nation. The myriad tropes of the foreign Other – as vector of disease, agent of subversion, corrupter of the moral order and debaser of the national identity – all trade on the exteriorization of threat and the foreigner as the embodiment of its infiltration. Canadian immigration history is replete with examples, ranging from the exclusion of racialized groups on grounds of inferiority and degeneracy, to the deportation of foreign-born labour and social activists in the inter-war years, to the persistent stereotype of immigrants as distinctively crime-prone.[30] In this symbolic order, the border of the state is akin to the pores of the national corpus, and expelling the foreign body serves to restore the health of the nation.

Viewed within a historical and semiotic frame, the equation of terrorism with foreignness follows almost axiomatically. Yet, the image of terror as a foreign import, something that adheres to foreigners as part of their personal/cultural baggage, was challenged by the revelations that Ahmed Ressam was recruited in Montreal. Some of the World Trade Centre perpetrators were apparently recruited in Hamburg.[31] The most scrupulous inspection or background check prior to admission to Canada or Germany would not have detected them as terrorists because they had yet to become terrorists.

Unlike the *Anti-Terrorism Act*, immigration legislation has consistently refused to actually define terrorism. The notorious difficulty of providing a neutral objective definition for such an inherently political concept has been thoroughly explored in the Canadian and international context by Sharryn Aiken and others.[32] Despite the ambiguity and imprecision of the term, its chilling effect on lawful expression and association by non-citizens, and the particularly dire consequences of its deployment against refugees, the Federal Court of Canada resolutely refused to define it or to strike it down as unconstitutionally vague. Mr. Justice Denault's comments in *Re Ahani*[33] are particularly noteworthy for the judge's eccentric approach to statutory interpretation:

In my view, since Parliament has decided not to define these terms, it is not incumbent upon this Court to define them ... I do not share the view that the word [member] must be narrowly interpreted. I am rather of the view that it must receive a broad and unrestricted interpretation. As to the word 'terrorism,' while I agree with counsel for the Respondent that the word is not capable of a legal definition that would be neutral and non-discriminatory in its application, I am still of the opinion that the word must receive an unrestricted interpretation.[34]

As Sharryn Aiken comments, Denault J's ruling effectively concedes that 'terrorism' is incapable of a definition that would meet the requirements of the rule of law and the *Charter* – neutrality and non-discrimination. Nevertheless – or perhaps therefore – the term must not only be applied, but warrants 'an unrestricted interpretation.'[35]

In the recently argued *Suresh*[36] and *Ahani*[37] appeals, the Supreme Court of Canada was called upon to find 'member' and 'terrorism' unconstitutionally vague. Whatever the Court's ruling on the terrorism issue, its impact will have been dissipated by the *Anti-Terrorism Act*, which does define terrorism. On the other hand, since membership in a terrorist organization is not criminalized in the *Anti-Terrorism Act*, the Supreme Court of Canada's ruling on this issue remains pertinent.

Why did the drafters of the *Anti-Terrorism Act* elect to exclude membership and define terrorism? I can only speculate that in the course of '*Charter* proofing' Bill C-36, the government recognized that prohibiting membership would likely violate freedom of association and 'terrorism' was indeed too vague to withstand constitutional scrutiny – at least where the rights of *citizens* were ostensibly at stake.

The truth is that laws that arouse deep concern about civil liberties when applied to citizens are standard fare in the immigration context. Critics of Bill C-36 point with alarm at the imprecision of the definition of terrorism (s. 83.01(1)(b)), non-disclosure of information to an accused (s.38.06) and warrantless, preventive detention (s. 83.3(4)). I have already noted the absence of any definition whatsoever of terrorism in immigration law, although I anticipate that the definition in the Anti-Terrorism Act will eventually be incorporated into regulations under the *Immigration and Refugee Protection Act*. Immigration law already permits automatic, indefinite warrantless, preventive detention of a non-citizen if the Minister of Citizenship and Immigration and Solicitor General sign a certificate declaring the person concerned to be a security risk.[38] The certificate process contained in Bill C-36 with its non-disclosure provisions, was inspired by the existing certificate process in immigration law.[39] Immigration lawyers have accumulated years of experience attesting to the near futility of trying to adequately represent an individual without proper access to the evidence against him or her. This certificate process, as applied against a permanent resident suspected of involvement in organized crime, survived a 1992 constitutional challenge in *Chiarelli* v. *Canada*.[40]

Under immigration legislation, the standard of proof required to trigger inadmissibility and deportation (including *refoulement*) is nothing more than 'reasonable grounds to believe,' as applied to past, present or future membership in organizations, and to the past, present or future activities of those organizations. This standard is even lower than the civil standard of balance of probabilities, and compounded in the case of membership by its double deployment. Conversely, conviction for a criminal offence related to terrorism will require proof beyond a reasonable doubt. Only non-citizens are subject to regulation by immigration law, but the *Criminal Code* applies to all.

Contrary to the exhortations of media pundits and anti-immigrant crusaders, the Constitution has proved a fairly thin cloak protecting non-citizens. The main exception is *Singh* v. *MEI*,[41] which guaranteed refugee claimants a right to an oral hearing in the determination of their claim. While it is technically true that most *Charter* rights apply to all persons physically in Canada,[42] in practice the courts have sharply circumscribed the nature and extent of those rights for non-citizens faced with removal. The jurisprudential rationale for these outcomes typically partakes of three related propositions:

1 Non-citizens have no unqualified right to enter or remain in Canada.
2 Therefore, deportation outside the refugee context does not engage any life, liberty or security of the person interest (s. 7), nor is it cruel or unusual treatment or punishment (s. 12).
3 Even if a s. 7 interest is violated by deportation, the intensity of the violation is diminished by the feeble quality of the non-citizen's right (see 1 and 2), such that the principles of fundamental justice demand no more than whatever the state has already elected to do in the circumstances.[43]

The fact is that immigration law has long done to non-citizens what the *Anti-Terrorism Act* proposes to do to citizens – without public outcry and with judicial blessing. Despite the demand from some quarters to invoke s. 33 of the Constitution to expel non-citizens from the shelter of the Charter,[44] proponents of the override are fighting a gratuitous battle.

This, of course, begs the question of what advocates of the notwithstanding clause believe its invocation would do to enhance security.

In any event, by shifting the locus of terrorism from immigration to criminal legislation, the Government has institutionally destabilized the figure of the foreigner as the paradigmatic source of danger to the security of the nation, and the border as the site for removal of the threat. Once terrorism is transposed to the criminal context, it becomes rather more difficult in principle to distinguish Timothy McVeigh the criminal from Mohammed Atta the terrorist. This transposition of terrorism to domestic criminal law arguably erodes the primacy of borders in securing the nation.

In one respect, this shift in emphasis represents a positive development for non-citizens. Where imprisonment for a criminal offence is at stake, citizenship is irrelevant to the *Charter* calculus: Non-citizens-R-Us. It is good news for non-citizens especially because, as any informed person knows, in practice the primary targets for surveillance, investigation, apprehension, detention and prosecution under the various provisions of the Anti-Terrorism Act will be persons born outside Canada, especially Arabs, Muslims and migrants from particular conflict ridden countries.[45] As one journalist commented shortly after Bill C-36 was introduced:

> ... most Canadians will not be terribly inconvenienced by Ms. McLellan's proposals. Instead, the costs will be borne by people who find themselves targets of police suspicion because of their ethnic background, radical political views or association with immigrant communities that have ties with groups deemed to be terrorist fronts.[46]

By extension, the organizations that will attract greatest scrutiny as potential 'terrorist groups,' (financial support of which will be deemed to facilitate terrorism), and the charities most likely to be deregistered, will be those serving communities connected to regions of conflict, repression, and civil strife. As the Canadian Council for Refugees recently submitted,

> groups that commit acts that may be characterized as 'terrorist' are often multi-faceted, and not necessarily limited to a single, violent purpose. People may be members of or associated with a group without being involved in or supporting 'terrorist' actions and perhaps even without knowing that they are being committed.

...

[Many immigrant communities] face the problem that the complexities of events in their home countries are little understood in Canada, with the result that support for a political option might be confused with support for violent actions.[47]

The security provisions in immigration law already have a chilling effect on lawful political expression, advocacy and association by diasporic communities. The temperature will only drop further under the security gaze of the *Anti-Terrorism Act*. It is sadly ironic that refugees attract particular suspicion, for as Reg Whitaker explains:

The very nature of a Convention Refugee claim: a 'well-founded fear of persecution for reasons of face, religion, nationality, membership in a particular social group or political opinion' arises out of political conflicts that are unlikely to be contained within the country of origin. Spread of such conflicts is always a fear, and in the age of international terrorism and the global telepolitics of violence, this fear is not always imaginary. There is always some suspicion that attaches to anyone who has had to flee one state on political grounds, a kind of irreducible aura of political instability that could potentially threaten the order of the host country.[48]

Members of diasporic communities, whatever their immigration status, will experience more than ever how boundaries demarcated by ethnicity, culture, religion and politicization emerge in sharp relief, while inclusion within the boundary defined by citizenship status recedes in import when viewed through the lens of the state's surveillance camera. Boundaries of membership and modes of exclusion can be (and regularly are) redrawn from within the nation. They trace themselves along fault lines that erupt along the surface of our pluralistic, multicultural, democratic country when stressed by real or perceived crisis.

Assuming they are prosecuted under the criminal law, non-citizens accused of terrorism-related offences can claim Charter protection *qua* accused, a status that attracts significantly greater judicial consideration than the status of non-citizen. Yet I strongly doubt that my assumption is valid. If the history of war crimes prosecutions provides any guidance, criminal prosecution for terrorism-related offences will prove difficult, if not futile, precisely because it must be done in a manner that respects fundamental rights and freedoms of accused. Wherever possible, I antici-pate that the state will take advantage of the broad investigative powers conferred under the *Anti-Terrorism Act* to gather evidence to have the person concerned declared a security risk under the *Immigration and Refugee Protection Act*. Simply put, it is easier in law to deport than to imprison. At present, this conclusion obtains even if the deportee has lived in Canada since infancy and, subject to the Supreme Court of Canada's judgment in *Suresh*, even if he or she faces torture or death upon return.[49]

There is an even more cynical reason for believing that non-citizens will be the primary target and immigration law will be the instrument of choice for state authorities: Security agencies sometimes play what Reg Whitaker labels 'intelligence games' with non-citizen subjects of investigation (especially refugees), dangling before them the prospect of secure immigration status in exchange for becoming 'co-operative' intelligence sources. Whitaker effectively captures the disjuncture between what security personnel believe they are doing and what the subject experiences:

> The agency sees no conflict with the official purposes of screening. This methodology simply allows them greater amplitude in carrying out their task to guard against threats to national security. From the point of view of the subject, however, the process may appear very different indeed, forcing crises of conscience and loyalty, and sometimes even involving dangerous, life threatening situations. The long-term psychological cost to someone who agrees to such an arrangement may be very debilitating, even where refuge and thus a degree of security has been purchased.[50]

Refugees are probably most vulnerable to this game, but since all non-citizens are subject to a minimal 'reasonable grounds to believe' standard of proof regarding conduct that is itself indeterminate, the genuine fear of deportation by genuinely innocent people makes non-citizens susceptible to pressure in a way that citizens are not. Only in the case of an immigrant who has acquired Canadian citizenship will resort to the criminal law be necessary. In practice, I forecast that reliance on immigration law will effectively reinscribe the border dividing citizens and non-citizens that Bill C-36 effaces in theory.

Taking seriously the proposition that terrorism transcends national borders invites another perspective on the instrumental choice between deportation and prosecution. If terrorist acts can be committed beyond the territory of the target state (US embassies in Kenya and Tanzania, the SS Cole), if anyone armed with a computer and a modem can wreak havoc on international financial markets, if anthrax can be mailed from anywhere, how much security can expulsion buy? It is not obvious that deporting a person who is determined to engage in acts of terror back to, say, Afghanistan, Sudan or Iraq will deny him the opportunity to pursue his objective at some later date, perhaps through other means. In other words, if the War Against Terrorism is indeed global, and the objective is to 'get the guilty "off the international streets,"'[51] then deporting the 'guilty' (in immigration terms, a person who there are reasonable grounds to believe is, was, or will be a member of an organization that there are reasonable grounds to believe is, was, or will be engaging in terrorism) to another neighbourhood is a singularly parochial and ineffectual reaction. It rather resembles the Not In My Back Yard phenomenon in zoning disputes, transposed to the global realm.

If prosecution is arguably a more coherent response than deportation, important questions arise regarding the relative merits of national versus international prosecution. I do not propose to embark on that inquiry here, except to suggest that if we understand our national and/or international quest for security as predicated on concerns and entitlements that derive from our common humanity, we are compelled to acknowledge that those who stand accused of perpetrating heinous crimes against our collective security must be judged according to norms and processes that also derive from our common humanity, and not from their citizenship status *vis a vis* any particular state.

Conclusion

I am not making a categorical claim that borders no longer matter. Nor do I wish to imply that the permeability of borders is irrelevant to security.

But to the extent that the functionality of geo-political borders is waning, one observes a displacement of their functions to other socio-legal processes and phenomena. Thus, Bill C-36 enlarges the scope for state practices that marginalize and stigmatize through heightened surveillance, harassment, ethnic profiling, and the like. These in turn may reverberate in discrimination in domains such as employment, financial relations and associational life. The effect is to alienate the subject from social citizenship, even if legal citizenship is already secured. And while many look to the criminal law to protect us from the enemy within, I urge us to attend to the law's role in producing the alien within. The history of this country gives one ample reason to worry about the extent to which an abstract, collective security will be purchased through the infliction of tangible insecurity on particular individuals and communities.

All this because of September 11. We have been told that the atrocity posed such a massive challenge to our collective security, an existential threat to our way of life, that we are virtually driven to adopt a response of the magnitude of Bill C-36. I do not agree. But rather than argue the point, I wish to recall another date, one that is perhaps less easily recognized: June 22. On that date in 1985, a flight that began in Vancouver exploded in mid-air off the coast of Ireland. Three hundred and twenty-nine people died, mostly Canadian citizens and permanent residents. The cause of the explosion was a bomb planted in luggage. Until September 11, it was the single deadliest terrorist attack in aviation history. And yet, I do not remember our elected officials denouncing the event as a fundamental assault on our nation, our values, our people. No foreign leader declared 'we are all Canadians.' I do not recall any public outcry for anti-terrorist legislation to protect us from the transnational, existential threat to our democratic polity. I am not suggesting that the correct response would have been to enact legislation of the sort before us now. But I do wonder what vision of the nation animated the drafters of Bill C-36, and whether that vision would include the passengers aboard Air India Flight 182.

Notes

* The author wishes to thank Andrew Brouwer for his excellent assistance, and Sharryn Aiken and Mariana Valverde for their comments and suggestions, and Elaine Gibson for her timely editorial assistance.
1 Bill C-11, *An Act respecting immigration to Canada and the granting of refugee protection to persons who are displaced, persecuted or in danger*, 1st Sess., 37th Parl., 2001, passed 1 November 2001.
2 Bill C-36, An Act to amend the Criminal Code, the Official Secrets Act, the Canada Evidence Act, the Proceeds of Crime (Money Laundering) Act and other Acts, and to enact measures respecting the registration of charities, in order to combat terrorism, 1st Sess., 37th Parl., 2001.
3 United States Embassies in Nairobi, Kenya, and Dar es Salaam, Tanzania, were bombed on August 7, 1998. [http://www.fbi.gov/majcases/eastafrica/summary.htm]; American soldiers were captured and killed by Somali warlords in Mogadishu in October 1993; The USS COLE (DDG 67) was attacked in the port of Aden, Yemen, on 12 October 2000. [http://www.defenselink.mil/pubs/cole20010109.html].

4 *See, generally*, Canadian Council for Refugees, 'Canadian Measures of Interdiction,' *CCR Task Force on Interdiction*, 1998.

5 C. Clark, 'Attempts to stem refugee flow bogged down – bureaucratic tensions delay imposition of visa rules for Hungarian claimants' *The Globe and Mail* (2 November 2001) at A13.

6 See Sharryn Aiken, 'Manufacturing Terrorists: Refugees, National Security and Canadian Law (Part 2), (2001) 19(4) *Refuge* 116 at 124. A recent government document actually proposes authorizing Canadian law enforcement officials to board ships on the high seas to deflect would-be migrants: A. Humphrey, 'Seizure of boats outside Canadian limits proposed,' *National Post*, November 2, 2001 http://www.nationalpost.com/news/story.html?f=/stories/20011102/767096.html

7 A. Thompson, 'Is Canada Really the Weak Link?,' *Toronto Star* (6 October 2001).

8 'When I talk about the perimeter, I'm talking about doing a better job as people come in from overseas,' he said. 'As people come in from overseas, we want to have these common security efforts, and the compatibility on security efforts would be helpful. But I don't think anyone is saying you have to have exactly the same immigration policies.' US Ambassador Paul Celluci in C. Clarke, 'Canada urged to do more about security' *The Globe and Mail* (1 November 2001) at A10.

9 A. Thompson, 'Canada, US edge toward joint screening,' *Toronto Star*, 31 October 2000.

10 'Some ministers, including John Manley, the Minister of Foreign Affairs, and Jean Chrétien, the Prime Minister, are leery of the word ["perimeter"]. They fear it implies an extraordinarily ambitious co-ordination of the two countries' security forces along the lines of the 13-nation 'Schengen Area' in Europe.' R. Fife and P. Wells, '"Perimeter" has Liberals drawing battle lines – Semantics split Cabinet' *National Post* (1 November 2001)

11 *Dublin Convention determining the State responsible for examining applications for asylum lodged in one of the Member States of the European Communities*, signed 15 June 1990, entered into force 1 September 1997, reprinted in G.S. Goodwin-Gill, The Refugee in International Law, 2d ed. (Oxford: Clarendon, 1996) at 454–63.

12 Presidency Conclusions, Tampere European Council (15 and 16 October 1999), reproduced in (1999) 11 *Int'l J of Refugee Law* 738.

13 'U.S. President George W. Bush took a step toward the creation of a North American security perimeter yesterday, ordering his officials to begin harmonizing customs and immigration policies with those of Canada and Mexico ... Mr. Bush ordered administration officials to work to ensure "maximum possible compatibility of immigration, customs and visa policies," according to a White House statement.' C. Clark, 'Bush aims to tighten continent's borders – U.S. bid to harmonize immigration and customs puts heat on Chretien' *The Globe and Mail* (30 October 2001) at A1. 'Paul DeVillers, chairman of the Liberal national caucus, is also on side, saying most Liberal MPs don't care whether "North American perimeter" is used when talking about common immigration and border security policies.' I think the concept that we have to have co-ordinated security measures so we have similar programs is generally acceptable within the caucus,' he said.' R. Fife and P.

Wells, '"Perimeter" has Liberals drawing battle lines – Semantics split Cabinet' *National Post* (1 November 2001)

14 Preliminary Draft Agreement Between the Government of Canada and the Government of the United States of America for Cooperation in Examination of the Refugee Status Claims from Nationals of Third Countries, 24 October 1995 [unpublished]. See generally J. Hathaway and A. Neve, 'Fundamental Justice and the Deflection of Refugees from Canada,' (1996) 34 Osgoode Hall LJ 213.

15 C. Clark, 'Bush aims to tighten continent's borders – U.S. bid to harmonize immigration and customs puts heat on Chretien' *The Globe and Mail* (30 October 2001) at A1. C. Clark, 'Canada in talks with U.S. on pact dealing with refugees, visitor visas,' *Globe and Mail*, 26 October 2001, A6 http://www.globeandmail.com/ servlet/GIS.Servlets.HTMLTemplate?tf=tgam/search/tgam/SearchFullStory.html& cf=tgam/search/tgam/SearchFullStory.cfg&configFileLoc=tgam/config& encoded_keywords=immigration&option=&start_row=9&current_row=9&start_ro w_offset1=&num_rows=1&search_results_start=1. I do not support a harmonization of refugee admission between Canada and the US, given that the procedural protections and substantive interpretation of the refugee definition differ between the two countries. Moreover, a recent article about the implementation of the *Dublin Convention* concludes that 'The basic problem with the Dublin Convention of 1990 is that it does not really work. Since its coming into force in September 1997 only a few states have been able to use it successfully to return asylum seekers to the first country of arrival within the European Union.' Nicholas Blake, 'The Dublin Convention and Rights of Asylum Seekers in the European Union,' in E. Guild and C. Harlow, eds., *Implementing Amsterdam: Immigration and Asylum Rights in EC Law*, (Oxford: Hart Publishing, 2001), 95.

16 Indeed, I understand anecdotally that Canadian police attribute the rise in urban shooting deaths in Canada to the ease with which US citizens can import guns (legal in the US) into Canada, where they are illegal.

17 See S. Bell, 'A conduit for terrorists' *National Post* (13 September 2001); Diane Francis 'Canada gets well-deserved U.S. snub – Our neighbour's upset over our loose refugee system.' *Financial Post* (22 September 2001). D. L. Brown, 'Attacks Force Canadians to Face Their Own Threat' *The Washington Post* (23 September 2001) at A36. J. Baglole et al. 'Pressure Rises on Canada to Get Tough with Foreigners Seeking Refugee Status,' *The Wall Street Journal*, September 24, 2001. Politicians on the right have also been quick to blame Canada. Since September 11, Canadian Alliance leader Stockwell Day has repeatedly argued that Canada's immigration and refugee policies are too lax. On October 26, 2001, he told the CBC: 'We've got to send a message around the world that Canada is prepared and able to screen and monitor people trying to get here ... (Criminals) say to themselves, "Where are the points of access, or where are the countries we know that aren't as tough as other countries?" And, unfortunately, Canada has some loopholes here.' [CBC News Online staff, 'Ports need more police: opposition,' http:// vancouver.cbc.ca/cgi bin/templates/view.cgi?category=Canada&story=/news/ 2001/10/26/ports_security011026]

18 My summary of the cases of Ahmed Ressam and Nabil Al-Marabh is distilled from various media accounts. Given that the media reports are not entirely consistent, I acknowledge the possibility that elements of my composite may eventually prove inaccurate. S. Bell et. al, 'Canada let loose terrorism suspect,' *National Post*, 21 September 2001. P. Cheney et al., 'The mystery of the invisible al-Marabh Terrorist kingpin or ordinary store clerk?,' *Globe and Mail*, 27 October 2001 at A1. 'Proposed law would provide better shot at fighting terrorism, CSIS says,' The Canadian Press, 1 October 2001. http://www.canoe.ca/NationalTicker/CANOE-wire.Terrorist-Cda-Immigration.html. CBC News Online, 'Nabil al-Marabh Timeline' http://www.cbc.ca/news/indepth/background/wtc_almarabh_timeline.html. CBC News, 'Trail of a Terrorist,' broadcast 21 September 2001.

19 Valerie Lawton and Allan Thompson, 'Still in Canada? No One Knows,' *Toronto Star*, 7 October 2001 (internet edition).

20 *Id.* Both countries have about a 15% removal rate on outstanding deportation orders.

21 'Defenders of the Canadian system also note that some 40–50% of refugee claim-ants come to Canada from U.S. soil, where they had been admitted as visitors and were free to carry out acts of terrorism before even knocking on Canada's door.' L. Chwialkowska, 'Bordering on harmonization: Why Canada faces pressure,' *National Post*, 1 October 2001 http://www.nationalpost.com/search/story.html?f=/stories/20011001/714752.html&qs=immigration.

22 *See* R. Whitaker, 'Refugees: The Security Dimension,' (1998) 2(3) *Citizenship Studies* 413, 414–417.

23 Convention relating to the Status of Refugees, 28 July 1951, 189 U.N.T.S. 2545 (entered into force 22 April 1954), supplemented by the Protocol relating to the Status of Refugees, 606 U.N.T.S. 8791 (entered into force 4 October 1967) [herein-after Refugee Convention].

24 Article XX of the Refugee Convention prohibits states party from returning an asylum seeker to their country of origin if they have a well founded fear of perse-cution for reasons of race, religion, nationality, membership in a particular social group or political opinion.

25 In its review of The Economic Component of the Canadian Immigration Program in its 2000 Annual Report, the Auditor General of Canada reported on the impact of cutbacks on service delivery:

> In the meantime, the federal government began its Program Review, resulting in large cuts to the budgets of several departments and agencies. Citizenship and Immigration was no exception; its operating budget was cut by $54 million, almost 20 percent, between 1996 and 1998. To be able to continue delivering its Immigration Program with fewer resources, the Department had to review several of its procedures, adopt new ways of doing business and make significant organizational changes ...

Auditor General of Canada, 2000 Report (http://www.oag-bvg.gc.ca/domino/reports.nsf/html/0003ce.html).

26 See P. Cheney, '"Never mix security and profit" – Passenger screening at airports is in chaos, leading to calls for Ottawa to take charge' *The Globe and Mail* (3 November 2001).

27 Citizenship and Immigration Canada, 'Strengthened Immigration Measures to Counter Terrorism' (News Release), 12 October 2001. G. Smith, 'Canada locks out hundreds of refugees,' *Globe and Mail*, 27 September 2001. http://www.globeandmail.com/servlet/ArticleNews/printarticle/gam/20010927/UREFUM

28 See K. Lunman, 'Waits at U.S. border hurting economy, B.C. Premier says – He urges PM to push for North American security perimeter' *The Globe and Mail* (17 October 2001); P. Kuitenbrouwer, 'Perimeter will save trade: CEOs – 74% say we need common security rules as worries mount over access to key market' *National Post* (29 October 2001).

29 *Immigration Act*, RSC 1985 c. 31, s. 19; *Immigration and Refugee Protection Act*, ss. 33,34. The interaction of s. 33 and s. 34(1)(f) of the *Immigration and Refugee Protection Act* create an ambiguity regarding whether past and future membership fall within the parameters of exclusion.

30 See, generally, M. Trebilcock and N. Kelley, *The Making of the Mosaic: A History of Canadian Immigration Policy* (Toronto: U of T Press 1998).

31 S. Komarow, 'Hijacking plan may have been bred in Hamburg' *USA Today* (18 September 2001).

32 Sharryn Aiken, 'Manufacturing "Terrorists": Refugees, National Security, and Canadian Law,' (2001) 19(3) *Refuge* 54.

33 [1998] F.C.J. No. 507 (T.D.).

34 Id.

35 Aiken, 'Manufacturing Terrorists' (Part 2) at 122. In a remark reminiscent of the US Supreme Court's notorious definition of obscenity, Teitelbaum J. stated in the Federal Court (Trial Division) decision in *Suresh* that there is no need to define terrorism because 'when one sees a 'terrorist act,' one is able to define the word.' For an exploration of the relationship between emergency powers and the rule of law, see Dyzenhaus, this volume.

36 *Suresh* v. *Canada (Minister of Citizenship and Immigration)*, [2000] 2 FC 592 (CA), appeal to Supreme Court of Canada heard 22 May 2001 (judgment reserved).

37 *Ahani* v. *R.* (1996) 37 CRR (2d) 181 (FCA), appeal to Supreme Court of Canada heard 22 May 2001 (judgment reserved).

38 *Immigration and Refugee Protection Act*, ss. 77, 83.

39 *Immigration and Refugee Protection Act*, s. 77.

40 [1992] 1 SCR 711.

41 [1985] 1 SCR 177.

42 Mobility rights extend only to citizens and permanent residents, and voting rights are guaranteed only to citizens.

43 *Chiarelli, supra.*

44 *See, for example*, T. Kent, 'Immigration Now: How to Regain Control and Use it Well,' *Policy Insights* (Kingston, ON: School of Policy Studies, Queen's University, October 2001) available online http://policy.queensu.ca/spspi/docs/tk1001.shtml

45 The same conclusion applies perforce to the other provisions of the *Anti-Terrorism Act* that deal with money laundering and charities registration.

46 Shawn McCarthy, 'Sweeping curbs on freedom in antiterrorism legislation likely to go to top court,' *Globe and Mail* (16 October 2001), A5.

47 Canadian Council for Refugees, 'Comments of the Canadian Council for Refugees on Bill C-36, *Anti-Terrorism Act*,' 5 November 2001.

48 Whitaker, *supra* at 416.

49 Article 3(1) of the *Convention Against Torture* (CAT) prohibits return of a person to another state where there are substantial grounds for believing the person will be tortured. Canada signed CAT in 1984 and ratified it in 1987. One of the issues in Suresh is whether Canada may *refoule* Mr. Suresh to Sri Lanka on grounds that he is a member of a terrorist organization. The evidence tendered by the appellant is that he faces a substantial risk of torture if returned to Sri Lanka.

50 Whitaker, supra, at 427–28.

51 Mark A. Drumbl, 'Terrorist Crime, Taliban Guilt, Retaliatory Strikes and Western Innocence,' *Washington & Lee Public Law and Legal Theory Research Paper Series*, Working Paper No. 01–13, September 2001 at 16.

52 See M. Valverde, 'Governing Security – Governing through Security' (this volume).

A Thousand and One Rights

ED MORGAN*
Faculty of Law
University of Toronto

The inclusion of non-disclosure provisions in Canada's new anti-terrorism legislation, Bill C-36,[1] has given rise to the concern that those accused of terrorism-related crimes will have no real opportunity to know and counter the case against them.[2] The speculation is that criminal process will eventually come to resemble existing procedures under the *Immigration Act*, in which national security certificates issued by the Solicitor General and the Minister of Immigration on the advice of the Canadian Security Intelligence Service ('CSIS') are admissible against a prospective deportee and are subject only to in camera and ex parte judicial review.[3] Scholarship dealing with similar deportation proceedings in the United States has suggested that this field of law is lacking in due process and consistently biased in favour of foreign policy interests.[4] The question addressed in this paper is whether Canadian law has done any better.[5]

The literary classic for which this article is named is an eclectic compilation of folk tales which have been spun around a unifying, but loose narrative structure. It seems an appropriate lens through which to gaze at national security and immigration law issues for a number of reasons, not the least of which is its sheer complexity. Not only is *A Thousand and One Nights* a lengthy piece of work – the very title suggests that it goes on forever[6] – but it is surprising in its ability to weave apparently disparate stories into an intricate web of tales that lead to further tales and whose subplots and asides are in themselves stories within stories. Moreover, it is not an easy work to characterize: it is populated with mythical figures who seem to be a mirage of smoke at a same time as they bear swords of steel; it is a work of fantasy at the same time as it is a detailed portrait of the medieval east of its authors and the medieval west of its translators.[7] It is fragmentary and unified, utopian and violent, spiritual and practical. As one scholar has pointed out, the entire work is as paradoxical as the genie of the first story, who both towers over the merchant and is so insignificant that the merchant has killed his son by hitting him when he spit out the pit of a date.[8]

The framework around which the *Nights* is built entails a young woman, Scheherazade, struggling to keep herself alive by relating a story a night to the oppressive monarch to whom she is betrothed. Likewise, in cases dealing with terrorism and national security, length and complexity often seem to be ends in themselves. Like so many appeals of motions within procedural and substantive motions, the *Nights'* tales are interwoven and imbedded into each other such that the 'story-telling is in itself a heroic and life-saving device.'[9] Similarly, one reads the case law spawned by the more renowned Canadian terrorism cases as a series of interlinked attempts to keep the process alive, the legal heroics being in the longevity of the entangled procedures rather than in the substantive result of any one of them.

Perhaps the most well known case of this genre is that of Mahmoud Mohammad Issa Mohammad, an admitted member of the Popular Front for the Liberation of Palestine who was convicted by a Greek court of taking part in a 1968 attack on an El Al airplane in Athens airport in which one passenger was killed.[10] Mohammad had served four months of his 17 year sentence in Greece when he was released in a hostage exchange following a hijacking of an Olympic airways plane with 155 passengers aboard; he came to Canada in 1987 as a landed immigrant, having failed to disclose the Greek conviction to Canadian officials at the embassy in Madrid where he applied for his visa.[11] A deportation inquiry was commenced against him in January 1988 when his presence in Canada came to the attention of the press,[12] and proceedings have continued in fits and starts ever since.

A brief summary of the Mohammad case should suffice to convey the trail of the Scheherazade-like narrative. Facing a deportation inquiry, Mohammad commenced an action in Federal Court in March 1988 seeking an order quashing the report and direction for inquiry, and an order prohibiting the deportation inquiry from proceeding.[13] The court dismissed the application, whereupon Mohammad immediately brought an application to stay the inquiry proceedings pending the outcome of his appeal of his initial application.[14] The stay application was dismissed, and in December 1988 the Federal Court of Appeal affirmed the dismissal of the initial application to quash as well.[15] The inquiry proceeded with one further procedural detour in the form of a challenge brought by Mohammad to the refusal of an RCMP officer to answer certain questions put to him during the course of the inquiry. The Federal Court dismissed this application for review, ruling that the immigration hearing did not include the absolute right of a defendant to be made aware of all the national security information in the possession of the Minister[16]

The route having been cleared for a deportation order, Mohammad then applied for refugee status in order to remain in Canada.[17] At the opening of the refugee determination hearing, he sought a media ban on reporting the proceedings on the grounds that he and his family would be endangered if details of his application were publicly known.[18] This motion to exclude the press was granted in the summer of 1989 by a single adjudicator, Joseph Kenney, without hearing evidence on the issue,[19] following which *The Toronto Star* and the *Hamilton Spectator* launched an appeal to the Federal Court.[20] In February 1990, the court quashed the ruling excluding the press, indicating that such a ruling should not have been made without the benefit of hearing evidence on point;[21] whereupon the adjudicator proceeded to hold an evidentiary hearing on the issue of risk to Mohammad and his family, eventually ruling that the evidence supporting the refugee claim should not be made available to the public.[22]

In November 1992 – seven months after commencement of a secret hearing in Niagara Falls – a two-member panel held in a confidential, 40 page decision that there was a 'credible basis' to Mohammad's refugee claim, and ordered a second hearing before the Immigration and Refugee Board.[23] At the same time, the panel ruled that the public may never hear any of the evidence of the closed-door sessions, nor may it have access to any reasons for the decision or reasons for holding the sessions in secret.[24] Thus, when the second hearing began in January 1993, it was also held under a veil of secrecy.[25] The two-member panel of the Immigration and Refugee Board sat intermittently until December 1994, and in its 80 page decision issued in the summer of 1995 it denied Mohammad refugee status and recommended him for deportation.[26] This decision was then appealed to the Federal Court, which in August 1996 upheld the Board's decision rejecting the refugee application.[27]

In the spring of 1999, the Board issued the final deportation order against Mohammad.[28] The brief reasons for judgment that were made available to the public indicated that there were a number of different grounds on which the deportation was affirmed[29] – i.e. that there were reasonable grounds to believe that Mohammad engaged in terrorism,[30] that he was a member of a terrorist organization,[31] that he had been convicted outside of Canada of an offense that would be punishable by a term of imprisonment of ten years or more if committed in Canada,[32] and that he had gained permanent resident status by means of misrepresentation of material facts.[33] A naive reader might have thought that the tale of Mohammad Issa Mohammad had reached its logical end.

The deportation was subsequently appealed up to the next link in the Board's adjudicative chain,[34] primarily on the theory that the order was issued under the terrorism section of the *Immigration Act*, which was itself enacted after Mohammad was granted permanent resident status. This retroactivity argument was, in turn, rejected by an adjudicator in November 2000,[35] although the full appeal of the deportation order remained under reserve for a year of undoubtedly careful contemplation.[36] The appeal was finally dismissed by the Appeal Division of the Board in November 2001, on the stated basis that after 13 years the case had begun to parody due process.[37] With potential avenues of appeal going up the Federal Court chain, however, the Mohammad story – already a tale of medieval complexity and heroic lawyering – remains an indeterminate work in progress.[38]

In one of the more famous of the *A Thousand and One Nights* sequences, 'The Porter and the Three Ladies of Baghdad,'[39] three women throw a debauched party in which they invite three one-eyed men and cavort eccentrically with three black dogs. In order to calm down the raucous affair, each of the guests tells a story. The three one-eyed gentlemen each relate tales that are strangely reminiscent of each other, in which princes are inevitably lost, found, metamorphized into animals, transformed back into humans, and lose an eye in the process.[40] The next morning, the eldest of the three hostesses is compelled to tell the story of the previous evening's unusual behaviour, and relates a winding tale of how her three sisters had a myopic vision of life and marriage in the quest of riches and were for their troubles transformed by a genie into the three black dogs that had played so central a role at the party (and whose own tales could, in turn, form further parts of the overall collection).[41] Like the *Mohammad* case and its multifaceted procedural history, the entire episode entails stories embedded within stories and sustains itself by multiplying its own possibilities with each new narrative turn. The *Nights* took centuries to collect,[42] but it seems to be contemporary immigration law which has truly brought the episodes alive.

The other notable characteristic of the *Nights* is that the tales tend to treat the real world as fantastic and the fantasy world as reality. In embarking on one of the many tales of dreams, magic and adventure, one never knows what version of 'reality' will dominate the narrative. As the Argentinian writer, Jorge Luis Borges, has said, the *Nights* contain the notion of hidden treasures as well as the notion of magic – anyone can discover at any time a causal relation other than those that we know. 'The genie is a slave who is also omnipotent and who will fulfills our wishes. It can happen at any moment.'[43] In similar fashion, the *Immigration Act* case law pertaining to national security and terrorism fluctuates between the expected and the unexpected. Each of the major issues – identifying 'terrorist organizations,' finding 'reasonable grounds' to believe that a person is a terrorist or national security risk, and evaluating the constitutionality of the various provisions – raises compound possibilities. The multiple causal relations pursued by the governing legal theory have given rise to a body of law in which anything truly seems able to happen at any moment.

By way of illustration, the question of whether a given violent group is a 'terrorist organization' for the purposes of the *Immigration Act*'s exclusionary category has produced a vexing body of legal doctrine. While in the main the authorities have followed the international definitions by focusing on irregulars and civilian groups that target non-combatants,[44] a sticking point has emerged with respect to uniformed or government-related forces. Here there is thought to be a direct competition between the right of the Canadian public to keep the nation free of foreign violence, and the right of the immigrant or applicant to have previously served his, albeit violent, foreign nation. Thus, in the case of *Balta*,[45] the Federal Court determined that the Bosnian Serb Army, a hybrid force of regulars and conscripts owing allegiance to a non-sovereign entity and frequently attacking civilian targets, could not properly be perceived as a terrorist organization.[46] In overturning the ruling of the Immigration and Refugee Board on this point, the court opined that while the Bosnian Serb Army 'may be utilizing terrorist means to achieve political ends, ... it is significant that there are political ends, namely Serbian control of Bosnia.'[47] In other words, the private right to engage in politics by force trumped the public right to have aggressive political commitments remain abroad.

A fruitful comparison might be made between the decision in *Balta* and that in *Ahani*.[48] In the latter case, the Federal Court of Appeal determined that the applicant, a member of Iran's Ministry of Intelligence and Security ('MOIS'), belonged to a terrorist organization engaged in the assassination of Iranian dissidents.[49] Drawing on case law that had defined as internationally illegal any organization 'principally directed to a limited, brutal purpose,'[50] the court concluded that the MOIS was a 'secret police' unit whose mandate was 'directed at silencing political dissidents who seek to bring about change through the exercise of free expression.'[51] As a working definition, the aims of the applicant's 'terrorist organization' were seen as 'seek[ing] political reform through the use of violence directed at an innocent civilian population.'[52] In other words, the public right to be free from politics by force trumped the private right to aggressive political commitments abroad.

Politics therefore leads the assessment of terrorist organizations in unpredictable directions. Accordingly, the focus of most cases raising the reasonableness of CSIS' assertions about the terrorist activity of an individual immigrant or refugee applicant has been on the competing duties to and rights of the nation. An example of this approach is a 1991 case reported under the pseudonym *Smith*,[53] in which the Federal Court quashed the Ministerial security certificate on the grounds that the applicants, who were Iraqi Shiites and admitted members of the al-Dawa party operating in Iran, Iraq, Kuwait and a number of other countries, were not likely to represent a threat to Canada's national security.[54] In concluding that CSIS had failed to establish reasonable grounds for their exclusion, the court took account of the 'state of war between the United Nations Alliance and Iraq'[55] and the fact that 'al-Dawa did not support the current Iraqi government.'[56] The implication of this was that activism in a fundamentally internationalist cause feeds the private right of the applicants to pursue their interests, all at minor risk to Canada and at the expense of their own home state.[57] In other words, the private right of internationalism trumped the public duties typically owed to nations.

Another fruitful comparison might be made between the decision in *Smith* and that of the Federal Court in *Mahjoub*.[58] The court acknowledged in *Mahjoub*, as it had in previous cases, that '[a]s Parliament did not define the term "terrorism" with respect to the *Immigration Act*, it is not incumbent upon this court to define it.'[59] It then went on to consider, and support, the summary of evidence provided by CSIS indicating that the applicant, allegedly a member of the Egyptian Al-Jihad and, by his own admission, a personal acquaintance and employee of those at the pinnacle of world terrorism, was a danger to the international community.[60] In the process, the court refused to characterize Al Jihad as limited to Egyptian actions such as the November 1997 killing of 58 tourists in Luxor, the August 1993 attempted assassination of Egypt's Interior Minister, the February 1993 bombing of a Cairo café, and the October 1981 assassination of Egyptian President Anwar Sadat;[61] rather, it focused on the 'communiqués whereby they have threatened Zionists and Americans.'[62] The court also took the opportunity to remind itself of CSIS' repeated assertion that 'there are more international terrorist groups active here than [in] any other country in the world.'[63] It was the internationalism of the allegations that effectively brought them home to roost. In other words, the public right of international law enforcement trumped the private right to aggressively engage one's nation.

Since nationhood is as unruly a principle as involvement in politics, the courts have looked to constitutional norms to provide an analytically coherent package. The problem with terrorism cases, however, is that much as 'one person's freedom fighter may be another person's terrorist,'[64] one person's right of expression or association may be another's crime against humanity.[65] Similarly, one state's reasonable limit on rights of expression and association may be another's undermining of the international humanitarian order.[66] The assortment of co-existing constitutional values is as difficult to untangle as anything else in this field.

It is revealing to compare the two leading constitutional cases, both of which raise claims of freedom of association. In one, an immigrant who 'was head of the PFLP [Popular Front for the Liberation of Palestine] in Abu Dhabi ... [and] was "involved" in a bomb attack on an Air Egypt office in the United Arab Emirates,'[67] gets an effective constitutional defense. The Federal Court determined that he could not be constitutionally excluded as 'a member of a group that might engage in acts that might endanger the safety of persons in Canada.'[68] In the other, an immigrant who was a 'member of the Liberation Tigers of Tamil Eelam (LTTE) ... [and who] was alleged ... to have collected funds on behalf of the LTTE in North America,'[69] achieves no constitutional protection. The Federal Court of Appeal upheld a ruling declaring him to be 'a member of ... an organization alleged to engage in terrorism within the Indian subcontinent.'[70] Constitutional rights in favour of the inclusive society and section 1 limits in favour of the protective polity seem to arise and trade places with ease.

The cases demonstrate that the scales may be tipped in favour of national rights over individual rights, or, conversely, the international struggles of persons everywhere might outweigh the value of the domestic community's peace. More than that, all of the 'rights' possibilities seem to coexist in suspension and intertwine with each other in the atmosphere of the case law, with the parties waiting to discover which right will be crystallized by court enforcement. To borrow a common aphorism of this field, 'Like beauty, [legal rights are] in the eye of the beholder.'[71] The cases seem to be political rather than principled or strictly rational, but one would also be hard put to actually identify a coherent form of bias.

One of the more fanciful episodes in the *Nights*, and one that illustrates the seemingly infinite possibilities of the stories as well as the law, is the tale of two dreamers, one in Baghdad and one in Cairo.[72] The man in Cairo dreams that a treasure waits to be found in Baghdad, and so sets off on an arduous journey only to fall among thieves and be arrested upon his arrival in the distant city. When he tells his tale to the local police, the officer chides him for being so gullible. 'Three times I have dreamed of a house in Cairo,' says the officer, 'behind which is a garden, and in the garden a sundial, and then a fountain and a fig tree, and beneath the fountain there is a treasure. I have never given the least credit to this lie.'[73] The Egyptian, of course, returns home to Cairo having recognized his own house in the officer's dream. He digs beneath the fountain in the garden beyond the sundial and next to the fig tree and finds the buried treasure.

Dreams and stories, like the manifold possibilities of legal rights, branch out, intertwine, and multiply with each narration. The rights of the public and those of the private person, the rights of the nation and those of the international community, the rights of the domestic community and those of individuals everywhere, all coexist as equal possibilities. The cases about rights, like the stories of the *Nights*, go on almost forever, each one potentially containing a buried treasure trove of other rights. They may be difficult to reconcile, fanciful and indeterminate, but they are not biased or consistently supportive of any government policy, and certainly do not lack in due process. Indeed, process is so due that it seems never due to end. The reasoning of the law may be poor, but if anything the seemingly infinite variations, the rights upon rights within rights, add up to an embarrassment of riches.

Notes

* Associate Professor, Faculty of Law, University of Toronto. Many thanks to Victoria Blond for her research assistance.
1 1st Session, 37th Parliament, 49-50 Elizabeth II, 2001, (1st Reading 15 October, 2001), Part I: Amendments to the *Criminal Code*, sections 83.05(6), 83.06(1),

86.06(3); Part III: Amendments to the *Canada Evidence Act*, sections 37(1), 37(4), 37(5); Part V: Amendments to the *Privacy Act*, section 70.1.

2 'A Better Anti-terror Law,' *The Toronto Star* (31 October, 2001), p. A30; Tesher, E., 'Police Don't Need Sweeping Powers,' *The Toronto Star* (30 October, 2001), p. A21; Harper, T., 'Big Brother Looms with Terrorism Bill: Watchdog,' *The Toronto Star* (24 October, 2001); Harper, T. and Madonik, R., 'What Price Freedom?,' *The Toronto Star* (27 October, 2001), p. K3.

3 *Immigration Act*, R.S.C. 1985, c. I-2, sections 40.1(4), 40.1(5), 40.1(10), 40.1(11), 117. The hearing is not entirely ex parte. The national security evidence is summarized and disclosed to the applicants on that basis.

4 See, e.g., Akram, Susan, 'Scheherazade Meets Kafka: Two Dozen Sordid Tales of Ideological Exclusion,' 14 Geo. Immigr. L.J. 51 (1999) (concluding that secret evidence leads to exclusion of immigrants on purely ideological grounds); Widden, Michael, 'Unequal Justice: Arabs in America and United States Antiterrorism Legislation,' 69 Fordham L. Rev. 2825 (2001) (suggesting that security concerns in immigration law has led to ethnic discrimination and denials of equal protection); Johnson, Kevin, 'The Case Against Race Profiling in Immigration Enforcement,' 78 Wash. U. L.Q. 675 (2000) (concluding that racial profiling would be unconstitutional in immigration law much as it is in criminal investigations).

5 Canadian literature on the subject of civil liberties and national security in the immigration context is sparse and somewhat ambivalent. See, e.g., Leigh, Ian, 'Secret Proceedings in Canada,' (1996) 34 Osg. Hall L.J. 113; and Bassan, Daniela, 'The Canadian Charter and Public International Law: Redefining the State's Power to Deport Aliens,' (1996) 34 Osg. Hall L.J. 583.

6 Thompson, Diane, 'Arabian Nights Study Guide,' http://novaonline.nv.cc.va.us/eli/eng251/arabstudy.htm. Tate, Karen D., 'One Thousand and One Nights: Title and Story History,' http://web.utk.edu/~gwhitney/tales/1001/title.htm ('The ancient Egyptians used the heiroglyph which stood for 1000 to mean "all." ') Borges asserts that, 'To say a thousand nights is to say infinite nights, countless nights, endless nights. To say a thousand and one nights is to add one to infinity.' Borges, Jorge Luis, 'The Thousand and One Nights,' [1984] Georgia Review 564, 566.

7 Although many of the stories of the *Thousand and One Nights* are set in India and Samarkand, they were for the most part written in either Arabic or Persian beginning around the year 1000. The embellishments by the western translators and editors, however, cannot be ignored, so that the standard versions of the work today reflect a compilation of eastern tales told through the narrative prism of the west. For example, in the well known 1885 English translation by Sir Richard F. Burton, a full 40% of the text is contained in footnotes although the original stories contained no footnotes at all. See, *Annotated Arabian Nights*, 'Introduction,' http://mfx.dasburo.com/an/a_index_commented.html.

8 Beaumont, Daniel, *Alf Layla wa Layla, or The 1001 Nights*, http://www.arabiannights.org/beaumont.html, 'Introduction.'

9 Ramadan, Hanan, 'Arabian Nights: Its Origins and Legacy,' http://www. middleeastuk.com/culture/mosaic/arabian.htm.

10 Oziewicz, E., 'Terrorist passes first test in claim for refugee status,' *The Globe and Mail* (24 November, 1992), p. A1.

11 Tenszen, M., 'Convicted terrorist closer to winning refugee status,' *The Toronto Star* (26 November, 1992), p. A10.

12 *Mohammad* v. *Canada (Minister of Employment and Immigration)*, [1988] 3 F.C. 308 (Fed. Ct. T.D.). See also, Oziewicz, *supra* note 10.

13 *Mohammad, ibid.*

14 *Mohammad* v. *Canada (Minister of Employment and Immigration)*, [1988] F.C.J. No. 235 (Fed. Ct. T.D.).

15 *Mohammad* v. *Canada (Minister of Employment and Immigration)*, [1989] 2 F.C. 363 (Fed. C.A.).

16 *Mohammad* v. *Canada (Minister of Employment and Immigration)*, [1988] F.C.J. No. 1078 (Fed. Ct. T.D.).

17 Bindman, S., 'Terrorist Denied Refugee Bid,' *The Toronto Star* (11 June, 1995), p. A1.

18 Tenszen, M. 'Convicted Terrorist Closer to Winning Refugee Bid,' *The Toronto Star* (26 November 1992), p. A10.

19 Watson, P., 'Ex-terrorist's Hearing Off Limits to Journalists,' *The Toronto Star* (22 November 1990), p. A2.

20 *Ibid.*

21 *The Toronto Star v. Kenney*, [1990] 1 F.C. 425 (Fed. Ct. T.D.).

22 Watson, P., 'Refugee Hearing Secrecy Challenged,' *The Toronto Star* (1 December 1990), p. A13.

23 Tenszen, *supra* note 18.

24 *Ibid.*

25 Bindman, *supra* note 17.

26 *Ibid.*

27 Levy, H., 'Canada Still Home to Convicted Terrorist,' *The Toronto Star* (29 August, 1996), p. A23.

28 'No Haven for Terror,' *The Toronto Star* (28 April 1999), p. A1.

29 *Minister of Citizenship and Immigration* v. *Mohammad*, File No. 0003-96-01804, Amended Reasons for Decision Available to the Public, May 5, 1999 (Immigration and Refugee Board).

30 Citing *Immigration Act*, section 19 (1)(f)(ii).

31 Citing *Immigration Act*, section 19(1)(f)(iii)(B). The constitutionality of this provision is currently before the Supreme Court of Canada in *Suresh* v. *Canada (Minister of Immigration)*, on appeal from the Federal Court of Appeal, [2000] 2 F.C. 592.

32 Citing *Immigration Act*, section 27(1)(a.1)(i).

33 Citing *Immigration Act*, section 27(1)(e).

34 'Terrorist Appeals,' *The Toronto Star* (3 June 1999), p. A1.

35 *Mohammad* v. *Canada (Minister of Citizenship and Immigration)*, [2000] I.A.D.D. No. 1941 (I.R.B., A.D.).

36 'Terrorist Remains Years after Deportation Order,' *The Toronto Star* (4 October 2001), p. A8.

37 For an account of the November 2, 2001 Appeal Division decision, see Cobb, C., 'Terrorist loses another appeal to stay,' *The Ottawa Citizen* (3 November 2001), p. A3 (To do otherwise [than to dismiss the appeal] ... would be a 'mockery of Canadian legislation.').

38 Scholars seem to agree that the 1001 figure is metaphoric, and that Shaherazade relates to her king an endless supply of tales. The earliest version is from the Persion collection *Hazar Afsana* ('A Thousand Legends'), and that the Arabic version of *Alf Layla wa Layla* ('One Thousand Nights and a Night') dates from 10th century Iraq in which its first known editor, al-Jahshiyari, compiled a near infinite number of tales from local storytellers. *Arab Gateway: The Thousand and One Nights*, http://www.al-bab.com/arab/literature/nights.htm. Borges points out that, 'The Arabs say that no one can read The Thousand and One Nights to the end. Not for reasons of boredom: one feels the book is infinite.' Borges, *supra* note 6, p. 570.

39 For an annotated version of this and several other selected stories from the *Nights*, see, http://www.techfak.uni-bielefeld.de/ags/ti/personen/mfreeric/m/an/a_index_commented.html

40 The three 'Kalandars' Tales,' *ibid.*

41 For the full text of 'The Eldest Lady's Tale,' see, http://www.techfak.uni-bielefeld.de/ags/ti/personen/mfreeric/m/an/a_night_8.html.

42 The corpus of *Nights* stories began to be collected around the year 1000. The first European edition was a 'free translation' into French by Abbé Antoine Galland in 1704. *Thousand and One Nights*, Encyclopedia entry, http://www.factmonster.com/ce6/ent/A0848596.html.

43 Borges, *supra* note 6, p. 570.

44 See, *A Brief Overview of the Current Global Threat Environment*, Canadian Security Intelligence Service, Public Report, June 1999, at: http://www.csisscrs.gc.ca/eng/-publicrp/pub1999e.html (identifying extremist forces in the Islamic world as 'the preeminent international terrorist threat'); and also Protocol Additional to the Geneva Conventions, 1949, and Relating to the Protection of Victims of International Armed Conflicts (Protocol I), art. 51(2), adopted June 8, 1977, 16 I.L.M. 1396, 1413 (condemning violent acts spreading terror among civilian populations); Council of Europe, European Convention on the Suppression of Terrorism, arts. 1, 2, 15 I.L.M. 1272, 1272-3 (1976) (terrorist acts excluded from 'political offense' exception to treaties between European states).

45 *Balta* v. *Canada (Minister of Citizenship and Immigration)*, [1995] F.C.J. No. 146 (Fed. Ct. T.D.).

46 Citing the U.N. Convention Relating to the Status of Refugees, 1951, 189 U.N.T.S. 150, article 1(F)(a) (excluding as refugees persons who have committed 'crimes

against peace, a war crime, or a crime against humanity, as defined in the international instruments drawn up to make provision in respect of such crimes.').

47 *Balta, supra* note 45, para. 14.

48 *Ahani v. Canada (Minister of Citizenship and Immigration)*, [2000] F.C.J. No. 53 (Fed. C.A.).

49 *Ibid.*, para. 18, relying on facts certified by the Solicitor General and the Minister of Immigration under section 40.1 of the *Immigration Act*, that the applicant was 'a member of an inadmissible class specific in the anti-terrorism provisions in subparagraph 19(1)(e)(iii), clause 19(1)(e)(iv)(C), subparagraph 19(1)(f)(ii), clause 19(1)(f)(iii)(B) and paragraph 19(1)(g) of the Act.' *Ibid.*, para. 8.

50 *Ramirez v. Canada (Minister of Employment and Immigration)*, [1992] 2 F.C. 306 (Fed. C.A.).

51 *Ahani, supra* note 48, para. 18.

52 *Ibid.*, quoting *Suresh v. Canada (Minister of Citizenship and Immigration)*, [2000] 2 F.C. 592, para. 65 (Fed. C.A.).

53 *Smith v. Canada (Minister of Employment and Immigration)*, [1991] F.C.J. No. 212 (Fed. Ct. T.D.).

54 *Ibid.*, para. 56, citing the need for a 'high degree of probability'in the assessment of risk, as set out by the House of Lords in *R. v. Secretary of State for the Home Department, ex parte Khawaja*, [1984] A.C. 74.

55 *Smith, ibid.*, para. 22.

56 *Ibid.*

57 *Ibid.*, para. 56 ('... it is not reasonable to consider that the applicants will engage in acts of violence that would endanger people in Canada ... it is possible that groups which are involved in terrorism, which it appears that al-Dawa might be in certain circumstances, are not monolithic ...').

58 *Canada (Minister of Citizenship and Immigration) v. Mahjoub*, [2001] F.C.J. No. 1483 (Fed. Ct. T.D.).

59 *Re Baroud* (1995), 98 F.T.R. 99, 109-110 (Fed. Ct. T.D.) (considering the status of the Fatah organization and the related Force 17).

60 *Mahjoub, supra* note 58, para. 63; see also para. 43, quoting the applicant's affidavit dated September 6, 2000, para. 46: 'Osama Bin Laden met me personally and told me that he had interviewed several people ... He specifically told me that he had interviewed 2 Egyptians and that he prefers to interview personally those people who will be in charge of projects and in positions such as project managers or assistant project managers.'

61 *Ibid.*, para. 52.

62 *Ibid.*, para. 53.

63 *Ibid.*, para. 22, quoting Submission to the Special Committee of the Senate on Security and Intelligence by Director Ward Elcock, June 24, 1998. The Elcock observation has been quoted in several other cases dealing with terrorism and international crime. See, e.g., *Suresh v. Canada (Minister of Citizenship and*

Immigration, [2000] 2 F.C. 592, 661-2 (Fed. C.A.), and *U.S.A.* v. *Kindler*, [1991] 2 S.C.R. 779.

64 *Ahani, supra* note 47, para. 18.

65 See, *Sivakumar* v. *Canada (Minister of Employment and Immigration)*, [1994] 1 F.C. 433 (Fed. C.A.) (crimes against humanity not protected under section 2(b) of the Charter).

66 Section 3 of the *Immigration Act*, which provides Parliament's objectives of the legislation for the purposes of a Charter section 1 justification, provides as follows:

(g) 'to fulfil Canada's international legal obligations with respect to refugees and to uphold its humanitarian tradition with respect to the displaced and the persecuted;

(h) to maintain and protect the health, safety and good order of Canadian society; and

(i) to promote international order and justice by denying the use of Canadian territory to persons who are likely to engage in criminal activity.'

67 *Al Yamani* v. *Canada (Minister of Citizenship and Immigration)*, [2000] 3 F.C. 433, para. 11 (Fed. Ct. T.D.).

68 *Al Yamani* v. *Canada (Solicitor General)*, [1996] 1 F.C. 174 (Fed. Ct. T.D.) (holding that section 19(1)(g) of the *Immigration Act* infringes section 2(b) of the Charter in applying to landed immigrants solely because of their membership in organizations posing a risk of violence).

69 *Suresh* v. *Canada (Minister of Citizenship and Immigration)*, [2000] 2 F.C. 592, para. 7 (Fed. C.A.).

70 *Ibid.*, applying sections 19(1)(e) and (f) of the *Immigration Act*.

71 *Mahjoub, supra* note 58, quoting *Re Baroud, supra* note 59, quoting counsel for the Minister ('Like beauty, the image of a terrorist is, to some extent, in the eye of the beholder.').

72 'The Ruined Man Who Became Rich Again through a Dream,' Burton, Richard F., trans., *The Arabian Nights* (1850), http://www.library.cornell.edu/colldev/mideast/arabnit.htm#RUINED.

73 *Ibid.* Some accounts place the story in Isfahan, Persia instead of Baghdad, although the garden dreamed of by the officer always seems to be in Cairo. See, Borges, *supra* note 6, p. 572.

The Intersection of Administrative Law with the Anti-Terrorism Bill

LORNE SOSSIN*
Osgoode Hall Law School

There are two complementary purposes which animate administrative law: first, to protect participatory rights in the public decision-making process; and second, to ensure accountability for public decision-making. Both purposes are contingent on the institutional and legislative contexts of administrative decision-making. Bill C-36 (the 'Anti-Terrorism Bill')[1] is ambitious and far-reaching. Its purpose, in part, is to 'prevent and suppress the financing, preparation, facilitation and commission of acts of terrorism, as well as to protect the political, social and economic security of Canada and Canada's relations with its allies.' Such sweepingly vague goals raise complex and important questions as to how participatory rights and accountability apply to administrative decision-making in the context of national security. The need for secrecy, confidentiality and flexibility in national security matters, accentuated in the wake of the attacks of September 11, 2001, seems at odds with administrative law goals of transparency, disclosure, justification and predictable procedures. Can one set of goals be achieved without sacrificing the other? The interaction of administrative law with the Anti-Terrorism Bill invariably will be one of tension and balance.

My aim in this short paper is to elaborate on this tension, and explore this balance. I will focus on the two purposes of administrative law set out above, and the way in which the Anti-Terrorist Bill intersects with each: first, I will examine the problem of procedural fairness in the context of national security decision-making; and second, I will examine the problem of accountability in relation to ministerial discretion in matters of national security.

There are many aspects of the Anti-Terrorism Bill which touch on administrative law. The Act authorizes a variety of new powers for executive officials, and in particular the Ministers of Justice, Defence, National Revenue and the Solicitor General. Delineating the scope and boundary of those powers will be a key concern for administrative law in the coming months. The new definition of 'terrorism' coupled with the absence of a definition of 'security' will likely give rise to ripple effects throughout a variety of administrative bodies, from the Parole Board to the Immigration and Refugee Board to the Commissioner of the Communications Security Establishment. Statutory powers mean little in the abstract. It is how they are exercised that matters in the context of administrative law.

The following analysis is based on a preliminary and partial reading of the Anti-Terrorism's implications for administrative law. Even a preliminary and partial review, however, gives rise to a recurring concern. The Act reflects the presupposition that providing adequate procedural safeguards for those affected by discretionary authority, and subjecting the exercise of discretion to meaningful forms of accountability, are luxuries that may, and sometimes must, be discarded in times of emergency or crisis, or where national security is at stake. Echoing David Dyzenhaus' arguments regarding the relationship between the rule of law and crisis,[2] I believe that it is precisely at junctures of crisis that administrative law's concern for the parties affected by government action, and for the integrity of government decision-making, become most needed. At a more functional level, the safeguards and supervisory scrutiny imposed by administrative law may well lead to more accurate, more effective and more just decision-making in matters of national security.

A. National Security, Terror and Fairness

Most of the criticism and concern directed at the Anti-Terrorism Bill has been focussed on its revisions to the *Criminal Code*,[3] and specifically the expanded powers for surveillance, arrest, detention and compelling testimony where suspected terrorists are involved.[4] While these criminal justice powers may be new and extraordinary, there is little new or extraordinary about sacrificing procedural fairness in the administrative decision-making process in the interest of policy goals such as national security. What is new, however, is the expansion of the administrative settings that are seen as warranting this sacrifice. One such new setting, the registration process for charitable organizations under the *Income Tax Act*, is examined as a brief case study below.

The duty of fairness arises wherever a person's rights, interests or privileges may be adversely affected by government decision-making. In *Baker v. Canada (Minister of Immigration and Citizenship*,[5] L'Heureux-Dubé J., writing for a unanimous Court on this issue, characterized the duty of fairness in the following terms:

> ... the purpose of the participatory rights contained within the duty of procedural fairness is to ensure that administrative decisions are made using a fair and open procedure, appropriate to the decision being made and its statutory, institutional, and social context, with an opportunity for those affected by the decision to put forward their views and evidence fully and have them considered by the decision-maker.[6]

In addition to the importance of procedural fairness as a goal of administrative justice, participatory rights also enhance the quality and accuracy of administrative decision-making, particularly where credibility is at issue. Allowing affected parties to test the veracity of the allegations against them, and to disabuse decision-makers of misapprehensions, false information or mistaken impressions, serves to minimize the risk of error and the opportunity for injustice. This point was underscored, for example, in *Haghighi v. Canada (Minister of Citizenship and Immigration)*,[7] in which the Federal Court of Appeal held that the duty of fairness required the disclosure by an immigration officer of a negative risk report relied upon by the officer in reaching a decision. Evans J.A. elaborated on the rationale for requiring disclosure in the following terms:

> In my opinion, the duty of fairness requires that inland applicants for [landing status based on humanitarian and compassionate grounds] under subsection 114(2) be fully informed of the content of the PCDO [post-claims determination officer]'s risk assessment report, and permitted to comment on it, even when the report is based on information that was submitted by or was reasonably available to the applicant. Given the often voluminous, nuanced and inconsistent information available from different sources on country conditions, affording an applicant an opportunity to comment on alleged errors, omissions or other deficiencies in the PCDO's analysis may well avoid erroneous H&C decisions by immigration officers, particularly since these reports are apt to play a crucial role in the final decision.[8]

In the context of national security, of course, there are countervailing concerns regarding procedural fairness generally, and disclosure in particular. If intelligence is gathered through covert means, or by informants, and this is disclosed to the party affected, the intelligence gathering networks may be compromised, investigations may be undermined, confidentiality arrangements with cooperating foreign governments may be breached and the lives of informants may be jeopardized.[9] Courts, for the most part, have accommodated the argument that the exigencies of certain institutional settings require flexibility when it comes to procedural fairness (whether raised as a common law challenge, a challenge under s.2(e) of the *Bill of Rights*,[10] or by way of a challenge under s.7 of the *Charter of Rights and Freedoms*[11]).[12] Courts have upheld reducing disclosure in prison settings, to take just one example, where the safety of an informant may be compromised.[13] The Supreme Court also has upheld abrogating disclosure rights when a deportee seeks to challenge a ministerial certificate in immigration proceedings in the interests of national security.[14] The power to issue a certificate under s.40 of the *Immigration Act* includes a reference procedure to a Federal Court judge similar to the procedure contemplated under various sections of the Anti-Terrorism Bill.[15] This procedure has been found not to violate the procedural fairness guarantee in the *Bill of Rights* or the principles of fundamental justice under the *Charter*.[16]

Where the Courts have not been sufficiently responsive to the concerns of government in interpreting the duty of fairness in national security settings, it remains open to Parliament to curtail procedural rights explicitly by legislation. The duty of fairness is a common law procedural requirement which can be modified or displaced by statute.[17] This is precisely what the Anti-Terrorism Bill does in a diverse array of settings. In the following section, I examine one such setting, that of the charities registration decision-making process, in more detail.

(1) *The Case of the* Charities Registration (Security Information) Act

One of the most significant and controversial legislative initiatives in the Anti-Terrorism Bill is the enactment of the *Charities Registration (Security Information) Act* (the 'CRSIA')[18] which, *inter alia*, empowers the Solicitor General and the Minister of National Revenue to sign a certificate which, in effect, renders an organization ineligible to become a registered charity, or if already registered, provides a basis for deregistration of the charity. While this aspect of the Bill is subject to a more probing analysis by David Duff elsewhere in this collection,[19] for the purpose of this paper, I believe it serves as an illustration of the broader phenomenon of how administrative settings, once reconceived as a site of national security, may be subject to a dramatic diminution of procedural protections.

It is perhaps ironic that while the Minister of National Revenue now has a statutory definition of 'terrorist' to apply, there remains no statutory definition of 'charity.' In other words, while Parliament has not seen fit to provide guidance as to what charitable activity is, the *CRSIA* provides substantial guidance on what a charitable activity is not. A charity cannot be an organization which has made, makes or will make available any resources, directly or indirectly, to a terrorist association.[20] This is a strikingly broad net, which has attracted widespread opposition.[21] To give but one of the many extreme examples one could imagine, a charity raising money in order to provide humanitarian assistance to Afghani refugees in Pakistan, could be deregistered if it is discovered that the food and medicine it plans to send will find their way to individuals considered to be members of terrorist groups. It is not overstating this power by much to conclude that the Solicitor General and the Minister of National Revenue, by the power to issue certificates on this basis, can withhold registration or revoke registration from virtually any organization at will. The potential for abuse is substantial and the only meaningful constraint on this discretion are the procedures to which the Ministers must abide.

Section 2 of the CRSIA states that its provisions are to be applied with two procedural principles in mind:

(a) maintaining the confidence of taxpayers may require reliance on information that, if disclosed, would injure national security or endanger the safety of persons; and
(b) the process of relying on the information referred to in paragraph (a) in determining eligibility to become or remain a registered charity must be as fair and transparent as possible having regard to national security and the safety of persons.[22]

The procedure provided by the CRSIA, as in other settings where ministerial certificates are authorized, is to deny affected parties any role in the process leading up to the ministerial determination to issue a certificate. Once a certificate is issued, it is referred to a Federal Court Judge for a determination as to whether the certificate is 'reasonable.'[23] While the applicant or registered charity is to be provided with a statement by the judge enabling it to be 'reasonably well-informed' and to afford it with 'a reasonable opportunity to be heard,' the *CRSIA* specifically authorizes the judge not to disclose to the affected party information which, in the judge's opinion, might injure national security or endanger the safety of any person, and to hear all or part of the evidence in the absence of the applicant or registered charity and any counsel representing it.[24] By limiting the role of the judge to assessing the reasonableness of the certificate, the significance of the parties' input is limited as well.[25]

The effect of these provisions is that it is possible to have a certificate signed and to have a judge uphold the certificate as reasonable, without the affected applicant or registered charity ever knowing what activity it is alleged to have engaged in, or an opportunity to test the credibility or veracity of the evidence underlying those allegations before the decision-maker. Once a certificate is upheld as reasonable by a judge, it cannot be appealed or reviewed by any Court on any grounds.

While this scheme appears to result in a potentially severe curtailment of procedural rights, the determination of whether an organization meets the requirements to be registered as a charity under the *Income Tax Act* has always contained a broad discretion subject to few procedural constraints.[26] In *Scarborough Community Legal Services* v. *The Queen*,[27] the Federal Court of Appeal upheld a denial of registration to an organization found to engage in 'political activities,' and rejected the argument that the organization was entitled to disclosure and an opportunity to be heard in the decision-making process. The majority differed on whether to characterize the decision as administrative or legislative but agreed that, in either case, it fell outside the ambit of the duty of procedural fairness.[28]

While the CCRA's practice has been to alert applicants to the potential for an adverse disposition by correspondence, and to provide a basis for this disposition to which the applicant may respond, it does not appear to be under a legal obligation to do so. Based on this analysis, it would appear that the *CRSIA*, curiously, may provide applicants with more procedural protection than they would otherwise be entitled to at common law. However, the determination that an organization had made, is making or will make resources availability to terrorist groups is arguably more serious than the mere determination that an organization does not meet the criteria for registration as a charitable organization, and therefore requires additional procedural guarantees. With respect to deregistration, by contrast, a duty of procedural fairness does apply, although it is unclear whether that duty would impose obligations beyond what that the *CRSIA* has provided.[29]

Ultimately, my concern with the procedures contemplated under the *CRSIA* is not that they violate the duty of fairness, but rather that they transform a setting for regulating charities into one for implementing national security policy. This transformation begs an important question. Why is the *CRSIA* necessary in the first place? Applicants may already be denied registration, or registered charities deregistered, on the basis of engaging in 'political activities,' or on the basis of not engaging in 'charitable activities,' which are standards sufficiently broad to encompass much if not all of what is now defined as terrorist activity under the Bill.[30]

I would suggest that the *CRSIA* has been incorporated into the Bill, for the most part, not to do things that could not have been done, or even to do them in a way that could not have been done, but rather to emphasize the political message that the government has undertaken a particular mission with respect to combatting terrorism and protecting national security, that this mission requires a legal environment of urgency, secrecy, and flexibility, and that procedural fairness, while a desirable feature of administrative decision-making, must be sacrificed if it conflicts with this mission.

B. Discretionary Power and National Security

The Anti-Terrorist Bill provides a number of Ministers with broad, new discretionary authority relating to national security decision-making. This raises an obvious administrative law concern regarding accountability for how these new powers are used. What safeguards or review mechanisms exist to ensure that discretionary authority relating to national security is not abused, or exercised arbitrarily or for ulterior purposes? This question should be seen against the backdrop of the *Charter*, which applies to the exercise of ministerial discretion, and of the rule of law, a central tenet of which is that no grant of discretion can be absolute.[31] However, these fundamental constitutional and administrative law constraints, in practice, may well have marginal application to the national security field given the principle of deference to ministerial decision-making. A broader approach to accountability in this setting may be required.

Based on my preliminary review, the Bill contains a number of ministerial powers that purport to be immunized from review. For example, the Bill amends the Access to Information Act to empower the Attorney General to at any time personally issue a certificate that prohibits the disclosure of information for the purpose of protecting international relations or national defence or security,[32] and similarly authorizes 'prohibition certificates' in the context of the *Personal Information Protection and Electronic Documents Act* and the *Privacy Act*.[33] Further, these amendments specify that the certificates are not to be published pursuant to the *Statutory Instruments Act*. Thus, not only would the public not have an opportunity to see the certificates justified, the public may not even know if a certificate had been issued.[34]

Several grants of discretionary power in the Anti-Terrorism Bill provide for judicial review, but specify that such review will take place in private, and with provision for excluding the affected parties and their counsel. One example of this procedure is discussed above in relation to the *CRSIA*. Another example is the discretion to create a 'terrorist list.' The Bill amends the *Criminal Code* to provide the Governor in Council, by regulation, to create a 'list of terrorists' based on the recommendation of the Solicitor General.[35] Judicial review is permitted, but subject to the aforementioned conditions, which may limit the ability of an affected party to respond to the allegations that it is a terrorist organization, and limit the government's accountability for the process employed to compile such lists.

In these and other sections of the Bill, where discretionary authority is granted, that authority is qualified in one phrasing or another by a requirement that the decision-maker have a 'reasonable' belief that the action taken is necessary on national security grounds. If challenged under the *Charter*, it may be necessary to determine whether such action could be justified as a 'reasonable limit' on *Charter* rights and freedoms. How is reasonableness to be assessed given the claim that national and international policy concerns influence decision-making in national security settings, and what level of deference should be accorded to Ministers and their delegates in making this decision-making? The following cursory discussion suggests that Courts will typically defer to government decision-makers when discretion in the area of national security policy is at issue, and thus may not provide adequate accountability for the exercise of that discretion.

(1) *Deference, Discretion and Accountability in Combatting Terrorism*

In most settings of ministerial discretion in the Bill, the question of accountability arises in how Ministers or their delegates have interpreted and applied the concept of 'terrorist activity' defined for the first time in the Anti-Terrorism Bill,[36] and the concept of 'security,' which remains undefined, except to include 'economic security.'[37] A review of the relevant case law suggests that the highest form of deference will apply to the judicial supervision of discretion related to national security. This has always been the case but will no doubt be a heightened concern in the post-September 11 era. As Lord Steyn recently opined in the House of Lords judgment in *Secretary of State for the Home Department* v. *Rehman*,[38]

> ... the Commission must give due weight to the assessment and conclusions of the Secretary of State in the light at any particular time of his responsibilities or of Government policy and the means at his disposal of being informed of and understanding the problems involved. He is undoubtedly in the best position to judge what national security requires even if his decision is open to review. The assessment of what is needed in light of changing circumstances is primarily for him.[39]

Courts maintain a constitutionally rooted, supervisory function over all administrative decision-making (which, at a minimum, gives courts the authority to ensure that impugned exercises of discretion were undertaken in good faith, and not for arbitrary, ulterior or discriminatory purposes, and for ensuring that the exercise of this discretion was within the jurisdiction of the decision-maker).[40] Beyond this analysis as to whether an exercise of discretion was *ultra vires*, courts will apply a pragmatic and functional analysis to determine the appropriate standard of review for courts supervising the exercise of discretion. This approach considers the wording of the statute, the purpose of the authority, the expertise of the decision-maker and the nature of the decision. In *Baker*, L'Heureux-Dubé J. described the relationship between deference and discretion in the following terms:

> Incorporating judicial review of decisions that involve considerable discretion into the pragmatic and functional analysis for errors of law should not be seen as reducing the level of deference given to decisions of a highly discretionary nature. In fact, deferential standards of review may give substantial leeway to the discretionary decision-maker in determining the 'proper purposes' or 'relevant considerations' involved in making a given determination The pragmatic and functional approach can take into account the fact that the more discretion that is left to a decision-maker, the more reluctant courts should be to interfere with the manner in which decision-makers have made choices among various options. However, though

discretionary decisions will generally be given considerable respect, that discretion must be exercised in accordance with the boundaries imposed in the statute, the principles of the rule of law, the principles of administrative law, the fundamental values of Canadian society, and the principles of the *Charter.*[41] (Emphasis added.)

In *Baker*, this analysis led the Court to apply a standard of reasonableness *simpliciter*. In other discretionary settings, a standard of patent unreasonableness has been applied where the discretion falls within the specialized expertise of the decision-maker.[42] Iacobucci J. in *Pezim* v. *British Columbia (Superintendent of Brokers)*,[43] held that where a tribunal is vested with a 'broad discretion' a reviewing court should not disturb the exercise of that discretion unless that tribunal has 'made some error in principle in exercising its discretion or has exercised its discretion in a capricious or vexatious manner'[44] While curial deference will often be given to specialized tribunals, even broader deference is normally accorded to the exercise of ministerial discretion where policy concerns motivate a decision.[45]

An example of the way in which deference may insulate ministerial decision-making where national security is said to be at stake is the Federal Court of Appeal's decision in *Suresh* v. *Canada (Minister of Citizenship and Immigration)*.[46] The Court rejected an appeal by Manickavasagam Suresh, a Tamil citizen of Sri Lanka, seeking to overturn a 'danger opinion letter' issued by the Minister of Citizenship and Immigration pursuant to s. 53(1)(b) of the *Immigration Act*, on the basis of which he could be deported to Sri Lanka notwithstanding the risk he would be subject to torture if returned.[47]

The Court first rejected a challenge to s.53(1)(b) under the *Charter*. While finding the provision violated the substantive due process requirement under s.7, the Court held this was a reasonable limit under s.1 given that the objective of the provision was to combat terrorism.[48] The Court also rejected another substantive due process argument that the absence of a definition of national security or terrorism under the *Immigration Act* rendered the Minister's danger opinion void for vagueness.[49] With respect to the administrative law challenge, the Court rejected this as well, concluding that it should defer to the Minister's judgment unless the decision was *ultra vires* her authority (i.e. unless the decision breached an implied limit on her discretion, was made in bad faith, or was based on irrelevant considerations or on a misapprehension of the facts). Based on cases such as *Suresh* (and subject to the Supreme Court's judgment in that case) it appears that deference to ministerial discretion in relation to national security will significantly circumscribe the extent to which the judiciary is prepared to hold government accountable for how the Anti-Terrorism Bill is applied and enforced.

Most observers would agree that the new forms of discretion contained in the Anti-Terror Bill could be subject to abuse. To cite just the most obvious danger, the discretion could be exercised disproportionately to the disadvantage of specific racial or ethnic groups or national communities in times of crisis or perceived crisis.[50] Not all would agree, however, how best to avoid such potential abuse from occurring. For some, the training, professionalism and internal accountability mechanisms of the national security bureaucracy will be sufficient safeguards.

In my view, these measure are necessary but are not sufficient. The most effective method of accountability is subjecting the exercise of discretion to public scrutiny. Often, this may be accomplished through judicial review. While the result of judicial challenges, more often than not, is to reiterate the court's broad deference to ministerial decision-making (and, perhaps, to legitimate these decisions by providing a judicial imprimatur of reasonableness for the decision-making process) subjecting a decision to a judicial challenge usually shines a spotlight on the decision, and its justification. While the Anti-Terror Bill includes a variety of important roles for judicial involvement, because this involvement may take place in secret, behind closed doors, and without an opportunity for further review or appeal, the judicial capacity to provide accountability for government decision-making is limited. In this context, it may be desirable to look beyond the Courts for sources of fuller accountability.

Judicial review, it should be emphasized, is not the only means of subjecting national security decision-making to public scrutiny (although it frequently may be the only way to protect the rights of those specifically affected by national security decision-making, and to uphold the rule of law). Through reports of the Auditor General,[51] public inquiries (e.g. the Somalia Inquiry), the reports to Parliament of the Inspector General of CSIS and Commissioner for the Communications Security Establishment, the oversight of the Security Intelligence Review Committee, as well as the Privacy and the Information Commissioners, and finally, through submissions to, and reports by, various Parliamentary committees, accountability for national security decision-making may be assessed with varying degrees of public disclosure. In the context of the Anti-Terrorism Bill, a potentially significant form of non-judicial accountability is contemplated by the three-year review.[52] More than ever now, these various forms of, and forums for reviewing the Anti-Terrorism Bill, and the action taken under it, need to be coordinated to ensure that accountability does not fall through the bureaucratic and adjudicative cracks.

Conclusion

The Anti-Terrorism Bill has wide application in administrative decision-making. To a large extent, the variable nature of the duty of fairness, and the deferential posture of courts to ministerial discretion, already provide administrative decision-makers with wide latitude and flexibility to act in matters of national security. This latitude must have fixed and enforceable limits. Procedurally, it will normally be unjustifiable to reach an adverse decision without providing the affected party with at least a gist of the basis for the decision and an opportunity to respond, even if in restricted circumstances. Substantively, it will normally be unjustifiable to have discretion exercised over which there is no public form of accountability whatsoever. If national security requirements may in rare and urgent cases justify departing from these constraints, such exceptional measures should be narrowly focussed, cautiously undertaken, and based on criteria that are open to public evaluation. The Anti-Terrorism Bill contains no indications that the provisions therein are to be applied or enforced with these limiting principles in mind.

There is a real danger that the flexibility and deference which characterize the procedural and substantive constraints imposed by administrative law are poorly suited to ensure participatory rights and accountability in decision-making relating to combatting terrorism and national security matters. As more settings of administrative decision-making become sites for implementing national security policy, the need to respect the principles of administrative law intensifies. The Anti-Terrorism Bill, despite its attempt at balance, neglects some of the most fundamental administrative law principles, and as a result, far more than national security will be at risk in its application.

Notes

* Assistant Professor, Osgoode Hall Law School, York University. I am grateful to Sharryn Aiken, David Dyzenhaus, Julia Hanigsberg, Gerald Heckman, Kent Roach and Katrina Wyman and for comments on an earlier draft of this paper.

1 First Session Thirty Seventh Parliament 49–50 Elizabeth II, 2001 (Bill C-36, 2001) (First reading, October 15, 2001).

2 See D. Dyzenhaus, 'The Permanence of the Temporary: Can Emergency Powers be Normalized?' in this collection.

3 R.S.C., 1985, c. C-46.

4 See K. Roach's contribution to this volume, 'The Intersection of the New Terrorism Offences and the Criminal Law.'

5 *Baker* v. *Canada (Minister of Immigration and Citizenship)*, [1999] 2 S.C.R. 817.

6 *Ibid.*, at para. 22. See also para. 28.

7 [2000] 4 F.C. 407 (C.A.).

8 Ibid. at para. 37.

9 Analogous concerns were recognized by the Supreme Court as justifications for curtailing procedural rights in *Canada (Minister of Employment and Immigration)* v. *Chiarelli*, [1992] 1 S.C.R. 711 at para. 48.

10 R.S.C., 1985, Appendix III.

11 Being Part I of the *Constitution Act, 1982*, Schedule B, *Canada Act* 1982, 1982, c. 11 (U.K.).

12 See D. Mullan, *Administrative Law* (Toronto: Irwin, 2001), pp. 265–79.

13 *Gallant* v. *Trono, Deputy Commissioner, Correctional Service Canada* (1989), 36 Admin. L.R. 261 (F.C.A.).

14 See *Prata* v. *Canada (Minister of Manpower and Immigration)*, [1976] 1 S.C.R. 376. See also s.40 of the *Immigration Act*, R.S.C., 1985, c. I-2, [as am. by S.C. 1992, c. 49, s. 32], authorizing the Minister of Immigration and Citizenship and the Solicitor General to issue certificates that a person is a member of an inadmissible class based on security and criminal intelligence reports not disclosed to the affected person. This provision has been invoked both before and after September 11, 2001 to justify the detention and deportation of suspected terrorists. See, for example, J. Gadd, 'Process Unfair, Lawyer Says: Man Facing Deportation Can't See Evidence' The Globe and Mail, November 2, 2001, A4.

15 The Federal Court judge is empowered to determine if the certificates were reasonable and to provide the affected person with a reasonable opportunity to be heard. See the discussion of the certificate power under the *Charities Registration (Security Information) Act*, infra.

16 Section 40 of the *Immigration Act* was found not to violate s.2(e) of the *Bill of Rights* or s.7 of the *Charter* due to the 'variable' and 'contextual' nature of the procedural fairness component of the principles of fundamental justice. One contextual factor cited by the Court was the lesser entitlement to fairness enjoyed by non-citizens relative to citizens. See *Ahani* v. *Canada*, [1995] 3 F.C. 669 (T.D.), affirmed by (1996) 201 N.R. 233 (F.C.A.), leave to appeal to the S.C.C. denied, [1996] S.C.C.A. No. 496.

17 This principle was recently affirmed in *Ocean Port Hotel Ltd.* v. *British Columbia (Liquor Control and Licensing Branch, General Manager)*, 2001 SCC 52. Statutes which modify or displace the common law duty of fairness remain subject to review under the *Charter* and *Bill of Rights*.

18 See Part 6, ss. 113–118 of the Bill. This Part incorporates much of the content of Bill C-16, which was introduced in March of 2001 and withdrawn with the introduction of Bill C-36.

19 D. Duff, 'Charitable Status and Terrorist Financing: Rethinking the Proposed *Charities Registration (Security Information Act)*' in this collection.

20 See section 4 of the *CRSIA*.

21 Submissions on Bill C-36 from both the Canadian Bar Association (see infra note 27) and Canadian Council For Refugees (November 5, 2001) strongly criticize this definition and recommend that the *CRSIA* be scrapped in its entirety.

22 Section 2(2) of the *CRSIA*.

23 Section 5(5) of the *CRSIA*.

24 Section 6 of the *CRSIA*.

25 Interpreting s.40 of the *Immigration Act*, one Federal Court judge characterized his role in the following terms: 'Mr. Rodrigues, I want to check whether you have explained to the witness the role that I am playing here. In other words, he is not on trial before me. I have to determine whether the people who signed the certificate had adequate or an appropriate amount of evidence to make that decision. If anybody is on trial, it is the people who signed the certificate.' See *Canada (Minister of Citizenship and Immigration)* v. *Jaballah*, [1999] F.C.J. No. 1681 at para. 6 per Cullen J.

26 For a discussion of the discretion of CCRA officials with respect to charitable registration and deregistration, see L. Sossin, 'Regulating Virtue: A Purposive Approach to the Administration of Charities' in J. Phillips et al. (eds.), 'Between State and Market' Essays on Charity Law and Policy in Canada (Montreal: McGill-Queen's Press, 2001), pp. 373–406

27 [1985] 1 C.T.C. (F.C.A.); leave to appeal to S.C.C. refused 87 N.R. note (S.C.C.) (hereinafter '*Scarborough Legal Services*').

28 *Scarborough Legal Services*, ibid at p. 42 (Q.L.).

29 See *Renaissance International* v. *M.N.R.*, [1983] 1 F.C. 860 (C.A.), in which the Federal Court of Appeal held that a charity was entitled to a 'reasonable' opportunity to be heard prior to revocation of a charitable registration.

30 See s.149.1(6.2) of the *Income Tax Act*. Some important distinctions should be noted. The present scheme does permit 'ancillary or incidental' political activity by charitable organizations, and does not contemplate denying registration or deregistration on the basis of future activity, nor would it necessarily capture indirect uses.

31 This principle was recognized by the Supreme Court in *Roncarelli* v. *Duplessis* [1959] S.C.R. 121; and recognized as an unwritten principle of the Canadian Constitution in *Reference re Secession of Quebec*, [1998] 2 S.C.R. 217 at 257, where the Court described the 'rule of law' in the following terms: '[t]he "rule of law" is a highly textured expression, importing many things which are beyond the need of these reasons to explore but conveying, for example, a sense of orderliness, of subjection to known legal rules and of executive accountability to legal authority.'

At its most basic level, the rule of law vouchsafes to the citizens and residents of the country a stable, predictable and ordered society in which to conduct their affairs. It provides a shield for individuals from arbitrary state action."

32 Section 87 of the Bill

33 Sections 103–104 of the Bill.

34 The Canadian Bar Association 'Submission on Bill C-36 (October 2001)' (www.cba.org) accessed November 2, 2001, characterizes this aspect of the amendments 'inconsistent with our notions of open and fair government.' (at p.43).

35 See section 83.05 of the *Criminal Code* in Part II.1 of the Bill.

36 In her article, 'Manufacturing Terrorists': Refugees, National Security and Canadian Law: (2001) 19 *Refuge* No. 3 54 at p.58, Sharry Aiken points to the absence of a statutory definition of 'terrorism' in the *Immigration Act* as a source of confusion, vagueness and potential injustice. However, she recognizes that attempting to define terrorism may be even less desirable. As many have and will note in this conference, yesterday's terrorist may be viewed as today's freedom fighter, just as today's terrorist may be viewed as tomorrow's defender of the downtrodden.

37 See s.83.01(b)(i)(B) of the *Criminal Code* in Part II.1 of the Bill.

38 [2001] UKHL 47. In this case, the House of Lords held that the deportation of a Pakistani national on the basis of his membership in an Islamic terrorist organization was justified given an expansive interpretation of the term 'national security.'

39 Ibid. at para. 26.

40 *Crevier* v. *A.G. (Quebec)*, [1981] 2 S.C.R. 220.

41 *Baker*, supra note 3, at para. 56. Most interesting in the emphasized portion of this passage is the term 'fundamental values of Canadian society' which, if seen as something other than statutory limits, the rule of law, the principles of administrative law and the *Charter*, suggest a potentially important new source of broader constraints may also operate on discretionary decision-makers.

42 See, for example, *Nanaimo (City)* v. *Rascal Trucking Ltd.*, [2000] 1 S.C.R. 342.

43 [1994] 2 S.C.R. 557.

44 Ibid. at 607.

45 See, for example, *Thorne's Hardware Ltd.* v. *The Queen*, [1983] 1.S.C.R. 106, where. Dickson J. (as he then was) held that generally, '[d]ecisions of the Governor in Council in matters of public convenience and necessity are final and not reviewable in legal proceedings.' (at 111) He observed that this deference was justified because 'governments may be moved by any number of political, economic, social or partisan considerations' (at 112–13). For an elaboration of deference in respect of ministerial discretion, see D. Mullan, 'The Role of the Judiciary in the Review of Administrative Policy Decisions: Issues of Legality' in *The Judiciary as Third Branch of Government: Manifestations and Challenges to Legitimacy* (eds. Mossman and Otis) (Montréal: Les Éditions Thémis, 2000) pp. 313–368.

46 [2000] 2 F.C. 592 (C.A.). The Supreme Court granted leave to appeal, and its judgment in this case is presently reserved.

47 While Suresh was recognized as a Convention refugee after entering Canada, and

had applied for landing status in Canada, a certificate was issued jointly by the Solicitor General of Canada and the Minister of Citizenship and Immigration alleging that he was a person inadmissible under section 19 of the *Immigration Act*, because he was a member of the Liberation Tigers of Tamil Eelam (LTTE), an organization alleged to engage in terrorism within the Indian subcontinent.

48 Ibid. at para. 118.

49 Vagueness was recognized as an aspect of the principles of fundamental justice under s.7 of the *Charter* in *R. v. Nova Scotia Pharmaceutical Society*, [1992] 2 S.C.R. 606 at 643 per Gonthier J.('a law will be found unconstitutionally vague if it so lacks in precision as not to give sufficient guidance for legal debate.'). In *Suresh*, the Federal Court of Appeal held that the impugned phrases, while not precise concepts, were capable of rational application. (at paras. 64 and 67).

50 For discussion, see Sujit Choudhry, 'Ethnic and Racial Profiling and the Charter' in this collection.

51 See for example, 'The Canadian Intelligence Community: Control and Accountability' *Report of the Auditor General of Canada, 1996* (Ottawa: Queen's Printer, 1996)

52 Section 145(1) and (2) of the Bill provide for a 'comprehensive review' of the 'provisions and operation of this Act' within three years from the date it received Royal Assent to be undertaken by a Parliamentary committee, which is under an obligation to report to Parliament within a year from the time of its review.

Concluding Comments from the Department of Justice

Ron Daniels

Let me introduce our two commentators from Justice. I am so pleased that you have both taken time from your schedules to join us and to participate in our deliberations. First, I am pleased to introduce Rick Mosley, who is the Assistant Deputy Minister at Justice with responsibility for Criminal Law Policy. He has been the principal architect of the legislation. I am also pleased to introduce Stan Cohen, who is General Counsel at the Department of Justice Human Rights Law Section. I have asked them to speak on behalf of Justice, and to respond to some of the themes that have been raised in the conference.

Richard Mosley

Thank you Dean Daniels. May I first express my appreciation for having an opportunity to address the conference but also more generally to the University of Toronto Faculty of Law for having put this on. I was unable to get here for yesterday's morning session but I did arrive for the afternoon and received a briefing on the presentations that were made yesterday morning. I must say that I have found those that I heard yesterday afternoon and this morning to be of great interest and I am sure they will be of great value to the parliamentarians who will be resuming their deliberations on this Bill in the near future. I must also of course make the usual caveats. Neither Stan nor myself are the Government. We are not members of the Government, we are employees of the Government, and there are limitations on the role that we can play in conferences such as this. We give our advice to the Government and of course we have to respect the restrictions that pertain to that advice. We are also not parliamentarians. Perhaps it is a statement of the obvious, but it is important for you to keep in mind that this Bill is in the hands of Parliament and it is parliamentarians who will ultimately determine its final form. We did work on the legislation. We worked through a very intense period of weeks leading to its introduction. I did want to comment a bit on the process because of questions that were raised by the gentleman yesterday and again today about how much of the legislation was 'in the can,' so to speak, before September 11th. I can tell you that those portions of the legislation relating to de-registration of charities had been drafted, as has been noted by speakers in the conference, and was before Parliament in the form of Bill C-16. We had done some work on the implementation of the UN Convention on the Suppression of Terrorist Bombing. In the normal course of events over this Fall, that work would have progressed to external consultation and ultimately to the introduction of the Bill in Parliament. The way that we normally work on criminal law reform projects is to develop options for consideration for Ministers and for consultation. We take those options out to, as somebody mentioned this morning, the 'usual suspects' – groups, national associations, organizations, individuals that would have a particular interest in the subject matter – and we consult on the nature, scope and effect of the proposals before they are finally drafted for introduction in Parliament. In these circum-stances, there was no opportunity for consultation of that nature.

We had also done some work on the modernization of the Official Secrets Act that had been kicked around over the course of four years progressing in fits and starts but it had never reached a stage where it had gelled into actual legislative form. We also worked on the Canada Evidence Act amendments and much of that had been drafted prior to September 11th. But we had done nothing on what is, I think people would agree, the core elements of this Bill – nothing on the implementation of the UN Convention on the Suppression of Terrorist Financing. That was in our work plan. We were to get to it probably sometime this winter, and we would have followed the normal course of developing options for implementation, consulting on them and then developing a proposal for Cabinet to approve. That process would certainly have taken months, and it could well have taken years.

Post September 11th, there was an immediate review of what legislation was in place in Canada within our legislative framework to address terrorism. A number of speakers have spoken to the already formidable body of law that we had in place on September 11th that could deal with much of the conduct that people feared might happen following the tragic events in New York. Those of you who follow these matters will recall that there was a debate in the House when its proceedings resumed on the 17th On the 18th the Minister of Justice spoke and indicated that she was proposing to move forward with amendments to implement the remaining UN Conventions dealing with terrorism, those being the Convention on the Suppression of Terrorist Bombing and the Con-vention on the Suppression of Terrorist Financing. She also referred to the reforms to the Official Secrets Acts and the Canada Evidence Act and so on. At that time, the work was not well advanced. We were dealing with a number of conceptual issues that had to be addressed before anything could take shape in the form of legislation and chief among those, I would suggest, is the question of definition. There has been a debate both domestically and internationally as to whether you should define or attempt to define terrorism and terrorist activities, and, if so, what would the definition look like? There are strong views on both sides of that question within Government and there are certainly many who would argue that Canada should have proceeded to implement the remaining Conventions without attempting to define terrorism, however, we within the Department of Justice arrived at the conclusion that it was essential to offer a definition to Parliament, for a number of reasons. One, a definition was needed to shape and circumscribe the scope of the criminal amendments that would be required to implement the Terrorist Financing Convention. These amendments were required despite the existing body of law, because without them we would not have been in compliance with the Convention. We debated the form of the definition right up until two days before the Bill was introduced when we had to put to bed the final print of the Bill. That was Saturday, October 13th that we were making final changes to the penultimate print of the Bill. We recognized that this was not going to be anywhere near the end of the debate and that it would then have to be addressed in a broader public context and also, of course, within Parliament as to what this definition should consist of. We were conscious as well that, during the oral argument on *Suresh*, the Supreme Court had signalled quite clearly that, in moving to criminalize the financing of terrorism, Canada would have to offer a definition of what terrorism was about. There are existing references to terrorism within a number of Federal Statutes. My favourite is in the *Blue Water Bridge*

Act, which I gather is somewhere down near Sarnia, and I'm not entirely sure why it's in there, but it's in there.

From the very beginning of this process the instructions we were operating under were to be open throughout the process to changes in this Bill. The Government was not going to go to Parliament with a Bill and be unreceptive to amendments. That was never signalled to us and certainly never signalled to Parliament during the debates. A controversy has arisen over whether the Prime Minister is open to amendments, and whether he is open to a sunset clause, which I think is a bit of an artificial controversy that has been whipped up by the media. Clearly, the Government embarked on this venture understanding that this Bill would be amended in the parliamentary process with the benefit and the wisdom that parliamentarians such as Irwin Cotler brought to bear on the subject.

One factor which has not been mentioned in this conference thus far is that while we were engaged in this work, the UN Security Council passed a Resolution, Resolution 1373 of September 28th. That resolution is binding on member states of the United Nations and it declares what member states must do to fight terrorism. It also requires a report back to the Security Council by the member states as to how they have implemented the resolution. That report is due 90 days after the adoption of the resolution, the end of December. We realized that for a number of reasons there was clearly a demand for quick legislative action on the part of the government. But we also realized that, in order to report back to the UN Security Council within that timeline and understanding the parliamentary timetable, this legislation had to be introduced early. Our initial target date was November 1st, and that was moved up to October 15th. I'm sure you can appreciate the pressure that puts on the process of trying to identify and refine the content of the Bill.

I'm just going to touch on a couple of issues and then turn over to Stan to discuss matters relating to justification. There has been reference made to controls in the Bill for the protection of information. Certainly, the certificate power it would give to the Attorney General of Canada is extraordinarily strong. Michael Code, I think, stated that the Courts would never allow someone to be convicted where Government is refusing to provide information relevant to the defence. I agree entirely with that: it will not happen. But in discussing the certificate power under s. 38(13) of the *Canada Evidence Act*, you have to go to the next section, 38(14). There is an express statement there to the effect that the Court can make any order that it deems necessary in order to ensure a fair trial and that could include, for example, a stay of proceedings. So the Government will have a hard choice to make in circumstances where it may wish to use a certificate. Does it want to protect that information at the cost of having the proceedings against the accused stayed?

Now Michael also suggested that the Government has control of the proceedings, but that fails to take into account, of course, the federal-provincial dynamic in Canada and circumstances in which the carriage of an action may well be in the hands of the provincial government as opposed to the federal Crown. Why does the federal Crown need to protect that information? Well, quite simply because much if not most of our foreign intelligence comes from other countries and those other countries do have mechanisms in place to protect their most sensitive information. For example, the U.K. legislation relating to freedom of information which was just enacted last year, and is still not in place, excludes the information held by MI5 and MI6. Those organizations share information with Canada and expect it to be protected or we will not receive it. If we do not receive it, we may not be in a position to take actions in support of the security of the country. I think I'll pause there and turn the floor over to Stan.

Stan Cohen

I'd like to begin by congratulating the University of Toronto and Dean Daniels again for what has been, I think, a wonderful contribution to the democratic process. I'm not saying that out of any sense of formality, but rather I think that this is something that will make a real contribution to democratic debate. I believe that this book that is going to be presented to all parliamentarians in a week is something that will be read. It isn't going to get lost in the shuffle and will be timely, and I think that everyone should recognize that this is really what the purpose of these kinds of conferences is all about. I'd also like to thank Dean Daniels for inviting me yesterday morning to speak. It came as a surprise to me, but in any event, I am happy to be here and I think that everyone who is here and has participated should be congratulated as well because this has been a critical and analytical forum for discussion of these matters.

I, like many of you, grew up in a time and in a place where people didn't have to lock doors to their houses. As children we used to go from home to home without much in the way of formality or impediments. Of course, in 2001 that world for the most part does not exist. Doors are locked and beyond ordinary locks, people have also installed burglar alarms. I regret the passing of that time and the sensibility that spoke to it, and I have no great affection for that which has replaced it. And I think now we see a similar phenomenon in the world that it has produced Bill C-36. We find ourselves in a conference where we hear phrases such 'acceptable levels of toxicity to democratic practices' and warnings about the permanent expansion of extraordinary state powers. I think it's undeniable that these are troubling and sobering times for anyone who considers themselves to be civil libertarians. Speakers have asked whether we have been too quick to accept what is permissible and have suggested that the bells and whistles of *Charter*-proofing should do little to quiet the anxiety that is felt about adopting extraordinary measures in extraordinary times. My friend and former colleague, also my professor, Irwin Cotler, yesterday described in a brief way the reality of responding to the invocation of the *War Measures Act* in 1970 and the absence of remedies and redress that was prevalent at that time. That was a time of arbitrary arrest and detention, of unreasonable search and seizure, and of curtailed due process. This too is a dark period, but we do have a *Charter of Rights and Freedoms* and I, for one, am glad of it. We all have to recognize the *Charter* does have its limits, but the values that are espoused in the *Charter* are fundamental and I don't believe are of a kind that should be denigrated. *Charter*-proofing is a nice phrase but I don't think it really captures what went on in this exercise. I say that for having been on the inside and I know that it is not great comfort for many people that the Minister of Justice might have used such a phrase, although I did not personally hear her say that this is *Charter*-proof, but I think she did say that there had been a great deal of scrutiny that has gone into the legislation with regard to compliance with the *Charter*. In any event, I would ask the question rhetorically whether consistency with the *Charter* is a defect? As David Dyzenhaus reminded us yesterday, the Supreme Court has now recast the rule of law as embodying a culture of justification. It is to the question of justification and the safeguards that have been created in this Bill that I wish to address my remarks to you today, but one last word on *Charter*-proofing.

Charter-proofing, if that is the term that can be used, is not a matter of establishing the outer limits, at least it is not in Canada a matter of establishing the outer limits of action. There is much to be learned by looking around us and seeing what has gone on in the world and to look at the examples and the legislation that exists in other part of the world. Look to the legislation of England or France or the United States or Australia, New Zealand and Germany, and what you will find is that in important respects the limits can be placed much further out than they have been in this Bill. Bill C-36, as I've mentioned, contains extraordinary measures that are designed to respond effectively to exceptional threats that are posed by global terrorism. Strong measures have been adopted or are in the process of being adopted, as I've mentioned, in other free and democratic societies, for that is the *Charter*'s term, around the world. There is naturally a certain symbiosis in the evolution of policies as affected states have brought forward their measures for combating this phenomenon. However, as Rick Mosley has told you, the measures that have been drafted with the Canadian reality in mind are in a sense 'made in Canada'. We are aware that the process that has brought it forward has been a contracted, compacted process subject to limitations that we would have preferred not to have lived under, but that has been the process and to a certain extent all of the actors within the Government of Canada have felt impelled to act at this time.

Now Rick Mosley can be called an architect of this legislation and I suppose you should regard me as the bricklayer, but in a sense, we have all participated in this and we're here to hear from you and to do what we can to assist in the refinement and improvement of this legislation if that can be the case. We know that the most controversial measures contained in Bill C-36 in one form or another can all expect to meet with challenges that are based on the Canadian *Charter of Rights and Freedoms*. We believe that these measures will ultimately successfully withstand these challenges and you have heard others speaking, uncomfortably I acknowledge, that they too have come to the conclusion that to a certain extent this is the probable result. Nevertheless, since these measures do have the capacity to impinge in a significant fashion upon individual liberties and civil rights, these challenges cannot and should not be regarded as being based on specious or trivial objections. It is expected that the Courts will find that the *Charter* is engaged when considering these objections, although it is possible that the courts may find that many if not all of these measures can be justified within the confines of the very right or freedom that is allegedly infringed. It is more useful for the purposes of this discussion to discuss these measures in terms of the kinds of justifications or, if one wishes to use the Section 1 terminology, the reasonable limits that might be offered in their defence.

An appropriate place to begin this examination is with the national security justification itself. This justification really has application to virtually all of the measures in the *Anti-Terrorism Act*, but that is not to say that these measures do not require their own individual justification. National security is arguably the most important justification that can be advanced in support of legislation since it springs from the necessity to safeguard and preserve the very existence of the state and its democratic institutions and ensure their continued survival. The need to safeguard the security of the nation can also be rooted in the ability of the state to take measures to protect the national interest, to conduct its national defence, or in the power to enact laws to ensure the peace, order and good government of Canada. The *Charter* itself begins with the preamble that states that Canada is founded upon principles that recognize the supremacy of God and the rule of law. The primacy of the rule of law, as we have been reminded, is a reference point for all Canadian legislation including those that address national security. While the rule of law comprehends the existence of and maintenance of public order through the systematized application or threat of force by a modern state, it is more than this. It is the position of all advanced democracies including Canada that our laws' claim to legitimacy also rests on an appeal to moral values many of which are embedded in our constitutional structure. The rule of law, therefore, is a principle that requires that all government action must comply with the law including the constitution. I'm not using words of my own there, I'm quoting from Supreme Court of Canada jurisprudence when I speak in those terms. The collective rights of all persons to whom the protections and guarantees of the *Charter* extend must include the right to peace and security. Order and security under law are preconditions to the maintenance of the rule of law. The rule of law again to quote the jurisprudence vouchsafes to the citizens and residents of the country a stable, predictable and ordered society in which to conduct their affairs. The ability of the state to take measures proportional to the threat posed in order to preserve itself and to ensure its continued survival is undoubted and is reflected in the doctrines of necessity and self-defence. International instruments including the International Covenant on Civil and Political Rights recognize, as Section 1 of our *Charter* does, that rights are not absolute. Rights may be subject to limits in accordance with such procedures as are established by law, as well as limits based on grounds of public order or national security. The ability of the state to take strong measures as part of national security, legitimate self-defence, and for protection against the threat of global terrorism is also well-recognized by a host of international instruments ratified by Canada.

I've already mentioned that other free and democratic societies have taken similar measures, in other cases stronger measures, in response to the threat of global terrorism. The need for strong measures does not abrogate the need to respect *Charter* principles and values. The *Charter* is a flexible instrument. Depending upon context, the notion of societal needs can result in the lowering or altering of *Charter* standards that might otherwise be applicable in a given situation. Even prior to Bill C-36, national security had been recognized as a valid justification for the adoption of special measures which may have the effect of abridging procedural rights that might otherwise accrue to individuals. Chief Justice Dickson in *Hunter v. Southam* says where the state's interest is not simply law enforcement, as for example where state security is involved, or where the individual's interest is not simply his expectation of privacy, as for instance where the search threatens his bodily integrity, the relevant standard might well be a different one.

I'm going to pass on to just a couple of observations about virtues of this legislation because we haven't really heard the word virtues used in the discussion to this point. One virtue of this legislation is there is no use of the notwithstanding clause, no override in the legislation itself. I say this is a virtue because the use of the notwithstanding clause actually contracts or shrinks the area of rights that are available and exercisable by a citizen. The virtue of this legislation is that it preserves for the citizen and for affected persons the right to question whether the legislation does in fact get it right. So this is something that cannot be understated, this is an important aspect of the legislation. Another significant safeguard in this Bill which is different from that which you will find in other places is in its deliberate limitation to terrorism and terrorist activity. I know that there has been a great deal of discussion about the definition but let's put that aside for the moment. I know that that's a difficult exercise in view of the changes that have been suggested including the deletion of one part of the terrorist activity definition, but there still is the rest of the definition even if you delete paragraph (e). To the extent possible in this legislative exercise, changes have been limited so as to preclude their extension to ordinary law enforcement powers and procedures. This is a federal state activity that allows for an effective response to the direct challenge that must be confronted while at the same time limiting opportunities for possible manipulation or abuse. If you have been watching developments in the United States, for example, there have been several endeavours to have anti-terrorism initiatives piggyback on law enforcement procedures and powers. That is not the case in this legislation here.

I will not deal with all of the controversial features of this legislation in order to demonstrate that there are safeguards that have been built into it, albeit that they are still controversial initiatives. I will deal with a couple that I know have captured the concern and imagination of people here.

The first that I would deal with is the preventive arrest or the 'recognizance with conditions' provision. This procedure allows for a period of detention prior to final judicial determination that effectively can run for up to three days. That has been amply stated. Provisions in other comparable jurisdictions are longer. Save for emergency or exigent circumstances, this substantial power of preventive arrest can only be invoked with the consent of the Attorney General. The section is modeled on the release or bail provisions in the *Criminal Code* and contemplates a judicial hearing within 24 hours. Additional safeguards include judicial supervision of the recognizance process, the 'reasonable grounds to believe that terrorist activity will be carried out' requirement, the requirement that an arrest without warrant can only be made where it is necessary to prevent the commission of a terrorist activity, and the ability by the person to have the recognizance terms and conditions varied.

Turning then to the investigative hearing, this order requires a witness to testify under oath at the early stages of an investigation. Despite impressions to the contrary, this procedure is not unprecedented. Compelled questioning exists in Securities law, and in public inquiries with regard to Fire Marshall and Coroner's inquests, and it is used extensively since 1988 in relation to the *Mutual Legal Assistance and Criminal Matters Act,* which means that other jurisdictions can come into Canada and compel people who are in Canada to answer questions pursuant to that *Act.* That *Act* has withstood judicial review and constitutional scrutiny. Under these new provisions, the citizen must answer questions put to him, but the legislation extends self-incrimination, subsequent use and derivative use immunity protections. Also while the individual is compelled to testify, laws relating to non-disclosure of information or privilege continue to apply. The right to counsel continues to apply. Also as regards cases of compelled testimony in relation to future events, as contrasted with instances where terrorist acts have already been committed, the prior consent of the Attorney General is required before an application for compulsory questioning may be brought. The standard on which an order is obtained is based upon a *Charter*-consistent 'reasonable grounds to believe' standard. There must also be reasonable grounds to believe that the person to be compelled has direct and material information that relates to the offence, or that reveals the whereabouts of the person whom the peace officer suspects may commit that offence. Reasonable attempts must have been made to obtain the information from the person. The legislation also provides a judge with the authority to include in the evidence gathering order terms and conditions to protect the interests of witnesses and third parties.

That really is as much as I would say. It is possible to look at other provisions here and enumerate safeguards dealing with standards of *mens rea*, right to counsel and judicial review and the like. I know that these measures have been described as measures that merely *Charter*-proof the legislation, but I am thankful that the *Charter* at least has had that much effect. Thank you.

Richard Mosley

I want to add a point that I should have made earlier – we are very concerned with the impact of this legislation on the ethno-cultural communities of Canada and, on the day of its tabling, we reached out to national organizations representing those communities and a few days later sat down to discuss with them their concerns about how it could have an impact on members of their communities. That was particularly with reference to the Arab, the Islamic, and the Afghan communities within Canada. We hope to continue that dialogue, and hope to set it up on a regular basis in order to get feedback as to how they see these provisions being administered against members of their communities. There is always the capacity for abuse with any piece of legislation. I don't think there is any naiveté about that going into this process. In addition to the bodies which are charged with oversight for the police and the security agencies, we hope to get that type of feedback and oversight review from the communities themselves.

Appendix A: Annotated and Selected Excerpts of Bill C-36 As Introduced in Parliament October 15, 2001[1]

Summary

This enactment amends the Criminal Code, the Official Secrets Act, the Canada Evidence Act, the Proceeds of Crime (Money Laundering) Act and a number of other Acts, and enacts the Charities Registration (Security Information) Act, in order to combat terrorism.

Part 1 amends the Criminal Code to implement international conventions related to terrorism, to create offences related to terrorism, including the financing of terrorism and the participation, facilitation and carrying out of terrorist activities, and to provide a means by which property belonging to terrorist groups, or property linked to terrorist activities, can be seized, restrained and forfeited. It also provides for the deletion of hate propaganda from public web sites and creates an offence relating to damage to property associated with religious worship.

Part 2 amends the Official Secrets Act, which becomes the Security of Information Act. It addresses national security concerns, including threats of espionage by foreign powers and terrorist groups, economic espionage and coercive activities against émigré communities in Canada. It creates new offences to counter intelligence-gathering activities by foreign powers and terrorist groups, as well as other offences, including the unauthorized communication of special operational information.

---

1 Extracts compiled and edited by Marylin J. Raisch, International and Foreign law Librarian, and Shikha Sharma, Reference Librarian, both of the staff of the Bora Laskin Law Library, Faculty of Law, University of Toronto

Part 3 amends the Canada Evidence Act to address the judicial balancing of interests when the disclosure of information in legal proceedings would encroach on a specified public interest or be injurious to international relations or national defence or security. The amendments impose obligations on parties to notify the Attorney General of Canada if they anticipate the disclosure of sensitive information or information the disclosure of which could be injurious to international relations or national defence or security, and they give the Attorney General the powers to assume carriage of a prosecution and to prohibit the disclosure of information in connection with a proceeding for the purpose of protecting international relations or national defence or security.

Part 4 amends the Proceeds of Crime (Money Laundering) Act, which becomes the Proceeds of Crime (Money Laundering) and Terrorist Financing Act. The amendments will assist law enforcement and investigative agencies in the detection and deterrence of the financing of terrorist activities, facilitate the investigation and prosecution of terrorist activity financing offences, and improve Canada's ability to cooperate internationally in the fight against terrorism.

Part 5 amends the Access to Information Act, Canadian Human Rights Act, Canadian Security Intelligence Service Act, Corrections and Conditional Release Act, Federal Court Act, Firearms Act, National Defence Act, Personal Information Protection and Electronic Documents Act, Privacy Act, Seized Property Management Act and United Nations Act. The amendments to the National Defence Act clarify the powers of the Communications Security Establishment to combat terrorism.

Part 6 enacts the Charities Registration (Security Information) Act, and amends the Income Tax Act, in order to prevent those who support terrorist or related activities from enjoying the tax privileges granted to registered charities.

Preamble

WHEREAS Canadians and people everywhere are entitled to live their lives in peace, freedom and security;

WHEREAS acts of terrorism constitute a substantial threat to both domestic and international peace and security;

WHEREAS acts of terrorism threaten Canada's political institutions, the stability of the economy and the general welfare of the country;

WHEREAS the challenge of eradicating terrorism, with its sophisticated and trans-border nature, requires enhanced international cooperation and a strengthening of Canada's capacity to suppress, investigate and incapacitate terrorist activity;

WHEREAS Canada must act in concert with other nations in combating terrorism, including fully implementing United Nations and international instruments relating to terrorism;

WHEREAS the Parliament of Canada, recognizing that terrorism is a matter of national concern that affects the security of the nation, is committed to taking comprehensive measures to protect Canadians against terrorist activity while continuing to respect and promote the values reflected in, and the rights and freedoms guaranteed by, the Canadian Charter of Rights and Freedoms;

AND WHEREAS these comprehensive measures must include legislation to prevent and suppress the financing, preparation, facilitation and commission of acts of terrorism, as well as to protect the political, social and economic security of Canada and Canada's relations with its allies;

NOW, THEREFORE, Her Majesty, by and with the advice and consent of the Senate and House of Commons of Canada, enacts as follows:

Proposed Amendments to the Criminal Code

[Editors' note: The definition section of this act is perhaps the key part of Bill C-36. The definition of terrorist activity in this section is incorporated in many of the new offences found elsewhere in the bill, as well as in the new investigative powers and provisions for listing terrorist organizations. A number of the essays focus in particular on the definition of terrorist activities found in s.83.01(1)(b)(i)(E.)]

s. 83.01(1)   Interpretation

Definitions

83.01 (1) The following definitions apply in this Part.

'terrorist activity' means

(a) an act or omission committed or threatened in or outside Canada that, if committed in Canada, is one of the following offences:

(i)   the offences referred to in subsection 7(2) that implement the Convention for the Suppression of Unlawful Seizure of Aircraft, signed at The Hague on December 16, 1970,

(ii)   the offences referred to in subsection 7(2) that implement the Convention for the Suppression of Unlawful Acts against the Safety of Civil Aviation, signed at Montreal on September 23, 1971,

(iii) the offences referred to in subsection 7(3) that implement the Convention on the Prevention and Punishment of Crimes against Internationally Protected Persons, including Diplomatic Agents, adopted by the General Assembly of the United Nations on December 14, 1973,

(iv) the offences referred to in subsection 7(3.1) that implement the International Convention against the Taking of Hostages, adopted by the General Assembly of the United Nations on December 17, 1979,

(v)   the offences referred to in subsection 7(3.4) or (3.6) that implement the Convention on the Physical Protection of Nuclear Material, done at Vienna and New York on March 3, 1980,

(vi) the offences referred to in subsection 7(2) that implement the Protocol for the Suppression of Unlawful Acts of Violence at Airports Serving International Civil Aviation, supplementary to the Convention for the Suppression of Unlawful Acts against the Safety of Civil Aviation, signed at Montreal on February 24, 1988,

(vii) the offences referred to in subsection 7(2.1) that implement the Convention for the Suppression of Unlawful Acts against the Safety of Maritime Navigation, done at Rome on March 10, 1988,

(viii) the offences referred to in subsection 7(2.1) or (2.2) that implement the Protocol for the Suppression of Unlawful Acts against the Safety of Fixed Platforms Located on the Continental Shelf, done at Rome on March 10, 1988,

(ix) the offences referred to in subsection 7(3.72) that implement the International Convention for the Suppression of Terrorist Bombings, adopted by the General Assembly of the United Nations on December 15, 1997, and

(x)   the offences referred to in subsection 7(3.73) that implement the International Convention for the Suppression of Terrorist Financing, adopted by the General Assembly of the United Nations on December 9, 1999, or

(b) an act or omission, in or outside Canada,

   (i) that is committed

      (A) in whole or in part for a political, religious or ideological purpose, objective or cause, and
      (B) in whole or in part with the intention of intimidating the public, or a segment of the public, with regard to its security, including its economic security, or compelling a person, a government or a domestic or an international organization to do or to refrain from doing any act, whether the person, government or organization is inside or outside Canada, and

   (ii) that is intended

      (A) to cause death or serious bodily harm to a person by the use of violence,
      (B) to endanger a person's life,
      (C) to cause a serious risk to the health or safety of the public or any segment of the public,
      (D) to cause substantial property damage, whether to public or private property, if causing such damage is likely to result in the conduct or harm referred to in any of clauses (A) to (C) and (E), or
      (E) to cause serious interference with or serious disruption of an essential service, facility or system, whether public or private, other than as a result of lawful advocacy, protest, dissent or stoppage of work that does not involve an activity that is intended to result in the conduct or harm referred to in any of clauses (A) to (C),

and includes a conspiracy, attempt or threat to commit any such act or omission, or being an accessory after the fact or counselling in relation to any such act or omission, but, for greater certainty, does not include an act or omission that is committed during an armed conflict and that, at the time and in the place of its commission, is in accordance with customary international law or conventional international law applicable to the conflict, or the activities undertaken by military forces of a state in the exercise of their official duties, to the extent that those activities are governed by other rules of international law.

'terrorist group' means

(a) an entity that has as one of its purposes or activities facilitating or carrying out any terrorist activity, or
(b) a listed entity, and includes an association of such entities.

Facilitation

(2) For the purposes of this Part, a terrorist activity is facilitated whether or not

(a) the facilitator knows that a particular terrorist activity is facilitated;
(b) any particular terrorist activity was foreseen or planned at the time it was facilitated; or
(c) any terrorist activity was actually carried out.

Financing of Terrorism

[Editors' Note: The following provisions provide new offences relating to the financing of terrorism.]

Providing or collecting property for certain activities

83.02 Every one who, directly or indirectly, wilfully and without lawful justification or excuse, provides or collects property intending that it be used or knowing that it will be used, in whole or in part, in order to carry out

(a) an act or omission that constitutes an offence referred to in subparagraphs (a)(i) to (ix) of the definition of 'terrorist activity' in subsection 83.01(1), or
(b) any other act or omission intended to cause death or serious bodily harm to a civilian or to any other person not taking an active part in the hostilities in a situation of armed conflict, if the purpose of that act or omission, by its nature or context, is to intimidate the public, or to compel a government or an international organization to do or refrain from doing any act,is guilty of an indictable offence and is liable to imprisonment for a term of not more than 10 years.

Providing, making available, etc., property or services for terrorist purposes

83.03 Every one who, directly or indirectly, collects property, provides or invites a person to provide, or makes available property or financial or other related services

(a) intending that they be used, or knowing that they will be used, in whole or in part, for the purpose of facilitating or carrying out any terrorist activity, or for the purpose of benefitting any person who is facilitating or carrying out such an activity, or

(b) knowing that, in whole or part, they will be used by or will benefit a terrorist group, is guilty of an indictable offence and is liable to imprisonment for a term of not more than 10 years.

Using or possessing property for terrorist purposes

83.04 Every one who

(a) uses property, directly or indirectly, in whole or in part, for the purpose of facilitating or carrying out a terrorist activity, or

(b) possesses property intending that it be used or knowing that it will be used, directly or indirectly, in whole or in part, for the purpose of facilitating or carrying out a terrorist activity, is guilty of an indictable offence and is liable to imprisonment for a term of not more than 10 years.

List of Terrorists

[Editors' note: The following provision provides for the listing of terrorist groups and a review mechanism. There are consequences throughout the act for a group that is listed as a terrorist organization and for those who deal with such a group.]

Establishment of list

83.05 (1) The Governor in Council may, by regulation, establish a list on which the Governor in Council may place any entity if, on the recommendation of the Solicitor General, the Governor in Council is satisfied that there are reasonable grounds to believe that

(a) the entity has carried out, attempted to carry out, participated in or facilitated a terrorist activity; or

(b) the entity is acting on behalf of, at the direction of or in association with an entity referred to in paragraph (a).

Recommendation

(1.1) The Solicitor General may make a recommendation referred to in subsection (1) only if the Solicitor General has reasonable grounds to believe that the entity to which the recommendation relates is an entity referred to in paragraph (1)(a) or (b).

Application to Solicitor General

(2) On application in writing by a listed entity, the Solicitor General of Canada shall decide whether there are reasonable grounds to recommend to the Governor in Council that the applicant no longer be a listed entity.

Deeming

(3) If the Solicitor General does not make a decision on the application referred to in subsection (2) within 60 days after receipt of the application, the Solicitor General is deemed to have decided to recommend that the applicant remain a listed entity.

Notice of the decision to the applicant

(4) The Solicitor General must give notice without delay to the applicant of any decision taken or deemed to have been taken respecting the application referred to in subsection (2).

Judicial review

(5) Within 60 days after the receipt of the notice of the decision referred to in subsection (4), the applicant may apply to a judge for judicial review of the decision.
Reference

(6) When an application is made under subsection (5), the judge shall, without delay

(a) examine, in private, any security or criminal intelligence reports considered in listing the applicant and hear any other evidence or information that may be presented by or on behalf of the Solicitor

General and may, at the request of the Solicitor General, hear all or part of that evidence or information in the absence of the applicant and any counsel representing the applicant, if the judge is of the opinion that the disclosure of the information would injure national security or endanger the safety of any person;

(b) provide the applicant with a statement summarizing the information available to the judge so as to enable the applicant to be reasonably informed of the reasons for the decision, without disclosing any information the disclosure of which would, in the judge's opinion, injure national security or endanger the safety of any person;

(c) provide the applicant with a reasonable opportunity to be heard; and

(d) determine whether the decision is reasonable on the basis of the information available to the judge and, if found not to be reasonable, order that the applicant no longer be a listed entity.

Publication

(7) The Solicitor General shall cause to be published, without delay, in the Canada Gazette notice of a final order of a court that the applicant no longer be a listed entity.

New application

(8) A listed entity may not make another application under subsection (2), except if there has been a material change in its circumstances since the time when the entity made its last application.

Review of list

(9) Two years after the establishment of the list referred to in subsection (1), and every two years after that, the Solicitor General shall review the list to determine whether there are still reasonable grounds, as set out in subsection (1), for an entity to be a listed entity and make a recommendation to the Governor in Council as to whether the entity should remain a listed entity. The review does not affect the validity of the list.

Completion of review

(10) The Solicitor General shall complete the review as soon as possible

and in any event, no later than 120 days after its commencement. After completing the review, the Solicitor General shall cause to be published, without delay, in the Canada Gazette notice that the review has been completed.

Freezing of Property

Freezing of property

83.08 No person in Canada and no Canadian outside Canada shall knowingly

(a) deal directly or indirectly in any property that is owned or controlled by or on behalf of a terrorist group;

(b) enter into or facilitate, directly or indirectly, any transaction in respect of property referred to in paragraph (a); or

(c) provide any financial or other related services in respect of property referred to in paragraph (a) to, for the benefit of or at the direction of, a terrorist group.

83.12 (1) Every one who contravenes any of sections 83.08, 83.1 and 83.11 is guilty of an offence and liable

(a) on summary conviction, to a fine of not more than $100,000 or to imprisonment for a term of not more than one year, or to both; or

(b) on conviction on indictment, to imprisonment for a term of not more than 10 years.

No contravention

(2) No person contravenes section 83.1 if they make the disclosure referred to in that section only to the Commissioner of the Royal Canadian Mounted Police or the Director of the Canadian Security Intelligence Service.

Forfeiture of Property

Application for order of forfeiture

83.14 (1) The Attorney General may make an application to a judge of the Federal Court for an order of forfeiture in respect of

(a) property owned or controlled by or on behalf of a terrorist group;
(b) property that has been or will be used, in whole or in part, to facilitate or carry out a terrorist activity; or
(c) currency and monetary instruments owned or controlled by or on behalf of an individual who has facilitated or carried out a terrorist activity, or is planning to do so.

Participating, Facilitating, Instructing and Harbouring

[*The following, in addition to the financing offences outlined above, are the main new offences to be added to the Criminal Code.*]

Participation in activity of terrorist group

83.18 (1) Every one who knowingly participates in or contributes to, directly or indirectly, any activity of a terrorist group for the purpose of enhancing the ability of any terrorist group to facilitate or carry out a terrorist activity is guilty of an indictable offence and liable to imprisonment for a term not exceeding ten years.

Prosecution

(2) An offence may be committed under subsection (1) whether or not

(a) a terrorist group actually facilitates or carries out a terrorist activity;
(b) the participation or contribution of the accused actually enhances the ability of a terrorist group to facilitate or carry out a terrorist activity; or
(c) the accused knows the specific nature of any terrorist activity that may be facilitated or carried out by a terrorist group.

Meaning of participating or contributing

(3) Participating in or contributing to an activity of a terrorist group includes

(a) providing, receiving or recruiting a person to receive training;
(b) providing or offering to provide a skill or an expertise for the benefit of, at the direction of or in association with a terrorist group;
(c) recruiting a person in order to facilitate or commit

    (i)   a terrorism offence, or

   (ii) an act or omission outside Canada that, if committed in Canada, would be a terrorism offence;

> (d) entering or remaining in any country for the benefit of, at the direction of or in association with a terrorist group; or
> (e) making oneself, in response to instructions from any of the persons who constitute a terrorist group, available to facilitate or commit

    (i)   a terrorism offence, or

   (ii) an act or omission outside Canada that, if committed in Canada, would be a terrorism offence.

Factors

(4) In determining whether an accused participates in or contributes to any activity of a terrorist group, the court may consider, among other factors, whether the accused

(a) uses a name, word, symbol or other representation that identifies, or is associated with, the terrorist group;

(b) frequently associates with any of the persons who constitute the terrorist group;

(c) receives any benefit from the terrorist group; or

(d) repeatedly engages in activities at the instruction of any of the persons who constitute the terrorist group.

Facilitating terrorist activity

83.19 Every one who knowingly facilitates a terrorist activity is guilty of an indictable offence and liable to imprisonment for a term not exceeding fourteen years.

Commission of offence for terrorist group

83.2 (1) Every one who commits an indictable offence under this or any other Act of Parliament for the benefit of, at the direction of or in association with a terrorist group is guilty of an indictable offence and liable to imprisonment for life.

Prosecution

(2) An offence may be committed under subsection (1) whether or not the accused knows the identity of any of the persons who constitute the terrorist group.

Instructing commission of offence for terrorist group

83.21 (1) Every person who knowingly instructs, directly or indirectly, any person to carry out any activity for the benefit of, at the direction of or in association with a terrorist group, for the purpose of enhancing the ability of any terrorist group to facilitate or carry out a terrorist activity, is guilty of an indictable offence and liable to imprisonment for life.

Prosecution

(2) An offence may be committed under subsection (1) whether or not

(a) the activity that the accused instructs to be carried out is actually carried out;

(b) the accused instructs a particular person to carry out the activity referred to in paragraph (a);

(c) the accused knows the identity of the person whom the accused instructs to carry out the activity referred to in paragraph (a);

(d) the person whom the accused instructs to carry out the activity referred to in paragraph (a) knows that it is to be carried out for the benefit of, at the direction of, or in association with a terrorist group;

(e) a terrorist group actually facilitates or carries out a terrorist activity;

(f) the activity referred to in paragraph (a) actually enhances the ability of a terrorist group to facilitate or carry out a terrorist activity; or

(g) the accused knows the specific nature of any terrorist activity that may be facilitated or carried out by a terrorist group.

Instructing to carry out terrorist activity

83.22 (1) Every person who knowingly instructs, directly or indirectly, any person to carry out a terrorist activity is guilty of an indictable offence and liable to imprisonment for life.

Prosecution

(2) An offence may be committed under subsection (1) whether or not

(a) the terrorist activity is actually carried out;

(b) the accused instructs a particular person to carry out the terrorist activity;

(c) the accused knows the identity of the person whom the accused instructs to carry out the terrorist activity; or

(d) the person whom the accused instructs to carry out the terrorist activity knows that it is a terrorist activity.

Harbouring or concealing

83.23 Every one who knowingly harbours or conceals any person whom he or she knows to be a person who has carried out or is likely to carry out a terrorist activity, for the purpose of enabling the person to facilitate or carry out any terrorist activity, is guilty of an indictable offence and liable to imprisonment for a term not exceeding ten years.

Proceedings and Aggravated Punishment

[*The following provisions, as well as s.83.2 outlined above provide for various forms of enhanced punishment for terrorism offences as well as the consent of provincial or federal Attorneys General for terrorism offences.*]

Attorney General's consent

83.24 Proceedings in respect of a terrorism offence or an offence under section 83.12 shall not be commenced without the consent of the Attorney General.

Jurisdiction

83.25 (1) Where a person is alleged to have committed a terrorism offence or an offence under section 83.12, proceedings in respect of that offence may, whether or not that person is in Canada, be commenced at the instance of the Government of Canada and conducted by the Attorney

General of Canada or counsel acting on his or her behalf in any territorial division in Canada, if the offence is alleged to have occurred outside the province in which the proceedings are commenced, whether or not proceedings have previously been commenced elsewhere in Canada.

Trial and punishment

(2) An accused may be tried and punished in respect of an offence referred to in subsection (1) in the same manner as if the offence had been committed in the territorial division where the proceeding is conducted.

Sentences to be served consecutively

83.26 A sentence, other than one of life imprisonment, imposed on a person for an offence under any of sections 83.02 to 83.04 and 83.18 to 83.23 shall be served consecutively to

(a) any other punishment imposed on the person, other than a sentence of life imprisonment, for an offence arising out of the same event or series of events; and

(b) any other sentence, other than one of life imprisonment, to which the person is subject at the time the sentence is imposed on the person for an offence under any of those sections.

Punishment for terrorist activity

83.27 (1) Notwithstanding anything in this Act, a person convicted of an indictable offence, other than an offence for which a sentence of imprisonment for life is imposed as a minimum punishment, where the act or omission constituting the offence also constitutes a terrorist activity, is liable to imprisonment for life.

Offender must be notified

(2) Subsection (1) does not apply unless the prosecutor satisfies the court that the offender, before making a plea, was notified that the application of that subsection would be sought by reason of the act or omission constituting the offence also constituting a terrorist activity.

Investigative Hearing

[The following sets out the procedures for investigative hearings, one of the most controversial investigative powers in the bill.]

Definition of 'judge'

83.28 (1) In this section and section 83.29, 'judge' means a provincial court judge or a judge of a superior court of criminal jurisdiction.

Order for gathering evidence

(2) Subject to subsection (3), a peace officer may, for the purposes of an investigation of a terrorism offence, apply ex parte to a judge for an order for the gathering of evidence.

Attorney General's consent

(3) A peace officer may make an application under subsection (2) only if the prior consent of the Attorney General was obtained.

Making of order

(4) A judge to whom an application is made under subsection (2) may make an order for the gathering of evidence if the judge is satisfied that the consent of the Attorney General was obtained as required by subsection (3) and

(a) that there are reasonable grounds to believe that

    (i) a terrorism offence has been committed, and

    (ii) information concerning the offence, or information that may reveal the whereabouts of a person suspected by the peace officer of having committed the offence, is likely to be obtained as a result of the order; or

(b) that

    (i) there are reasonable grounds to believe that a terrorism offence will be committed,

    (ii) there are reasonable grounds to believe that a person has direct and material information that relates to a terrorism offence referred to in subparagraph (i), or that may reveal the whereabouts of an individual who the peace officer suspects may commit a terrorism offence referred to in that subparagraph, and

(iii) reasonable attempts have been made to obtain the information referred to in subparagraph (ii) from the person referred to in that subparagraph.

Arrest without warrant

(4) Notwithstanding subsections (2) and (3), if

(a) either

(i) the condition exists for laying an information under subsection (2) but, by reason of exigent circumstances, it would be impracticable to lay an information under subsection (2), or

(ii) an information has been laid under subsection (2) and a summons has been issued, and

(b) the peace officer suspects on reasonable grounds that the detention of the person in custody is necessary in order to prevent the commission of an indictable offence, where the act or omission constituting the offence also constitutes a terrorist activity, the peace officer may arrest the person without warrant and cause the person to be detained in custody, to be taken before a provincial court judge in accordance with subsection (6).

Duty of peace officer

(5) If a peace officer arrests a person without warrant in the circumstance described in subparagraph(4)(a)(i), the peace officer shall, within the time prescribed by paragraph (6)(a) or (b),

(a) lay an information in accordance with subsection (2), or
(b) release the person.

When person to be taken before judge

(6) A person detained in custody under subsection(4) shall be taken before a provincial court judge in accordance with the following rules:

(a) if a provincial court judge is available within a period of twenty-four hours after the person has been arrested, the person shall be taken before a provincial court judge without unreasonable delay and in any event within that period, and

(b) if a provincial court judge is not available within a period of twenty-four hours after the person has been arrested, the person shall be taken before a provincial court judge as soon as possible, unless, at any time before the expiry of the time prescribed in paragraph (a) or (b) for taking the person before a provincial court judge, the peace officer, or an officer in charge within the meaning of Part XV, is satisfied that the person should be released from custody unconditionally, and so releases the person.

How person dealt with

(7) When a person is taken before a provincial court judge under subsection (6),

(a) if an information has not been laid under subsection (2), the judge shall order that the person be released; or

(b) if an information has been laid under subsection (2), the person shall be dealt with in accordance with sections 515 to 524, those sections being applied subject to the following:

    (i) such modifications as the circumstances require,

    (ii) the word 'justice' shall be read as meaning a provincial court judge only, and

    (iii) the person may not be detained in custody by virtue of this section for longer than forty-eight hours following the appearance before the provincial court judge under subsection (6).

Recognizance with Conditions

[The following is sometimes referred to as the "preventive arrest" provision of the bill, another of the more controversial investigative procedures in the bill.]

Attorney General's consent required to lay information

83.3 (1) The consent of the Attorney General is required before a peace officer may lay an information under subsection (2). Terrorist activity

(2) Subject to subsection (1), a peace officer may lay an information before a provincial court judge if the peace officer

(a) believes on reasonable grounds that a terrorist activity will be carried out; and

(b) suspects on reasonable grounds that the imposition of a recognizance with conditions on a person, or the arrest of a person, is necessary to prevent the carrying out of the terrorist activity.

Appearance

(3) A provincial court judge who receives an information under subsection (2) may cause the person to appear before the provincial court judge.

Arrest without warrant

(4) Notwithstanding subsections (2) and (3), if

(a) either

   (i) he condition exists for laying an information under subsection (2)but, by reason of exigent circumstances, it would be impracticable to lay an information under subsection (2), or

   (ii) an information has been laid under subsection (2) and a summons has been issued, and

(b) the peace officer suspects on reasonable grounds that the detention of the person in custody is necessary in order to prevent the commission of an indictable offence, where the act or omission constituting the offence also constitutes a terrorist activity, the peace officer may arrest the person without warrant and cause the person to be detained in custody, to be taken before a provincial court judge in accordance with subsection (6).

Duty of peace officer

(5) If a peace officer arrests a person without warrant in the circumstance described in subparagraph (4)(a)(i), the peace officer shall, within the time prescribed by paragraph (6)(a) or (b),

(a) lay an information in accordance with subsection (2), or

(b) release the person.

When person to be taken before judge

(6) A person detained in custody under subsection (4) shall be taken before a provincial court judge in accordance with the following rules:

(a) if a provincial court judge is available within a period of twenty-four hours after the person has been arrested, the person shall be taken before a provincial court judge without unreasonable delay and in any event within that period, and

(b) if a provincial court judge is not available within a period of twenty-four hours after the person has been arrested, the person shall be taken before a provincial court judge as soon as possible, unless, at any time before the expiry of the time prescribed in paragraph (a) or (b) for taking the person before a provincial court judge, the peace officer, or an officer in charge within the meaning of Part XV, is satisfied that the person should be released from custody unconditionally, and so releases the person.

How person dealt with

(7) When a person is taken before a provincial court judge under subsection (6),

(a) if an information has not been laid under subsection (2), the judge shall order that the person be released; or

(b) if an information has been laid under subsection (2), the person shall be dealt with in accordance with sections 515 to 524, those sections being applied subject to the following:

(i) such modifications as the circumstances require,

(ii) the word 'justice' shall be read as meaning a provincial court judge only, and

(iii) the person may not be detained in custody by virtue of this section for longer than forty-eight hours following the appearance before the provincial court judge under subsection (6).

Hearing before judge

(8) The provincial court judge before whom the person appears pursuant to subsection (3) may, if satisfied by the evidence adduced that the peace officer has reasonable grounds for the suspicion, order that the person

enter into a recognizance to keep the peace and be of good behaviour for any period that does not exceed twelve months and to comply with any other reasonable conditions prescribed in the recognizance, including the conditions set out in subsection (10), that the provincial court judge considers desirable for preventing the commission of a terrorism offence.

Refusal to enter into recognizance

(9) The provincial court judge may commit the person to prison for a term not exceeding twelve months if the person fails or refuses to enter into the recognizance.

Conditions – firearms

(10) Before making an order under subsection (8), the provincial court judge shall consider whether it is desirable, in the interests of the safety of the person or of any other person, to include as a condition of the recognizance that the person be prohibited from possessing any firearm, cross-bow, prohibited weapon, restricted weapon, prohibited device, ammunition, prohibited ammunition or explosive substance, or all of those things, for any period specified in the recognizance, and where the provincial court judge decides that it is so desirable, the provincial court judge shall add such a condition to the recognizance.

Surrender, etc.

(11) If the provincial court judge adds a condition described in subsection (10) to a recognizance, the provincial court judge shall specify in the recognizance the manner and method by which

(a) the things referred to in that subsection that are in the possession of the person shall be surrendered, disposed of, detained, stored or dealt with; and
(b) the authorizations, licences and registration certificates held by the person shall be surrendered.

Reasons

(12) If the provincial court judge does not add a condition described in subsection (10) to a recognizance, the provincial court judge shall

include in the record a statement of the reasons for not adding the condition.

Variance of conditions

(13) The provincial court judge may, on application of the peace officer, the Attorney General or the person, vary the conditions fixed in the recognizance.

Other provisions to apply

(14) Subsections 810(4) and (5) apply, with any modifications that the circumstances require, to recognizances made under this section.

First Degree Murder

Section 231 of the Act is amended by adding the following after subsection (6):

Murder during terrorist activity

(6.01) Irrespective of whether a murder is planned and deliberate on the part of a person, murder is first degree murder when the death is caused while committing or attempting to commit an indictable offence under this or any other Act of Parliament where the act or omission constituting the offence also constitutes a terrorist activity.

New Offence of Mischief to Religious Property

Section 430 of the Act is amended by adding the following after subsection (4):

Mischief relating to religious property

(4.1) Every one who commits mischief in relation to property that is a building, structure or part thereof that is primarily used for religious worship, including a church, mosque, synagogue or temple, or an object associated with religious worship located in or on the grounds of such a building or structure, and the commission of the mischief is motivated by bias, prejudice or hate based on religion, race, colour or national or ethnic origin,

(a) is guilty of an indictable offence and liable to imprisonment for a term not exceeding ten years; or
(b) is guilty of an offence punishable on summary conviction and liable to imprisonment for a term not exceeding eighteen months.

Peace Bonds

(1) Subsection 810.01(1) of the Act is replaced by the following:

Fear of criminal organization offence or terrorism offence

810.01 (1) A person who fears on reasonable grounds that another person will commit a criminal organization offence or a terrorism offence may, with the consent of the Attorney General, lay an information before a provincial court judge.

(2) Subsection 810.01(3) of the Act is replaced by the following: Adjudication

(3) The provincial court judge before whom the parties appear may, if satisfied by the evidence adduced that the informant has reasonable grounds for the fear, order that the defendant enter into a recognizance to keep the peace and be of good behaviour for any period that does not exceed twelve months and to comply with any other reasonable conditions prescribed in the recognizance, including the conditions set out in subsection (5), that the provincial court judge considers desirable for preventing the commission of an offence referred to in subsection (1).

811. A person bound by a recognizance under section 83.3, 810, 810.01, 810.1 or 810.2 who commits a breach of the recognizance is guilty of

Proposed Amendments to Canada Evidence Act

[Editors' Note: These proposed amendments relate to restrictions on the disclosure of information in legal proceedings.]

Objection to disclosure of information

37. (1) Subject to sections 38 to 38.16, a Minister of the Crown in right of Canada or other official may object to the disclosure of information before a court, person or body with jurisdiction to compel the production of information by certifying orally or in writing to the court, person or body that the information should not be disclosed on the grounds of a specified public interest.

Obligation of court, person or body

(1.1) If an objection is made under subsection (1), the court, person or body shall ensure that the information is not disclosed other than in accordance with this Act.

Objection made to superior court

(2) If an objection to the disclosure of information is made before a superior court, that court may determine the objection.

Objection not made to superior court

(3) If an objection to the disclosure of information is made before a court, person or body other than a superior court, the objection may be determined, on application, by

(a) the Federal Court-Trial Division, in the case of a person or body vested with power to compel production by or under an Act of Parliament if the person or body is not a court established under a law of a province; or

(b) the trial division or trial court of the superior court of the province within which the court, person or body exercises its jurisdiction, in any other case.

Limitation period

(4) An application under subsection (3) shall be made within 10 days after the objection is made or within any further or lesser time that the court having jurisdiction to hear the application considers appropriate in the circumstances.

Disclosure order

(4.1) Unless the court having jurisdiction to hear the application concludes that the disclosure of the information to which the objection was made under subsection (1) would encroach upon a specified public interest, the court may authorize by order the disclosure of the information.

Disclosure order

(5) If the court having jurisdiction to hear the application concludes that the disclosure of the information to which the objection was made under subsection (1) would encroach upon a specified public interest, but that the public interest in disclosure outweighs in importance the specified public interest, the court may, by order, after considering both the public interest in disclosure and the form of and conditions to disclosure that are most likely to limit any encroachment upon the specified public interest resulting from disclosure, authorize the disclosure, subject to any conditions that the court considers appropriate, of all of the information, a part or summary of the information, or a written admission of facts relating to the information.

Prohibition order

(6) If the court does not authorize disclosure under subsection (4.1) or (5), the court shall, by order, prohibit disclosure of the information.

When determination takes effect

(7) An order of the court that authorizes disclosure does not take effect until the time provided or granted to appeal the order, or a judgment of an appeal court that confirms the order, has expired, or no further appeal from a judgment that confirms the order is available.

Introduction into evidence

(8) A person who wishes to introduce into evidence material the disclosure of which is authorized under subsection (5) but who may not be able to do so by reason of the rules of admissibility that apply before the court, person or body with jurisdiction to compel the production of information may request from the court having jurisdiction under subsection (2) or

(3) an order permitting the introduction into evidence of the material in a form or subject to any conditions fixed by that court, as long as that form and those conditions comply with the order made under subsection (5).

Relevant factors

(9) For the purpose of subsection (8), the court having jurisdiction under subsection (2) or (3) shall consider all the factors that would be relevant for a determination of admissibility before the court, person or body.

Special rules

37.21 (1) A hearing under subsection 37(2) or (3) or an appeal of an order made under any of subsections 37(4.1) to (6) shall be heard in private.

Representations

(2) The court conducting a hearing under subsection 37(2) or (3) or the court hearing an appeal of an order made under any of subsections 37(4.1) to (6) may give

(a) any person an opportunity to make representations; and
(b) any person who makes representations under paragraph (a) the opportunity to make representations ex parte.

Protection of right to a fair trial

37.3 A judge presiding at a criminal trial or other criminal proceeding may make any order that he or she considers appropriate in the circumstances to protect the right of the accused to a fair trial, as long as that order complies with the terms of any order made under any of subsections 37(4.1) to (6) in relation to that trial or proceeding or any judgment made on appeal of an order made under any of those subsections.

Notice to Attorney General of Canada

38.01 (1) Every participant who, in connection with a proceeding, is required to disclose, or expects to disclose or cause the disclosure of, information that the participant believes is sensitive information or potentially injurious information shall, as soon as possible, notify the Attorney General of Canada in writing of the possibility of the disclosure, and of the nature, date and place of the proceeding.

During a proceeding

(2) Every participant who believes that sensitive information or potentially injurious information is about to be disclosed, whether by the participant or another person, in the course of a proceeding shall raise the matter with the person presiding at the proceeding and notify the Attorney General of Canada in writing of the matter as soon as possible, whether or not notice has been given under subsection (1). In such circumstances, the person presiding at the proceeding shall ensure that the information is not disclosed other than in accordance with this Act.

Notice of disclosure from official

(3) An official, other than a participant, who believes that sensitive information or potentially injurious information may be disclosed in connection with a proceeding may notify the Attorney General of Canada in writing of the possibility of the disclosure, and of the nature, date and place of the proceeding.

During a proceeding

(4) An official, other than a participant, who believes that sensitive information or potentially injurious information is about to be disclosed in the course of a proceeding may raise the matter with the person presiding at the proceeding. If the official raises the matter, he or she shall notify the Attorney General of Canada in writing of the matter as soon as possible, whether or not notice has been given under subsection (3), and the person presiding at the proceeding shall ensure that the information is not disclosed other than in accordance with this Act.

Military proceedings

(5) In the case of a proceeding under Part III of the National Defence Act, notice under any of subsections (1) to (4) shall be given to both the Attorney General of Canada and the Minister of National Defence.

Exception

(6) This section does not apply when

(a) the information is disclosed by a person to their solicitor in connection with a proceeding, if the information is relevant to that proceeding;

(b) the information is disclosed to enable the Attorney General of Canada, the Minister of National Defence, a judge or a court hearing an appeal from, or a review of, an order of the judge to discharge their responsibilities under section 38, this section and sections 38.02 to 38.13, 38.15 and 38.16;

(c) disclosure of the information is authorized by the government institution in which or for which the information was produced or, if the information was not produced in or for a government institution, the government institution in which it was first received; or

(d) the information is disclosed to an entity listed in the schedule.

Exception

(7) Subsections (1) and (2) do not apply to a participant if a government institution referred to in paragraph (6)(c) advises the participant that it is not necessary, in order to prevent disclosure of the information referred to in that paragraph, to give notice to the Attorney General of Canada under subsection (1) or to raise the matter with the person presiding under subsection (2).

Schedule

(8) The Governor in Council may, by order, add to or delete from the schedule a reference to any entity, or amend such a reference.

Disclosure prohibited

38.02 (1) Subject to subsection 38.01(6), no person shall disclose in connection with a proceeding

(a) information about which notice is given under any of subsections 38.01(1) to (4);

(b) the fact that notice is given to the Attorney General of Canada under any of subsections 38.01(1) to (4), or to the Attorney General of

Canada and the Minister of National Defence under subsection 38.01(5);

(c) the fact that an application is made to the Federal Court-Trial Division under section 38.04 or that an appeal or review of an order made under any of subsections 38.06(1) to (3) in connection with the application is instituted; or

(d) the fact that an agreement is entered into under section 38.031 or subsection 38.04(6).

Exceptions

(2) Disclosure of the information or the facts referred to in subsection (1) is not prohibited if

(a) the Attorney General of Canada authorizes the disclosure in writing under section 38.03 or by agreement under section 38.031 or subsection 38.04(6); or

(b) a judge authorizes the disclosure under any of subsections 38.06(1) to (3) or a court hearing an appeal from, or a review of, the order of the judge authorizes the disclosure, and either the time provided to appeal the order or judgment has expired or no further appeal is available.

Authorization by Attorney General of Canada

38.03 (1) The Attorney General of Canada may, at any time and subject to any conditions that he or she considers appropriate, authorize the disclosure of all or part of the information and facts the disclosure of which is prohibited under subsection 38.02(1).

Military proceedings

(2) In the case of a proceeding under Part III of the National Defence Act, the Attorney General of Canada may authorize disclosure only with the agreement of the Minister of National Defence.

Notice

(3) The Attorney General of Canada shall, within 10 days after the day on which he or she first receives a notice about information under any of

subsections 38.01(1) to (4), notify in writing every person who provided notice under section 38.01 about that information of his or her decision with respect to disclosure of the information.

Disclosure agreement

38.031 (1) The Attorney General of Canada and a person who has given notice under subsection 38.01(1) or (2) and is not required to disclose information but wishes, in connection with a proceeding, to disclose any facts referred to in paragraphs 38.02(1)(b) to (d) or information about which he or she gave the notice, or to cause that disclosure, may, before the person applies to the Federal Court-Trial Division under paragraph 38.04(2)(c), enter into an agreement that permits the disclosure of part of the facts or information or disclosure of the facts or information subject to conditions. No application to Federal Court

(2) If an agreement is entered into under subsection (1), the person may not apply to the Federal Court-Trial Division under paragraph 38.04(2)(c) with respect to the information about which he or she gave notice to the Attorney General of Canada under subsection 38.01(1) or (2).

Disclosure order

38.06 (1) Unless the judge concludes that the disclosure of the information would be injurious to international relations or national defence or security, the judge may, by order, authorize the disclosure of the information.

Disclosure order

(2) If the judge concludes that the disclosure of the information would be injurious to international relations or national defence or security but that the public interest in disclosure outweighs in importance the public interest in non-disclosure, the judge may by order, after considering both the public interest in disclosure and the form of and conditions to disclosure that are most likely to limit any injury to international relations or national defence or security resulting from disclosure, authorize the disclosure, subject to any conditions that the judge considers appropriate, of all of the information, a part or summary of the information, or a written admission of facts relating to the information.

Order confirming prohibition

(3) If the judge does not authorize disclosure under subsection (1) or (2), the judge shall, by order, confirm the prohibition of disclosure.

Introduction into evidence

(4) A person who wishes to introduce into evidence material the disclosure of which is authorized under subsection (2) but who may not be able to do so in a proceeding by reason of the rules of admissibility that apply in the proceeding may request from a judge an order permitting the introduction into evidence of the material in a form or subject to any conditions fixed by that judge, as long as that form and those conditions comply with the order made under subsection (2).

Relevant factors

(5) For the purpose of subsection (4), the judge shall consider all the factors that would be relevant for a determination of admissibility in the proceeding.

Special rules

38.11 (1) A hearing under subsection 38.04(5) or an appeal or review of an order made under any of subsections 38.06(1) to (3) shall be heard in private and, at the request of either the Attorney General of Canada or, in the case of a proceeding under Part III of the National Defence Act, the Minister of National Defence, shall be heard in the National Capital Region, as described in the schedule to the National Capital Act.

Ex parte representations

(2) The judge conducting a hearing under subsection 38.04(5) or the court hearing an appeal or review of an order made under any of subsections 38.06(1) to (3) may give any person who makes representations under paragraph 38.04(5)(d), and shall give the Attorney General of Canada and, in the case of a proceeding under Part III of the National Defence Act, the Minister of National Defence, the opportunity to make representations ex parte.

38.12 (1) The judge conducting a hearing under subsection 38.04(5) or the court hearing an appeal or review of an order made under any of subsections 38.06(1) to (3) may make any order that the judge or the court considers appropriate in the circumstances to protect the confidentiality of the information to which the hearing, appeal or review relates.

Court records

(2) The court records relating to the hearing, appeal or review are confidential. The judge or the court may order that the records be sealed and kept in a location to which the public has no access.

Prohibition certificate

38.13 (1) The Attorney General of Canada may at any time personally issue a certificate that prohibits the disclosure of information in connection with a proceeding for the purpose of protecting international relations or national defence or security.

Military proceedings

(2) In the case of a proceeding under Part III of the National Defence Act, the Attorney General of Canada may issue the certificate only with the agreement, given personally, of the Minister of National Defence.

Service of certificate

(3) The Attorney General of Canada shall cause a copy of the certificate to be served on

(a) the person presiding or designated to preside at the proceeding to which the information relates or, if no person is designated, the person who has the authority to designate a person to preside;

(b) every party to the proceeding;

(c) every person who gives notice under section 38.01 in connection with the proceeding;

(d) every person who, in connection with the proceeding, may disclose, is required to disclose, or may cause the disclosure of, the information about which the Attorney General of Canada has received notice under section 38.01;

(e) every party to a hearing under subsection 38.04(5) or to an appeal of an order made under any of subsections 38.06(1) to (3) in relation to the information;

(f) the judge who conducts a hearing under subsection 38.04(5) and any court that hears an appeal from, or review of, an order made under any of subsections 38.06(1) to (3) in relation to the information; and

(g) any other person who, in the opinion of the Attorney General of Canada, should be served.

Filing of certificate

(4) The Attorney General of Canada shall cause a copy of the certificate to be filed

(a) with the person responsible for the records of the proceeding to which the information relates; and

(b) in the Registry of the Federal Court and the registry of any court that hears an appeal from, or review of, an order made under any of subsections 38.06(1) to (3).

Effect of certificate

(5) If the Attorney General of Canada issues a certificate, then, notwithstanding any other provision of this Act, disclosure of the Information shall be prohibited in accordance with the terms of the certificate.

Statutory Instruments Act does not apply

(6) The Statutory Instruments Act does not apply to a certificate made under subsection (1).

Protection of right to a fair trial

38.14 The person presiding at a criminal proceeding may make any order that he or she considers appropriate in the circumstances to protect the right of the accused to a fair trial, as long as that order complies with the terms of any order made under any of subsections 38.06(1) to (3) in relation to that proceeding, any judgment made on appeal from, or review of, the order, or any certificate issued under section 38.13.

Fiat

38.15 (1) If sensitive information or potentially injurious information may be disclosed in connection with a prosecution that is not instituted by the Attorney General of Canada or on his or her behalf, the Attorney General of Canada may issue a fiat and serve the fiat on the prosecutor.

Effect of fiat

(2) When a fiat is served on a prosecutor, the fiat establishes the exclusive authority of the Attorney General of Canada with respect to the conduct of the prosecution described in the fiat or any related process.

Fiat filed in court

(3) If a prosecution described in the fiat or any related process is conducted by or on behalf of the Attorney General of Canada, the fiat or a copy of the fiat shall be filed with the court in which the prosecution or process is conducted.

Fiat constitutes conclusive proof

(4) The fiat or a copy of the fiat

(a) is conclusive proof that the prosecution described in the fiat or any related process may be conducted by or on behalf of the Attorney General of Canada; and
(b) is admissible in evidence without proof of the signature or official character of the Attorney General of Canada.

Military proceedings

(5) This section does not apply to a proceeding under Part III of the National Defence Act.

Regulations

38.16 The Governor in Council may make any regulations that it considers necessary to carry into effect the purposes and provisions of sections 38 to 38.15, including regulations respecting the notices, certificates and the fiat.

Communications Security Establishment

[Editors' Note: These provisions are a statutory recognition of the Communications Security Establishment]

273.62 (1) The part of the public service of Canada known as the Communications Security Establishment is hereby continued.

Chief

(2) The Chief of the Communications Security Establishment, under the direction of the Minister or any person designated by the Minister, has the management and control of the Establishment and all matters relating to it.

Appointment of Commissioner

273.63 (1) The Governor in Council may appoint a supernumerary judge or a retired judge of a superior court as Commissioner of the Communications Security Establishment to hold office, during good behaviour, for a term of not more than five years.

Duties

(2) The duties of the Commissioner are

(a) to review the activities of the Establishment to ensure that they are in compliance with the law;

(b) in response to a complaint, to undertake any investigation that the Commissioner considers necessary; and

(c) to inform the Minister and the Attorney General of Canada of any activity of the Establishment that the Commissioner believes may not be in compliance with the law.

Annual Report

(3) The Commissioner shall, within 90 days after the end of each fiscal year, submit an Annual Report to the Minister on the Commissioner's activities and findings, and the Minister shall cause a copy of the report to

be laid before each House of Parliament on any of the first 15 days on which that House is sitting after the Minister receives the report.

Powers of investigation

(4) In carrying out his or her duties, the Commissioner has all the powers of a commissioner under Part II of the Inquiries Act.

Employment of legal counsel, advisors, etc.

(5) The Commissioner may engage the services of such legal counsel, technical advisors and assistants as the Commissioner considers necessary for the proper performance of his or her duties and, with the approval of the Treasury Board, may fix and pay their remuneration and expenses.

Directions

(6) The Governor in Council may issue directions to the Commissioner respecting the carrying out of his or her duties.

Transitional

(7) The Commissioner of the Communications Security Establishment holding office immediately before the coming into force of this section shall continue in office for the remainder of the term for which he or she was appointed.

273.64 (1) The mandate of the Communications Security Establishment is

(a) to acquire and use information from the global information infrastructure for the purpose of providing foreign intelligence, in accordance with Government of Canada intelligence priorities;
(b) to provide advice, guidance and services to help ensure the protection of electronic information and of information infrastructures of importance to the Government of Canada; and
(c) to provide technical and operational assistance to federal law enforcement and security agencies in the performance of their lawful duties.

Protection of Canadians

(2) Activities carried out under paragraphs (1)(a) and (b)

(a) shall not be directed at Canadians or any person in Canada; and

(b) shall be subject to measures to protect the privacy of Canadians in the use and retention of intercepted information.

Limitations imposed by law

(3) Activities carried out under paragraph (1)(c) are subject to any limitations imposed by law on federal law enforcement and security agencies in the performance of their duties.

Ministerial authorization

273.65 (1) The Minister may, for the sole purpose of obtaining foreign intelligence, authorize the Communications Security Establishment in writing to intercept private communications in relation to an activity or class of activities specified in the authorization.

Conditions for authorization

(2) The Minister may only issue an authorization under subsection (1) if satisfied that

(a) the interception will be directed at foreign entities located outside Canada;

(b) the information to be obtained could not reasonably be obtained by other means;

(c) the expected foreign intelligence value of the information that would be derived from the interception justifies it; and

(d) satisfactory measures are in place to protect the privacy of Canadians and to ensure that private communications will only be used or retained if they are essential to international affairs, defence or security.

Ministerial authorization

(3) The Minister may, for the sole purpose of protecting the computer systems or networks of the Government of Canada from mischief, unauthorized use or interference, in the circumstances specified in

paragraph 184(2)(c) of the Criminal Code, authorize the Communications Security Establishment in writing to intercept private communications in relation to an activity or class of activities specified in the authorization.

Conditions for authorization

(4) The Minister may only issue an authorization under subsection (3) if satisfied that

(a) the interception is necessary to identify, isolate or prevent harm to Government of Canada computer systems or networks;
(b) the information to be obtained could not reasonably be obtained by other means;
(c) the consent of persons whose private communications may be intercepted cannot reasonably be obtained;
(d) satisfactory measures are in place to ensure that only information that is essential to identify, isolate or prevent harm to Government of Canada computer systems or networks will be used or retained; and
(e) satisfactory measures are in place to protect the privacy of Canadians in the use or retention of that information.

Personal Information Protection and Electronic Documents Act

4.1 (1) The Attorney General of Canada may at any time personally issue a certificate that prohibits the disclosure of information for the purpose of protecting international relations or national defence or security.

Prohibited information

(2) This Part does not apply to information the disclosure of which is prohibited by a certificate under subsection (1).

Registration of Charities – Security Information

[Editors' Note: The following are provisions governing taking away charitable status from charities which support terrorist groups.]

The Charities Registration (Security Information) Act is enacted as follows: An Act respecting the registration of charities having regard to security and criminal intelligence information

SHORT TITLE

Short title

11. This Act may be cited as the Charities Registration (Security Information) Act.

PURPOSE AND PRINCIPLES

Purpose

2. (1) The purpose of this Act is to demonstrate Canada's commitment to participating in concerted international efforts to deny support to those who engage in terrorism, to protect the integrity of the registration system for charities under the Income Tax Act and to maintain the confidence of Canadian taxpayers that the benefits of charitable registration are made available only to organizations that operate exclusively for charitable purposes.

Principles

(2) This Act shall be carried out in recognition of, and in accordance with, the following principles:

(a) maintaining the confidence of taxpayers may require reliance on information that, if disclosed, would injure national security or endanger the safety of persons; and

(b) the process for relying on the information referred to in paragraph (a) in determining eligibility to become or remain a registered charity must be as fair and transparent as possible having regard to national security and the safety of persons.

INTERPRETATION

Definitions
3. The following definitions apply in this Act.

'applicant'

'applicant' means a corporation, an organization or a trust that applies to the Minister of National Revenue to become a registered charity.

'judge'

'judge' means the Chief Justice of the Federal Court or a judge of the Trial Division of that Court designated by the Chief Justice.

'Minister'

'Minister' means the Solicitor General of Canada.

'registered charity'

'registered charity' means a registered charity as defined in subsection 248(1) of the Income Tax Act.

CERTIFICATE BASED ON INTELLIGENCE

Signature by Ministers

4. (1) The Minister and the Minister of National Revenue may sign a certificate stating that it is their opinion, based on security or criminal intelligence reports, that there are reasonable grounds to believe

(a) that an applicant or registered charity has made, makes or will make available any resources, directly or indirectly, to an entity that is a listed entity as defined in subsection 83.01(1) of the Criminal Code;

(b) that an applicant or registered charity made available any resources, directly or indirectly, to an entity as defined in subsection 83.01(1) of the Criminal Code and the entity was at that time, and continues to be, engaged in terrorist activities as defined in that subsection or activities in support of them; or

(c) that an applicant or registered charity makes or will make available any resources, directly or indirectly, to an entity as defined in subsection 83.01(1) of the Criminal Code and the entity engages or will engage in terrorist activities as defined in that subsection or activities in support of them.

Statutory Instruments Act

(2) A certificate is not a statutory instrument for the purposes of the Statutory Instruments Act.

JUDICIAL CONSIDERATION OF CERTIFICATE

Notice

5. (1) As soon as the Minister and the Minister of National Revenue have signed a certificate, the Minister, or a person authorized by the Minister, shall cause the applicant or registered charity to be served, personally or by registered letter sent to its last known address, with a copy of the certificate and a notice informing it that the certificate will be referred to the Federal Court not earlier than seven days after service and that, if the certificate is determined to be reasonable, the applicant will be ineligible to become a registered charity or the registration of the registered charity will be revoked, as the case may be.

Restriction

(2) The certificate and any matters arising out of it are not subject to review or to be restrained, prohibited, removed, set aside or otherwise dealt with, except in accordance with this Act.

Non-publication or confidentiality order

(3) Notwithstanding subsection (2), the applicant or registered charity may apply to a judge for an order

(a) directing that the identity of the applicant or registered charity not be published or broadcast in any way except in accordance with this Act; or

(b) that any documents to be filed with the Federal Court in connection with the reference be treated as confidential.

No appeal

(4) An order on an application referred to in subsection (3) is not subject to appeal or review by any court at the instance of a party to the application.

Filing in Federal Court

(5) Seven days after service under subsection (1), or as soon afterwards as

is practicable, the Minister or a person authorized by the Minister shall

(a) file a copy of the certificate in the Federal Court for it to make a determination under paragraph 6(1)(d); and

(b) cause the applicant or registered charity to be served, personally or by registered letter sent to its last known address, with a notice informing it of the filing of the certificate.

Reference

6. (1) When the certificate is referred to the Federal Court, the judge shall, without delay,

(a) examine, in private, the security or criminal intelligence reports considered by the Minister and the Minister of National Revenue and hear any other evidence or information that may be presented by or on behalf of those Ministers and may, on the request of the Minister or the Minister of National Revenue, hear all or part of that evidence or information in the absence of the applicant or registered charity and any counsel representing it, if the judge is of the opinion that disclosure of the information would injure national security or endanger the safety of any person;

(b) provide the applicant or registered charity with a statement summarizing the information available to the judge so as to enable the applicant or registered charity to be reasonably informed of the circumstances giving rise to the certificate, without disclosing any information the disclosure of which would, in the judge's opinion, injure national security or endanger the safety of any person;

(c) provide the applicant or registered charity with a reasonable opportunity to be heard; and

(d) determine whether the certificate is reasonable on the basis of the information available to the judge and, if found not to be reasonable, quash it.

No appeal or review

(2) A determination under paragraph (1)(d) is not subject to appeal or review by any court.

EVIDENCE

Admissible information

7. For the purposes of subsection 6(1), the judge may, subject to section 8, admit any relevant information, whether or not the information is or would be admissible in a court of law, and base the determination under paragraph 6(1)(d) on that information.

Foreign information obtained in confidence

8. (1) For the purposes of subsection 6(1), in private and in the absence of the applicant or registered charity or any counsel representing it,

(a) the Minister or the Minister of National Revenue may make an application to the judge for the admission of information obtained in confidence from a government, an institution or an agency of a foreign state, from an international organization of states or from an institution or an agency of an international organization of states; and

(b) the judge shall examine the information and provide counsel representing the Minister or the Minister of National Revenue with a reasonable opportunity to be heard as to whether the information is relevant but should not be disclosed to the applicant or registered charity or any counsel representing it because the disclosure would injure national security or endanger the safety of any person.

Return of information

(2) The information shall be returned to counsel representing the minister who made the application and shall not be considered by the judge in making the determination under paragraph 6(1)(d) if

(a) the judge determines that the information is not relevant;

(b) the judge determines that the information is relevant but should be summarized in the statement to be provided under paragraph 6(1)(b); or

(c) the minister withdraws the application.

Use of information

(3) If the judge decides that the information is relevant but that its

disclosure would injure national security or endanger the safety of any person, the information shall not be disclosed in the statement mentioned in paragraph 6(1)(b), but the judge may base the determination under paragraph 6(1)(d) on it.

Ineligibility or revocation

9. (1) A certificate that is determined to be reasonable under paragraph 6(1)(d) is conclusive proof, in the case of an applicant, that it is ineligible to become a registered charity or, in the case of a registered charity, that it does not comply with the requirements to continue to be a registered charity.

Publication

(2) The Minister shall, without delay after a certificate is determined to be reasonable, cause the certificate to be published in the Canada Gazette.

REVIEW OF CERTIFICATE

Review of certificate

10. (1) An applicant or former registered charity in relation to which a certificate was determined to be reasonable under paragraph 6(1)(d) and that believes that there has been a material change in circumstances since that determination was made may apply in writing to the Minister for a review of the certificate by the Minister and the Minister of National Revenue.

Notice to Minister of National Revenue

(2) The Minister shall, without delay, notify the Minister of National Revenue of an application for review.

Information for review

(3) For the purpose of a review, the Ministers may consider any submission made by the applicant or former registered charity that applied for the review and any security or criminal intelligence reports that are made available to the Ministers.

Time for decision

(4) The Ministers shall make their decision on an application for review within 120 days after receipt of the application by the Minister.

Decision on review

(5) The Ministers may decide that, since the time the certificate was determined to be reasonable,

(a) there has not been a material change in circumstances, in which case the Ministers shall deny the application; or

(b) there has been a material change in circumstances, in which case the Ministers shall determine whether there are reasonable grounds as provided in subsection 4(1) and, accordingly,

    (i)   continue the certificate in effect, or

    (ii) cancel the certificate as of the date of the decision.

Automatic cancellation

(6) If no decision is made within a period of 120 days after receipt of the application, the certificate is cancelled on the expiration of that period.

Notice to applicant or charity

(7) As soon as a decision is made or the certificate is cancelled under subsection (6), the Minister or a person authorized by the Minister shall cause the applicant or former registered charity that applied for the review to be served, personally or by registered letter sent to its last known address, with notice of the decision or cancellation.

Application for review

11. (1) An applicant or former registered charity that applied for a review under subsection 10(1) may, after giving written notice to the Minister who in turn shall notify the Minister of National Revenue, apply to the Federal Court for a review of a decision made under paragraph 10(5)(a) or subparagraph 10(5)(b)(i).

Review by Court

(2) The Court shall carry out the review in accordance with section 6, with any adaptations that may be required.

Referral to Ministers

(3) If the Court quashes a decision of the Ministers made under paragraph 10(5)(a), it shall refer the application to the Ministers for a decision under paragraph 10(5)(b).

Cancellation of certificate

(4) If the Court quashes a decision of the Ministers made under subparagraph 10(5)(b)(i), the certificate is cancelled as of the date the decision is quashed.

No appeal

(5) The determination of the Court is not subject to appeal or judicial review.

Publication of spent certificate

12. The Minister shall, in a manner that mentions the original publication of the certificate, cause to be published in the Canada Gazette notice of the cancellation of a certificate by reason of

(a) a decision made under subparagraph 10(5)(b)(ii);
(b) the operation of subsection 10(6); or
(c) a determination of the Federal Court referred to in subsection 11(4).

Term of a certificate

13. Unless it is cancelled earlier, a certificate is effective for a period of seven years beginning on the day it is first determined to be reasonable under paragraph 6(1)(d).

Regulations

14. The Governor in Council may make any regulations that the Governor in Council considers necessary for carrying out the purposes and provisions of this Act.

R.S., c. 1 (5th Supp.)

Appendix B: Public Order Regulations, 1970 SOR/70–444

[Editors' Note: Reference is made in a number of papers to the following regulations which were enacted on October 16, 1970 in response to the terrorism of the October Crisis.]

Whereas it continues to be recognized in Canada that men and institutions remain free only when freedom is founded upon respect for moral and spiritual values and the rule of law;

And Whereas there is in contemporary Canadian society an element or group known as Le Front de Libèration du Quèbec who advocate the use of force or the commission of crime as a means of or as an aid in accomplishing a governmental change within Canada and who have resorted to the commission of serious crimes including murder, threat of murder and kidnapping;

And Whereas the Government of Canada desires to ensure that lawful and effective measures can be taken against those who thus seek to destroy the basis of our democratic governmental system on which the enjoyment of our human rights and fundamental freedoms is founded and to ensure the continued protection of those rights and freedoms in Canada.

Therefore, His Excellency the Governor General in Council, on the recommendation of the Prime Minister, pursuant to the War Measures Act, is pleased hereby to make the annexed Regulations to Provide Emergency Powers for the Preservation of Public Order in Canada.

REGULATIONS TO PROVIDE EMERGENCY POWERS FOR THE PRESERVATION OF PUBLIC ORDER IN CANADA

Short Title

1. These Regulations may be cited as the Public Order Regulations, 1970.

Interpretation

2. In these Regulations,

'communicate' includes the act of communicating by telephone, broadcasting or other audible or visible means;

'peace officer' means a peace officer as defined in the Criminal Code and includes a member of the Canadian Armed Forces;

'statements' includes words spoken or written or recorded electronically or electromagnetically or otherwise, and gestures, signs or other visible representations; and

'the unlawful association' means the group of persons or association declared by these Regulations to be an unlawful association.

General

3. The group of persons or association known as Le Front du Libèration du Quèbec and any successor group or successor association of the said Le Front de Libèration du Quèbec or any group of persons or association that advocates the use of force or the commission of crime as a means of or as an aid in accomplishing governmental change within Canada is declared to be an unlawful association.

4. A person who

   (a) is or professes to be a member of the unlawful association,
   (b) acts or professes to act as an officer of the unlawful association,
   (c) communicates statements on behalf of or as a representative of the unlawful association,
   (d) advocates or promotes the unlawful acts, aims, principles or policies of the unlawful association

(e) contributes anything as dues or otherwise to the unlawful association or to anyone for the benefit of the unlawful association,

(f) solicits subscriptions or contributions for the unlawful association, or

(g) advocates, promotes or engages in the use of force or the commission of criminal offences as a means of accomplishing a governmental change within Canada is guilty of an indictable offence and liable to imprisonment for a term not exceeding five years.

5. A person who, knowing or having reasonable cause to believe that another person is guilty of an offence under these Regulations, gives that other person any assistance with intent thereby to prevent, hinder or interfere with the apprehension, trial or punishment of that person for that offence is guilty of an indictable offence and liable to imprisonment for a term not exceeding give years.

6. An owner, lessee, agent or superintendent of any building, room, premises or other place who knowingly permits therein any meeting of the unlawful association or any branch, committee or members thereof, or any assemblage of persons who promote the acts, aims, principles or policies of the unlawful association is guilty of an indictable offence and liable to a fine of not more than five thousand dollars or to imprisonment for a term not exceeding five years or to both.

7. (1) A person arrested for an offence under section 4 shall be detained in custody without bail pending trial unless the Attorney General of the province in which the person is being detained consents to the release of that person on bail.

   (2) Where an accused has been arrested for an offence under these Regulations and is detained in custody for the purpose only of ensuring his attending at the trial of the charge under these Regulations in respect of which he is in custody and the trial has not commenced within ninety days from the time he was first detained, the person having the custody of the accused shall, forthwith upon the expiration of such ninety days, apply to a judge of the superior court of criminal jurisdiction in the province in which the accused is being detained to fix a date for the trial and the judge may fix a date for the beginning of the trial or give such directions as he thinks necessary for expediting the trial of the accused.

8. In any prosecution for an offence under these Regulations, evidence that any person

   (a) attended any meeting of the unlawful association,
   (b) spoke publicly in advocacy for the unlawful association, or
   (c) communicated statements of the unlawful association as a representative or professed representative of the unlawful association is, in the absence of evidence to the contrary, proof that he is a member of the unlawful association.

9. (1) A peace officer may arrest without warrant

   (a) a person who he has reason to suspect is a member of the unlawful association; or
   (b) a person who professes to be a member of the unlawful association; or
   (c) a person who he has reason to suspect has committed, is committing or is about to commit an act described in paragraphs (b) to (g) of section 4.

   (2) A person arrested pursuant to subsection (1) shall be taken before a justice having jurisdiction and charged with an offence described in section 4 not later than seven days after his arrest, unless the Attorney General of the province in which the person is being detained has, before the expiry of those seven days, issued an order that the accused be further detained until the expiry of a period not exceeding twenty-one days after his arrest, at the end of which period the person arrested shall be taken before a justice having jurisdiction and charged with an offence described in section 4 or released from custody.

10. A peace officer may enter and search without warrant any premises, place, vehicle, vessel or aircraft in which he has reason to suspect

    (a) anything is kept or used for the purpose of promoting the unlawful acts, aims, principles or policies of the unlawful association;
    (b) there is anything that may be evidence of an offence under these Regulations;
    (c) any member of the unlawful association is present; or
    (d) any person is being detained by the unlawful association.

11. Any property that a peace officer has reason to suspect may be evidence of an offence under these Regulations may, without warrant, be seized by a peace officer and held for ninety days from the date of seizure or until the final disposition of any proceedings in relation to an offence under these Regulations in which such property may be required, whichever is the later.

12. These Regulations shall be enforced in such manner and by such courts, officers and authorities as enforce indictable offences created by the Criminal Code.